CANADIAN ORGANIZED CRIME

CANADIAN ORGANIZED CRIME

Stephen Schneider

CANADIAN
SCHOLARS

Toronto | Vancouver

Canadian Organized Crime
Stephen Schneider

First published in 2017 by
Canadian Scholars
425 Adelaide Street West, Suite 200
Toronto, Ontario
M5V 3C1

www.canadianscholars.ca

Library and Archives Canada Cataloguing in Publication
Schneider, Stephen, 1963-, author
    Canadian organized crime / Stephen Schneider.

Includes bibliographical references and index.
Issued in print and electronic formats.
ISBN 978-1-77338-024-7 (softcover).--ISBN 978-1-77338-025-4 (PDF).--
ISBN 978-1-77338-026-1 (EPUB)
    1. Organized crime--Canada--Textbooks. 2. Organized crime--
Textbooks. 3. Textbooks. I. Title.
HV6453.C3S338 2017   364.1060971   C2017-906370-7
                                             C2017-906371-5

Text and cover design by Elisabeth Springate
Cover photo: *Kid Oblay, Montreal, Quebec – Opium and Narcotic Drug Act.* © Government of Canada. Reproduced with the permission of Library and Archives Canada (2017). Source: Library and Archives Canada/Royal Canadian Mounted Police fonds/Vol. 3309, file 1925-HQ-189-4-C-1

Printed and bound in Canada by Marquis

Canada

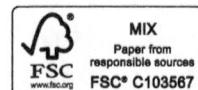

CONTENTS

PREFACE

In 2014, Criminal Intelligence Service Canada (CISC) estimated there were 672 organized crime (OC) groups in Canada. CISC defines organized crime as "a crime committed by any group of at least three people that involves the commission of a serious offence in pursuit of profit." The breadth of this definition reflects how the term has simultaneously been used to denote criminal groups and networks as well as serious, profit-oriented illegal activities.

OC has a long history in Canada. The antecedent to the modern criminal syndicates of the twentieth and twenty-first centuries can be traced back centuries to pirates who operated off the Atlantic coast. During the nineteenth century, criminal groups were organized around smuggling, bank robberies, whiskey trading, currency counterfeiting, and cattle rustling. The modern era of OC in North America finds its genesis in the early part of the twentieth century when various intoxicating substances—opium, heroin, cocaine, marijuana, and liquor—were criminalized for the first time in the United States and Canada. Outlawing these substances drove their production and distribution into underground markets, and some of the suppliers evolved into sophisticated and powerful criminal groups. The increased use of illicit drugs and other outlawed products and services in the post-war years continued to fuel the proliferation of OC and illegal markets in Canada and throughout the world. In addition to the supply of illicit goods and services, OC groups and networks also engage in a wide range of predatory crimes (those that leave a victim behind), including extortion, theft, fraud, human trafficking, and counterfeiting. Today, the most profitable OC activities in Canada—drug trafficking, contraband cigarettes, gambling, counterfeiting, fraud, smuggling, and human trafficking—are carried out by a diverse range of offenders, highly structured organizations, and loosely knit networks that have emerged from different parts of the country and the world.

In Canada, the impact of OC is measured in the billions of dollars in economic losses to citizens, business, and governments, not to mention the loss of life due to drug overdoses and gangland violence. To some, OC no longer simply constitutes a criminal problem, but is also a threat to national and international security. The containment of OC through the criminal justice system remains a highly elusive, and some would argue unattainable, goal. As CISC puts it, "Organized crime poses a serious long-term threat to Canada's institutions, society, economy, and to individual quality of life. Exploiting opportunities across the country, organized crime groups create sophisticated transnational networks that facilitate criminal activities and challenge law enforcement efforts" (Criminal Intelligence Service Canada, 2014).

Public fascination with OC has been uninterrupted for decades, and it is a popular topic for novels, true crime non-fiction, movies, the news media, Internet websites, and video games. This issue has also come under the scrutiny of the academic community. Despite this attention, OC remains difficult to define or conceptualize and a wide divergence of definitions, descriptions, theories, research findings, and opinions have emerged. As von Lampe (2016: xiii) writes, "organized crime is not something that lends itself easily to scientific scrutiny. It is not a coherent empirical phenomenon but first and foremost a construct, reflecting social reality as much as the emotions, prejudices, and ideologies of those involved in the construction process."

Like crime in general, the social construction of organized crime has been influenced (and distorted) by fictionalized Hollywood portrayals, sensationalized media reporting, self-serving politicians and enforcement agencies, and questionable academic research, all of which has resulted in simplistic, stereotypical, xenophobic, over-exaggerated, and panic-inducing accounts of the causes, scope, nature, and impact of OC. Thus, "in the absence of an agreed definition and the constructionist nature" of the term *organized crime*, "there exists an ontological vacuum which is constantly exploited" to such an extent that "the border between fiction and reality has become seriously distorted" (Rawlinson, 2012: 294). The subject of OC is controversial in both theoretical terms (how it is defined and conceptualized, and its hypothesized causes, scope, and impact) and in applied terms (especially in how to control it). Both also share a historically evolving nature: not only has OC "evolved substantially in terms of its definition, but there have also been considerable changes in the way it is dealt with" (Carrapiço, 2012: 19).

OBJECTIVES OF THIS TEXTBOOK

The over-arching goal of this textbook is to provide an introductory, yet in-depth examination and critical analysis of organized crime and its control in Canada. This goal will be met by exploring, advancing, and critically analyzing definitions, descriptions, theories, research, case studies, criminal justice policies, and enforcement approaches related to OC in this country. The textbook will also endeavour to dispel the enduring myths, sensationalized portrayals, and chronic misinformation that have engulfed this topic for so many years. Indeed, an ancillary goal of this textbook is to contribute to the development of students' analytical and critical thinking skills. The study of organized crime is highly conducive to nurturing these important cognitive skills because of its highly secretive and enigmatic nature; the challenges in obtaining accurate information; the diverse range of competing theories, definitions, and descriptions; and its sensationalized coverage in popular culture. As such, throughout this textbook, readers are challenged to analyze and think critically about various issues related to the topic of OC. This means scrutinizing any and all information presented in the textbook, which includes assessing how a particular source—be it academic, the news media, politicians, law enforcement, or other government agencies—socially constructs the subject of OC. For von Lampe (2016: xv), "Any endeavor intended to contribute to a better understanding of organized crime is faced with two considerable challenges. The first challenge is to emancipate the audience from stereotypical and mythical imagery created and promoted in the media and—unfortunately—also in some of the academic literature. The second challenge is to overcome the confusion that stems in part from the diversity of conceptualizations in the public and scholarly debate on organized crime and in part from the diversity of the empirical phenomena that are associated with organized crime."

Like any criminological topic, an understanding and critical analysis of OC in Canada should engender a broader perspective; that is, efforts should be made to understand how OC is situated within broader structural and systemic forces and institutions in Canada and the rest of the world. This includes understanding how these forces and institutions give rise to the onset and persistence of organized criminality, the symbiotic relationship between organized crime and Canadian society, and how OC is part of (not alien to) Canada. For Albini (1992: 79), the study of OC portends to a broader sociological and even existential area of inquiry:

> It is a study that calls forth an understanding of the entire realm of human behavior as manifest in varying cultures and societies. It is a study of the structure of personality and the many ways individuals go about fulfilling their daily and lifelong needs. It is a study of social values and the socialization processes by which individuals make choices. It is the study of corruption, fraud, and deception; of how friendships form and how people become enemies. It is the study of business enterprises and the many forms such enterprises can take, legal as well as illegal. It is the study of love and of hate. It is the study of why and how people engage in activities that society acknowledges but pretends to know nothing about. It incorporates the realm of mythology and the study of how mythology develops and is perpetuated. Above all, the study of organized crime is the study of social interaction, an interaction that cleverly weaves its way through the legal and illegal pathways of social existence.

Based on Albini's epistemology, the study of OC in Canada should not just be a criminological endeavour, it must also entail a historical, sociological, political, economic, and cultural exploration. Canada is lauded globally as a law-abiding, peaceful country. Yet, there is an illuminating parallel history to the one generally accepted and taught in our schools. A central theme of this book is that OC in Canada has resulted, in part, from historical developments, dominant institutions, government policies, as well as social conditions, norms, values, and vices that are indigenous to this country. In other words, Canadian society has helped give birth to and shaped OC domestically, which has reciprocated by influencing this country, its institutions, and the lives of its people. Despite the many harms that OC has inflicted on Canada,

Canadians have a symbiotic relationship with criminal syndicates and underground markets by readily consuming black market goods and services to satisfy their many vices. Given the long history of organized criminality in Canada and its complex relationship with Canadian society, readers are encouraged to examine critically this phenomenon as a reflection of the history, institutions, and even the collective identity of Canadian society. In short, this book and its readers are challenged to ask such questions as: How is OC reflective of Canada? How is it a product of domestic forces, developments, institutions, and social norms? How is it reflective of and a product of our political system, our economic system, and specific policy areas, like immigration or the criminalization of certain goods and services? How does our free market system and integration into the global economy encourage OC? Answers to these questions transcend the limited terrain of criminology, which means the study of OC is simply about "individuals and groups breaking the law but rather about actors and institutions that emerge, evolve, and disappear under certain historical conditions" (Volkov, 2014: 160). The final chapter of this book will attempt to determine whether it is possible to formulate and conceptualize a version of OC that is distinctively Canadian (or at the very least encapsulates how domestic and international forces have conspired to shape OC in Canada).

The purpose of this textbook is not to reduce OC to one explanatory concept; OC is a complex social phenomenon that is constantly changing as it adapts to evolving circumstances and opportunities. The reader should come away from this textbook with a vivid appreciation and understanding of the multifaceted nature of OC, how this complexity is a product of many factors both domestically and internationally, and how such complexity gives rise to vociferous debates and much disagreement about its causes, character, scope, and impact.

Given the above, the broad goals of this textbook can be summarized as follows:

- Provide readers with information on the topic of OC and its control in Canada (and the world), both historically and in recent years
- Help them understand the complex nature of this phenomenon and its varied treatment in academic literature, popular culture, and government enforcement policies and programs
- Challenge readers to view OC as the product of broader structural forces within and outside of Canada and how it is embedded in, reflective of, and symbiotic with Canadian society
- Help readers determine if there is a distinctively Canadian OC, which is distinguishable from that of other countries
- Encourage and nurture readers' ability to critically analyze the topic of OC and its control and to scrutinize any information presented on this subject

SOURCES

In order to provide a descriptive, analytical, and critical assessment of OC and its control in Canada, this textbook draws upon a number of disciplines and sources of information. From a scholarly perspective, the empirical and theoretical literature used to inform this book is grounded primarily in the field of criminology. However, given the importance of situating OC within the broad parameters of Canadian society, this book also draws upon other relevant academic disciplines, including sociology, economics, history, political science, psychology, and criminal law. That such a diverse range of disciplines has contributed to the study of OC is a testament to its complex nature.

In addition to scholarly sources, this textbook also relies on the news media, true crime non-fiction, as well as government reports and law enforcement documents. Notwithstanding the various sources used, any book covering OC must acknowledge the challenges of obtaining dependable and timely information, given the obstacles to gathering rigorous empirical data on this subject. Della Porta (2012: xiv) highlights the "methodological challenges" inherent in scholarly research into OC, writing, "fieldwork is difficult and often dangerous; quantitative data banks are biased. Thus, collecting information remains complicated. Social and political scientists need to rely on the investigative capacity of other actors who (as the police or the judiciary) have other priorities, as well as their own constraints." For Marvelli and Finckenauer (2012: 510), the "ability to measure the criminal markets that criminal organizations participate in has remained elusive for both practitioners and scholars. In large part, this inability to measure criminal activity is hindered by the secretive nature of the activity. In the parlance of criminologists, the 'dark figure' of crime poses the greatest challenge to measuring organized crime. The true amount of narcotics or numbers of people trafficked into the US, for instance, are largely unknown. At best, we have rough estimates." Research methods typically used in the social sciences, such as surveys, questionnaires, focus groups, structured interviews, or experiments, are extremely difficult to administer in relation to organized crime and underground markets. And while some researchers have gathered reliable information using rigorous research methods, "their inherent limitations leave much of our understanding of organized crime to popular culture." In other words, the "public's perception of and reaction to organized crime is largely shaped by the media's representation of it" (Chambliss & Williams, 2012: 52).

Among other sources, this textbook relies on the news media for descriptive case study information on OC in Canada. This reliance is due to the widespread coverage and timely reporting of pertinent issues, events, and developments by the news media collectively combined with the paucity of scholarly research on organized crime in Canada (there are not enough scholars in this country to cover, in a timely and comprehensive manner, the extensive scope of organized criminality). Nonetheless, consumers of this textbook are exhorted to critically analyze journalistic accounts of OC. The news media has been disparaged for its superficial, simplistic, saturated, and sensationalized coverage of OC, not to mention a proclivity for ethnic and racial stereotyping. Lyman and Potter (2014: 59) accuse journalistic accounts of providing "very little substantive knowledge or analysis of organized crime" because they fail to cover "the complexity of organized crime and paints a simplistic picture of an entity that is at odds with the elegant complexities of the real illicit market and the organizational dynamics of real organized crime groups." Critics charge that the news media coverage of OC tends to be sensational in that it focuses overwhelmingly on notorious, exotic, exciting, or violent individuals and events. To this end, "news coverage of organized crime is usually treated by the media more as entertainment for popular consumption than as serious news" (Lyman & Potter, 2014: 57).

The news media has also been chastised for relying too heavily on information provided by police and other government agencies and for reporting on this information uncritically. As a result, the social reality of OC created by journalistic accounts "closely reflects the state's view of organized crime" (Lyman & Potter, 2014: 58). As with news media sources, particular scrutiny needs to be applied when reading reports prepared by law enforcement agencies and other state actors. They can be a treasure trove of data for researchers, primarily because law enforcement officials or government commissions are accorded such invasive data collection powers (through criminal investigations, surveillance, witnesses, confidential informants, etc.). Police and prosecutors also have a stake in ensuring information is collected in a rigorous manner and is accurate (it must be for criminal trials). Subsequent chapters in this book detail how state actors—including politicians and civil servants, government commissions, and law enforcement agencies—have used their role and powers to become highly influential in the social and political construction of organized crime. However, their views on OC may be biased and deliberately distorted or subtly influenced by specific perspectives or ideologies. Furthermore, access to state-collected information is not always possible for external researchers, "and law enforcement agents do not always cooperate with researchers seeking information. After all, the primary goal of law enforcement agents is to prosecute offenders, rather than to assist theorists and researchers. In addition, it is highly unlikely that an official law enforcement agency would give researchers information contradicting its official position on organized crime" (Lyman & Potter, 2014: 5). Researchers also encounter difficulty when trying to corroborate, through other sources, information provided by state actors.

A final word about sources used for this textbook: many are from the United States, which may be unexpected for a book on Canadian OC. The use of American sources is inevitable given the limited body of scholarly work on OC from Canadian researchers combined with the large amount of American scholarship and government data. At the very least, the American theories and empirical research serve a unique purpose for a book on OC in Canada: they can be applied to the Canadian environment to discern if they are in fact applicable to this country and may even help with the construction of a distinct Canadian conception of OC. Once again, readers are challenged to critically assess whether the application of American scholarship to Canada is appropriate and informative. In the same vein, they should be cognizant of the "Americanization" of OC information and control strategies in Canada and the world. In this context, two distinct but intertwined dynamics are at play: (1) the export of American concepts, definitions, and theories on organized crime, and (2) the adoption of American enforcement policies in other countries (often under intense pressure by the US government) (Grayson, 2003; Woodiwiss, 2003). As such, readers of this textbook should be ready to critically analyze and determine whether Canada has been unduly influenced by American depictions of OC, not to mention this country's acquiescence to adopting American-style enforcement strategies (including the war on drugs).

WHAT CONSTITUTES ORGANIZED CRIME?

As will be discussed in chapter 2, one of the most contentious ontological debates surrounding OC is what offenders and what crimes should be included in this omnibus category of criminality. This debate will never end simply because of the complexity of the topic and the many differences of opinion in how OC should be defined and conceptualized. For example, should street gangs be included under the moniker of organized crime? We know that corporations, state actors, and other elites in society are involved in criminal behaviour that carry many of the hallmarks of OC. Should these forms of "elite" or "organizational" crime be included in a textbook on organized crime? The same question can be asked of terrorist groups, many of which commit profit-oriented crimes like drug trafficking, smuggling, and fraud to help fund their violent political and social change mandate.

While the first chapter delves whole-heartedly into this debate, for the most part the textbook does not conceptualize OC to include other varieties of organizational crime. As a result, this book uses only a limited number of case studies in which elite or organizational crimes are held out as examples of organized crime. The rationale for this decision is partially due to space limitations (the book is already long enough!). More importantly, it is due to the book's fervent effort to retain some conceptual boundaries and clarity; if every form of organizational crime is defined and conceptualized as OC, the term becomes highly ambiguous and largely meaningless. With that said, readers are once again encouraged to consider for themselves whether or not street gangs, corporate crime, state crime, and political extremism should fall within the rubric of organized crime.

ETHNICITY AND THE ORGANIZATION OF CRIMINAL OFFENDERS

As will be evident throughout this book, crime syndicates in Canada and abroad are often organized around ethnicity and nationality. Ethnicity—defined as a distinct ancestry or culture of a particular group of people—has long been assumed to be a key determinant in the membership of criminal syndicates, in part because it serves as a binding force, whether through a shared birthplace, language, or experience. This textbook does depict ethnicity and nationality as one way that serious criminal offenders organize themselves. This is evident in part II of the book, which largely demarcates different organized crime actors or "genres" based on ethnicity (e.g., Italian, Chinese, Nigerian, or English- and French-Canadian motorcycle gangs).

But readers should be cognizant of the controversies that accompany any effort to highlight ethnicity and nationality as an organizational core for serious criminal offenders and as a scientific basis to analyze OC. Given these controversies, several caveats should be kept in mind when evoking ethnicity in the study of organized crime. First, categorizing OC genres based on ethnicity or nationality does not suggest that there is a causal relationship between the former and organized criminality. Almost every ethnic community or nationality in Canada is represented by some form of organized criminal element. Second, ethnicity and nationality are not necessarily the most important factors in determining the ties that bind offenders in an organized criminal conspiracy. As described in more detail in chapter 3 (which examines the ties among criminal offenders involved in OC), "ethnic homogeneity" may simply be a "superficial characteristic" of criminal groups and networks that, in fact, are organized around family, friendship, shared language, or local community ties. In other words, "only rarely is the explicit claim made that shared ethnicity rather than anything else is what brings co-conspirators together" (von Lampe, 2012: 193). Numerous other factors unique to different organized crime genres may also play a more significant binding force than ethnicity. For example, while members of outlaw motorcycle gangs are primarily white, most of these gangs originated out of their shared affinity for motorcycles (with a requirement for membership being ownership of a Harley-Davidson).

Arguments against an ethnocentric basis for analyzing how criminal offenders organize themselves are also supported by evidence that the world of OC is increasingly characterized by a network or syndicated approach, which has abandoned most traditional restrictions on participation—in particular ethnicity or nationality. Instead, the main criterion that qualifies an individual to become part of a criminal syndicate is the ability to contribute to its revenue-generating goal. As a binding force for modern organized crime networks, ethnicity and nationality has taken a back seat to revenue maximization, which means that organized criminal conspiracies frequently involve offenders from a wide range of backgrounds, all of whom join together for one purpose: to make money. According to Albanese (2015: 12), "ethnicity is not a very powerful explanation for the existence of organized crime" for the following reasons: "Organized crime is committed by a wide variety of ethnic groups, making ethnicity a poor indicator of organized crime activity. Evidence shows that often organized crime activities are not carried out within the boundaries of a specific ethnic group, making it inter-ethnic. Other variables, such as local market conditions and criminal opportunities for certain products and services, may be much better indicators of organized crime than ethnicity" (Albanese, 2015: 12). Moreover, while biographical attributes, such as ethnicity, may help in describing the makeup and even the ties that bind a criminal group, "they do little to explain that person's or group's behavior (especially when compared to other members of that ethnic group who do not engage in organized crime activity)" (Albanese, 2015: 12).

While acknowledging that ethnicity or nationality have no causal relationship with (organized) criminal behaviour, this book contends that in Canada the core of the dominant organized crime "genres"—in particular, the Mafia-style criminal organizations in which there is a core group of inducted members (the Sicilian Mafia, the Calabrian 'Ndrangheta, Chinese triads, as well as English- and French-Canadian motorcycle gangs)—continue to be organized (although not exclusively) around ethnicity. There is considerable empirical evidence that formal membership in these organizations is largely dictated by one's ethnicity (including outlaw motorcycle gangs, like the Hells Angels, which have a ban on black members). This textbook also readily acknowledges that the core members of these Mafia-style criminal organizations do work with external associates from a diverse range of ethnicities and nationalities.

Other organized crime scholars continue to identify ethnicity and nationality as a binding force in the organization of criminal offenders (Abadinsky, 2013; Allum & Gilmour, 2012; Finckenauer & Albanese, 2014; Lyman & Potter, 2014; Reichel & Albanese, 2014). At the same time, there are those who have refuted this ethnocentric basis for criminal associations, arguing that it masks more significant binding ties, such as familial relationships (Albanese, 2014; von Lampe, 2016). Notwithstanding the ethnic-based demarcation of OC genres in the textbook's second part, emphasis is placed throughout on discussing the multi-ethnic nature of many ongoing criminal conspiracies and how the networked approach to OC has increasingly supplanted the ethnic-based Mafia-style organization.

TEXTBOOK OUTLINE

To facilitate a systematic examination of organized crime in Canada, the material presented in the textbook is broken down into four major themes. The first part of the book consists of four chapters that provide a historical, empirical, and theoretical overview of OC. This includes definitions and descriptions, theories on the causes and structures of OC, and a brief history of OC in Canada. The second part of the book also consists of four chapters, each of which examines a different OC "genre" in Canada. This includes three chapters on what is considered the most dominant OC genres in this country (past and present): Italian OC (the Sicilian Mafia and Calabrian 'Ndrangheta), English- and French-Canadian outlaw motorcycle gangs (the Hells Angels in particular), and Chinese triads and criminal networks. The final chapter in part II discusses other OC genres in Canada that may not be as widespread, but are nonetheless active in this country. These secondary organized criminal genres include Indigenous criminal groups and gangs, organized street gangs, South Asian organized crime, Vietnamese crime groups, Middle Eastern organized crime, and Nigerian criminal enterprises. A website accompanying this textbook includes sections on two other dominant OC genres: Russian/Eastern European organized crime and Latin American cocaine-trafficking organizations (focusing on the Colombian cartels of the 1980s and 1990s).

The third part of the book explores the business of organized crime—the illegal (and legal) activities carried out by criminal enterprises. Chapter 9 begins by examining the key conceptual aspects of organized crime activities and then discusses a range of organized predatory activities carried out in Canada, including extortion, theft, fraud, counterfeiting, human trafficking, as well as labour and business racketeering. Chapter 10 explores consensual crimes commonly carried out by criminal organizations, focusing on gambling, smuggling, and loansharking. The final chapter in part III discusses in detail the one criminal activity that has become the biggest revenue source for and synonymous with organized crime: drug trafficking.

The final part of the book examines OC control, with particular emphasis on the traditional criminal enforcement model. Chapter 12 outlines OC control in conceptual terms, focusing on principles, theories, objectives, and strategies. The subsequent chapter describes and examines OC control in Canada, examining criminal justice policies (law and legislation) as well as agencies tasked with combatting this criminal problem.

PEDAGOGY

The textbook emphasizes an active learning approach that advocates techniques to help students learn through greater interactive engagement with the subject matter. The following summarizes the different ways this active learning pedagogy is used in this book:

- Each chapter begins with an outline of its structure and contents, its learning objectives, and a summary of its contents.
- Case studies taken from the news media, true crime non-fiction books and articles, scholarly sources, and Canadian law enforcement agencies are presented throughout each chapter to provide illustrative examples of concepts, theories, and other relevant issues being discussed.
- Critical thinking questions are also scattered throughout each chapter to challenge students to scrutinize and analyze particularly contentious information and debates.
- The end of each chapter includes a list of key concepts and terms presented in that chapter, review questions that should help students reflect on major themes and issues, and a short bibliography of relevant readings.

Internet resources have also been created to accompany the textbook and can be found at www.stephenschneider.ca. These resources include further information on OC in Canada, as well as supplemental material to facilitate the instruction of the textbook material and to enhance the learning experience of students. As a resource for students and instructors, this website includes:

- Additional chapters
- Links to other web pages and videos on topics of relevance to each respective chapter
- Links to annotated bibliographies on the subject of organized crime
- Links to recent news media stories on organized crime in Canada
- Supplemental resources (PowerPoint slides, assignments, exam questions) for instructors using this textbook in a course

PART I

INTRODUCTION TO ORGANIZED CRIME IN CANADA: A HISTORICAL, EMPIRICAL, AND THEORETICAL OVERVIEW

The first part of this textbook consists of four chapters that provide a historical, empirical, conceptual, and theoretical overview of organized crime (OC). We begin in chapter 1 with a brief history of OC in Canada, which is meant to provide some descriptive context as well as important historical reference points for the analyses to come in subsequent chapters. Chapter 2 discusses different definitions and conceptualizations of OC and includes comparisons with other forms of organizational crimes, such as corporate crime, state crime, street gangs, and terrorism, among others. Chapter 3 provides a more detailed description of what constitutes a criminal organization or network by enumerating key characteristics presented in a taxonomy created for this textbook. The fourth and final chapter in this part explores theories that help to explain those factors that have led to the onset and proliferation of OC in Canada. Theories and conceptual models on the different structures of organized criminal associations are also presented. In sum, part I addresses these key questions:

- What are some of the key developments in the history of OC in Canada? How has it evolved over the years? How has it stayed the same?
- How has OC been defined and conceptualized?
- What are some of the key characteristics of OC as identified by definitions and conceptualizations? Are there any universal characteristics?
- What are some of the theorized causes of organized crime? How do they compare to theories of crime generally?
- What are the different conceptual models on how organized criminal associations are structured?
- What are the some of the challenges, critiques, and controversies that have accompanied these definitions, theories, and conceptual models?

- What are the similarities and differences between OC and other types of crimes, including "disorganized" crimes (committed by individuals acting alone or in small groups) as well as other forms of organizational crime (street gangs, corporate crime, state crime, terrorism)?
- What kind of harms stem from OC? Why are these harms considered more detrimental when compared to disorganized crime?
- To what extent does an understanding of the definitions, conceptualizations, theories, and a history of OC in Canada contribute to a distinctively Canadian conceptualization of OC? In other words, is there a Canadian organized crime that can be distinguished from that of other countries?

1

A BRIEF HISTORY OF ORGANIZED CRIME IN CANADA

CHAPTER OUTLINE

- Introduction and Overview
- Pre-nineteenth Century: Pirates and Privateers off the Atlantic Coast
- Nineteenth Century: Land Pirates, Thieves, Smugglers, and Counterfeiters
- Late Nineteenth and Early Twentieth Centuries: The Genesis of Modern Organized Crime
- 1920 to 1933: Prohibition
- The 1930s to the 1980s: The Ascendance of the Italian Mafia
- The 1980s to the Present: The Proliferation, Diversification, and Internationalization of Organized Crime
- Conclusion: What Does History Tell Us about Canadian Organized Crime?

LEARNING OUTCOMES

After reading this chapter, you should have a thorough understanding of the following:

- The history of organized criminality (broadly defined) in Canada
- The different epochs in the history of OC in this country
- How OC has evolved over the centuries and how it has stayed the same
- How modern OC in the twentieth and twenty-first centuries find its precedence in the criminal activities and groups of previous centuries
- How smuggling represents a historical mainstay in organized criminality affecting Canada
- How dominant institutions and characteristics that have shaped Canada have also contributed to and shaped OC in this country
- The extent to which a history of OC sheds light on a distinctively Canadian organized crime

INTRODUCTION AND OVERVIEW

The term *organized crime* was not popularized until the modern criminal organization emerged during Prohibition in the 1920s. Yet even before the nineteenth century there existed within North America different forms of criminal conspiracies that exhibited the hallmarks of OC (multiple offenders, continuing enterprise, serious profit-oriented crimes, etc.). Many of these conspiracies can be viewed as antecedents to modern OC.

Pirates were the first criminal organizations operating in North America. During the nineteenth century, criminal gangs were formed around robberies (banks and trains mostly), cattle rustling, smuggling (liquor, cigarettes, opium, and people), and currency counterfeiting. The criminalization of heroin (and then cocaine and marijuana) in the first quarter of the twentieth century was a significant catalyst for OC in North America. The genesis of the so-called Italian Mafia in Canada can also be found in the early part of the twentieth century in the form of secret societies made up of expatriate Italians who extorted their fellow countrymen.

Prohibition was perhaps the single most important turning point in the evolution of OC in North America. Outlawing liquor in the 1920s and early 1930s drove its production and distribution into the underground market where it was supplied by increasingly sophisticated and powerful criminal groups. The "dry years" were a catalyst in the creation of modern OC and spurred criminal organizations to focus on consensual crimes that catered to the vices of the public. Because Canada was the main supplier of booze to a dry America, Prohibition gave rise to an unprecedented level of organized criminality and corruption in this country while drawing Canada further into the web of American OC.

Immediately following the repeal of temperance laws in the 1930s, criminal organizations turned their attention to other profitable consensual crimes—in particular, illegal gambling (through clandestine casinos) and bookmaking (taking bets on horse racing and sporting events). It was also during the 1930s that Italian OC in the United States began to mutate into the distinct crime groups and, by the 1940s, Mafia families located in New York City, Buffalo, and Detroit had established their own subsidiaries in Quebec and Ontario.

Throughout the post-war years, the ever-increasing demand for illegal drugs would fuel the proliferation, wealth, internationalization, and power of criminal organizations in Canada and throughout the world. With the assistance of their crews in Canada, Italian-American Mafia families became part of some of the largest heroin-trafficking conspiracies in the world. Trafficking in heroin, cocaine, marijuana, and synthetic drugs also helped ferment the rise of a diverse range of criminal organizations.

By the start of the twenty-first century, OC in Canada consisted of hundreds of groups and networks comprised of thousands of individuals. Among the most dominant are the Italian Mafia (Montreal's Rizzuto family and the various 'Ndrangheta clans of Ontario), English- and French-Canadian motorcycle gangs (in particular, the Hells Angels), as well as Chinese criminal networks.

As the number of crime groups multiplied, so did the range of organized criminal activities carried out. Crimes that catered to the public's demand for illegal or highly regulated goods and services—in particular, drugs, cigarettes, liquor, counterfeit goods, migrant smuggling, and gambling—were the biggest money-makers. Since at least the early 1990s, there also appears to have been a significant uptick in well-organized predatory crimes, including fraud and counterfeiting. Thefts were becoming more organized as evidenced by sophisticated vehicle theft, cargo theft, and even identity theft. As the twenty-first century progresses, criminal organizations throughout the world have become a leading force behind cybercrimes.

PRE-NINETEENTH CENTURY: PIRATES AND PRIVATEERS OFF THE ATLANTIC COAST

It can be said that the first criminal organizations in North America were **pirates** operating off the Atlantic Coast. To be able to hunt down and pillage their victims, pirate ships required many of the essential trappings that would come to define OC: multiple offenders, a focus on profit-oriented crimes, the use of intimidation and violence, a code

Photo 1.1: Blackbeard the Pirate, 1724

Source: Engraved by Benjamin Cole (1695–1766), via Wikimedia Commons

of secrecy among the conspirators, access to black markets to sell their stolen wares, and connections with the political elite to protect and even sanction their predatory activities. Pirates captured and plundered their "prizes" by outnumbering and overpowering the victims, so ships that could carry large crews were preferred. Regardless of the size of their vessels, pirate captains had to constantly enlist crew members. Some of these recruits joined willingly while others were "press-ganged" (forced) into the occupation.

Pirate ships relied heavily on intimidation to steal from other ships, whether it was the sight of a fully manned deck and a well-armed hull of a pirate ship or the raising of a pirate flag. Whenever a pirate ship was ready to attack, the **Jolly Roger** would be hoisted at the top of the mainsail to signal their intentions and to scare victims into submission. Hundreds of years later, similar tactics would be adopted by the Hells Angels and other motorcycle gangs, by donning their menacing "colours" to intimidate "citizens." The Hells Angels' trademarked winged-head death skull insignia is nothing more than a latter-day version of the pirates' skull and crossbones.

The master pirate had to be a ruthless warrior, a competent sailor, and an astute navigator and tactician in order to locate and track down lucrative prey, as well as a disciplinarian to keep order among a rough, unruly, and potentially mutinous crew. To help ensure order while at sea, pirate captains had to implement rules, regulations, and a code of conduct, a practice that would be emulated by such twentieth-century criminal descendants as the Italian Mafia, the outlaw motorcycle gangs, and the Russian *vory v zakone*.

Like their modern-day criminal counterparts, pirates were wholly concerned with financial gain, and a few of the most successful pirate captains were able to live a life of luxury, and even buy their way into nobility with the riches they harvested from their unlawful ventures. Available to pirates were numerous revenue-generating opportunities; the most common, of course, was to rob ships of their cargo. Port towns were also targeted, not only for their valuables but to refit ships, restock supplies, and to recruit crew members. Some pirates were also known to use extortion, such as blockading harbours and trade routes and then charging a fee for any merchant vessel that wished to pass.

The great age of piracy coincided with the colonization of the New World between the fifteenth and eighteenth centuries. Not long after the Spanish and the Portuguese began to explore and lay claim to South America, pirates were attacking and looting merchant and naval vessels, which were filled with gold, silver, and other precious metals. Most of these pirate ships sailed from English and Caribbean ports, often with the

CRITICAL THINKING EXERCISE

Reflect on the comparison between pirates and modern organized crime. In addition to the similarities noted in this chapter, what are some of the main differences? In your opinion, did pirates set a precedent for OC in Canada or is this assertion too simplistic?

blessing of the British monarchy. While a ship carrying gold or silver was the pirate's greatest prize, other commodities were highly sought after, including wine from Spain or Italy, fur from New France, cured fish from Newfoundland, and spices, sugar, fruits, tobacco, and molasses from the West Indies. In addition to their cargo, ships that fell victim to pirates were often stripped bare of their sails, navigational equipment, weapons, and anything else of value.

To dispose of their seized bounty, some pirates were part of a network of black marketers. These mercantilist fences included prominent merchants and traders, including some from nobility, who sold or bartered stolen goods and captured ships. As Michael Woodiwiss (2002: 29) writes, piracy was an occupation that was "well protected" by the economic and political powers of France, England, and other European countries. "Pirates could not have carried on their trade without the support of merchants, gentlemen and officials, especially admiralty officials, and measures taken against such abettors of piracy were, for the most part, ineffective since all too frequently those responsible for executing the law were themselves notorious offenders."

Newfoundland became a major epicentre for pirates during the seventeenth and eighteenth centuries because of its profitable fishing industry, growing reservoir of manpower, evolving infrastructure to service and supply seagoing vessels, and strategic location astride the navigation route between Europe and the New World. Fishing vessels, merchant ships, and coastal towns were repeatedly targeted by pirates. Pirate ships also came to Newfoundland to rest, repair, pick up supplies, and conscript seamen. The earliest record of a pirate ship off the Grand Banks was in 1517. The *Mary Barking* and the *Barbara*, two British ships that had been outfitted for the Newfoundland fishery, turned to piracy as soon as they arrived in the New World. Soon, the main draw of Newfoundland for pirates was as a staging area for excursions into the more profitable waters of the Caribbean and South America. Because Spanish ships followed the Gulf Stream when sailing from South America to the old country, they often came within a few hundred miles of the Newfoundland coast. Thus, it was in seventeenth-century Newfoundland, according to Harold Horwood and Ed Butts, that the "pirate captains set up forts, careenages, docks; recruited shipwrights, sail-makers, iron-workers, deckhands by the thousands; then sailed south, well equipped to deal with the merchant ships of all nations, including their own." As the authors note, there were three classes of English pirates during this period: those who attacked only the ships of their enemies, those who attacked ships of any foreign power, and those who attacked anything, including the ships of England (Horwood & Butts, 1984: 2, 13).

By the mid-eighteenth century, Nova Scotia would surpass Newfoundland as British North America's centre for seafaring thieves and, for the next 70 years, it would be both a victim of and a staging ground for pirates and privateers during times of war. Between 1750 and 1815 Nova Scotia was at the front and rear of naval battles staged off the Atlantic coast during a succession of wars involving Great Britain (including those against France and Spain, as well as the American revolutionaries). During the eighteenth and early

Case Study: The "Notorious Pyrate" Peter Easton

One of the most successful pirates operating from Newfoundland was Captain Peter Easton, whose criminal pursuits also took him to the Caribbean, the Spanish Main, and the English Channel. Easton originally came to the eastern seaboard of North America in 1602 after he was commissioned by Queen Elizabeth I to take three British warships to Newfoundland (when England was at war with Spain) to protect the Newfoundland fishing fleet from Spanish attacks. When James I came to the throne in England in 1603, he decreased the size and power of the English navy, and Easton's commission was terminated. As a result, Easton and the members of his crew were stranded in Newfoundland without pay. It was then that Easton began to organize pirate crews. Along with his officers, they commandeered the naval vessels and set out to plunder ships and coastal communities.

By 1610, Easton was being described by his contemporary Captain Henry Mainwaring (the man commissioned by the English Crown to capture Easton) as a "notorious pyrate" (Manwaring, 1920: 6–7). At any one time, Easton was said to have commanded between six and ten ships and had hundreds of men in his employ. The Spanish colonies of the Caribbean and their treasure galleons were among Easton's favourite prey, but he also victimized ships and settlements along the Newfoundland coast. A letter from John Guy, the first governor of the English colony of Newfoundland, dated July 29, 1612, reported on Easton's activities at Harbour Grace, a scant 15 miles by sea from the new colonial settlement in Cupid's Cove. "Captain Easton remained in Harbor Grace, there trimming and repairing his shipping and commanding not only the carpenters of each ship to do his business; but hath taken victuals, munition, and necessaries from every ship, together with about one hundred men out of the Bay, to man his ships, being now in number six" (Purchas, 1907: 150–51). That summer, Easton invaded harbours along the Newfoundland coast with a fleet that was described by Sir Richard Whitbourne (1870) in his 1622 book as "ten sayle of good ships well furnished and very rich." Easton plundered 30 English vessels in St. John's Harbour and robbed French, Portuguese, and Flemish fishing vessels at Ferryland. As part of these latest raids, Easton recruited or forced into his service some five hundred men (Galgay & McCarthy, 1989: 3; Gosse, 1976: 129).

Easton also plied his trade back in his home country. From the mouth of the River Avon in Bristol, he extorted ships moving into and out of the Bristol Channel by demanding a fee for their safe passage. Easton's predatory services had been secured by Sir John Killigrew, the vice admiral of Cornwall, who secretly financed Easton's trip back to England and took a cut of the money he wrung from merchant vessels. The **extortion** operation that Easton and Killigrew carried out would become a hallmark of OC groups throughout the twentieth century.

Easton's cunning was so remarkable that despite the efforts of the British Admiralty, he was never captured. Today, Peter Easton is considered a folk hero in Newfoundland and a monument has been erected to his memory at the site of his old fort in Harbour Grace (Galgay & McCarthy, 1989; Gosse, 1976; Horwood & Butts, 1984; Hunt, 2000; Manwaring, 1920; Purchas, 1907; Schneider, 2016: 12–15; Whitbourne, 1870).

nineteenth centuries, Nova Scotia produced some of the most successful war-time **privateers** in the world. In essence, privateers were pirates who were issued licences (called "Letters of Marque") by the sovereign or government of their country that empowered them to rob merchant ships belonging to enemy countries in times of war. These mercenary commerce-raiders sailed on armed, privately owned ships that acted either as a substitute for, or an adjunct to, a state navy and attacked the ships of enemy nations at virtually no cost to the sovereign. "Privateering was an essential element to marine warfare," Maritime historian Dan Conlin wrote, "especially in colonial theatres like Nova Scotia, where it was seamlessly integrated with colonial commerce and complemented state navies such as the Royal Navy" (Conlin, 1998: 79). During the War of 1812, privateers were the principal line of defence that prevented Upper and Lower Canada, New Brunswick, and Nova Scotia from becoming the property of the United States of America.

Privately owned vessels sailing out of Halifax, Liverpool, Shelburne, and Annapolis Royal roamed the North Atlantic and even ventured as far south as the Spanish Main in search of French, Spanish, and American enemy merchant ships. A privateering cruise from Nova Scotia began when merchants, risking their own capital, petitioned the colonial governor for permission to launch a ship in search of prizes. Private ships of war sailing out of Nova Scotian harbours and other British colonies operated under strict regulations established by the Crown. No vessel could officially go prize-hunting without first obtaining a letter of marque from the governor. A regular account of captures and proceedings had to be kept in a logbook and any valuable information obtained by the privateer about the enemy had to be recorded and reported to the Vice Admiralty Court. All prisoners were also to be turned over to the court. Privateers were forbidden to kill in cold blood, torture, maim, inhumanely treat, or ransom any prisoner (Marsters, 2004: 6; Nichols, 1908: 112).

Crews of Nova Scotian privateer ships averaged between 40 and 50 men and most ships were manned by locals, including experienced fishermen. Among the most important of the crew members were the **prize masters** who were responsible for sailing captured enemy vessels back to port while the mother ship continued her search for more victims (Kert, 1997: 157).

Photo 1.2: The *Liverpool Packet*, which sailed during the War of 1812, was one of Nova Scotia's most successful privateer vessels, capturing hundreds of American merchant vessels

Source: Reprinted with permission from the Queen's County Museum, Nova Scotia

Privateering in Nova Scotia began in earnest around 1756 with British excursions against the French during the Seven Years' War. During the war, 15 privateer ships were armed and fitted out at the Halifax port, most of which sailed against French merchant ships in southern waters. The next great surge of privateering activity on the eastern seaboard began with the outbreak of the American Revolution in 1775. Although paling in comparison to the number of American privateers, colonial authorities in Nova Scotia granted at least 75 letters of marque to Loyalists, who ended up capturing more than 80 American vessels during the revolutionary period (Conlin, 1998: 80). The last great spate of privateering activity in North America began when US President James Madison declared war against Great Britain on June 18, 1812. As in the Revolutionary War, American naval forces quickly overwhelmed the British colonies and less than a month after war was declared, newspapers were already reporting heavy losses. While not as quick off the mark as the Americans, the Loyalists launched 40 privateering ships before the war ended, although few of these ships were specifically built for this purpose.

The people of Atlantic Canada realized significant economic benefits from privateering, more than making up for the disruptions to trade that usually accompanies war. As Faye Kert states, privateering became "a major component of the Atlantic coastal economy. Entrepreneurs and merchant ship owners found an outlet for investment capital that would otherwise have laid idle, experienced seamen found employment, shore-based industries such as shipbuilding, rope making, and chandlery prospered, and the courts and auctions provided work for an array of clerks, prize agents, lawyers, and notaries." Privateering also contributed heavily to government coffers. "Buoyed by wartime speculation, military contracts, a steady supply of prize cargoes, and a populace willing to engage in trade under licence or under cover, the provinces of New Brunswick and Nova Scotia prospered" (Kert, 1986: 9, 80, 128–29).

Within the context of Canada's historical development, privateering was more than an economic activity; it provided a locally managed defence and offence, especially given the Royal Navy's neglect of the Canadian colonies during periods of war. As maritime writer Thomas Raddall observed, "The privateers of Nova Scotia were the first warships to be built, owned, manned and commanded on the high seas entirely by Canadians. In them, the Royal Canadian Navy had its humble beginning" (Raddall, 1958: 7). For Horwood and Butts, "the War of 1812 was Canada's war of independence when native Canadians, led by small groups of British regulars, fought off the one major attempt to take their country by force of arms." And it was the privateers, mainly those sailing out of Nova Scotia, who were "the principal line of defence that prevented Upper and Lower Canada, New Brunswick, and Nova Scotia from becoming American territories and eventually American states." Out-capturing their American counterparts by a four-to-one ratio, Canadian privateers "won the war at sea" (Horwood & Butts, 1988: 72–73).

The War of 1812 was the last international conflict in history where private navies played a significant role. By the middle of the century, most nations agreed to abolish privateering. As naval enforcement increased throughout the nineteenth century, the pirate ship also became a relic of the past. While the last hanging in Canada for piracy took place in Halifax in 1809, future organized criminals would have an ample amount of pirate in them.

CRITICAL THINKING EXERCISE

Maritimers are very proud of their privateering history and the role it played in resisting annexation by the American revolutionary forces. Do you believe that privateers should be considered as organized crime? In your attempt to answer this question, consider whether today's standards and definitions should be applied to historical periods. In other words, privateering was a legal activity before 1825, so it would not have been considered a criminal occupation back then.

NINETEENTH CENTURY: LAND PIRATES, THIEVES, SMUGGLERS, AND COUNTERFEITERS

By the mid-nineteenth century, the sea pirate was replaced by the frontier outlaw as the fabled criminal of the epoch. The "spread of crime in the rural districts of this province, is daily more alarming," warned a February 6, 1846, article in the *Toronto British Colonist*. "We hear of gangs of horse thieves, and of burglars of every description, prowling about the country in organized gangs, and the peaceable inhabitants have to guard themselves and their properties against the nocturnal depredations of these bandits." For the next year, newspapers in southern Ontario would be filled with stories on the Markham Gang, an "extensive and organized gang of rogues" responsible for "a great many daring burglaries and other crimes" in and around the township of Markham (*Toronto British Colonist*, February 30, 1846).

During the time the Canadian West was being settled in the nineteenth century, organized criminality centred around illegally distilling and selling liquor. By the 1860s, Western Canada was inundated with whiskey traders. Like the fur traders in New France two centuries before, this parasitic profession was forged on the drunken and dead bodies of Indigenous people who were given cheap liquor in return for valuable buffalo pelts. At first, the independent whiskey traders operated from wagons and horseback. As business increased, they built forts, which were fortified with rifle ports and small cannons. A few of the names of the forts located in Canada even suggested the unsavoury character of these outposts. Fort Standoff was named for the time a band of smugglers "stood off" an American marshal who had pursued them over the border. Fort Slideout received its name after the occupants "slid out" one night to escape a war party of Blood Indians determined to kill the men who had been poisoning their people. Another post was simply called Robbers' Roost.

Of all the whiskey posts, the most notorious and successful was Fort Whoop-Up. Built in 1869, a few kilometres from what is now the city of Lethbridge, Alberta, it was the brainchild of Al Hamilton and Johnny Healy. Fort Whoop-Up was open for business in the fall of 1870, financed mostly by Isaac Gilbert Baker, a wealthy American fur trader based in Montana. The fortress, which was built by 32 men under the supervision of a former Hudson's Bay Company master carpenter, featured heavy timbers and thick walls loopholed for rifles and a stockade. Windows were fitted with iron bars while a cannon was mounted on one bastion and a howitzer on the other. The exterior walls were over four metres high and topped with sharpened stakes. Heavy log roofs were laid across the partitions and covered with earth to protect the buildings from flaming arrows. Three wickets were carved out of the walls to facilitate trade, and a large gate made of oak was built to admit wagonloads of supplies. At any one time, dozens of men worked at the fort trading homemade liquor for furs, rifles, and cash (Berry, 1953: 32; Horwood & Butts, 1984: 167–84).

Case Study: The Markham Gang

Between 1844 and 1846, a criminal gang made of British expatriots operating in the Markham Township of Ontario became well known for their armed robberies, residential burglaries, horse theft, pickpocketing, counterfeiting, and violence. In a June 13, 1845, article, the *Toronto British Colonist* estimated that at any one time the gang included as many as 19 men, although 6 were considered the group's leaders or more chronic offenders. The so-called Markham Gang represented one of the more sophisticated predatory criminal groups at the time. A notable feature of the gang was the systematic planning and careful reconnaissance that preceded its crimes. "From the nature of the robberies committed by them, the parties were evidently quite familiar with the habits and mode of living of those they have robbed," the *Toronto British Colonist* reported in 1845. "They always watched the most favourable opportunity to enter the houses, so as to escape detection and save their booty." The gang relied on a network of informants and spies who roamed the countryside and townships gathering information on potential victims. Some of the gang's operatives were travelling salesmen or tradesmen who scouted on a part-time basis. One even gained entrance into a home on the pretext of being a roaming Methodist minister. He read psalms and prayed with the family in exchange for food and lodging, all the while trying to determine the location of their valuables (Arculus, 2003: 19).

The well-organized and disciplined nature of the criminal group was reinforced by a strict code of secrecy and loyalty. Each member pledged "to adhere to their rules and never to betray their secrets on the pain of certain death," the *Toronto British Colonist* newspaper stated in an article dated July 9, 1846. Gang members also had to follow strict rules to avoid incrimination. They were never to take stolen items to their own homes or to try to fence the goods in their own community and, if captured, they could not reveal the identity of their co-conspirators. All communication among gang members had to be oral and special horseback messengers were employed to talk over long distances. Violence and intimidation were also used to deter anyone from "taking proceedings against the robbers, from the fear that the greater evils of fire and murder would be inflicted upon them by this desperate gang" (*Toronto British Colonist*, July 9, 1846). Even judges, police constables, and jurors were not immune to these intimidation tactics; some magistrates were accused of refusing to sign arrest warrants against gang members for fear of reprisals (Arculus, 2003; *Toronto British Colonist*, June 13, 1845, July 9, 1846).

Photo 1.3: Exterior of Fort Whoop-Up, with Blood Indians

Source: Courtesy of the Glenbow Archives, NB-9-7

In exchange for pelts, Indigenous traders could receive blankets, guns, pots, axes, ammunition, and other supplies, although the item that was in most demand was whiskey. An employee of the fort would stand at the trading window, with a tub of "whoop-up wallop" at his side, and dole out tin cups of the noxious brew. One buffalo pelt fetched two cups of whiskey. The fort was tremendously successful, collecting upwards of nine thousand buffalo hides in less than a year. At the peak of the whiskey boom in the early 1870s, the trading post pulled in an annual revenue that has been estimated as high as $500,000 (Cruise & Griffiths, 1996: 121; *Dawson News*, March 22, 1908; Neuberger, 1953: 32).

Rival traders took notice of Fort Whoop-Up's success and the number of whiskey forts throughout southern Alberta and Saskatchewan swelled. Their proliferation and infamy were also attracting the attention of Dominion government officials in Ottawa. The scope of the illicit whiskey trade was perceived to be so destructive to the frontier and the Indigenous population that the government was compelled to form the North-West Mounted Police, which would become responsible for curbing the liquor trade and policing the western part of the country (and would eventually evolve into the Royal Canadian Mounted Police).

During the 1880s, construction crews building the Canadian Pacific Railroad produced another ready-made market for illegal whiskey merchants, not to mention prostitutes, con artists, and crooked gamblers, "all bent upon fleecing the poor railway man of his hard earned gains" (Clark, 1942: 406). The various gold rushes during the latter half of the century in British Columbia and the Yukon also fuelled a cornucopia of outlawed consensual vices. In 1863, a correspondent for the *British Columbian* newspaper reporting from the gold-rich Cariboo admonished government authorities for turning a blind eye to the well-organized and omnipresent games of chance:

> The openness and extent to which gambling is carried on in the Cariboo is a matter of general remark and surprise. Right under the very nose of the officers of the law, without the slightest show of concealment, are gambling tables daily opened,— covered with gold and surrounded with professionals and their unsuspecting dupes. In almost every public house licensed for the sale of liquors these tables are to be seen and are seen, by those whose business it is to suppress such vices; and the very openness with which the profession is pursued is the best evidence that it is winked at by authority. (*The British Colombian*, July 25, 1863)

Another form of commercial piracy began to imbed itself on the Canadian landscape in the mid-nineteenth century: **counterfeiting**. Based on police and media reports, currency counterfeiting appears to have begun in earnest in the 1850s, and for many years following, Canada was a significant source of US counterfeit cash or "green goods." On August 1, 1854, for instance, two groups of counterfeiters were arrested in Sherbrooke, Quebec. When government authorities searched one of the premises they found a printing press, 26 platters for paper money, an 800-pound machine for stamping gold and silver coins, various engravers' tools, 24 moulds for running hard-money dies, ink, paper, and thousands of dollars in fake money. The *New York Times* proclaimed, "this is probably the most important arrest of the kind ever made on this continent" (*New York Times*, August 10, 1854).

Despite the predatory nature that characterized the early versions of OC in Canada, **smuggling** is the most historically rooted, persistent, and widespread form of organized non-compliance perpetrated by Canadians. Contraband smuggling foreshadowed the future of OC in Canada and abroad—a reliance on profit-oriented illegal activities that did not prey on people, but was consensual in nature, supplying goods and services demanded by the public. While smuggling can be carried out on a small scale by individuals for personal consumption, it has also been one of the most organized forms of illegal behaviour affecting this country. Historical documents make note of the dramatic escalation and increased organization of smuggling into Britain's North American colonies throughout the 1700s. This was due to the precipitous rise in duties applied to goods imported into the colonies. Tea was, without a doubt, the most popular **contraband** during this time because of its inflated costs in the colonies, which in turn was the result of exorbitant duties and the monopoly handed to the British-controlled East India Company over the sale of tea throughout the empire.

The stifling consumer taxes would become an economic noose around commerce in the British colonies. Thus, "smuggling activities promoted an institutionalization of crime in the colonies in order to ensure their commercial survival" (Chambliss, 2005: 12). The

American colonies ultimately responded to Britain's heavy-handed mercantilist policies by dumping cases of British tea into Boston harbour and then rebelling against the unjustness of taxation without representation. The expression of defiance by the mother country's subjects north of the 49th parallel was more subdued—they simply evaded the taxes by bringing in shiploads of contraband. Customs historian Dave McIntosh goes so far as to say, "the only reason Canada and the Maritime colonies did not join the revolution was that they were expert smugglers and consequently were not as enraged by customs duties as were the Americans." The contraband market flourished as "Canadians showed no remorse for disregarding trade regulations imposed by a faraway imperial authority without their consent" (McIntosh, 1984: 34).

Smuggling only increased after the United States became an independent country. While travelling through the northern United States and Upper Canada during the 1790s, the noted French writer François de la Rochefoucauld alluded to the repercussions of British mercantilist policies on her Canadian colonies following the founding of America. "The high duty laid by England upon all the commodities exported from her islands proves a powerful encouragement to a contraband trade with the United States, where, in many articles, the difference of price amounts to two-thirds" (de la Rochefoucauld, 1799: 247). By the start of the nineteenth century, America became the single largest source of contraband coming into Canada. In their 1908 book *The King's Custom*, Atton and Holland estimated the proportion that contraband made of consumer goods in the Maritimes by the end of the eighteenth century: "nearly all the tea; three-quarters of the wine; nine-tenths of the spirits; seven-eighths of the soap and candles; most of the indigo, starch, mustard, tobacco and cottons; and all the nankeens, sailcloth, cordage and anchors" (Atton & Holland, 1908: 36).

The lucrative profits of the contraband trade quickly expanded the ranks of the professional smuggler and, as McIntosh (1984: 282) writes, "armed gangs of smugglers were not uncommon on the Eastern Townships border of Lower Canada and on the St. Lawrence and Niagara frontiers of Upper Canada." An 1865 *Globe* newspaper article describes correspondence sent by customs officers stationed along the St. Lawrence that documented the "many instances" in which "officers have been personally assaulted by bands of smugglers while in the performance of their duties" (*The Globe*, December 21, 1865).

CRITICAL THINKING EXERCISE

As you read through the remainder of the textbook, compare and contrast the historical instances of smuggling with more current examples. To what extent do smuggling and contraband markets in Canada before the twentieth century set a precedent for organized criminality in the subsequent years? In your opinion, is it accurate to say that smuggling is the most persistent form of organized crime in this country?

As the nineteenth century drew to a close, tobacco products became the most popular contraband in Canada, due to the imposition of an import duty to protect Canadian cigarette manufacturers. In February 1865, a 50 percent tariff on opium imported into the colony of British Columbia was imposed, far exceeding the usual 12.5 percent applied to most other imports (*The British Colombian*, February 18, 1865). The substantial tariff prompted the widespread smuggling of opium into Canada, helping the legal substance take its first baby steps into the nether region of the criminal underworld. Less than a few months after the tariffs were imposed, colonial customs officials in BC began seizing contraband opium, most of which was being smuggled aboard steamer ships from Hong Kong or San Francisco. **Migrant smuggling** also flourished during the latter half of the nineteenth century as thousands of Chinese migrants were illegally transported into Canada *en route* to the United States. In 1884, law enforcement authorities in British Columbia captured 14 fishing ships engaged in human smuggling, each one realizing "handsome profits for their owners," as the *New York Times* put it. "As high as $80 per head for women and $80 for Chinese men are now paid to Captains of boats for running them across the boundary line." Over an eight-week period, more than "1,000 Chinamen [sic] have crossed over voluntarily" (*New York Times*, September 28, 1884).

LATE NINETEENTH AND EARLY TWENTIETH CENTURIES: THE GENESIS OF MODERN ORGANIZED CRIME

While predatory crimes like theft, extortion, and fraud continued into the new century, it was becoming clear that the greatest source of illicit revenue was to be accumulated by providing people with the goods and services they demanded, but which were outlawed or strictly controlled by the government. Gambling, drugs, liquor, and prostitution would increasingly be driven into the receptive environs of the criminal underworld by powerful reformist movements, panicked over the growth in society's vices, the breakdown of Victorian moral values, and the threat posed to the racial and religious purity of white, Protestant society by the flood of new immigrants. Only too happy to oblige the powerful prohibition lobby were politicians who enacted laws regulating and criminalizing the supply and consumption of society's most popular turpitudes. The consequence of these actions would be the creation of immensely profitable underground markets, widespread law breaking, and the launching of OC to a new level of wealth, sophistication, violence, and power.

While there continued to be plenty of freelance prostitutes in the first quarter of the twentieth century, it was during this period that the sex trade became much more organized in North America. The heightened demand for sex trade workers fuelled by the immigration of thousands of single men into North America resulted in the aggressive recruitment and procurement of young women who were often forced into

DANGEROUS AMUSEMENTS—THE BRILLIANT ENTRANCE TO
HELL ITSELF
Young girls who have danced at home a little are attracted by the blazing lights,
gaiety and apparent happiness of the "dance halls," which in many instances lead to
their downfall.

Photo 1.4: Illustration, originally published in 1910, depicting methods used to seduce young women into the "white slavery" of prostitution

Source: Unknown artist; originally published in Bell, E., ed. (1910). *War on the White Slave Trade: Fighting the Traffic in Young Girls.*

sexual servitude. Prostitution became organized and international in scope as women were brought over from Eastern European countries to work in the sex trade in North America. Many others became addicted to opium, heroin, or morphine and had to resort to prostitution to finance their habits. The increased organization of the sex trade and the forced conscription of women into the profession prompted a deliberately frightening new term in the public's lexicon—the **white slave trade**. While not all of those forced into prostitution were Caucasian, the term was deliberately coined to arouse a moral indignation among the dominant white, Anglo-Saxon, Protestant public.

Illegal gaming also became more predominant and organized beginning in the late nineteenth century. Long before governments in Canada began legalizing gambling, anyone wishing to partake in a professionally run game of chance had to visit an underground **gambling** den, while those who preferred to bet on the horses or a hockey game had to consult with their local bookmaker. During the 1890s, the *Toronto Daily Star* ran several stories on the illegal gambling parlours in the city. The most popular destinations for gamblers in Toronto during this time were the "poker joints" (*Toronto Daily Star,* May 21, 1894). **Bookmaking** was another growing source of revenue for underground entrepreneurs who took bets primarily on horse racing. Taking advantage of the telegraph service, off-track betting operations or "bucket shops" soon emerged throughout many Canadian cities to take bets on horse races from all over North America. By the 1920s, large-scale bookmaking consortiums were operating in Canada's major cities, most of which had ties to American gambling syndicates. In Toronto, the independent, small-time **horse-book** operators were gradually pushed out or absorbed by organized gambling syndicates based out of Buffalo. As gambling operations became better organized, a division of labour began to emerge, which included such positions as runners (who took bets), collectors (who collected cash), enforcers, bankers (who controlled the money, paid winners, and bribed police), technicians (who installed the wire service), operators (who decoded the information coming over the wire), and controllers (mid-level managers who hired and supervised all of the above).

The international underground trade in both legal and illegal narcotics was also growing steadily during the first quarter of the twentieth century. While opium had been introduced into North America as early as the 1850s, during the first decade of the next century, numerous well-organized opium-smuggling syndicates operating in Hong Kong, China, Vancouver, Toronto, and the eastern seaboard of North America were broken up by police. In 1908, the smuggling and sale of **opiates** in Canada was driven further underground and became even more organized when Parliament passed the *Opium Act*, which criminalized the import, manufacture, and sale of opiates, except for medical use. For the first time in Canadian history, a narcotic was now criminalized, a historical milestone in the creation of the modern illegal drug trade in Canada. By the end of First World War, demand for opiates had spiked due to the return of soldiers who had become addicted to morphine in Europe. A review of year-end reports by the RCMP during the 1920s shows that the trafficking of opiates had become a significant law enforcement problem in many of Canada's larger cities. In 1922, the federal Opium and Narcotic Drug Branch declared that the illegal opium traffic "is controlled almost altogether by large drug rings, which employ numerous agents to distribute the drug" (City of Vancouver Archives, MSS. 69: 4). It was during the 1920s that Montreal became a central conduit through which opium from Southwest Asia and morphine from Europe began to be illegally transported to New York. Vancouver was also established as a major port of entry for **opium** from Southeast Asia and a trans-shipment point for other markets in the Pacific Northwest of the United States and as far east as Toronto.

The early part of the twentieth century was also a time that stories about the existence of secret societies, extortion activities, and vendetta-based violence began to emerge from within the expatriate Italian communities in North America. Secret societies were formed by Italian immigrants who had already been inducted as members of "honoured societies" in their native country. Other aspiring **Mafiosi** in North America had no such past but endeavoured to create their own secret organizations in the United States or Canada. Still, others who did not bother with such formalities

CRITICAL THINKING EXERCISE

What are the major factors that differentiate organized crime in the first part of the twentieth century compared to that of previous years? What are some of the events and developments during the early twentieth century that helped lay the foundation for future organized crimes, criminal organizations, and illegal markets?

carried out rudimentary extortion rackets that preyed upon their fellow Italian immigrants. Most notable of the early twentieth-century Italian criminal operations was the **Black Hand**, which existed in numerous American and Canadian cities. The Black Hand was never a formal organization with any kind of national or international scope, but more a system of local extortion rackets perpetrated against other Italian immigrants. An anonymous letter would be sent—usually to a well-to-do Italian immigrant, who in most cases was a storeowner—threatening various types of violence if cash was not forthcoming.

1920 TO 1933: PROHIBITION

In 1920, the Eighteenth Amendment to the American Constitution took effect. This amendment prohibited the production and consumption of liquor in that country. It was the failed experiment of **Prohibition** that irrevocably transformed the criminal underworld in North America. Not only did it launch crime and criminals toward an unprecedented level of revenue, wealth, sophistication, and symbiosis with the public, it also represented the single most important impetus for modern-day OC on the continent. Before Prohibition, crime and criminals in North America were petty, parochial, and operated from a narrow base (Lupsha, 1986). The widespread demand for outlaw booze meant small-time neighbourhood gangs evolved into or were replaced by larger criminal groups and networks that operated on a regional and even international level. At the same time, prior to Prohibition, most criminal offenders did not accumulate a great deal of money, power, or influence. "Criminals had always belonged to the flotsam and jetsam of society, not to the economic elite," C.W. Hunt wrote in his book *Booze, Boats and Billions*. "Now, prohibition and the enormous illegal profits it made possible was changing this perception and leading to the emergence of a new phenomenon in Canadian society—the millionaire criminal" (Hunt, 1988: 49).

The implications of Prohibition to the organization of crime in North America was articulated in a 1929 article in *Canadian Forum* magazine. "What has actually happened is that prohibition has given a new rallying point and a new coherence to the criminal element. There is a demand to be satisfied, and the legal sources of supply have been stopped. The result is an illicit trade that has reached the basis of an established industry" (McInnis, 1929: 414). Prohibition would have a profound effect on organized crime in Canada as illegal Canadian liquor became the lifeblood of a thirsty and receptive American population. While contraband liquor would flow into the United States from a diverse number of countries, Canada was by far the greatest source for dry Americans, outstripping all other countries combined. Estimates of Canada's share in the total illegal liquor entering the United States ranged from 60 to 90 percent (Allen, 1961: 253). Despite provincial temperance laws, the production of liquor in Canada, which is federally regulated, was never banned. Canadian distilleries, breweries, rumrunners, moonshiners, bootleggers, and a supporting cast of thousands

Photo 1.5: Sam Bronfman, circa 1936

Source: Illustration by Ben Frisch

repeatedly skirted America's temperance laws and Canadian export laws by bringing in the highest quality "hooch," which was greatly preferred over the "bath tub gin" being produced surreptitiously in the United States. In southern Ontario, Rocco Perri became Canada's "King of the Bootleggers." Henry Reifel was British Columbia's largest supplier of illegal liquor and allegedly worked with Joseph Kennedy, the father of future president John F. Kennedy. The single largest supplier of booze to the United States during Prohibition, however, was the Seagram Distillery Company and its CEO, the legendary Canadian businessman Samuel Bronfman.

Prohibition was a formative event that spurred Canada's nascent distilling industry to reap hundreds of millions of dollars in revenues. The role of this industry in helping to demonstrate the futility of Prohibition cast these companies in a unique position as far as

Case Study: Sam Bronfman and Seagram's Distillery

By the time he died in 1971, Samuel Bronfman was a billionaire who had built one of the world's largest liquor empires, at one point supplying more than one-fifth of the US liquor market. The foundations for this empire were laid during Prohibition.

Sam was one of eight children in the Bronfman family, which emigrated from the Bessarabian region of Russia to Saskatchewan in 1889. After trying their luck in farming, wood fuel delivery, and even horse trading, the family entered the hotel business. It wasn't long before Sam realized that the true money-making potential

Continued

of hotels was in the sale of booze. The family's road to its global liquor empire initially appeared to be blocked early on by provincial prohibition laws enacted in 1916. Undaunted, Sam and his older brothers, Harry and Abe, embarked on what at the time could be considered an inauspicious and ill-timed business move: they entered the whiskey trade. Yet this decision was simply an early indication of the cunning and opportunistic business sense of the Bronfman brothers. They recognized that while the temperance laws in Manitoba and Ontario prohibited the local sale of liquor there was a loophole in their laws that allowed booze to be imported from outside provincial boundaries. With this in mind, Abe Bronfman, the oldest brother, moved to Ontario where he set up a liquor mail-order house that catered to the Winnipeg market and later established a mail-order company in Montreal to supply liquor to eastern Ontario.

The enactment of national Prohibition in Canada during the First World War virtually wiped out the Bronfman's mail-order liquor business. But true to form, Sam and Harry took advantage of another loophole in provincial legislation. They realized that Saskatchewan still allowed the sale of liquor for medicinal purposes. So in 1919, Harry obtained a provincial licence to establish a wholesale drug company in Yorkton, Saskatchewan, which Bronfman biographer Michael Marrus called "a thinly disguised liquor outlet that soon pumped more whiskey into retail drugstores than any other wholesaler in Saskatchewan" (Marrus, 1991: 58, 68). This new business venture was another crucial turning point for the career of the Bronfmans. No longer were they simply taking advantage of legal loopholes. They were now breaking the law. In addition to importing and legally supplying medicinal alcohol to doctors and pharmacies in that province, the same liquor would be flavoured, bottled, and then labelled for underground markets in Canada and the United States. Their next move was to use the family's wholesale drug firm to obtain a bonded warehouse licence from the federal government. With both licences, the Bronfman's could now import and export raw alcohol and distilled spirits to and from Canada. When Prohibition in the United States took effect in 1920, the Bronfman brothers established export companies to ship to the United States, hired sales agents to drum up orders there, and set up a string of "boozoriums" along the Saskatchewan–North Dakota border from which American customers could conveniently purchase their liquor.

Despite the vast profits already rolling in for the family, the brothers realized that even more money could be made in liquor production. The Bronfman family was now in the distilling business. While Harry was in charge of producing whiskey, Sam travelled about the country, establishing a network of connections with Canadian and American bootleggers and smugglers. In the mid-1920s, Sam moved to Montreal where he established the headquarters of his ever-expanding liquor conglomerate. In 1924, he founded Distillers Corporation Limited and built what would become one of the world's largest distilleries. In 1928, Sam purchased Joseph E. Seagram's and Sons Ltd. and its historic distillery in Waterloo, Ontario. After merging numerous corporate entities, Seagram's became the world's largest producer of spirits.

By this time, the Bronfmans controlled all aspects of their contraband liquor business from distilling, to export, to distribution. They expanded to the east coast, where they acquired bonded warehouses in Saint John and Halifax. Around 1930, when the Canadian government began banning liquor shipments to the United States, the Bronfmans set up a warehouse on the French Island of St. Pierre and Miquelon, located just off the coast of Newfoundland. The Northern Export Company was established on the island as a Seagram's distribution facility and catered almost exclusively to American bootleggers.

The Bronfman brothers become the most sophisticated of all Canadian liquor suppliers during American Prohibition, setting up elaborate systems of distribution, utilizing a labyrinth of real and shell companies, fictitious names, export companies conveniently located along the US-Canada border, a myriad of ports from which to export, and an elaborate money laundering operation to hide their ill-gotten revenue. Their illegal liquor shipments to the United States were facilitated by Canadian and foreign customs agents who were on the Bronfmans' payroll. These crews and other rum-running employees were well protected by the Bronfmans as the bail and legal expenses of various individuals charged with Prohibition-related offences were put up by the family's many subsidiaries.

As the 1920s drew to a close, their many years of covert activities began to catch up with the Bronfmans. A Royal Commission investigating smuggling and corruption in Canada's Customs and Excise Department had placed the Bronfmans' family businesses under an unfavourable light. In 1929, government authorities in Saskatchewan laid corruption charges against Harry, and in 1934, the Canadian government laid charges relating to their evasions of duties on liquor exported from Canada. The Bronfmans were acquitted on all charges after the RCMP could not gather sufficient information from Seagram's headquarters. (Accusations quickly surfaced that Sam Bronfman ordered the destruction of thousands of incriminating papers, "almost certainly with a view to shielding their early operations from inquisitorial eyes," according to a 1935 article in the *Globe* newspaper.) Other Bronfman companies used for smuggling purposes conveniently went out of business and their assets were transferred off-shore.

By the time American Prohibition ended in 1933, Seagram's was one of the largest suppliers of (legal) liquor in the world. On July 10, 1971, Sam died of cancer, leaving the empire in the hands of his family (*The Globe*, December 20, 1929; Gray, 1972: 110–11; Marrus, 1991; Newman, 1978; Royal Commission on Customs and Excise: 1928, 52; Siekman, 1966: 196).

the history of OC in Canada is concerned. There is often a fine line separating legitimate from illegitimate businesses, and this was epitomized by Seagram's and the many other legal distilleries that knowingly produced and distributed liquor for the underground market in the United States and Canada.

The Canadian government also reaped a huge tax windfall from liquor production during American Prohibition and never implemented any prohibitive laws on the manufacture of alcohol in Canada. Despite the benefits that American Prohibition provided to the Canadian economy and government coffers, the indifferent and often obstructionist position taken by the Canadian government toward American and provincial temperance laws fermented extensive lawlessness, organized criminality, violence, and corruption in Canada. As Allen (1961: 254) wrote, "It took half a dozen years or more before Canada fully comprehended the impossibility of providing both an operating base and the raw materials for a multi-billion-dollar criminal industry while itself remaining untouched by the crimes involved." Through the charity extended to liquor smugglers, the Canadian government was instrumental in creating an environment that tolerated widespread law-breaking. Corruption and internal conspiracies within the custom and excise department had become so endemic that the federal government was forced to convene a Royal Commission to investigate.

By the end of the 1920s, the Canadian government was "waking up to the disagreeable fact that smuggling *into* Canada was on the increase, with a consequent breakdown in Canadian law enforcement and the loss of considerable revenue. American bootleggers, who were already breaking the laws of one country, saw no reason to observe those of Canada. Where once they went back to Canada with empty cars and boats, they now found double profits from smuggling in both directions" (Everest, 1978; 14). The Minister of Customs himself stated in 1925 that at least $50 million worth of smuggled goods entered Canada annually. As a 1926 article in *Maclean's* magazine reported, "Truck-loads of liquor are running to the United States, and truck-loads of silks, denims, radio supplies—even jewellery—are run into Canada, on the return trips. Smugglers soon learned that the primary principle of economics of transportation is that it does not pay to return empty" (McKenzie, 1926: 24).

When American Prohibition ended in 1933, the liquor smuggling trade reversed course; contraband liquor was now being illegally shipped from the United States into Canada due to the much higher liquor taxes in the latter country. Liquor smuggling into Canada continues unabated to this very day and has resulted in billions of dollars of tax losses to the federal and provincial governments and, ironically, is partially blamed for the implosion of Canada's distilling industry.

One of the most significant repercussions of the great social experiment is the legacy of OC that still can be felt today. The revenue that was generated from bootlegging provided the initial wealth that launched Italian-American organized crime into its grand ascendance over the next four decades. It also ushered in an unparalleled level of corruption among politicians, law enforcement, and other government officials, which would become a central tactic for OC in years to come. As importantly, Prohibition demonstrated that outlawing vices would not necessarily curtail demand or supply; it simply forces these vices underground where they are serviced by criminal entrepreneurs. As such, gangsters learned an invaluable lesson from Prohibition: there was far more money to be made in satisfying the vices of a receptive public than cheating, extorting, or stealing from the tenderloin citizen. From that period forward criminal entrepreneurs would focus overwhelmingly on consensual crimes—including gambling, prostitution, loansharking, smuggling, illegal migration, and the most profitable of all, drug trafficking.

THE 1930S TO THE 1980S: THE ASCENDANCE OF THE ITALIAN MAFIA

The end of Prohibition coincided with the start of the Great Depression and, for Richard Hammer (1975: 125), the climate of the Depression was in some ways superior to that of the Roaring Twenties for "racketeers were the dispensers of recreation, dreams and escape—in the form of liquor, gambling, drugs, and sex ... " The 1930s ushered in the dawn of a radically different criminal underworld in North America. Organized crime was now more widespread, more entrepreneurial, and more geared toward consensual crimes. The period following the repeal of Prohibition also witnessed a meteoric expansion and consolidation of the so-called Italian Mafia in North America. And while the Mafia did not have a monopoly over black markets in the United States or Canada, they became synonymous with OC. The scope and influence of the Italian Mafia in North America were deemed so great during the post-war years that some (erroneously) believed it constituted a single monolithic organization whose threat to the legal, economic, and moral values of democratic societies was second only to that of Communism. To investigate and counter this threat, there were at least five presidential or congressional commissions formed in the United States and at least six provincial or federal commissions in Canada between the end of the war and the early 1980s.

With the legalization of liquor in the United States, gambling soon emerged as the most profitable illegal activity in North America. The money from the gambling operations also helped Mafia families branch out into different rackets, including loansharking, labour racketeering, organized theft, and drug trafficking. While legend has it that a few heads of the Italian-American crime families prohibited their members from engaging in the drug trade, most could not resist the opportunity. Beginning in the 1950s, crime groups in the United States, Italy, Canada, and France orchestrated the largest heroin importation conspiracy the world had seen up to this point. Dubbed the **French Connection**—due to the involvement of French Corsicans and the use of the port of Montreal as a major conduit for heroin entering North America— the conspiracy helped to establish the Montreal Mafia in the world of OC. The French

Connection was significant for many reasons. It was the largest international heroin conspiracy to date and turned Mafia groups in New York and Quebec into the largest heroin importers in North America. In addition, it helped cement a significant international commercial relationship among Italian OC groups in Sicily, the United States, and Canada. It also heralded a new era where organized criminals began to look beyond their own local communities and work with like-minded crime groups in other countries. This provided the foundation for the future internationalization of (organized) crime and the rise of the transnational criminal organization.

From the 1950s until the 1970s, the Montreal Mafia, led by Vic (The Egg) Cotroni earned millions from gambling, loansharking, prostitution, fraud, business racketeering, union racketeering, and drug trafficking. For many years, the Cotroni crime group was not a Mafia family itself; instead, it was wing of New York's Bonanno Mafia family. While Quebec was considered the fiefdom of the Bonanno family, southwestern Ontario fell under the influence of the Detroit mob, while the rest of Ontario's underworld became the fiefdom of Buffalo's Mafia boss Stefano Magaddino. Among the infamous Canadian mobsters who were made members of Magaddino's Mafia family were Giacomo Luppino, John Papalia, and Paul Volpe. The subordination of the Mafia in Canada to that in the United States would be a hallmark for Canadian OC for much of the twentieth century (see chapter 5 for more details).

THE 1980S TO THE PRESENT: THE PROLIFERATION, DIVERSIFICATION, AND INTERNATIONALIZATION OF ORGANIZED CRIME

By the mid-1980s, a number of significant trends in the world of OC were becoming apparent. One of the most discernible was the proliferation of criminal groups, which began in the early 1970s and gathered speed during the 1980s and 1990s. While the Italian Mafia was still very much active during the post-war years, by the start of the new millennium a plethora of other criminal groups representing a diverse range of ethnicities and nationalities were active. Foremost among these new OC "genres" in Canada were the English- and French-Canadian motorcycle gangs, Chinese crime groups and networks, Colombian cocaine cartels, and Eastern European OC. Soon to be ingrained in the annals of Canadian criminal history were crime groups sporting such names as the Hells Angels, the Outlaws, the Rock Machine, the West End Gang, the Kung Lok Triad, the Big Circle Boys, the Medellin Cartel, and the Cali Cartel.

In its 2007 annual report, Criminal Intelligence Service Canada (CISC) estimated there were 950 known organized crime groups in the country, an increase of nearly 20 percent over the previous year (Criminal Intelligence Service Canada, 2007, 14). In British Columbia alone, the estimated number of OC groups more than doubled—from

52 in 2003 to 108 in 2005. In a public speech, the assistant commissioner in charge of the RCMP in the province said that this increase was largely fuelled by marijuana production. He added that limited law enforcement resources mean "only 30 percent of known organized crime groups can be targeted every year" (Royal Canadian Mounted Police "E" Division, 2005; *The Province*, December 4, 2005).

Crimes that catered to public vices—drug trafficking, cigarette and liquor smuggling, migrant smuggling, gambling, and loansharking—continued to be major money-makers for criminal groups. By the 1990s, predatory offences, such as extortion, fraud, human trafficking and theft, were also gaining more prominence in the repertoire of many existing and budding crime groups, and there was considerable growth in the scope, variety, sophistication, and regularity of fraud and counterfeiting crimes being carried out. This was exemplified by the growth in organized bankcard crimes, which entail the theft of personal data from a debit or credit card, the creation of counterfeit cards, and then the fraudulent use of such cards. Traditional street-level crimes, such as automobile theft, were also becoming more organized. The sexual slave trade that was such a cause of concern in the early part of the century re-emerged with a vengeance in the 1990s, as prostitution, migrant smuggling, and human trafficking coalesced to form a transnational and highly profitable trade in women.

Organized crime in Canada and worldwide also displayed a strong propensity to capitalize on emerging technology and the Internet in particular. This has led to what arguably has become one of the greatest threats posed by criminal organizations in the twenty-first century: cybercrime. Bedroom-cloistered teenaged hackers have been supplanted by tech-savvy groups with university trained computer programmers and engineers who are behind the digital hacking of banks, credit card companies, and retail giants. As a result, billions of dollars have been stolen and millions of personal identities of clients and customers have been compromised. In 2014, the RCMP published a report on cybercrime in Canada, concluding that cybercrime has been expanding in this country due in part to the increased involvement of criminal organizations (Royal Canadian Mounted Police, 2014).

Another characteristic that came to define OC beginning in the 1980s was its transnational nature. For much of the century, most criminal groups were confined

CRITICAL THINKING EXERCISE

Law enforcement and criminal intelligence agencies in Canada have attempted to gauge the scope of OC by estimating the number of criminal groups in existence. Scrutinize the accuracy of these estimates. What are the methodological problems confronting police in trying to make these estimates? Do police and law enforcement have a vested interested in inflating such numbers?

to or controlled a well-defined local or regional territory or market. Any large-scale international movement of drugs or contraband was conducted by two or more different groups, each of which was located in a different country (as personified by the French Connection). In the last few decades, the world's major OC genres—the Chinese triads, outlaw motorcycle gangs, the Colombian cartels, and Eastern European criminal groups—have become truly multinational in scope, with cells located in various countries. Canada has not been immune to the globalization of crime and serves as a branch plant for transnational criminal organizations and a transit point for the international movement of illegal goods. According to the US Department of State's 2002 International Narcotics Control Strategy Report, "heroin, cocaine, and MDMA (ecstasy) are trafficked through Canada, as international drug traffickers take advantage of Canada's proximity to the United States, less stringent criminal penalties as compared to the U.S., and the constant flow of goods across the U.S.-Canada border" (United States Department of State, 2002). Canada is also a conduit for undocumented immigrants, primarily from Asia, who are illegally entering the United States.

In addition, Canada is an international supplier of illegal and contraband goods. This tradition began when British Columbia became a major producer of smokable opium in the early part of the century and which found new life in the 1970s when outlaw biker gangs such as the Satan's Choice, the Outlaws, and the Hells Angels established this country as a major producer of synthetic drugs. By the start of the new millennium, Canada was a source of high-grade marijuana, methamphetamines, and ecstasy for the United States and other Pacific Rim countries. In its 2013 report on international narcotics trafficking, the US State Department notes that Canada is now "the primary foreign source of ecstasy to the United States" and "also supplies Japan, Australia and New Zealand" (United States Department of State, 2013: 118). Canada has also become an international centre for mass marketing fraud and the counterfeiting of currency, bank cards, and digital entertainment products. These developments reflect how various OC groups in Canada "have taken great advantage of opportunities to diversify their criminal activities, enabling them to swiftly advance from domestic trafficking to global distribution" (Royal Canadian Mounted Police, 2007: 1).

Another significant trend in the world of organized crime has been an increase in the co-operation and networking among different criminal groups. While competition and violence still mark inter-group relationships, different crime groups are known to coordinate their illegal activities—in particular, drug smuggling and trafficking. Gangs that were once sworn enemies now work together. Family ties, ethnicity, nationality, and language are no longer barriers to collaboration; making money is the only thing that matters. In a Statistics Canada survey of police agencies, the respondents indicated that 93 percent of the criminal organizations they investigated in this country had links with other crime groups (Sauvé, 1999). The purposes

Case Study: Project Loquace

In 2012, more than 1000 police officers took part in a series of raids targeting a massive drug-trafficking syndicate operating across Quebec, Ontario, and British Columbia that was smuggling cocaine from Mexico via the United States into Canada and exporting synthetic drugs to the United States. The multi-agency investigation, codenamed "Project Loquace," resulted in the arrest of 103 people in different parts of Canada and the seizure of 158 kilograms of cocaine, more than 46,000 methamphetamine pills, and 13 barrels of a banned solvent used to produce gamma-hydroxybutyrate (GHB), the so-called date rape drug. Also confiscated were 161 guns, 291 other prohibited weapons, 1486 explosives, and 50 detonators.

Police said that the drug-trafficking network, which they called a "consortium," involved members of the Hells Angels, the Italian Mafia, and the West End Gang, mostly from Quebec. It had been under investigation for about six months and in that short time managed to generate an estimated $50 million in revenue. The cooperation of individuals from some of the country's largest crime groups demonstrates "that the country's criminal underworld is as interconnected as it is unstable," Sûreté du Québec Inspector Michel Forget told the media. "A criminal partnership that started in British Columbia migrated to Quebec last spring and developed ties with several criminal groups in order to distribute Mexican cocaine across the country" (Canadian Press, November 1, 2012; CBC News, November 1, 2012; *Montreal Gazette*, May 15, 2015; *The Province*, November 1, 2012; QMI Agency, November 2, 2012; *Vancouver Sun*, November 1, 2012, November 3, 2012).

of these linkages are to combine expertise; share personnel, facilities, or smuggling routes; exchange goods and services; and to expand into new markets. Drug trafficking epitomizes the networked structure of OC in that few, if any, criminal groups independently carry out all the essential functions of the drug trade, from production to street-level distribution. Most transnational criminal activities are carried out by collaborative networks of smaller groups and individual criminal offenders located in different countries, each of which specializes in one or more aspects of the trade, such as supplying the raw material or processed product; arranging financing; brokering the purchase, transportation, or distribution; physically transporting the goods; or storing, wholesaling, and retailing the product.

The Project Laquace case study is notable because it embodies some recent trends and developments in the Canadian drug trade: the increase in poly-drug trafficking (the handling of numerous kinds of illegal drugs by criminal groups and networks), the production of synthetic drugs in Canada (and their subsequent export to other countries), the involvement of Canadian crime groups in the northbound smuggling of cocaine into Canada and the southbound smuggling of Canadian-produced drugs, as well as the co-operation among different criminal groups in these illegal ventures.

CONCLUSION: WHAT DOES HISTORY TELL US ABOUT CANADIAN ORGANIZED CRIME?

Broadly defined, organized crime in Canada spans more than 500 years and is a part of some of this country's most important historical developments and enduring institutions. Pirates were among the first arrivals in the settling of Newfoundland and Labrador while privateers helped to protect Canada from American invading forces during the revolutionary war and the War of 1812. Smuggling between the United States and Canada is part of and help forged trade and broader economic relations between the two countries. The fur trade "exercised a profound influence in the sculpting of the Canadian soul," Peter C. Newman wrote (1985: 18), and "more than virtually any other single experience, is the primary matrix out of which modern Canada emerged." The early fur trade also "became a focal point for widespread law-breaking" (Carrigan, 1991: 16). One of the great institutions in Canadian history, the Hudson's Bay Company (HBC) was founded in 1668, and during its early history it operated in an extremely unscrupulous manner. HBC was the first to supply Indigenous hunters with cheap liquor in return for expensive pelts. In its ravenous appetite for profits and a quest to monopolize the fur trade, it readily turned to violence when faced with competition, especially from its rival North West Company, which was founded in 1783. As Carrigan (1991: 115–16) writes, "Murder, theft, destruction of property, arson intimidation, and assault marked the commercial rivalry. Raids on each other's posts were common." The founding of the legendary North-West Mounted Police was promoted by well-organized whiskey traders. Canada's distilling industry, once the envy of the world, would never have had come to fruition without the impetus provided by Canada's role in supplying the United States during Prohibition.

William Lyon Mackenzie King was the driving force behind the criminalization of opium in Canada and used this as a springboard to become Canada's longest serving prime minister. During his tenure as prime minister he signed the 1924 Convention to Suppress Smuggling with the United States, the "first international treaty Canada negotiated without Britain's involvement, one signalling the start of made-in-Canada foreign policy … " Moreover, "the catalyst for the famous 1925 King-Byng constitutional crisis— the power struggle between Canada's prime minister and its governor-general—was a vote of no-confidence in the government of Mackenzie King for allowing liquor smuggling and corruption to run rampant in the department of customs and excise" (Konkel, 2009).

These historical touchstones reinforce the argument that OC is not foreign to Canadian history and culture, but a part of it. A historical overview also refutes one of the most enduring and endearing of all Canadian folklore: that the historical development of this country was free of crime and lawlessness. As this chapter has demonstrated, the idyllic picture painted by some revisionist historians and nationalists belies the historical reality.

Another constant in the history of organized crime in Canada is the realization that its eradication—or even containment—through the criminal justice system remains a highly elusive and, some would argue, unattainable goal. While numerous criminal groups and illegal markets have been disrupted, and gangland bosses and their underlings put behind bars, organized crime will be with us for some time to come. Within a historical context, OC must be viewed as an ephemeral and flexible social phenomenon that easily and opportunistically adapts to changes and external circumstances (including changes in public preferences, technological advances, government policies, and law enforcement strategies). The resilience of OC stems from the fact that, like crime in general, it is very much rooted in the institutions and cultures of the societies it inhabits, making it an enduring historical fixture on the Canadian landscape.

KEY TERMS

Black Hand	Migrant smuggling
Bookmaking	Opiates
Contraband	Opium
Counterfeiting	Pirates
Extortion	Privateers
French Connection	Prize masters
Gambling	Prohibition
Horse-book	Smuggling
Jolly Roger	White slave trade
Mafiosi	

REVIEW QUESTIONS

1. What are some of the key developments in the history of organized crime in Canada?
2. How has OC changed over the centuries? How has it stayed the same?
3. To what extent does "modern" OC in the twentieth and twenty-first centuries find its precedence in the criminal activities and criminal groups of previous centuries?
4. What is the importance of smuggling in the historical context of OC in Canada?

5. How have historical Canadian developments, institutions, and characteristics shaped OC in this country? To what extent has OC been present in or influenced historical developments and institutions in this country?
6. To what extent does this history shed light on a distinctively Canadian organized crime?

FURTHER READINGS

Carrigan, D.O. (1991). *Crime and Punishment in Canada: A History*. Toronto: McClelland & Stewart.

Edwards, P., & Auger, M. (2012). *The Encyclopedia of Canadian Organized Crime: From Captain Kidd to Mom Boucher*. Toronto: McClelland & Stewart.

Fox, S.R. (1989). *Blood and Power: Organized Crime in Twentieth Century America*. New York: W. Morrow.

Horwood, H., & Butts, E. (1984). *Bandits and Privateers of Canada: 1610 to 1932*. Toronto: Doubleday.

Schneider, S. (2016). *Iced: The Story of Organized Crime in Canada*. Toronto: HarperCollins.

2 DEFINING AND CONCEPTUALIZING ORGANIZED CRIME

CHAPTER OUTLINE

LEARNING OUTCOMES

After reading this chapter, you should have a thorough understanding of the following:

- The various definitions and conceptualizations of OC that have emerged over the years and their historical context
- The challenges and controversies inherent in trying to define and conceptualize OC, including why many argue that OC is a "social construct"
- The similarities and differences between OC and other forms of "organizational" crime, as well as the overlap among different forms of organizational crime
- How definitions and conceptualizations distinguish Canadian OC
- The nature and scope of harms to Canadian society attributed to organized crime and how they are amplified compared to "disorganized crimes"

INTRODUCTION AND OVERVIEW

One of the great challenges that has confronted the academic community in the study of organized crime is elucidating a definition that is able to capture its complexity. The problem with the term *organized crime* may be the term itself, as it has been criticized as a vague umbrella concept that is of little value as a basis for theory-building, empirical analyses, or policy-making. Some argue that the term is more of a social construct that attempts to make sense of a complex social reality and, as such, can mean different things to the many entities involved in constructing a definition.

No consensus has emerged on a definition, which has led some to assert that it may be best simply to identify its immutable characteristics. To this effect, some of basic characteristics that "organize" crime and criminals include the involvement of multiple offenders; a structure and purpose to the relationship among the offenders; the commission of serious, profit-oriented criminal offences; continuity (i.e., an ongoing relationship among offenders and/or the execution of multiple offences over a period of time); and a relatively high level of planning, rationality, and sophistication.

Conceptually, the term *organized crime* has been used to differentiate a specific manner of criminality from **disorganized crime**—forms of personal and property crimes typically committed by individuals working alone or in pairs or small groups (such as residential burglaries, automobile theft, vandalism, crimes of passion, and so on). The term has simultaneously been used to describe any the following: groups and networks that carry out these illegal offences, specific types of illegal activities, or how illegal activities are carried out (rationally, on an ongoing basis, involving multiple offenders, etc.).

Conceptually, OC has traditionally been distinguished from other types of organizational crime, such as state crime or corporate crime, as well as groups that may persistently be involved in serious illegal activities, including street gangs or terrorist groups. Despite these conceptual differences, in reality there is an increased overlap between OC and the other aforementioned forms of organizational crime.

Older definitions and conceptualizations of OC that were highly ethnocentric and focused on a hierarchical organizational profile of crime groups have evolved toward those that recognize a more multi-ethnic, networked approach to organized criminality. This conceptual evolution is a reflection of the historically evolving nature of how serious profit-oriented criminal activities are organized.

DEFINITIONS OF ORGANIZED CRIME

Throughout the years, various attempts have been made to define OC. Definitions have been developed by scholars, legal experts, public policy makers, criminal justice agencies, and inter-governmental organizations, such as the United Nations. Definitions of

OC are needed, and not simply to contribute to a better conceptual understanding. They have also been crafted to help guide government policy makers and criminal justice agencies in combatting this problem through laws and legislation as well as operational strategies. This section begins with an overview of some of the many definitions of OC that have arisen over the years. Each definition is accompanied by a brief analysis that identifies some of its key elements, as emphasized by its source. The definitions are presented in chronological order and include a description of the relevant historical context that helped influence a particular definition. Presenting the various definitions in chronological order also helps to discern if there has been any evolution or other changes that have occurred through the years (and whether definitions have kept up with the evolving nature of OC). This section concludes with a critical analysis on the matter of defining OC. This analysis identifies the challenges inherent in defining such a complex and ever-changing phenomenon as well as critiques of the definitions and how they are not necessarily reflective of the reality of OC, but instead have been constructed to advance a particular agenda.

Organized Crime: A Chronology of Definitions and Descriptions

Given that modern OC has been heavily (but not exclusively) influenced by the American experience, it is not surprising that the term *organized crime* was originally coined in the United States. As von Lampe (2016: 15) notes, the "concept of organized crime as it is used today is essentially a U.S. invention. While its origins go back to at least the 19th century, it was not until the early 20th century, in the United States, that a more or less consistent meaning was attached to the combination of the words organized and crime." There appears to be some consensus that the term was first used in the 1896 annual report of the New York Society for the Prevention of Crime, which "employed it to refer to gambling and prostitution operations that were protected by public officials" (Paoli & Vander Beken, 2014: 15).

Chicago City Council Committee on Crime (1915)
One early attempt to define and describe OC was contained in a 1915 report by the Chicago City Council Committee on Crime and alludes to a particular **criminal organization** operating in Chicago around that time:

> While this criminal group is not by any means completely organized, it has many of the characteristics of a system. It has its own language; it has its own laws; its own history; its traditional customs; its own method and techniques; its highly specialized machinery for attacks upon persons and property; its own highly specialized mode of defense. These professionals have interurban, interstate, and sometimes international connections. (As cited in Maltz, 1976: 344)

The committee noted that while this criminal group may be systematic, it also shares some traits with more rudimentary criminals (i.e., "not completely organized"). With that said, the definition notes that the group has characteristics that make it unique within the criminal milieu (its history, customs, methods, techniques, and use of "specialized machinery" for violence). The definition also identifies another trait that separates the group from the common criminal element: its multi-jurisdictional nature.

National Commission on Law Observance and Enforcement (1931)

Because of the increased organization and sophistication of the illegal liquor traffic in the 1920s and 1930s brought about by American Prohibition laws, "the understanding of organized crime changed significantly" (von Lampe, 2016: 20), and it was during this period that "commentators and academics began to make serious efforts to define and discuss organized crime" (Paoli & Vander Beken, 2014: 15–16). According to von Lampe (2016: 20), by the end of the 1920s, organized crime referred to "'gangsters and racketeers' who were organized in 'gangs,' 'syndicates,' and 'criminal organizations,' following 'big master criminals' who functioned as 'powerful leaders of organized crime'." Similarly, Paoli and Vander Beken (2014: 15–16) write that during this period, "organized crime was made synonymous with racketeering, another loose expression that usually referred to extortion, predatory activities, and the provision of a variety of illegal goods and services, ranging from illegal drugs and liquor to gambling and counterfeit documents."

Amidst the widespread lawlessness that accompanied Prohibition, the US government convened the National Commission on Law Observance and Enforcement. While charged with the mandate of assessing the enforcement of national Prohibition laws, the commission observed that the outlawing of liquor gave rise to an increase in the organization of crime and criminals. The commission did not use or define the term *organized crime* in its 1931 report, although it does consistently refer to the suppliers of illicit booze as "highly organized" or "elaborately organized." At one point, it also described the illegal importation of liquor into the United States in commercial terms—"a well organized exceedingly profitable business, admitting of lavish expenditure for protection and corruption, and of employing the best talent in design, construction, and operation of apparatus and equipment" (National Commission on Law Observance and Enforcement, 1931: 43). The above quotation is notable for its depiction of this organized criminal behaviour as a "business," which includes an elaborate division of labour and the corrupting of public officials to sustain and protect the illegal liquor enterprises.

Special Committee to Investigate Organized Crime in Interstate Commerce (1951)

By the 1950s, according to Paoli and Vander Beken (2014: 16), "the understanding of organized crime as a set of criminal entrepreneurial activities with the frequent involvement of legal businesses and government representatives was abandoned after World War II. From the late 1940s on, conceptualizations of the problem focused on foreign career criminals who allegedly constituted well-structured and powerful criminal organizations representing a threat to the integrity of American society and politics." Adds von Lampe (2016: 20), throughout the Prohibition era, the term *organized crime* "had no ethnic connotation. This changed dramatically in the 1950s and 1960s with the resurgence of the imagery of Italian mafia groups having taken root in the United States." In short, beginning in the early 1950s, the depiction of OC changed in three significant ways. First, it took on a decidedly ethnic tone as it was equated almost synonymously with the so-called Italian Mafia. Second, it "no longer appeared to be primarily a local problem but instead one that existed on a national scale and threatened local communities from the outside" (von Lampe, 2016: 20). Third, conceptually, OC was depicted as a rationally structured, hierarchical organization—in effect, a criminal corporation.

This emergent conceptualization was attributed largely to the work of the US congressional Special Committee to Investigate Organized Crime in Interstate Commerce and its chairperson, Senator Estes Kefauver. As part of its high-profile investigation into organized crime, which included televised hearings, "the committee set out the terms of an Italian mafia-centered view of OC that remained the US official standpoint for almost three decades. This identified OC with a nationwide, centralized criminal organization dominating the most profitable illegal markets, which allegedly derived from an analogous parallel Sicilian organization and largely consisted of migrants of Italian (and specifically Sicilian) origin" (Paoli & Vander Beken, 2014: 16). Despite the scarcity of evidence to back up its arguments, the committee concluded in a 1951 report that numerous criminal groups throughout the United States were tied together by "a sinister criminal organization known as the Mafia" (United States Congress, 1951: 2). The merger of the concepts of OC and the Mafia in the official discourse of American government officials and federal law enforcement was buttressed in 1963 with another congressional committee that spotlighted testimony from Mafia member Joe Valachi (Paoli & Vander Beken, 2014: 16–17). This ethnic-based, Mafia-centred view of OC in America was perpetuated throughout the 1960s and 1970s via other federal government commissions and conferences, the increased and disproportionate media attention paid to the Italian Mafia in the United States, as well as through popular culture, including the publication of the novel *The Godfather* by Mario Puzo in 1969 and the 1972 Academy award–winning film adaptation directed by Francis Ford Coppola.

CRITICAL THINKING EXERCISE

Read *The Godfather* novel or watch the first (or all three) of the *Godfather* films and then think about how Italian-American OC is depicted in fictional terms. To what extent do you believe definitions and the public's understanding of OC have been influenced by the *Godfather* franchise?

Photo 2.1: Actor Marlon Brando as the fictional "Godfather," Vito Corleone

Source: Aggiorna, via Wikimedia Commons

The Oyster Bay Conference on Organized Crime (1965)

One of the first conferences among America law enforcement officials that focused on organized crime was held in Oyster Bay, New York, in 1965. This conference was a significant step toward a general definition of OC. Conference participants defined OC as "the product of a self-perpetuating criminal conspiracy to wring exorbitant profits from our society by any means—fair or foul, legal and illegal. Despite personnel changes, the conspiratorial entity continues ... It survives on fear and corruption. By one or another means, it obtains a high degree of immunity from the law. It is totalitarian in its organization; a way of life, it imposes rigid discipline on its underlings who do the dirty work while the top men of organized crime are generally insulated from the criminal act and the consequent danger of prosecution."

Some of the salient features of this definition include the profit-oriented nature of OC (from both illegal and legal activities); how it is "self-perpetuating" regardless of its membership; the existence of a hierarchical command structure; and its ability to insulate the group and its leadership from law enforcement actions. Conference participants ultimately concluded that OC is an illicit profit-oriented business venture, operating much like a corporation, but which uses persuasive (illegal) tools—in particular, internal discipline, fear, intimidation, murder, and corruption—to generate revenue. At the same time, the definition implies that OC (i.e., the Mafia) is more than just a business; it is a "way of life."

The Oyster Bay conference also recognized the inherent difficulties in generalizing about OC, noting the diversity of organizational structures and levels of sophistication (which includes a spectrum-based conceptualization whereby youth gangs and shoplifting rings constitute lower forms of OC).

> In the broad sense, the phrase "organized crime" may include criminal organizations in a wide variety of sizes and types of unlawful enterprises. At its lowest levels, it includes youth gangs, which have as their principal purpose the systematic commission of crime, or other small loosely-knit groups which engage in single or multiple crimes, such as shoplifting, burglary, and confidence games. At its highest level, of course, it includes hard-core activities such as professional gambling, the importation and distribution of narcotics, loan sharking, or labour racketeering. Indeed, "organized crime" is often identified solely with these hard-core activities. This, however, is a mistake. Like the similar phrase "white-collar crime," organized crime properly refers not so much to the activity as to the status of the people who engage in it. (As cited in Herbert & Tritt, 1984: 8)

The above depiction bestows an elite status on those who participate in criminal organizations. This perspective appears to be based on the characterization of the "white-collar" criminal as a person "of respectability and high social status," which was put forth in Edwin Sutherland's 1949 book on this subject (see the section on white-collar crime later in this chapter). The main point that is made by conference participants is that one cannot define OC by the illegal activities undertaken, but apparently by the high underworld status of those who undertake the crimes.

President's Commission on Law Enforcement and Administration of Justice, Task Force Report: Organized Crime (1967)

This presidential commission, which ran from 1965 to 1969, was formed in response to the dramatic increase in crime in the United States during the 1960s and the challenges facing American law enforcement and policy makers in containing this growing problem. Nine different task forces made up the commission, including the Task Force on Organized Crime, which defined OC as

> ... a society that seeks to operate outside the control of the American people and their governments. It involves thousands of criminals, working within structures as complex as those of any large corporation, subject to laws more rigidly enforced than those of legitimate governments. Its actions are not impulsive but rather the result of intricate conspiracies carried on over many years and aimed at gaining control over whole fields of activity in order to amass huge profits. (President's Commission on Law Enforcement and Administration of Justice, 1967: 187)

The commission's influential characterization of OC claimed the presence of a highly structured, highly organized, nationwide crime conspiracy in the United States. Other important traits apparent in this definition include its continuity, efforts to monopolize legitimate and illegal markets, and profit-oriented nature. Like the other federal commissions before it, it created a description that was formed primarily with Italian-American Mafia in mind, which the commission claimed consisted of 24 groups with approximately 5000 members of all whom are of Italian origin.

Donald Cressey (1969)

Based on his consulting work with the presidential commission, in 1969 the noted criminologist Donald Cressey published a book entitled *Theft of a Nation* that provided more credence to the depiction of the Italian-American Mafia as consisting of many rationally structured organizations. In particular, he defines "an organized crime as any crime committed by a person occupying an established division of labour, a position designed for the commission of crime, providing that such division of labour also includes, at least, one position for a corrupter, one position for a corruptee, and one position for an enforcer" (Cressey, 1969: 319). While limited, this definition is notable for the emphasis that Cressey places on the use of corruption, violence, and intimidation by criminal groups—tactics used to support the revenue-generating nature of criminal organizations and how these

Photo 2.2: Professor Donald Cressey, 1960

Source: Associated Students, University of California, Los Angeles, via Wikimedia Commons

functions are specialized within a hierarchical Mafia organization. In addition, he combines the traditional conceptualization of OC as a group of criminals with the alternative that depicts OC as the organization of criminal activities ("organized crimes"). Cressey's primary interpretation of OC as rationally designed, hierarchical Mafia groups conveyed the message that OC "should be dealt with as organizations, not merely as collections of individual criminals, and any 'attack' on them must deal with organizational structures and the social contexts in which the structures thrive"(Cressey, 1972: 22).

The idea that ethnic Italian crime groups monopolized serious, profit-oriented crime, like drug trafficking, gambling, and loansharking, in the United States through a "near-corporate structuring principle" (Sheptycki, 2003: 125) and a nationwide conspiracy was debunked in later years as over-exaggerated, sensationalized, and based on dubious evidence. However, at the time, the aforementioned government and scholarly depictions were highly influential and a significant catalyst in increasing federal law enforcement resources and prompting the introduction of punitive legislation directed toward organized crime in the United States.

The United States' Omnibus Crime Control and Safe Streets Act (1968)

In 1968, the US Congress passed the *Omnibus Crime Control and Safe Streets Act*, which defined OC as " ... the unlawful activity of the members of a highly organized, disciplined association engaged in supplying illegal goods and services, including but not limited to gambling, prostitution, loan sharking, narcotics, labour racketeering, and other unlawful activities of members of such organizations." While continuing to equate OC with the Italian Mafia (the "disciplined association"), this definition is most notable for its emphasis on how consensual illegal activities are at the core of modern organized criminal conspiracies.

Quebec Police Commission (1975)

Up until the 1970s, definitions of OC in Canada (by Canadians) were noticeably lacking. This was due, in part, to the refusal of politicians and senior law enforcement officials to even acknowledge the problem existed in this country. This began to change in the mid-1970s when the Quebec government initiated hearings into OC and corruption in that province. The final report contained the following broad definition of OC: " ... this new class of the underworld is a group of individuals continuously and secretly conspiring together on a permanent basis with a view to profiting from several types of crimes" (Quebec Police Commission, 1975: 13). Like in the United States, many of the earliest reports issued by the Quebec Police Commission equated OC with the Italian Mafia, which had become entrenched in Montreal as a wing of New York City's Bonanno crime family.

National Advisory Committee on Criminal Justice Standards and Goals, Task Force on Organized Crime (1976)

In 1976, this American task force recognized the dangers in trying to concisely define OC due its complexity and ever-evolving nature. In fact, the committee argued, "no single definition is believed inclusive enough to meet the needs of the many different individuals and groups throughout the country that may use it as a means to develop an OC effort." Instead, the task force identified the characteristics of organized criminal activity:

- It is a conspiratorial crime.
- It has profit as its primary goal.
- It is not limited to illegal enterprises or unlawful services but includes sophisticated legal activities as well.
- It is predatory, using intimidation, violence, corruption, and appeals to greed.
- The conspiratorial groups are well disciplined and incorrigible.
- It is not synonymous with the Mafia and knows no ethnic bounds.
- It excludes political terrorists, being politically conservative, not radical (as cited in Bynum, 1987: 4).

President's Commission on Organized Crime (1986)

According to Carrapiço (2012: 24), by the 1980s definitions and conceptualizations of OC in America "shifted in a new direction as a result of the over-ethnicization in the perception of organized crime and its reported lack of empirical basis." The President's Commission on Organized Crime, which was struck by the Regan administration, acknowledged that "the histories of American organized crime have been ordinarily drawn too narrowly in that they have focused nearly exclusively on the Mafia or La Cosa Nostra" (President's Commission on Organized Crime, 1987: 176). As a result, the subsequent "strategy pursued by American government institutions was to broaden the definition of organized crime to include other criminal organizations involved full-time in the supply of illegal commodities in demand by the general populace" (Paoli and Vander Beken, 2014: 19). To this end, the commission's report also discussed outlaw motorcycle gangs, prison gangs, Chinese triads and tongs, Vietnamese gangs, Colombian cocaine traffickers, as well as Irish, Russian, and even Canadian OC.

Howard Abadinsky (1990)

In one of the first textbooks published on OC in the United States, criminologist Howard Abadinsky continued the traditional depiction of the highly structured criminal organization. At the same time, he fleshes out his definition with what he views as the core characteristics of OC:

Organized crime is a non-ideological enterprise involving a number of persons in close social interaction, organized on a hierarchical basis, with at least three levels/ranks, for the purpose of securing profit and power by engaging in illegal and legal activities. Positions in the hierarchy and positions involving functional specialization may be assigned on the basis of kinship or friendship, or rationally assigned according to skill. The positions are not dependent on the individuals occupying them at any particular time. Permanency is assumed by the members who strive to keep the enterprise integral and active in pursuit of its goals. It eschews competition and strives for a monopoly on an industry or territorial basis. There is a willingness to use violence and/or bribery to achieve ends or to maintain discipline. Membership is restricted, although non-members may be involved on a contingency basis. There are explicit rules, oral or written, which are enforced by sanctions that include murder. (Abadinsky, 1990: 6)

This is certainly one of the more comprehensive definitions developed to date. Abadinsky first emphasizes the non-ideological nature of OC, inferring it is not interested in social or political power, but making money. He also notes that there exists an organizational hierarchy, which includes specialized functions that can be allocated based on either the association a member has with the leadership of the group (kinship ties) or based on that member's particular skills. Either way, these functions are like jobs in a legitimate enterprise: they are not linked to any one member of the group, but can be filled by different people. Similarly, he notes that one of the roles of the group members is to help ensure the organization persists over times, which is done by continuously making money. Abadinsky also characterizes criminal organizations as monopolistic (they don't like competition within a particular industry or territory). Finally, he also points out that while some criminal groups have a formal membership, they also are reliant upon non-members outside the group to perform certain legal or illegal tasks.

United Nations Convention against Transnational Organized Crime (2000)

For the purposes of the UN convention, an "[o]rganized criminal group shall mean a structured group of three or more persons, existing for a period of time and acting in concert with the aim of committing one or more serious crimes or offences established in accordance with this Convention, in order to obtain, directly or indirectly, a financial or other material benefit." The convention defines a "structured group" as "a group that is not randomly formed for the immediate commission of an offence and that does not need to have formally defined roles for its members, continuity of its membership or a developed structure" (United Nations, 2000: 25–26). The UN definition contradicts earlier definitions somewhat in that it does not view members of an organized crime group as having "formally defined roles" (i.e., a well-defined division of labour that includes specialization). However, it does ascribe a systematic nature to a criminal organization in that it is purposively (not randomly) formed and persists over a "period of time."

Criminal Code of Canada (1997/2002)

With the 1997 enactment of *An Act to amend the Criminal Code (criminal organizations) and to Amend Other Acts in Consequence*, the *Criminal Code of Canada* now provides a (broad) definition of a criminal organization. The definition is part of a section of the

Criminal Code that deals specifically with offences associated with criminal organizations (e.g., committing an offence on behalf of a criminal organization, recruiting, or counselling another to commit to joining a criminal organization). Section 467.1(1) of the *Criminal Code* (as amended in 2002) defines a criminal organization as follows:

> ... a group, however organized, that
>
> (a) is composed of three or more persons in or outside Canada; and
>
> (b) has as one of its main purposes or main activities the facilitation or commission of one or more serious offences that, if committed, would likely result in the direct or indirect receipt of a material benefit, including a financial benefit, by the group or by any of the persons who constitute the group.
>
> It does not include a group of persons that forms randomly for the immediate commission of a single offence.

It is no coincidence that there are great similarities between the *Criminal Code* definition and that provided by the UN convention; as a signatory to the convention, federal Parliament amended this section of the *Criminal Code* in 2002 in part to ensure the definition was in compliance with that developed by the UN.

Reconceptualizing Organized Crime

The definitions of OC by Abadinsky and the United Nations are a throwback to a time when OC was viewed as being synonymous with highly structured organizations. By the 1990s, there was a growing discontent among academics with this depiction, which resulted in "a re-conceptualization of organized crime as a much looser association of individuals ... " This network-based model "pushed for the abandonment of the concept of organized crime as an entity, by proposing it to be understood as a complex set of connections" among criminal offenders. There was also a shift in focus from criminal actors and entities to how profit-oriented illegal activities are organized (Carrapiço, 2012: 24). Both of these important shifts in thinking could be traced to the mid-1970s when Dwight Smith published his groundbreaking book *The Mafia Mystique*. Smith argued for the need to move the focus away from criminal organizations to organized criminal activities and, in so doing, argued that the latter should be understood as an extension of a typical commercial operation and entrepreneurship but carried out in illegal markets (see chapter 4 for more on Smith's spectrum-based theory of a criminal enterprise).

European Union (2001)

As part of its efforts to determine penalties for participating in a criminal organization, the Commission of the European Communities and EUROPOL (2001: 42) developed their own definition: "A criminal organisation shall mean a structured association, established over a period of time, of more than two persons, acting in concert with a view to committing offences which are punishable by deprivation of liberty of a maximum of at least four years or a more serious penalty; whether such offences are an end in themselves or a means of obtaining material benefits and, where appropriate, of improperly influencing the operation of public authorities." The European Union (EU) definition is predicated on that originally developed by the United Nations. However, what delineates their definition from that of the UN and the ones developed by the US government commissions is that it uses the broader term *association* to depict the relationship among offenders, instead of the more restrictive word *organization* (which implies a corporate-like hierarchical structure). Other important attributes of OC highlighted in this definition are continuity over time, multiple officers that commit serious profit-oriented criminal offences, and the use of corruption.

US Department of Justice (2008)/Jay Albanese (2015)

Like the EU, the US Department of Justice avoids a strict adherence to any one organizational model when it defines transnational organized crime (TOC) as "self-perpetuating *associations* of individuals who operate internationally for the purpose of obtaining power, influence, monetary and/or commercial gains, wholly or in part by illegal means, while protecting their activities through a pattern of corruption and/or violence" (United States Department of Justice, 2008: 2; emphasis added). Similarly, criminologist Jay Albanese also avoids the term *organization* when he defines OC as "a continuing criminal *enterprise* that rationally works to profit from illicit activities that are often in great public demand. Its continuing existence is maintained through the use of force, threats, monopoly control, and/or the corruption of public officials" (Albanese, 2015: 4; emphasis added).

CHALLENGES AND CONTROVERSIES IN DEFINING AND CONCEPTUALIZING ORGANIZED CRIME

Definitions and conceptual models of OC have evolved from those that were highly ethnocentric and formed around a well-structured organizational profile to those that recognize the alternative multi-ethnic, networked approach. It is important to acknowledge, however, that both broad depictions are equally valid, given the wide diversity of organized criminal conspiracies historically and in recent years. While the more current definitions, descriptions, and conceptual models are increasingly evidence-based, this does not mean that the more rigorous depictions of OC are without limitations. The word *organized* is central to all efforts to define and describe the reality of organized crime because by organizing themselves to commit profit-oriented crime, offenders expect that they will be maximizing revenues, while minimizing the risks of getting caught and being punished (McIntosh, 1975: 14). The organization of crime and criminals is also meant to delineate more sophisticated, complex, profit-oriented criminal behaviour from the more rudimentary types of property and interpersonal crimes. Thus, for Lyman and Potter (2014: 14), "to understand organized crime we have to get away from the view of the individual perpetrator. Organizational structure, the way in which individuals join together and coordinate their activities to engage in criminal enterprises, becomes the vital consideration."

Yet, as many have noted, the etymological problem with the term *organized crime* may be the term itself. For Lyman and Potter (2014: 6), "Perhaps the greatest problem in understanding organized crime is not with the word crime but with the word organized. In fact, although the public, criminologists, and the research literature often agree as to what constitutes criminal behavior, little agreement exists regarding what constitutes organized criminal activity." Albanese (1985: 4) agrees, writing, "there appears to be as many descriptions of organized crime as there are authors," while Savona (1999: 2) points out, "traditionally, attempts to define organized crime have caused much controversy and contention."

The problem may lie with the sheer diversity of phenomena that has been subsumed within the term *organized crime*. It has variously referred to a wide range of criminal activities (and not simply profit-oriented ones), criminal markets (illegal and legal), and societal actors (professional criminals, street gangs, terrorist groups, state actors, legitimate corporations). Empirical research reveals a complex mix of criminal offenders ranging from sophisticated "specialists" to "opportunists"—all operating in the same field (Beare, 2003a: xxii). Carrapiço (2012: 25) notes that an important part of the scientific literature "has encouraged the development of a theoretical debate on organized crime, arguing that it is necessary to clarify it conceptually and to reduce it to a more objective definition...." However, "despite efforts to narrow down the definition of TOC, we have, instead, witnessed the enlargement of the concept, which seems to be continuously enriched with new types of activities and organizational structures. The danger associated with expanding concepts lies in the possibility of over-stretching them to a point where they risk losing their meaning and coherence" (Carrapiço, 2012: 25). Making a similar point, Paoli and Vander Beken (2014: 13) contend, "Whereas the term organized crime still has strong evocative power, which undoubtedly explains its political success, the many different criminal actors and activities that have been subsumed under this label make it a vague umbrella concept that cannot be used, without specification, as a basis for empirical analyses, theory-building, or policymaking."

Beare argues that the term *organized crime* is already "overused" and "excessively broad" (2003a: xxii, xxiv). She asserts that the expansive definition put forth by the United Nations and codified in Canadian legislation may in fact be intentional for self-serving political and enforcement purposes. "The concept of organized crime has been stretched and mythologized to the point of total distortion, rendering it useless for anything but political mileage and the bargaining for resources by law enforcement bodies leading some critics to suspect that those results might have been the objective" (Beare, 2003a: xxv). Moreover, "the accepted definition includes virtually all economically motivated serious crime that is committed by more than one person. Obviously, the wider the definition, the more 'organized crime' there can be claimed to exist" (Beare, 2003a: xxiv), which in turn serves as a basis for more punitive laws and expanded law enforcement resources and powers. Law enforcement agencies have been accused of advancing specific conceptualizations of OC when it suits their needs. For Paoli and Vander Beken (2014: 17), "the myth of a powerful and centralized mafia organization representing a threat to America's political, economic, and legal systems long continued to be resorted to whenever police budgets had to be raised or new legislation increasing federal jurisdiction had to be passed." Politicians have also misrepresented and inflated the scope and threat of OC in pursuit of their own political ambitions, an accusation most famously levelled at US Senator Estes Kefauver (see the alien conspiracy theory in chapter 4). In short, OC has become a "political construct that serves a particular set of functions for the state" (Hobbs & Antonopoulos, 2014: 99).

Even intellectuals have not been spared the accusation of professional bias when weighing in on the definition of OC. For Allum and Gilmour (2012: 8–9), "Researchers are not and cannot be neutral as their opinions and preferences are constructed by their different experiences, education, disciplines and geographical location, for example." This explains why economists, political scientists, lawyers, and sociologists are all going to define organized crime differently. Albanese uses the age-old analogy of the blind men who attempt to identify an elephant, each of whom arrive at a different answer by touching different parts of the animal. Similarly, the result "of efforts to model OC invariably reflects the perspective of the investigator. Economists model it in terms of economic factors. Government investigators model OC as a hierarchical government-like enterprise. Social scientists view it as a social phenomenon. In too many cases the perceptions are based in reality, but the conclusions drawn are either inaccurate or over-generalized" (Albanese, 2015: 106).

This analogy elucidates a point made by Vander Beken (2012: 83), who writes, "organized crime is not a 'natural' crime phenomenon that can be observed, counted and classified like other crimes. More than most other types of crime, organized crime is a **social construct** that strongly reflects policy choices and beliefs." von Lampe (2016: 12) agrees that OC "is a construct, an attempt to make sense of a complex social reality." According to Carrapiço (2012: 26), OC is "not as the result of a simple observation of an independent reality but as a labelling process amounting to a political and/or moral act. It can be considered so in the sense that such labelling encompasses a political and/or moral message, regarding for instance how society should be managed, which order it should follow, what is normal and what is not, and which values should·be protected." When viewed from this perspective, the labelling of OC "as a very serious threat is directly related to the actor performing the labelling, rather than to the object being labelled" (Carrapiço, 2012: 26). Put more bluntly, Beare (2003a: xxi) states, "Discussions related to organized crime and transnational crime—about the factors leading to the creation of illegal markets, about the size of the 'threat' and about the passing of extraordinary legislation to attack the problem— are steeped in politics."

Finckenauer (2005: 68) explains why a reliance on social and political constructs of OC may be dangerous, especially in the absence of agreed-upon, rigorous, empirical research and theoretical models: "the problem of [how] organized crime is defined goes a long way toward determining how laws are framed, how investigations and prosecutions are conducted, how research studies are done, and, increasingly, how mutual legal assistance across national borders is or is not rendered." The fact that "the concept, definition and popular understanding of organized crime and, more recently, transnational organized crime has been skewed and misrepresented over and over again throughout the twentieth century" (Chambliss & Williams, 2012: 52) makes it all the more difficult to effectively combat the problem. This is particularly true when state actors in North America define OC exclusively in terms of the Italian Mafia (and ignore numerous other criminal threats, allowing them to operate and grow unfettered). Similarly, framing OC "as a common external enemy, which is endangering society and the lives of citizens, is very different from defining it as the result of individuals' local demands for illegal products/services, stemming from the core of society itself. The first one might lead to concerted responses ranging from criminalization processes to military interventions, whereas the second one would possibly result in comprehensive and tailor-made solutions, more directed at the roots of the issue rather than at the symptoms" (Carrapiço, 2012: 26–27).

Finally, it should be noted that the social construction of OC has also taken on a distinctly American flavour as definitions and conceptualizations promulgated by state actors

CRITICAL THINKING EXERCISE

Considering the Canadian definitions of OC presented in this section, as well as any others you may have identified in your own research, to what extent do you believe they have been socially constructed? To what extent have legislators and law enforcement in Canada defined OC for political purposes? Within this context, what are the pros and cons of the broad, UN-derived definition of a criminal organization that is now codified in Canada's *Criminal Code*?

in the United States have spread to other countries and international organizations—despite the fact that the nature, scope, and threat of OC varies greatly from one country to the next. As explored in more detail in chapter 13, critics charge that the Americanization of the concept of OC internationally has been part of a broader effort by the United States to export its enforcement strategies and policies to other countries. Carrapiço (2012: 24) claims this began in the early 1960s, when "the political and academic debate on organized crime" began to "spread beyond US borders and to permeate international fora such as the United Nations (UN), the G8 and the Council of Europe."

In sum, critics of how OC has been socially and politically constructed do not mean to say that this problem doesn't exist in the real world or that it does not pose particular dangers. The critiques suggest that OC is such a complex phenomenon that it is averse to concise, commonly understood definitions. And because the conceptual framing of OC has become so politicized, one may not be able to trust definitions or conceptual models put forth due to the bias or ulterior motives of those behind the definitions or models. In the absence of rigorous, agreed-upon, and empirically supported definitions, concepts, and theories of OC, powerful (state) actors may hijack the concept for their own self-serving purposes. This means the problem may not be addressed sufficiently or state actors may use extraordinary punitive measures that may result in even more damage to society than the criminal conspiracy or activity itself (for instance, see chapter 13 for a critique of the war on drugs).

COMPETING CONCEPTUALIZATIONS OF ORGANIZED CRIME

In addition to attempts to concisely define OC, scholars have also been engaged in a vigorous debate over some of its fundamental elements. In effect, these debates have contributed to the development of distinct ideas on how best to conceptualize this phenomenon. Like the various definitions that have emerged over the years, there are also numerous ways to conceptualize OC. This section summarizes some of the more significant debates, in particular those that attempt to determine if OC is best characterized as follows:

- The **organization of criminals** or the **organization of crimes**
- Highly structured criminal organizations or more loosely structured criminal networks
- A limited number of large organizations that monopolizes criminal markets and territories or many smaller groups and individual criminal entrepreneurs who compete in **disorganized illegal markets**
- A system of governance or a system of criminal activities

None of these competing positions are either completely right or completely wrong; OC is so diverse and complex that any of the above ideas are applicable in a particular historical and contemporary context.

Organization of Criminals versus Organization of Crimes

One of the more fundamental binaries through which OC has been conceptualized is (1) a set of associations or organizations in which members and associates systematically engage in crime, versus (2) a set of serious criminal activities, most of which are carried out for monetary gain. As Paoli and Vander Beken (2014: 14) put it, "some authors as well as national and international policy and law enforcement agencies have emphasized the 'Who,' that is, the individual offenders and their variable partnerships, whereas others have given more relevance to the 'What,' that is, the criminal activities conducted."

Many of the aforementioned definitions of OC focus on how criminal offenders organize themselves. According to von Lampe, (2016: 32), the concept of OC has traditionally been concerned with "the ways criminals are connected to other criminals" and "one of the main challenges in the study of OC is to sort through the myriad social relations of criminals and to understand how these relations influence and shape criminal behavior" (von Lampe, 2016: 5). Thus, when conceptualizing OC in this manner, "it is not so important what offenders do or how they do it but how offenders are linked to and associated with each other. Organized crime, then, is about some form of organization of criminals in contrast to lone, independently operating offenders" (von Lampe, 2016: 27). At the same time, von Lampe (2016: 3) writes, "Much of what is commonly associated with the term organized crime has to do with the provision of illegal goods and services." In other words,

> organized crime is primarily about crime. Many definitions in essence state that organized crime is crime. Organized crime, therefore, is seen as a specific type of criminal activity. What makes crime organized is either the nature of these activities or the criminals behind them. Criminal activities are regarded as being organized, for example, because of a certain level of sophistication, continuity, and rationality, or by a certain level of harm.

van Duyne (1996: 203) also emphasizes that OC is inherently shaped by the dynamics of criminal activities and, more specifically, illegal markets: "What is organized crime without organizing some kind of criminal trade; without selling and buying of forbidden goods and services in an organizational context? The answer is simply nothing." Paoli and Vander Beken (2014: 18) write that conceptualizing OC as a conglomerate of criminal activities has now become the *de rigueur* approach in the United States: "Organized crime has, thus, become a synonym for illegal enterprise. That is, the involvement in criminal market activities has become nowadays the basic requirement of virtually all definitions of organized crime in the US scientific and official discourse, and this view is shared by both supporters of the mafia-centered understanding of organized crime and its critics." Some believe that criminal activities and illegal markets are so central to the understanding and constitution of OC that it should be alternatively referred to as "enterprise crime" (Smith, 1975, 1980), the "organization of crime for gain" (Paoli & Vander Beken, 2014: 20) or simply "organising crime" (Block & Chambliss, 1981).

According to Paoli (2014a: 2–3), determining whether OC is conceptualized as an association of offenders or the organization of crimes is influenced by the extent to which a particular country has experienced large, powerful, structured criminal organizations: "The general public, the media, and most policy-makers primarily use the expression 'organized crime' to refer to criminal organizations, such as the Sicilian and American Cosa Nostra, the Japanese Yakuza, Colombian and Mexican drug cartels, and other large-scale criminal groups around the world thought to have a hierarchical and lasting structure. Particularly in countries with no direct experience of such large-scale crime groups, however, scholars, law enforcement officials, and some policy-makers relate OC to trafficking in illegal drugs and human beings, gambling, and the provision of other goods and services that are fully criminalized or heavily restricted."

For some, the two concepts are critically interconnected in the sense that they influence one another. In this regard, there is a key question that must be asked: Does the association of offenders influence the illegal activities they carry out or do the illegal activities carried out by a group of offenders influence how this association is structured? More broadly, Smith (1994: 121) asks, "Does an organization determine its actions, or do actions determine an organization?" In answering Smith's question, von Lampe (2016: 59–60) believes that "to a large extent, the latter is the case." Albini (1971: 49) also claims that "criminal groups are dynamic entities, not static ones," and that "they change with the nature of the criminal acts they commit." He later elaborated on this comment, writing "A growing body of evidence indicates that OC groups revolve around specific illicit activities rather than the opposite. Desirable illicit activities, made desirable due to public demand, the local market, or other opportunity factors, appear to dictate how and what type of criminal group will emerge to exploit the opportunity"

CRITICAL THINKING EXERCISE

Do you believe Paoli's argument that countries with direct experience with large criminal organizations are more apt to conceptualize OC as an association of offenders is relevant to Canada? Why or why not? Would you say that Canada has a historical tradition of well-organized illegal activities but only a relatively short history of large, hierarchical, lasting criminal organizations? Which conceptualization of OC do you believe is most applicable to Canada's history: as a set of criminal organizations or as a set of criminal activities?

(Albanese, 2015: 14–15). van Duyne (1996: 203) says criminal groups or networks are an "outcome" rather than a precondition for organized criminal activities.

In sum, the term *organized crime* has been used to simultaneously refer to both criminal activities and criminal organizations. A more in-depth discussion and analysis of how criminal offenders and criminal activities are organized is presented in part II (Organized Criminal Genres) and part III (Organized Criminal Activities), respectively.

Structured (Mafia-style) Criminal Organization versus Criminal Network

As discussed in the definitions section of this chapter, one of the debates in the study of OC is over how criminal offenders are organized. This debate pits those who view OC as made up of hierarchical organizations and those who believe that criminals are organized around a networked approach. The hierarchical model views criminal groups as highly structured and tightly controlled organizations with various levels of bosses, lieutenants, and soldiers. The network model does not view OC as a monolithic, self-contained organization but as a loosely knit, fluid association of like-minded independent **criminal entrepreneurs** and small groups, none of whom has any long-term authority over the others. (The different conceptual models on the structure of organized criminal associations are discussed in more detail in chapter 3.) Conceptual models regarding how organized criminal conspiracies are structured have important implications for the relationships among the participating offenders. The relationships within hierarchical structures are based on power (e.g., there are layers of positions, including an all-powerful boss) while in the case of networks, the relationships are more symmetrical—largely based on the expertise of or resources available to a particular participant.

Decker and Pyrooz (2014: 277) argue, "there is a major division of opinion among scholars of organized crime, with some who see organized crime groups in ways that are consistent with networking theory and others who describe them in terms consistent with hierarchical theory." Suffice to say, both conceptual models have some degree of accuracy. In historical and contemporary terms, there are examples of rationally structured hierarchical criminal organizations and there also are numerous examples of networked criminals. As Bouchard and Morselli (2014: 293) succinctly state, the degree of organization can vary greatly from one criminal conspiracy to another. Studies examining taxonomies of drug-trafficking conspiracies, for example, "described a wide-ranging spectrum of organizational complexity, from very loose and changing partnerships, to corporate-like organizational structures."

Some organized criminal conspiracies are in fact hybrids of the two structures. Italian-American Mafia families, Chinese triads, outlaw motorcycle gangs, and Colombian cocaine cartels as well as other international drug-trafficking or human-smuggling conspiracies all integrate some aspects of both the hierarchical and network models. The local chapter of an outlaw motorcycle gang, for example, has a hierarchical structure in which lower echelon members are answerable to the chapter president. At the same time, the full-patch member of a chapter will have a network of associates outside of the chapter that he works with to carry out illegal activities. Notwithstanding this hybrid model, there is a growing consensus that over the years the structure of OC has moved in the direction of a more networked approach.

Large Mafia Organizations that Monopolize Criminal Markets and Territories versus Disorganized Illegal Markets with Numerous Small Operators

The debate over how criminal offenders are structured as part of an organized criminal conspiracy is often accompanied by a related question: Is OC characterized by large highly organized, Mafia-style criminal organizations that dominate and even monopolize illegal markets or specific territories, or are illegal markets and territories disorganized in that they are made up of a number of individual criminal entrepreneurs and small groups competing against one another (and sometimes co-operating) for market share? There are two overlapping components to this debate: one is about how large and well organized an association of criminal offenders is while the other is about how organized or disorganized criminal markets are. The two components are interconnected in that if one believes OC is made up of large well-organized groups, then presumably they tend to dominate or monopolize illegal markets or territories. Conversely, if OC is made up of smaller, less organized groups, then illegal markets are more disorganized (i.e., more competitive).

Some of the earliest and most powerful ideas around OC in America were that illegal markets were monopolized by criminal organizations, and Italian Mafia groups in particular. As Paoli and Vander Beken (2014: 14) put it, "from the 1950s onward, in fact, the assumption spread in the United States that criminal organizations were responsible for most serious criminal activities for gain." Inherent in this view are the following assumptions: (1) large criminal organizations maintain a criminal monopoly in the marketplace, and (2) these conspiracies are controlled by bosses at the top of a criminal hierarchy, with a chain of command through which orders related to specific criminal tasks are passed down to the low-level soldiers (Lyman & Potter, 2014: 72).

Subsequent research has shown this argument to be largely false, in both historical and contemporary terms, in North America. While there have been large, hierarchical criminal groups, most illegal markets are made up of a number of smaller fleeting groups with little organizational profile. The turning point in this debate can be attributed to Peter Reuter's 1983 book *Disorganized Crime*. In his study of illegal gambling and loan-sharking in New York City, Reuter found that both illicit industries were populated by small operators with little or no organization. In other words, no one group—including none of the city's major Mafia families—monopolized these markets or exercised any significant control over independent gambling operators or loansharks. His research found each of these industries to be fragmented and highly competitive. Reuter concluded that because criminal entrepreneurs are always at risk of police enforcement and cannot seek the assistance of the courts in enforcing contracts, illegal markets tend to be populated "by localized, fragmented, ephemeral, and undiversified enterprises" (Reuter, 1983: 131).

Lyman and Potter (2014: 55) elaborate on the practical reasons why small groups are the norm in most illegal markets: "small size and segmentation reduce the chances that the enterprise will be caught and members prosecuted. Because employees in illicit industries are the greatest threat to these operations and make the best witnesses against them, organized crime groups must limit the number of people who have knowledge of the groups' operations." Moreover, because all criminal enterprises operate in uncertain, unstable, and relatively hostile environments (as a function of their illegality), they are more likely to remain small in size, flexible, loosely structured. They will also have little organizational complexity or formality (i.e., formal rules, procedures, chains of command) (Bouchard & Morselli, 2014; Lyman & Potter, 2014). As a result of all of the above factors, "It follows that the larger the organization, the more vulnerable it is to infiltration by law enforcement" (Bouchard & Morselli, 2014: 289). In short, "'Small is beautiful' appears to be the norm by which illegal entrepreneurs operate their businesses. Small groups are considered to be safer, easier, and more efficient than larger organizations" (Bouchard & Morselli, 2014: 289).

Research in the United States, Canada, and other countries has corroborated how illegal markets and organized criminal activities tend to be characterized by small groups competing against one another. Bouchard and Morselli (2014: 288) allude to "how researchers have often referred to the mass of small and ephemeral groups that form in any given criminal market as opportunistic operators and less organized (or disorganized) forms of criminal operations." Similar findings were made in more recent studies of domestic drug markets, including those in Canada. Research by DesRoches (2005) concerning convicted drug traffickers who operated at the wholesale level concluded that the illicit drug trade in Canada, with the exception of a few large groups such as outlaw motorcycle gangs, is characterized by open competition among a large number of small criminal networks. Based on a sample of imprisoned drug traffickers in Quebec, Bouchard (2006) found that 60 percent were active in organizations of less than 10 members, while only 13.7 percent had more than 20 members (as cited in Bouchard & Morselli, 2014: 292).

The frequency of small group operators even extends into transnational criminal activities, such as drug trafficking, which most experts believe are characterized by a

CRITICAL THINKING EXERCISE

Read through the subsequent chapters of this textbook that deal with case studies of organized crime in Canada and identify examples where criminal organizations attempted to dominate or monopolize a particular illegal market or territory in Canada. Were they successful? If so, why? If not, why not? Also identify current and historical examples of illegal markets that are highly competitive.

network of small autonomous operators responsible for separate functions in the international chain. As Lyman and Potter (2014: 55) write, in international drug trafficking, "the production, importation, distribution, and retail activities are kept as discrete functions, often performed by completely different organized crime groups, most of which are both temporary and small." Indeed, OC has increasingly been characterized by the network structure due to small group specialization in distinct functions. "Rather than global Mafias, this international trade has stimulated small, flexible, discrete networks. This makes perfect sense. First, smaller networks enhance profitability by reducing production and corruption costs. Second, smaller networks better control the flow of information about what a criminal group is doing and how it is doing it, reducing the risk of law enforcement interference in the daily business of organized crime" (Lyman & Potter, 2014: 14). Justifying this argument, van Dijk and Spapens (2014: 215) point to how "the notoriously powerful Cali and Medellin cartels have since long been disbanded and superseded by hundreds of smaller, more flexible, and more sophisticated cocaine-trafficking organizations."

This growing conceptualization of (transnational) organized crime "has been highly influential, sometimes to the point that it seems to have been misconstrued to represent a natural law according to which large, complex criminal organizations do not and cannot exist" (von Lampe, 2016: 45–46). Lyman and Potter (2014: 13) appear to agree with this "natural law" when they write, "In moving toward this newer conceptualization, we recognize the fact that the older traditional forms of organized crime, such as Mafia-type organizations, if they ever existed, are now an endangered species, no longer useful in a globalized world economy. Just like legitimate corporations, organized crime groups today are actually loose networks of entrepreneurs." Bouchard and Morselli (2014: 293) cite examples of a "few studies" of street gangs, outlaw motorcycle gangs, and Mafia groups that "certainly confirm that organizations that are larger than usual exist in almost every setting. However, they remain the exception rather than the rule, and they rarely manage to dominate an illegal market, except on a limited territorial base." In fact, research shows that most serious, profit-oriented crime is not carried out by well-organized criminal groups nor do Mafia-style criminal organizations monopolize a particular market of illegal goods or services with a particular territory. "Empirical evidence is substantial that opportunistic and small criminal groups are the predominant form of operating unit in organized crime" (Bouchard & Morselli, 2014: 290).

Organized Crime as a System of Governance versus Organized Crime as Criminal Activities

Popular notions of OC as an association of criminals or as a set of serious criminal activities are joined by a third conceptualization that emphasizes governance and power over people. According to von Lampe (2016: 27), "there is a view that organized crime does not have to do primarily with specific forms of criminal activities or specific forms of criminal organization but with the concentration of illegitimate power in the hands of criminals."

> This third basic dimension of the study of organized crime, illegal governance, has to do with the amassing and use of power in a way that is more akin to government and politics than to market-based or predatory crime. There are two spheres of society where the power amassed and exercised by criminals may come to bear: underworld and upperworld. In the underworld, that sphere of society where the state has no ambition to regulate behavior other than to suppress it because it is illegal, forms of self-regulation may develop that can take on the form of an underworld government. Individuals or groups may emerge that, as indicated before, set and enforce rules of conduct and settle disputes among criminals and in turn demand a share of illegal profits. Such influence can also extend into the legal spheres of society, especially where the state is weak. This typically occurs in the form of an alliance of criminal, business, and political elites. The overriding question in both cases is how it is possible that crime, the quintessential violation of commonly shared norms and values, can create order, sometimes even enjoying a high degree of legitimacy, as ethically twisted as this order may be. (von Lampe, 2016: 32)

In short, "In one scenario, criminals create an underworld government that controls, regulates, and taxes illegal activities. In another scenario, criminals gain influence in legitimate society by either replacing legitimate government or by entering into alliances with corrupt members of political and business elites for the purpose of manipulating the constitutional order in their favor" (von Lampe, 2016: 27–28). The first scenario is grounded in theories and empirical evidence regarding how criminal groups and powerful criminal offenders, such as the Italian Mafiosi, present themselves as a patron to and even an alternative underworld government for their "clients." These clients may include other criminals (who are looking for help in brokering an illegal transaction) or more "legitimate" citizens who cannot or will not turn to the government or police for help (e.g., immigrants to North America who may be suspicious

CRITICAL THINKING EXERCISE

Analyze whether this view of OC as a form of underground governance applies to any of the Canadian Mafia groups and leaders discussed in chapter 5. To what extent did these leaders view themselves as some form of underground government? To what extent does this fit into their own view of the role of the Mafiosi in society? How did this view embolden their efforts to carry out protection schemes and extortion?

of government). When providing such services, the Mafiosi often demand a monetary payment, which essentially functions as a tax.

As von Lampe articulates, the influence of OC in governance and the corridors of power also extends into the legitimate spheres of society (the "upperworld"). This typically occurs when individual criminal entrepreneurs or groups establish some form of connection or alliance with state actors, such as politicians. To some extent, von Lampe is describing how OC uses the tool of corruption to amass power. However, this portrayal of OC transcends the mere bribing of public officials and extends into a type of co-governance where the criminal gang exercises power in the legitimate world of politics through the influence that this corruption brings.

DIFFERENTIATING ORGANIZED CRIME FROM OTHER CRIMINAL CONSPIRACIES

One way to understand OC conceptually is to differentiate it from "disorganized" crime. OC should also be distinguished from other types of criminality, which may have confusingly similar titles (such as "organizational crime") or which may share some of the central tenets of OC, such as ongoing conspiracies involving multiple individuals (e.g., street gangs or terrorist groups). This section compares OC with "disorganized crime," street gangs, white-collar crime, corporate crime, state crime, and terrorism. One of the goals of this section is to determine if other forms of organizational crime should fall under the conceptual and legal rubric of OC. The implications of including these various categories of criminality under the rubric of OC are not just conceptual; it could have significant legal implications as well. Prosecuting street gang members or the executives of a felonious corporation under organized crime legislation would mean the offenders could be charged with criminal offences that carry very punitive penalties.

Organized versus Disorganized Crime

Organized crime should not be defined strictly by the type of illegal activities that is carried out, for many of these criminal activities can also be carried out by offenders working alone or in small groups. Instead, OC can best be characterized by *how* illegal activities are carried out. As Albanese (2015: 61) succinctly puts it, "The act of preparing or organizing to commit crimes is what distinguishes organized crime from most street crimes." More specifically, according to von Lampe (2016: 31), organized crimes are "committed on a continuous basis involving planning and preparation as opposed to impulsive, spur-of-the moment criminal acts. Organized can also mean that a crime is not a simple, one-dimensional act, like the snatching of a purse, but an endeavor that requires the coordinated completion of interlocking tasks."

In contrast, "disorganized" or "unorganized" crime can be characterized as crimes carried out by individuals working alone or in small loosely knit groups. These crimes can range from the rudimentary (e.g., shoplifting) to the serious (e.g., sexual assault) and can include both predatory crimes (e.g., burglaries) and consensual crimes (e.g., small-time, retail drug trafficking or prostitution). Disorganized and organized crimes can be placed on opposite ends of a continuum; at one extreme are "spontaneous, impulsive, isolated acts," while on the other end are "criminal endeavors that follow a rational plan, involve the combination of different tasks, and extend over long periods of time" (von Lampe, 2016: 31). This is not to say that OC syndicates or their individual participants do not act impulsively, irrationally, opportunistically, or haphazardly. On the whole, however, the very nature of some organized criminal activities requires planning, coordination, sophistication, and rationality.

Organized Crime versus Youth/Street Gangs

There are theoretical and empirical grounds to characterize street gangs as OC. This is especially true if OC is conceptualized as a continuum that ranges from localized, rudimentary gangs all the way to highly sophisticated transnational criminal syndicates. **Youth or street gangs** incorporate some of the fundamental tenets of OC: two or more people involved; a structure to the relationships between the individuals; and a continuing enterprise that engages in (multiple) criminal activities, including profit-oriented ones. The "instrumental-rational perspective" of gangs, as described by Decker and Curry (2000: 474), holds that gangs "have a vertical structure, enforce discipline among their members, and are quite successful in defining and achieving group values." Other indicators of "an instrumental-rational gang include age-graded levels of membership, leadership roles, regularly attended meetings, coordinated drug sales, written rules and codes of conduct, expansion in legitimate business operations, and ties and influence in the political process" (Decker & Pyrooz, 2014: 274). Because some street gangs are more organized than others, Decker and Pyrooz (2014: 275) suggest that is "useful to conceptualize gangs along a normal distribution of organization, with informal-diffuse at one end and instrumental-rational at the other." There is evidence that some street gangs have evolved into well-organized, fairly sophisticated, and widespread entities that are no longer confined to a particular city, let alone a particular neighbourhood. Although if "a gang becomes so organized and institutionalized" it stops being a street gang and "enters into the definitional parameters of an 'organized crime group'" (Decker & Pyrooz, 2014: 275). Even if this is the case, street gangs may retain some of their initial characteristics, including a grounding in a certain neighbourhood, which may lead to the use of the hybrid term *organized street gang*.

Howell (2007: 40–41) dispels the "instrumental-rational perspective" of street gangs (the "myth of the formal organization"), which claims that American street gangs are becoming large, powerful criminal organizations, arguing that very few youth or street gangs in America meet the essential criteria for classification as OC. The contrary "informal-diffuse perspective" holds that gangs "are diffuse, self-interested and self-motivated aggregations of individuals, most of whom sell drugs for themselves" (Decker & Curry, 2000: 474). Street gangs can be distinguished from OC in numerous ways. First, they are generally confined to adolescents and young adults, while most OC groups or networks are made up of adults, some of who are older and are career criminals. Second, the illegal activities of street gangs are not simply or exclusively profit-oriented in nature; youth gang activity may revolve around nuisance crimes such as vandalism. Gangs are said to be less about making money and doing crime, and more about fulfilling "a variety of symbolic functions, such as friendship, revenge, and peer affiliation, that are largely independent of instrumental concerns such as making money" (Decker & Pyrooz, 2014: 275). Street gangs and their activities are confined to a well-defined area, such as a neighbourhood, which contrasts with OC syndicates, which may be multi-jurisdictional, national, and international in scope. For Decker & Pyrooz (2014: 282), by their very nature gangs are oriented to the street, which means their criminal activities tend to be limited to such crimes as car theft, robberies, assaults, and retail drug sales. These street crimes, not to mention "the expressive motivation of much gang crime—retaliation, marking territory,

Case Study: Organized Street Gangs and Human Trafficking in Canada

In July 2014, 11 people were charged in connection with an alleged human trafficking and prostitution ring that stretched from Toronto to Montreal. According to police, teen girls were forced to work as prostitutes out of hotels and motels in the Greater Toronto Area and Montreal by associates of the Galloway Boys gang, which is based in Scarborough, a suburb of Toronto. Victims were typically recruited in their neighbourhood, police allege. Each person arrested as part of Project Dove faced multiple charges, including trafficking of a person under the age of 18 and living on the avails of juvenile prostitution (*Scarborough Mirror*, July 7, 2014). In October of the same year, police in Ontario reported that another organized street gang—North Preston's Finest, which is based out of Nova Scotia—was actively recruiting girls and women from the Maritimes and forcing them into a life of prostitution in Toronto and other cities across Canada. According to the CBC, "The notorious gang, with roots in the small Nova Scotia community of North Preston, northeast of Halifax, was first identified by police in Toronto in the early 1990s. A spokesperson for the York Regional Police, which is responsible for policing Scarborough, said it's common to encounter pimps as from North Preston as well as sex trade workers who have been transported from the Maritimes to the GTA" (CBC News, October 8, 2014).

expressing dominance," not only sets them apart from OC but also contributes to a visible and public "brand" that more sophisticated, professional criminals try to avoid (except for outlaw motorcycle gangs). OC groups are about making a profit, not making a statement. "It is quite difficult to imagine a transnational organized crime group identifying its crimes in the way that street gangs 'brand' their activities" (Decker & Pyrooz, 2014: 282). In sum, Decker and Pyrooz (2014: 277) list four broad areas that distinguish gangs from other forms of criminal associations:

> These include: (1) differences in goals, with symbolic ends as opposed to economic ends, being more important to street gangs, (2) organizational structure that is looser, reflecting the age structure of gangs, (3) fluctuating levels of cooperation, leadership, and structure in sporadic profit-making activities in contrast to OC groups, terrorists, and smugglers, where the constant presence of profit making leads to as much organization as is necessary to complete the crime without cueing law enforcement, and (4) the importance of a particular turf, territory, or place to gangs.

Organized Crime versus Elite Crime

Conspicuously absent from traditional narratives of OC is **elite crime**—crimes carried out by affluent and powerful individuals in society, such as lawyers, politicians, and corporate directors and executives, among others. History is replete with examples of individuals who have used their professions, and to some extent their social status, to orchestrate well-organized serious crimes, some of which have brought lucrative monetary and political benefits to them while inflicting considerable harm on many unsuspecting victims (shareholders, consumers, taxpayers, government, the environment). In this sense, most elite crime is predatory in that there usually is a victim involved.

Exclusion of these "elite" white-collar, corporate, and state criminals from the rubric of OC is criticized for the following reasons. First, their crimes have many of the hallmarks of OC (multiple offenders, serious profit-oriented offences, organizational continuity, etc.). Second, corporations and state actors have become involved in offences traditionally associated with OC (smuggling, corruption, fraud, theft, counterfeiting, money laundering, tax evasion, and even drug trafficking in the case of some pharmaceutical companies). Third, the crimes undertaken by elite actors, in particular corporations and the state, can inflict a great deal of harm on society as a whole—and may inflict an even far greater harm than traditional organized criminal activities. Fourth, the impact of predatory crimes committed by powerful individuals and entities goes beyond the immediate and direct harms it inflicts on societies. As Hammer (1975: 3) writes, the tone for organized and white-collar criminality within a society "is inevitably set by those at the top." Corrupt politicians and corporate criminals send the message that on the way to accumulating wealth, power, and affluence, the end justifies the means. Finally, corporate and state actors have long been implicated, and even been willing participants, in criminal schemes involving traditional organized crime groups. As Woodiwiss (2003: 15) succinctly states, history shows that "Politicians, public officials, professionals, and other representatives of the 'respectable' classes were clearly part of the problem of organized crime, not passive victims or tools of distinct gangster-dominated entities." The following sections compare OC with forms of elite crime, which raises the question: Should crimes committed by corporate and state elite be considered organized crimes? In Canadian legal terms, the answer would be no. To be designated a criminal organization in Canada, Section 467.1(1) of the *Criminal Code* specifies that the individuals or entity in question must be involved in serious criminal offences as one of its "main purposes or main activities." This emphasis would delineate criminal organizations from corporations, state agencies, fraternal groups, or other entities that may engage in crime as a deviation from or a small part of their normal activities.

Organized Crime versus White-Collar Crime

The term **white-collar crime** is attributed to the criminologist Edwin H. Sutherland, who defined it as "a crime committed by a person of respectability and high social status in the course of his occupation" (Sutherland, 1949: 9). Sutherland viewed white-collar crime as a crime committed as part of the offender's usual commercial or professional responsibilities. Within this context, white-collar crime encompasses the embezzlement and misapplication of funds, fraud, stock market manipulation, and bribery, to name just a few.

When the term *white-collar crime* is restricted to Sutherland's narrow application, one can clearly differentiate it from OC because the former is carried out by legitimate business people, professionals, or government officials, and not by career criminals. Today, the term is defined more broadly, referring to financially motivated, non-violent crimes that involve the theft of money through fraud and misrepresentation (i.e., the betrayal of the victim's trust). Thus, modern white-collar crimes include various types of consumer and investor fraud, insider trading, embezzlement, copyright infringement, identity theft, forgery, and even cybercrime. At the same time, this broader definition means that white-collar crime is no longer viewed as the exclusive purview of people who occupy "high social status" and/or who commit such financial crimes in the course of their occupation. Indeed, non-violent, white-collar crimes are committed by a range of occasional and career offenders, including those who are not part of the economic elite.

Perhaps the qualities of white-collar crime that best distinguish it from OC are that the former can be carried out by individuals acting alone and generally does not rely on violence. Yet, there is considerable overlap between white-collar crime and OC because criminal syndicates have long been involved in various forms of fraud, stock market manipulation, cybercrime, copyright infringement, counterfeiting, and money laundering, to name a few. For some, the distinction between white-collar crime and OC is an arbitrary one when it comes to fraud and other types of non-violent, financially motivated crimes. As one criminologist put it, "organized crime in business is usually referred to as white collar crime, except when committed by racketeers who enter into business, in which case it is called organized crime, even though the criminal acts may be identical" (Maltz, 1976: 340).

Organized Crime versus Corporate Crime

John Braithwaite coined the term *organizational crime*, which includes crimes committed by corporations, governments, and other organizations during the course of their legitimate activities (Braithwaite, 1989). While some may want to cast chronically malfeasant corporations as OC, the main argument against doing so is that most **corporate crime** is a deviation from the legitimate and legal commercial activities of a company. Another difference is how the state responds to corporate crime, relative to street crime or OC. von Lampe (2016: 234) writes that "corporate and other elite offenders are less likely to be investigated and apprehended. And if they are brought to justice, sanctions tend to be less severe. In fact, it may be the case that fines are set so low that corporate crimes remain profitable even if they are detected." Beare (2003b: 184) speculates that one reason corporations typically do not qualify as organized criminals is "that they have the financial backing to sue anyone who would try to extend a definition of serious, continuous, organized criminal activity to include their corporate business policies." Corporations can also count on powerful politicians to protect them from criminal prosecution or lawsuits (politicians who coincidentally accept campaign donations from the same corporations).

With that said, distinctions between OC and corporate crime have become blurred. While criminal groups are involved in white-collar crime, legitimate companies have also been implicated in serious crimes that have led to the widespread victimization of consumers, investors, and society at large through the use of deception, fraud, misrepresentation, and even intimidation. Some of America's original business tycoons, such as John Jacob Astor, Leland Stanford, John D. Rockefeller, Cornelius Vanderbilt, and J. Pierpont Morgan, have been referred to as "robber barons" because they amassed their fortunes by monopolizing such essential industries as oil, railroads, liquor, cotton, and other textiles in the early period of American capitalism. They also were known to have liberally used intimidation, price-fixing, collusion, violence, bribery, fraud, and smuggling to accumulate their unprecedented wealth (Abadinsky, 2013).

The construction of the railway system in Canada during the latter half of the nineteenth century was a magnet for powerful and dishonest businessmen who manipulated stock prices, swindled settlers out of their land, and offered bribes for government contracts. On the receiving end of the bribes were politicians, some of whom were in a gross conflict of interest as they sat on parliamentary committees that awarded contracts to firms in which they had a financial interest. During the early part of the twentieth century, pharmaceutical producers and distributors in Europe, America, and Canada regularly diverted legal drugs like morphine to the black market. During the era of Prohibition, giant liquor producers in Canada sold huge quantities of liquor to smugglers and gangsters.

In later years, research and federal investigations in the United States revealed that automobile manufacturers knowingly refused to reveal or even repair dangerous car defects despite their knowledge of resulting deaths, while tobacco and firearm manufacturers hid research that clearly indicated the widespread number of deaths that resulted from their products. In part, these cases led the National Advisory Committee on Criminal Justice Standards and Goals to remark in its 1976 *Report of the Task Force on Organized Crime* that "the perpetrators of organized crime may include corrupt business executives, members of the professions, public officials, or members of any other occupational group, in addition to the conventional racketeer element" (p. 213). Tobacco companies in North America have also been implicated in numerous illegal schemes that diverted legal products to the black market.

In more recent years, many of the world's largest banks and investment firms have engaged in one or more business practices that have breached criminal and even national security laws. These offences include the laundering billions of dollars of drug money, facilitating tax evasion by clients, misleading marketing of financial products, and conspiring to manipulate foreign currency exchange rates. The world's largest financial institutions were overwhelmingly responsible for the 2008 financial crisis, which causes a global recession, due to their excessive risk taking, reckless and predatory lending practices, and marketing of toxic products, often through fraud and misrepresentation (Schneider, 2015a, 2015b).

In sum, a particularly contentious issue in the study of criminology is the extent to which corporations should be labelled as organized crime when they are involved in perpetuating serious criminal acts on an ongoing basis. Conceptually, at least, one must make the distinction between organizations that form expressly to commit illegal offences (organized crime) from organizations that are formed for legitimate business purposes and commit illegal acts as an aberration from their legitimate business. However, once the law-breaking occurs, some argue it is "difficult to draw any clear lines between

CRITICAL THINKING EXERCISE

Do you believe there are forms of corporate crime that should be classified and prosecuted as organized crime? Research specific cases of corporate crime in Canada and identify any traits that you think are characteristic of organized crime. Do you believe that corporate executives should be charged with criminal organization offences?

Case Study: Involvement of Tobacco Companies in Cigarette Smuggling

In the early to mid-1990s, Canada was in the midst of perhaps its worst experience with tobacco smuggling from the United States due to a substantial increase in Canadian taxes on cigarettes (although no taxes were applied to exported cigarettes). One man who profited greatly from the contraband tobacco trade was Larry Miller, an American businessman from Las Vegas. Through a company called LBL Importing Ltd., cigarettes were imported into the United States from Canada tax-free and then smuggled back across the border through the Akwesasne reserve. At the height of his smuggling operation in 1995, Miller had an average of 26 tractor-trailers packed with contraband cigarettes crossing the border every day. Most of the smokes imported by LBL were the popular Canadian brand Export "A," which was produced by RJR-MacDonald, of Canada, a subsidiary of RJR Reynolds based in Winston-Salem, North Carolina. Police later learned that the management of the parent company and its Canadian subsidiary conspired with the Miller organization.

A subsidiary of RJR-MacDonald, called Northern Brands International, was incorporated, and Leslie Thompson, a director of Canadian sales for RJR, was appointed to work with Miller to export the tax-free cigarettes to the United States and then smuggle them back to Canada. Northern Brands sold tax-free Export "A" to LBL and another Miller-connected company. Canadian and American customs authorities were told that the cigarettes would be stored in bonded warehouses on the American side of the Akwesasne reserve and then legally transported to Estonia and Russia. Instead, they were smuggled into Canada.

During its first year in business, Northern Brands was earning an average weekly profit of US $1.3 million, making it the single most lucrative unit of RJR Reynolds. Les Thompson later claimed in an interview on the CBS news program *60 Minutes* that more than five billion cigarettes from RJR-MacDonald and its new subsidiary were smuggled into Canada every year, and at one point, 60 percent of RJR's business in Canada was from the sale of contraband cigarettes. Thompson said executives at RJR Reynolds appointed him to oversee the smuggling scheme and were well aware of the illegal operation.

In December 1999, Miller was sentenced in a US court to 12.5 years in prison and agreed to forfeit to the government up to $160 million in personal assets. Also sentenced that month was Leslie Thompson who received five years and was fined $20,000. In December 1998, Northern Brands International Inc. pleaded guilty to conspiracy offences in the United States and was fined $15 million. In February 2003, the RCMP laid six counts of fraud and one count of conspiracy against JTI-MacDonald (the subsidiary of Japan Tobacco Inc. that had purchased RJR-MacDonald in 1999) and eight of its former executives. By 2006, one former vice-president of sales for RJR-MacDonald from the early 1990s was convicted and sentenced to eight months of house arrest resulting from the RCMP investigation. In the summer of 2008, the tobacco companies pleaded guilty to federal charges and were forced to pay $1.5 billion in criminal fines and civil penalties. This followed repeated unsuccessful attempts by the Canadian government to sue the US-based tobacco companies under the *Racketeer Influenced Corruption Organizations Act*, American legislation typically used to combat organized crime (Schneider, 2016: 364–65).

legitimate and illegitimate businesses or markets," given "they all seek to enhance profits by breaking, neglecting or avoiding the law" (Croall, 2010: 679). von Lampe (2016: 232) adds, "Corporate crime does not fit the stereotypical imagery of organized crime. Accordingly, the two tend to be treated as separate phenomena. Upon closer inspection, however, this distinction is rather artificial." In regard to the aforementioned tobacco smuggling case study, Beare (2003b: 201) says it is "tempting to view the alleged corporate criminals in these criminal processes as somehow still 'outside' organized crime— useful to organized crime but 'different' from it. However, the conduct that has been alleged, if proven in court, is organized crime activity."

Perhaps one of the most striking similarities between corporate and organized crime, according to von Lampe (2016: 233), "is that criminal activities and criminal structures can be found to be embedded in a subculture conducive to crime. Corporate crime has been attributed to the organizational culture of specific companies and more broadly to 'deviant subcultures' that encompass business sectors and the entire capitalist market system. Research has found a cultural environment within companies that is fostered by the top management and which induces unethical and criminal behavior by employees ... These criminogenic cultures, in turn, are seen to be embedded in a broader cultural environment in which ruthless profit seeking, even if it involves law breaking, is condoned."

Organized Crime versus State Crime

Williams (2010a) defines **state crime** as "a state organised act or failure to act that breaks either the internal criminal laws or public international laws or is a form of organised deviance (by omission or commission) involving the violation of human rights or the destruction either of the interests of peoples or of their economies." Chambliss (1989: 184) defines *state crime* simply as "acts defined by law as criminal and committed by state officials in pursuit of their jobs as representatives of the state."

State actors include elected and appointed officials, civil servants, and the institutions and agencies comprising the apparatus of the state and its governments (Ross, 2000). The types of crimes carried out by state actors are varied and can include human rights abuses, illegal violence (by the military or police, including kidnapping, torture, and genocide), tax evasion by politicians, electoral fraud, unlawful surveillance, espionage against foreign states and corporations (including state-sponsored cybercrime), overthrowing of elected leaders, and illegal invasion or annexation of other countries. This section focuses primarily on criminal activities carried out by state actors that result in some kind of financial benefit to them. This focus will facilitate a direct comparison

---

Case Study: State Crime as Organized Crime in Canada

Compared to other countries, state actors in Canada have traditionally been less corrupt, at least according to international comparative corruption indexes (Transparency International website, n.d.). This is not to say that there have not been historical or contemporary instances of state crime in this country. Some of the earliest crimes sanctioned by the state took place while the country was still a colony of Great Britain. This is particularly true if privateers—mercenaries licensed by the sovereign or government to steal from the merchant ships of Britain's war-time enemies—can be considered criminal.

One of the first major corruption scandals that emerged in Canada following confederation involved the first prime minister, Sir John A. MacDonald, and centred on the construction of the Canadian Pacific Railway. Opposition politicians and newspapers uncovered evidence that Sir Hugh Allan, a prominent railway baron and shipping magnate, had channelled $350,000 to Macdonald and his Conservative party right before the 1872 election. In return, Allan's consortium

Photo 2.3: The building of the Canadian Pacific Railway in the late nineteenth century was engulfed in controversy due to allegations of political corruption

Source: Thomas Hill, via Wikimedia Commons

was promised the contract to build the railway. Few believed the prime minister's protestations that the political donations and the awarding of the contract were unrelated, and MacDonald was censured by a parliamentary commission.

Because smuggling into and out of Canada has been so historically rampant, there are a litany of cases where border officials and other law enforcement officers have been caught and charged with taking bribes. This corruption reached its apogee during the era of Prohibition when massive amounts of liquor was smuggled out of Canada into the United States. Corruption within the Canadian Department of Customs and Excise was so endemic that a Royal Commission was convened in 1926. In fact, the entity that benefited financially the most from Prohibition in America was the Canadian government, which made billions of dollars in revenue from liquor excise taxes (Schneider, 2016: 216–19).

During the 1920s and 1930s, corruption was also prevalent within municipal police departments and governments. Many purveyors of gambling dens, bookmaking operations, or bawdy houses were protected by municipal police agencies and politicians, sometimes in return for generous compensation. Prostitution and gambling were often viewed as harmless vices by police and politicians; as such, they could rationalize taking a bribe. Beginning in the 1930s, criminal offenders were often recruited by political parties to help rig elections, which usually meant intimidating voters or stuffing ballot boxes (Schneider, 2016: chapter 4).

Perhaps the most high-profile instance of "state organized crime" in Canada in recent years occurred in Quebec when it was discovered that the tendering of public construction contracts in Montreal was rigged through a collusion of a consortium of construction firms, municipal government officials, municipal political parties, and the Rizzuto Mafia family. Two of the highest profile individuals implicated in this corruption saga were mayors of Montreal, both of whom were accused of financially benefiting from the rigged bids. More significantly, in 2013, Gilles Vaillancourt, the mayor of the Montreal suburb of Laval, was arrested and charged by police with 12 counts of conspiracy, fraud, breach of trust, and participating in a criminal organization, all *Criminal Code* offences. He was arrested along with other senior bureaucrats after being accused of accepting bribes and kickbacks from a number of construction firms in exchange for public contracts. Police said Vaillancourt warranted the criminal organization charges because he was running an organized network of corruption and collusion in the acquisition of municipal contracts in Laval. In 2015, Vaillancourt's lawyers said that he would not contest the criminal organization charges laid against him (*Montreal Gazette*, October 15, 2015; *La Presse*, August 19, 2015; *Toronto Star*, May 9, 2013).

CRITICAL THINKING EXERCISE

Research the case of Gilles Vaillancourt more fully, which should include examining the charges laid against him and the rationale provided by police for these charges. Do you believe that Vaillancourt deserved to be charged with participation in a criminal organization?

with OC, which in turn is meant to help determine whether state crimes can be conceptualized as organized crimes.

Perhaps the most dominant form of revenue-generating state crime is corruption in which state actors accept bribes. As Karstedt (2014: 311) notes, "economic gains are a prevalent motive in widespread corruption or in the capture of state institutions for illegal exploitation by powerful groups." While the general perception is that honest politicians and public servants are the ones corrupted by powerful groups, history is replete with examples whereby the state actor instigates the corrupt relationship. This is even the case where the corrupt relationship exists between the state actor and a criminal entity. In this relationship, the bribe is provided to the criminal offender for one of two reasons: (1) a promise of preferential treatment in a private sector or public sector transaction (e.g., guarantees they will receive a contract by the government), or (2) protection from arrest and prosecution. In sum, according to Lyman and Potter (2014: 350), "It has been common throughout the history of OC for a series of exchanges between the underworld and upperworld to develop into a long-term corrupt relationship."

Some corrupt state actors are more than the mere recipients of graft money. They can also be the actual organizers of profit-oriented organized crimes (Lyman & Potter, 2014: 350). There are plenty of historical examples of state actors, including those at the pinnacle of power, who are central organizers of criminal activities such as drug trafficking, theft, extortion, or fraud.

Arguments against classifying (some types of) state crime as OC is predicated on the same one that serves to exclude corporate crime from such a designation: unlike criminal organizations, states and governments are not wholly concerned with criminal activities, and such crimes are a deviation from their legitimate governance mandate and activities. While equating state crime with OC is open to debate, what is clear is that state crime and organized crime (not to mention corporate crime and terrorism) all have the potential to result in widespread harm. According to Karstedt (2014: 305), "given the power that the modern state is capable of exerting over its citizens (and abroad), state crimes are crimes of extraordinarily serious nature, as they have the potential of affecting large groups of victims and causing great harm in terms of life, health, and economic and social well-being." Williams (2010a: 741) concurs, writing, "Throughout

CRITICAL THINKING EXERCISE

Karstedt (2014: 303) notes that in reports on OC issued by state governments and inter-governmental agencies, including the United Nations and Europol, "the state as actor on its own account or even only as facilitator of organized crime is conspicuously absent ... To the contrary, the state is seen as a victim of organized crime with its economy, society, and even polity being affected by 'infiltration' and 'influence' from organized crime groups." What vested interest do government agencies have in excluding state crime from their reports on OC? Review the definitions on OC by government commissions and agencies documented earlier in this chapter and determine if there is any mention of state involvement in OC. Conduct your own research into government and inter-governmental reports on OC and determine the extent to which these reports provide any indication that the state may be a major organized criminal actor (or at the very least complicit in OC).

history states have committed crimes which dwarf those of 'conventional' offenders or even organised criminal groups; their actions have often been costly, exceptionally violent and destructive of both property and people."

Organized Crime versus Terrorism

The fundamental difference between OC and **terrorism** lies in the respective goals of each. The goal of OC is economic in nature, its primary purpose being the pursuit of profits. Terrorism, on the other hand, is concerned with political or social change. In this sense, one of the fundamental differences between the two is that terrorism is highly ideological in nature while OC is not. Gendron (2012: 406) discusses two other distinctions. First, "Criminal groups operate with maximum anonymity. They do not thrive upon the attention from the media craved by terrorist groups." Second, the "optimal 'business environment' objective of criminal groups is unlikely to coincide with the aims of terrorist groups. Terrorist groups seek to destroy the status quo while criminal groups seek to create a stable business environment within existing structures."

Despite these distinctions, there are some commonalities between the operational aspects of terrorist groups and OC groups. According to Gendron (2012: 406), "Both types of group operate outside the law and are willing to use violence to advance their objectives; they engage in money-laundering to move and protect illegally acquired assets; they resort to similar security methods including false documentation and counter-surveillance techniques; and the organizational structure of both is changing in ways that give individual actors more freedom to operate independently of any centralized headquarters." There is also growing evidence of an overlap or relationship between criminal organizations and terrorist groups. The relationship between OC and terrorist groups can be divided into five categories, as detailed below.

1. The flow of goods and other types of support from criminal syndicates to terrorist groups—OC syndicates have been involved in funnelling arms and other strategic materials to extremist groups. The greatest concern today is that criminal organizations are providing terrorist groups with the material to conduct biological and even nuclear warfare.

2. Protection provided by extremist groups to OC groups—South American and Asian crime groups that are involved in coca and opium production respectively have been protected by well-armed extremist groups. In return, the extremist groups take a cut of the profits of the illicit drug-trafficking trade as a protection fee.

3. The financing of extremist groups by organized criminal activities—The distinction between OC and terrorism is becoming blurred, in part because terrorist groups are heavily involved in profit-oriented criminal activities to finance their political objectives. According to a 2001 RCMP report entitled *Narcoterrorism and Canada*, the sale of illegal narcotics has long been used by OC and terrorist groups as a means of generating revenue to support armed conflict (as cited in *Vancouver Sun*, February 16, 2002). While drugs continue to be a source of revenue for extremist groups, it is now clear that a wide range of profitable criminal activities is used to fund terrorism. This includes contraband tobacco trafficking, migrant smuggling, human trafficking, counterfeiting, extortion, fraud, theft, kidnapping, and organized automobile theft (Gendron, 2012). (See chapter 8 for details on how Tamil extremist groups raised millions of dollars in Canada through extortion and other criminal activities.)

4. The use of terror tactics by OC groups—Violence and intimidation have been used by criminal groups as a means to terrorize populations and even state actors in order to undermine any opposition. In this context, Gendron (2012: 405) concludes, "Transnational criminal networks too are a potential threat to democracy and like terrorists, exploit the vulnerabilities, fears and powerlessness of others and engage in activities that are corrosive beyond the immediate damage from criminality." Drug-trafficking groups in Colombia and more recently Mexico have long used violent terrorist tactics, including mass killings of innocent civilians and state officials. In Canada, during the 1990s, the Quebec Hells Angels began a campaign to murder journalists as well as criminal justice officials as a means to intimidate them and destabilize the criminal justice system in Quebec (Sher & Marsden, 2003).

5. The transformation of political extremist groups into OC groups—Some terrorist groups are so focused on raising funds to finance their operations that a

revenue-generating orientation is no longer a means to an end, but an end in itself. In other words, their original extremist political or social goals are replaced by revenue-maximization goals. Makarenko (2012: 237) identifies "the three main catalysts that have the potential to transform a politically motivated terrorist group into one that is motivated primarily by profit maximization: the destruction of the leadership structure; political transformations 'that debunk the ideological basis of the group'; and 'opportunities for financial gain so great that they subsume ideological motives'."

The first two categories are concerned with the daunting issue of how terrorist groups and OC groups may collaborate. Makarenko (2012) concludes the relationship between transnational organized crime and terrorist groups can take several forms, which she classifies as alliances, appropriation of tactics, convergence (integration and hybrid), and transformation. Alliances are when terrorist groups actively work in conjunction with criminal groups or networks. Appropriation of tactics refers to instances when "terrorist groups appropriate (i.e., internalize) criminal operations, and criminal groups appropriate terror tactics as part of their operational strategy." Convergence refers to two scenarios: first, when a terrorist and organized group merges together (integration), and second, the merging of criminal and political goals in one group (a hybrid criminal-political entity). Transformation is when the ultimate goals and motivations of the group are changed so radically that politically oriented terrorist groups become profit-oriented criminal groups and *vice versa* (Makarenko, 2012).

THE HARMS STEMMING FROM ORGANIZED CRIME

The harms that OC inflicts on Canadian society are manifold and consequential. They include the corruption of public officials; the exploitation of women and children for illicit sex; the massive costs incurred by companies, government, and private citizens due to thefts and fraud; injuries and deaths resulting from the sale of dangerous counterfeit and contraband goods (such as knock-off prescription drugs), from arms trafficking, and from innocent bystanders getting caught in the crossfire of gangland conflicts; billions of dollars in evaded income taxes and excise taxes; not to mention the billions of dollars spent every year by governments, companies, and individuals to combat OC and to deal with its aftermath. Porteous (1998) categorizes the many harms inflicted on Canada as socio-political, economic-commercial, health and safety, violence generation, and environmental.

The human, social, and economic impact of illegal drugs alone is well documented. Illegal drug use causes crippling addictions and overdoses (including fatal ones); can lead to other severe health problems; facilitates the spread of diseases, such as hepatitis and AIDS; contributes to higher levels of property crime, retail drug trafficking, prostitution, and violent crime (committed by addicts); and disrupts personal, familial, and legitimate economic relationships. Drug trafficking and drug use can have a devastating impact on local neighbourhoods, contributing to significant decline in the local economy, health, vibrancy, and physical infrastructure. Illicit drug use in Canada results in billions of dollars in crime, health, and lost productivity costs: "The public bears much of the burden of these indirect costs because it finances the criminal justice response to drug-related crime, a public drug-treatment system, and anti-drug prevention programs" (Rhodes, Layne, & Hodik, 2000: 3).

The victims of predatory OC are deprived of their money, their security, their livelihood, and their physical and psychological well-being. Even the consumers of illegal goods and services—drug users, inveterate gamblers, illegal migrants, and recipients of high-interest loans—can be considered victims as their personal vices and addictions are exploited and exacerbated. In indirect societal terms, it is the public-at-large that is also victimized by OC as "billions of dollars of tax revenue from organized crime go uncollected," which results in higher tax rates for law-abiding citizens. Moreover, "expenses related to law enforcement, criminal prosecution, and imprisonment of convicted members create a substantial drain on the economy of any community" (Lyman & Potter, 2014: 23).

The Royal Canadian Mounted Police (2009) also illuminates the wide-ranging social (and monetary) costs of OC:

> In terms of economic-related crimes, it is estimated that organized crime costs Canadians $5 billion every year; that's $600 a year for a family of four. This amount, however, does not include costs related to the many other crimes (i.e. drugs, counterfeit goods) that organized crime groups are involved in ... Organized crime affects our basic Canadian rights to peace, order and good government. Acts of violence and intimidation in our communities, potential corruption in our political systems and government greatly diminish quality of life, compromise our personal security and disrupt our private life.

The harms inflicted by OC, relative to disorganized, street-level crimes, are considered greater due to the former's heightened level of organization (the hundreds of kilos of heroin imported by a criminal group will obviously have far greater impact on society than the grams or ounces sold by the street-level trafficker). "The distinguishing feature is that it is 'organized,'" according to Vander Beken (2012: 83), "suggesting that the threat and seriousness of the phenomenon only stem from the way that such crimes are committed." Albanese (2015: 1) agrees, writing that there is "something inherently more dangerous about crimes committed by two or more people." Apart from the level of organization, it is also the serious nature of the crimes carried out by OC that makes it such a threat to Canada and other societies. The detrimental impact of illegal drug trafficking and use on societies is well known. Other organized criminal activities—fraud, human trafficking, extortion, and violence—all exact considerable tolls as far as human suffering and economic losses are concerned. The use of corruption within public and private sector institutions also inflicts a level of harm to the functioning of a society that most rudimentary, disorganized crimes do not carry.

"As a consequence," Carrapiço (2012: 19) writes, organized crime "is no longer considered simply an economic problem; on the contrary, it is understood as having obtained the capacity to destabilize (economically, socially and politically) the countries where it operates. In other words, because it has managed to reach a level of power reserved, in the past, only for State actors, this phenomenon is currently framed as a 'threat' to the safety of citizens and to the existence of countries themselves (that is to say, as a security issue rather than a crime problem)." In contrast, some have argued that the national security threat posed by OC to countries like Canada has been over-exaggerated (van Duyne & Nelemans, 2012; Woodiwiss, 2012).

CONCLUSION

After reviewing this chapter, most readers should have a better understanding of the different ways OC has been defined and conceptualized, how it compares with other forms of criminality, and its impact on Canadian society. At the same time, readers should come away with an appreciation of how difficult it is to define, conceptualize, and distinguish this complex and mutable criminal phenomenon. Perhaps the most significant conundrum is determining exactly what constitutes OC and what does not.

Given the challenges in trying to define and conceptualize this topic and the various critiques of the term *organized crime*, more rigorous and exacting terms have been suggested. Those who focus on criminal actors use such terms as criminal entrepreneurs, racketeers, organized crime group, criminal association, criminal organization, criminal group, illegal enterprise, criminal network, continuing criminal enterprise, or Mafia. Those who emphasize criminal activities speak of organized crimes, racketeering, organizing crime, the organization of crime for gain, or profit-driven crime. There are even hybrid terms that can refer to both, such as enterprise crime, syndicated crime, or organized criminal conspiracy.

No one engaged in the study of OC should be expected to reach a definitive conclusion on its definitional and conceptual boundaries. What readers should recognize is how the challenges inherent in defining and conceptualizing OC are the result of (1) the multifaceted and complex nature of this phenomenon, and (2) how definitions are highly influenced by the perspectives, biases, and position of the individual or entity behind the definition. All of the above is applicable to the study of OC in Canada. Historically, there have been only a limited number of attempts to define or conceptualize OC in this country by state actors (including politicians and criminal justice officials). This was partially due to the refusal of many government or law enforcement officials to even acknowledge the presence of OC in this country as well as the limited community of criminology researchers in Canada. Unlike the United States, there was a hesitancy to view the Italian Mafia or any OC group as a nation-wide conspiracy in Canada, which may reflect a greater tendency by Canadian officials to avoid over-exaggerating the scope of the problem for self-serving purposes. At the same time, Canadian politicians and criminal justice officials have been criticized for not responding in a timely and forceful manner to OC, which allowed it to expand.

When Canadian politicians and criminal justice officials began to publicly acknowledge the problem of OC around the early 1960s, it was almost entirely equated with the Italian Mafia. With that said, police and media representations of drug trafficking in Canada throughout much of the twentieth century also tended to disproportionately equate organized criminality with ethnic Jewish and Chinese offenders, which was a product of stereotyping and blatant racism. A closer look at official criminal justice records and media accounts show that in both historical and contemporary times drug traffickers and other criminal entrepreneurs in Canada have been represented by an array of ethnicities and nationalities (although it is difficult to find any large organized criminal conspiracy in this country that did not somehow involve Anglo-Canadian offenders in some capacity).

Like in the United States, there was a tendency in this country to characterize the association among organized criminal offenders as a rationally constructed, hierarchical, continuous corporate-like body (especially in regards to the Italian Mafia, Chinese triads, and outlaw motorcycle gangs). Yet, perhaps even more so than the United States, a closer look at Canadian OC historically and in more recent times indicates that the structure reflects a networked approach.

By the 1980s and 1990s, official state definitions of OC began to emerge in Canada, but they were so broad that they were of no real value in fostering a better conceptual understanding of this phenomenon. In 1997, the *Criminal Code* officially adopted the UN definition of OC, which was intentionally broad to allow police and prosecutors the opportunity to case their net wide when charging offenders with criminal organization offences. However, as in the United States, there has been resistance by lawmakers to equate elite crimes—in particular, corporate and state malfeasance— with OC. This may account for why these two forms of criminality have not been an enforcement priority in this country. Today, Canadian lawmakers and criminal justice officials do not define OC much differently than the US government. This may be the direct result of pressure placed on Canada by American officials to take OC more seriously and to adopt American definitions, conceptualizations, and enforcement policies and strategies.

KEY TERMS

Corporate crime

Criminal entrepreneurs

Criminal organization

Disorganized crime

Disorganized illegal markets

Elite crime

Organization of crimes

Organization of criminals

Social construct

State crime

Terrorism

White-collar crime

Youth or street gangs

REVIEW QUESTIONS

1. What are some definitions of organized crime and how have they changed over the years?
2. What are the common characteristics of organized crime identified in the various definitions that have emerged over the years?
3. What are the challenges inherent in trying to define and characterize organized crime?
4. What are the main critiques of organized crime definitions? What does it mean when critics charge that organized crime is a "socially constructed" phenomenon?
5. What are the differences and similarities between organized crime and other forms of organizational crimes?
6. What are the harms inflicted on society by organized crime? Why is it that organized crimes are said to have a greater impact on society relative to disorganized (street) crimes?

FURTHER READINGS

Finckenauer, J.O. (2005). Problems of definition: What is organized crime? *Trends in Organized Crime*, 8(3): 63–83.

Hagan, F.E. (2006). "Organized Crime" and "organized crime": Indeterminate problems of definition, *Trends in Organized Crime*, 9(4): 127–37.

Maltz, M.D. (1994). Defining organized crime, in R.J. Kelly, L. Chin, & R. Schatzberg (Eds.), *Handbook of Organized Crime in the United States* (pp. 21–37). Westport, CT: Greenwood Press.

Varese, F. (2010). What is Organized Crime?, in F. Varese (Ed.), *Organized Crime: Critical Concepts in Criminology* (pp. 1–33). London: Routledge.

von Lampe, K. (2016). *Organized Crime: Analyzing Illegal Activities, Criminal Structures, and Extra-legal Governance*. Los Angeles: Sage.

3 DESCRIBING ORGANIZED CRIME: IDENTIFYING AND CLASSIFYING DOMINANT CHARACTERISTICS

CHAPTER OUTLINE

- Introduction: Identifying Key Characteristics of Organized Crime
- Previous Efforts to Systematically Identify the Characteristics of Organized Crime
- A Comprehensive Taxonomy of the Characteristics of an Organized Crime Conspiracy
- Conclusion

LEARNING OUTCOMES

After reading this chapter, you should have a thorough understanding of the following:

- Key characteristics of OC
- The challenges of identifying common characteristics of OC
- How an analysis of OC characteristics contributes to a better understanding of Canadian organized crime

INTRODUCTION: IDENTIFYING KEY CHARACTERISTICS OF ORGANIZED CRIME

As the previous chapter demonstrated, there is no consensus on how best to define or conceptualize OC. The myriad of definitions that have emerged over the years reveals the great challenge in trying to encapsulate the diversity and complexity of OC in a concise definition or conceptual model. As such, some have argued that a robust understanding of OC may be better achieved by systematically identifying its various characteristics. Abadinsky (2013: 2) states, "a number of attributes have been identified by law enforcement agencies and researchers as indicative of the phenomenon" of OC. He also makes the point that identifying the different traits of OC "has a practical dimension: the attributes provide a basis for determining if a particular group of criminals constitutes organized crime and, therefore, needs to be approached in a way different from the way one would approach terrorists or groups of conventional criminals or a group of persons that forms for the immediate commission of a single offense."

Some characteristics of OC are universal in the sense that most experts agree they should be present in any description or conceptual model of OC (e.g., more than two people involved, committing a serious criminal offence for profit, etc.). Other characteristics may not be universally applied to organized criminal associations (e.g., exclusive membership, is hierarchically structured, specialization, large size, etc.). Given the diversity of OC conspiracies, the discretionary characteristics exceed the universal traits.

This chapter begins by identifying previous efforts to systematically identify the characteristics of OC (including what could be considered universal traits). It then presents a comprehensive taxonomy of OC characteristics developed for this textbook. Particular emphasis is placed on identifying and examining what constitutes a criminal organization.

PREVIOUS EFFORTS TO SYSTEMATICALLY IDENTIFY THE CHARACTERISTICS OF ORGANIZED CRIME

In his textbook on organized crime, Albanese (2015) dissects definitions provided by 15 scholars over a 15-year period. Based on this review, he identifies 11 attributes of OC. Table 3.1 lists these attributes and the number of scholars who identified this trait in their definition of OC.

To elucidate its own definition (presented in the previous chapter), the European Union also identifies 11 fundamental traits of a criminal organization:

1. Collaboration of more than two people
2. Each person has own appointed tasks
3. In operation for a prolonged or indefinite period of time

4. Using some form of discipline and control
5. Suspected of the commission of serious criminal offences
6. Operating at an international level
7. Using violence or other means suitable for intimidation
8. Using commercial or business-like structures
9. Engaged in money laundering
10. Exerting influence on politics, the media, public administration, judicial authorities, or the economy
11. Determined by the pursuit of profit and/or power

What makes the European Union's taxonomy particularly useful, from both a conceptual and an operational perspective, is their caveat that not every organized criminal conspiracy encompasses all 11 of these traits. To be deemed a criminal organization for law enforcement and prosecution purposes, a criminal conspiracy need only exhibit 6 of the 11 traits. Yet, the EU also argues there are core characteristics that are present in all types of criminal organizations. Thus, among the six characteristics that must be proven to establish whether a group of offenders constitutes a criminal organization, four must constitute the following traits: (1) collaboration of more than two people, (3) in operation for a prolonged or indefinite period of time, (5) suspected of the commission of serious criminal offences, and (11) pursues profit and/or power.

Table 3.1: Attributes of Organized Crime as Identified in the Scholarly Literature

Attribute	Number of Scholars Using This Attribute in Their Definition
Organized hierarchy continuing	15
Rational profit through crime	12
Use of force or threat	11
Corruption to maintain immunity	11
Public demand for services	6
Monopoly over particular market	5
Restricted membership	3
Non-ideological	3
Specialization	3
Code of secrecy	3
Extensive planning	2

Source: Albanese, J. (2015). *Organized Crime in America*. New York: Routledge, p. 4.

Strategic **threat assessment** models have also been developed to identify and rank the attributes of different criminal organizations in order to measure and grade their potential and real impact on society. Constructing and applying numeric threat assessment models makes it possible to develop an estimate of the relative threat posed by a crime group to society, which can then be used to prioritize tactical law enforcement resources. Klerks (2000), for example, constructed a model to estimate a criminal group's threat to society at multiple levels. Using a complex scoring system, Klerks identifies 31 dimensions to define the character, threat, and impact of a particular organized crime group on society. Each of these dimensions has its own unique weight and scale, the sum of which, when compared against other groups, provides a relative threat ranking. A similar threat assessment model, entitled Project Sleipnir, has been developed by the Royal Canadian Mounted Police (2000b). This model identifies 19 attributes of a criminal organization, each of which is defined, weighted, and has a set of values that together are

Table 3.2: Criminal Organization Threat Assessment Attributes

Klerks	RCMP
Local or global	Corruption
Purposes and ambitions	Violence
Output	Infiltration
Diversity	Expertise
Sophistication	Sophistication
Innovative capacities	Subversion
Violence and deadly violence	Strategy
Intensity and variety in the use of weapons	Discipline
	Insulation
Level of finances (gross)	Intelligence gathering
Possessions (consolidated)	Multiple enterprises
Size of group	Mobility
Working with other groups	Stability
Dependence on a larger group	Scope
Political affiliations	Monopoly
Presence and influence in the "upper world"	Group cohesiveness
	Continuity
Accessibility for law enforcement	Links to other organized crime groups
Use of defensive counter-strategies	Links to criminal extremist groups
Use of offensive counter-strategies	
Dominance over non-criminals	
Access to scarce knowledge and means	

Table 3.3: Organized Crime Group Attributes

Intent	Capability
Desire	*Resources*
Discipline	Corruption
Intelligence gathering	Size of group
Deadly violence	Working with other groups
Violence	Local or global
Monopoly	Scope
	Level of finances
	Mobility
Confidence	*Knowledge*
Sophistication	Expertise
Risk attitude	Infiltration
Accessibility for law enforcement	Continuity
Strategy	Multiple enterprises
Insulation	

Source: Black, Vander Beken, & De Ruyver. (2000).

used to judge the relative threat to Canadian society posed by a specific organized crime group. Each attribute has five possible values: High, Medium, Low, Nil, or Unknown. A value is defined for each attribute (except "Unknown"). The risk and impact attributes for assessing and ranking organized crime groups developed by Klerks and Project Sleipnir are summarized in Table 3.2.

Black et al. (2000) loosely adopt the attributes of a criminal organization developed by Project Sleipnir in constructing their own four-point qualitative scale for each attribute. They divide the threats posed by criminal groups into two broad categories: intent and capability. Under these two headings, they further divide a number of attributes into four mutually exclusive categories (desire, resources, confidence, and knowledge) as shown in Table 3.3.

A COMPREHENSIVE TAXONOMY OF THE CHARACTERISTICS OF AN ORGANIZED CRIME CONSPIRACY

Building upon the OC definitions and traits identified thus far, as well as the broader literature on this subject, the remainder of this chapter presents a comprehensive taxonomy

Table 3.4: A Comprehensive Taxonomy of the Characteristics of an Organized Crime Conspiracy

Organizational	Commercial	Behavioural
1. Multiple offenders	11. Profit-oriented criminal activities	17. Chronic and serious offenders (career criminals)
2. A systematic pattern to the relationship among the offenders	12. Serious illegal acts	18. Rationality
3. Specialization/Division of labour	13. Consensual and Predatory crimes	19. Subcultural norms/ Contempt for civil society
4. Insulation against law enforcement	14. Multiple enterprises	20. Sophistication
5. Specialized channels and modes of communication	15. Monopolistic ambitions	21. Non-ideological
6. Limited or exclusive membership	16. Operational tactics that support commercial activities (corruption, violence, money laundering, etc.)	22. Rules, regulations, and codes of conduct
7. Recruitment		23. Discipline
8. Continuity/Continuing enterprise		
9. Multi-jurisdictional/ Transnational in scope		
10. Secrecy		

of an organized crime conspiracy. The traits that make up this taxonomy are summarized in Table 3.4 and detailed on the following pages. The taxonomy is meant to be flexible in its attempt to balance competing conceptualizations of OC identified in chapter 2, in particular: (1) an organization of criminals versus an organization of crimes, and (2) a well-structured (Mafia-style) criminal organization versus a loose criminal network. To this end, the term *organized crime conspiracy* as used in this taxonomy may encompass an organization, a network, or a collection of illegal activities (and uses the *Criminal Code* definition of "**conspiracy**").

This taxonomy of characteristics is meant to be the most comprehensive (yet flexible) one constructed to date. It was developed by this author for conceptual purposes,

CRITICAL THINKING EXERCISE

Scrutinize each of the characteristics and determine for yourself whether they should be part of a taxonomy on OC. Moreover, determine for yourself whether certain traits should be designated as mandatory (universal to all OC conspiracies) or as optional (may be present in only some OC conspiracies).

but also as part of his work as an expert witness in criminal court cases to determine whether defendants are part of a criminal organization. It should also be emphasized that very few (if any) criminal groups or networks in the world encompass every one of the traits listed in this taxonomy. However, as inferred by the European Union, a definition, conceptual model, or taxonomy concerning an organized crime conspiracy must include at least some core characteristics. Thus, this author has established the following parameters when using the above taxonomy to determine whether a particular group of offenders or criminal activities does constitute an OC conspiracy:

- It must satisfy at least 10 of the characteristics
- The following six characteristics are considered universal to any organized criminal conspiracy and, as such, must be present: (1) multiple offenders, (2) a systematic and purposive pattern to the relationship among the offenders, (11) the commission of profit-oriented criminal activities, (12) the commission of serious illegal acts, (16) the use of at least one tactical support activity, and (21) a non-ideological purpose.
- In addition to the six mandatory characteristics, at least one more characteristic must come from each of the three categories.

Any entity that does not meet the aforementioned criteria would not be considered an OC conspiracy based upon this conceptual model.

The development and application of this flexible taxonomy is a recognition of the complexity of OC conspiracies and how their characteristics can alter over time and vary between different conspiracies. As such, this model adheres to Albini's argument that we must view OC "on a vast continuum allowing for freedom of analyzing and defining a given particular criminal group as an entity in itself possessing a variety of characteristics, as opposed to a rigid classification based upon certain specific attributes. Viewed from this wide perspective, there are many forms which organized crime can take, with variations, of course, to be found within each form" (Albini, 1971: 37–38). In short, some OC conspiracies in Canada encompass all of the traits listed in this taxonomy, such as the Italian Mafia in Quebec, the 'Ndrangheta in Ontario, or the Hells Angels. However, most historical or contemporary organized criminal conspiracies do not encompass all of the attributes. This is why the majority of the traits listed in the taxonomy are considered as discretionary when determining whether a particular criminal conspiracy constitutes an OC conspiracy.

Organizational

This category includes traits that are concerned with the structure and organization of those involved in an OC conspiracy. As discussed in chapter 2, OC is frequently conceptualized as an "organization of criminals," which leads Albini (1971: 35) to stress that "the most primary distinguishing component of organized crime is found within the term itself, mainly, organization."

Multiple Offenders

One of the core traits of OC is that it involves multiple offenders. Generally speaking, the more people involved in a profit-oriented criminal conspiracy, the greater the requirement that these people and the activities they carry out are organized.

A Systematic Pattern to the Relationship of the Offenders

To constitute an OC conspiracy, there must not only be multiple offenders, there must also be a systematic pattern to the relationship among these offenders. For Albini, a key characteristic of the organizational nature of OC is "interaction" among participants. Yet, "a mere aggregation of individuals performing a criminal act in the presence of one another would not, in itself, constitute an organized act" (Albini, 1971: 35). In other words, this pattern of relationships (i.e., interaction among offenders) must have some structure that is deliberately and functionally purposive for the offences being carried out and/or the broader goals of the criminal conspiracy. This systematic pattern of relationships separates OC from other forms of collective (but disorganized) criminal action, such as riotous mobs or even street gangs.

In sum, OC is defined by the pattern to the relationship of multiple offenders, not just the involvement of multiple offenders. This pattern must be deliberate, systematic, and purposive to the criminal activities being carried out or the goals of the criminal association, and ultimately this systematic and purposive pattern of relationships culminates in some coherent and discernible structure.

Within the context of OC, von Lampe (2016) refers to the pattern of relationships among offenders as "criminally exploitable ties," which he describes as "interpersonal relations that enable an individual to interact with other individuals in the furtherance of criminal activities whenever the need or opportunity arises." One of the more controversial debates in the study of OC concerns the nature of the relationships among the offenders and how these "criminally exploitable ties" are structured. There is no single pattern or source of such relationships, just as there is no one type of organizational structure. The pattern of relationships may be based on kinship, friendship, or fraternal or business ties, while the structure of an organized criminal conspiracy may be hierarchical (based on power relations among the offenders involved) or more symmetrical (based on the specialized tasks carried out by or resources available to each of the participants).

In his seminal study of criminal syndicates in New York City, Ianni (1974) identified two basic forms of relationships among the offenders. The first is **associational networks**, which are held together by close personal relationships among the offenders and includes a strong sense of mutual trust. Examples of these personal relationships are kinship and shared ethnicity, as embodied by the Italian Mafia "family." von Lampe (2012: 193) argues that ethnicity is in fact "a superficial characteristic" of criminal networks that are instead "based on family, friendship or local community ties." He contends that family ties "are commonly regarded as the strongest basis for criminal networks" while "ritual kinship ties created by fraternal associations" such as outlaw motorcycle gangs, Chinese triads, and Mafia groups "are even more likely to foster the cross-border networking of criminal entrepreneurs." van de Bunt, Siegel, and Zaitch (2014: 330) agree, writing, "The use of kinship, family, and locality ties, more than ethnicity per se, has consistently been found across all ethnic minorities and immigrant groups, providing a fertile ground for 'bounded solidarity,' enforceable trust, cooperation, loyalty, and secrecy needed to protect and enforce illegal operations." While it may appear that ethnicity is the "bounded solidarity" that binds criminal offenders, it may in fact mask the real (albeit more nuanced) ties. This includes "instrumental" ties (pragmatic use of blood and artificial kinship by, for instance, the Italian Mafia or Colombian cocaine cartels), "tribal affiliation" (as in the case of Nigerian criminal enterprises), or "large extended families" as in the case of Albanian, Romanian, or Hungarian crime groups (van de Bunt, Siegel, & Zaitch, 2014: 330). If there is a common ethnic tie among participants in an organized criminal conspiracy in North America, it may be due more to the involvement of immigrants "who come from production or transit areas from where illegal goods (drugs, etc.), services (prostitution), or people (human smuggling and trafficking) originate" (van de Bunt, Siegel, & Zaitch, 2014: 331).

In their rejection of ethnicity as an organizational basis for OC, van de Bunt, Siegel, and Zaitch (2014: 323) highlight the importance of **social embeddedness** in determining how criminal offenders are organized. Based on the understanding that "criminal cooperation does not exist in a social vacuum," this concept refers to how criminal ties are often built on existing familial, social, and professional relationships.

> Criminal activities cannot be separated from the social relations between the participants and the institutional environments in which their interactions take place. These relationships usually involve more aspects than just committing crimes. "Partners in crime" are first and foremost partners who are bound by relatively strong social ties. Criminal cooperation is usually embedded in existing friendly, familial, or work-related relationships. Collaborating in illicit operations relies heavily on mutual trust ... Everything comes down to trust because there is little to no protection from opportunistic behavior. This is why criminal cooperatives are often characterized by strong internal relationships. Criminals prefer working with family members or friends in order to ensure the smooth running of their operations. (van de Bunt, Siegel, & Zaitch, 2014: 323)

The second form of relationship among organized criminal offenders put forth by Ianni (1974) follows an **entrepreneurial model**, where the bond among the offenders is less personal and more determined by business interests. The relationship among the offenders is either hierarchical, such as that between a boss and an employee, or more symmetrical, such as that between two business partners.

It is important to note that each of Ianni's models may be applicable to the same criminal genre or group, depending on one's perspective. For example, at the core of the traditional Italian Mafia family are such binding relations among members as kinship, nationality, and ethnicity. However, when the made members deal with criminal associates outside the family, the relationships may be more characterized by business interests. In general, the historical trend in OC in Canada has seen business relationships replacing associational networks as the principal binding force among the offenders involved. With that said, the structure of relationships among participants in an organized criminal conspiracy may be both associational and entreprenurial. von Lampe (2016) describes how the different relationships among criminal offenders in the context of an organized crime conspiracy result in different functions being performed:

> Entrepreneurial structures enable criminals to pool resources and to coordinate their activities to achieve material gain through market-based or predatory crimes. Associational structures provide status, cohesion, and mutual support, and they provide a forum for communication, thereby strengthening deviant values. Quasi-governmental structures regulate the behavior of criminals in the areas under their control. They enforce certain rules and settle disputes, and they may neutralize law enforcement through centralized corruption, thereby reducing the risks and uncertainty that criminals face in committing crimes and interacting with other criminals. (von Lampe, 2016: 123)

Specialization/Division of Labour

Many organized criminal conspiracies have a division of labour whereby the participating offenders undertake one or more general or specific functions (Abadinsky, 2013: 5). In a hierarchical Mafia-style criminal organization, this division of labour often corresponds to the position one assumes in the power structure (i.e., those in the lower echelons must physically carry out the day-to-day criminal activities). If the binding ties of the offenders are associational in nature (e.g., kinship ties), an offender's responsibility is often dictated by one's relationship with the central coordinating power within the network (e.g., the Mafia don). For example, the son of the head of a Mafia family will often have greater power and stature than someone who is not related by blood ties and, as such, will be delegated more prestigious tasks and/or leadership responsibilities. In a more symmetrical networked criminal association, each offender's role and specialization may be based on particular skills or resources. Specialized functions within an organized criminal conspiracy appear to be particularly paramount in the networked approach to OC. In its 2006 annual report, Criminal Intelligence Service Canada detailed how many "crime groups" are made up of temporary alliances of individual criminals who merge their *particular skills* to better achieve success in specific criminal enterprises. Once a specific criminal venture is completed, these individuals may continue to collaborate on further criminal activities, or the group may dissolve. Although the individuals may go their separate ways, they sometimes reform into new groups based upon the *skill requirements* of new criminal opportunities. The nature and success of such networks *are largely determined by individual characteristics and skills* among those who act as their component parts. (Criminal Intelligence Service Canada, 2006: 6; emphasis added)

One of the most intricate divisions of labour within an ongoing OC conspiracy can be seen in the Cali and Medellin cocaine cartels that were dominant during the 1980s and 1990s. As part of their complex organizational structures, there was a well-established division of labour in which each individual (or a group of individuals) carried out one specific function. Some of the specialized functions included refining the raw coca into cocaine, transporting goods, bribing government officials, money laundering, distributing wholesale, and managing "stash" houses in destination countries. Cells operating in Canada exhibited a distinct division of labour based on both power relations (e.g., cells operating in the country were run by managers called *Calenos*) and by specific tasks (production, transportation, storage, enforcement, corruption of public officials, money laundering, etc.). (See the chapter on Latin American drug-trafficking organizations on this textbook's website for more details.)

Insulation against Enforcement and Prosecution

Regardless of how an OC conspiracy is structured, the utility of the organizational structure is truly maximized when it can serve to protect its members from arrest and prosecution. Moreover, this insulating function is not simply to protect individual offenders, but also to fortify the criminal group or network against law enforcement actions. The importance of this organizational insulation stems from the belief within traditional criminal groups, such as the Mafia family or the outlaw motorcycle club, that the organization itself is supreme and more important than the lives of individual members.

A hierarchical organizational structure helps to insulate the upper echelons of a criminal group from law enforcement by relegating the hands-on execution of activities to those at the lowest level of the organization or even by individuals who are outside of the organization. For example, the Italian Mafia in Montreal was well known for delegating criminal tasks to "associates," while outlaw motorcycle gangs throughout Canada use "prospects," "hangers-on, "puppet clubs," or street gangs to carry out their dirty work. In 2001, CISC reported that Asian crime groups in BC's Lower Mainland were targeting high schools with large English-as-a-second-language populations "as labour pool for a variety of lower-level criminal activities, as a source of recruits and as insulation to shield senior members from the attentions of rival gangs or law enforcement" (Criminal Intelligence Service Canada, 2001: 19). The more buffers between those who physically carry out crimes and those in the upper echelons of the organization, the more the latter will be insulated from arrest and prosecution.

The insulation of criminal syndicates is fortified by implicit or explicit oaths taken by participants not to implicate their superiors or anyone else in the syndicate if they are arrested. This is an extension of the broader "code of the street" where members of gangs, criminal groups, or those in the criminal subculture refuse to co-operate with police. For the Italian Mafia family, the insulation of made members, the upper echelons of the family, and ultimately the family itself, is codified in the sacrosanct code of *omerta*. At the most practical level, *omerta* is about secrecy: keeping the operations of the family secret from non-members and, ultimately, protecting the family and its leaders from law enforcement by refusing to co-operate with police. For decades, members of the Italian Mafia in the United States escaped prosecution because of their commitment to this code. The once-powerful Italian Mafia has been decimated in the United States in part because members increasingly turned their back on the code of *omerta* by becoming witnesses for the state (Reppetto, 2007).

Lower-echelon members of some criminal groups may be rewarded for taking the rap for the criminal activities directed by their leaders through cash payments, advancement in the organization, preferential treatment while incarcerated, or "welfare" payments to their wives and families. Conversely, insulation is also enforced by a brutal system of punishment—including death—if an offender co-operates with law enforcement and "rats out" his bosses or anyone else involved in the conspiracy.

Specialized Modes and Channels of Communication

Because of the danger of electronic eavesdropping by police, those taking part in organized criminal conspiracies must often be very guarded about how they communicate and what they say to avoid providing law enforcement with evidence that can be used in court. Communication can be protected in one of two ways. First, the offenders can structure their communications so it cannot be interpreted by police, which is largely accomplished by talking in abstract codes. Second, criminal groups may undertake measures to ensure that their conversations are not intercepted by police. This may involve "patting down" anyone involved in a criminal conspiracy to guard against surreptitious recording devices, playing loud background music to obstruct an audio recording, using electronic devices that can detect recording bugs, encrypting digital communication, or using multiple disposable cellular phones.

In addition to the mode of communication, some criminal organizations are also characterized by structured channels of communication, whereby the lower echelons of a criminal organization can only communicate with certain other group members, generally those directly above them in the hierarchy. The main purpose of these strict channels of communication is to insulate the leaders of the crime group from arrest and criminal prosecution.

Limited or Exclusive Membership

"Limited or exclusive membership" (Abadinsky, 2013: 3) refers to the restrictions some OC groups place on who can become a member. Membership in traditional crime groups may be based on such factors as ethnicity, nationality, kinship, or criminal record (and in the case of the outlaw motorcycle gang, ownership of a modified Harley Davidson).

Membership in traditional OC groups is not merely symbolic. Once a member of a Mafia family, the "made guy," "wiseguy," or "good fella" can now oversee his own crew and/or has jurisdiction over a particular area to carry out his criminal activities. Membership may also grant him greater access to criminal markets as well as government, private sector or union officials, and other resources that generally are not available to most ordinary criminals. Joseph Bonanno, the long-time boss of the New York Mafia family that bears his name, emphasized that the advantage of an official membership is that it "places the family member in a society of friends who can help each other through a network of connections" (Bonanno & Lalli, 1983: 149). More importantly, being a member of a criminal syndicate, such as a Mafia family or an outlaw motorcycle gang, bestows an unprecedented level of affluence, prestige, and credibility upon individuals within the criminal underworld.

Today, the world of OC is characterized by a network or syndicated approach that has abandoned most traditional restrictions on membership. Instead, the main criterion is one's ability to contribute to the revenue-generating goals of a particular OC conspiracy. In recent years, the membership of some criminal groups has grown quite slowly or even stagnated as much of the criminal activities are farmed out to associates who remain outside the confines of group membership.

Recruitment

In order for localized gangs and OC groups to survive, Donald Cressey (1969: 236) writes, they must have "an institutionalized process for inducting new members and inculcating them with the values and ways of behaving ... " Traditional criminal syndicates in Canada, such as the Italian Mafia, outlaw motorcycle gangs, or Chinese triads, have been known to actively recruit members who join willingly, and in some cases, unwillingly. Recruitment has become increasingly important for modern organized criminal groups and networks because of the need for specialized skills or resources. According to CISC (2009: 13), "where critical skills necessary to facilitate criminal activities are absent within a criminal group, skilled outsiders are recruited or exploited to provide this service. The individual may be considered an outside contractor or part of the criminal network."

Continuity/Continuing Enterprise

The *Criminal Code of Canada* recognizes OC as a continuing enterprise by emphasizing that a criminal organization "does not include a group of persons that forms randomly for the immediate commission of a single offence." Many dominant criminal organizations have persisted through time and have lasted beyond the life of individual members, including its leadership (Abadinsky, 2013: 4). The interests of the individual offenders are subordinate to those of the organization, which itself has "a specified purpose over a period of time" and most personnel can be replaced as a matter of course (Lyman & Potter, 2014: 44). There is a line of succession to leadership and, as a rule, there are no indispensable members (Salerno, 1967: 7). The continuing nature of some organized criminal associations is epitomized by the five major New York Mafia families, as well as the Montreal-based Mafia, which have survived for more than 75 years. In the United States, the Hells Angels have officially existed since the 1950s, with roots stretching back to the immediate post-war period, while the first Canadian chapter was established in 1977. The self-perpetuating nature of these groups highlights their resilience, especially in the face of numerous successful law enforcement actions that have put many members, including those in leadership positions, behind bars.

Yet, the large Mafia-style organizations that perpetuate over many years may be the exception to the rule, especially in more recent years as the networked organizational structure has increasingly replaced the monolithic hierarchical structure. "The empirical research clearly demonstrates that very few criminal enterprises last for long periods of time, so they are certainly not continuous" (Lyman & Potter, 2014: 10).

Case Study: The Resilience of the Quebec Hells Angels as a Continuing Criminal Enterprise

In April 2009, police in Quebec raided 16 separate properties, including numerous clubhouses of the Hells Angels Motorcycle Club (HAMC) as part of the massive police operation, codenamed SharQc, which targeted the biker gang and its associates. More than 150 people were arrested and charged, including an unprecedented number of full-patch members of the HAMC—111 in total. The various charges laid included murder, conspiracy to commit murder, drug trafficking, and participation in a criminal organization. "With SharQc 2009, our objectives were to prosecute nearly all the [Hells Angels] of Quebec and their main collaborators, and to bring them before court—as well as dismantle their five chapters and seize their headquarters," Steven Chabot, deputy director general for the Quebec provincial police, told the media. Operation SharQc eventually culminated with the arrest of almost every member of the Hells Angels in Quebec; it effectively crippled the motorcycle club in that province, leaving most chapters without the minimum number of members required by the HAMC charter. By June 2015, 101 of the accused had pleaded guilty to various charges.

Despite this enforcement success, the Hells Angels in Quebec demonstrated a remarkable pliability by regrouping and even re-opening chapters that had been closed due to the jailing or death of its members. Their resurrection was facilitated in part through the recruitment of new members and the creation of affiliated and subservient outlaw motorcycle (puppet) clubs. The Hells Angels were also able to survive in Quebec due to support from chapters in other provinces. In particular, some of the 13 HAMC chapters in Ontario were responsible for ensuring the presence and viability of chapters in Quebec and Nova Scotia where the motorcycle club was hit hard by law enforcement actions. As Detective Sergeant Len Isnor of the Ontario Provincial Police Biker Enforcement Unit said in a 2015 interview, the Quebec HAMC chapters were sustained "because Ontario members of the outlaw biker gang have held down the fort in Quebec." This included helping to establish a number of puppet clubs in the province (CBC News, May 30, 2015; Langton, 2015; *Montreal Gazette*, May 7, 2015; *Toronto Star*, March 5, 2015).

In August 2016, more than 100 members and associates of the Hells Angels and its puppet clubs attended the funeral of one of its members in Quebec who was killed in a highway accident. According to organized crime researcher Pierre de Champlain, the funeral doubled as a strategic display of strength and resilience for the HA: "It was a chance for the bikers to show that they're close to each other and at the same time, a demonstration of their strength to other bikers who are their enemies." Added Guy Ryan, a former investigator with Montreal police, "These guys are returning ... They will start reconquering their territory and selling drugs" (CBC News, August 14, 2016).

Multi-jurisdictional/Transnational in Scope

Albanese (2015: 19) believes "the greatest change in organized crime over the past decade has been the transition from a focus on local crime groups and impacts to transnational organized crime." Despite the historical prevalence of well-organized smuggling across national borders, up until the 1970s most criminal groups were confined to local territories and usually did not attempt to operate outside their sphere of influence. This was even true of the major Mafia families in New York and other urban centres in the United States and Canada, each of which operated in a well-defined territory and, with some exception, did not conduct criminal activities outside their jurisdiction. Today, many of the dominant OC genres are now transnational in scope, including the 'Ndrangheta groups, Latin American cocaine cartels, Chinese triads, Eastern European crime groups, Nigerian criminal enterprises, and outlaw motorcycle gangs. The Hells Angels motorcycle club has chapters in more than 50 countries on almost every continent, some of which co-operate across national borders as part of their criminal and fraternal endeavours. Arsovska (2012: 307) writes "the Russian Mafia is active in at least twenty-six foreign countries, Albanian organized crime groups dominate some criminal markets on five continents, and the 'Ndrangheta is present in almost twenty countries." Paoli (2014b: 124) states that the 'Ndrangheta, while historically based in the Calabrian region of Southern Italy, is a "confederation of about 150 groups located outside its home region, most specifically in northern Italy and particularly in the regions of Lombardy, Piedmont, and Liguria, as well as in several foreign countries, most prominently Germany, Canada, and Australia."

The transnational nature of OC is also reflected in the many criminal activities that now cross national borders. Even those criminal activities that do not necessarily require any cross-border movement—such as telemarketing fraud, bank card fraud, currency counterfeiting, product piracy, auto theft, and money laundering—have increasingly crossed national boundaries. Based on a survey of member countries, the United Nations (1995) identified 18 categories of transnational offences, which were found to have direct or indirect effects in two or more countries. This UN list is broad and includes money laundering, terrorist activities, theft of art and cultural objects, theft of intellectual property, illicit trafficking in arms, aircraft hijacking, sea piracy, land hijacking, insurance fraud, computer crime, environmental crime, human trafficking, trade in human body parts, illicit drug trafficking, fraudulent bankruptcy, infiltration of legal business, and the corruption and bribery of public officials, party officials, and elected representatives. The unprecedented frequency with which criminal groups and activities now cross national boundaries, combined with the global structure and reach of some crime groups, has led to the spectre of **transnational organized crime**.

Notwithstanding the above arguments and evidence, Fijnaut (2014: 87–88) cautions that "organized crime is not always transnational in nature—not by any means. Extortion in black or legitimate markets is usually a very local affair." Moreover, the increasingly networked approach of OC also means that there are few criminal groups that are transnational in scope (the aforementioned examples are the exception to the rule). Instead, an international drug-trafficking conspiracy often entails numerous small groups or independent criminal entrepreneurs situated in different countries that coordinate with one another (and may never leave that country or even a local jurisdiction). Production and distribution of illegal goods and services are also localized in nature (Fijnaut, 2014: 87–88).

Secrecy

Ensuring a criminal syndicate and its activities remain shrouded in secrecy is of obvious importance. While secrecy is paramount in most criminal activities, organized criminal offenders may take more concerted, more comprehensive, and more lethal steps to ensure their activities and those performing them are protected from law enforcement detection and interdiction. Organized crime syndicates safeguard their secretive nature through violence, intimidation, insulation, corruption, as well as rules and even established codes of conduct. As discussed previously, the importance of maintaining the secrecy of an OC group is personified by the Mafia's code of *omerta*, in which a Mafioso is defined in part by his ability to conceal the existence and operations of the family, especially in the face of law enforcement interdiction.

Commercial

As discussed in chapter 2, a dominant way to conceptualize organized crime is by depicting it as the organization of criminal activities, which is the focus of this category.

The heading "Commercial" derives from the revenue-generating, profit-oriented nature of organized crimes.

Profit-oriented Criminal Activities

In its definition of a criminal organization, the *Criminal Code of Canada* emphasizes that such organizations are involved in offences that "would likely result in the direct or indirect receipt of a material benefit, including a financial benefit, by the group or by any of the persons who constitute the group." The profit-oriented nature of OC distinguishes it from many other types of criminal behaviour, including interpersonal violence, crimes of passion, vandalism, and terrorism, to name just a few. Organized crime groups are exceptionally opportunistic and are involved in wide range of money-making ventures. Drug trafficking appears to be the biggest money-maker, and Criminal Intelligence Service Canada has estimated that 80 percent of all identified OC groups in Canada are involved in the illegal drug trade (2007: 13, 2009: 9). Human trafficking is considered by some to be second only to drug trafficking in terms of the amount of revenue generated for criminal entrepreneurs (International Labour Office, 2012; United Nations Office on Drugs and Crime, 2012b).

Serious Illegal Acts

The *Criminal Code* states that to constitute a criminal organization, it must have "as one of its main purposes or main activities the facilitation or commission of one or more *serious* offences ..." While the seriousness of a crime may vary from country to country, it is usually equated with crimes that carry lengthy sentences. In Canada, a serious crime is one that is classified as an **indictable offence**, which generally carries a minimum sentence of two years and a maximum of life imprisonment. The illegal acts committed by criminal organizations are considered serious in the sense that they exact significant harm on victims and society as a whole (e.g., drug trafficking, extortion, human trafficking, fraud, violence, etc.). The serious nature of organized criminal activities are distinguished from those revenue-generating crimes that are considered less harmful to a victim or society as a whole (e.g., thefts from homes, vehicles, or retail stores below $5000).

Consensual and Predatory Crimes

Revenue-generating organized criminal activities include both consensual and predatory crimes. A consensual crime is one where no victim exists; that is, two or more individuals willingly engage in an illegal commercial transaction. Common consensual organized crimes include drug trafficking, gambling, prostitution, human smuggling, and the supply of contraband or counterfeit products. The main business of OC has been described as providing goods and services that are in demand by the public, but have been made illegal or are tightly regulated by the state because they are deemed immoral or destructive. Predatory crimes are those in which a victim suffers a direct physical or financial loss. Common predatory crimes carried out on an organized basis include extortion (protection rackets), theft, human trafficking, currency counterfeiting, and various types of fraud. More sophisticated predatory crimes appear to have increased in recent years and include bank card fraud, cybercrimes, organized automobile theft, and identity theft. The fact that criminal organizations are involved in both consensual and predatory crimes reveal a relationship with the broader society that is, at the same time, symbiotic and parasitic.

Multiple Enterprises

Another common characteristic of many OC syndicates is that they carry out more than one profit-oriented (legal or illegal) activity. It is not uncommon for members of an outlaw motorcycle gang, an Italian-Canadian Mafia clan, or a Chinese triad to be involved in drug trafficking, gambling, telemarketing fraud, prostitution, credit card counterfeiting, and extortion, to name just a few. The notable exception to this rule is the Colombian drug-trafficking cartels that were dominant in the 1980s and 1990s and that focused almost exclusively on cocaine trafficking.

Monopolistic Ambitions

Some OC groups have demonstrated a clear ambition to seek a monopoly over the sale of a particular good or service or in a particular geographic area. As Abadinsky (2013) puts it, "An organized crime group eschews competition. It strives for hegemony over a particular geographic area (a metropolitan area or section of a city), a particular 'industry,' legitimate or illegitimate (for example gambling, trucking, loansharking), or a combination of both (for example, loansharking in a particular area or the whole-sale cocaine market in a city)." These monopolies are typically sought and maintained through violence, the threat of violence, or by corrupt relationships with government, businesses, or union officials (Abadinsky, 2013: 4). A bloody conflict between the Hells Angels and its rivals during the 1990s, which cost the lives of more than 150 people, was over efforts by the Hells Angels to monopolize the lucrative cocaine trade in Quebec (Sher & Marsden, 2003). It should be noted that a distinction should be made between "monopolistic ambitions" and actually achieving a monopoly over a particular illegal market or territory. As described in chapter 2, few, if any, illegal markets are actually monopolized by any particular criminal entity.

Operational Tactics that Support Commercial Activities

While most organized crimes directly generate revenue, others are carried out to facilitate the profit-making enterprises of the criminal syndicate. Like a legitimate corporation, criminal groups and networks must undertake certain activities to support the production, distribution, and marketing of its products and services. Common tactical illegal activities used as part of OC conspiracies include corruption, violence, money laundering, and intelligence gathering. The corruption of public officials has historically been an integral tactical imperative of OC. In addition to politicians, OC syndicates have also used graft in relation to civil servants, criminal justice officials (police, prosecutors, the judiciary), labour union leaders, as well as management and other employees of private sector companies. Violence is a constant in Canada's criminal underworld and is used rationally by crime groups to ensure that certain individuals—usually competing gangsters, victims, witnesses or informants, and in some cases government officials—do not obstruct the criminal organization from reaching its objectives. Violence (or the threat thereof) is also used to maintain internal discipline within crime groups. Money laundering refers to the process of converting and legitimizing illegally earned revenue and has become an important function for criminal groups that accumulate large amounts of illicit cash. Another operational support tactic used by more sophisticated crime syndicates is intelligence gathering and counter-surveillance, which includes the use of eavesdropping technology or placing gang associates inside enforcement agencies or other government agencies, to gather information.

Behavioural Characteristics

This final category of characteristics is concerned with the traits of individual OC actors as well as the norms, values, and codes that govern the attitudes and behaviour of many of those involved in OC conspiracies and illegal markets.

Chronic and Serious Offenders (Career Criminals)

One of the reasons some OC conspiracies persist over time is that the offenders involved are career criminals. In criminological terms, they would be considered **chronic and serious offenders** in that they are habitually engaged in committing a variety of (serious) criminal offences. They may also be labelled "life-course persistent offenders" (Moffitt, 1993) in that their criminal offending occurs over much of their lifetime (often beginning during adolescence). At the very least, well-established criminal groups are disproportionally populated by people who have criminal records. For official membership in some traditional crime groups, a criminal record may, in fact, be a prerequisite. An agreed statement of facts that came out of a court case in London, Ontario, indicated that as of 2014, a dozen full-patch members of the London chapter of the Hells Angels and three "hangarounds" had 105 criminal convictions between them (QMI Agency, October 22, 2014). Even after accumulating considerable wealth or spending long periods of time in jail, many of those involved in criminal syndicates continue with their life of crime.

Research that contradicts this characterization was conducted among individuals convicted of drug trafficking in Canada who operated at the wholesale level. DesRoches (2005) found that most were not career criminals; they transitioned into illegal drug trafficking later in life from a legitimate business background and live relatively prosocial lifestyles apart from their involvement in drug trafficking.

Rationality

Criminology's rational choice theory contends that most offenders are perceived as self-maximizing decision-makers who carefully calculate the advantages and disadvantages associated with specific criminal acts. In other words, offenders make rational choices in their decision to commit crimes (Clarke & Cornish, 1985). Organized crime represents one of the most rational forms of criminality. This is exemplified by the consensual criminal activities carried out by criminal entrepreneurs, who, generally speaking, are responding to the forces of the free market—in particular, the laws of supply and demand. In other words, because OC conspiracies are profited-oriented, they have to act rationally in their illegal business enterprises. Organized criminal entrepreneurs are also said to operate rationally because they are motivated by financial benefits and the relatively low risk of being caught (and if they are caught and penalized, this is considered as a rational cost of doing business).

The rational choice theory of offender decision-making places a premium on how criminal offenders, in the course of planning and carrying out a criminal act, make decisions based on opportunities that become available to them. As the study of OC has shown, criminal entrepreneurs and groups are very opportunistic. For Lyman and Potter (2014: 55), "Organized crime is made up of a series of highly adaptive, flexible networks that readily take into account changes in the law and regulatory practices, the growth or decline of market demand for a particular good or service, and the availability of new sources of supply and new opportunities for distribution. This ability to adapt allows organized crime to persist and flourish."

Rationality is often reflected in the structure of a criminal organization itself. According to Cressey (1969: 34–35), the structure of American crime syndicates is based on "a rational design for safety and profit." Criminal groups "selling illicit goods and services must, if they are to capitalize on the great demand for their wares, expand by establishing a division of labour ... The next rational move is consolidation and integration of separate divisions of labor into a cartel designed to minimize competition and maximize profits. Such a monopolistic move is, of course, a rational decision for peaceful coexistence." In short, criminal organizations are structured rationally to maximize their revenue-generating function. Even violence is used for rational ends by criminal groups, regardless of how grisly and wonton it may seem, because it is used to support their end goals. The rational nature of OC can be contrasted with more emotionally driven crimes (e.g., domestic violence) or impulsive (irrational) crimes committed by a collective of people, such as riots.

Subcultural Norms/Contempt for Civil Society

Members of traditional OC groups, such as the Italian Mafia, Japanese Yakuza, the Russian *vory v zakone*, and outlaw motorcycle gangs, openly rebel against conventional social rules and values that govern civil society and organize their behaviour according to the norms of their criminal group. This particular trait of OC is associated with subculture theories of criminality and violence. These theories argue that serious and chronic offenders adhere to values and norms that are learned through their immersion in a deviant subculture and that are at odds with the dominant law-abiding culture (Ferracuti & Wolfgang, 1967). The OC subculture and its contempt for mainstream society is exemplified by the term *wiseguy*, which is what some members of Italian-American Mafia groups have used to refer to one another. From their perspective, a Mafioso is superior to everyone else in mainstream society; a wiseguy believes that anybody who follows the commonly accepted rules and laws of civil society deserves to be victimized. In his book on the Italian Mafia in New York and New Jersey, Pileggi adeptly captures the wiseguy's attitude toward American society:

> They lived in an environment awash in crime, and those who did not partake were simply viewed as prey. To live otherwise was foolish. Anyone who stood waiting his turn on the American pay line was beneath contempt. Those who did—who followed the rules, were stuck in low-paying jobs, worried about their bills, put tiny amounts away for rainy days, kept their place, and crossed off workdays on their kitchen calendars like prisoners awaiting release—could only be considered fools. They were timid, law-abiding, pension-plan creatures neutered by compliance and awaiting their turn to die. To wiseguys, "working guys" were already dead. (Pileggi, 1985: 32–33)

Similarly, the *vory v zakone* or "thief in law" is a high-ranking, well-respected OC figure in the old Soviet underworld and the new Republic of Russia. Akin to the Italian Mafia, the code of the "Thieves World" emphasizes one's willingness to separate oneself from conventional society. A *vory* rejects traditional social norms, including legitimate work, paying taxes, having a family, and is particularly disdainful of government authority.

Sophistication

Some OC conspiracies can be quite sophisticated. In the context of criminal activity, sophistication is measured by "the degree of preparation and planning for the crime and how much skill and knowledge are needed in order to commit the crime" (Marvelli & Finckenauer, 2012: 510). The level of sophistication in both the organization of criminal offenders and crimes separates the larger transnational criminal conspiracies from smaller, localized, more rudimentary gangs of offenders. In Canada, CISC states, "Only a small number of organized crime groups are capable of operating elaborate criminal operations."

> These groups are engaged in diverse and complex activities. For the most part, they operate out of the largest urban areas but have secondary operations or criminal influence in other cities or rural areas. These groups are distinguished by

sophisticated operations, often involving the importation, manufacture, or distribution of a wide range of illicit commodities as well as the ability to commit complex frauds, money laundering, or financial schemes. In addition, many of these groups display the capability to target, coerce, or employ individuals in legitimate business, professionals, such as lawyers and accountants, and other community members in order to facilitate their criminal activities. Many of these groups are difficult to target as they strategically insulate themselves from law enforcement. (Criminal Intelligence Service Canada, 2007: 14)

The sophistication of some criminal syndicates is very much reflected in their use of technology. Police have uncovered counterfeiting technologies that produce almost exact replicas of credit cards, passports, currency, and consumer goods. Submarines have been used to smuggle cocaine from South America (*New York Times*, September 10, 2012). Some crime syndicates possess the computer technology to steal identification and other data directly from bank cards or through the Internet. Computer hackers who are able to decode complex security systems and firewalls of corporations

Case Study: The Cali Cartel

The sophisticated transnational criminal organization is perhaps epitomized by Colombia's cocaine wholesaling Cali Cartel. According to Ron Chepesiuk, "at the height of its power in the early 1990s, the Cali Cartel was running its criminal empire more on the model of a multinational corporation than a criminal enterprise. It treated its members like company employees, hired the best person for the job, used business strategy to market its illegal product [cocaine], and shifted operations from one locale to another as economic and political conditions necessitated" (Chepesiuk, 2006). Reporting to Gilberto Rodriguez Orejuela, the acknowledged CEO of the cartel, were his senior vice-presidents responsible for finance, supply, production, transportation, marketing, sales, and enforcement. Under these men was a cadre of regional directors who headed importation and distribution cells located in different jurisdictions in the United States, Canada, and Western Europe (Chepesiuk, 2006). As the US Drug Enforcement Administration put it, the "Cali leaders ran an incredibly sophisticated, highly structured drug trafficking organization that was tightly controlled by its leaders in Cali" (United States Drug Enforcement Administration, n.d.c). The advanced nature of the Cali Cartel was also evident in their use of white-collar professionals, including lawyers, accountants, and financial consultants, to support their criminal activities. They also used advanced technology to help their criminal operations including mainframe computers, sophisticated telecommunications, and counter-surveillance equipment.

have been increasingly linked to organized criminals whose intentions are theft for financial gain (Lennon, 2015; *NetworkWorld.com*, May 9, 2007; Verizon Business Risk Team, 2009). "Cybercrime groups" even develop and market "crimeware"—malicious software specifically designed to steal confidential personal and financial information (Criminal Intelligence Service Canada, 2010: 12). Some crime syndicates have engineered intricate encryption codes and software to communicate surreptitiously online, while others possess the technology to conduct radar sweeps of drug surveillance planes to map out gaps in coverage.

Non-ideological

Organized crime syndicates are not motivated by political ideologies, religious dogma, or a desire for social change. Their goal is the accumulation of money and other material benefits. This non-ideological stance distinguishes criminal organizations from terrorist groups in which the illegal activities are driven by the goal of social and political change.

Rules, Regulations, and Codes of Conduct

Like many legitimate organizations, some traditional criminal groups have rules and regulations that members are expected to follow (Abadinsky, 2013: 3). These rules are mostly implicit, while for some OC genres (e.g., the Italian 'Ndrangheta or outlaw motorcycle gangs), they are explicit and actually written out. Rules are a control mechanism that regulates relationships within the criminal group and between the group and the outside world. "Control systems of this sort begin with values that define what is 'good' and what is 'bad,' what is expected in behaviour and what is condemned" (Ianni, 1974: 300). These rules exist more as a value system, however, "rather than a formally organized set of operating instructions for guiding the bureaucratic organization" (Lyman & Potter, 2014: 48).

Because criminal organizations explicitly operate outside the accepted norms, standards, and laws of civil society, their own rules and codes have evolved to regulate behaviour within the underworld. Ironically, while the Hells Angels originally stressed wild, anarchistic behaviour, all of its chapters are governed through formal by-laws that establish a rigid set of rules and regulations as well as the penalties for non-compliance. By-laws regulate how patches are to be worn, require all members to own a Harley Davidson motorcycle, restrict members from using drugs involving needles, forbid them from stealing from other members, and mandate all members to attend all chapter meetings and biker runs.

Other rules and codes have evolved to protect the individual member and, more importantly, the criminal organization. To this end, the two most important and intertwined codes that members of criminal fraternities must follow are secrecy and loyalty. The code of secrecy is paramount, given the illegal nature of the activities undertaken by the criminal organization. Loyalty is similarly critical and stems from the primacy that the criminal organization assumes in the life of the individual members. The member of a traditional OC group must demonstrate his loyalty to the

Case Study: The Rules, Rites, Rituals, and Structure of the *Honorata Società*

In 1971, while Toronto police were searching the home of a suspected member of the Canadian cell of an Italian 'Ndrangheta crime group, they found a 27-page document, handwritten in an antiquated Italian script, in his kitchen cupboards. Experts from Canada and Italy would later conclude that the papers outlined the rules, rites, rituals, and structure of the *Honorata Società*. This document would prove to be a significant breakthrough in efforts by police to prove the existence of a secret criminal society in Canada with roots to southern Italy's Calabrian province.

The heading on the first page was *Come Formare una Società* ("How to Form a Society") and the preamble partially reads, "My stomach is a tomb, my mouth a bleated work of humility." Another section dictates the initiation rites of an inductee who symbolically vows to take "a bloody dagger in my hand and a serpent in my mouth" should he betray the Honoured Society. A 1972 *Globe and Mail* article described the remainder of the document as "a tangle of centuries old archaic Italian, the phrases laced with flowery, mystic imagery" dealing with such matters as the structure of an 'Ndrangheta cell, the punishment of members who don't surrender their guns at meetings, initiation rituals for new members, and the importance of secrecy.

The papers outlined the basic structure of an 'Ndrina cell, which includes three levels or ranks: *camorrista*, the highest rank; *picciotto*, a middle rank; and "youths of honour," the lowest rank. There were also references to the pledges and obligations of members, the most important being a vow of silence. An Italian expert on the Mafia pointed out that the Italian word *d'umilta* appears throughout the document and should be interpreted the same as the word *omerta*, the Sicilian Mafia's oath of secrecy. The document also refers to the term *mastro di sgarru*, another important obligation of members that has to do with vendettas against enemies of the Society. Another term found in the document was *baciletta*, which was interpreted as "extorted money" collected by Society members that should be "given to the ones who need it, the ones who have been arrested, for the defence lawyers, to help the people the police are looking for" (Dubro, 1986: 114–15; *Globe and Mail*, June 2, 1972; Schneider, 2016: 314–15).

organization, first and foremost, although, in some hierarchical groups, the leadership demands that ultimate loyalty be paid to it. In more colloquial terms, Cressey (1969) lists the following rules of conduct that must be followed by members of Italian crime groups in the United States:

Be loyal to members of the organization. Do not interfere with each other's interests and do not be an informer.

Be a man of honor and always do right. Respect women and your elders. Do not rock the boat.

Be rational. Be a member of the team. Do not engage in battle if you cannot win.

Be a stand-up guy. Keep your eyes and ears open and your mouth shut. Do not sell out.

Have class. Be independent. Know your way around the world. (As cited in Lyman & Potter, 2014: 48)

The creation of rules and codes of conduct within the criminal underworld is part of what von Lampe calls the "quasi-governmental" role played by OC groups, which is meant to "support illegal entrepreneurial activities by creating a more predictable and more secure environment in a sphere that the legitimate government is unwilling or unable to regulate" (von Lampe, 2016: 103). To this end, the rules of conduct extend into the ever-important commercial aspects of illegal markets, such as dealings between a buyer and a seller.

Discipline

In order to ensure that the rules and regulations of the criminal group are obeyed, forms of discipline based on loyalty, a code of honour, and the fear of reprisals may be imposed. Disciplinary actions can include removal from the organization, demotion, physical beatings, and even death.

CONCLUSION

This chapter is meant to contribute to a better understanding of (Canadian) organized crime through a comprehensive enumeration of common characteristics. The

---

CRITICAL THINKING EXERCISE

Are the OC characteristics presented in this chapter complete? Can you think of any characteristics that may have been missed? Are there certain characteristics that you believe are universal to OC, but are not deemed so in this conceptual model? Are there certain characteristics you believe should be removed from this taxonomy?

taxonomy presented in this chapter revolves primarily around OC as an association of offenders, although it recognizes that any characterization of OC must include a focus on criminal activities and how these activities are carried out. As should be apparent by now, given the diversity of criminal groups and networks, combined with the controversies over how to define and conceptualize OC, there are only a few traits that could be deemed universal.

The taxonomy presented in this chapter was built using empirical evidence and case studies. Many of these cases are drawn from Canada, which shows how OC in this country collectively encompasses most, if not all, of the OC traits identified in the extant literature. This may suggest that as far as characteristics are concerned there is really nothing distinctive about Canadian organized criminal associations relative to other countries.

KEY TERMS

Associational networks

Chronic and serious offenders

Conspiracy

Entrepreneurial model

Indictable offence

Social embeddedness

Threat assessment

Transnational organized crime

REVIEW QUESTIONS

1. What are the key characteristics of organized crime that make it a unique type of criminality?
2. Is there any agreement on common or universal characteristics?
3. Is it possible to distinguish Canadian organized crime based on an analysis of key characteristics?

FURTHER READINGS

Abadinsky, H. (2013). *Organized Crime* (10th Ed.). Beverly, MA: Belmont.

Albanese, J.S. (2015). *Organized Crime: From the Mob to Transnational Organized Crime* (6th Ed.). New York: Routledge.

Black, C. (2000). *Measuring Organised Crime in Belgium: A Risk-based Methodology.* Antwerp: Maklu.

Commission of the European Communities & EUROPOL. (2001). *Towards a European Strategy to Prevent Organised Crime*. Brussels: Commission of the European Communities. March.

Maltz, M. (1990). *Measuring the Effectiveness of Organized Crime Control Efforts.* Chicago: University of Illinois at Chicago, Office of International Criminal Justice.

Royal Canadian Mounted Police. Criminal Intelligence Directorate. (2000). *Project Sleipnir: The Long Matrix for Organized Crime.* August. Ottawa: RCMP.

4 THEORIES OF ORGANIZED CRIME

CHAPTER OUTLINE

- Introduction and Overview
- Etiological Theories of Organized Criminal Behaviour
- Administrative Criminology and the Organization of Crimes
- The Organization of Criminals: Theoretical Models on the Structure of Organized Crime Associations
- Conclusion

LEARNING OUTCOMES

After reading this chapter, you should have a thorough understanding of the following:

- Theories that explain the existence of organized crime
- Etiological theories that explain criminal behaviour, including the differences among the following:
  - Theories that blame exogenous forces and actors versus theories that blame social conditions indigenous to North America
  - Sociological versus economic versus political theories
  - Theories that locate the root causes of criminal behaviour in society and the social environment versus theories that focus on human agency and decision-making by the individual offender
- Theories on how crimes are organized
- Theoretical models on how criminal offenders are organized
- Strengths and weaknesses (critiques) of the theories covered in this chapter
- The applicability of the mostly American theories of organized crime to Canada and a critical analysis of this application

INTRODUCTION AND OVERVIEW

This chapter explores various theories that attempt to explain the existence of organized crime. This will involve applying contemporary criminological theories as well as theories developed specifically in relation to organized crime. The first set of theories tries to help us to understand the causal factors that contribute to the existence of organized crime. These etiological theories are particularly concerned with explaining the onset and persistence of criminal behaviour among those who are habitually engaged in serious, profit-oriented, multiple, planned crimes and/or those who participate in criminal groups and networks. Alien conspiracy theory argues that organized crime in North America is the result of the importation of foreign secret criminal societies made up of chronic offenders. In contrast are those theories that emphasize the factors native to North America that give rise to, and facilitate, the onset and growth of organized crime. In general, this latter category of theories applies basic criminological theories and concepts—such as strain, differential association, social disorganization, social control, and subcultures—to help explain the causal factors underlying organized criminal behaviour. Taken together, these sociological theories argue that North American society, through conflicts and contradictions between its goals and the means to attain them, exerts pressure on some people to behave in a deviant rather than conformist ways (strain theory). However, a criminal orientation is not solely based on blocked aspirations; the individual must also exist in an environment where criminal behaviour can be learned and emulated, primarily through associations with individuals who are involved in criminal activities (differential association theory). This is generally found in neighbourhoods where there is a high level of "social disorganization." Particularly vulnerable in these neighbourhoods are youth who have either been "under-socialized" in the accepted norms of civil society or "over-socialized" in the norms and values of the deviant criminal subculture (social disorganization theory). Similarly, ethnic succession theory contends that the ethnic basis of many organized crime groups in North America is the result of immigrant and minority groups being shut out of legitimate avenues of social mobility (due to discrimination, for example) and then turn to innovative, albeit illegal ways, to achieve the American dream. Radical and critically oriented structuralist theories view crime and criminal behaviour as rooted in capitalism (and the support for capitalism by the state), which promotes organized crime in society by placing a premium on income generation and the ensuing conflict between the working class and those who control the free market system. Unlike sociological theories, an economic analysis does not view organized crime as pathological in nature, but as a highly rational system, which can be seen as an extension of the free market economy. In other words, an economic approach to understanding organized crime contends its existence is due to the basic laws of supply and demand. The related state-centred "protection theory" argues that organized crime arises in circumstances where the state is quite weak and/or corrupt.

The second set of theories discusses hypotheses, theories, and tools that facilitate an analysis of how serious and profit-oriented crimes are organized. Particular emphasis is placed on analyzing the discipline of administrative criminology, which argues that individuals become involved in organized crime through a rational, opportunistic decision-making process.

The third set of theories attempt to explain how criminal offenders are organized, that is, the organizational structures of criminal conspiracies. The bureaucratic/hierarchical model contends that criminal organizations resemble the hierarchical structure of legitimate organizations, such as a corporation or a government body. The kinship model asserts that the structure of the Italian-American Mafia family is based on a traditional social grouping that has been patterned by cultural traditions and organized around kinship relationships. The patron–client model envisions the structure of organized crime groups as a loose system of power relationships where members of criminal groups become a patron or broker to others by providing the right contacts, influence, and direction. The network model views organized crime as made up of symmetrical business partnerships among many different offenders, each of whom contributes a particular expertise, contact, or resource in the context of a particular criminal event (e.g., a cocaine importation conspiracy).

Within the context of scientific inquiries, a theory can be defined as an idea or set of ideas that attempts to explain a phenomenon in terms of deeper or more fundamental processes. An important criterion of a theory is that it has to be amenable to testing using rigorous scientific methods. Not all the explanations provided in this chapter live up to these standards and therefore cannot be considered theories *per se*. Some are, in fact, academic disciplines or schools of thought that provide a particular perspective on organized crime. Others are analytical models that advocate a certain approach to understanding organized crime. Still, others are merely conjectures or speculation. Regardless, all are presented as explanations of why and how organized crime exists (i.e., the root causes of organized criminal behaviour, how crimes are organized, and how offenders are organized).

ETIOLOGICAL THEORIES OF ORGANIZED CRIMINAL BEHAVIOUR

Willie Sutton, one of America's most prolific bank robbers, was once asked why he robbed banks. He reportedly replied, with an incredulous look, "That's where the money is!" (Sutton, 1976: 160). While a tad flippant, his answer does nonetheless help us to appreciate why some people become involved in crime: "For the money!" Without a doubt, pure unadulterated greed and a penchant for material pleasures are a driving force behind organized criminality as well as white-collar criminality (especially among the wealthy criminal elite or corporate fraudsters who cannot cry poverty as a reason that drives their actions). The pursuit of the almighty illicit dollar, however, does not answer one perennial question often at the root of etiological theories of criminality: Why do some people resort to crime, while others—who may encounter similar opportunities, face the same temptations, share demographic characteristics, and come from the same environment—do not? This section explores etiological theories that can help explain the existence of organized crime generally and organized criminal behaviour specifically (the word *etiology* can be defined as the assignment of cause or reason to help explain a certain phenomenon). Etiological theories of organized crime attempt to answer such questions:

- Why does organized crime exist?
- What are its root causes?
- What are the factors that contribute to organized crime and illegal markets?
- What are the factors that contribute to the onset and persistence of organized (serious, chronic, entrepreneurial) criminal behaviour?
- Why do certain individuals become involved in organized crime, while other individuals, under similar circumstances, do not?

There are various theories that try to explain the causes of organized crime and criminality in North America. The theories presented below approach the subject from a number of different disciplines, including sociology, criminology, psychology, economics, political science, and public administration. That organized crime has been analyzed from such diverse disciplines is a testament to the wide-ranging nature and scope of this social phenomenon (not to mention the need to rely on a multidisciplinary approach to understanding it).

Some of the theories are specific to organized crime, while others are based on general etiological theories of crime and criminality that have been adapted to organized crime. This in and of itself raises the important question of whether "the causes of

CRITICAL THINKING EXERCISE

As you read the different explanations presented below, critically analyze each to discern those factors that influence them, such as the following:

- The source of the theory (e.g., state actors, scholars, journalists)
- The broader discipline or paradigm from which this theory came (e.g., sociology versus economics, administrative criminology versus critical criminology)
- Assumptions underlying the theory (e.g., offenders are to blame versus society is to blame)
- Political ideologies that may have predisposed the explanation (socialist versus liberal versus conservative)

organized crime are different from the causes of other types of crime" (Albanese, 2015: 89). As Albanese notes, "some have argued that explanations of crime should be universal, whereas others argue that different manifestations of crime may require different explanations. In either case, it is obvious that different people commit different crimes for different reasons. Therefore, more than one explanation is likely needed to explain the crimes of many diverse people" (Albanese, 2015: 87).

Alien Conspiracy Theory

One theory of organized crime that has been developed in United States is referred to as the **alien conspiracy theory**. This school of thought has been used primarily to explain the origins and scope of Italian organized crime in that country. However, it may be applied to other ethnic-based organized crime groups in North America that may have originated in other countries. The basic argument underlying this theory is that organized crime in the United States is the result of the importation of secret criminal societies from other countries. Alien conspiracy theory rests on the view that OC does not emerge from the norms, values, and institutions of American culture, but rather has been thrust upon the country by foreign cultures. In other words, the roots of OC can be found in norms values antithetical to those of American society and are imported via the cultural transmission of specific immigrant groups. The theory originally contended that a secret society originating in Sicily made its way to the United States during the Italian diaspora that took place in the late nineteenth and early twentieth centuries. This secret society then grew to a monolithic nationwide criminal conspiracy—made up of about two dozen Mafia "families" of Italian lineage all of which were governed by a national commission—which is anti-government and serves to subvert and erode the fundamental law-abiding values of American society.

Alien conspiracy theory was not originally developed by scholars but was initially promoted in the early 1950s by the Special Senate Committee to Investigate Organized Crime in Interstate Commerce, chaired by Senator Estes Kefauver. This committee reached a number of conclusions based on its examination of illegal gambling and other rackets in the United States:

- "There is a sinister criminal organization known as the Mafia" operating throughout the United States with ties to similar organizations in other countries. The Italian-American Mafia is a direct descendant of a secret criminal society of the same name that originates on the island of Sicily (United States Congress, 1951: 2).
- "Its leaders are usually found in control of the most lucrative rackets in American cities," including drug trafficking (p. 131).
- "There are indications of a centralized direction and control of these rackets," but leadership appears to be in a group rather than in a single individual (i.e.,

the nationwide conspiracy is directed by a national commission made up of the heads of different Mafia families) (p. 150)

- The Mafia is the cement that helps to hold together the various syndicates that are spread throughout the country (p. 150).

In 1963, the McClellan Committee, another US Senate inquiry into organized crime, heard testimony from Joseph Valachi, a low-level soldier in New York's Genovese family which he claimed was part of the national criminal conspiracy called *la Cosa Nostra* (Maas, 1968; United States Senate, 1965). Valachi was the first made member of an Italian-American Mafia family to testify before to a government commission. The testimony of Valachi was later exposed as inaccurate, sensationalized, vague, confusing, and inconsistent (Peterson, 1983: 425). While Valachi did not provide credible evidence of a powerful national syndicate, his testimony was taken as gospel due to the fervent efforts by the US government and law enforcement agencies to promulgate the belief that a nationwide criminal organization existed and to characterize the Italian Mafia as an alien threat (Albanese, 1996; Smith, 1975). Hawkins (1969) goes so far to contend that Valachi was coached by the FBI so the government could create a self-fulfilling prophecy of a national organized criminal conspiracy.

Photo 4.1: Frank Costello, reputed Mafia member accused of being a senior member of the LCN's national commission, appearing before the Kefauver Commission, March 1951

Source: Al Aumuller, World Telegram staff photographer, via Wikimedia Commons

This conspiratorial theory was also present in the conclusions of the President's Commission on Law Enforcement and Administration of Justice (1967), which was later replicated in a book by the commission's principal consultant on organized crime, criminologist Donald Cressey. The shared conclusions of the commission and Cressey were that a "nation-wide illicit cartel and confederation" was formed during the 1930s when organized crime units across the United States linked themselves together in a monopolistic cartel. The subtitle of Cressey's 1969 book, *Theft of a Nation*, epitomized the language used to overestimate and sensationalize the scope of and threat posed by Italian organized crime in America.

Alien conspiracy theory has been roundly criticized. Its detractors contend the theory is rooted in racist doctrines and fails to ignore the social, political, and economic environment of the United States that helps foment organized crime there. The theory is also undermined by a reliance on anecdotal and biased evidence provided by law enforcement agencies and unreliable informants.

Subsequent scholarly research and evidence gathered by criminal justice agencies refute the two main pillars of alien conspiracy theory: (1) that organized crime was a product of secret criminal societies imported from other countries; and (2) there was a nationwide, monolithic, interconnected conspiracy known as *la Cosa Nostra*. First, according to Lyman and Potter (2014: 62), "virtually every U.S. city had well-developed organized crime syndicates long before the large-scale Italian immigration of the late nineteenth and early twentieth centuries. If Italians and other immigrants played a major role in developing organized crime, they were only joining and augmenting widespread crime corruption already native to the United States." As will be explained in more detail in chapter 5, a secret criminal organization called the Mafia was never imported from Italy to North America (although some relevant Sicilian cultural traditions that later influenced Italian-American organized crime were brought over from the old country). The ethnic Italian crime groups that predominated the United States found their real genesis in the urban immigrant ghettos of such cities as New York, Buffalo, New Orleans, Chicago, Cleveland, and Philadelphia, among others. Lupsha (1981: 8) also rejects the "alien" underpinnings of this theory noting that the leadership of *la Cosa Nostra* in the United States was "for the most part, American born or raised." And while "volumes have been written on the Sicilian roots of organized crime," he emphasizes that "organized crime is a product of America. It is not Italian, Sicilian, Jewish, German, Polish, or Russian. Its leaders were American born or socialized, and the context of the American economic and political system affected them" (8). In short, "organized crime is a true product of American values and American culture. It is an American crime" (4).

The second major criticism of this theory is that there is little evidence of a truly nationwide Mafia criminal conspiracy with centralized control. There were many Italian-American Mafia families spread across North America and they were linked through ethnicity subcultural norms, methods, illegal networks, and criminal activities. Some influential LCN members, such as Charles (Lucky) Luciano, even attempted to create a national "commission" that would coordinate and regulate the competing interests of the various Italian crime groups and there were, at times, meetings held among senior members of different families from across the country. However, a national commission never fully materialized, and most groups worked independently in their own cities, with sporadic cooperation (and conflict) (Albini, 1971; Smith, 1975). The so-called Mafia Commission was largely confined to the state of New York and had only limited power over the crime families there.

These conspiratorial theories were systematically refuted in a 1975 book by Dwight C. Smith called *The Mafia Mystique*. Smith argues that alien conspiracy theory arose, in part, because of the public's fascination with organized crime and crime in general. Hard-boiled "pulp fiction" novels, sensationalized newspaper and magazine articles, Hollywood movies, and self-serving governmental commissions and law enforcement reports all presented portraits that were largely devoid of sound factual evidence on the nature and scope of Italian-American organized crime and inflated the threat that it posed to safety and security of Americans. This theory is particularly distorted because of the political agenda that was behind its original formulation; it was most vigorously promoted by American politicians, who were using the issue to advance their political careers. In his book *Kefauver and the Politics of Crime*, Moore (1974) points out that Senator Kefauver helped to foster the belief in this nationwide conspiracy, partially to raise his national profile in his bid to be a candidate for US president. Law enforcement agencies, the FBI in particular, were strong promoters of this theory because of their desire to secure greater enforcement resources and powers (Albanese, 1996: 92). Critics also charge that politicians and law enforcement agencies enthusiastically promulgated alien conspiracy theory because by "externalizing the problem of organized crime," they were able to downplay "the involvement of police, judges and politicians in racketeering" (Arsovska, 2012: 313). In other words, the theory is part of a broader narrative in which "organized crime is defined as a problem of 'outsiders,' while the involvement of 'insiders' and the ways societies create and promote organized crime opportunities themselves is neglected" (Kleemans, 2014: 33).

Despite the many critiques, the principle tenets of this theory—that organized crime can be blamed on outsiders; in particular, ethnic immigrant minority groups—continue to be both an implicit and explicit foundation of popular natavist narratives in North America and other continents. According to Kleemans (2014: 33), strains of this theory is evident in other countries, in part due to the tendency to speciously blame specific immigrant and ethnic minority groups for "constituting the main problem of organized crime or the central players in specific criminal activities...." This is particularly true in Western Europe: "When the Soviet Union imploded and travel restrictions between eastern and western Europe faded away, worries emerged in many European countries that they would be flooded by Russian and eastern European organized crime groups" (Kleemans, 2014: 33).

CRITICAL THINKING EXERCISE

Read the passage below and determine for yourself the following: Is alien conspiracy theory applicable to Canada? Does such an application resurrect discredited theories? Are the arguments below xenophobic and/or racist?

Like the United States, Canada is a nation of immigrants and, beginning in the early part of the twentieth century, became home to secret Italian societies, Black Hand extortions, and later Sicilian and Calabrian Mafia groups (see chapter 5). A history of organized crime in Canada may also reveal how other criminal groups have been organized around ethnicity, which falls outside the dominant Anglo-Saxon Protestant culture and which may have been imported from other countries. This list includes Jewish drug-trafficking groups in Montreal in the early twentieth century, as well as Chinese criminal entrepreneurs and groups that trafficked in opium and ran illegal gambling operations in Vancouver, Toronto, and Montreal. More recently, the organized crime landscape in Canada has included criminal groups in which the principal offenders are Vietnamese, Jamaican, Nigerian, Persian, Hungarian, Haitian, and Somali, respectively. Within the Canadian context, alien conspiracy theory could even be applied to the Hells Angels and other outlaw motorcycle gangs, which were imported into Canada from the United States. Proponents of this theory would argue during their emigration to Canada, immigrants from different ethnic groups and nationalities bring with them norms and values, not to mention actual criminal societies, which are antithetical to the law-abiding, peaceful, deferential nature of Canada (as symbolized by the country's motto of "peace, order and good government").

As in the United States, critics would counter this theory's applicability to Canada by arguing that the forces contributing to the onset and persistence of organized crime, and crime in general, are rooted in Canadian culture and society. Racism, discrimination, and segregation have long excluded immigrant ethnic groups from economic and educational opportunities, and integration into mainstream Canada society, which may help to explain why members of ethnic immigrant groups turned to crime. Moreover, as should be clear from

Continued

the first chapter, organized criminality in Canada (and British North America) existed long before the so-called ethnic immigrant groups began to arrive in Canada. Indeed, the origins of most pirates, privateers, as well as most nineteenth-century outlaws, smugglers, fraudsters, counterfeiters, and traffickers in Canada were English.

When applied specifically to Italian-Canadian organized crime, it is true that many of the early Italian criminal societies in this country were made up of immigrants who brought with them some basic ideologies and criminal methods from Sicily and Calabria. However, Italian-Canadian organized crime evolved and prospered in this country due to the same indigenous conditions that existed in the United States. In addition, there is no evidence that a national Italian-Canadian organized crime conspiracy, with a centralized command and control function, ever existed in this country.

While there was never any nationwide confederation of Italian crime groups in Canada, a *Camera di Controllo* was established in Ontario in the 1950s. Made up of the heads of the various 'Ndrangheta cells in that province, the goal of this "board of control" was to ensure co-operation, to avoid territorial infringement, and to resolve any problems that may arise among the different cells. The board, which answered to Buffalo's Stefano Magaddino, who controlled most of the Mafia groups in Ontario, was loosely based on the commission founded in the United States.

Indigenous Social and Cultural Systems Theories

The alien conspiracy theory has been criticized because it erroneously views the relationship between organized crime and North American society as antagonistic, instead of seeing it as an organic outgrowth of complex social forces on the continent that give rise to crime and criminality. Alternative etiological theories of organized crime in America have been developed over the years that place greater emphasis on indigenous factors that contribute to the onset and growth of organized crime. This perspective is epitomized by the adage: "every society gets the crime it deserves." In one of the earliest critiques of alien conspiracy theory, Tyler (1962: 325) argues that the roots of organized crime lie deep within the American culture, "drawing nourishment from the traditional virtues as well as the popularized vices of our civilization."

This section describes and examines theories that situate the root causes of organized crime within American and Canadian societies. These include etiological theories that have been applied to explain crime and criminality in general (strain theory, differential association theory, control theory, social disorganization theory), theories specific to organized crime (ethnic succession theory), as well as subculture theory, which straddles both general and specific theories. The theories presented in this section are complementary in that collectively they explain the causes of (organized) criminality at the macro/mass societal level (strain theory, ethnic succession theory, critically oriented theories), the meso/neighbourhood level (social disorganization theory), and the micro/individual and family level (control theory, differential association theory). This section does not purport to apply every etiological theory to organized crime. Instead, it examines etiological theories that are particularly dominant in the discipline of criminology and particularly applicable to explaining the causes of organized criminality.

Strain and Culture Conflict Theory

Building on a concept originated by the nineteenth-century French sociologist Émile Durkheim, Robert Merton (1938) postulated a highly influential explanation for deviant behaviour in the United States. **Strain and culture conflict theory** suggests that American society, through conflicts and contradictions between its goals and the means to attain them, exerts a pressure on some people to behave in criminal rather than conformist ways. Strain results when people are confronted by the contradiction between goals and the opportunities available for them to reach those goals. As a result, individuals "become estranged from a society that promises them in principle what they are deprived of in reality" (Merton, 1964: 218). The basic argument is that when the channels of vertical mobility are closed or narrowed in a society that places a high premium on economic affluence and social advancement, those who are denied such opportunities turn to illegitimate means to achieve them. This is of central importance in understanding the motives and drives of those situated in America's underclass—the poor, ethnic, or racialized minority groups; immigrants; and others who feel the pain of exclusion—who have, at the same time, embraced the cultural values of material success. The "American Dream" urges all citizens to succeed, yet the opportunity to succeed is distributed unequally (resulting in significant socioeconomic inequalities). Merton says that people at the bottom of the economic ladder may resort to crime to succeed if their sense of frustration is acute enough and their drive to succeed is sufficiently strong. Rudimentary criminal acts generally do not lead to any significant level of economic success, however (Taylor, Watson, & Young, 1973: 97). Innovation is required, which means one must often adopt entrepreneurial crimes that hold the greatest potential to generate wealth.

Ethnic Succession Theory

When viewed in the context of organized crime, strain theory has most often been applied to the blocked aspirations of immigrant minority ethnic and racial groups within

North American society. **Ethnic succession theory** contends that when ethnic minority immigrant groups are disproportionately involved in organized crime, it is because of the barriers they routinely encounter in the pursuit of the American Dream (Bell, 1953; Ianni, 1974). For this theory, the ethnic basis of organized crime groups in the United States is not tied to the importation of foreign criminal cultures or secret societies but results from minority groups struggling for a place in their adopted country. Each successive immigrant group experiences certain strains in American society (such as unemployment, lack of political power, discrimination, violence, etc.), and some members of these groups react by becoming involved in criminal activities. As time passes and as legitimate and socially acceptable avenues of mobility open up to these ethnic groups, the strain subsides, they integrate more fully into mainstream society, and they rely less and less on crime for upward mobility. This, in turn, creates an opportunity for succeeding immigrant groups to fill the criminal void in their own attempts to climb the ladder of success (i.e., ethnic succession).

In his 1953 article, "Crime as an American Way of Life," Daniel Bell criticizes the Kefauver Commission for failing to understand and assimilate salient facts that have created social, political, and economic cleavages within American society. These cleavages and the extraordinary American talent for "compromise in politics and extremism in morality" (132) combine to create what Bell refers to as "one of the queer ladders of social mobility in American life" (133). This ladder represents a shortcut to success in the United States for ethnic and racial groups that do not have access to the legitimate means of power. In short, organized crime persists, in part, because it provides for the upward mobility and assimilation of ethnic and racial minority groups that they cannot always find in mainstream society (Bell, 1953). Individuals or entire ethnic groups that are implicated in organized crime are not intrinsically committed to a deviant subculture but are merely using available, albeit illegal, opportunities to achieve economic success. Thus, involvement in organized crime is simply a rational response to blocked opportunities.

Francis Ianni (1974: 13–14) provides early historical examples of the successive movement of different ethnic (immigrant) groups into and out of organized criminality in the United States, which appear to corroborate this theory:

> The Irish came first, and early in this century, they dominated crime as well as big-city political machinations. As they came to control the political machinery of large cities, they won wealth, power, and respectability through subsequent control of construction, trucking, public utilities, and the waterfront. By the 1920s and the period of Prohibition and speculation in the money markets and real estate, the Irish were succeeded in organized crime by the Jews, and Arnold Rothstein, Lepke Buchalter and Gurrah Shapiro dominated gambling and labor racketeering for over a decade. The Jews quickly moved into the world of business and the professions as more legitimate avenues to economic and social mobility (A dream of

one of America's most successful Jewish gangsters, Meyer Lansky, was to see his son graduate from West Point Military Academy.) The Italians came next.

Ianni and Reuss-Ianni (1972: 193) document another example of ethnic succession theory at the micro-level, in the form of an Italian-American Mafia family they researched. Of those in the fourth generation of the family, "only four out of twenty-seven males are involved in the family business organization. The rest are doctors, lawyers, college teachers, or run their own businesses." In a later book, Ianni (1974: 25) insinuates support for ethnic succession theory when he writes, "the Italians are leaving or being pushed out of organized crime [and] they are being replaced by the next wave of migrants to the city: blacks and Puerto Ricans." According to Kelly (1987: 20), since the 1970s, evidence support Ianni's prediction: ethnic, racial, and other minority groups who are marginalized in American society—African-Americans, Latinos, and Asians— appear to be inheriting or seizing illicit businesses that helped propel the Irish, Jews, and Italians into success and power in the past.

Critics of ethnic succession theory assert that Italian-Americans remained active in organized crime long after they were integrated into North American society. Lupsha (1981: 22) contends that Italian-American organized crime figures who gained economic status were not leaving the underworld and, in many instances, their progeny followed in

Case Study: Can Ethnic Succession Theory Be Applied to Canada?

The history of organized crime in Canada may offer some support for ethnic succession theory. In the mid- to late nineteenth century, Irish immigrants were disproportionately represented in violent criminal gangs in Upper and Lower Canada, in part because they were relegated to the second class by the English and Scots who held most positions of power. During the first half of the twentieth century, Irish gangs were eclipsed by more sophisticated Jewish criminal entrepreneurs who focused on consensual crimes and appeared to be dominant in such rackets as gambling and drug trafficking (particularly in Montreal where anti-Semitism was rife). Around the same time, Chinese merchants in British Columbia were some of the leading purveyors of opium, gambling, and prostitution. Their clientele was the Chinese immigrant labourer, who found refuge in such vices in the face of constant racial hatred, ethnicity-based herding, violence, and legislative disenfranchisement by the larger white population. The era of Prohibition and the post-war years witnessed the rise of the so-called Italian racketeers, many of whom were discriminated against in Canada due to their ethnicity and Catholic religion. By the 1970s, Italian-American crime groups were in decline, with the resulting void filled by other ethnic groups that had recently immigrated to North America.

their footsteps. Lupsha writes that a criminal lifestyle is a highly personal choice "based on individual skills and a personal rationalization which perverts traditional American values and culture" (4). The possibility of making big money by catering to American vices in tandem with "personal choice, not career blockage or frustration with legitimate mobility paths" provides the opportunity structure for immigrants and others in America to become involved in entrepreneurial crime (14). Further, "they turned to crime because they felt the legitimate opportunity structure was for 'suckers'" (15). In other words, those who become involved in organized crime are in it for the money and are committed to the deviant lifestyle; they are not in it for social mobility in legitimate society.

Potter (1994) concludes that historically, ethnic succession appears to be a dubious concept; members of immigrant ethnic and racialized groups may turn to organized crime, but they do not necessarily replace older groups. Moreover, while encounters with strain, such as racism and limited economic opportunity, may certainly compel members of ethnic minority groups toward criminal activities, it does not explain why middle-class, white, Anglo-Saxon men become involved in organized crime (including the overwhelmingly white, Anglo-Saxon outlaw motorcycle gangs). Nor does it explain why organized economic crimes by the wealthy and the powerful continue to be a major problem in North America.

Radical and Critically Oriented Theories

Strain and ethnic succession theories can be viewed as **structuralist theories** because they situate the causes of organized crime within a broader overarching political and economic system or structure that is said to ostensibly influence human behaviour, and the causes of criminal behaviour specifically. The more radical or critically oriented structuralist theories are influenced by **Marxist** philosophies and **critical criminology**. While there are important differences between the two schools of thought in how they view the structural causes of crime, both generally agree that capitalism (and the support for free markets by the state) promotes organized crime in capitalist societies. As Albanese (2015: 95) puts it, "In this view, capitalism promotes organized crime by placing a premium on income generation and the ensuing conflict between the working class and those who control the legitimate market." Further, when viewed within the context of the capitalist system, there is really no difference between crimes committed by corporations or criminal organizations. Critically oriented structuralists "argue that the American capitalist ideology, which equates success with income accumulation, encourages people to disregard the rights of others who stand in their way. The line between a successful business person, a white-collar criminal, and an organized crime offender, according to this view, is narrow indeed, distinguished only by the method (legal or illegal) by which the money was obtained, not by who may have been exploited in garnering it" (Albanese, 2015: 95).

Schneider and Schneider (2012) argue, "The formation of criminal organizations in the nineteenth and early twentieth centuries owes a great deal to capitalist development and Western European colonial expansion. First, the dynamics of capital accumulation and colonialism dislocated many rural populations, eliminating their rights to use commonly held resources, dispossessing them from land, and, often, taking away their livelihoods. Energized by ideas of just retribution, bandits, gangsters, pirates and other 'outlaws' pursued careers of predatory payback, out of which grew various (and variously extortionist) mechanisms for privately protecting persons and property" (Schneider & Schneider, 2012: 355).

Albanese critiques this radical or critical structuralist approach, writing, "if the capitalist ideology lies at the root of organized crime, it can be argued that socialist economies would have less organized crime because of less pronounced disparities in income and opportunities within society. However, this does not appear to be the case. Organized crime, corruption, and smuggling have been reported to be widespread in many different kinds of socialist countries" (Albanese, 2015: 96).

Differential Association Theory

Strain theory, ethnic succession theory, and critically oriented theories sketch out the general structural contradictions that may precipitate the rise of (organized) crime. Yet it leaves unanswered the following question: Why do some people suffering from strain turn to criminal innovation, while others do not? Edwin Sutherland provides one answer: **differential association**. According to his differential association theory of deviance, criminal behaviour is not simply an impulsive reaction to thwarted opportunities or an instinctive response to situations that produce frustration. Sutherland (1973) argued that just as individuals will tend to conform if their socialization emphasizes a respect for prevailing norms, so too would they become deviant if their socialization emphasizes contempt for these norms. For Sutherland, a criminal orientation is not solely based on blocked aspirations; the individual must also exist in an environment where criminal behaviour can be learned and emulated, primarily through associations with individuals who are involved in criminal activities.

The more a neophyte is surrounded by individuals who are contemptuous of and regularly violate prevailing cultural norms and laws, the greater the probability that he or she will become criminal. They are at risk of such behaviour because of their sustained contact with those already committed to law breaking and because of the relative isolation from those who obey the law (Kelly, 1987: 19). Abadinsky (1983: 71) sums up how strain and differential association are relevant to organized crime:

> Socioeconomic conditions relegate persons to an environment wherein they experience a sense of strain—anomie—as well as differential association. In the environment that has traditionally spawned organized crime, this "strain" is intense. Conditions of severe deprivation, with extremely limited access to ladders of legitimate success, are coupled with readily available success models that are innovative (e.g., racketeers). Thus, participation in organized crime requires anomie and differential association.

However, learning the techniques of sophisticated criminality also requires the proper environment—ecological niches where this education is available.

Robert Lombardo (1979: 18) points out that the prospective members of Italian-American organized crime groups "typically come from communities which share collective representations and moral sentiments which allow them to recognize the pursuit of a career in the underworld as a legitimate way of life." Young men from these areas dress in a certain style and congregate in social clubs and nightspots where they are able to associate with the men who have already been allowed entry into an organized crime group. They are ready and eager to show their mettle by accepting

---

Case Study: Applying Differential Association Theory to Vito Rizzuto

Vito Rizzuto, who headed the Montreal Mafia from the early 1980s until his death in 2013, may have very well epitomized differential association theory. Throughout his life, Vito was surrounded by men who upheld the values of the Sicilian Mafia and, from an early age, he was indoctrinated into this criminal culture. Vito was born in the small Sicilian town of Cattolica Eraclea, located in the province of Agrigento, a Mafia stronghold. By the time of his birth, his father, Nicolo (Nick) Rizzuto, had married into the local Mafia family, which was led by his new father-in-law, Antonio Manno. When he immigrated to Canada with his wife and children in 1954, Nick renewed contact with his Mafia family members and other Sicilian Mafiosi who had already relocated to Montreal. Nick became a member of the Montreal wing of the Bonanno family sometime in the late 1950s or early 1960s while it was under the leadership of Vic Cotroni.

From an early age, Vito was groomed by his father to become a made member of the Mafia. During this time, Vito was learning the tricks of the trade from his father, who was a prolific international drug trafficker. Vito himself would later become one of Canada's biggest drug importers and wholesalers. After Nick staged a coup that overthrew Vic Cotroni as leader of the Montreal Mafia, Nick installed his son as the head, where he became one of Canada's most powerful and successful criminals.

The case of Vito Rizzuto demonstrates that one does not have to be raised in poverty or poor neighbourhoods to be negatively socialized (surrounded and influenced by anti-social individuals). Vito was raised in wealth and privilege and it could be said that the attraction of the Mafia lifestyle was positively reinforced for a youthful Vito as he observed the wealth and power his father and other Mafiosi accrued through their criminal ventures.

assignments from these "goodfellas" (Abadinsky, 2000: 38). Donald Cressey (1969: 263) argues that local gangs and organized crime groups encourage deviance among youth. In order for an organized crime group to survive, it must have "an institution-alized process for inducting new members and inculcating them with the values and ways of behaving of the social system." In addition, "in some neighbourhoods, all three of the essential ingredients of an effective recruiting process are in operation: inspiring aspiration for membership, training for membership, and selection for membership."

Social Disorganization Theory

Notwithstanding the case of Vito Rizzuto, instances where young people learn and organize their behaviour according to the norms of a delinquent or criminal group are more likely to occur in local environments characterized by **social disorganization**. These are typically poor, marginalized, high-crime neighbourhoods. Clifford Shaw and Henry McKay, sociologists at the University of Chicago, used their city as a laboratory to study of patterns of crime and delinquency during the 1920s and 1930s. Their analysis of where anti-social youth lived in Chicago showed a concentration in inner-city areas characterized by low rent and physical deterioration. The question that Shaw and McKay attempted to answer : What was it about the environment of these neighbourhoods that made them criminogenic? Their answer was that in such neigh-bourhoods, which they called "zones of transition," there was also a rapid turnover of the local population, which led to a chronic problem of "social disorganization." In turn, this undermined social cohesion, informal social control, and the positive socialization of children and youth. As a result of this social pathology and the weak-ening of local informal social controls, children and young people were ineffectually socialized, which gave rise to delinquency.

Shaw and McKay also found that socially disorganized neighbourhoods main-tained a high level of delinquency and criminality over many years despite local pop-ulation turnover and changes in the ethnic composition of the neighbourhood. Such neighbourhoods are characterized by attitudes and values that are conducive to pro-moting an ecosystem of delinquency and crime that is transmitted from one local generation to the next, in much the same way that language and other social forms are transmitted. "The heavy concentration of delinquency in certain areas means that boys living in these areas are in contact not only with individuals who engage in a pro-scribed activity but also with groups which sanction such behavior and exert pressure upon their members to conform to group standards." Moreover, the presence of a large number of adult criminals in socially disorganized neighbourhoods "means that chil-dren there are in contact with crime as a career and with the criminal way of life, sym-bolized by organized crime" (Shaw & McKay, 1972: 174). In short, like differential association theory, social disorganization theory suggests that it is one's social envi-ronment where deviant norms and values, as well as techniques of (organized) criminal behaviour, are transmitted culturally, interpersonally, and intergenerationally.

Case Study: Social Disorganization and Gangs on First Nation Reserves

It could be argued that some of the most socially disorganized communities in Canada are First Nations reserves. Compared to non-Indigenous communities, First Nations reserves are more likely to have much lower standards of living and higher rates of poverty and unemployment, substandard housing, boil water advisories, family dysfunction and break up, child physical and sexual abuse, substance abuse, preventable diseases, mortality, and youth dropping out of school. In short, First Nations reserves are rife with factors that contribute to criminality.

This social disorganization is the result of a complex interaction of many historical and contemporary factors: colonialization, the destruction of cultures and languages, herding historically nomadic cultures into reserves, historically ingrained racism and discrimination by the dominant white culture, as well as the deleterious repercussions of the residential school system.

It should be no surprise then that some of the worst crime and violence in Canada take place on First Nations' reserves. Some of the most feared criminal gangs in the Prairies, such as the Indian Posse, the Manitoba Warriors, and the Native Syndicate, are made up of young people from province's colonialized Indigenous population who live in socially disorganized neighbourhoods in Regina and Winnipeg or First Nations reserves in these provinces.

Subculture Theory

The assumption that the negative socialization of young people contributes to the onset of criminal behaviour presupposes that the offender is attached to values and norms that are at odds with the mainstream, law-abiding culture. Collectively, chronic and serious offenders belong to a subculture made up of people who have rejected many of the central tenets and norms of the prevailing culture. This is the basis of the **subculture theory** of crime.

The term *culture* refers to a source of patterning in human conduct; it is the sum of patterns of social relationships and shared meanings by which people give order, expression, and value to common experiences. A subculture implies there is a social value system that stands apart from a larger or central value system in a society (Wolfgang & Ferracuti, 1967: 99). Organized crime comprises a deviant subculture into which offenders are immersed, some of whom making a lifelong commitment. Instead of conforming to conventional social norms, chronic and serious organized criminal offenders openly rebel against them and orient their behaviour according to the norms of the subculture and/or the criminal group to which they belong or with which they identify. They reject the very obedience to traditional rules, regulations, and laws that govern civil society. This rejection forms the basis of an organized crime subculture that is promoted,

Photo 4.2: One-percenter diamond patch worn by members of outlaw motorcycle clubs

Source: Icedragon, via Wikimedia Commons

perpetuated, and even cherished by those in the underworld. As one member of New York's Gambino crime family succinctly said to a reporter, "[W]e don't want to be part of your world. We don't want to belong to country clubs" (as cited in Brenner 1990: 181).

The subcultures manifest themselves in secret societies and criminal organizations that are characterized by anti-social norms and even rules of conduct that promulgate such norms. The values and norms of the organized crime subculture inculcate a contempt for civil society that is reflected in the belief that only "suckers" work legitimate jobs (Lupsha, 1981: 22). Exemplifying this attitude is the term used by some American Mafiosi to refer to one another. As noted in chapter 3, a "wiseguy" believes that anybody who follows commonly accepted rules and laws is a sap and deserves to be victimized. In his biography, Henry Hill infers how his boss, Paul (Paulie) Vario, a made member of the Lucchese crime family, represents a cogent example of a wiseguy:

> Paulie was always asking me for stolen credit cards whenever he and his wife, Phyllis, were going out for the night. Paulie called stolen credit cards "Muldoons," and he always said that liquor tastes better on a Muldoon. The fact that a guy like Paul Vario, a capo in the Lucchese crime family, would even consider going out on a social occasion with his wife and run the risk of getting caught using a stolen credit card might surprise some people. But if you knew wiseguys, you would know right away that the best part of the night for Paulie came from the fact that he was getting over on somebody. (Pileggi, 1985: 20)

An anti-establishment subculture is also a defining characteristic of outlaw or "one-percenter" motorcycle gangs. Reveling in their image as social outcasts, they purposively cut themselves off from the majority culture (and other motorcycle enthusiasts) through their label "one-percenter," which refers to "the one percent of us who has given up on society" (Bandidos MC website, n.d.). Motorcycle gangs are "particularly attractive to individuals who display deviant behaviour because the group is mutually supportive of all relevant deviant acts whether it is drug dealing or rape. The group returns recognition for feats of macho-daring and coddles the individual in a strange sociopathic mutual exchange of supportive psychological tribal needs" (Royal Canadian Mounted Police, 1987a: 9).

Summary: Indigenous Social and Cultural Systems Theories

In sum, strain alone may not be sufficient to explain one's participation in organized criminality. What may be necessary is cultural transmission through differential association, which is often (but not always) found in families and neighbourhoods where there is a high level of social disorganization (including poverty, transience, crime, and deviant subcultures). Particularly vulnerable in these environments are youth who have been either under-socialized in the accepted norms of civil society, or over-socialized in the norms and values of the deviant subculture by family members, peers, or other role models. What each of the aforementioned theories has in common is the belief that (organized) crime is rooted in the institutions of a society and arises from disruptions and malfunctioning of these social systems, which results in the negative socialization of young people. Indeed, what many of these theories also have in common is that chronic and serious criminal behaviour often finds its root causes in childhood and adolescence. Furthermore, such criminal behaviour does not have a single cause—its roots are complex and multifaceted, meaning that more than one of the aforementioned theories may be applicable to a particular (organized) criminal offender. The more criminogenic risk factors a child or adolescent faces and the more severe the risk factors are, the greater the chance that the young person will be involved in serious criminal offending later in life.

CRITICAL THINKING EXERCISE

Conduct biographical research into one or more offenders that have been involved in organized crime in Canada. Try to apply two or more of the preceding etiological theories to explain how this individual became a serious and chronic offender. You should also be prepared to critically analyze the application of these sociological theories to the offenders you are researching.

Economic Theories of Organized Crime

In addition to sociological concepts and theories, organized crime has also been ex-plained through economic theories and analyses. An economic approach focuses on how criminal groups and illegal markets come into existence to supply goods and services that are demanded by the public, but which have been declared illegal or are strictly regulated by the state, such as drugs, gambling, counterfeit goods, alcohol, cigarettes, or weapons. As history has shown, outlawing a good or service simply drives it into under-ground markets, where it is sold by criminal entrepreneurs.

Like sociological theories, economic analyses situate the cause and contributing factors of organized crime within the societies where it operates. However, an econom-ic perspective avoids explanations that define organized crime in pathological terms. Indeed, an economic analysis views OC and illegal markets as a rational system that operates according to the laws of supply and demand. Kleemans (2014: 33) refers to this as **illegal enterprise theory**, which posits that "illegal activities are quite similar to legal activities and that illegal entrepreneurs (and illegal enterprises) may be best viewed as calculating individuals (or enterprises) operating in illegal markets in a similar way as in legal markets."

The implication of this economic perspective is that organized crime is not alien to the societies in which it operates, but a part of the many commercial markets within a society. Instead of viewing organized crime as an alien parasite that preys upon society and gives nothing in return, an economic analysis recognizes there is a symbiotic rela-tionship between criminal organizations and illegal markets (as suppliers) and the larger society (as consumers) (Dickie & Wilson, 1993: 216; Martens & Miller-Longfellow, 1982: 4). In short, organized crime fulfills certain commercial functions for society (Lotz & Gillespie, 1975).

Economic theories of organized crime view the underground economy as an exten-sion of the legitimate economy. As such, an economic analysis of organized crime and illegal markets draws parallels with legitimate economic institutions and commerce. Some argue that illegal markets can be explained through the same concepts, theo-ries, and assumptions that explain commerce in the legitimate marketplace. Research has shown that the price of illegal or contraband commodities is related to supply and demand. This means, for example, if the local cocaine supply is plentiful, the price will be low, but if the local supply is limited, the price will usually rise (Caulkins & Reuter, 2010; Office of National Drug Control Policy, 2004; Royal Canadian Mounted Police, 2007). Simply put, organized crime and illegal markets operate according to the same fundamental assumptions that govern entrepreneurship in the legitimate marketplace and, as such, "the laws of supply and demand play an important role in the willingness of a criminal group to enter into criminal behavior" (Lyman & Potter, 2014: 79). Once in an illegal market, the criminal group endeavours to maintain and extend their share of the market (Smith, 1980).

Of course the parallels between legal and illegal enterprises end when certain characteristics of illegal markets are taken into consideration; criminal groups often use illegal means to enter a market or to maintain or increase their profits (e.g., corruption, violence), and participants always run the risk of getting caught by police or being killed by competitors. Yet, these factors are part of the economic analysis of organized crime and illegal markets and are also taken into consideration by the rationally minded criminal entrepreneur.

The laws of supply and demand are implicitly recognized by police and researchers who often use the current retail or wholesale price of drugs to gauge the current level of supply. This economic perspective also has significant implications for efforts to control organized crime and illegal markets. Schelling (1967) concludes that if society is unwilling to restructure the laws and regulations that are instrumental in creating the protected markets of organized crime, then perhaps the legalization of organized crime businesses will produce benefits for society because supply will now take place in legal, regulated markets.

Smith's **spectrum-based theory of enterprises** is an explicit recognition that profit-driven illegal enterprises operating in black markets can be equated to profit-driven companies in the legitimate economy. His theory, in fact, places illegal and legal enterprises at the opposite ends of the same continuum (or spectrum) of legitimacy (with legal enterprises that periodically engage in criminal conduct situated somewhere in the middle of the spectrum). As Smith (1975: 335) writes, "illicit enterprise is the extension of legitimate market activities into areas normally proscribed—i.e., beyond existing limits of law—for the pursuit of profit and in response to a latent illicit demand." Placing illegal and legal enterprises on the same spectrum reflects Smith's contention that there are no differences between criminal organizations and legal corporations that engage in criminal conduct. Instead, any profit-making venture can be placed somewhere on this spectrum based on the scope and nature of criminal wrongdoing (i.e., a legal corporation that engages in fraud may be situated on the same point on the spectrum as a criminal group conducting the same sort of fraud).

CRITICAL THINKING EXERCISE

Critically analyze the economic approach to understanding organized crime. Do you believe this analysis contributes to a better understanding of why organized crime exists? Do you believe that an economic analysis is an accurate depiction of how illicit markets form and operate? Apply an economic analysis to the black market for an illegal good or service in Canada. To what extent does this analysis capture why criminal entrepreneurs may want to become involved in this black market?

In sum, according to von Lampe (2016: 45), examining organized crime through the lens of economic theory "implies three basic assumptions: (a) that organized crimes are a form of economic activity, aimed at generating profits, (b) that the individuals and groups involved in these activities resemble enterprises that are in many ways similar to their legitimate counterparts, and (c) that these enterprises sell their illegal products to customers in a market setting dictated by the laws of supply and demand."

One criticism of this economic perspective is that illegal markets are highly distorted relative to legitimate markets. Naylor (2004: 21) contends, "the facile analogy between legal and illegal firms is at best a serious oversimplification, at worst simply wrong. In illegal markets that are highly segmented, decisions are personalized, information flows constricted, capital supplies short-term and unreliable, objective price data lacking, and the time horizons (indeed the very existence) of enterprises coterminous with those of the entrepreneurs." Furthermore, the application of traditional economic theory to organized crime only captures consensual crimes and ignores predatory criminal activities such as theft, hijacking, kidnapping, extortion, and fraud. These predatory crimes are also significant revenue generators for criminal groups and do not correspond to the laws of supply and demand (i.e., there is not much consumer demand for extortion or kidnappings).

The State, Public Policy, and Organized Crime

This section examines how the state and governments contribute to the creation of illegal markets and the fermentation of organized crime. This includes (1) the role that public policies make in creating illegal markets, and (2) how organized crime is fostered in countries or regions characterized by weak and or corrupt states and state actors.

The Role of Public Policy in Creating Illegal Markets and Organized Crime

Whether goods or services are to be made available in either the legal or illegal market (or both) depends primarily on laws and regulations created by the state. In general, there are three scenarios in which government policies create illegal markets for products and services. The first is when a government passes laws prohibiting the sale and consumption of a particular good or service in demand by the public, which often drives supply to the underground market. This creates an opportunity for criminal entrepreneurs to monopolize that product or service. Second, illegal markets are created when governments place significant controls or restrictions on the supply and consumption of certain goods, because this creates a limited supply or a high price of these products in the legitimate markets. One pertinent example of this scenario is prescription drugs, which is tightly controlled and regulated by the state, but which is also widely sold in black markets.

Case Study: OxyContin and Illegal Markets

In the fall of 2004, eight men in Cape Breton, Nova Scotia, were charged with more than 20 offences after allegedly selling the prescription drug OxyContin to an undercover RCMP officer during a four-month police operation. Most of the OxyContin pills, which addicts inject or sniff after crushing them, were sold to police in 40- or 80-milligram doses. The pills sell on the streets for an average $1 per milligram. Police have said that people involved in low-level retail sales of the drug are either using their own prescriptions to make money, are stealing the pills from drug stores or homes, are buying pills from regional (illegal) wholesale dealers, or receiving shipments from outside the province through organized crime networks (*Chronicle Herald*, October 28, 2004).

Third, illegal markets are often created by the state through taxation policies. When governments place a tax on legal consumer goods and services, this generally drives up their retail prices. A black market is created in this circumstance if this tax creates a price disparity between different jurisdictions; that is, if the good or service can be obtained cheaper elsewhere (i.e., a jurisdiction with lower taxes). International and domestic smuggling of legal products are usually the result of a disparity in the level of taxes that have been applied to a product by different jurisdictions. Black market cigarettes are perhaps the most cogent example of how taxes contribute to smuggling and illicit markets in Canada and globally. The higher taxes that are levied on cigarettes by federal and provincial governments in Canada relative to those in the United States has created great disparities in the retail price and has produced a burgeoning trade in contraband cigarettes smuggled into Canada from the United States.

Regardless of whether the good or service is criminalized, tightly controlled, or heavily taxed by the state, the argument is that public policies help create and perpetuate illegal markets. (Ironically, governments in Canada are in competition with organized crime groups over the supply of certain goods and services, in particular liquor and gambling, both of which generate revenues in the billions of dollars annually for both governments and criminal organizations.) One implication of this public policy perspective is that in order to control organized crime and minimize illegal markets, the state should legalize certain goods and services that are currently criminalized. In its policy manual for the 2015 federal election in Canada, the Liberal Party relied partially on this rationale for its proposed policy of legalizing marijuana, pledging, "To ensure that we keep marijuana out of the hands of children, and the profits out of the hands of criminals, we will legalize, regulate, and restrict access to marijuana" (Liberal Party of Canada, n.d., 55).

There is some evidence that when certain criminalized goods and services are legalized, the illegal market for these goods and services are diminished because they can be obtained legally, which in turn often means that criminal entrepreneurs withdraw

Photo 4.3: Government policies that criminalize society's vices help to create and sustain organized crime

Source: Saffron Blaze, via Wikimedia Commons

from the illegal market. After Prohibition laws were repealed in the United States in 1933, the illegal liquor market contracted significantly and criminal organizations moved into other illegal markets created by government criminal policies, in particular gambling and drugs. Following Prohibition, government taxation policies in Canada created a significant domestic black market in liquor because they increased the price of booze relative to that of the United States, which became the main source of the cheaper contraband liquor north of the border. Even when government policies reduce the size of an illegal market, it does not impact on the overall problem of organized crime as criminal entrepreneurs and groups adapt to policy changes and opportunistically pursue other profitable illegal activities and markets.

A criticism of this public policy perspective is that it only partially explains the causes behind organized crime and illegal markets. It does not explain why certain individuals become involved in illegal markets or organized crime. Those who support the criminalization of certain drugs also argue that legalization policies do not necessarily mean that harmful substances are no longer available in illegal markets. If the price of legal marijuana is high, if availability is limited, or if there are (age) restrictions on purchasing the drug, there stands a good chance that illegal markets for pot will continue to exist. There is already a precedent in which criminal entrepreneurs and groups have infiltrated the legal market for medicinal marijuana in Canada. Police cases have documented the involvement of criminal groups in the production and retailing of legal medical marijuana, which includes the illegal diversion of pot from licensed medical marijuana production facilities to the black market (Canadian Press, July 3, 2013; *Vancouver Sun*, February 18, 2014). One criticism of the Liberal Party's marijuana legalization policy that is specific to Canadian circumstances is that it will not affect organized crime's involvement in the marijuana trade in Canada because a good proportion of the pot produced in this country is exported for foreign markets. If pot is legalized in Canada, producers may simply focus more on export markets. Finally, from a policy perspective, there is a fear that if certain consensual crimes are legalized, criminal organizations will focus more on predatory crimes.

The Connection between Weak States and Organized Crime

In addition to government policies, the creation and proliferation of organized crime has also been attributed to a weak state presence in a particular country or region. van Dijk and Spapens (2014: 215) write that Mafia-type criminal syndicates "seem to have developed, and may still thrive, in countries where state authority is weak, corruption levels are high, and consequently, enforcement is lax." In these circumstances, "dominant criminal groups may even develop into an alternative for the state, by offering protection to citizens." Gambetta was one of the first to advance this idea through his **protection theory**, which was initially applied to explain the rise of the Mafia in Sicily. Gambetta argues that the Sicilian Mafia originally arose from the weak central government in Rome, creating the opportunity for private enforcers called "gambellottos" or "mafiosos" to fill the void. The Mafia in Italy is said to operate as "an industry which produces, promotes, and sells private protection" (Gambetta, 1993: 1). The demand for protection, according to von Lampe (2016: 47) "typically arises in a market where there is a lack of trust between market participants and where their interests are not sufficiently safeguarded by the state. This applies to illegal markets, where the state, by definition, does not assume a regulatory function but also to legal markets if and when the state fails to provide effective protection. Criminal organizations then step in, for example, to enforce contracts or to keep new competitors out of a market in exchange for a share of the profits." According to Kleemans (2014: 36), Mafia-style groups gain control of markets and territories as "alternative governments" and generate revenue "by taking over two traditional state monopolies: the use of violence and taxation." The two are interconnected in that violence and intimidation are often used to coerce people and businesses to pay a fee, tribute, or tax (see chapter 9 for more on the protection racket).

States and their governments may also promote organized crime by becoming susceptible to or even initiating corruption. "Large and strong criminal organizations cannot develop if the government is strongly organized," Sutherland (1934: 188) claims. He goes so far to assert, "Modern law enforcement agencies cooperate with criminal organizations because they are under the control of politicians who are either criminals in the usual sense of the word, grafters, and bribe-takers (specialized forms of criminals), or have sympathetic relations because of common membership in the underworld" (as cited in Fijnaut, 2014: 75).

Gambetta's protection theories have been applied to other countries with weak, unstable, and/or corrupt state actors. The rapid rise of organized crime in Russia has been attributed in part to government instability and corruption that accompanied the collapse of the Soviet Union. In particular, extortion and other protection rackets perpetrated against emergent private sector firms became endemic during the period of rapid transition away from the totalitarian state, and it was this "evaporating centralized state control" that presented "opportunities for Mafia groups" (Kleemans, 2014: 36). Weak and corruptible states have also been blamed for the rise of crime groups in Latin American countries, and the emergence of powerful multinational drug-trafficking cartels in Colombia and Mexico specifically. Volkov (2014: 160–61) relates how the involvement of Mafia-style Yakuza crime groups in Japan's "real estate foreclosure, bankruptcy adjudication, and debt recovery are examples of organized crime profiting from inadequate state regulation."

According to Paoli (2014a), the "American Cosa Nostra rose in the early twentieth century when the U.S. government still had limited authority in the Italian ethnic community." This limited authority stemmed in part from the lack of experience that Sicilian immigrants had with formal governments. The "limited authority" that American state actors had over criminal offenders from the Italian immigrant community also stemmed from corrupt government officials that "preferred to come to terms with, rather than prosecute, Cosa Nostra bosses and other criminal entrepreneurs fostered by Prohibition" (Paoli, 2014a: 3). Kleemans (2014: 36) notes that Gambetta's protection theory has been applied to "the dominance of Italian-American Mafia families in New York, in the building sector, the waste disposal industry, the Fulton Fish Market, the unions, and the harbor, among others."

Critics of Gambetta's protection theory note that it may only apply to a limited number of countries or organized crime cases. Many OC conspiracies find their origins and continue to operate in countries and regions where there is a strong state presence. Another "weak aspect of protection theory is that the analogy between Mafia groups and states is ill-conceived." In other words, Mafia groups do not replace the state in illegal markets because states "generally neither guarantee illegal transactions in illegal markets nor illegal operations in legal markets" (Kleemans, 2014: 37).

CRITICAL THINKING EXERCISE

Based on the passage below, as well as other cases described in this textbook, determine if the Gambetta's protection theory—and the broader argument of the weak and corruptible state—can be applied to explain the onset and proliferation of the Italian Mafia and organized crime generally in Canada. Other than the

Continued

examples provided below, can you identify any others? What critiques do you have of the examples provided below?

It can be argued that organized criminality arose in what is now Canada during a time when there was a weak state presence in British North America or New France. This was particularly true when pirates first began roaming the seas off Newfoundland in the 1700s. The organized whiskey pedlars of the nineteenth century flourished in the Canadian prairies before any formal government presence was established there (in fact, the destructive presence of the illegal whiskey merchants precipitated the formation of the North-West Mounted Police in the Prairies by the Dominion government). During the 1920s and 1930s, organized crime flourished in many Canadian urban centres due to endemic corruption within municipal, provincial, and federal government agencies (including police and customs agencies). During the 1950s, corruption among municipal government officials and police subsided somewhat, which resulted in "removing police protection from illegal markets such as prostitution, gambling, and late-night drinking." The result was that these markets were suddenly left unprotected. The unintended consequences of police reform provided an opening for the Italian crime groups, especially in Montreal and Toronto, giving them "a golden opportunity to become entrenched as suppliers of services of dispute resolution and protection in place of the corrupt police officers" (Varese, 2014: 349).

The rise of outlaw motorcycle gang has been attributed, not necessarily to weak or corrupt states, but a delayed response by lawmakers and police to the rise of violent biker gangs beginning in the 1970s. Like most other countries, the state does little to regulate illegal markets in Canada and it can be argued that powerful criminal groups like the Hells Angels or the Montreal Mafia have tried to fill this void by attempting to monopolize illicit markets and control other criminal actors through coercion or negotiation. One final example may be the corruption that has permeated Montreal's public sector construction contracts, which is a function of corruption at the provincial and municipal levels as well as the Rizzuto Mafia family's adherence to its role as a provider of protection (in this case to construction companies) and a broker of illicit contracts.

ADMINISTRATIVE CRIMINOLOGY AND THE ORGANIZATION OF CRIMES

Administrative criminology differs from sociological, economic, or political theories in that it is unconcerned with the causes of organized crime or related criminal behaviour. Instead, its focus is on the actual commission of the criminal event in a specific time and place by rationally thinking offenders who take advantage of opportunities presented to them within a particular environment. Specifically, administrative criminology asserts three main hypotheses concerning crime:

1. Most criminal acts require convergence of motivated offenders and potential victims at a particular time and place (Cohen & Felson, 1979).
2. Many types of crime are opportunistic; that is, offenders take advantage of certain opportunities they perceive can be exploited within a particular physical and human environment (Brantingham & Brantingham, 1981, 1998).
3. Criminal behaviour is purposive in the sense that it is intended to meet an immediate or long-term need of the offender and may also be characterized as a rational decision-making process whereby the offender calculates the advantages and disadvantages of a specific criminal act (although administrative criminologists recognize that not all offenders act rationally) (Clarke & Cornish, 1985).

One methodological tool used to facilitate a situational analysis on how criminal acts unfold is a **crime script,** which is meant to provide a way of "generating, organizing and systematizing knowledge about the procedural aspects and procedural requirements of crime commission" (Cornish, 1994: 151). Crime script analysis draws attention to the procedural aspects of rational criminal offending that are goal-oriented and which consist "of a sequence of steps or sub-goals" (Cornish, 1994: 158). To this end, the application of the script process "enables one aspect of the rational choice perspective on criminal behavior—the unfolding of criminal events—to be developed further, and captures something of the routinized quality, yet flexibly responsive nature of criminal decision making" (Cornish, 1994: 155–57). In short, a crime script analysis recognizes that, situationally, every criminal act is the result of sequential events and analytically identifies and organizes these steps as such. "By drawing attention to the way that events and episodes unfold," Cornish (1994: 155) writes, "the script concept offers a useful analytic tool for looking at behavioral routines in the service of rational, purposive, goal-oriented action."

A situational approach to understanding organized crime is focused mostly on the organization of crimes and, more specifically, a particular criminal event (or interlocking series of criminal events). Crime scripts are conducive to a situational analysis of organized criminal events because the latter, by definition, often entails many potential sequential steps, offenders, and decisions. Operating on an assumption that offenders involved in organized crimes make rational decisions, the scripts of experienced and professional criminals tend to be more complex compared to those of rudimentary street crimes. Therefore, the scripts for organized crimes attempt to model the experience, sophistication, and adaptability of organized criminal offenders. As Cornish (1994: 177) puts it, "as offenders become more experienced and as specific offenses are committed by more people, elaboration occurs in a variety of ways as the result of: performance and practice; rehearsing and flaw-hunting; neutralizing the risks: overcoming the obstacles and barriers encountered while offending; and debriefing and sharing accounts of failures with others." One skeletal example of a crime script applied to the inbound smuggling of drugs through a Canadian marine port is summarized below.

Outline of a Crime Script: The Smuggling of Drugs through a Canadian Marine Port

1. Preparation—Preparing the illegal goods and shipping container for export to Canada
   - Physically breaking down the drugs into smaller quantities for concealment
   - Concealing drugs
   - Loading legitimate goods (and illegal drugs) onto a shipping container
   - Completion of (misrepresentative) paperwork

2. Receiving—Delivery of marine container to exporting marine port
   - (Foreign) marine port logistical operations

3. Unloading and storage—Placing the container in a known and recorded location at a marine port so it may be retrieved when it is needed
4. Staging—Preparing a container to leave the marine port terminal; containers to be exported are identified and organized so as to optimize the loading process
5. Loading—Placing the container on the ocean-going vessel
6. Exit—Departure of vessel from foreign marine port
7. Transportation
8. Preparation—Preparing for the arrival of illegal goods from a foreign country by conspiring criminal offenders in Canada
9. Arrival at Canadian marine port
10. Receiving
11. Storage
12. Staging
13. Loading (of inter-modal land transport vehicle)
14. Exit—Departure of inter-modal carrier from Canadian marine port

Source: Presidia Security Consulting Inc., & Schneider, S. (2011). *A Study of the Vulnerability of Marine Port Operations to Organized Crime.* Report submitted to Public Safety Canada.

THE ORGANIZATION OF CRIMINALS: THEORETICAL MODELS ON THE STRUCTURE OF ORGANIZED CRIME ASSOCIATIONS

As noted in previous chapters, a predominant way to view OC is as an association of criminal offenders. Thus, a defining characteristic of OC is a systematic pattern to the relationship among the offenders, which in turn helps define the organizational structure of a particular criminal conspiracy. Within this context, four theoretical models capture the different types of offender relationships and organizational structures: (1) the bureaucratic/hierarchical model, in which there is a vertical power structure and one's role in the organization is dictated by where one fits in this hierarchy; (2) the kinship model, in which the crime group is portrayed as being structured around familial ties and blood relationships; (3) the patron–client model, where the Mafioso and other professional criminals become patrons to others by providing contacts, resources, influence, and direction; and (4) the network model, which is characterized by a fluid association of like-minded offenders who are connected through symmetrical business partnerships based on complementary areas of specialization or resources. As von Lampe (2016: 93–94) notes, different structures may be in place to achieve different goals: "some structures help criminals successfully commit crimes, some structures foster social bonds between criminals, and yet other structures regulate and control the behavior of criminals." Each of these different theoretical models is discussed below. Mention will be made of how different structures accomplish different goals; however, what all of these structures have in common is a shared purpose of making money through illegal means.

The Bureaucratic/Hierarchical Model

A bureaucracy is an organization that has certain defining characteristics, such as a hierarchical power structure, a division of labour, and formal channels of communications. What makes it most distinctive from other social groupings is that it has been rationally and deliberately designed and constructed (rather than randomly or culturally patterned) to achieve specific goals. It also has the ability to reconstruct itself, including reorganizing its structure, transferring or substituting personnel, or reordering its priorities to increase its effectiveness and efficiency in striving toward its goals (Ianni & Reuss-Ianni, 1972: 152). Most organizations in the public sector (government departments, police agencies, the military) and private sector (in particular, corporations) are structured hierarchically, with power concentrated among a few executives at the top and various levels of administrative and operational units below them.

The **bureaucratic/hierarchical model** of organized crime views criminal groups as rationally and purposively designed, highly structured, and tightly controlled organizations. Similarly, some criminal organizations have also been conceptualized through the "corporate model," because they are structured hierarchically like a corporation while also sharing the same profit-making motives. In both models, the criminal organization is viewed as having an all-powerful boss at the top, one or more mid-level managerial or supervisory positions, and a larger number of individual offenders at the bottom of the hierarchy who are expected to take orders from their superiors and carry out the day-to-day criminal activities. These lower-echelon offenders may specialize in a particular function (e.g., drug sales, bookmaking, enforcement, money laundering) or they may be generalists (i.e., they are expected to perform a variety of tasks).

This model was initially conceived for Italian-American organized crime groups (Cressey, 1969; President's Commission on Law Enforcement and Administration of Justice, 1967). In his book *Theft of a Nation*, Cressey acknowledges that the American *Cosa Nostra* did have the trappings and rituals of a traditional Mafia family (initiation, *omerta*, blood ties, etc.), yet he nonetheless envisioned the structure of modern Mafia group as resembling a business corporation. In particular, he argues that a typical Mafia family in the United States incorporated a complicated hierarchy, an extensive division of labour, positions assigned on the basis of skill, recruitment on the basis of proven abilities, responsibilities carried out in an impersonal manner, extensive rules and regulations, and communications passed down through the hierarchy. Cressey says this organizational structure evolved during Prohibition and was firmly in place by the beginning of the 1930s. He wrote "to use an analogy with legitimate business, in 1931 organized crime units across America formed into monopolistic corporations and these corporations, in turn, linked themselves into a monopolistic cartel" (Cressey, 1969: 35). A depiction of the Italian-American Mafia organizational structure based on the work of Cressey is presented in Figure 4.1.

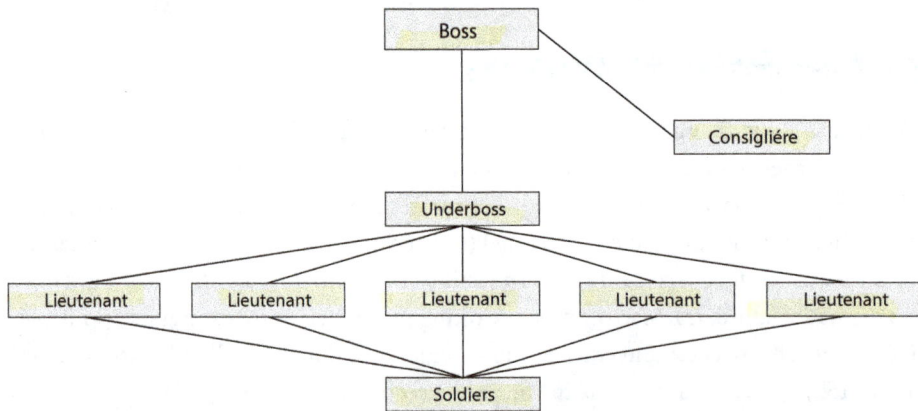

Figure 4.1: Depiction of a hierarchical structure of an Italian-American Mafia family, based on the research of criminologist Donald Cressey

Source: Cressey, D.R. (1969). Theft of a Nation: The Structure and Operations of Organized Crime in America. New York: Harper and Row.

In Canada, the ethnic Italian criminal organizations that predominated during the 1950s through to the early 1980s also appeared to have a hierarchical structure, although it was somewhat flatter than that envisioned by Cressey. During the late 1960s and early 1970s, for example, the Montreal wing of New York City's Bonanno crime family was headed by Vic Cotroni. Underneath him at any one time were four or five senior lieutenants. Each lieutenant was in charge of a particular geographic region of Montreal and had his own crew made up of several soldiers who, in turn, were in charge of, or had business ties with, a number of other people outside of the Cotroni group (Charbonneau, 1975; Edwards, 1990; Quebec Police Commission Inquiry on Organized Crime, 1977a).

Many experts have been critical of the application of the bureaucratic/hierarchical model to the Italian Mafia in North America. Ianni and Reuss-Ianni state that the bureaucratic analogy arose as "honest attempts to explain syndicate organization in terms that are familiar to the public" (1972: 110). There was also "another, more suspect motivation" behind this model, which was its support of the government-promoted theory that the Mafia was a national conspiracy, which "demands the existence of a national organization." Critics also charge that many aspects of a bureaucracy, such as lengthy chains of command, rigidity, and a well-defined division of labour, do not apply to Italian Mafia families in the United States and Canada.

Despite the criticisms, this model may be applied to other criminal organizations. Albanese (2015: 109) proclaims that it was during the 1980s that information became available showing "conclusively that the hierarchical model accurately portrayed at least some manifestations of organized crime." This quote may be most applicable to the Medellín and Cali cocaine cartels from Colombia. During the 1980s and 1990s, they had become the world's largest cocaine trafficking organizations and the epitomes of transnational organized crime—both of which were facilitated by their complex, hierarchical organizational structures. Some have concluded that these cartels emulated multinational corporations and were structured so they could control every step required in processing, exporting, and wholesaling cocaine. To facilitate this vertical integration, "each of the trafficking groups in Medellin, Bogota, and Cali contain various sections, each with a separate function, such as manufacturing, transportation, distribution, finance and security," according to the President's Commission on Organized Crime (1984a: 562). The managers of each section reported to their bosses in Colombia who were at the very top of the supposed corporate hierarchy.

Chambliss and Williams (2012: 61) conclude that "there do exist some criminal associations that are highly organized and bureaucratic, where the decision-making is centrally concentrated and subordinates execute activities. However, these groups are anomalies in the global underworld." Paoli (2014a: 3) agrees, writing,

> Large, stable, structured criminal organizations operate in a number of countries, engaging in a plurality of money-making activities and usually also claiming some sort of control over the political, economic, and social life of their home areas of

settlement. Contrary to popular perceptions, however, these organizations are a rarity. They consolidated and have survived in contexts in which government structures are weak or the latter's representatives are willing to enter into pacts with the bosses of criminal organizations. The oldest and most established among them, such as the Chinese Triads, Japanese Yakuza, and the two main Southern Italian mafia organizations, Cosa Nostra and 'Ndrangheta, for example, go back to the 18th and 19th centuries.

Kinship Model

Albini (1971) as well as Ianni and Reuss-Ianni (1972) argue that the structure of an Italian-American Mafia group has nothing to do with modern bureaucratic or corporate principles, but rather is primarily a social grouping shaped by culture, patterned by tradition and structured around kinship relationships. Italian-American crime families are just that: structures that parallel families interconnected by blood or marriage (and in some cases, simply a shared ethnicity). The so-called **kinship model** originally derived from a study of one Italian-American crime group by Ianni and Reuss-Ianni (1972), who found that members of the Lupollo family (a pseudonym) were sustained by kinship and not criminal activities or the operation of a secret society. The family operated as a "social unit with social organization and business functions merged," and all "leadership positions, down to 'middle management' level," were assigned on the basis of kinship (Ianni & Reuss-Ianni, 1972: 106).

Ianni and Reuss-Ianni (1972) outline some of the differences between Mafia families and more formal organizations, like corporations. Formal organizations are composed of positions, not personalities. The duties and rights of a corporate executive, for instance, are clearly delineated so that the organization can swiftly replace an incumbent who dies or resigns. In some Mafia families, however, particular members are indispensable because they possess special skills or have established highly personal contacts. The death of a member who acts as a "corrupter" may significantly disrupt the functioning of the family's criminal operations because no immediate substitute has the same level of political connections. Formal organizations are also supposed to be rationally organized with persons rising to leadership because of their demonstrated skill, intelligence, dedication, and expertise. Ianni and Reuss-Ianni (1972) argue that family standing and tradition are equally important—maybe more important than the criteria of merit—in determining which family members will assume leadership roles. In the Lupollo crime family, power accrued to an individual not because he is the best qualified, but because kinship or tradition demanded it. This may also have been evident with the Rizzuto mafia family in Montreal where, in the early 1980s, the reins of power were handed down from father to son.

The structure of the Italian-American Mafia family can be traced to the traditions and experiences in Sicily, where a Mafia group was simply an immediate or extended family that revolved around a Mafioso, a man of respect who protected his family, often through violent means. The Mafioso has the authority of a ruler, but, traditionally, also served as a quasi-father figure; the respect that accrues to this position in the old Sicilian family structure reinforces the authority of the boss in his role as head of the Italian-American criminal organization (Tepperman, 1976: 132). His power and authority are so incontrovertible that to family members and other constituents, as already discussed, he rivals the state in stature and operates as an unofficial parallel system of government. Upon being transplanted in North America, immigrants from Sicily continued to preserve their important cultural models—their family system with filial respect for the mother and the father and their antagonism to police and the state (Ianni & Reuss-Ianni, 1972: 49). In both Italy and North America, Mafia families found it necessary or convenient to supplement and extend family ties by taking in members who were not relatives. While such alliances are commonly used in peasant societies as a means for extending the influences and increasing the wealth of the family, in North America such tactics were essential to establishing and perpetuating the criminal Mafia "family."

Patron–Client Model

For Ianni and Reuss-Ianni (1972), the ongoing criminal operations of the Italian-American Mafia family involve a loose system of power, interpersonal and "business" relationships built around a central symbiotic relationship between the "patron" and a "client." This **patron–client** model was first proposed by Joseph Albini (1971). At the centre of the patron–client conceptualization of the Mafia is the head of the family: the *capo*. Unlike the head of a corporation, the role of the *capo* is less a chief executive officer and more of a patron to his family and associates; he is the focal point of a network of family and business relationships. Over time, the patron comes to dominate a network of individuals in a geographic area (Ianni & Reuss-Ianni, 1983).

The *capo*, and the Mafiosi more generally, is a provider of services, especially for those who can't or won't turn to the government. The role of the *capo* is to help ensure the welfare and security of his family, friends, and associates, such as putting up start-up capital to assist new enterprises, handling the flow of graft money to politicians, regulating the use of violence, and resolving disputes (Albini, 1971; Gambetta, 1993; Hess, 1973). Thus, a particularly important role of the *capo* is to serve as an intermediary, whether it is a commercial agent who brings legitimate businessmen or criminals together to make a deal, a political power broker who helps friends get elected to public office, or a mediator who arbitrates a conflict between two parties.

As seen in Figure 4.2, the *capo* is at the centre of this patron–client structure, immediately surrounded by members of the crime family to whom he acts as a patron (and receives a monetary tribute from each). In addition, each made member of the Mafia family is given a great deal of autonomy as far as making money for the family is concerned. To this end, he cultivates his own network of clients, including his own crew of made members as

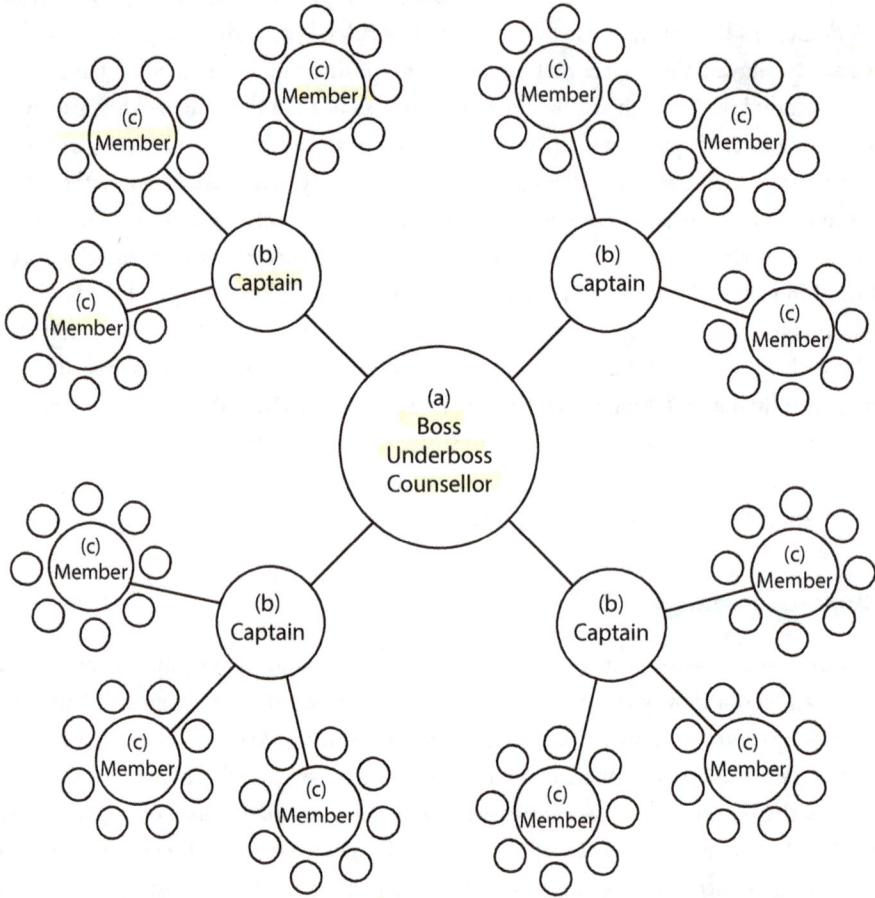

(a) At the centre of each organized crime family (*famiglia*: Family) is the boss (*capo*). He is assisted by an underboss (*sottocapo*) and a counsellor (*consigliére*).

(b) Surrounding the boss are his clients, the captains (*capiregime*).

(c) Orbiting around each captain are his clients, the lowest ranking members who have been formally initiated into the Family (*soldati*: "made guys").

(d) The members act as patrons to nonmember clients.

(e) Each unit is tied to other Families throughout the country by the *capo*, whose sovereignty is recognized by the other bosses.

Figure 4.2: Depiction of the structure of an Italian-American Mafia organization based on patron–client theory

Source: Ianni, F., & Reuss-Ianni, E. (1972). *A Family Business: Kinship and Social Control in Organized Crime*. New York: Russell Sage Foundation.

well as associates and others who are external to the family. These external clients may represent a wide spectrum of society, including other criminals, politicians, law enforcement officials, judges, businessmen, and union leaders (Albini, 1971). The functional benefit of the patron–client structure is the potential to cultivate a wide range of connections, which is essential to carrying out profitable criminal activities.

In short, Albini (1971: 288) argues, rather than encompassing a rigid corporate structure where decision-making is centralized and orders passed down through the chain of command, an Italian-American criminal syndicate "consists of a system of loosely structured relationships functioning primarily because each participant is interested in furthering his own welfare." While the patron–client model was developed primarily to describe Italian-American organized crime, it also appears to have some relevance to other organized crime groups. For example, members of outlaw motorcycle gangs or Chinese triads are known to have an extensive network of associates whose criminal activities revolve around a particular member.

Network Model

The **network model** does not view organized crime as made up of monolithic, hierarchically structured organizations or kinship-based clans, but as a loosely knit, fluid network of like-minded criminal entrepreneurs, none of whom has any long-term authority over the others. A network model of organized crime views the patterns of relationships among the offenders as symmetrical business partnerships based on complementary areas of specialization that contribute to one particular deal or a series of ongoing criminal conspiracies. In a network, the structure of the relationship among the offenders is not defined by power, but by the particular function that the individual performs in the criminal conspiracy and/or by a financial investment made by a "business partner" in that venture. Finckenauer (2005: 65) writes that most contemporary organized crime conspiracies are "loosely affiliated networks of criminals who coalesce around certain criminal opportunities. The structure of these groups is much more amorphous, free-floating and flatter, and thus lacking in a rigid hierarchy." In its 2006 annual report, CISC characterized the nature of relationships among criminal entrepreneurs that make up modern organized crime in Canada as one increasingly based on a networked model:

> ... law enforcement is identifying crime groups that are based on temporary alliances of individual criminals who merge their particular skills to better achieve success in specific criminal enterprises. Once a specific criminal venture is completed, these individuals may continue to collaborate on further criminal activities, or the group may dissolve. Although the individuals may go their separate ways, they sometimes reform into new groups based upon the skill requirements of new criminal opportunities. The nature and success of such networks are largely

determined by individual characteristics and skills among those who act as their component parts. (Criminal Intelligence Service Canada, 2006: 6)

In his research into organized crime in Canada, Morselli (2005, 2009) also identifies a number of networked aspects of contemporary organized crime: the personal contacts and social networking among offenders, the "flexible order" of criminal conspiracies that make them resistant to law enforcement targeting and enforcement, and the centralizing coordinating role of "brokers" within loosely structured organized criminal ventures.

According to Bjelopera and Finklea (2012: i), "Modern organized criminals often prefer cellular or networked structural models for their flexibility and avoid the hierarchies that previously governed more traditional organized crime groups such as the Cosa Nostra. Fluid network structures make it harder for law enforcement to infiltrate, disrupt, and dismantle conspiracies. Many 21st century organized crime groups opportunistically form around specific, short-term schemes and may outsource portions of their operations rather than keeping it all 'in-house.'" For Kleemans (2014: 40), the nature of criminal networks helps explain why they are resilient: "In networks, nobody is really irreplaceable; even important persons, such as investors, organizers, and facilitators, can be substituted by others. Perhaps this is the main reason why criminal networks often seem to suffer little damage from arrests or seizures: links may be lost, but the chain is easily repaired." Hignett (2012: 288) also identifies a number of advantages of a looser organizational profile "for criminals working across national borders including the provision of higher levels of mobility, adaptability, flexibility and fluidity. The greater 'stretch' between core and periphery in transnational networks requires an organizational structure that facilitates the flow of information across far greater geographical distances." Hignett (2012: 288) states that a network structure also "allows the criminal 'core' to draw on more specialist 'support networks' on a more ad hoc basis, such as forgers to provide documentation for illegal immigrants; financial experts to assist with money laundering; trained chemists for amphetamine production and even professional assassins and contract killers hired for occasional 'necessary' jobs." In short, "organized crime (or a criminal market) is largely a resource pooling process that is built around individuals who are connected (or socially embedded) with each other in various ways beyond co-membership in a criminal organization" (Bouchard & Morselli, 2014: 297). Albanese (2015: 120) posits that the "more fluid, less formal, and temporary associations" of modern criminal networks "reflect a wider characteristic in society in general, where long-term relationships in families and the workplace are increasingly rare, reducing personal loyalty and commitment among individuals and institutions."

The network model is applicable to large-scale drug importation and trafficking conspiracies, which rarely are carried out by a single organization. A good example of the network model for large-scale international drug trafficking was the legendary French Connection beginning in the 1940s, which consisted of partnerships between Turkish

Case Study: The Networked Structure of an Auto Theft "Ringing" Operation in Montreal

In their research into an organized auto theft conspiracy in Montreal, Morselli and Roy (2008) conclude that the "ringing" operation was a loosely structured network. The data sources for their analysis came from a law enforcement task force in Quebec that was in operation between 1993 and 2005 and which targeted stolen cars that were resold domestically or exported through the Port of Montreal for resale in other countries. Applying a crime script analysis, the study divided the crime's organization into five stages: (1) the theft of the vehicle, (2) storing (concealing) the stolen vehicle, (3) physically modifying the vehicle, (4) forging vehicle registration numbers and forms, and (5) exporting or reselling domestically the vehicles.

Within each of these phases, numerous individuals were involved as part of the larger network, all of whom operated more-or-less as independent contractors (professionals and amateurs) applying their particular expertise and available resources. The thieves who stole the cars were separate from those who modified the vehicles, who in turn were detached from individuals who obtained blank vehicle registration forms from the registration bureau of Quebec. The forms were subsequently completed (fraudulently) by other individuals while another group took care of dispatching the vehicles to foreign and local buyers.

The study shows that even in the context of a loosely structured criminal network, centralization is an important component. The centralized function was performed by so-called brokers who coordinated and linked the various phases, components, and participants. The brokers were also critical to ensuring the criminal operation was sufficiently flexible and creative in dealing with and avoiding problems. "The stolen-vehicle ringing operations studied here were centralized and resilient because they contained brokerage features that increased the degree of flexibility for achieving the collective goal. Removing the main brokers would have decreased this flexibility to the extent that each crime script no longer would be functional" (Morselli & Roy, 2008: 91).

farmers, who cultivated the opium; Istanbul-based brokers, who trafficked the morphine; French Corsican gangsters, who processed the morphine into heroin in France and then moved the final product across the Atlantic; American and Canadian Mafia groups, who coordinated its importation and wholesale distribution in North America; and a diverse list of individuals and groups who sold the drugs at the retail level (Charbonneau, 1976; Naylor, 2004). More contemporary research into international drug smuggling summarized by Decker and Pyrooz (2014: 279) suggests they are "horizontally organized" involving "discrete cells" of offenders at different levels of the international supply chain from the production in a source country all the way to the retail distribution in the United States.

Illegal Enterprise
Cicero Enterprises 1925–1930

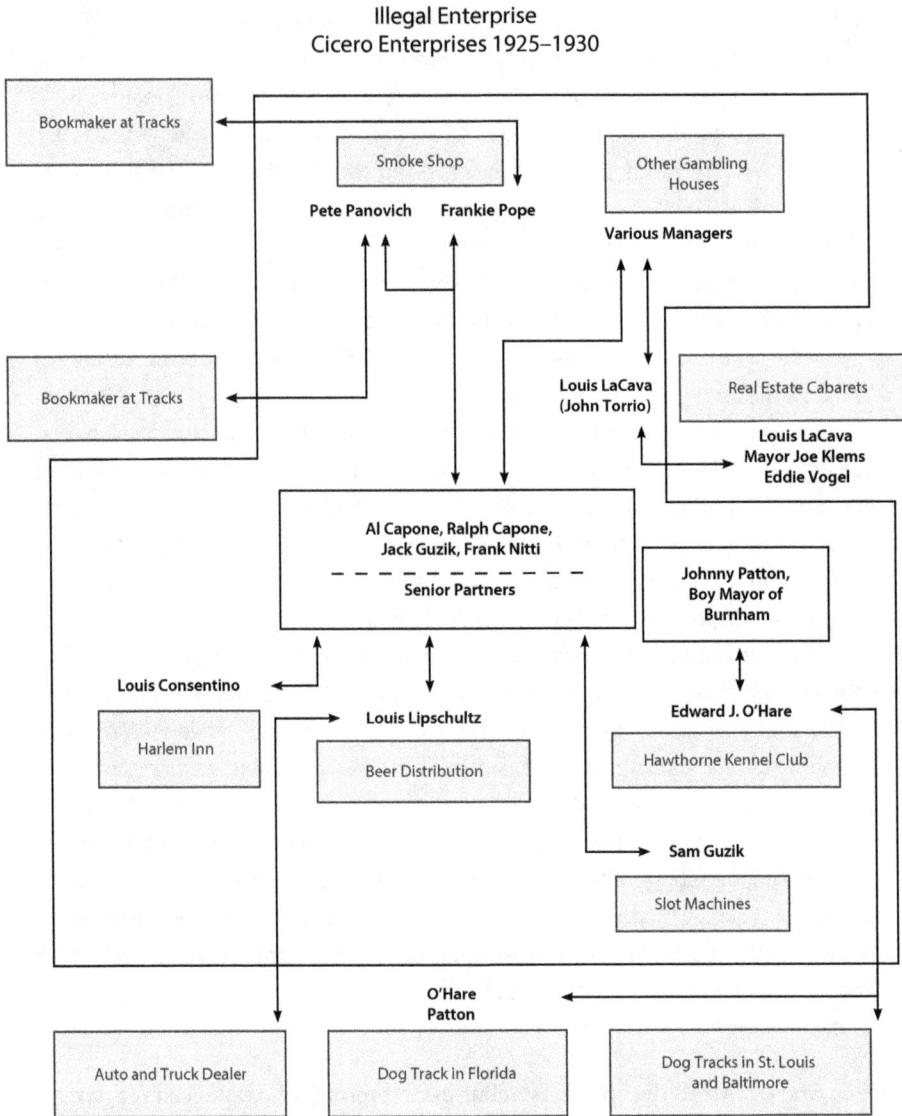

Figure 4.3: Al Capone's organized crime network

Source: Haller, M. (1990). Illegal enterprise: A theoretical and historical interpretation, *Criminology*, 28(2): 207–34; at p. 207.

The authors cite various studies into international human smuggling and trafficking made up of "small networks of individuals that function largely without a hierarchy or system of internal discipline" (Decker & Pyrooz, 2014: 279).

Haller (1990) uses Al Capone's criminal empire as a historical case study of the network model, arguing that Capone was at the centre of an expansive web of associates and entities (which is depicted in Figure 4.3). The various enterprises associated with Capone during the 1920s and 1930s did not operate as part of a monolithic corporation he headed, but as a complex set of business partnerships. At the core of these partnerships were four men who Haller calls "senior partners"—Al and his older brother Ralph, their cousin Frank Nitti, and Jack Guzik. The four shared more or less equally in their joint income and acted as equals in looking after their varied business interests. The senior partners, in turn, made investments into and formed partnerships with a variety of other individuals to launch numerous illegal and legal enterprises, mainly in Cicero, a suburb of Chicago. Many of the partners were themselves entrepreneurs who carried on other business enterprises, legal and illegal, independently of the four men (Haller, 1990: 221). Each enterprise—including contraband liquor, prostitution, illegal gaming, bookmaking, and assorted legitimate business—operated independently from the other; the only common denominator was that the operations were financed or co-managed by one of the four senior partners.

In short, the traditional bureaucratic/hierarchical/corporate model of organized crime stresses centralized control, while the network model envisions greater decentralization. In addition to rendering an illicit enterprise less vulnerable to law enforcement, Haller (1990: 222) writes that decentralization also makes sense for another important reason: "criminal entrepreneurs generally have had neither the skills nor the personalities for the detailed, bureaucratic oversight of large organizations. They are, instead, hustlers and dealers, for whom partnership arrangements are ideally suited. They enjoy the give and take of personal negotiations, risk-taking, and moving from deal to deal."

Summary: Theoretical Models of Organizational Structures

Table 4.1 provides a summary of the aforementioned theoretical models and how each compares to one another based on some of the key organizational attributes of OC from the taxonomy presented in chapter 3.

While each of these models is conceptually distinct from one another, the organizational structures of a particular OC enterprise may integrate different aspects from each model. Research by Morselli and Roy (2008) intimates that the significant role of the broker in the decentralized organized auto theft operation they studied means there are parallels between the criminal network model and the patron–client model. In her analysis of Chicago crime groups, Anderson (1979) concludes that the network model may be viewed as a combination of the bureaucratic/hierarchical model, the kinship model, and the patron–client model. She argues that well-defined criminal

Table 4.1: Summary of Attributes of Theoretical Models of Organizational Structures

	Theoretical Model			
	Bureaucratic/ Hierarchical	**Kinship**	**Patron–Client**	**Network**
Relationship pattern among offenders	Asymmetrical power relations	Kinship, blood ties, or ethnic ties	Brokerage relationship between crime group members and their associates	Symmetrical, fluid business partnerships based on skills, resources, and duties performed
Organically or purposely created	Purposely	Organically	Organically and purposely	Purposely
Limited or exclusive membership	Yes	Yes	Yes (crime group members) and No (associates)	No
Specialization/ Division of labour	Yes	No	No (crime group members are generalists) and Yes (associates are specialists)	Yes
Continuity/ Continuing enterprise	Yes	Yes	Yes	No

organizations do exist and that some entail a hierarchical structure, but they also include various associates who were not true members themselves. These associates carry out many activities (both legal and illegal) necessary for the success of the group and enter into patron–client type arrangements with the members of the criminal group.

The structure of the Cotroni–Violi Mafia group in Montreal during the 1960s and 1970s is an example of one hybrid organizational model. It was, to some extent, hierarchical; however, senior positions within that hierarchy were often dictated by blood lines (Vic Cotroni, the head of the Mafia group, appointed his brothers as senior lieutenants) and ethnicity (those from the Calabrian province of Italy were often senior to those from Sicily). The patron–client model was also quite applicable in that the various heads of the group—in particular, Paolo Violi—saw the Mafiosi as a patron to his many associates, clients, and partners both inside and outside the group. The network model is also relevant because of the many extended and fluid partnerships between members of the group and associates external to the group.

One of the key lessons of this chapter is the great diversity of organizational structures and the hazard inherent in trying to develop a universal model of organized criminal associations. As Levi (2002: 881) writes, "Why, after all, should an organisational model of crime that applies to parts of Italy in some historical periods apply to the north-eastern US; and even if it accurately depicts crime there, why should it apply throughout, or indeed in any part of the UK, Germany or Canada?" Some definitions of organized crime now eschew any mention of any specific or universal organizational structure. As the United States Department of Justice (2008: 2) emphasizes, "there is no single structure under which transnational criminals operate; they vary from hierarchies to clans, networks, cells, and may evolve to other structures." Sheptycki (2003: 124) points out that the conceptual models can be placed on a continuum ranging from the rigid bureaucratic/hierarchical model to the more fluid network model.

The United Nations Office on Drugs and Crime (UNODC) also recognizes the diversity of criminal organizational structures and developed a typology that attempts to reflect this diversity. The typology was built using data provided by UN member states who were asked to provide information on "the three most prominent organized criminal groups in their country." The UN collected data on 40 groups from 16 countries from all over the world. The groups analyzed were seen as representative of their countries by national experts (United Nations Office on Drugs and Crime, 2002a: 11). Based on the data, UN experts identified five different types of criminal organizational structures, distinguished primarily by the degree to which they exhibit a hierarchical structure:

1. *Standard rigid hierarchy*—This type of group is characterized by a centralized authority structure (a single leader), a clearly defined hierarchy, several units or divisions, strong system of internal discipline, multiple criminal activities, and the use of violence. A standard hierarchical group may be identifiable by a name (e.g., Cali Cartel), often have a strong ethnic or social identity, and usually operate in clearly defined geographical areas. Members of the group often come from the same ethnic background or a similar background experience (e.g., prison gangs). A third of the 40 groups identified by the survey fall into this category and includes criminal organizations from Italy, China, Colombia, and Eastern Europe.

2. *Regional hierarchy*—This type includes all or most of the attributes of the standard hierarchy group structure except there is some autonomy at regional level, meaning there are regional sub-units, with their own hierarchy, that enjoy some degree of independence. A notable example of such regional hierarchical groups are outlaw motorcycle gangs such as the Hells Angels, which have chapters in different countries, all of which operate autonomously. In Canada, there is no formal national Hells Angels leadership. Power may be centralized in one chapter in each province, although each chapter in a province may have considerable independence.

3. *Clustered hierarchy*—This organizational structure is characterized by a number of relatively autonomous small groups or cells that are interconnected under a common system of governance, coordination, and control that encompasses all illegal activities in which these groups engage. These groups have formed within a specific social/historical context and are relatively rare.

4. *Core group*—This type is characterized by a relatively tightly organized, yet unstructured, group of offenders, surrounded by a loose network of other offenders. The hierarchical structure in the core group is relatively flat in that power is shared equally among its members. The small size of the core group and surrounding network helps to maintain internal discipline. Neither the core group nor their network of associates have a common ethnic identity.

5. *Criminal network*—This type of organizational structure is made up of individuals who are loosely and fluidly connected and often "constitute themselves around a series of criminal projects" (United Nations Office on Drugs and Crime, 2002a: 34). In other words, the specific structure of the network is influenced by the type of criminal activity being perpetrated and the network structure will change depending upon the criminal activities undertaken and those who take part (Albanese, 2015: 218; Aronowitz, 2012: 225; Lyman & Potter, 2014: 18–22; Smith, 2014: 121; United Nations Office on Drugs and Crime, 2002a; van Dijk & Spapens, 2014: 214).

Attempts to understand how organized crime groups are structured is not simply an academic exercise: it has significant implications for broad efforts to control OC and interdict a particular organized criminal conspiracy. The foremost characterization of organized crime as made up of centralized, hierarchical, corporate-like structures not only "confuses an already complex subject" but also undermines law enforcement strategies, Chambliss and Williams (2012: 62) write. For years, American law enforcement authorities tailored their efforts toward a mythical creature—the nationwide, rationally structured, centrally coordinated Mafia corporation. Hindsight indicates that enforcement strategies should have had a more localized orientation, which reflect the limited geo-spatial scope of most Italian-American Mafia groups (Woodiwiss, 2012: 101). "Perhaps the biggest problem with the hierarchical model of organized crime is that it leads to the conclusion that prosecution of the 'bosses' and others in control will make organized crime less prevalent and less threatening," Albanese (2015: 111) writes. However, "once these entrepreneurs are removed by arrest or incarceration, others emerge because the demand remains, as do the opportunities for criminal exploitation of the legitimate marketplace." Despite the different organizational structures, there appears to be a consensus that organized crime is increasingly structured in a network format, which has significant implication for organized crime enforcement domestically and internationally.

CONCLUSION

One of the holy grails of criminologists is an integrated, all-encompassing theory of the causes behind crime. Yet as Kleemans (2014: 48) notes, "Organized crime theory lacks such general theories, perhaps because many authors realize that no theory could ever encompass the diversity of different criminal groups and the diversity of different criminal activities that are often labeled as 'organized crime'." There are various theories that explain the existence of organized crime—some of which are diametrically opposed to one another, some of which complement one another. Explanations that are in direct opposition to one another tend to come from different paradigms or schools of thought on how crime, criminality, and social problems generally are created. In North America, for instance, there has long been the debate between those who view organized crime as the product of other countries that export traditional secret societies and criminal ways through immigrants and contrasting theories who view organized crime as the product of factors indigenous to the United States and Canada. Similarly, at one extreme, OC is viewed as an abnormal, subcultural phenomenon that is a deviation from mainstream norms, values, and institutions, and preys on society; at the other extreme, it is viewed as a product of the dominant norms, values, and institutions of the two countries.

Other binary delineations of OC theories echo broader debates in criminology. Those in the field of developmental criminology view criminal behaviour as a product of criminogenic risk factors (e.g., poverty, marginalization, inequality in society), while administrative criminologists tend to view crime as a product of rationally thinking offenders who take advantage of an opportunity to make money. A similar debate occurs between classical and neo-classical criminologists, on the one hand, who tend to blame the offender as pathological, versus sociologists, structuralists, and critically oriented criminologists who blame factors outside of the individual's control, including the immediate social environment as well as broader structural forces that are rooted in modernity, capitalism, and the state. The broader context for these differences is the perennial debate over whether society and individual human behaviour are dictated by broad social forces versus those who believe society and human behaviour are more influenced by purposive decisions made by people individually and collectively. None of these competing theories or perspectives are completely right and none are completely wrong. The world of organized crime and those involved is so diverse and complex that different theories can be applied to different offenders, groups, and circumstances. Once again, it is up to the reader to critically analyze each explanation and its underlying assumptions, sources, and influences.

Throughout this chapter efforts have been made to adapt the mostly American theories to organized crime in Canada, with the ostensible goal of determining whether such theories can explain why organized crime exists and persists in this country and whether there are unique conditions here that give rise to and perpetuate this criminal phenomenon. There is no one etiological theory or causal explanation that would sufficiently account for the presence of organized crime in Canada, although some of the answers can be found in the theories discussed in this chapter.

Despite its original xenophobic tenets, it would be naïve for Canadians to dismiss alien conspiracy theory outright as some of the dominant organized crime genres in Canada originated in other countries. Ethnic Italian organized crime in Canada has traditionally been characterized as a branch plant of Italian-American Mafia families or the 'Ndrangheta in southern Italy. The same could be said for Colombian, Russian, and Nigerian cells that are located in this country but are linked to broader criminal syndicates in Colombia, Russia, and Nigeria, respectively. Even outlaw motorcycle gangs are an import from the United States. However, none of the above would have taken root in Canada without the many social, economic, and political factors indigenous to this country that gives rise to organized crime and illicit markets.

Some have argued that Canada's relatively lax criminal laws are to blame for the proliferation of OC in this country, although this rationale fails to explain a similar increase in other countries with much more punitive criminal justice systems, such as Russia, China, or even the United States. Those who characterize Canada's criminal laws as too lenient are often the same ones who blame the country's liberal immigration laws for allowing an influx of criminal offenders into Canada. The long tradition of government prohibitionist policies in Canada has certainly served as a catalyst for the creation and persistence of organized crime and illegal markets here. Historically, organized smuggling into and out of Canada has been precipitated by the mercantilist policies of the British government of the eighteenth and nineteenth centuries, excessive duties on imported opium in the late nineteenth century, the criminalization of drugs and liquor in the early twentieth century, as well as hikes in cigarette taxes during the 1990s. Government prohibition policies help create OC and underground markets while the laws of supply and demand perpetuate their existence.

Another indisputable element that contributes to organized crime in this country is the symbiotic relationship between criminal entrepreneurs and illicit markets on the one hand and the Canadian public on the other. The former would not exist in this country if it were not for the indefatigable demand for illegal drugs, other outlawed goods and services, as well as cheap cigarettes or counterfeit consumer fashions by Canadian consumers. Foreign demand for illicit Canadian products, such as marijuana, synthetic drugs, and counterfeit goods, has also played a role in the growth of organized crime in this country.

Economic theories suggest that organized crime is simply an extension of Canada's free market system. From an economic perspective, illegal markets are a capitalist's dream: an unfettered market of pure competition with no government regulation. Canada's tripartite roles as a consumer of illicit goods produced elsewhere, an international transit country for drugs and illegal migrants, and an international supplier of domestically produced goods is reflective of this country's integration into the global economy and its dependency on international trade.

The post-war political economy has helped forge the structural preconditions for crime, the geo-spatial concentration of crime, and the root causes of criminality in Canada by fuelling socioeconomic disparities and the concentration of poverty and other hardships. Canadian gangs and criminal groups are populated by an underclass of disenfranchised young men, often from disadvantaged environments, who become involved in a subculture of crime and violence due, in part, to the lack of other legitimate opportunities in their lives. Census data and numerous studies show that the wealth of most Western nations, including Canada, is held by a shrinking number of individual and corporate elites, the gap between the rich and the poor has been widening, urban centres have become segregated along socioeconomic lines, and poverty has become ever more concentrated in certain neighbourhoods, communities, and racialized groups. These trends and developments are leading developed nations like Canada toward what critical criminologist Jock Young calls a "dystopia of exclusion," where "the poor are isolated in inner-city ghettos, in orbital estates, and in ghost towns" (Young, 2001: 20). This spatial concentration of poverty and marginalization has led to the spatial concentration of crime and violence in many Canadian cities and First Nations reserves. In a Statistics Canada study examining the distribution of crime and violence in Winnipeg, the researchers concluded the "level of socioeconomic disadvantage of the residential population in a neighbourhood was most strongly associated with the highest neighbourhood rates of both violent and property crime" (Fitzgerald, Wisener, & Savoie, 2001: 8).

The multi-ethnic character of organized crime in Canada is a reflection of the multicultural nature of Canadian society. Ethnic succession theory may help shed some light on the historically rooted racism in Canada whereby certain "ethnic" immigrant groups—the Irish, Jews, Chinese, Italians, Hispanics, Jamaicans—have been shut out of legitimate economic opportunities *en masse*. As strain theory advocates, individuals within these groups have turned to the underground economy to eke out a living. Thus, the ethnic basis of some organized crime groups in Canada is not tied to the importation of foreign criminal cultures or secret societies but results from minority groups struggling for a place in this country, often in the face of discrimination and marginalization. This helps explain why the growing underclass of racialized young men make up a disproportionate number of gang members in many cities in Canada.

In sum, the origins of organized crime in Canada are complex and multifaceted. Broadly speaking, one can situate the origins of organized crime in both indigenous and external factors. With that said, any serious examination of the origins and proliferation of organized crime in this country must begin and end with an examination of Canadian society itself.

KEY TERMS

Administrative criminology

Alien conspiracy theory

Bureaucratic/hierarchical model

Crime script

Critical criminology

Differential association

Ethnic succession theory

Illegal enterprise theory

Kinship model

Marxist

Network model

Patron–client model

Protection theory

Social disorganization

Spectrum-based theory of enterprises

Strain and culture conflict theory

Structuralist theories

Subculture theory

REVIEW QUESTIONS

1. What are the various theories that explain the causes of organized crime? What are the similarities among these etiological theories? What are the contrasting features of these theories? What are the strengths and weaknesses of these different theories?

2. What are the various explanations for how crimes become organized? What methodological tools can contribute to a better understanding of organized crimes? What contributions do the following make to a better understanding of how crimes are organized: Administrative criminology? Economic analysis? Public policy impetus? What are the strengths and weaknesses of these different theories?

3. What are the various theoretical models that explain how criminal offenders are organized? What are the strengths and weaknesses of these different models?

4. To what extent can organized crime in Canada be better understood by applying the mostly American theories of organized crime? Is it possible to develop an integrated theory of organized crime that explains its genesis and proliferation in Canada? If so, what would this integrated theory entail?

FURTHER READINGS

Abadinsky, H. (2013). *Organized Crime* (10th Ed.). Belmont, CA: Wadsworth Publishing.

Albanese, J. (2015). *Organized Crime: From the Mob to Transnational Organized Crime.* (7th Ed.). New York: Routledge.

Lyman, M.D., & Potter, G.W. (2014). *Organized Crime* (6th Ed.). Boston: Pearson.

Naylor, R.T. (1997). Mafias, myths, and markets: On the theory and practice of enterprise crime, *Transnational Organized Crime*, 3(3): 1–45.

Southerland, M.D. (1993). Applying organization theory to organized crime, *Journal of Contemporary Criminal Justice*, 9(3): 251–67.

PART II

ORGANIZED CRIME GENRES

This section explores different organized crime "genres" in Canada as well as the dominant criminal groups and networks within these genres. The first three chapters describe and analyze specific organized criminal associations that have been designated by the RCMP as Tier I criminal organizations in Canada, indicating that they pose the highest threat to Canadian society. The genres that are included in this category are Italian organized crime (the Montreal Mafia and the ' in Ontario), outlaw motorcycle gangs (in particular the Hells Angels), and Chinese organized crime. The final chapter in this section explores other organized crime genres in this country: Indigenous organized crime, organized street gangs, South Asian criminal groups, Vietnamese criminal groups, Middle Eastern organized crime, and Nigerian Criminal Enterprises. (Chapters on two other major organized crime genres—Latin American drug-trafficking groups and Russian/Eastern European organized crime—can be found on the textbook's website.)

The Tier I group is made up of traditional, Mafia-style criminal organizations characterized by official and restricted membership, binding ties among members that are both associational and entrepreneurial (i.e., the ties are both fraternal and geared toward revenue generation) (Ianni, 1974), some semblance of an organizational hierarchy, continuity of the organization over time, and the existence of initiation rituals as well as explicit organizational rules and regulations that members must follow. The genres and groups discussed in chapter 8 are more representative of a networked approach to organized crime: they eschew a traditional hierarchical structure and a restricted membership, the ties that bind members are less associational and more entrepreneurial, there is less organizational continuity, and there are no initiation rituals or rules and regulations. With that said, the complexity and diversity of organized crime in Canada means that these generalizations have some important exceptions. For example, while there is some organizational hierarchy in the Mafia-style organizations, they too have very much embraced a more networked approach. Nigerian criminal enterprises may also share characteristics with some of the Tier I crime groups—like the Hells Angels, the Kung Lok, or the Rizzuto Mafia family—including a central hierarchy that also includes a networked cellular appendage, and a transnational presence.

For each of the aforementioned genres, a historical overview is first provided. This is followed by a brief discussion of the social, political, legal, and economic factors that helped ferment the genesis and proliferation of this OC genre outside and within Canada. This may include applying etiological models from chapter 1. The analysis of each genre and specific criminal group also includes a description of its significance within the history and study of OC in Canada. Finally, an analysis of OC genres and specific criminal organizations will entail applying the "comprehensive taxonomy of organized crime characteristics" from chapter 3.

CRITICAL THINKING EXERCISE

This part of the book demarcates organized crime genres largely based on ethnicity. As detailed in the preface and chapter 2, categorizing organized crime genres and groups by ethnicity is highly controversial, in part because it implies that the dominant binding force that brings criminal offenders together in an organization or network is ethnicity. As you read through this part of the book, determine for yourself: (1) whether the categorization of organized crime by ethnicity and nationality is a valid way to conceptualize different types of organized criminal syndicates in Canada, and (2) whether ethnicity is a significant binding force that brings criminal offenders together organizationally. Specifically, some questions you should ask yourself include the following:

- Does the empirical data presented in the chapters (in particular the case studies) provide sufficient support for this ethnocentric categorization of organized crime in Canada?
- Can you think of a better way to categorize how criminal offenders are organized (consider the other typologies presented in chapter 2)?
- Are there instances where certain criminal groups are organized around ethnicity while others are not?
- For those groups that appear to be organized around ethnicity, can you identify other more nuanced factors that may provide an alternative explanation for the ties among the criminal offenders? Does such an ethnicity-based classification bolster alien conspiracy theory? In other words, does it suggest that organized crime in North America is dominated by ethnic minority groups and is a product of foreign cultures? Is this ethnicity-based categorization racist (especially since the categories are dominated by ethnic minority demographic groups)? In contrast, are those who are opposed to an ethnic-based categorization being too politically correct?

5 ITALIAN ORGANIZED CRIME

CHAPTER OUTLINE

- Introduction and Overview
- History of Italian Organized Crime in North America
- Italian Organized Crime in Ontario
- Italian Organized Crime in Quebec
- Describing and Analyzing Italian Organized Crime: The Montreal Mafia

LEARNING OUTCOMES

After reading this chapter, you should have a thorough understanding of the following:

- The origins and history of Italian organized crime in Italy and North America, including the factors that helped ferment their genesis and proliferation
- The historical interconnections between Italian organized crime in Canada and the United States
- The different categories of Italian criminal organizations in North America (in particular, the Sicilian Mafia and the Calabrian 'Ndrangheta)
- The characteristics of the Montreal Mafia, based on the theoretical model from chapter 3
- The significance of Italian organized crime in the study of Canadian organized crime

INTRODUCTION AND OVERVIEW

For many, organized crime is synonymous with what is commonly referred to as the Italian Mafia. For decades, Italian crime "families" had a presence in many of North America's largest cities, including Toronto and Montreal. The scope and threat of Italian organized crime (IOC) in the United States was perceived as so great that during the 1950s and 1960s the prevailing belief was that there was a nationwide monolithic conspiracy, complete with a national structure and a ruling commission. There have also been at least five presidential or congressional inquiries formed in the United States and, at least, seven provincial or federal inquiries in Canada to address IOC over the last 75 years (including the most recent Charbonneau Commission, which issued its report in November 2015).

Figure 5.1: Map of southern Italy indicating origins of secret criminal societies

Source: Map by Devon Rogers

IOC was considered so dominant and such a standard-bearer for organized crime that law enforcement officials in Canada began referring to it as "traditional organized crime." Before this label was created, another distinctive moniker—*la Cosa Nostra* (LCN)—was applied by US law enforcement to the Mafia in America in the early 1960s. Roughly translated from Italian as "this thing of ours" or "our thing" (the abstract way Mafia members referred to their secret criminal society; they never used the term *Mafia* themselves), this sinister-sounding designation was reportedly created by the FBI to help scare the public into supporting the war against organized crime. In Canada, most government officials were less alarmed by the threat posed by the Italian Mafia. In fact, for many years, the attitude of Canadian politicians and some senior police officers was to deny that the Mafia even existed in this country. Technically, they were correct. Unlike the United States, where membership in LCN families was restricted to those who traced their roots to Sicily, most Mafiosi in Canada were from Calabria, or, at least, could trace their roots to the Italian province. As such, the secret Italian criminal societies that arose in Canada beginning around the turn of the century were mostly influenced by the traditions of the **'Ndrangheta** (although for the most part there is little difference between the customs, traits, and criminal operations of the Sicilian and Calabrian Mafia).

The Criminal Intelligence Service Canada's annual report on organized crime for 2002 indicated that IOC in Canada is composed primarily of three main groups: the Sicilian Mafia, the 'Ndrangheta, and the Canadian arm of the LCN (Criminal Intelligence Service Canada, 2002: 14). While the 'Ndrangheta heavily influenced IOC in Canada, so did the American LCN; since at least the late 1930s, most IOC groups in Canada were branches of Mafia families in New York, Buffalo, or Detroit. Beginning in the 1980s, however, the subordination of Canadian Mafiosi to American crime families began to dissipate. This was especially true of the Montreal-based Mafia, which began as a crew of New York's Bonanno family but then, under the command of Vito Rizzuto, became a family in its own right.

For years, the Montreal Mafia was made up of members who were from (or traced their heritage to) Sicily and Calabria. Up until the 1980s, the Bonanno family's crew in Montreal was headed by Calabrians. That was until the Sicilian Nick Rizzuto launched a *coup d'etat* and then handed power over to his son, Vito. From that point forward, not only did Vito Rizzuto turn the Montreal Mafia into an independent family, but its scope, power, and wealth would eclipse that of any Italian Mafia family in the United States. With the death of Vito Rizzuto in December 2013, the Montreal Mafia is now in disarray and under attack from rivals looking to supplant its influence in Quebec's criminal underworld.

Many observers believe that the greatest threat to the Montreal Mafia is the 'Ndrangheta. Now considered the most powerful IOC faction in Canada, the Calabrian Mafia has numerous cells in southern Ontario. Since the early 1950s, the Greater Toronto Area has been home to what police originally called the "Siderno Group," which is made up of 'Ndrangheta clans that owed their allegiance to criminal groups in the Siderno region of Calabria.

While the genesis of IOC in North America can be traced to some extent to Sicily and Calabria, its growth in Canada resulted from a complex mix of customs and traditions associated with these secret societies, the imperialistic ambitions of the American LCN, as well as social, cultural, political, and economic conditions in North America. IOC in North America has long been shrouded in mystery, misunderstanding, and stereotypes, due in part to sensationalized media reports and Hollywood films. This chapter will attempt to foster a more accurate understanding of the origins, history, structure, scope, and activities of IOC in Canada.

HISTORY OF ITALIAN ORGANIZED CRIME IN NORTH AMERICA

This section provides a historical overview of IOC in Canada, which includes tracing its connections to that in Italy and the United States, both of which influenced the origins and development of the Italian Mafia in this country. This section begins by tracing the origins of IOC in Italy, while also discussing the etymology and meaning of the term *Mafia*, as well as the cultural significance of the Mafia subculture, which shaped IOC in Italy and North America for decades to come.

Defining and Conceptualizing the Sicilian Mafia

As a reflection of its secretive nature, the Mafia has been defined, conceptualized, characterized, and mythologized in any number of ways. Some have argued that the Mafia is a worldwide criminal organization headquartered in Italy with cells located throughout the world. Others dispute this but suggest there is an interconnected international criminal conspiracy of Mafia groups in different countries, with the same historical origins, overlapping memberships, and the same codes and membership rites of passage (McSweeney, 1988; Reid, 1952). Others have argued that LCN in the United States and its branches in Canada are separate and distinct in its origins and operations from organized crime groups in Italy (Cressey, 1969; Turkus & Feder, 1952; United States Congress, 1965). Some scholars stress that the terms *Mafia* or *'Ndrangheta* should not be used as nouns to describe a particular secret society or criminal conspiracy. Instead, they represent (similar) philosophies that are based in historical Sicilian and Calabrian cultural traditions (Albini, 1971). Finally, there are those who reduce this debate to a simple question of semantics: whether one calls it the Mafia, 'Ndrangheta, the honoured society, *la Cosa Nostra*, the Syndicate, or any other name, it involves a group of men, mostly (but not exclusively) of Italian heritage, that are involved in ongoing criminal conspiracies.

There are a number of sociological and anthropological explanations for the origins and meaning of the Mafia and its significance in Sicilian society and culture. For Hess (1986: 113), the term describes a phenomenon far more complex "than the headlines about a vaunted, secret criminal association suggest." It refers to a philosophy, a behaviour, and, indeed, a way of life that emerged from historically rooted subcultures in Sicily and dictates how powerful men are to conduct themselves and the role they are to play in society or at least in their own subterrain of society. According to Inciardi (1975), the principles behind the Mafia as a subculture and the word itself comes from Sicilian historical and literary works and denotes a state of mind, a style of behaviour, a cultural pattern, and a way of life. Specifically, the word *Mafia* is Sicilian-Arabic in its origins and is derived from terms meaning "to protect and to act as guardian; a friend or companion; to defend and preserve; power, integrity, strength" (Inciardi, 1975: 112–13). Various definitions of the word that began surfacing in nineteenth-century Italy included superlatives that reflected the traditional ideals of manhood and manliness: power, superiority, bravery, bravado, boldness, self-confidence, revenge, respect, honour, and vainglory. In turn, the meaning and ideals of the word were personalized and embodied in the **Mafioso**, who is known and admired for his ability to protect and provide essential services to his kin, his friends, and his associates because he is a man of respect and a **man of honour** (Ianni & Reuss-Ianni, 1976: 45). He is able to get things done and defend himself and his kin because he has friends and associates who will rally to his aid.

Hess (1973) notes that the Mafioso succeeds because he commands a *partito*, a network of relationships whereby he acts as an intermediary or a broker. As the centre of this network, he views himself as a *padrone* (patron) to his clients. In this role, he is a provider of services, especially for those who cannot or will not turn to the government for help (Albini, 1971; Gambetta, 1993; Hess, 1973). He plays the parts of a middleman who brings legitimate businessmen or criminals together to make a deal, a political power broker who helps friends get elected to public office, and a mediator who arbitrates a conflict between two parties. "He acts as a guarantor so that persons who do not trust one another can transact business with a significant degree of confidence; this refers to legitimate entrepreneurs and, most particularly, the illegitimate, persons who cannot turn to the police or courts to remedy their grievances" (Abadinsky, 2013: 111). Cesare Mori, who was appointed by Italian dictator Benito Mussolini to root out Mafia organizations in the 1920s, wrote that a Mafioso is in a position of power to provide "protection where the state is unwilling or unable; arbitration services superior to those available from local judges, especially to the poor person who cannot afford a lawyer, or for those whose justice is of a social, not a legal, nature—the pregnant daughter whose seducer refused to marry." The Mafioso, and, in particular, *capomafioso* (the head of a Mafia family), "can put it all right and his services are speedy and final" (Mori, 1933: 69). In short, as Abadinsky (2013: 111) puts it, the Mafioso is "a provider of protection broadly defined."

When the word *Mafia* is used as a noun, it denotes an organization—an unofficial, unrecognized, and secret system of government headed by unelected yet influential men who seek to control a particular jurisdiction. And much like a legitimate government, the Mafioso applies a tax to any transaction he brokers or is carried out in his jurisdiction. Put another way, as a *padrone*, he expects the payment of a **tribute**—either cash or a material possession—from the members of his mafia family and other constituents. Hobsbawm (1976) brings all these conceptualizations together when he summarizes the three overlapping meanings of the Mafia: (1) a general code of behaviour and attitude toward the state in a weakly governed society, (2) a system of patronage which substituted for the strong state power, and (3) a community situation in which a secret society controls all aspects of life. In short, the term *Mafia* has been defined as an attitude, a state of mind, a philosophy of life, a conception of society among Sicilians, a group of men, a criminal organization, and a secret unofficial government society that provides for and protects its constituents (Cressey, 1967: 48).

Origins and Early History of the Sicilian Mafia

There is evidence to suggest that the Mafia as an organization began as a patriotic clandestine sect in Sicily that fought to throw off the respective foreign rule of the Saracens, Spaniards, the Normans, and the French. Some have speculated that the origins of the Mafia—as a term, a philosophy, and a secret society—began when the French invaded Sicily in 1282. Many of the patriotic Sicilians retaliated with their own motto: *Morte alla Francia Italia anela*! ("Death to the French is Italy's cry!"—M.A.F.I.A.). Another popular explanation is that it was applied to Sicilian resistance movements after a mother screamed out "*Ma fia, ma fia*!" ("My daughter, my daughter!") while witnessing her daughter being dragged away by invading forces.

Regardless of its exact origin, the Mafia became a nationalistic symbol to the repressed and conquered Sicilian people. Resistance fighters were made to swear an oath under the penalty of death that they would never reveal their underground movement to outsiders and the official ruling elite. In turn, this gave rise to what has evolved into an inviolable norm for the historical and contemporary Mafia subculture: **omerta**, which symbolized manliness, self-control in the face of adversity, the use of vengeance and vendettas against those that wrong members of the Mafia, defiance to government authorities, and the importance of secrecy. The code of *omerta* would serve to bind Mafia members and organizations and help insulate and protect its operations from forces invading Sicily. As the Mafia evolved into a criminal organization in the nineteenth and twentieth centuries, *omerta* would become the most sanctified code of secrecy to which all members must abide, in part to protect the organization from law enforcement.

Following the fifteenth century, as the influence of foreign forces waned in Italy, the social role of the Mafia evolved from a clandestine rebellious force to an unparalleled political and economic institution in rural Sicily. The Mafioso was a patron to his peasants; he controlled their access to scarce resources, such as farmland, and mediated disputes. In rural Sicily, the Mafiosi (plural of Mafioso) essentially became the ruling class in relation to the peasantry. A Mafioso did not invoke state law; instead, his power was derived from the respect granted to him by his constituents and by winning a reputation for toughness, courage, and honour (Hobsbawm, 1976: 92). The Mafioso soon evolved into the local (unofficial) government in many parts of Sicily, which had very weak local governing institutions (exacerbated by the island's distance from the central government in Rome). The Mafioso was the police, the judge, the jury, and the executioner. A rigid code of right and wrong, of guilt and innocence, became established and was enforced by the *compieri* (armed guards), who were recruited because they were men of respect—meaning that they were quick to use violence and people feared them (Abadinsky, 2013: 108).

The origins of the social grouping that would serve as a basis for the Mafia as a criminal organization emerged alongside the Mafioso's rise to power in Sicily during the eighteenth century. Modelled after the extended family, which was the ideal of Sicilian social institutions, most of the early Mafia clans were formed around kinship because it was only blood relatives—*sangu de me sangu* ("blood of my blood")—where true loyalty could be found. When an exclusive reliance on kinship proved to be too restricting, the *famiglia* began to be augmented through the custom of *comparatico* or *comparragio* (fictional kinship or godparenthood), in which outsiders became members to help increase the clan's strength and power. Over time, standardized rituals were adopted to induct new members into the family, and all inductees had to swear allegiance to their *famiglia* and pledge their commitment to the principle of *omerta*.

Around the same time, the heads of each family (*capomafioso or* **capo di famiglia***)* began networking with one another and, in some parts of Sicily, came together to form a *cosca*, a small, localized clique whereby member-families supported one another to pursue mutual objectives, divide up territories, and arbitrate disputes amongst themselves. The typical *cosca*, writes Arlacchi (1987), rarely had more than 15 or 20 members, at the centre of which four or five were blood relatives. The *cosca* was devoid of any rigid organization and was simply referred to as *amici degli amici* ("friends of friends"). The members of a *cosca* were known as *aregli uomini qualificati* ("qualified men" or "men of honour"). A *zio* ("uncle") or *capo* ("head") was recognized as the leader of these informal, secretive networks, and whoever rose to this esteemed position truly personified the attributes of the Mafioso. Anton Blok (1974) states that one became a member of a *cosca* gradually, and not through formal initiation. Another level of organization was the *consorteria*, an alliance made up of two or more *coscas*. One *cosca* was recognized as supreme within the *consorteria* and its head was anointed as the **Capo di tutti Capi** ("the boss of bosses"). This happens when one *cosca* head is recognized as the most powerful, has more men, more friends, more money, or more high-ranking protectors (Arlacchi, 1987; Gambino, 1974: 3; Hess, 1986: 119–22; Ianni & Reuss-Ianni, 1976: 45).

As time passed, the family-based groups evolved in the direction of a formal organization. Each family controlled a particular activity, such as the sale of cattle or the control of water rights, and so avoided competition with one another. While separate from the state, the Mafioso was also able to wield his power by serving as a procurer of votes for political candidates who of course, once elected, would be beholden to him and would reciprocate by granting favours when requested (Albini, 1992: 86). By the middle of the nineteenth century, much of Sicily was under the control of Mafia groups. They held sway over a large portion of the rural population, had influence over local government, and controlled a number of vital industries on the island. According to Hobsbawm (1976), standardized rituals began to be developed in the 1870s. Young Sicilian men were indoctrinated into Mafia clans, on the proviso that they would become wholly subservient to the organization and its reigning don. Members were taught to abhor all formal authority, except for the Catholic Church, which was to be tolerated.

As the nineteenth century drew to a close, many of the Mafia groups became involved in predatory and criminal activities. The protective service offered by the Mafiosi would soon become an excuse to extort peasants and shopkeepers by forcing them to pay a tax to protect them from unforeseen calamitous events that may befall them, their family, or their business. Violent deaths began to be the norm for any- one betraying a Mafia group. By the end of the nineteenth century, the Mafia had been transformed from a protector of the Sicilian people to their subjugators and they perpetuated this dominance through intimidation, violence, and almost dictatorial powers. Incorporating criminal activities into their traditional role contributed to the forging of a complex and paradoxical social, political, economic, and criminal force in Sicily. As Peter Robb noted in his 1996 book *Midnight in Sicily*, "The Mafia was outlawed, but tolerated, secret, but recognizable, criminal but upholding of order. It protected and ripped off the owners of the great estates, protected and ripped off the sharecroppers who worked the estates, and ripped off the peasants who slaved on them" (Robb, 1996: 48).

CRITICAL THINKING EXERCISE

The origins of the Mafia in Sicily are complex and controversial. The above depic- tion will no doubt generate considerable disagreement among the experts. As with any attempt to document and explain the origins and history of an organized crime genre, students must ensure that they critically analyze the information presented to them. Based on your own research, what are the historical origins of the Mafia in Sicily? Can the term *Mafia* be traced back as far as the late thirteenth century, as some sources have argued?

Origins and Early History of the 'Ndrangheta

In addition to the Sicilian Mafia, a subculture with similar structures, rituals, and norms was forming and evolving into violent criminal fraternities in the southern Italian province of Calabria. According to the FBI, the 'Ndrangheta originated in the 1860s with Sicilians who were banished by the Italian government from their native island, an explanation that suggests the Calabrian Mafia grew out from the rib of the Sicilian Mafia (Federal Bureau of Investigation, n.d.). In contrast, Nicaso and Lamothe (2005) believe the origins of 'Ndrangheta were indigenous to Calabria; it began as a defence mechanism for impoverished rural peasants against their aristocratic landlords.

Regardless of its origins, as in Sicily, weak local governing institutions and the remoteness of Calabria from Rome helped pave the way for the emergence of power-hungry men bent on unofficially controlling all facets of local life, while financially wetting their beaks. For Nicaso and Lamothe (2005: 10), "Some leaders were beneficent; others were tyrannical. But all were violent, having to first prove their manliness through homicide, preferably in public, and preferably being acquitted of the ensuing charges." Like the Mafia, the term *'Ndrangheta*—which is derived from the Greek word *andragathía*, meaning heroism, cunning, virtue, and manliness—is imbued with deeper meanings as to how powerful men should conduct themselves.

Variously referred to as "the Honoured Society," "the Calabrian Mafia," *Fibbia*, or *N'drina*, signs of this secret society began to emerge in southern Italy by the end of the nineteenth century. In 1888, the Prefect of the city of Reggio, Calabria, received an anonymous letter alerting him to the existence of "a sect that fears nothing" (*The Guardian*, June 8, 2006). Four years later, more than 250 men from several villages throughout Calabria and southern Italy were investigated for Mafia-like activities (Nicaso & Lamothe, 2005: 10).

Origins of the Mafia in North America: Late Nineteenth and Early Twentieth Century

The origins of Italian-American organized crime in North America have long been debated, although there appears to be a consensus that it began to emerge just before the turn of the twentieth century, not long after the diaspora of Italian immigrants to North America began in the latter half of the nineteenth century. At the core of the contentious debate is whether a secret criminal conspiracy, methods, and infrastructure were exported from Italy to North America or, alternatively, whether the origins of IOC on this continent are found in factors indigenous to the United States and Canada. Most likely, the answer lies somewhere in between. While members of the Italian secret societies did make their way to North America as part of the massive immigration of Italians, the IOC groups that emerged in the first half of the twentieth century in the United States and Canada developed autonomously from the Sicilian Mafia and the

CRITICAL THINKING EXERCISE

Based on your understanding of etiological theories presented in chapter 4, do you believe that strain theory is a credible explanation for why Italian criminal societies formed in North America during the early part of the twentieth century? Conversely, do you believe that the causes of IOC should not be blamed on broader social forces (such as discrimination) but on deliberate choices by some Italian immigrants to turn to crime as a more expedient way to make money?

Calabrian 'Ndrangheta. The origins of *la Costa Nostra* in North America was the result of a potent mix of customs and traditions associated with the Calabrian 'Ndrangheta and Sicilian Mafia combined with the social, legal, and economic environment of the United States and Canada into which immigrants were acculturated.

During the early part of the twentieth century, evidence began to emerge of secret societies within the small but growing Italian population in some parts of the United States and Canada. Many of the Italians immigrating to North America during this period were poor peasants from the southern portions of the country, including Calabria and Sicily. Once they arrived, they moved to the urban areas where they lived in the most deprived social and economic circumstances, helping to populate large ethnic urban ghettos. If strain theory is applied, one could argue that many Italian immigrants saw the prosperity that surrounded them but felt impotent to achieve it due to the prejudice and discrimination they experienced. The largely agrarian roots of the immigrant Italians, combined with their lack of education and business experience, as well as an unfamiliarity with the urban environment, contributed to the slow or non-existent social mobility of the early Italian immigrants.

At the same time, the traditions and philosophies of the Mafia and 'Ndrangheta were imported by some Italian immigrants and were reproduced in the cities in which they settled. While the basic traditions and norms of the Mafia were carried over to North America, there is little evidence to suggest that entire Mafia groups were transported from Sicily to the continent.

Secret Societies: 1900 to 1930

According to Nelli (1976: 136), by the late nineteenth century, there were Italian secret societies in every American city that had a sizable Sicilian population, "feeding off the common labourer's honest toil and claiming to serve as a means of easing the adjustment to American society." Most of these societies were formed in North America and played a schizophrenic role in the Italian community; they provided much needed services to Italian immigrants, but also preyed upon them, primarily through extortion. Some secret societies were becoming a force in the cities where sizeable Italian immigrant populations resided, such as New York, Philadelphia, Cleveland, New Orleans, Montreal, and Hamilton. The earliest versions of secret Italian societies in Canada were loosely structured groups, influenced by the Sicilian Mafia and the Calabrian 'Ndrangheta. Within the expatriate Italian communities, they were simply referred to as "The Society" and were "much whispered about" before they came to the attention of the media or law enforcement (Nicaso & Lamothe, 2005: 11–12). Some of these societies followed the original philosophical credo of the Mafiosi and provided a range of services to Italian immigrants, such as helping to bring over family members, locating accommodations, finding jobs, providing money, and fostering social relationships. This was all conducted within the context of the traditional *partito*, where the *padrone* served as a provider of services to his Italian clients in the new country. Many of the *padrones* who founded these societies, however, regularly abused their positions of power and trust and devolved into criminal piranhas who forced Italian immigrants to join their society and pay dues.

The Black Hand: 1905 to 1927

Another early manifestation of IOC that grew and flourished in North American cities was the *Mano Nera* (the **Black Hand**), which almost exclusively revolved around the extortion of Italian immigrants. The extortion was often carried out by individuals involved in the secret Italian societies, yet the Black Hand was not an organization *per se*. Instead, it was a label applied by the media during the early part of the century to the highly publicized extortions carried out within the expatriate Italian communities. A Black Hand extortion attempt invariably began with a letter addressed to an intended victim. As Jay Robert Nash writes, these extortion schemes were not just prosaic, but highly intimidating and potentially lethal:

> An anonymous Black Hander would threaten various types of violence to extort money from one, usually well-to-do, victim. These threats most often involved kidnapping a family member, threatening to blow up a business or shop, or to attack, injure, or kill a family member or the recipient of the Black Hand note. These notes were crudely written in broken English … and boldly demanded a certain amount of money, with specific instructions as to how the cash was to be delivered. The note would usually be decorated with a number of horrific symbols and images— daggers dripping blood, a bomb exploding, a gun smoking at the barrel, a skull and crossbones, a body dangling from a rope tied about the neck. The signature of the sender was invariably a hand imprinted in heavy black ink, thus the sobriquet, *La Mano Nera* (The Black Hand). (Nash, 1993: 56)

In 1903, the *New York Herald* newspaper published what is believed to be the first story of an extortion letter received by a shopkeeper that was signed with the imprint of a black hand. Soon thereafter, a number of extortion rings in New York, New Jersey, Pennsylvania, Ontario, Manitoba, and British Columbia were being reported during the early 1900s, some of which culminated in violent deaths. In February 1904, a Newark, New Jersey, man named Michael Rossati received a letter threatening to kill him and his wife if he did not pay $400. The signature was a black ink imprint of a hand (*New York Times*, February 29, 1904). In December of the same year, a New Yorker named Joseph Pagano received a letter demanding $100 or his life. The letter, written in Italian, bore a skull and crossbones (*New York Times*, December 12, 1904). In May of 1905, the fruit store and home of an Italian immigrant in Monessen, Pennsylvania, was dynamited after he allegedly refused to pay $5000 demanded in two previous extortion letters (*New York Times*, May 23, 1905). Numerous other bombings of Italian shopkeepers followed in Pennsylvania and New York City.

Some of the extortion attempts were carried out by the secret Italian societies under the guise of "membership fees." In 1905, the *New York Times* reported that Italian men working on the dams in New York's Winchester County were threatened with violence if they did not pay a membership fee to the local society. "Every pay day at the different dams agents of the Black Hand band demand all the way from $1 to $5 from each man, and if refused a note threatening him with death is left at his home the next day" (*New York Times*, July 9, 1905). Those forced to join a society were also often compelled, under the threat of violence, to carry out further extortion operations against their fellow countrymen.

Numerous extortion attempts were reported in Ontario between 1905 and 1910. Extortionists turned up at the work and camp sites of Italian labourers toiling on construction projects. Some were so brazen that they stood at the paymasters' wickets to collect their cut of the cash wages paid to their victims (Nicaso & Lamothe, 2005: 15). In 1906, Italian workers arriving in Toronto from Port Colborne, located in the southern portion of the Niagara Peninsula, told stories about one labourer who had been terrorized into paying $30, and another who disappeared after persuading a friend to guarantee the payment of a similar amount. Under the title, "Are there Black Hand Italians at Port Colborne?" a reporter for the *Toronto Daily Star* wrote the following in a 1906 article: "It is said that a number of the thriftier Italians have been threatened with dire penalties should they fail to pay the specified amounts. Letters have been written, but frequently the prospective victims are seen in person and significant threats used" (*Toronto Star*, May 4, 1906). In North Bay, Ontario, where a large Italian community supplied labour for railroad, dam, and sewer construction, a local society was considered so active that "there has been a spirit of unrest manifest in the Italian colony," resulting in "a revolt among the victims" (*Toronto Star*, January 9, 1909).

Case Study: Early Italian Secret Society in Ontario

Events leading to one of the first police investigations into a "Society" in Canada began on December 7, 1908. It was on this day that Louis Belluz, a baker in Fort Francis, Ontario, received a letter written in red ink. The letter demanded $100 and, according to a police summary of a statement made by Belluz, if payment was not forthcoming, "his buildings were to be burned and himself burned to death." After Belluz reported the extortion attempt, police traced the letter to Nicholas Bessanti and a fellow Italian immigrant who went by the name of Joe Ross (some Italians anglicized their names in order to avoid incidents of bigotry). Bessanti told police that he wrote the letter on behalf of a secret society he was forced to join in Fort Francis. He estimated total membership in this group at 15 or 16 people. His fee to join was $25, but Bessanti disclosed that he only paid $10. He spoke of an initiation ceremony where a closed circle of men crouched over a large stiletto knife and chanted oaths that consisted of arcane Italian poetry and at the end, they hugged and kissed one another. "In joining the Society," Bessanti told police, "we took a solemn oath that we would obey our leader's orders: would rob, burn or kill as he directed; that we would protect one another from the hands of the law; to disobey these orders we would expect to be punished by death or otherwise as decide upon by the Society." Bessanti explained that the group "met every Saturday night in the west end of freight shed and there they decided what to do to raise money."

Bessanti also informed police that he attended a meeting where it was decided "the Baker Louis Belluz must pay over some money to them" and if he "did not put up, at least, $50.00, they would burn his house up and him in it." Bessanti was warned by leaders of the society that he would suffer the same fate as the baker if the letter was not delivered. The letter Bessanti wrote was dictated to him by the society's founder Francesco Tino. By the time police had begun to close in on Tino, he and Frank Muro, who helped organize the Fort Francis society, had crossed the border into the United States. After warrants were issued by Canadian authorities, American police arrested the two men in the town of Hibbing, located in northern Minnesota. Tino and Muro were brought back to Canada and following a trial were convicted, along with Bessanti, of theft and other charges. Tino received the harshest sentence of five years (Archives of the Province of Ontario, RG 4-32, File No: 1909-651; Nicaso & Lamothe, 2005: 18–22; *Toronto Telegram*, May 6, 1909).

The Black Hand extortions were not only in Ontario. The town of Fernie, located in the Kootenay region of British Columbia, was reeling under allegations that Black Handers were extorting the local Italian population, most of whom had immigrated to the area from southern Italy in the late 1890s in search of work in the mines or in railway construction. In 1908, a petition signed by dozens of Fernie citizens and sent to the provincial government requested that action be taken against the "Black Hand Society," which has "for its object, extortion of money; the wounding of persons who do not yield to its requests, and in many cases, it commits murder" (Provincial Archives of British Columbia, GR-0429, Folio Nos: 3052/08, 3039/08). Following a police investigation, 12 men were arrested and charged with conspiracy to obtain money by threats. Police had obtained statements from at least five of the arrested men that they were compelled to become members of the society and forced to pay an initiation fee. Based on their evidence, police identified the two ringleaders as Stephen Bruno and Frank Albernesse, who had come to Fernie from Spokane, Washington, expressly to organize a "Society" (*The Fernie Free Press*, July 3, 1908).

The era of the Black Hand in Canada came to an end in 1928 with a highly publicized case that was played out in a courtroom in Welland, Ontario. On February 21, 1928, Giuseppe (Joe) Italiano was found guilty on eight counts of extortion and related charges. He was sentenced to nine years' imprisonment, 18 strokes of the lash, and deportation at the expiration of his prison term. Italiano was arrested and charged with threatening Frank Mango, the owner of a shoe shop in Niagara Falls. In November 1927, Mango received an extortion letter postmarked in Buffalo and written in Italian, complete with a death threat and numerous expletives, demanding $4,000. The letter, which was translated into English for the trial, promised, "We sure going to clean you out, even the cats, your house. Your house is going to be blown up like a balloon. Your time is short, one week or 15 days at least if you like to save yourself and family." The letter cautioned Mango to "Be sure not to open your mouth. I think you know what we are talking about. If you don't do that, we blow your building up all over the river and all you have in Canada." The letter was signed, "The President of Vendetta, we will destroy you." At the bottom of the letter was a crudely drawn picture of a grave (with "Your Grave" written underneath) as well as two daggers pointing at a heart (subtitled with "You die the knife go through your heart and mouth Better keep your mouth shut."). On November 7, Mango's house was rocked by an explosion, which police determined was caused by dynamite that had been placed on his front porch. Ten days later, Mango received a visit from Italiano, who told him, "The Brotherhood wants the money." Mango replied that he did not have $4,000 but agreed to pay $400 in four installments. Italiano accepted the offer, but unbeknownst to the Black Hander, Mango had previously been in contact with police, who had his house under surveillance. When Italiano left Mango's home, with $400 in his hand and threatening letters in his pocket, he was arrested, charged, and later convicted (Archives of Ontario, RG 22, File No: RG-22-392-0-8947; *The Globe*, February 27, 1928; Nicaso, 2001a).

Although it was not known at the time, the Italiano case represented the end of the Black Hand era in Canada. It was a fitting end, given that the case typified the elementary and brutish tactics of early IOC in Canada and the United States. Yet, evidence continues

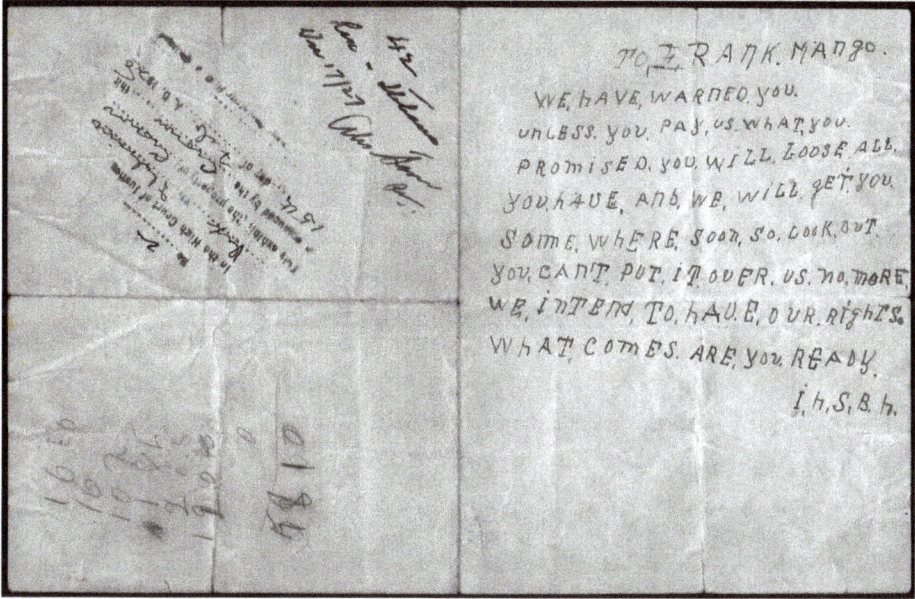

Photo 5.1: Actual extortion letter sent to Frank Mango

Source: Reprinted with permission from the Archives of Ontario, File No. RG 22-392-0-6308, Container 167

to mount that some of the Black Handers in places like North Bay, Hamilton, Toronto, Winnipeg, and Fernie were connected to secret societies, complete with ceremonies, rituals, and a rudimentary organizational hierarchy, that were influenced by the Sicilian Mafia and Calabrian 'Ndrangheta. While the era of the Black Hand may have ended, extortion would continue to be a stock-in-trade for Italian criminal groups in Canada for at least the next five decades. The Black Hand label, and the term *extortion*, would now be replaced with a new and grossly misleading designation: "protection" (see chapter 9).

Prohibition: 1920 to 1934

While extortion continued to be used by Italian criminal groups, predatory money-making ventures increasingly lost ground to consensual crimes. By the 1920s, the highly profitable trade in drugs, gambling, and prostitution made it clear that the greatest source of illicit money was to be made in satisfying the vices of receptive consumers. It was the outlawing of liquor, however, that launched IOC in North America into the modern era of organized crime. Prohibition presented an unequalled money-making opportunity for many criminal entrepreneurs in North America, but it represented a particularly seminal turning point for IOC. While the clientele of the Italian bootleggers were primarily their fellow countrymen, they soon began supplying the larger population, thereby allowing them to break out of the confines of "Little Italy" and operate in the wider society. Members of the Italian community were also in an advantageous position to capitalize on temperance laws. They already had in place an infrastructure, a wide social network, experience in producing liquor (as wine makers), and an existing market in the immigrant Italian population. Thousands of Italian immigrants continued to stream into North America, including numerous Mafiosi who had been run out of Italy by Mussolini, and who quickly recognized the money to be made in bootlegging. Italian criminal groups were also populated with some of the most ambitious gangsters, who worked their way to the forefront of the underworld through their cunning, organizational skills, innovation, ruthlessness, and a penchant for violence. It was because of Prohibition that such criminal luminaries would emerge in the United States, including Charles Luciano, Johnny Torrio, Frank Costello, Joe Bonanno, and Al Capone. On the Canadian side of the border was a man who would eventually be anointed as Canada's own Al Capone and the Canadian "King of the Bootleggers"—Rocco Perri.

Case Study: Rocco Perri (1890–1944)

Rocco Perri not only established himself as one of southern Ontario's most prolific bootleggers during Prohibition, he was also one of the most influential Calabrian crime bosses in the region during the 1920s. His organizational infrastructure and criminal operations represented a significant forerunner for OC syndicates to come in Canada. Perri was born in Reggio, Calabria, in 1890. He immigrated to Canada at the age of 13, where he joined thousands of young Italian immigrants toiling at low-paying manual labour jobs. In 1912, Perri moved to Toronto where he fell in love with Bessie Starkman, the wife of his landlord, and soon thereafter stole Bessie from her husband. In 1915, the two moved to Hamilton, where Perri worked in a pasta factory. While in Hamilton, Perri immersed himself in the Italian population and quickly become one of the community's best-known personalities.

By 1916, Perri, with the help of Starkman, ran a small grocery store in Hamilton, where they sold olive oil and Italian specialties. It was also through this store that the Perri's bootlegging career was born. The *Ontario Temperance Act* restricted the consumption of liquor in that province, and Perri quickly took advantage of the pent-up demand by selling whisky from the back of his store for 50 cents a shot. By 1918, Perri was the largest bootlegger in Hamilton, and under the guise of a travelling salesman for the Superior Macaroni Company, he traversed the province arranging liquor sales for his many customers (Dubro & Rowland, 1988: 48).

In 1920, Prohibition had come into effect in the United States, and Perri was well-placed to take advantage of this even greater opportunity. While Bessie handled the domestic bootlegging operations, Rocco moved into the liquor export business, using his Calabrian connections in southern Ontario and northern New York to find customers and establish shipping routes. Perri eventually owned or leased dozens of fishing boats on Lake Erie that were used to run booze to the

United States, facilitated by customs agents paid to conveniently look the other way (Hunt, 1988: 143). Perri also reportedly operated an estimated 40 trucks that delivered booze to a network of bootleggers stretching from Niagara Falls to Kitchener, Ontario (Hunt, 1988: 170). Many of his vehicles were modified to carry capacities of up to 300 gallons at a time.

Perri reportedly had more than 200 employees on either side of the border (McNulty, 1923: 125), many of whom were Calabrians who swore blood ties and faithful allegiance to him. "There is not an Italian in Hamilton who would give this man away," the RCMP Officer commanding western Ontario during Prohibition was quoted as saying. "He is the 'King-pin' directing all operations but the members of his gang when caught, shoulder the responsibility and pay the penalty" (National Archives of Canada, RG 16: Records of the Department of National Revenue, Vol. 789). Perri's ability to avoid capture was also due to his liberal use of graft; those purportedly on his payroll included local police, liquor licence inspectors, customs officers on both sides of the border, and judges. His ascendance was also based on his use of violence, which he honed through his active role in hijacking liquor shipments.

Perri's sources of liquor were plentiful. He became a regular customer of the Gooderham and Wort's Distillery of Toronto, Seagram's in Waterloo, the Kuntz Brewery in Kitchener, and the Hiram Walker Distillery in Windsor (Dubro & Rowland, 1988: 12). Perri was buying cases of 60-proof whiskey at distilleries in Toronto for as little as $18 a case and reselling them in the United States for $120 a case (Dubro, 1985: 269). During a boastful interview with the *Toronto Star*, Perri admitted that he sometimes sold as many as 1000 cases of whisky a day. Police investigators later uncovered several bank accounts—with over $900,000 on deposit—opened by Bessie Starkman under various names. This was in addition to their impressive portfolio of other assets, including speakeasies, hotels, a fleet of boats and trucks, and their expensive 19-room Hamilton mansion. A 1927 Royal Commission that investigated corruption in Canada Customs as a result of the illegal liquor trade estimated that Perri grossed close to $1 million annually.

Perri soon became a top priority of law enforcement. On November 18, 1927, the Royal Commission laid eight counts of perjury charges against Perri and Starkman based on their less-than-forthcoming testimony. Following a short trial, in 1928 both were convicted and served six-month sentences.

When Perri was released from jail, he re-entered a changed and hostile world. The *Ontario Temperance Act* was repealed, taking away their large domestic market for bootlegged liquor. Competition over the American market became fiercer and more violent—a fact that brutally hit home for Rocco and Bessie. On the night of August 13, 1930, the couple was returning home from a party when two unidentified assailants pulled shotguns and fired over 100 bullets into the body of Bessie

Continued

Photo 5.2: Rocco Perri following the funeral of his wife, Bessie Starkman

Source: Milford Smith Collection, Hamilton Public Library

Starkman. The gangland-style murder of Bessie fuelled speculation that she was the real brains behind their operations. Perri himself would be targeted later years, including two attempts on his life in 1938, which he escaped with only minor cuts. However, his luck ran out on April 23, 1944. While visiting a cousin, he stepped outside for some air and was never seen again.

The Ascendance of Italian Organized Crime in North America: The 1930s to the 1960s

By the time Prohibition was repealed in the early 1930s, a radically different criminal underworld had arrived in North America. Organized crime was now more widespread, more sophisticated, more transnational, and more entrepreneurial. For the next 50 years, the so-called Italian Mafia would become the most infamous organized criminal force in North America. Replacing the lost revenue from bootlegging, Mafia groups expanded into other illegal activities, including gambling, loansharking, prostitution, labour racketeering, and drug trafficking. According to Robert Stewart (1980: 6), ICO emerged from the Prohibition era with an empowering legacy, including a purpose, structure, and methodology that transcended any single crime; adhering members and associates who shared deep subcultural bonds, values, and goals and were comparatively disciplined, loyal, energetic, and resourceful; and a protocol that enabled members, who were often strangers, to collaborate on joint business ventures in a framework of mutual trust. IOC in the post-Prohibition years also profited from capable, ambitious, and visionary leadership who stressed a business-like, entrepreneurship approach and the timely exploitation of any illegal or legal business opportunity that had the potential to make money. American and Canadian Mafia groups also effectively incorporated the essential tactics of organized crime—in particular, the use of intimidation, violence, and corruption—while the code of *omerta* ensured other crucial tenets of a criminal organization—loyalty, discipline, and silence—were maintained to protect members from arrest and prosecution. In addition, Mafia families benefited greatly from the partnerships they formed with other like-minded criminal entrepreneurs, regardless of their race, religion, ethnicity, nationality, or location.

Perhaps most importantly, the Mafia families in North America learned the lessons of Prohibition better than anyone else: the biggest criminal profits were to be made by satisfying society's vices and, more specifically, by controlling the manufacture or whole-saling of illicit goods. Italian crime groups emerged from Prohibition with a substantial financial war chest that was re-invested into a number of illegal and heavily regulated goods and services that were in high demand. The end of Prohibition had little effect on Mafia groups in Canada; they quickly capitalized on the increased costs of booze in this country by providing a cheaper tax-free product that was produced in secret underground distilleries or was shipped in from abroad.

It was illegal gambling and bookmaking, however, that became the single greatest source of income for IOC in the years immediately following Prohibition. Like booze, gambling enjoyed a popularity that cut across social classes and ethnic groups. The demand for commercial gambling outlets fuelled a dramatic increase in underground casinos, floating card games, illegal lotteries, and bookmaking operations. In the United States, casinos financed by LCN families sprang up all over the country. The enormous profits made from gambling were then loaned back to gamblers at usurious rates, making loansharking second only to gambling in terms of profit during the 1930s.

If any one individual can take credit for the LCN's invasion of Canada, it was Charles (Lucky) Luciano, the far-sighted and ambitious American mobster who has been widely credited as the father of modern organized crime. Inspired by the Roman Empire, Lucky Luciano sought a comparable criminal dynasty and in 1933 even created a governing Mafia Commission in the United States. Made up of the heads of the major Mafia families in New York and other American cities, the commission acted as a sort of board of directors for the LCN. Although it had little formal power, it was respected enough to mete out binding decisions in disputes that arose between different families. Luciano's grand vision also reportedly resulted in the partitioning of the United States and Canada into 24 regions, each of which would be under the jurisdiction of a particular Mafia family. The implication for Canada was that it would be treated as a protectorate of the American Mafia. As a result, Montreal came under the fiefdom of New York's Bonanno family and southwestern Ontario fell under the influence of the Detroit mob, while the rest of Ontario's underworld belonged to Buffalo mob boss Stefano Magaddino.

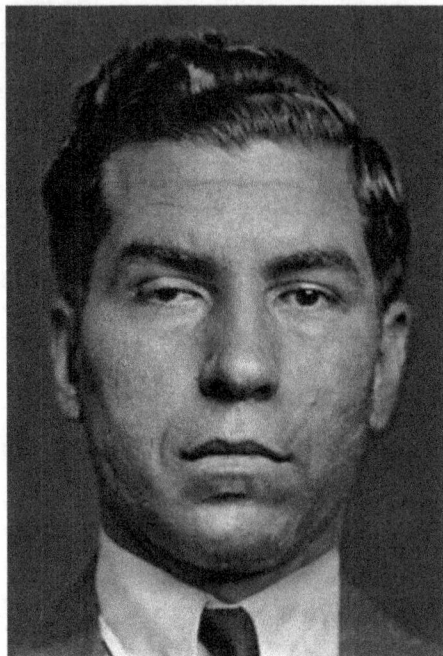

Photo 5.3: Charles "Lucky" Luciano

Source: New York Police Department, via Wikimedia Commons

The servitude of Italian-Canadian crime groups to their American counterparts escalated in the early 1950s when a crackdown on organized crime in the United States prompted Mafia leaders in that country to relocate many of their illegal gaming operations to Quebec and Ontario. Independent professional gamblers and bookmakers in Canada were put out of business, or at the very least were forced to pay a percentage of their revenues to their new bosses. Canada was also established as a major lay-off centre for the American Mafia's bookmaking operations (a "lay-off man" takes bets from other bookmakers who are trying to insure against heavy losses—if one horse or sports team receives heavy betting—by placing bets on the favourite with the lay-off man). Through their expansion into Canada and Cuba, their move into Las Vegas, as well as shrewd investments in national and international wire services (which instantaneously transmitted information on sporting events), the American Mafia families created an international gambling and bookmaking network the likes of which had never been seen. As Alan Phillips wrote in a 1964 *Maclean's* article, "this underworld federation is first and foremost a gambling cartel, a monopoly so well-concealed that some policemen refuse it credence. Gamblers call it 'The Combination.' Through a network of affiliates, a small bettor in Saskatchewan can bet on a fight in Sweden, a dog race in Florida, or a horse running on any track in America" (Phillips, 1964: 3).

RCMP Commissioner Clifford Harvison confirmed the American Mafia's move into Canada in a well-publicized address to the Canadian Club in Toronto on November 6, 1961: "The American syndicates are showing an increased interest in Canada and they are moving to take over direct control of some existing criminal organizations and to expand their criminal activities. They are already active in the field of gambling, narcotics trafficking, counterfeiting, and in the protection rackets. There are some indications and there is some evidence that the syndicates have already started to treat Canada as an area for expansion of their activities" (Ontario Police Commission, 1964: 1, 2). Commissioner Harvison's comments prompted President John F. Kennedy to remark in 1962 that his administration's war against organized crime must be succeeding if so many gangsters were fleeing to Canada (*Toronto Star*, October 11, 1962).

Italian Organized Crime and Narcotics Trafficking: The 1940s to the 1980s

Not only was the American *Cosa Nostra* integrating Canada into its continental gambling network, it was also situating its northern neighbour as an integral part of an international pipeline for heroin smuggled into the United States (see chapter 11 for more historical details on narcotics trafficking affecting Canada). In the post-war years, the production, smuggling, and wholesale distribution of heroin became concentrated in the hands of a confederation of criminal syndicates—the French *L'Union Corse*, the Sicilian Mafia, the American LCN and its Canadian affiliates—that collectively would become one of the largest and longest-lasting international heroin trafficking conspiracies of all time.

At the start of the 1940s, Italian Mafia families in the United States and Canada became the largest illegal dispensers of opiates and, for the next 40 years, they held an almost complete monopoly over the wholesale distribution of Turkish heroin in both countries. Their main suppliers were French Corsicans, who had become the world's biggest heroin producers, with much of the world's supply being produced in France. Quebec's cultural, commercial, and linguistic ties to the mother country, the subservience of the Mafia in the province to New York's Bonanno family, as well as Montreal's inviting seaports and close proximity to New York, made the city a major entry point for heroin being shipped into North America. Over the course of the next 30 years, police in the United States and Canada investigated dozens of major importation conspiracies that brought in thousands of kilos of almost pure Turkish heroin and led to the conviction of more than 300 people in the two countries. Many of these were members or associates of Canadian and American Mafia groups (The McClellan Committee, 1976: 199). One of the legacies of this international heroin trafficking network was that it gave Canada and Canadian mobsters a pivotal role in the heroin trade in North America while further pulling the country's criminal underworld into the orbit of the American *Cosa Nostra*.

ITALIAN ORGANIZED CRIME IN ONTARIO

The Magaddino Family

Rocco Perri's disappearance signalled the end of an era for Ontario's criminal underworld. The independent mobster who achieved power during Prohibition was now being replaced by a tightly knit group of men, many of who also hailed from Calabria and whose criminal roots were much more firmly planted in the traditions of the 'Ndrangheta. They also had less autonomy in that they were answerable to Mafia families in the United States. Most notable among the new Calabrian crime bosses in Ontario were Anthony (Tony) Sylvestro, Calogero Bordonaro (a.k.a. Charles Bardinaro), and Santo Scibetta (euphemistically referred to as the "Three Dons").

Photo 5.4: Stefano Magaddino

Source: Walter Albertin, World Telegram staff photographer, via Wikimedia Commons

Their rise to power, which began after the repeal of Prohibition in the United States, was bolstered by their close association with the Magaddino crime family in Buffalo. At the top of the family hierarchy sat Stefano Magaddino. Following the repeal of Prohibition, Magaddino put together his own Mafia family and moved into loansharking, extortion, labour racketeering, fraud, theft, gambling, and drug trafficking. Illiterate, but with a strategic mind and a ruthless demeanour, Magaddino and his wealth and power were recognized when he was awarded a seat on the Mafia's ruling commission. As part of the partitioning of North America by the commission, Magaddino was granted jurisdiction over much of Ontario, which he jealously guarded until his death in 1974.

The alliance the Three Dons forged with Magaddino was instrumental in fuelling the re-emergence of IOC in the province and its growing dominance in gambling, bookmaking, and drug trafficking. Starting around the mid-1930s, Ontario's Mafia groups helped fuel the expansion of the opium and heroin trade there. By the 1940s, classified reports from the US Bureau of Narcotics and the RCMP documented the flow of Mexican brown heroin from Buffalo to Hamilton and then on to Toronto and Vancouver, as well as Turkish heroin that was moving from Ontario to Buffalo and then to the eastern seaboard (National Archives of Canada, RG 29, File no: 323-2-6).

While Magaddino controlled much of southern Ontario, Windsor was considered the jurisdiction of Detroit's Mafia families. Southwestern Ontario was of strategic benefit for the Detroit mob, especially when it came to smuggling. In the 1950s, Windsor and the surrounding area became a launching pad for heroin imported into Detroit and served as a staging ground for the smuggling of illegal Italian immigrants into the United States (*New York Times*, December 5, 1970; *Toronto Telegram*, April 28, 1961). Ontario was also key to the American Mafia's consolidation of gaming and bookmaking operations throughout North America. In 1948, Detroit police commissioner Harry Toy stated publicly that Windsor was a "central wire service" that supplied all the bookie establishments in Detroit (*Toronto Star*, February 27, 1948). Outside of Windsor, the Magaddino family was behind the LCN's takeover of gambling in southern Ontario.

Case Studies: John Papalia and Giacomo Luppino

John (Johnny Pops) Papalia was the son of Rosie Italiano and Anthony Papalia, who had immigrated to Canada from Calabria around the beginning of the twentieth century and settled in Hamilton. Sometime in the 1920s, Anthony Papalia began bootlegging liquor and continued to do so for years following the repeal of Ontario's temperance laws. Born on March 18, 1924, John Papalia grew to be a skinny, often sickly looking kid, but had a tough reputation, even at a young age. He dropped out of school around the age of 13. It was as a young teenager that Papalia embarked on a criminal career, first becoming involved in theft and bootlegging before moving on to more violent crimes, such as extortion and muscle-for-hire. By 1943, Papalia had relocated to Toronto where he began running with a gang of other young toughs. While in Toronto, he received a four-month sentence for a residential break-in, the first of many convictions that would see him in and out of jail for the rest of his life. Before the end of the decade, he was pushing heroin for one of Toronto's biggest traffickers, Harvey Chernick, who was supplied by Anthony Sylvestro. In 1949, he was imprisoned for two years less a day for trafficking in heroin. When he was released, he went to Montreal where he worked as an enforcer for Carmine Galante, a captain in New York's Bonanno family. Over the next four years, Papalia would complete his apprenticeship and be accepted as a made member of the Magaddino Mafia family. When he settled back in Hamilton in 1955, his Mafia connections would help him rise to the top of Hamilton's criminal underworld.

During the 1950s, Papalia also began to make a move on gambling operations in other parts of southern Ontario, including Toronto. His first move was to tell each of the operators that he was going to take a cut of those profits. Soon all the gambling operations in the Toronto–Hamilton area were paying protection money to Papalia. In 1955, Papalia branched out into loansharking and the operation of vending machine companies in Hamilton and Toronto. Police later claimed that Papalia's vending machines were often put into the businesses of people who owed him gambling debts, and those store owners who would not accept the machines occasionally were threatened with violence. As the Sicilian and Italian-American Mafia families increased their heroin operations during the 1950s and 1960s, the Magaddino family tightened its control over drug smuggling through Ontario. Papalia, the acknowledged leader of Magaddino's crew in the province, became active in helping to smuggle heroin into New York and Ontario. In 1961, he was convicted in a New York courtroom on charges of conspiracy to import US $150 million worth of heroin into the United States and received a 10-year sentence.

When Papalia was released from jail in 1968, he faced competition from a number of other mobsters, in particular Paul Volpe, another member of Magaddino's Ontario crew who was attempting to take control of the entire province. On

Continued

Photo 5.5: John Papalia

Source: Illustration by author, based on 1960s newspaper photo

November 14, 1983, the bullet-torn body of Toronto mobster Paul Volpe was found stuffed into the trunk of his wife's leased BMW at the Toronto International Airport. Immediately police suspected Papalia; however, to this day, the murder has never been solved. For the next 14 years, Papalia remained a major Mafia figure in the province, yet, he was never able to re-impose his supremacy. In May 1997, Papalia was gunned down by on orders from Pat and Angelo Musitano, leaders of a rival Mafia group in Hamilton.

During the mid-1950s, John Papalia would be joined in Hamilton by another powerful Mafioso and future Magaddino family member named Giacomo Luppino. Born in 1900 in the village of Oppido in Calabria, Luppino came to Canada in 1955, already a member of an 'Ndrangheta clan in Italy. Settling in Hamilton, he would go on to be Magaddino's most trusted and reliable Ontario lieutenant. While little is known about Luppino's initial years in Canada, it was around the late 1950s or early 1960s that he and Santo Scibetta were chosen by Magaddino to oversee his Ontario interests, largely to replace John Papalia who at the time was under indictment in the US.

Influenced by his Calabrian roots, the organization Luppino set up in Ontario reflected the structure, rules, and codes of the 'Ndrangheta. He became the *capo decina* of the Hamilton wing of the Magaddino family but was also in charge of Mafia crews or *decinas* (literally a set of ten) in other regions of Ontario. In keeping with 'Ndrangheta organizational tradition, different areas of the province were broken into *aubbocatos*, distinct territories that separated different families or wings of a family. Luppino became the *capo di tutti capi* over all of Magaddino's branches in Ontario, putting him in charge of *decinas* operating in such *aubbocatos* as Hamilton, Guelph, Oakville, and Toronto (*Hamilton Spectator*, August 31, 1984).

Following the lead of the Mafia's ruling commission in the United States, Luppino also established *La Camera di Controllo*. Made up of the heads of the various *decinas* in Ontario, the goal of this "board of control" was to ensure cooperation, to avoid territorial infringement, and to resolve any problems that may arise. The board, which answered to Magaddino, was reflective of Luppino's great reverence toward his boss and his adherence to the traditional role of the Mafioso as a mediator and arbitrator. Luppino has been described as "a master strategist" who built bridges and brokered deals among different Mafia leaders. He was frequently consulted by Mafia members from throughout North America and intervened to settle numerous disputes that arose over the years. By setting up the *Camera*, he forged strong relationships with other 'Ndrangheta leaders in Ontario and also maintained ties with the Montreal Mafia (Charney, 1979: 28; *Hamilton Spectator*, August 31, 1984; Talese, 1971: 62–63; *Toronto Star*, March 23, 1987). Luppino was a Mafioso in the classical sense in that he lived a modest life, believing that it was not wealth, but respect and honour that defined the worth of any man. In one conversation with his like-minded son-in-law Paolo Violi, both complained about how the American Mafia, with its emphasis on making money, had lost the "old country ways of operation" and conflicted with the traditional ways of the Mafiosi (*Globe and Mail*, July 6, 1986).

Beginning in 1967, police embarked on a five-year surveillance operation on Luppino, which included wiretapping his Hamilton home. Information gleaned from Operation Orbit provided great insight into the life of the Mafia don and the existence and structure of his criminal organization. Luppino did follow some time-honoured 'Ndrangheta customs. Made members had to pay dues and pass along a percentage of all profits from criminal or legal activities to him. He was also recorded discussing how one obligation of an 'Ndrangheta group was to make financial contributions to a "welfare assistance program" to help its members through difficult times. Despite his paternalistic nature, Luppino was still the head of a criminal group that made money from extortion, loansharking, fraud, counterfeiting, migrant smuggling, drug trafficking, and murder. Although his reign lasted for more than 30 years, up to his death in 1987, Luppino was never charged with a criminal offence in Canada (*Globe and Mail*, July 6, 1986; *Hamilton Spectator*, July 6, 1982, July 7, 1982, July 10, 1982; *Toronto Star*, July 7, 1982, March 23, 1987).

Stefano Magaddino backed the Sylvestro and Cipolla families in establishing Guelph as an important link in a cross-border bookmaking network that Guelph police estimated took in $15,000 to $30,000 a day in illegal bets (*Toronto Telegram*, April 24, 1961). Magaddino also took a cut of the revenue from gambling operations in Hamilton and Toronto run by members of the crews he had established there.

The early 1960s continued to be high-profile for organized crime in Ontario. In 1963, the US Senate Committee on Organized Crime heard Mafia turncoat Joseph Valachi proclaim that the LCN stretched into Ontario. At the same hearings, senior officers with the Buffalo Police Department testified that in Toronto, Hamilton, Guelph, and Niagara Falls, Ontario, there were at least 20 members of a crime syndicate headed by the "irrefutable lord paramount" Stefano Magaddino. The presentation was accompanied by an organizational chart entitled "The Magaddino Empire of Organized Crime." On the right hand of the chart, in a square marked "Canada," were the names of the Vito and Alberto Agueci, Charles and Frank Cipolla, Dan Gasbarrini, John Papalia and his two brothers, as well as Paul and Albert Volpe (*Globe and Mail*, October 17, 1963; United States Congress, 1965: 581–88).

The Siderno Group

While Luppino ruled his criminal fiefdom with the backing of Stefano Magaddino, Toronto was also home to 'Ndrangheta clans that were connected to Antonio Marci, the *capo crimini* (boss of all bosses) in Calabria, Italy. During the 1950s and 1960s, Marci forged a loose network of 'Ndrangheta cells in the United States, Canada, Germany, Switzerland, South America, and Australia, in part to facilitate his international heroin smuggling operation (Nicaso & Lamothe, 1995: 62–69). Each cell was based on 'Ndrangheta tradition: a small family of blood relatives formed the nucleus, while other members and associates were related through marriage or godparenthood. While each cell generally followed this template, and worked with one another, for the most part they operated autonomously from Marci. Some of the original members of the Toronto cell, which was founded in the late 1950s, had already been inducted into the Honoured Society in Italy, while their sons and other younger recruits took the ritual oath in Toronto. Because most of the Society men that were transplanted in Toronto hailed from a small port on the eastern coast of Reggio di Calabria called Siderno Marina, police began to refer to the Toronto cell as the Siderno Group.

The undisputed head of the Siderno Group up until his death in 1980 was Michele Racco. Born on December 12, 1913, in Siderno Marina, Racco was already a member of the 'Ndrangheta before he immigrated to Canada in the early 1950s. Upon arrival, Racco established a cell in Toronto that grew steadily as he recruited men of Calabrian descent locally and from Italy. By the early 1960s, Racco established a local commission (a *Crimini*) that settled disputes and maintained discipline among the city's 'Ndrangheta members. As the head of this ruling board, Racco became the *capo crimini* for Toronto.

From his small bakery on St. Clair Avenue in the city's Italian district, Racco oversaw a secret criminal society that at any one time included between 50 and 100 members who were involved in bootlegging, counterfeiting, extortion, immigrant smuggling, and drug trafficking. The bakery was also a popular meeting place for members of the Honoured Society and, like Luppino, Racco played the role of the traditional Mafia don. He rarely became directly involved in criminal activities; instead, his job was to help create opportunities for other Siderno Group members. He valued respect and honour over money and saw himself as a *padrone* to his constituents, providing jobs and loans to community members and safe passage to Canada for Italian immigrants. Racco was much sought after for advice or to solve disputes and maintained strong ties with like-minded *compares*, among them Giacomo Luppino in Hamilton and Vic Cotroni in Montreal, as well as leaders of other 'Ndrangheta cells in the United States and abroad. Police intercepted one telephone call from the United States in which the man on the other end solicited Racco's advice on how to resolve a territorial dispute between two 'Ndrangheta clans in New York (*Globe and Mail*, August 18, 1982). Although Racco preferred mediation to violence, he is suspected of sanctioning the death of two Toronto 'Ndrangheta members in the late 1960s.

Like the Sicilian Mafia, traditional 'Ndrangheta groups in Canada are also based on family relationships, either through blood, marriage, or the custom of *comparatico*. All members must go through an initiation ceremony, which consists of a series of vague questions and answers, obscure symbolic gestures, the invocation of mythical knights, and references to violence and the supremacy of the 'Ndrangheta clan to which the inductee is expected to make a life-long commitment. In 1985, police video cameras captured an undercover RCMP officer as he was inducted into an 'Ndrangheta cell during a ceremony held in a Greater Toronto apartment. After gathering the inductee and six made members into a circle, the leader of the cell welcomed the new member into "the Honoured Society of Calabria" and "the Family." The ceremony was described by long-time RCMP officer and organized crime expert Reginald King:

Photo 5.6: Michele Racco

Source: Illustration by Ben Firsch

A 'Ndrangheta group voted three times to accept the initiate into the organization. "I swear on the tip of this knife to forget father, mother, all the family, at whatever call, to answer to 'Corp of the Society'," the inductee was instructed to repeat. "There is a dark tomb wide and deep under the depth of the sea. Whoever uncovers it shall die with four knifings to the breast," the vow continued. Later, the leader explained some of the rules, the "codes of the court," as he called them. Cooperation, communication, dividing of profits, and punishment are crucial elements. "If we make a penny, a penny ... is what is divided amongst us. If (one of us) is in trouble, we are all in trouble. These are not things that are discussed with anyone," the leader said. "You are older than my brother, but because he entered (the Society) before you ... you have to respect him. I will tell you something. When one does a swearing in, they have to do a swearing in that will last. It is not a swearing in that you can say you want to leave ... If he does (a profitable activity) and I don't know but if I find out, if he does something light, small, there are other methods in which he can pay. And you don't pay with words ... You know how it is paid? With death, that's how it is paid." And finally, catchall words of wisdom: "If you are respectful, you are respected by all. When one has respect, the other things will come." The leader did not speak of punishment without pointing out benefits, including the connections that came with being a made member. (King, n.d.)

Italian Organized Crime in Ontario: The 1980s to Present

In 1984, a member of the Liberal Party of Ontario demanded a public inquiry into IOC in that province arguing, it "appears to be a completely runaway situation in organized crime" (*Vancouver Sun*, January 28, 1984). By this time, Ontario's Mafia underworld had become fractured and factionalized. In reference to the attempts by John Papalia and the rest of Magaddino's Ontario crew to dominate Toronto's criminal underworld, Dubro and Roy wrote in 1985 that the city "was always considered too large, disparate, and broken up to be handled by one family, and hence it became a more opportune ground for independents and new Mafia groupings; and Italians then, as now, were not the only ones interested in or organized enough to run effective organized crime operations" (Dubro & Roy, 1985: 21). In short, Toronto and, to a lesser extent, Hamilton, were "open cities" in that they were "open to many different mob groups operating simultaneously in different areas" (Dubro, 1985: 46–47).

Whatever power the American LCN did have in Ontario ended in the 1980s. The symbolic conclusion came with the 1987 death of Giacomo Luppino at the age of 88. The 150-car procession at his funeral was the last great Mafia burial to be held in Canada, yet few mob leaders attended. His sons tried to take the place of their father, but simply did not have the clout or the connections he enjoyed. John Papalia was spending so much time in jail that he was unable to wield any real power. By the time Giacomo Luppino had passed away, a new chapter in the history of organized crime in Ontario and Canada was already under way. The power vacuum created in the late 1980s opened the door for an even greater fractionalization of Ontario's organized crime scene as a diverse range of professional criminals, including Chinese triads, outlaw motorcycle gangs, Russian criminal groups, Colombian "cocaine cowboys," and organized street gangs crowded the criminal underworld. Yet, ethnic Italian criminal organizations continued to be a powerful force in southern Ontario.

These groups were much more aligned with Mafia groups in Calabria as opposed to America where the LCN had been weakened through intensive law enforcement actions. In 1985, CISC described how in Ontario the 'Ndrangheta continued to operate "a number of loosely structured 'cells,' which are branches of crime families based in Calabria, Italy. These cells exist in the London, Hamilton, Ottawa, and Toronto area" (Criminal Intelligence Service Canada, 1985: 7). A 1990 report by the Canadian Association of Chiefs of Police (CACP) (1990: 40) noted that members of the 'Ndrangheta cells in Toronto were behind a large-scale counterfeiting ring that was distributing fake

American one hundred dollar bills in the Toronto area. "Many members" of the 'Ndrangheta in the Toronto area were also "heavily involved in drug trafficking between Toronto, New York, and Italy," according to the report. In fact, the Calabrian Mafia in Canada was a central player in an international heroin trafficking conspiracy that linked 'Ndrangheta groups on the eastern shores of Calabria, which supplied the heroin, and those in New York state, which were the recipients of most of the heroin. The group also supplied cocaine that was traded for the heroin and destined for European markets (Canadian Association of Chiefs of Police, 1990: 40). By 1992, the CACP acknowledged that 14 "traditional organized crime groups" were active in Ontario. "Members of these organizations are established in Toronto, Windsor, Hamilton, Ottawa, and the Niagara Region," according to the report. "All of these groups associate with their counterparts in Quebec, the United States, and Italy. Connections have been confirmed between the American LCN in Detroit, Michigan and organized crime groups in Ontario" (Canadian Association of Chiefs of Police, 1992: 19).

At the dawn of the new millennium, the 'Ndrangheta emerged as the most powerful Mafia faction in Italy and one of the most dominant criminal organizations in Europe. It had become that continent's largest cocaine importer, supplied in part by Mexican drug cartels, and had influence over numerous marine ports in Europe to expedite the smuggling of cocaine and other drugs into the continent. In Canada, the 'Ndrangheta had risen to a Tier I national threat, Superintendent Kevin Harrison of the RCMP was quoted as saying in 2012. Around the same time, the *Toronto Star* printed condemnations from senior Italian law enforcement officials who accused Ontario of becoming an international "penal colony" for alleged members of the 'Ndrangheta who had fled Italy for the sanctity of Canada. As part of a sweeping investigation into the 'Ndrangheta in Italy, prosecutors there presented documents alleging there were at least seven Calabrian Mafia cells in Ontario. In their 2015 book on Italian organized crime in Canada, Edwards and Nicaso (2015: 99) claim 15 Mafia groups were located Ontario, most of which were 'Ndrangheta clans: "Nine of those Mafia groups were 'Ndrangheta families based around Toronto, mostly in York Region." Each clan or *locali* is grouped around a nucleus of family, with strong ties to clans in their native Italy. The boss of each *locali* also has a seat on the influential *La Camera di Controllo* (board of control) in Ontario (*Toronto Star*, September 22, 2012). Nicola Gratteri, the chief anti-Mafia prosecutor in Calabria, was quoted in the Canadian media in 2013 saying there were at minimum nine 'Ndrangheta cells in Toronto alone, meaning "there are hundreds of members, as each *locali* has at least 51 members." For Gratteri, while the 'Ndrangheta operates in numerous continents and countries around the world, he said the "foreign country where the 'Ndrangheta is the most present is in Canada … Mostly in Ontario, especially Toronto, and also in Montreal" (CBC News, June 28, 2013). Other Italian prosecutors were quoted as saying the Canadian 'Ndrangheta cells had climbed "to the top of the criminal world," by becoming dominant players in the global drug trade and by establishing a "continuous flow of cocaine" from Argentina. "Canada is a virgin land for the 'Ndrangheta," opined Roberto DiPalma, a senior prosecutor for

Italy's Direzione distrettuale antiMafia (Anti-Mafia Directorate). "It's a strategic place because it's very close to the U.S. and it has been chosen by the 'Ndrangheta as a very important point for the international affairs. It's a very good place for laundering money and a very good place for re-investing the money in the legal economy" (*National Post*, September 20, 2012).

In June 2015, the 'Ndrangheta was the target of a sweeping police investigation in the Greater Toronto Area. According to a Combined Forces Special Enforcement Unit (CFSEU) press release, on the morning of June 2, 2015, the unit "arrested 19 men for numerous offences related to criminal activity of several cells of a criminal organization, the 'Ndrangheta." The arrests were part of Project Ophoenix, an investigation that began in May 2013 and targeted "the highest levels of the 'Ndrangheta criminal organization operating within the GTA." The CFSEU said it dismantled two alleged cells of the 'Ndrangheta that were involved in importing drugs, trafficking firearms, "extreme violence," and extortion. Most of those arrested were charged with drug trafficking, extortion, possession of the proceeds of crime, and committing an offence for a criminal organization. "The lengthy, challenging, two year, joint-forces investigation revealed several specific organized crime cells that were involved with such criminal offences as drug importation and trafficking, firearms trafficking, extortion, possession of the proceeds of crime, laundering the proceeds of crime and organized crime related offences." One of the cells targeted by the investigation was previously led by Carmine Verduci, who was shot dead outside the Regina Sports Café in Woodbridge, Ontario, in April 2014. Before his death, Verduci was the subject of an arrest warrant issued by Italian authorities for his involvement in Mafia activities in that country (Combined Forces Special Enforcement Unit—Ontario Press Release, June 3, 2015; *Toronto Star*, June 3, 2015).

ITALIAN ORGANIZED CRIME IN QUEBEC

Throughout the Great Depression, World War II, and the post-war years, Montreal was home to Canada's largest vice economy. Despite judicial inquiries, new laws, and intensified police enforcement, the city's reputation as a "wide-open town," the "vice capital of Canada," and the "Paris of North America" remained intact. As Alan Phillips wrote in his 1963 exposé on organized crime in Canada, the city's "two hundred night clubs offered entertainment second only to New York. Its bordellos were famous. Its wide-open dice games drew an international clientele. You could bet any sum on a game or a horse through fifty-some wire-serviced bookmakers" (Phillips, 1963a: 10). Montreal's reputation as a sink of iniquity was bolstered during the post-war years with the invasion of American mobsters, who brought with them scores of bookmakers, crooked stockbrokers, strong-arm crews, and heroin importers. At the vanguard of the American criminal invasion in the 1940s and 1950s were senior members of the LCN, who carried across the border ambitions to take over and consolidate Montreal's rackets. Three men would lead the American Mafia's takeover of Montreal's vice industry: Joseph Bonanno, Carmine Galante, and Vincenzo Cotroni. In the process, the three would establish one of the most powerful, lucrative, and durable criminal organizations in Canadian history.

Giuseppe Carlo (Joseph) Bonanno was the head of one of New York's five Mafia families and under his control, his family prospered. Bootlegging, tax fraud, and drugs would be his family's stock and trade, but Bonanno also invested heavily in legitimate businesses include clothing factories, cheese producers, moving and storage, pizza parlours, espresso cafes, ca-

Photo 5.7: Joe Bonanno

Source: Illustration by Ben Firsch

tering, and funeral parlours. Whatever business Bonanno was involved in he was constantly looking to expand. When he made it clear that Quebec fell within his realm of influence, competing crime boss Stefano Magaddino angrily accused Bonanno of "planting flags all over the world."

Bonanno ruled his Quebec fiefdom from New York but sent senior lieutenants to Montreal to establish a wing of his crime family there. Of all the American gangsters who arrived in Montreal during the post-war years, none was more powerful, more ruthless, and more influential than the man called "Mr. Lilo." In 1953, Carmine Galante relocated from Brooklyn to Montreal to run the Bonanno family's bookmaking and gambling operations in the city. But this was not enough to satiate his Machiavellian ambitions; he wanted a cut of all criminal rackets in Montreal.

Galante was the most senior American Mafioso to be stationed in Montreal, and it was not long after his arrival that he began organizing the city's underworld on behalf of the New York families. Galante began by demanding protection money from the city's gambling dens, bookmakers, drug traffickers, brothels, nightclubs, thieves, and shady stockbrokers—as much as $300 a week from each plus 25 percent of their revenue. Those who refused to pay were faced with violent attacks, arson, or police raids. By 1954, Galante was extending his influence to Montreal's legitimate businesses by investing in nightclubs, bars, and restaurants. Galante also established a local *decina* of the Bonanno family, swearing in fellow Italians as members and establishing himself as the *capo decina*. One of those Galante initiated into the Bonanno family was Vic Cotroni. Although he was Calabrian, not Sicilian, Cotroni quickly impressed Galante and the two became friends and later godfathers to each other's children. Cotroni's standing in the Montreal *decina* accelerated quickly to the point that he would take over from Galante, paving the way for his long career as one of Canada's most powerful criminals (Charbonneau, 1976: 81–82; Edwards, 1991: 24–26; Nash, 1993: 171; *New York Times*, February 20, 1977; Phillips, 1963a: 12–13, 41; Robinson, 1999: 32).

Vincenzo Cotroni was born in 1911 in the small Calabrian village of Mammola. In 1924, he, along with his parents, two sisters, and younger brother Giuseppe, immigrated to Canada and settled in Montreal. Rather than attend school, Vic worked briefly as a carpenter's apprentice and then as a wrestler under the name "Vic Vincent." He became a student of Armand Courville, a well-known local wrestler and coach who gave lessons to aspiring young pugilists and who also had financial interests in various bars, speakeasies, and gambling houses. It was Courville who introduced Vic to Montreal's seamier side and, before long, his student was involved in bootlegging, petty theft, cheque kiting, passing counterfeit money, and working as a political goon that stuffed ballot boxes and terrorized voters on election day. The two would become good friends, business partners, and criminal associates for the next 50 years. By his early twenties, Vic had already accumulated a criminal record.

In 1942, Armand and Vic bought the Café Royale, a popular nightclub located in the heart of the red light district and frequented by many of Montreal's criminal elite. Cotroni, Courville, and other investors also became partners in a number of gambling operations, which they ran out of apartment buildings. In tandem with Courville, Vic entered the corrupt world of Quebec politics and in 1947 he was charged with and later acquitted of voter impersonation.

As Vic rose through the ranks of the Montreal Mafia, he now had a number of men reporting to him, and his influence in the Montreal *decina* grew even more when Galante was deported from Canada in 1954. After a succession of lieutenants sent from New York to Montreal to manage the Bonanno family affairs were exiled back to the United States by the Canadian immigration department, Vic and Luigi Greco were appointed as joint heads of the Montreal wing. However, Vic would quickly outmaneuver

CRITICAL THINKING EXERCISE

The intimate and long-lasting business partnership between the Italian immigrant Vic Cotroni and the French-Canadian Armand Courville is indicative of the multi-ethnic nature of organized crime in Montreal. While Courville could never be a made member of the Bonanno family, he was Cotroni's most trusted associate and Cotroni often assigned members of the family to Courville's supervision. Conduct research into and critically examine the extent to which the Montreal Mafia was multi-ethnic in composition. What does this say about the label "Italian Organized Crime" and about the organization of criminal offenders in Quebec generally?

Greco for sole possession of the *capo decina* position. By the end of the 1950s, Cotroni had grown quite wealthy from his interests in a wide variety of profitable enterprises, including extortion, gambling, bookmaking, labour racketeering, prostitution, and loansharking. Also joining him as made members of the *decina* were his two younger brothers Giuseppe (Pep) and Francesco (Frank). Neither would ever rise to the heights of their older brother, although both would become key players in the American LCN's international drug trafficking network.

By this time, plans were already afoot to establish Montreal as a major portal for the entry of heroin into North America. As part of the French Connection, the task of managing heroin importations into Montreal was entrusted to the Cotroni brothers, who established direct connections with the Corsican suppliers. By 1956, it was estimated that at least half of the heroin supplied to North America was entering the continent through Montreal (Edwards, 1990: 29–30).

Photo 5.8: Mug shot of a young Vic Cotroni

Source: Wikimedia Commons

In 1959, Pep Cotroni was arrested, along with dozens of other people in Canada and the United States, for drug trafficking and later convicted and sentenced to 10 years in jail. The second trial, the one against the American co-conspirators, ended in the summer of 1962 with the conviction of, among others, Carmine Galante, who was sentenced to 20 years.

The Montreal Mafia in the 1960s and 1970s

Throughout the 1960s, the LCN continued to be the biggest heroin importers in North America. For years to come, the Montreal *decina* would send millions of dollars to New York, generated from the heroin trade and other highly profitable criminal activities. Vic Cotroni's stature as a powerful and respected *capo decina* was also evident; while his brother and other members of the Montreal and New York Mafia were being convicted on drug-trafficking charges, all strictly adhered to the code of *omerta* and shielded Vic from arrest and prosecution. The Cotroni *decina* was also pulling in money from other illicit sources. By the mid-1960s, their gambling interests alone were multifaceted: Montreal continued to be a major bookmaking centre for North America, and Vic oversaw numerous gambling operations in the city while expanding into the Ottawa–Hull region. They were also now offering gambling junkets from Montreal to mob-controlled Las Vegas. In addition, money continued to pour in from extortion and protection rackets, loansharking, and labour racketeering. Cotroni also controlled a number of highly profitable, legally incorporated businesses in Montreal, including construction companies, food importing firms, ice cream manufacturing and distribution operations, as well as hotels, restaurants, and bars.

To carry out his numerous criminal and semi-legitimate business ventures, Vic built a productive and sturdy crew. At the core of his organization was some 20 "men of honour." During the 1960s and early 1970s, Vic's most senior lieutenants were Luigi Greco, Nicola Di Iorio, Frank Cotroni, and Paolo Violi. While full-fledged membership in the Montreal Mafia was available only to those of Italian descent, there was no discrimination based on what part of Italy someone hailed from. Testifying before the Quebec Organized Crime Commission in 1975, Dr. Alberto Sabatino, a senior official with the Italian national police, stated that the Montreal Mafia was an "exceptional" mixture of Calabrian and Sicilian men and that it was "unusual" to see the two regional groups working as one Mafia organization. "Such a mixture of Calabrian and Sicilian gangsters does not occur in Italy," Dr. Sabatino said (*Montreal Star*, December 3, 1975). What Sabatino did not know at the time was that cleavages did exist between the Sicilian and Calabrian factions, which would soon result in a wholesale transformation of the organization's leadership and hierarchy.

One of the men at the centre of this conflict was Paolo Violi, who would eventually share power with Cotroni and then contribute to a coup that would remove both him and Vic from the leadership of the *decina*. Born on February 6, 1931, in Sinopoli, a rural village on the Calabrian peninsula, Paolo's father was accused by Italian police of being the boss of the local 'Ndrangheta and was once even exiled from the village under that country's anti-Mafia laws. By the late 1960s, Paolo was making his move to take over the Cotroni *decina* and by the end of the decade, he shared power with Vic.

The 1970s would become one of the tumultuous decades for the Cotroni–Violi *decina* as Nick Rizzuto, who headed up the Sicilian wing of the Montreal Mafia, began to chafe under the authority of the Calabrians, Cotroni and Violi. Rizzuto had already become a major drug trafficker in his own right, helping to oversee a global heroin and cocaine trafficking network that brought in millions for the Bonanno family. As Rizzuto became wealthier and more powerful, he refused to follow the orders of Cotroni and Violi. As Edwards and Nicaso (1993: 66) write, "Rizzuto glibly ignored them, doing whatever he pleased, whenever he pleased. Worse yet, newly arrived Sicilian mobsters in Montreal gravitated toward him, while ignoring the old Calabrian leadership." Vic Cotroni and Paolo Violi felt so betrayed by Rizzuto's contemptuous actions that they moved to have him formally expelled from the Montreal *decina* and even considered seeking permission from senior Bonanno family officials to have him killed. But Violi was smart enough to know that New York would never sanction such an extreme move, especially given the drug trafficking revenues that Rizzuto was generating. In September 1972, two ranking members of the Bonanno family arrived in Montreal to try to settle the dispute and, after sitting down with each side, decided that Rizzuto should stay in the Montreal *decina*. This decision infuriated Cotroni who, in one police wiretap recording, fumed that he had the power to kick Rizzuto out: "Me, I'm capo decina. I got the right to expel" (Quebec Police Commission Inquiry on Organized Crime, 1977a: 73–74).

Photo 5.9: Paolo Violi

Source: Illustration by Ben Firsch

But Vic and Paolo were not about to challenge the authority of New York and, while both lost face as a result of the decision, they exacted some revenge when Paolo was named interim head of the family in 1974 after Vic was imprisoned for refusing to appear before the Quebec Police Commission hearings. This was the final affront for Rizzuto, who fled to Venezuela to join his fellow Sicilian drug-dealing associates in Caracas. Rizzuto's wayward behaviour infuriated Violi, who constantly complained about his lack of respect for the leadership of the *decina* (Quebec Police Commission Inquiry on Organized Crime, 1977a: 93).

Despite his distance from Quebec, Rizzuto had no intention of forsaking his membership in the Bonanno family or its Montreal *decina*. While he was establishing an international base in Caracas, his son Vito remained in Montreal to help coordinate the importation of heroin and cocaine and to maintain a foothold in the city and the local Bonanno wing until such time as the opportunity presented itself to launch a coup. With the retirement of Vic Cotroni in the late 1970s, Nick Rizzuto slipped back into Montreal and waged war on Violi, which would end up costing the lives of several men, including Violi who was killed in 1978. With Violi dead, Nick Rizzuto and his son Vito assumed control of the Mafia in Montreal. For the Rizzutos, the elimination of Cotroni and Violi removed the last obstacle to Sicilian control of the Mafia in Quebec.

Nick and Vito did build a working relationship with members of the Calabrian faction. However, it was Nick's network of Sicilian recruits and associates that would form the nucleus of this new chapter in the Montreal Mafia's history. With much of his ambitions realized, Nick Rizzuto passed the reins of power to his capable son, Vito, and returned to Venezuela. Together, the two ensured that Montreal would continue as a major gateway for drugs imported into North America, whether it was heroin now being processed in Sicily, cocaine from South America, or hashish from Pakistan and Lebanon.

The murder of Carmine Galante on July 12, 1979—who was shot dead as part of the New York Mafia's ongoing power struggles and as a direct result of his own unrelenting ambition to become the *capo di tutti capo*—marked another turning point for the Montreal Mafia insomuch as the Rizzutos began to seek greater independence from New York. While the Rizzutos did not immediately cut off ties with the Bonanno family, over the years they gained considerable autonomy to the point where they were no longer considered simply a *decina*, but an autonomous family in their own right. As for Vic Cotroni, his life was spared because of the status he enjoyed in Montreal's gangland, but also because it was only a matter of time before his cancer-riddled body would cease to function. On September 16, 1984, Vincenzo Cotroni died at the age of 74. Over the next two decades, Vito Rizzuto would entrench his position as Canada's most powerful Mafia don, and perhaps the most powerful criminal in all of Canada, while increasingly asserting his independence from the Bonanno family.

The Rizzuto Family: The 1990s to Present

Under Vito Rizzuto, the Montreal Mafia was accumulating a fortune through a maze of lucrative gambling and bookmaking operations that generated hundreds of millions of dollars a year. Rizzuto also expanded his gaming interests to include video lottery terminals, which were fast becoming the most lucrative form of gambling in Quebec. The wealth, power, and prestige of the Montreal Mafia as a global criminal network also came from the financing, smuggling, and trafficking of large quantities of hash, heroin, and cocaine. Vito Rizzuto had become a made member of the Bonanno family sometime during the 1970s, but he was determined to be much more than simply the head of one its crews. Rizzuto paid homage to his bosses in New York and was sending millions of dollars in tribute annually, while patiently planning for the day that he would run his own autonomous family. As Lamothe and Humphreys (2006: 208) write, "Few fully recognized the growing influence of the Sixth Family"—a title that alludes to the independence and power of the Montreal Mafia under the Rizzutos by equating it with the five New York families. "Fewer still understood that what was once a small, outpost of subservient gangsters had grown into an independent and powerful entity that could hold its own in any underworld on any continent." Lamothe and Humphreys also identified some reasons why the Montreal Mafia under Vito Rizzuto was able to achieve success during the 1980s and 1990s, a time when other Mafia groups throughout the United States were imploding:

The Sixth Family blends the traditions of the Sicilian Mafia with a modern corporate structure, building a rugged durable, ever-expanding corporate Mafia. It maintains the secretiveness of the Mafiosi tradition but keeps its inner circle more tightly controlled than in the American Mafia. The Sixth Family has shed the old militaristic organizational structure of the Five Families—which has soldiers answering to captains who answer to a boss. It has been replaced with a structure that is, even more, ancient—the family. It is not merely a Mafia initiation ceremony that binds its core, but rather, almost without exception, marriage vows and blood ties. It is far more effective at engendering loyalty and trust; for protecting the organization from betrayal and infiltration. (Lamothe & Humphreys, 2006: 306)

As the leader of the Montreal Mafia, Vito evolved into what Nicaso and Lamothe (2005: 44) called the "epitome of the modern global gangster." He had outposts and cells strategically placed throughout Canada and abroad and was forging a global organized criminal conglomerate that would surpass the reach, wealth, and power of any of the five New York families. While the Montreal Mafia may have only had 20 or so made members, Rizzuto could count on hundreds of associates around Canada and the world. In its 2001 annual report on organized crime, Criminal Intelligence Service Canada (2001: 57) asserted that the Rizzuto family "remains one of the most influential and powerful criminal organizations in the Montreal area, exerting extensive influence over other criminal organizations operating in Montreal." Rizzuto was well respected in Quebec's criminal underworld and his power so unchallenged that he was credited with playing a major role in persuading the leaders of the Hells Angels and the Rock Machine motorcycle clubs to negotiate a truce to their bloody war in Quebec. Indeed, Rizzuto revelled in the traditional role of the Mafioso as a broker or *padrone*. In this regard, he forged ties with Mafia families in Sicily, 'Ndrangheta clans in Canada and Italy, the Hells Angels, the West End Gang (which had significant influence over Montreal's marine ports), and Colombian cocaine suppliers.

A 2001 CISC report noted that the Montreal Mafia's "influence may be spreading beyond its Québec base." Rizzuto was making regular trips to Ontario to check up on his business investments. To some, his frequent visits were also a signal that he was intent on expanding his criminal enterprises into the province. One indication of this inter-provincial growth was revealed in April 2001 when a $200-million gambling operation in Montreal, Ottawa, Hamilton, and Toronto was disrupted by the arrest of 54 people in Quebec and Ontario. The 10-month investigation zeroed in on a high-tech bookmaking operation, linked to Rizzuto, to take bets on sporting events from across North America. Police also discovered a parallel loansharking operation and heard from one bettor who was given a loan to pay off his $75,000 gambling debt, but then had to deal with interest that totalled around $60,000 (Criminal Intelligence Service Canada, 2001: 57; *Hamilton Spectator*, April 12, 2001; *Ottawa Citizen*, April 12, 2001; *Toronto Star*, April 12, 2001).

In 2004, police and prosecutors in the United States accomplished something that eluded Canadian police for years: they laid serious criminal charges against Vito Rizzuto that would eventually stick. On January 20, the 57-year-old Rizzuto was picked up by Canadian police in response to an American warrant stemming from his alleged involvement in three murders that dated back to 1981. Rizzuto was one of 30 men arrested, most of whom were members of the now-reeling Bonanno family. An official with the federal district attorney's office in New York called the arrests "the broadest and deepest penetration ever of a New York City-based organized crime family." Rizzuto was accused of being the lead gunman in the May 1981 murders of three high-ranking members of the Bonanno family, who were killed as part of an internal power struggle. US federal officials quickly began extradition proceedings against the man they described as "the most influential Bonanno family member in Canada, the only family with a significant presence in Canada" (as cited in the *Globe and Mail*, January 21, 2004). Rizzuto was eventually deported from Canada and, on May 4, 2007, he pleaded guilty to racketeering charges in a New York courtroom. As part of a plea agreement, he was given a 10-year sentence to be followed by a three-year supervised release. The plea bargain required that Rizzuto confess to his role in the murders. "I was one of the guys who participated in this. My job was to say that it was a holdup so [the captains] would stand still," Rizzuto told the judge. "The other guys came in and started shooting" (*Montreal Gazette*, May 5, 2007).

For the next five years, Rizzuto would languish in a maximum security prison in Colorado. He was far from his home and family in Montreal and was rendered largely powerless to guide and protect an increasingly enfeebled criminal empire that was under attack from all sides. The Quebec police task force Operation Colisée had resulted in jail time for senior Mafia members and associates of the Rizzuto family, while the Montreal Mafia had become a central theme in the Charbonneau Commission, a public inquiry investigating corruption in Montreal's public sector construction industry. Rizzuto also had to deal with the many aspiring criminal interlopers who were circling to fill the void in Montreal's criminal underworld created by his incarceration. Not only were competing groups trying to take over Rizzuto's rackets in Montreal, but other Mafiosi were aiming to replace him as the *capo* of what had become North America's most successful Mafia organization. During the years Rizzuto spent in prison, numerous members of his Mafia family were killed, including his son, his father, and Agostino Cuntrera, who had reportedly taken over the reins of the family while Vito was in jail.

Speculation was rampant that the Ontario-based 'Ndrangheta were behind the murders as well as the disappearance of Vito's brother-in-law, his neighbour, his *consigliére*, and Paolo Renda. Targeting these four men was certainly strategic: it was clearly meant to pare the group's leadership in Montreal. In Vito's absence, the 'Ndrangheta clans in Ontario apparently had already begun encroaching on the Rizzuto family's rackets in Montreal, including gambling, bookmaking, and extortion, and were using street gangs as their muscle (Cédilot & Noël, 2011: 469).

In October 2012, amidst all the violence in Montreal's underworld, Vito Rizzuto was deported back to Canada from the United States after serving six years of his manslaughter sentence. It was not too long thereafter that he resettled in Montreal and began working to reclaim control of his criminal empire and exact revenge against his enemies. In addition to the violence engulfing his Mafia family, Rizzuto also had to contend with almost around-the-clock surveillance by police as well as other unwanted government attention. On November 19, Quebec police served Rizzuto with a subpoena to appear before the Charbonneau Commission. The inquiry had already heard extensive testimony about how construction firms colluded to determine who would be the successful bidder on public infrastructure tenders issued by the City of Montreal. The Rizzuto crime family was alleged to have facilitated the collusion, and Vito himself

Photo 5.10: Vito Rizzuto

Source: Illustration by author, based on newspaper photo

was accused of choosing which construction firm would be the winning bidder on a contract. In return, the crime family would receive a cut of between two and five percent of the contract. It was estimated that the collusion drove up the price of public construction contracts in the Montreal region by 35 percent more than they should have cost (Canadian Press, September 25, 2012, September 26, 2012; *Montreal Gazette*, September 27, 2012). Rizzuto would never appear before the Charbonneau inquiry. He died on December 23, 2013, at Sacré-Coeur Hospital in Montreal. The 67-year-old had been admitted that day for pulmonary problems, and the hospital later announced he died of lung cancer. His family asked that no autopsy be performed, fuelling some suspicions that the causes of his death were anything but natural.

DESCRIBING AND ANALYZING ITALIAN ORGANIZED CRIME: THE MONTREAL MAFIA

The preceding historical overview provides some indication of the characteristics of IOC groups in Ontario and Quebec. Using the taxonomy created in chapter 3, this section of the chapter will identify and examine in more detail the salient characteristics of the

Montreal Mafia. This includes an analysis of the group during the years it was under the leadership of the Calabrian faction (Vic Cotroni and Paolo Violi), as well as the years it was led by the Sicilians (Nick and Vito Rizzuto).

Organizational

Multiple Offenders

At any one time, the Montreal Mafia boasted numerous made members as well as dozens of associates that supported them through their involvement in criminal activities. If one looks at the Montreal Mafia in a historical sense, there were hundreds of individuals involved in the criminal activities it carried out, although at any one time the organization had only between 20 and 30 made members.

Limited or Exclusive Membership/Recruitment

Like most traditional Mafia groups, membership was restricted to those of Italian heritage. However, unlike Mafia groups in Sicily or America (where membership was restricted to Sicilians) or the 'Ndrangheta clans in Italy (where membership is restricted to Calabrians), the Montreal Mafia is unique in that it has a mix of both.

A number of criminals of non-Italian descent were associated with the Cotroni–Violi *decina*, including French-Canadians, Anglo-Saxons, Irish, Jews, Slavs, Blacks, and others. However, because most were not Italian, they could never become members. Paolo Violi confirmed this on May 10, 1974, when speaking of one French-Canadian who worked as an enforcer for him, "Yeah, but you gotta know that the guy who was with us, he's a good '*picciotto*,' a French '*picciotto*.' He's good … Yeah, but he's not one of ours …" (Quebec Police Commission Inquiry on Organized Crime, 1977a: 36).

In order to become a "man of honour," prospects of Italian heritage had to persevere through a lengthy probation period. According to the Quebec Police Commission, "a system of recruitment, apprenticeship and rigorous selection of members" is characteristic of the Montreal Mafia:

> There are officially recognized regular members, that is, those who, after a trial period, are selected according to the rules. Others, even though admitted to the family after probation, must wait for openings to be officially accepted. Then there are trainee members of outside families who come to Montreal to work with the local family and who must submit to a trial period regardless of their rank outside. Finally, there are local trainees, without status, who must make their mark in order to move up in the organization … In short, not everyone who wants to may enter the Cotroni–Violi family. The strict, selective method of admitting new members, which indicates that recruiting is done on a fairly systematic basis, points to the fact that this group constitutes more than an ordinary criminal gang. (Quebec Police Commission Inquiry on Organized Crime, 1977a: 35, 37)

Under Vito Rizzuto's leadership, there is some indication that he diverted from the age-old Mafia tradition of inducting only men of Italian heritage. One close associate of Rizzuto was Juan Ramon Fernandez, who was gunned down in a planned ambush in Casteldaccia, just outside Palermo, Sicily, in 2013. Fernandez, a Spaniard by birth, was Rizzuto's main representative in Ontario, where he coordinated various rackets for his boss. Before he was killed, Fernandez was overheard on police wiretaps in Sicily bragging about how he was a "man of honour," having been personally inducted into the Montreal Mafia by Rizzuto (*National Post*, May 8, 2013, May 9, 2013, May 10, 2013). There is also some speculation that French-Canadian Raynald Desjardins, one of Vito's top lieutenants and close drug-trafficking associate, was also a "man of honour" in the Mafia family, again personally inducted by Rizzuto.

A Systematic Pattern to the Relationships among Offenders

According to the Quebec Police Commission Inquiry on Organized Crime (1977a), individuals associated with the Cotroni *decina* can be grouped into four categories: (1) regular members, (2) unestablished, regular members, (3) hopefuls, and (4) non-member associates. At the core of this crime organization was the made members who, in the words of Carrigan (1991: 182), were "cemented together by family ties, friendship, common ethnic origins, and a strict code of loyalty and silence." Blood ties were an important factor in the membership of the *decina*: made members advanced through the ranks, not necessarily by their skill, but based on their blood ties to Vic. Both of Vic's brothers were high-ranking lieutenants, while two of his nephews were also made members. "We can therefore say that in many respects the Cotroni–Violi gang is a true family unit" (Quebec Police Commission Inquiry on Organized Crime, 1977a: 37). Similarly, Nick Rizzuto appointed his son to lead the Montreal Mafia, while two of Vito's sons reportedly became made members. The kinship ties of the Cotroni *decina* was extended to other Mafiosi through intermarriages and godparenthood. Wiretaps revealed frequent contact between Paolo Violi and John Papalia, who was the godfather of Violi's second son. Violi himself married the daughter of Ontario crime boss Giacomo Luppino. Joe Gentile, allegedly a leading Mafioso in Vancouver, was the godfather to one of Violi's daughters, while Vic Cotroni was godfather to Violi's first-born son.

Common ethnic ties were also a binding force for the Montreal Mafia. While the criminal group included both Sicilians and Calabrians, when the Calabrians (Vic Cotroni and Paolo Violi) were in charge, secondary leadership roles were most frequently filled by fellow Calabrians. When the Rizzutos took over, their lieutenants were more likely to be Sicilian in heritage. Several members of the Cotroni *decina* came from the same village or area in Calabria, which was deemed important for a ranking position. Similarly, the Rizzutos worked closely with and elevated to prominent positions individuals who hailed from the same part of Sicily. The *decina* also served as the infrastructure for a larger criminal organization, which included partners and associates from all types of ethnic backgrounds and who were involved in numerous illegal enterprises and legal businesses.

In short, regardless of who led the Montreal Mafia, there was a systematic pattern to the relationship among the offenders. Based on Ianni's (1974) model, the relationship among made members was "associational" (held together by close personal relationships such as kinship and shared ethnicity), while the relationship between the made members and associates was "entrepreneurial" in the sense that the bond was less personal and more determined by business interests. The structure of the Montreal Mafia is also reflective of the patron–client model. At the centre of these relationships was the *capo decina*—Vic Cotroni, Paolo Violi, and Vito Ruzzuto—who all considered themselves a patron to their constituents, brokering business transactions, connecting buyers with suppliers, providing protection, and mediating disputes if they arose. The power of the Cotroni *decina* bosses to mediate disputes and dispense justice and protection was documented at the Quebec Police Commission hearings in the 1970s. Because of his clout and reputation, Paolo Violi "was called on to intervene in disputes which had no connection with the criminal activities of his family. People outside the criminal world went on their own to ask Violi's help. Violi settled these disputes in the traditional manner of the underworld, substituting his 'justice' for that of legal institutions." In a discussion with high-ranking members of the Sicilian Mafia on April 22, 1974, Violi himself defined the obligations of a Mafioso. Speaking to Pietro Sciarra, he said, "Uncle Petrino, we're here to do the thinking, to arrange things for this one and that one ... and our job, all the time, is to straighten things out ... " (Quebec Police Commission Inquiry on Organized Crime, 1977a: 65).

By all accounts, Vito Rizzuto also saw his role as one of a *padrone* or at the very least a broker whose job was to arrange business opportunities, either by financing them or facilitating partnerships among different individuals. Rizzuto's brokerage role was cited during a public inquiry into allegations of corruption in Quebec's construction industry (the Charbonneau Commission) that began in May 2012. A police investigation into mob ties to Quebec's construction industry accused Rizzuto of determining which construction firm would be the winning bidder. In return, the family would receive a cut of the contract (Canadian Press, October 16, 2009). Lino Zambito, the president and co-owner of one construction firm testified to the commission that Rizzuto became directly involved in a dispute over who should win a bid for renovating Montreal's Acadie Circle (*Chronicle Herald*, November 14, 2014; *Hamilton Spectator*, October 2, 2012; *Montreal Gazette*, September 28, 2012).

Specialization/Division of Labour and Channels of Communication
According to the Quebec Police Commission Inquiry on Organized Crime (1977a), there were two kinds of ranks and degrees of power in the Cotroni *decina*: (1) a formal hierarchy, consisting of a well-defined line of command; and (2) an informal hierarchy, based mainly on personality and the conduct of the members toward each other. The formal line of command included an internal division of labour among members. At the time of the Quebec Police Commission Inquiry on Organized Crime report (1977a: 48), the leaders

of the group were recognized as Vic Cotroni and Paolo Violi, both of whom had "complete authority to commit the group's resources for given objectives." The Quebec Police Commission concluded that the power inherent in the *capo decina*—and Vic Cotroni in particular—was absolute (although for the most serious matters he had to defer to his bosses in New York). Relying on police evidence, the Quebec Police Commission Inquiry on Organized Crime (1977a: 54) stated that big operations and major projects of the gang were always first submitted to Vic Cotroni for approval. "He took no orders from anyone at the local level, called or cancelled meetings with lieutenants, set priorities, picked the men who carried out jobs, and settled differences. Vincent Cotroni, in short, set policy for the family. He regularly and faithfully, at fixed days and hours, met with a few select members such as Paolo Violi, Nicholas Di Iorio, Luigi Greco, and his younger brother Frank Cotroni, who for their part, clearly showed their power over other members and partners of the family by taking orders from Vincent Cotroni."

It was also clear that Paolo Violi enjoyed a great deal of power in the Cotroni *decina* and in Montreal's criminal underworld in general during the 1970s. Violi also expected that he be accorded the power and respect consistent with the stature of a Mafioso. As journalist Pierre Beauregard wrote on November 21, 1975, "The all-powerful Paolo Violi is party to all the plots, shares in all the rackets, and draws profits from all the criminal acts that take place within the reach of his long arm" (as cited in the Quebec Police Commission Inquiry on Organized Crime, 1977a: 59).

Assisting the *decina* leadership was an underboss, which from the late 1940s to his death in 1972 was Luigi Greco. Violi then assumed this position and was Cotroni's underboss before he was promoted to co-leader. Below the underboss were several lieutenants to whom a measure of authority was delegated. While there was a division of labour, most of the made members of the Cotroni *decina* did not specialize in any one particular criminal endeavour, but were in charge of or worked in a particular geographic district in Montreal (although they were also involved in drug-trafficking conspiracies that took place outside their local district). With such names as the "St-Laurent Gang" or the "Sorrento Gang," each cell was headed by a high-ranking member who had several *picciottis* (soldiers) under his command (Quebec Police Commission Inquiry on Organized Crime, 1977a: 50). Underneath the soldiers, and outside the membership ranks of the family, were prospects who were eligible for membership in the Montreal *decina* of the Bonanno Mafia Family. As mentioned, outside of the *decina* were associates or partners, many of whom were not Italian in heritage, and as such could never be a made member of the Bonanno Family.

Alongside the formal *decina* hierarchy, there appeared to be an informal power structure that ranked each member, and even external partners of the Montreal Mafia, at a different level of authority and importance. Not all members of the same formal rank were necessarily equal. A *picciotti* who had unique skills or contacts or made the *decina* a lot of money had more stature than his official rank indicated (Quebec Police Commission Inquiry on Organized Crime, 1977a: 51).

In general, the established hierarchy was accompanied by a channel of communication where, in most cases, only Cotroni's underboss and top lieutenants would meet with him to discuss business. Several made members and external associates answered directly to Cotroni or Violi, either because the bosses wished to supervise their work directly or because these particular individuals had sufficient stature and/or served some function that justified a direct link to the top leadership. In some instances, associates external to the Cotroni *decina* were deemed more important that made members and even had *picciottis* or prospects in the *decina* working for them. A case in point is Armand Courville, whom the Quebec Police Commission of the 1970s cited as "one of the most influential and respected non-Italian partners of the Cotroni-Violi family." (Quebec Police Commission Inquiry on Organized Crime, 1977a: 39).

It was the external associates of the Cotroni *decina* where one can begin to truly identify areas of specialization. In fact, it was the ability to specialize in functions deemed critical to the *decina* that made some of the external partners close to the leadership. Certain partners specialized in the all-important functions of enforcement and money laundering, which made them particularly valuable. For many years, Leslie Coleman, a black man, worked for underboss Luigi Greco as a bodyguard and specialized in enforcement roles. After Greco's death in 1972, Coleman attached himself to his replacement, Paulo Violi. Because of his loyalty and many years of service to the family, Coleman was assigned to the Ottawa–Hull region in 1973 to "intimidate people in his efforts to control the gambling and betting houses, as well as the bookmakers." Nick Maturo, a former *piciotti* of the Cotroni *decina*, told the Quebec Police Commission that Violi had sent him on several occasions to Ottawa where he was to obey Coleman's orders (Quebec Police Commission Inquiry on Organized Crime, 1977a: 45). William (Willie) Obront, the Cotroni *decina*'s brilliant financier and money launderer, was another example of how men external to the *decina* undertook important functions. Obront first came to police attention when he assumed the position as Vic Cotroni's chief financial consultant. His job was to launder and re-invest the illegal revenues into both legitimate and illegal business ventures. Obront also ran a thriving loansharking business for the *decina* that generated millions of dollars in profit. In late 1973, Obront took over all gambling in the Ottawa–Hull area for the *decina* (Quebec Police Commission Inquiry on Organized Crime, 1977b: 148).

Insulation against Law Enforcement

The hierarchy and division of labour of the Cotroni *decina* was structured to ensure that Vic Cotroni was shielded from arrest and prosecution primarily by delegating the hands-on criminal activities to the soldiers and associates external to the *decina*. This was fortified by the group's norms that included the principle of *omerta* as well as the reverence and respect paid to the *capo decina*. This would help explain why Vic Cotroni was never convicted of a serious offence, even when his own brothers were convicted of major drug-trafficking offences carried out on his orders. The same could be said of Vito

Rizzuto, who was never convicted of an indictable offence in Canada, despite the arrest and conviction of some of his top lieutenants and associates. In fact, his conviction and imprisonment in the United States was the result of testimony by senior members of New York's Bonanno family who became state witnesses in order to protect themselves from the death penalty. Thus, it was not Rizzuto's underlings that broke the sacred oath of *omerta*, but his superiors in New York.

Continuity/Continuing Enterprise

Like many other IOC groups, it was clear that the Montreal Mafia was an ongoing criminal conspiracy designed to persist through time, beyond the life of its current membership. In fact, the origins of the criminal organization can be traced back to the 1930s. Despite the loss of influential leaders—including Carmine Galante, Vic Cotroni, Paolo Violi, and Vito Rizzuto—and the constant turnover in personnel (due to retirement or death), the criminal group continues to function.

Multi-jurisdictional/Transnational in Scope

The scope and activities of the Cotroni *decina* was restricted to Quebec. As such, the group itself was not transnational in scope. However, for years the Montreal Mafia was considered a wing of New York's Bonanno family, which would make the family international in scope. Moreover, the *decina* had extensive ties with other criminal organizations in Sicily, France, Brazil, and Venezuela, which were originally forged to facilitate international heroin trafficking. Beginning in the 1940s, the Cotroni brothers forged strong business relationships with French Corsican suppliers of heroin and also had close relationships with members of Mafia groups in Sicily. These ties were largely *ad hoc* and based primarily on business partnerships (and drug-trafficking ventures in particular). The Quebec Police Commission also turned up evidence that ties were forged with other Mafia families in Sicily to discuss and even expedite certain procedural matters internal to the Montreal Mafia. According to the Police Commission Report, "most of these conversations dealt with the internal running of the Mafia, both in Montreal and in Sicily" (Quebec Police Commission Inquiry on Organized Crime, 1977a: 87).

On May 10 and 13, 1974, Paolo Violi, Carmelo Salemi, and Giuseppe Cuffaro discussed Mafia membership at great length, particularly the conditions for admission to the Montreal *decina* following the dispute caused by the appointment of a Montreal native (of Italian descent) to a position in the Sicilian Mafia hierarchy. According to the Quebec Police Commission, it was quite clear from the comments exchanged that Mafia members in Italy and in Montreal are all "friends," and people who belong to the same association. Violi made reference to this in a May 10, 1974, conversation with Carmelo Salemi, "Some people who come from Italy have the same privileges when we know they're 'residents' from over there. They come here … they're recognized by everybody." To which Salemi replied, "In our mob, it's a friend and we gotta recognize a friend and that's that" (Quebec Police Commission Inquiry on Organized Crime, 1977a: 88–89).

Despite the international operations and partnerships forged under the leadership of Cotroni and Violi, it was Vito Rizzuto who turned the Montreal Mafia into a transnational criminal organization. This was expedited by Rizzuto's strong ties to the Caruana–Cuntrera families, which for years coordinated one of the world's largest drug-trafficking operations. Collectively, the drug-trafficking and money-laundering activities associated with the Caruana–Cuntrera–Rizzuto network stretched to New York, Switzerland, England, and Venezuela. As Peter Edwards writes, under Rizzuto, the Montreal Mafia was transformed from a neighbourhood-based group that "mediated community disputes" to a "multi-national drug trafficking conglomerate" (Edwards, 1990: 177).

Commercial

Over the many years of its existence, the business of the Montreal Mafia entailed a diverse range of serious, profit-oriented criminal activities, including both predatory and consensual illegal activities as well as illegal and legal goods and services. The consensual criminal activities include gambling, liquor smuggling and bootlegging, loansharking, drug trafficking, and prostitution. Its predatory crimes include protection rackets, muscle-for-hire, theft and fencing of stocks and bonds, mass-marketing fraud, stock market manipulation, and counterfeiting. The Cotroni *decina* also controlled a number of legally incorporated businesses in Montreal, which were used to carry out both legitimate and illegitimate commerce. These businesses operated in such industries as construction, food wholesaling, hotels, restaurants, bars, ice cream parlours, vending machines, and hotels. William Obront, along with two associates, also managed the only meat storage facilities on the Expo '67 site, which sold tainted and spoiled meat to Expo '67 concessionaires.

The monopolistic ambitions of the Cotroni *decina* is perhaps most evident in relation to their legitimate businesses. According to Edwards (1990: 6), the group's reach into legitimate businesses in Quebec was so long, "It was possible to bite into a pizza, every ingredient of which had been supplied by businesses run by Cotroni or his associates. And if you wanted spumoni ice cream for dessert, you were again enriching the Cotronis. During Canada's centennial year, Cotroni enterprises managed to monopolize fast-food contracts at Expo '67 allowing Cotroni to fill thousands, perhaps millions of stomachs from across the world with diseased hot dogs." Cotroni, Violi, and associates like Armand Courville gained a monopoly over the sale of Italian ice creams in the north end of Montreal through force and intimidation. One witness before the crime commission testified there were only two firms making Italian ice cream in the Montreal area, "and the second wasn't allowed to sell it because Violi didn't want it to" (*Montreal Gazette*, November 29, 1975).

Outside of these semi-legitimate interests, there is no indication that the Cotroni *decina* attempted to monopolize criminal activities in Montreal. In fact, it was counterproductive to do so because of the so-called patron–client tradition, in which the Mafioso tolerates freelance criminals in their jurisdiction as long as they pay a tax or tribute. The

Cotroni *decina* also tacitly tolerated competing drug-trafficking groups in Montreal, such as the French-Canadian Dubois Brothers gang, the only other crime group that could seriously rival the strength and scope of the Cotroni clan during the 1960s and 1970s. The Mafia's lack of appetite to take on the Dubois Brothers was due to a realistic assessment of the damages this group could inflict on the *decina* if they were to engage in a protracted war. Vito Rizzuto also showed little appetite for monopolizing any particular territory or criminal activity. This stemmed in part from his own predilection toward co-operating with other criminal groups to maximize revenues and to avoid conflict. Rizzuto also saw himself as a financier and frequently became involved in criminal activities, such as drug trafficking, with other groups by fronting the much-needed capital.

Tactical Support Activities

Corruption has long been a dominant tactical criminal activity employed by the Montreal Mafia. In the 1950s, a police search of the home of Frank Petrula, an associate of underboss Luigi Greco, found a notebook that contained a list of funds (almost $100,000) used by the *decina* to finance the campaign of a particular candidate for mayor the group favoured. Petrula's payroll included the names of six newspapermen and a radio journalist who had accepted money to denounce and discredit the reform-minded Civic Action League and its mayoralty candidate Jean Drapeau, who was running on a platform to clean the city of vice and gangsters during a recent municipal election (Carrigan, 1991: 176–77; Charbonneau, 1976: 83–85; Phillips, 1963a: 13).

The corrupting influence of the Cotroni *decina* also extended to labour unions in Quebec and had particular influence over the Hotel and Restaurant Employees International. Vic Cotroni used union officials not only to ensure peace within the family's own hotel and restaurant businesses but also to try to stir up union dissent in competing businesses. Police once observed Frank Cotroni sharing drinks with union officials and when Cotroni associate Claude Faber came to Toronto, Local 75 of the union was billed for his room, meals, drinks, and closed-circuit movies. Vito Rizzuto was also active in corrupting officials within the private and public sectors. Most famously, there is substantial evidence that he orchestrated the collusion and price-fixing among private sector construction firms bidding on public infrastructure tenders issued by the City of Montreal.

Violence is also used by the Montreal Mafia to protect its commercial interests and its power. Many of their businesses were established (and prospered) through the liberal use of intimidation and violence against competing businesses. This allowed Cotroni and other members and associates to control the distribution of various foodstuffs that was distributed to local restaurants and stores. Intimidation and violence, in fact, serves a number of purposes for the Mafioso: to protect his kin and territory, to sustain his criminal activities, to ensure secrecy and obedience, and as a means to gain and reinforce respect, honour, and power. "The instant a Mafioso cannot protect those around him with violence, his respect evaporates and he becomes a target himself.

Murder is considered an honourable means of gaining and guarding power, respect, and territory" (Edwards & Nicaso, 1993: 2, 7). Paolo Violi could be particularly violent, especially if someone did not display the respect he believed he deserved. In 1969, Mauro Marchettini, who had recently arrived in Canada from Italy, decided to open a poolroom on Jean-Talon Street, some 400 feet from Paolo Violi's establishment, the Reggio Bar. Having not paid tribute to Violi, Marchettini was refused delivery of goods he had ordered. He was advised to leave the area and when he declined, Paolo's brother Frank beat him savagely (Quebec Police Commission Inquiry on Organized Crime, 1977a: 61).

The *decina* also employed a number of individuals—including many non-Italians who worked outside family membership—as enforcers and hired assassins. One of the most infamous of these was Réal Simard, who admitted to carrying out five murders on the orders of Frank Cotroni (Simard & Vastel, 1988). The Cotroni *decina* was also rocked by internal violence, in particular, the murder of Paolo Violi and other senior Calabrian members as part of the *coup d'etat* orchestrated by Nick Rizzuto.

Despite Vito Rizzuto's reputation as a man who preferred negotiation and dialogue over violence, when it was necessary he did not shy away from using the latter. This was especially true when his family came under attack while he was in prison in the United States. Following an ongoing barrage of violence, which resulted in the murder of numerous members of his crime group and family—including his son and father—Vito allegedly exacted revenge when released from prison. For instance, on November 4, 2012, less than a month following Vito's return to Canada, Joe Di Maulo was gunned down outside his house, about 45 minutes north of Montreal. Like other recent gangland murders in the province, police made no arrests in Di Maulo's murder; however, there was numerous conjectures that his death was ordered by Vito as payback for Di Maulo's apparent co-operation with the 'Ndrangheta groups in Ontario to depose him as leader of the Montreal Mafia.

Money laundering was also a regular tactic used by the Cotroni *decina* given the vast revenues it was generating. One of the most prolific money launderers in Canadian mob history was William Obront, who rose to prominence in the organization as Vic's chief "financial advisor." The Quebec Police Commission Inquiry on Organized Crime (1977b) estimated that over the course of 1974 and 1975 alone, Obront had handled more than $80 million for the Montreal Mafia and its associates.

Behavioural

Chronic and Serious Offenders (Career Criminals)
In 1977, the Quebec Police Commission Inquiry on Organized Crime report noted that most members of the Montreal Mafia, "are in fact professional criminals. Recruits come largely from the underworld and related circles" (Quebec Police Commission Inquiry on Organized Crime, 1977a: 35).

Rationality/Non-ideological/Sophistication

The Montreal Mafia was run as a highly rational, non-ideological criminal enterprise in the sense that it focused primarily on profit-oriented criminal activities and semi-legitimate businesses. While relying on rudimentary and localized predatory criminal activities, such as extortion or theft, the Montreal Mafia was also a sophisticated criminal organization under the leadership of Vic Cotroni and Paoli Violi. In addition to coordinating the import of hundreds of kilos of heroin into Montreal every year, the Cotroni *decina* also became involved in a number of commercial crime activities, including stock market fraud and telemarketing fraud. The money-laundering activities overseen by Willie Obront were particularly sophisticated for the time and included opening numerous bank accounts and incorporating a myriad of fake and legitimate companies to hide, legitimize, and invest vast amounts of dirty money. Obront was well at ease in the business world and, between 1950 and 1975, he was involved in 38 companies, as owner, shareholder, or director (Quebec Police Commission Inquiry on Organized Crime, 1977a: 69, 73, 84; *Toronto Star*, January 21, 1977).

The sophisticated nature of the Montreal Mafia was taken to an even greater level under Vito Rizzuto, in part because of the need to develop an intricate international network to expedite the extensive transnational drug operations that were being conducted under his watch. The 1992 annual report of Criminal Intelligence Service Canada (1992: 20) observed that the "sophisticated structure of this crime group enables members to oversee the entire drug importation operation from source country to street level trafficking ensuring maximum profit." The multi-million-dollar bookmaking operations under his control, which used the Internet and smartphones to take bets on sporting events from across North America, were also some of the most elaborate and technologically sophisticated the country had ever seen.

Subcultural Norms

Members of the Cotroni *decina* stayed true to many of the prevailing beliefs, principles, and norms associated with the Mafia. Paramount among these was the importance of respect, honour, secrecy, and loyalty. The Mafioso was a man of honour and deserved the utmost respect from his family members and associates. On January 4, 1975, for example, some members of the *decina* were discussing fundraising among friends of Frank Cotroni to help pay his growing legal bills. But neither Vic Cotroni or Paolo Violi were pleased they went outside the *decina* for money, because, as Violi explained, "It dishonours the family when people go round asking for money to help one of their own" (Quebec Police Commission Inquiry on Organized Crime, 1977a: 77).

Secret police recordings of Violi revealed a man who was obsessed with the concept of respect and how it served as the underpinning of the "man of honour." One journalist described Violi as a "benevolent feudal monarch," who emphasized the "necessity of reciprocal respect between the leader and his subordinates" (Charney, 1979: 30). Violi personified Edwards and Nicaso's characterization of the Mafia's "twisted concept of honour." As a man of honour, the Mafioso "cannot stand the slightest offence and reacts violently when a *sgarro* (insult) is done to him. A man of honour knows he is capable of exercising violence in such a way that he frightens others into giving him deferential treatment." In other words, it does not matter to the Mafioso how he obtains honour or respect; it could be forcibly extracted through threats, intimidation, extortion, revenge, or violence. In this regard, habitual criminals like Violi and other Mafiosi "feel the need to call themselves 'Men of Honour,' much the way those with the worst body odour in Elizabethan times often wore the most perfume" (Edwards & Nicaso, 1993: 2, 7).

Of course, supreme importance was also placed on loyalty and secrecy. During a long discussion with a Mafioso from Sicily on May 10, 1974, Paolo Violi was quite explicit about the importance of *omerta* in the affairs of the *decina*. When Giuseppe Cuffaro asked whether as an associate of the *decina* he could do business with "friends" from other Mafia families, Violi answered: "You can, but you can't talk to them about affairs of the family ... " (Quebec Police Commission Inquiry on Organized Crime, 1977a: 78–79).

Rules, Regulations, and Codes of Conduct/Discipline

The Quebec Police Commission Inquiry on Organized Crime also documented how discipline was used in the Cotroni *decina* if rules of conduct were broken. At one end of the discipline spectrum was expulsion from the family while at the other extreme was murder. On several occasions, Vic Cotroni and Paolo Violi spoke of their intention to expel Rizzuto from the ranks of the family and to even have him killed due to his independent ways and the lack of respect he displayed toward Cotroni.

KEY TERMS

Black Hand

Capo decina

Capo di famiglia

Capo di tutti Capi

Capomafioso

Crimini

Decina

Famiglia

Mafioso

Man of Honour

'Ndrangheta

Omerta

Partito

Padrone

Tribute

REVIEW QUESTIONS

1. What are the origins of Italian organized crime in Italy? In the United States? In Canada?
2. What are the factors that helped foment the genesis and proliferation of IOC in North America? What etiological theories presented in chapter 4 can be used to explain the origins and spread of IOC in Canada?
3. What is the scope of IOC in North America, in historical and contemporary terms?
4. How has IOC in Canada been influenced by that in the United States?
5. Compare and contrast between IOC in Quebec and Ontario. What are the three main IOC factions in Canada?
6. In general, how are IOC associations in North America structured? What organizational models presented in chapter 4 are most applicable to explain how COC is structured?
7. What criminal activities do IOC groups engage in?
8. What are the characteristics of IOC, based on the application of theoretical models from chapter 3?
9. What is the significance of IOC when examining organized crime in Canada?

FURTHER READINGS

Albanese, J. (2014). The Italian-American Mafia, in L. Paoli (Ed.), *The Oxford Handbook of Organized Crime* (pp. 142–58). Oxford, New York: Oxford University Press.

Cédilot, A., & Noël, A. (2011). *Mafia Inc.: The Long, Bloody Reign of Canada's Sicilian Clan*. Toronto: Random House Canada.

Dubro, J. (1985). *Mob Rule: Inside the Canadian Mafia*. Toronto: Macmillan of Canada.

Edwards, P., & Nicaso, A. (2015). *Business or Blood: Mafia Boss Vito Rizzuto's Last War*. Toronto: Random House Canada.

Gambetta, D. (1993). *The Sicilian Mafia. The Business of Private Protection*. Boston: Harvard University Press.

Paoli, L. (2014). The Italian Mafia, in L. Paoli (Ed.), *The Oxford Handbook of Organized Crime* (pp. 121–41). Oxford, New York: Oxford University Press.

6

CHINESE ORGANIZED CRIME

CHAPTER OUTLINE

- Introduction and Overview
- Chinese Triads
- The Origins and Early History of Chinese Organized Crime in Canada
- The Post-war Years: Drug Trafficking, People Smuggling, and Gambling
- Chinese Organized Crime in Canada in the 1990s and Beyond
- Analyzing Chinese Organized Crime

LEARNING OUTCOMES

After reading this chapter, you should have a thorough understanding of the following:

- The origins and history of Chinese organized crime in Canada
- The social, political, legal, and economic factors that helped ferment the genesis and proliferation of Chinese organized crime as well as applicable etiological theories
- Recent trends and developments in Chinese organized crime
- The characteristics of Chinese organized crime based on the application of theoretical models from chapter 1
- The significance of Chinese organized crime when examining organized crime in Canada

INTRODUCTION AND OVERVIEW

Chinese organized crime (COC) is not new to Canada. The first Chinatown in Victoria became home to illegal gambling halls, brothels, and opium dens, and Chinese merchants in British Columbia were behind some of the largest opium smuggling and trafficking rings in the early part of the twentieth century. The original Canadian branches of Chinese triad societies operated as political and benevolent associations and were not criminal or secret in nature. However, as the twentieth century wore on, some of these societies in Vancouver, Toronto, and Montreal were used by powerful members for such illegal endeavours as extortion, prostitution, gambling, opium trafficking, and people smuggling.

Beginning in the early 1970s, Southeast Asian heroin began to flood North America, and before long Chinese drug trafficking syndicates had surpassed the French Corsicans and the Italian Mafia as Canada's biggest heroin suppliers. By the mid-1970s, a rash of extortions within Toronto's Chinese community exposed the presence of Canada's first modern triad. The Kung Lok was established solely for criminal purposes and initially blended a traditional triad structure with a network approach to carrying out crimes. Around the same time, Chinese street gangs emerged in Vancouver. At the end of the 1980s, a network of professional criminals originally made up of ex-military from Mainland China and called the *Dai Huen Jai* (**Big Circle Boys**) were blamed for a series of violent robberies, home invasions, and pickpocketing in Vancouver and Toronto. Within ten years, this loose association of offenders would evolve into one of the largest and most sophisticated criminal networks in the country.

When examining the origins of COC in Canada, various etiological theories can be applied. Alien conspiracy theory is somewhat applicable in that triad societies, the Big Circle Boys, and other forms of COC originated outside the country. Strain theory, as well as its offshoot ethnic succession theory, is applicable because historically the Chinese have been discriminated against and persecuted in this country, which has blocked legitimate means for individual members to integrate into mainstream society. As the legitimate channels of social mobility were cut off to the Chinese in this country, some turned to organized crimes. Like any criminal genre that is symbiotic with the larger society, COC has thrived in Canada because it caters to the vices of their own community as well as broader Canadian society.

While the Italian Mafia and the Hells Angels may be Canada's most visible criminal organizations, COC now constitutes the most widespread, diverse, and sophisticated criminal conspiracy in Canada today. Their geographic strongholds are the Lower Mainland of British Columbia and the Greater Toronto Area (GTA) in Ontario, but their reach extends into almost every province. Contemporary COC in Canada is characterized by its networked structure that includes triad members, youth gangs, professional criminals, and semi-legitimate businesspeople. The sources of revenue for Chinese criminal syndicates include extortion, gambling, prostitution, illegal immigration schemes, and the drug trade. In addition to importing heroin from Southeast Asia, COC is the biggest producer of synthetic drugs (crystal meth and ecstasy) in Canada, which is trafficked domestically and exported to the United States and other countries. COC is active in more sophisticated and technological-based crimes as well, including the counterfeiting of credit cards, digital technology, and consumer products. They are also involved in the lucrative contraband tobacco market, where they are involved in illegally importing counterfeit cigarettes and are also suspected of operating unregulated cigarette manufacturing plants on First Nations reserves in Quebec and Ontario. COC in Canada has strong links to both Hong Kong and China, which is a source country for counterfeit goods, contraband tobacco, and chemicals used to produce synthetic drugs, as well as migrants who are smuggled into this country.

CHINESE TRIADS

The word **triad** has often been used generically to describe Chinese organized crime. However, COC also includes non-triad groups and networks that originated in Hong Kong, Taiwan, and the People's Republic of China as well as groups that focus almost exclusively on specific criminal activities like drug trafficking or people smuggling. While distinctions can be made between these different variations of Chinese organized crime, today there is an overlap among them all in the sense that one individual offender or a small criminal group may fall into all of these categories; this underscores the extensive co-operation, coordination, and networking that occurs within COC.

The so-called triads are the oldest and most infamous of the Chinese criminal organizations, and there is probably no organized crime genre whose origin is more shrouded by myth and obfuscation. Some have traced their beginnings back to the White Lotus Society, which was founded by monks in the twelfth century who revolted against the Mongol occupation of China during the thirteenth and fourteenth centuries. Others place the triads' beginnings in seventeenth-century China, where covert societies tried to overthrow the Manchu rulers of the Qing Dynasty (which ruled from 1644 to 1911) in order to return the country to the Ming Dynasty (in power from 1368 to 1644), which represented the majority ethnic Han Chinese. By the early nineteenth century, numerous rebel groups were operating in mainland China, such as the *Tian Di Hui* (Heaven and Earth Society), *San Tian Hui* (Triple Dot Society), and the *San He Hui* (Triple Unit Society). Collectively, these secret societies were referred to as the **Hong Men** (Hong refers to "Hongwu," the reign designation of the first Ming Emperor, Zhu Yuanzhang). The avowed revolutionary aims of these societies made them outlaw organizations in the eyes of the Qing rulers and any known member was subject to death (Chan, 1983: 122; Lintner, 2003: 42; McKeown, 2007; Murray & Biaoqi, 1994: 16–36).

Like the terms *Mafia* or *la Cosa Nostra*, the *triad* appellation is a Western concoction. It was reportedly coined in the 1820s by Dr. William Milne, a British educator working in Asia who, in his writings about the secret societies, recognized the importance of the number three in their names and rituals. The number three symbolizes how the founders of the early Hong Men societies viewed the metaphysical philosophy underlying their movements: united by and living in harmony with the three primary forces of the universe: heaven, earth, and man. For years, the number three (in all its mathematical permutations) saturated the many ritual aspects of the organizational structure, member initiation, and criminal operations of the secret societies and their future criminal reincarnations, including those operating in Canada (Murray & Biaoqi, 1994: 92).

While the intentions of the original triads were political in nature, others were formed by clans or tradesmen as mutual aid societies (the revolutionary groups also incorporated benevolent services into their mandate to varying degrees). As with the Italian Mafia, some of these groups began to incorporate criminal activities, such as extortion, kidnapping, and piracy, to help fund their operations. By the mid-nineteenth century, the Hong Men societies had spread throughout Southeast Asia, including Hong Kong, which was formally ceded to Britain by the Treaty of Nanking in 1842. Colonial records from this time suggest that the secret societies continued as both a political and criminal force under British rule. As one colonial official wrote in 1845, "Hong Kong has been infested by members of the Triad Society, the members of which under the shelter of a political maxim … perpetrate the grossest of enormities" (Main, 1991: 147).

Like the Qing rulers in China, the British colonial government vowed to crush the "Black Societies." The English and Chinese administrators in Hong Kong did not distinguish among those societies that functioned as revolutionary, criminal, or benevolent groups, and in 1845 an ordinance for the "Suppression of the Triad and Other Secret Societies" was enacted. But the outlawing of these societies simply drove them further underground, while prompting them to surreptitiously infiltrate legitimate workers' guilds and merchant associations (Lintner, 2003: 118; Main, 1991: 148). The evolution of triads into modern criminal entities began in earnest in Hong Kong and mainland China during the early part of the twentieth century. During this period, the Hong Men societies threw their support behind the revolutionary leader Dr. Sun Yat-sen, who himself was a member of the Tian Di Hui triad, one of the major financiers of his republican movement in China. (Some have speculated that he became a triad

CRITICAL THINKING EXERCISE

What is unique about the origins of triad societies compared to those of other organized crime genres discussed in this part of the textbook? Can you discern any similarities between the origins of Chinese triads and those of the Italian Mafia? What properties of the triads made them conducive to future criminality? Compare and contrast this to how the origins of the Sicilian Mafia influenced its future criminality.

member to take advantage of the vast membership and resources of the societies for his revolutionary ambitions.) In 1911, the Republicans, with strong support of the triad societies, staged a revolt in the city of Canton (now called Guangzhou, the largest city of Guangdong province in southern China), which spread rapidly throughout southern China. On January 1, 1912, the Republic of China was born.

The overthrow of the Qing Dynasty signalled the birth of the new modern criminal triad, and the revolutionary purpose of some societies was replaced with criminal endeavours that included extortion, illegal gambling, and drug trafficking. The influence of triads in republican China became all-pervasive and many triad society members went on to be powerful members and financiers of the Chinese National Party or **Kuomintang**, a political group founded in 1912 from a collection of revolutionary groups that had overthrown the Qing Dynasty. In order to rise in the party, civil service, or armed forces, one had to be a triad "brother," while merchants, bankers, and businessmen discovered that triad membership oiled the machinery of commerce. Triad societies also allied themselves with the various warlords in China and had great influence in the Chinese military under the command of another triad member, General

Photo 6.1: Sun Yat-sen

Source: Wikimedia Commons

Case Study: Tu Yueh-sheng

Tu Yueh-sheng (Big-Eared Tu) was the leader of a triad syndicate known as the Green Gang, which operated out of Shanghai from the early 1900s to the late 1940s. The precedent for triad involvement in drug trafficking was set by Tu; at that time, the Green Gang dominated the extremely lucrative opium trade in Shanghai, then a major seaport of several million people and the gateway to China. He was also active in extortion and prostitution.

Big-Eared Tu aided Chiang Kai-shek's rise to power by supplying the Kuomintang with much-needed funds. In the late 1920s, Tu also aided the Kuomintang's nationalist cause through a vicious crackdown against Shanghai's Communist Party organizers and labour activists. His pact with Chiang Kai-shek strengthened the Green Gang's influence with the Nationalist government in China, and Tu became one of the most powerful men in the country during the 1920s and 1930s. After Mao rose to power following the Chinese Civil War, Tu went into exile in Hong Kong and remained there until his death in 1951 (Booth, 1999; Martin, 1996; Wakeman, 1988; Wasserstein, 1999).

Photo 6.2: Tu Yueh-sheng

Source: Wikimedia Commons

Chiang Kai-shek. Between 1914 and 1939, Hong Kong became completely "triadized" with more than 300 such societies established during this time (Main, 1991: 148). "The Triads, in turn, grouped themselves into seven or eight different cartels. Each cartel operated in a particular section of the city and coordinated the activities of the member Triads in the various economic sectors from its 'headquarters'" (Fijnaut, 2014: 58).

During the immediate post-war period, triads re-established themselves in Hong Kong and began to expand to other parts of Southeast Asia and even to North America, primarily through the immigration of triad members. The 1949 takeover of mainland China by the Mao's Communists, who shared with the Qing and British rulers the same antipathy toward the triads, sparked an exodus of society members to Hong Kong, which helped cement the colony as triad central for decades to come. According to Fijnaut (2014: 59), the triads capitalized on "the weakened position of Britain's postwar colonial administrators" and "quickly regained control not only of the labor market and ports, but also of opium trafficking and prostitution in the city." They also became active in extortion, illegal gambling, and loansharking. "They were, of course, able to develop and run their criminal operations thanks to their close relationship with the authorities. According to estimates, for example, some 30 percent of all Chinese police officers in Hong Kong were members of a Triad in the early 1970s" (Fijnaut, 2014: 60).

Taiwan also emerged as a hotbed for the secret societies, when members of the triad-infested Kuomintang fled to the island. Other remnants of the Kuomintang nationalist army took refuge in Burma's northern hills and became active in the opium and heroin trade (with support from the CIA, which for years worked with opium growers and heroin traffickers in the so-called **Golden Triangle** of Burma, Laos, and Thailand to help finance their joint efforts with Chiang Kai-shek to destabilize Communist China). From this point onwards, Southeastern Asia would become one of the biggest sources of heroin in the world.

As Chinese immigration to North America increased over the first half of the twentieth century, triad influence began to spread beyond Asia, and many became involved in extorting money and operating illegal gambling houses and opium dens in the Chinatowns of Canada and the United States. The criminal networks associated with the Hong Kong triads continued to expand internationally in the 1960s, exploiting the growth of expatriate Chinese communities as well as the rapidly expanding heroin markets in North America. Throughout the 1970s and 1980s, the Chinese population in North America soared, and the presence of triads and associated criminal activity increased. During the 1990s, immigration of Hong Kong residents to Canada escalated dramatically due to the impending handover of the British colony to the People's Republic of China in 1997. According to the United States Drug Enforcement Administration (2001), during the late 1990s, Vancouver "emerged as a key operational headquarters for ethnic Chinese criminal elements" (United States Drug Enforcement Administration, n.d.b).

In 2000, the US National Security Council stated that there were 50 triad groups and subgroups in the world with an estimated membership of between 50,000 and 100,000. Even if these numbers are accurate, only a fraction of the groups and members are criminally active. Some triads are said to have as many as 25,000 members worldwide, but this is most likely an inflated number that includes members who are not active, members that are not involved in criminal activities, and individuals only loosely associated with the group, such as "quasi-legitimate businessmen involved in an array of criminal enterprises" (United States National Security Council, 2000). According to Fijnaut (2014: 58) "a considerable number" of Hong Kong triad members do "not belong to the Triad hard core. Of the 10,000 members of a particular cartel, only about 30 percent qualified as such. The rest joined mainly because the cartel had the power to mediate in such matters as social security and employment." The membership estimates may also include many who were forced to pay membership fees, a form of extortion.

In more recent years, only around a dozen or so triad societies remain active in Hong Kong. Among the largest and most criminally active are the Sun Yee On, the Wo Shing Wo, the 14K, the Wo On Lok, and the Wo Hop To. Founded in the early 1950s, the **Sun Yee On** (meaning "New Righteousness and Peace") is considered the largest of the Hong Kong triads, with an estimated 55,000 members worldwide, including those located in the United States, Canada, the United Kingdom, and parts of Western Europe. While this may again be an inflated number, some members and associates of the Sun Yee On carry out a wide range of crimes and use the society's infrastructure to work with other criminal offenders and groups. These criminal activities include gambling operations, heroin trafficking, counterfeiting, prostitution, smuggling, extortion, and what the Sun Yee On is perhaps best known for—its infiltration of Hong Kong's entertainment industry and the extortion of entertainers, promoters, and production company executives.

The **14K** grew out of the Hong Fat Shan Society, which was founded in Guangzhou in the late 1940s, supposedly on the orders of General Chiang Kai-shek. Originally made up of former Chinese nationalists, Hong Fat Shan was created as an alliance of existing triad societies to fight Communist forces. It later became known as the 14K in reference to the street address of the original headquarters of the alliance at 14 Po Wah Road in Canton. When Mao's Communists came to power in China in 1949, many of its members fled to Hong Kong. At one point, its worldwide membership was said to total 20,000, although its structure can best be described as a loose-knit network that is made up of at least 30 subgroups that share approximately 1000 criminally active members. Collectively, the 14K is heavily involved in heroin trafficking and migrant smuggling. Taiwan's largest triad is the **United Bamboo,** which was formed by a mix of native Taiwanese and triad members who fled Communist China in the mid-1950s. They operate internationally with cells in the United States, Canada, and throughout Asia, and are involved in drug trafficking, extortion, bank fraud, illegal gambling, prostitution, migrant smuggling, and gun-running (Dubro, 1992: 28; Lintner, 2003: 122; United States Congress, 1992: 1–11).

Photo 6.3: Chiang Kai-shek

Source: National Archive Press (Chung Hua Min Kuo Tsi Hua), via Wikimedia Commons

THE ORIGINS AND EARLY HISTORY OF CHINESE ORGANIZED CRIME IN CANADA

Around the early 1850s, word began to spread in China about a wondrous new land that was opening up opportunities for anyone willing to work, regardless of race, creed, or colour. Gold was discovered along California's Sacramento River in 1848, and thousands of Chinese fortune seekers crossed the Pacific Ocean to join in the quest for instant riches. Once the California gold mines were exhausted, many of the Chinese migrants began to work as labourers along the thousands of kilometres of railroad track being laid in the American West. Others turned to mining and some became merchants, many of whom set up shop in San Francisco, where the continent's first Chinatown took root.

By the late 1850s, another "gold mountain" was discovered along the west coast, this time in the Fraser River Valley of British Columbia. Chinese prospectors making their way north from California were joined by others emigrating to the province directly from China. All were looking to pan for gold in the Caribou gold fields during the 1860s or to help construct the Canadian Pacific Railway lines starting in the early 1880s. The 1885 Royal Commission on Chinese Immigration estimated that 15,701 Chinese nationals entered Canada from 1861 to 1884 (Royal Commission of Chinese Immigration, 1885: v). By the early 1870s, at least a third of all Chinese residents in British Columbia were living in Victoria, and the city's growing Chinatown district was a beehive of economic and cultural activity. Dry goods stores, restaurants, shoemakers, tailors, and launderers were opening on and around Johnson Street, while Chinese business, fraternal, and cultural organizations were being formed.

It wasn't long after Chinese immigrants arrived in British Columbia that Hong Men societies were established in the province. While the original Canadian branches pursued the same political objectives as their predecessors, they were also formed as a united bulwark against the discrimination they experienced at the hands of the larger white society. As such, some of the societies became a surrogate government for Chinese expatriates, providing a quasi-legal system that dispensed justice and mediated disputes, provided social welfare services, helped protect members against white vigilante justice, and offered recreational activities for the largely male population, such as gambling, prostitutes, and opium. The first known Chinese triad society in Canada was formed in 1863 in Barkerville, a small gold mining town in northeastern British Columbia. Founded by Chinese miners, it was called the Hong Shan Tang and was believed to be a branch or at least an offshoot of a similarly named society in San Francisco, which itself was associated with Hong Men societies in the Guangdong province of southern China (Booth, 1999: 313; Con & Wickberg, 1982: 30–31; Dubro, 1992: 54–55; Lyman, Willmott, & Ho, 1964: 530–39; Payne, 1997: 9–11).

Other triad societies in British Columbia followed. Most notable was the Chih-kung T'ang. Known as the CKT for short, the society was founded in 1876 in Quesnel. The goal of the CKT was to contribute to the overthrow of the Qing Dynasty back in China, but it was a fraternal association founded to promote harmonious relations among Chinese immigrants, promote their advancement through business and work, and also provide protection, mediation services, social welfare assistance, and even lodging to its members in British Columbia (Con & Wickberg, 1982: 31; Payne, 1997: 91). By 1885, according to Payne, "there were over 40 Chih-kung T'ang chapters in the province" (Payne, 1997: 12).

From the very beginning, the Hong Men chapters in British Columbia do not appear to have been shrouded in the level of secrecy that characterized their forebears in China. Some even erected lodges or temples that had the name of the society on the exterior and where members openly congregated (the English-language media were apt to call all Chinese societies *tongs*, which means "hall" or "gathering place" in Chinese).

The public nature of the Canadian societies did not stop the anti-Chinese lobby from stereotyping them as secret, subversive, criminal organizations. There is also no evidence to suggest that the early Chinese societies in British Columbia were formed or operated as criminal organizations. However, because some of the societies were

Photo 6.4: The Barkerville Chee Kung Tong Building circa 1960

Source: Image F-07470, courtesy of Royal British Columbia Museum, British Columbia Archives

controlled by Chinese merchants, who were emerging as suppliers of opium, gambling, and prostitution, the societies were increasingly equated with crime and vice. While members of local Hong Men societies were catering to the recreational needs of the migrant Chinese bachelors, the societies themselves acted as a sort of moral regulator and enforced a code of behaviour the society expected its members to follow so as not to give it a bad name. The constitution even threatened "severe punishment" for those who caused trouble in brothels or gambling houses (Payne, 1997: 11). While some triad societies in British Columbia did operate secretly due to their continued opposition to Qing rule in China, the media of the day failed to understand their complex nature. An 1885 resolution on the "Chinese Question" tabled in the legislature of British Columbia referred to "a system of secret societies, which encourages crime amongst themselves, and which prevents the administration of justice" (*The Globe*, March 25, 1885).

A CKT branch was first established in Vancouver in 1892 and, according to Terry Gould, by 1923 there were 54 societies in the city's Chinatown (Gould, 2004: 10). The most prominent of the BC societies was the Chinese Consolidated Benevolent Association (CCBA), which was founded in Victoria in 1884 after 31 local Chinese societies came together to establish an umbrella organization that provided loans and facilitated business opportunities for budding Chinese entrepreneurs while offering social assistance to the less fortunate. The CCBA was also a political advocacy group that

spearheaded opposition to the anti-Chinese movements and the racist government policies that were being introduced. In keeping with its paternalistic intentions, the association's original constitution pledged to provide financial and legal aid to any member who
was beaten, robbed, or owed money, or unjustly accused of criminal or bad behaviour
by whites. The CCBA also advanced a moral code for its members, provided assistance
to anyone in the Chinese community convicted of a criminal offence, and pledged to
combat one of the most serious social problems within the overseas Chinese population:
the trafficking of Chinese women (Chan, 1983: 86–88, 92–93).

Chinese Organized Crime in the Late Nineteenth and Early Twentieth Century

Notwithstanding the efforts of CCBA, a vice industry did emerge within the local
Chinese communities in British Columbia to cater to the demands of the predominately
male population. Forced to return from their low paying menial jobs to crowded, dis-
mal, unsanitary rooming houses, many lonely and despondent Chinese bachelors in BC
turned to gambling, prostitution, and opium smoking. Since the Chinese residents could
not patronize the white man's "houses of ill-fame," a handful of Chinese merchants in
Victoria and Vancouver began to cater to this demand (Chan, 1983: 84).

"From the days of the gold rush in 1858," Anthony Chan wrote, "gambling had been
an important part of Chinatown life. Leisure moments away from the sand bars and, later, the railroads, were spent at games of chance." At first, most of the early professional
Chinese gambling operations were transient in nature, catering to the scattered migrant
labourers by moving from one work camp to another. As the Chinese population became more sedentary and urban, so did the gambling parlours. After the completion of
the Canadian Pacific Railway in 1884, Victoria's "Fantan Alley"—which stretched one
city block and was named after the popular Chinese game of chance—boasted around
12 separate gaming establishments. "Most of the gambling dens were small and could
accommodate a few dozen gamblers at most," according to Chan, while "some of the
larger establishments could hold up to one hundred bettors" (Chan, 1983: 77–79). As
early as 1860, Victoria newspapers began to report on gambling houses catering to the
local Chinese population.

Another service that could be found in Victoria's Chinatown was prostitution,
which flourished due to the disproportionate number of Chinese males immigrating
to Canada. The first prostitutes brought to Victoria came via San Francisco, which had
become the centre for the international trade in Chinese women. The trafficking of
Chinese women was escalating so rapidly in North America that procurers scoured the
impoverished villages of rural China for families willing to sell their young daughters.
The women and girls would be either taken to an underground auction block in San
Francisco or sold directly to a Chinese merchant or group of merchants in Canada or the
United States (Chan, 1983: 80–81; Kobayashi, 1978: 7).

As the century drew to a close, the Chinese sex trade was becoming more orga-
nized in British Columbia. Testimony before the 1885 Royal Commission on Chinese
Immigration estimated there were "150 Chinese women prostitutes" in British
Columbia around this time (Royal Commission on Chinese Immigration, 1885: 83; *The
Globe*, March 25, 1885). Women and girls from the provinces of Guangdong, Jiangsi,
and Zhejiang were now bypassing San Francisco and arriving directly in Victoria and
Vancouver. Lee Mon-kow, a Chinese interpreter at the customs house in Victoria,
testified to the 1902 Royal Commission on Chinese and Japanese Immigration that
a contract would be drawn up between a Chinese woman and a Chinese merchant
or brothel operator who agreed to pay the woman's head tax, passage fees, and other
expenses. Lee even cited a bill of sale for one woman that cost a merchant $302 plus
$7 for clothing and $4 for her leather trunk. In return, he "had the right to her body
service." As part of the contract, the woman agreed "to pay a certain sum at a certain
time, to repay the passage money and the head tax and seven percent interest." When
this amount was paid off through revenue generated by the sexual services provided by
the woman, she would be "freed" from her indentured existence (Royal Commission
to Investigate Chinese and Japanese Immigration into British Columbia, 1902: 39).
Once in North America, the young women would be placed in one of two types of
Chinese brothels that were distinguished by the colour and class of the clientele. The
"parlours" were the more opulent establishments that catered to Chinese merchants
and white customers, and the women working there were generally more beautiful and
better paid (Kobayashi, 1978: 7).

Another vice closely associated with the Chinese population was opium smoking. While opium's medicinal use as an anaesthetic and all-round elixir was legal and
well-established among the white population, it wasn't until the arrival of the Chinese
immigrant that the recreational smoking of opium was introduced in North America.
Whether the opium was ingested by white, upper-middle-class housewives or Chinese
migrant labourers, it was legal in Canada and the United States during the nineteenth
century and was imported from the British colony of Hong Kong. Between 1870 and
1908, Chinese merchants opened a number of factories in Victoria and BC's Lower
Mainland to convert raw gum opium into the smokable form. Much of the processed
opium stayed in BC, although some was shipped east to Winnipeg, Toronto, and
Montreal and south to Seattle, California, and even Hawaii. By the 1880s, British
Columbia was the main North American importer, producer, and exporter of black tar
opium. Opium production was a competitive business; by 1901, however, three Victoria
firms with 18 partners had established a virtual monopoly over the manufacture of
opium in the province (Chan, 1983: 77).

The Chinese were also the first to open commercial opium dens in Canadian cities.
Like taverns and saloons, they were legal, accessible to adult males, and stocked with
an assortment of brands and smoking paraphernalia. The opium dens were the principal
clients of the opium factories, although Caucasian-operated pharmacies were quickly

Photo 6.5: Opium den in San Francisco, early twentieth century

Source: Photo by A. & E.O. Tschirch & Von Lippmann, via Wellcome Library, London

becoming lucrative customers as many were now selling smokable opium to white and Chinese smokers alike. The colonial, provincial, and Dominion governments also benefited from the early opium trade in Canada. They received licensing fees from manufacturers and taxes were imposed on the retail sale of opium, although the real government money was made from tariffs imposed on opium imports. In February 1865, a 50 percent tariff on opium imported into the BC colony was imposed, far exceeding the usual 12.5 percent applied to most other imports (*The British Colombian*, February 18, 1865). The new tariff incited the widespread smuggling of opium into Canada.

British Columbia's role as a manufacturer and exporter of processed opium increased substantially in 1890 when the US Congress imposed its own prohibitive tariffs on opium and morphine imports. The result was that even larger amounts of raw opium were being brought into Canada (legally and covertly), processed through BC-based opium factories, and then smuggled into the United States to avoid the tariffs.

CRITICAL THINKING EXERCISE

Examine the origins of drug trafficking by Chinese criminal entrepreneurs in North America. Compare and contrast the origins and early history with that of heroin trafficking by Italian organized crime and more specifically North America's LCN groups.

Opium and Heroin Trafficking in the Early Twentieth Century

Much of the opium and heroin imported through the west coast of Canada in the first quarter of the century came from Asia and was smuggled into the country by both white and Asian crew members of passenger ocean liners. Following the criminalization of opium and heroin in Canada in 1908 (see chapter 11), some of the biggest illegal suppliers were (white) doctors and pharmacists who wrote and filled prescriptions mainly for the Caucasian population. With that said, many importers and wholesalers of illegal opium and heroin in Canada were Chinese merchants, who took delivery of the drugs from crew members (National Archives of Canada, RG 18, Files of the Royal Canadian Mounted Police, Volume 3288, File No. HQ-189-E-1). One police investigation in the early 1920s led to the arrest and conviction of J.J. Wing, who the Crown alleged "to be one of the ringleaders in the narcotics trade of the city" (*The Vancouver Sun*, November 24, 1923). Other confidential RCMP documents from 1923 indicated that Wing had been "carrying on a very large and presumably well-protected system of import and distribution, both by a system of runners and also by the use of the mails." The RCMP estimated that Wing had "30 or 40 Runners" working for him in Vancouver (National Archives of Canada, RG 18: Files of the Royal Canadian Mounted Police, Volume 3167, File No. G494-1; *The Province*, December 13, 1923).

Now focusing primarily on major smuggling and trafficking conspiracies, the RCMP and the Dominion Customs Service on the west coast continued to make a number of significant drug seizures and arrests during the late 1920s and early 1930s. On July 14, 1927, Lore Yip, who the RCMP described as the third most important narcotics dealer in Vancouver, was arrested after police found 43 pounds of opium, morphine, and cocaine concealed in the paneling between two walls of his apartment at the Sherman Hotel in Chinatown (Royal Canadian Mounted Police, 1929: 23; *Vancouver Sun*, July 15, 1927). At the time, it was the single largest drug seizure in BC history.

Opium was also being illegally imported into Canada through Montreal's marine ports. In June 1918, a police raid on an old farmhouse on the outskirts of the city turned up approximately 70 pounds of raw and processed opium. Along with 240 copper boxes containing varying amounts of the drug, police also found a small manufacturing plant

CRITICAL THINKING EXERCISE

The preceding passages reveal a considerable interaction and co-operation between the Chinese community and English-Canadians (including those in positions of power) in drug smuggling. Identify the different forms of interaction and co-operation described above. What does this say about early "Chinese organized crime" on the west coast? What does this say about organized crime generally in Canada?

to turn the gum opium into the smokable variety. As the *Montreal Gazette* reported, "The boilers, machinery and raw material found in another of the rooms constituted the biggest drug plant that the police have yet raided. The quantity of opium found in the house is claimed to be the largest ever seized in Montreal." The house was also equipped to manufacture opium pipes, a number of which were seized by police. Two Chinese men were arrested at the scene, and it was clear they had prepared for a long stay; there was enough food and liquor in the house to meet the needs of the occupants for over a year, police told the media. "Several revolvers and many boxes of cartridges were also found, the men evidently being prepared for any raid which might occur" (*Montreal Gazette*, June 12, 1918). Less than a year later, police discovered 180 pounds of opium in the home of Lee Jee, a Chinese merchant with a store on La Gauchetière Street in Montreal. Eighteen packages, each one containing 10 pounds of opium, were seized. The packages had been shipped east from British Columbia via parcel post (*The Globe*, June 21, 1919).

Organized Gambling

In addition to drugs, gambling became a major money-maker for organized criminal interests in Canada's Chinese community. In Toronto, the Kuomintang (which supported the Republican cause back in China) "ran a police-protected gambling house that was in fierce competition with one run by a pro-Monarchist group who opposed the Nationalists in China and were in alliance with a rival underworld group in Toronto's Chinatown" (Dubro, 1992: 83). In one month alone, police conducted 90 raids on Chinese gambling halls in Toronto (Chan, 1983: 134).

Vancouver's Chinatown was a hotbed for both Chinese and white gamblers. In 1918, the *Globe* newspaper estimated "there are over forty gambling dens in Chinatown today, and that many of these have advertisements in their windows for 'fantan' as above stated" (*The Globe*, May 23, 1918). Chinatown came under the microscope of a 1928 judicial inquiry into vice and government corruption in Vancouver, with one police official providing the inquiry a list of 30 addresses that he said were operating as gambling dens between 1921 and 1928. Among the biggest gambling house operators in Vancouver's Chinatown was Chow Wong Lun (a.k.a. Georgie Chow), who ran one so large that it was described by a police officer as "an enormous barn of a gambling place," and Joe Won Lum, who admitted to being the "bossman" of a Chinese lottery at 846 Main Street and a gambling hall outside of Chinatown on Davie Street. The inquiry was told that Lum was "dealing with pretty well high up English people" and in order to better serve his white clientele Lum sent out runners with lottery tickets that his customers could mark at their leisure. This innovative service, which saved the affluent Caucasian gamblers the indignity of frequenting a Chinese gaming establishment, helped to modernize the numbers racket in the city and made Lum a tidy profit. According to ledgers seized by police, Joe Won Lum's gambling hall at 615 Davie Street took in as much as $1440 a month in bets, while only paying out winnings of

Case Study: Shue Moy—The King of the Gamblers

Shue Moy was the self-proclaimed Potato King—a moniker derived from his ownership of the largest potato ranch in Canada—but he was best known as Vancouver's "King of the Gamblers." Moy had come to British Columbia from China in 1899 and would go on to have an eclectic career in the province. In addition to farming potatoes, he owned a grocery store, sold lumber in Victoria, and served as the postmaster in a small interior town. Although he was never convicted of a criminal offence, Moy was accused of operating several gambling houses, running a brothel, trafficking opium, overseeing protection rackets, and providing generous bribes to city officials, including the chief of police and the mayor of Vancouver.

In his testimony at the 1928 judicial inquiry into vice and police corruption in Vancouver, officials with the Vancouver police department stated that Moy did not outright own any gambling halls, but had an interest in four of them located in and around Chinatown (City of Vancouver Archives, Vancouver Police Fonds, Series 181, Vol. 9, 4670–74). When put on the stand, Moy tried to characterize himself as nothing more than a patron of Chinatown's gambling operations, but quickly confessed to having an interest in several gambling joints in the city. Testimony at the inquiry also provided evidence of preferential treatment that Moy appeared to be receiving from the mayor's office and senior police officials. Georgie Chow complained that while police frequently raided his gambling joints on Cardova Street, those operated by Moy located just down the street were unmolested. According to Chow, Inspector Jackson of the Vancouver police once told him, "Shue Moy 'is a good friend to the mayor. He can do anything he wants." Jackson corroborated this in his own testimony to the inquiry. When asked if he could think "of one single place of Shue Moy's in Chinatown that was raided in 1927," Jackson replied, "Offhand I cannot tell you, no." In response to another question, he simply said, "The Mayor did not want us to bother about it. I have told you that before and that is as far as I can go" (City of Vancouver Archives, Vancouver Police Fonds, Series 181, Vol. 6, 2570, 2572–73).

Evidence presented before the commission, including testimony by Moy himself, showed that he visited the mayor's home on several occasions and had also made a number of financial contributions to his political campaigns. Other witnesses provided more damning evidence. Ah Kim, a partner with Moy in one gambling house, testified that he paid $300 a month to the mayor so that Moy could keep his main gambling house at 54 Cordova West open. Although Moy denied he ever paid protection money to the mayor or police, he did admit it was "a Chinese custom" to give "gifts" to officials (Dubro, 1992: 61–62; *Vancouver Sun*, May 2, 1928, May 16, 1928).

$34. Lum also confessed that he was a partner with Georgie Chow in other gambling operations (City of Vancouver Archives, MSS. 54, 2064-2065; *Vancouver Sun*, May 16, 1928, May 18, 1928a, May 18, 1928b).

Police detectives explained to the inquiry that gambling operations in Chinatown were rarely owned solely by one person, but controlled by groups of investors, through companies, benevolent societies, or other types of association. As Detective Ricci of the Vice Squad told the judicial inquiry, "these certain people come from China from a certain district; they get together; they are like a bunch of brothers. They call themselves cousins and brothers and they get a little money and chip in and start a gambling house" (City of Vancouver Archives, Vancouver Police Fonds, Series 181, Vol. 9, 4670–74). In his testimony before the inquiry, Joe Won Lum confirmed that most Chinese gambling halls were run as partnerships. He asserted that joint ventures were essential to ensuring the solvency of the gambling houses and explained to the inquiry the system by which large bets were handled. Amounts too big for the smaller operations were turned over to a "clearing house" that was itself a partnership among Chinatown merchants (*Vancouver Sun*, May 18, 1928a; May 18, 1928b). Detective Ricci concurred with this assessment, stating that the amount of capital required for some of the larger gambling halls to cover potential losses was greater than any one man could invest: "There is no gambling joint existing in Chinatown unless there is 10,000, 20,000 or 30,000 dollars in the bank and there are very few lottery joints that start with less than $10,000" (City of Vancouver Archives, Vancouver Police Fonds, Series 181, Vol. 5, 2064).

Discussion and Analysis: Strain Theory as an Explanation for Early Chinese Organized Crime

The racist, xenophobic, anti-Chinese, and anti-immigrant media of the early twentieth century had a field day with the numerous police reports of Chinese involvement in gambling, prostitution, and drug trafficking, and used the information as a basis to push for a ban on any further emigration of Chinese nationals to Canada. In 1907, *The Victoria Times* referred to the Chinese in BC as "a vast alien colony," unassimilated, uncultured, and "bound together in a secret and defensive organization with fewer wants and a lower standard of living than their neighbours, maintaining intact their peculiar customs and characteristics, morals and ideals of home and family life," and which, by the pressure of their very numbers, can only serve to undermine "the very foundations of the white man's well being" (as cited in Appleton & Clark, 1990: 6). A 1902 *Toronto Star* article called Chinese immigrants "jackal-like" for retaining their ancestry while in their adopted country (*The Toronto Star*, February 15, 1902). Chinese immigrants were even accused of "driving the white people out of British Columbia, and if they are not stopped will soon drive them out of Alberta, Saskatchewan and Manitoba" (*The Globe*, August 27, 1908). Anti-Chinese sentiments were not restricted to the media. A 1885 resolution presented in the British Columbia Legislature that urged the Dominion Government to curtail Chinese immigration argued, "The Chinese are alien in sentiment and habits" and the migrant labourers were nothing more than "the slaves or coolies of the Chinese race, accustomed to live on the poorest fare, and in the meanest manner, and hence their presence tends to the degradation of the white labouring classes" (as cited in *The Globe*, March 25, 1885).

The greatest fear among the white population was that the seemingly rampant vices within the Chinese community would spread to the broader Canadian society. In 1885, *The Globe* newspaper wrote that opium smoking appeared to be extending "throughout the province to the demoralization of the native races," a calculated strategy by the Chinese to "encourage the use of this drug amongst others of our own raising population" (*The Globe*, March 25, 1885). The Chinese were viewed not simply as consumers of opium, but as the exclusive purveyor of the narcotic. According to the 1885 Royal Commission of Chinese Immigration, "Opium is the Chinese evil" and "is used in every Oriental house...." Further, "the evil is growing with whites" and the commission claimed to have been told, "on good authority that white girls of respectable parents use it. The Chinese have taught white men and women, and boys and girls, to smoke opium" (Royal Commission on Chinese Immigration, 1885: 14, 48). As Canadian Magistrate Emily Murphy disgorges in her 1922 book *The Black Candle*, the peddling of opium beyond their own race was part of a "well-defined propaganda among the aliens of color to bring about the degeneration of the white race" (Murphy, 1922a: 188–89).

The reality of the early Chinese experience in North America, of course, was quite the opposite of the dreadfully stereotypical and racist portrayals put forth by newspapers, politicians, and "Anti-Asiatic" groups. Like many racialized ghettos, the various Chinatowns of Canada and the United States have wrongly been held out as symbols of the insular and clannish Chinese community. Instead, they were formed as the first and subsequent waves of Chinese settlers banded together for protection in the face of racial hatred, ethnicity-based herding, violence, and legislative disenfranchisement. Some cities went so far as to adopt restrictive by-laws to prevent the Chinese from buying property beyond the boundaries of the Chinatown enclave. Chinese labourers were excluded from unions, paid lower wages than their white counterparts, driven out of small towns and work camps, denied licences in certain professions (medicine, law, and teaching), and in some provinces forbidden to work on government-funded construction projects. Fears that the Chinese male was out to anaesthetize, seduce, and corrupt white women prompted laws in numerous jurisdictions prohibiting the latter from working in Chinese businesses. Chinese-Canadians were denied the federal vote until 1947 and the provincial vote in BC until 1949. Of all the immigrant groups arriving in Canada, only the Chinese had to pay a fee to settle here, the infamous "head tax" that was initially set at $50 in 1885, and then rose to $100 in 1902 and $500 in 1903. In 1923, the *Chinese Immigration Act* (which has been more accurately referred to as the *Exclusion Act*) prohibited Chinese immigrants from entering Canada with a few

CRITICAL THINKING EXERCISE

Given the above, do you believe that strain theory can be applied to explain the onset of organized criminal behaviour in Canada's early Chinese community? What critiques do you have of the application of this theory? Are there other theories from chapter 4 that you believe are applicable to help explain organized criminality within Canada's Chinese community?

exceptions. Anyone of Chinese descent already living in the country, including those who were born here, had to register with the Dominion government.

All of this provides some empirical backing to the application of strain theory to explain the rise of Chinese organized crime in Canada in the early part of the twentieth century. Institutionalized racism in Canada and the United States limited the legitimate economic opportunities of the Chinese population, denied them political power, and prohibited them from integrating into the broader society. In should also be noted that it was the laws of Canada that criminalized vices, which in turn helped give rise to organized criminality within the expatriate Chinese community.

THE POST-WAR YEARS: DRUG TRAFFICKING, PEOPLE SMUGGLING, AND GAMBLING

While there is little evidence that the Chinese benevolent societies in Canada were extensively involved in organized criminal activities, police investigations following the end of World War II did reveal that Chinese merchants, working in cartel-like partnerships, were active in opium trafficking and people smuggling. The Second World War greatly curtailed the supply of opium to North America. Following the end of the war and the Communist takeover of China in 1949, however, imports of heroin processed from Southeast Asian opium began to steadily rise on the west coast of Canada and the United States. As the Kuomintang nationalist army retreated to the opium-rich hills of Burma and Thailand, they began financing their attacks on Red China by supplying the Hong Kong triads with opium and heroin. When it became clear that their CIA-backed insurgency was failing, many former officers and soldiers turned to opium production and heroin processing full time. In their 1965 annual report, the RCMP made note of the spike in the potent "white" heroin in Canada that "has always been the choice of addicts" (Royal Canadian Mounted Police, 1965: 19). The RCMP drug units on the west coast were kept particularly busy investigating the importation of what would be known as "China White" (Booth, 1999; Martin, 1996; Wasserstein, 1999).

As triad members were fleeing China and Hong Kong, police in Canada began to suspect that some were illegally entering the country and settling in Vancouver and Toronto. Their fears were stoked by what appeared to be an upsurge in the illegal immigration of Chinese nationals into Canada. By the end of the 1950s, the RCMP launched a number of investigations into well-organized illegal immigration schemes. The problem had escalated to such a point that they set up a special unit, later known as the Passport and Visa Fraud Section. The RCMP estimated that between 1950 and 1959, upwards of 11,000 Chinese nationals may have entered the country illegally, using false pretences and forged documents. They soon discovered that most of the illegal immigrants were being brought to Canada by a sophisticated smuggling operation coordinated by Hong Kong–based syndicates. The federal government was particularly worried that Communist Chinese intelligence agents were among those taking advantage of these services (Harvison, 1967: 259–60).

A 1959 article in the *Toronto Telegram* quoted unnamed police sources who said that between 70 and 90 percent of the Chinese entering Canada from Hong Kong in the previous ten years had done so illegally. The illegal migration scheme took advantage of a legal loophole in restrictive Canadian immigration regulations that allowed members of the immediate family of Chinese-Canadians to settle in the country. Brokers working for criminal syndicates in Hong Kong offered Chinese-Canadians a cash payment and an all-expense-paid trip to Hong Kong to fake a marriage with a prospective immigrant, who had already paid a cash fee to the broker. Once in Hong Kong, the "newlyweds" were provided with forged marriage papers. "So clever and so expert are the forgeries that Canadian immigration officers have been unable to prove the fraud even though suspected," the *Telegram* reported (*Toronto Telegram*, October 23, 1959).

In 1960, the RCMP located several hundred illegal Chinese immigrants in the country, who were referred to the Department of Immigration for deportation. Among these were 16 Chinese nationals whom the RCMP called the "principal agents" behind the immigration scheme and who were charged with 79 criminal and immigration counts (Harvison, 1967: 259–60; Royal Canadian Mounted Police, 1961: 19–20). In a *Maclean's* magazine article published in 1962, entitled "The Criminal Society that Dominates the Chinese in Canada," Allan Phillips wrote that Chinese immigrants were being smuggled into the country "in junks with lockers concealing up to 200" (Phillips, 1962). He named the Chee Kung Tong as the Canadian organizers of the illegal immigrant conspiracy and contended that triads operating in Canada were recruiting prospective members from Hong Kong, who were then smuggled into the country. Phillips labelled the CKT as "the overseas branch of the Triad society" and backed up his claim by citing an RCMP investigation "that uncovered two books explaining the secret Triad ritual, reprinted by a Chee Kung Tong official in Toronto." While the CKT began as a triad society in British Columbia and continued to practise some traditional rituals, by this time it could no longer be considered a triad, let alone a criminal organization. With that said, some members of Canadian tongs were involved in the smuggling of Chinese immigrants to Canada. As Phillips notes, "three days after one Hong Kong broker was arrested, his Canadian agent flew out to take charge in the Triad-controlled area. Two Canadians, Wong Lai-yap and Chen Ping-hsuin, were among those convicted in Hong Kong as agents."

Phillips reported, "Uncle Jack" Wong, the long-time president of the Chee Kung Tong in Montreal, "is also boss of the biggest Chinese gambling joint in the city, the Victoria Sporting Club. Last year three young Chinese walked into his club and smashed it up" (Phillips, 1962: 47–48). Phillips was correct in that Wong controlled a number of illegal gambling clubs in Quebec in the 1950s and 1960s, some of which were vandalized on the orders of a rival Chinese gang leader who was attempting to extort Wong. Uncle Jack's foe was found murdered just a few weeks later. Wong continued as the "King of the Gamblers" in Montreal until the mid-1970s when police finally closed his illegal clubs (Dubro, 1992: 86–87).

Back in Vancouver, police raided six Chinese gambling clubs in 1979 and charged 33 people, who were collecting a rake-off that ranged from two to five percent. No one was convicted, however (*Vancouver Sun*, September 6, 1986). The Chinese Freemasons were also accused by law enforcement agencies of housing "active criminals" and their early history as a triad society was dredged up to help substantiate these assertions. A 1979 report from Criminal Intelligence Service Canada stated:

> ... consistent with the past, major Chinese criminals are operating from with-in a local legitimate ethnic fraternal organization, "The Vancouver Chinese Freemason Society." Present total membership is approximately 453; of this number approximately 45, or 10%, have been identified as active criminals. Members of the Chinese Freemasons are also covertly identified as "Hung Mun." The "Hung Mun" is the true Triad operating in South East Asia. Because it is now outlawed, they are also referred to as, "The Black Society." Locally the "Hung Mun" adopted the title, "Vancouver Chinese Freemason Society" to gain acceptance and respectability in Canada. The fraternal nature of this society (blood oaths) leads investigators to suspect that certain "respectable" members of this society have financed some large heroin transactions and other criminal endeavours. It should be noted that not all members of the Chinese Freemasons are criminals, but it is obvious that the majority of major criminals are members of this society.

The CISC report also alleged that "the four major Chinese social (gambling) clubs" in Vancouver's Chinatown are "primarily operated and controlled by members of the Chinese Freemasons. Many of these members have been, and in some instances still are involved in the following crime categories: 1) heroin importation and trafficking; 2) illegal gambling; 3) procuring; 4) loansharking; and 5) stolen property" (Criminal Intelligence Service Canada, 1979: 39).

Photo 6.6: Chinese freemason house in Vancouver, circa 1920s

Source: Oargos, via Wikimedia Commons

The Kung Lok

While Chinese merchants and society members in Toronto, Vancouver, and Montreal were linked by police to illegal activity, there were no triads that were exclusively criminal in the country before 1970. Chinese-Canadian organized crime began its own great leap forward in the early 1970s, due in part to the relaxation of immigration laws in Canada in the 1960s. Tens of thousands of immigrants, mostly from Hong Kong, came to Canada, including a small minority of career criminals who saw the country as a land of opportunity and began secret societies and gangs in major urban centres. Not only did triad leaders from Hong Kong receive landed status in Canada under new immigrant categories (in particular, the entrepreneur category), but the influx of Chinese immigrants greatly expanded the number of potential victims for their extortion activities as well as customers for gambling operations. A sizable majority of the new Hong Kong immigrants were young people, many of whom were sent to be educated in Canada while their parents remained in Hong Kong. This created a population highly vulnerable to the triads and youth gangs, either as new recruits or as victims of extortion.

The man behind the first known modern triad group that was established expressly for criminal purposes in Canada was Lau Wing Kui, who founded chapters of the

Luen **Kung Lok** in Toronto and Ottawa during the mid-1970s. Born in Hong Kong on April 19, 1929, Lau became a member of Hong Kong's Tung Lok Society, a sub-group within the larger Luen Kung Lok triad. He ran a number of legitimate businesses in Hong Kong, including a legal casino, and through the Luen Kung Lok he became involved in illegal gambling, extortion, loansharking, and drug trafficking. He was also known to have collected graft money for corrupt Hong Kong police officers. Lau arrived in Canada with his wife and two daughters on December 22, 1974, after being granted entrance under the entrepreneur category (thanks in part to the suppression of his voluminous police files by corrupt Hong Kong police officials). He told Canadian consular officials in Hong Kong that he wanted to open a restaurant in Toronto. His real motive was to start a criminal triad society. He no doubt recognized the city's Chinatown as virgin territory where he could make a lot of money by exploiting the traditional codes of silence and mistrust of police by the immigrant population.

Photo 6.7: Lau Wing Kui

Source: Illustration by Ben Firsch

By 1976, he had established the Kung Lok—which means "the house of mutual happiness"—in Toronto, with a subgroup in Ottawa under the leadership of Cheang Chi Wo (a.k.a. Danny Cheang). According to a 1984 CISC report, Lau's Canadian chapters operated with a certain amount of autonomy, "but ultimate control and direction came from the parent group in Hong Kong." Using his Fair Choice Restaurant in Toronto's Chinatown as a front, he actively recruited and initiated a number of young immigrant Chinese men into the triad society (which masqueraded as a Kung Fu club). Among the 13 "elder brothers" recruited by Lau were Mo Shui Chuen (a.k.a. Danny Mo), a martial arts expert who became the triad's fierce "Red Pole" enforcer; Leung Kin-hung (a.k.a. Peter Leung), who was given the position of Straw Sandal (responsible for internal communications and collecting extorted money); Kwan Yee Man (a.k.a. Charlie Kwan), the group's treasurer; and Yue Kwok Nam (a.k.a. "Big John" Yue), who operated his own youth gang before being initiated into the Kung Lok. Each of Lau's lieutenants was expected to recruit others and operate their own criminal cells. Lau also applied traditional triad numerical labels to the various positions within his criminal society: as the Dragon Head, he was assigned the supreme number of "489," his Straw Sandal was assigned "432," and the Red Pole was "426." The lowest ranking members were referred to as "49" (see the final section of this chapter for details on the significance of these numerical designations in a triad).

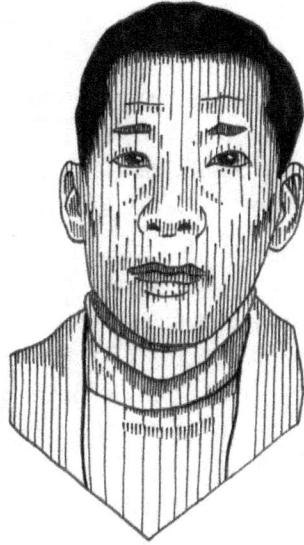

Before long, the Kung Lok was a criminal force in Toronto's Chinatown, running illegal gaming clubs, forcing existing clubs to pay protection, and extorting money from Chinese immigrants and businesses. While the group was most active in southern Ontario, it had connections in Montreal, Vancouver, and Saint John, New Brunswick. By 1980, the Kung Lok had a core membership in Toronto of about 150, but could count on another 250 associates across the city and country (Criminal Intelligence Service Canada, 1984: 7; Dubro, 1992: 111–20; Malarek, 1989: 86–87; *Toronto Star*, January 14, 1982, September 6, 1986).

Toronto police first became aware of the Kung Lok in 1976; an intelligence report that year described how six of its "elder brothers" met regularly in a Lombard Street restaurant (*Toronto Star*, September 18, 1983). Over the next two years, the Kung Lok would be joined in Toronto's Chinatown by a chapter of another Hong Kong triad, the 14K, as well as the Ghost Shadows, a non-triad Chinese gang that was first reported in New York City in the early 1970s and which extorted Chinese restaurants, merchants, and entertainers in Manhattan while protecting the gambling operations of the On Leong Tong (*Wall Street Journal*, August 18, 1980). A 1977 article in the *Toronto Star* reported, "the Toronto-New York connection" of the Ghost Shadows "has been confirmed by police in both cities." One robbery that year in Toronto that was typical of the Ghost Shadows saw three Chinese youths, armed with handguns and a machete, steal nearly $2000 from patrons of an underground Chinatown gambling hall (*Toronto Star*, July 15, 1977).

Following an upsurge in robberies, extortions, assaults, and shootings in Toronto's normally quiet Chinese community, Project Quay, a joint forces unit made up of the Metro Toronto Police, the OPP, and the RCMP was established. Between November 29, 1977, and May 1, 1978, the new unit made more than 100 arrests on a wide range of charges, including extortion, assault, obstruction of justice, impersonation, theft, possession of stolen goods, operating a common betting house, and offences against the *Immigration Act*. The enforcement actions and ongoing surveillance of the Kung Lok and the Ghost Shadows "has sharply limited their criminal activities," the 1979 CISC report read. "It has also prevented open street warfare between them. Unit vigilance has visibly upset the gangs and it is reported the Kung Lok are disorganized and breaking up. The Ghost Shadows remain strongly united but have been frustrated to a point that they admit they have to operate outside of Toronto" (Criminal Intelligence Service Canada, 1979: 40–41). While police did enjoy some success against both gangs, the optimism of the CISC report was premature.

Despite the considerable intelligence information the police task force collected on Lau Wing Kui, he was not one of those arrested. On January 11, 1980, however, Lau was ordered deported under Section 40 of the *Immigration Act*, which at the time allowed the federal cabinet to expel any landed immigrant who, based solely on law enforcement intelligence information, was considered to have criminal associations or posed a danger to

Canada. Lau left the country before he could be served the deportation notice and went to the Dominican Republic, where he had gained citizenship in 1978. He eventually returned to Hong Kong, and later began working for millionaire gambling magnate Stanley Ho at the Hotel Lisboa on the island of Macau, located off the coast of Hong Kong.

The Kung Lok's extortion attempts were generally successful (in that few victims went to police) in part because most victims were immigrants from Hong Kong who were already well versed in triad tactics and traditions. Members of the Kung Lok used this to their advantage and frequently demanded quantities of money that reflected the ritualistic numerical tenets of the triad societies. Demands for payments of $36.30, $72, and $1080 were common. Charles Chan, a 26-year-old waiter at a Chinese restaurant in Scarborough, was one of the few victims of the Kung Lok that did file a complaint with police. On May 13, 1981, two lower-level "49" members of the Kung Lok were charged with attempted extortion and assault after trying to rob $1080 in "lo mo" from Chan. When Toronto police searched the house of one of the accused, Wilson Tang, they found a 100-year-old book on the history of Chinese secret societies. With it was a scribbler, which contained handwritten notes in Chinese describing the initiation ceremonies for the Kung Lok. A translation of the text showed that the ceremony closely followed the ancient rituals of the original Hong Men societies and included a description of how to set up the room in which the initiation was to be conducted. Tang testified in court that the book was given to him four years earlier by Danny Mo. Both defendants, who were accused in court by the Crown of belonging to a secret Chinese crime syndicate, were convicted of extortion and sentenced to two years each (*Toronto Star*, May 14, 1981, September 1, 1983, September 13, 1983).

Despite the fear the Kung Lok had instilled in the local Chinese community, they were not immune to violence themselves. On July 12, 1981, 34-year-old Richard Castro—the part-Chinese, part-Portuguese Kung Lok treasurer who also ran small gambling and loansharking operations—bled to death after his throat was slashed with a broken drinking glass in a parking lot in Chinatown. His attacker, 30-year-old Wing-Chan Lo, who was in the country illegally and who had an extensive criminal record, was convicted of manslaughter and sentenced to six years (Dubro, 1992: 170–71; *Toronto Star*, July 17, 1981).

The Kung Lok was delivered another blow in 1985 when police shut down five gambling halls the triad either controlled or received money from through extortion or robberies. Despite a 1986 police intelligence report that said the Kung Lok continues to be "a principal threat to law and order in the Chinese community in Toronto," its days were now numbered (as cited in Lavigne, 1991: 133). Not only was it a high priority for police, but violent Vietnamese gangs began pushing the Kung Lok out of Chinatown's most lucrative rackets. This resulted in a considerable loss of face for Mo and his gang. Danny Mo's high-profile arrest and trial were also causing dissension in the ranks of the Kung Lok and an internal power struggle ensued.

Case Study: Danny Mo

Lau Wing Kui's abrupt departure prompted an internal power struggle among some of the Kung Lok's elder brothers. The man who quickly came out on top was Danny Mo. Described as a natural criminal leader who possessed "a skilful blend of personality and brutal force," Mo was from an affluent Hong Kong family. Before he became involved in crime on a full-time basis, he was the part owner and maître d' of a restaurant in Toronto (Dubro, 1992: 167–68). When he took over the reins of the Kung Lok, he embarked on an expansion drive through the forced recruitment of Chinese visa students and by importing gang members from New York and Boston. He was also busy extending the reach and influence of the gang through his contacts with Hong Kong triad leaders and other triads and Asian gangs in Montreal, Vancouver, San Francisco, Los Angeles, Boston, and New York. A federal immigration intelligence report dated November 8, 1980, states, "some form of alliance may have been established between the Kung Lok of Toronto and the On Leong of New York. It has in fact been reported that the Kung Lok is now referring to itself as the 'On Lok'" (National Archives of Canada, RG 76: Files of the Department of Immigration and Citizenship, Vol. 1447).

Under Mo, the Kung Lok's extortion racket victimized Chinese businesses and underground gambling clubs throughout Metro Toronto while wringing "membership fees" from immigrant Chinese students in Toronto, Ottawa, London, and Windsor. The victims were often asked to pay "lo mo" (short for "lucky money") or to make a "donation." Police gathered evidence indicating that one member of the Kung Lok extorted $20,000 to $30,000 from various students within a couple of months. Restaurant owners or managers were asked by gang members to "drink tea" with them, yet another euphemism for extortion (Canadian Broadcasting Corporation, November 8, 1983; *Toronto Star*, July 15, 1977, January 14, 1982, January 15, 1982, August 31, 1983, September 18, 1983).

In 1984, Mo was charged with two counts of armed robbery. The charges arose from a March 21 robbery, in which $15,000 worth of tickets for a show promoted by Wilson Tang of Vancouver were stolen at knifepoint from a Toronto ticket agent by two men

Photo 6.8: Danny Mo

Source: Illustration by Ben Firsch

wearing stocking masks. Toronto police later arrested two Kung Lok members and charged them with robbery. During his trial, the Crown told the court that Mo assumed he had the exclusive rights to bring Hong Kong entertainers into Toronto, which prompted him to order the two men to steal the tickets (Dubro, 1992, 185–86; *Globe and Mail*, December 17, 1986; *Toronto Star*, June 4, 1985, June 7, 1985).

By the mid-1980s, a number of senior members of the Kung Lok had achieved their own level of success and fortune, erecting fronts as respectable businessmen while overseeing such traditional rackets as extortion, robbery, and gambling. Some were also branching into more ambitious operations, like counterfeiting, heroin trafficking, and migrant smuggling (*Globe and Mail*, December 17, 1986). In keeping with a general trend where triads were assuming a decentralized form, Mo's lieutenants began operating more independently than ever, with some even breaking away and forming their own gangs. In 1988, CISC estimated the Kung Lok membership in Toronto at 400, although only between 80 and 100 were active members. Two years later, the number of active members had dwindled to around 50 (Canadian Association of Chiefs of Police, 1988: 22, 1990: 36). The autonomous branches set up by elder brothers meant that by the start of the new decade, the illegal enterprises of the Kung Lok had "shifted from the traditional crimes of extortion, gambling and robberies, into new areas such as the manufacturing of fraudulent credit cards, alien smuggling and the illegal sale of alcohol and cigarettes," according to a 1992 report from the Canadian Association of Chiefs of Police (CACP). In addition, some cells were now trafficking in cocaine, which they reportedly obtained from Italian Mafia sources.

The new decade also signalled the presence of more criminal triads in Canada. The 1992 CACP report noted "an increase in the number of Triad members and criminal associates in Canada over the past several years, most noticeably in British Columbia, Alberta and Ontario" (Canadian Association of Chiefs of Police, 1992: 25, 39). In addition to the Kung Lok and 14K, a 1993 classified federal intelligence report discusses the Canadian presence of the Sun Yee On, Wo Hop To, and Wo Shing Wo triads from Hong Kong, as well as the Taiwanese United Bamboo. "Many of these triads have apparently maintained links with their parent societies in Hong Kong or Taiwan and almost all utilize Vietnamese street gangs to undertake much of their street-level drug trafficking," the report said. The members of these triads "are hardened, professional criminals who use the triad mystique to glorify themselves." In 1988, CISC estimated the number of members in Toronto's 14K chapter at 150, although only 40 were criminally active, mostly in heroin trafficking, migrant smuggling, gambling, theft, and extortion. Four years later, CISC estimated its active criminal membership in Ontario at approximately 50 (Canadian Association of Chiefs of Police, 1988: 23, 1992: 25).

The Big Circle Boys

In 1993, the Coordinated Law Enforcement Unit of British Columbia released a report that examined police and court data related to criminal gangs in Greater Vancouver. As of 1990, there were 28 gangs and 976 "gang subjects" in the Lower Mainland, according to the report. Asian gangs accounted for 44.7 percent of all "gang subjects," non-Asian gangs accounted for 38.8 percent, while 16.5 percent were not associated to any particular gang. The age of gang members ranged from 13 to 65 years, with the average age being 23. Fifty-two percent of gang members were born outside Canada and the majority (73.3 percent) came from Asia—in particular, Vietnam, China, or Hong Kong. Twenty percent of the foreign-born gang subjects entered the country as refugees (Coordinated Law Enforcement Unit, 1993: i–v). By the mid-1980s, the Lotus Family, the Red Eagles, the Jung Ching, and the Viet Ching had become less of a street-level collection of gangs and more of what Simon Fraser University criminology professor Robert Gordon called "criminal business organizations"—criminal groups that exhibit a formal hierarchical structure that includes a mix of adult leaders in their twenties, thirties, and even forties and the rank-and-file members in their teens and early twenties (*Vancouver Sun*, December 22, 1998). The younger gang members were expected to carry out such lower-level "street activities" as theft, arson, auto theft, and buying and selling handguns for older gang leaders or other established crime groups in Vancouver. "We know they have ties with gangs in San Francisco, Toronto, Edmonton, Calgary, Hong Kong," Peter Ditchfield of the Vancouver police said in a 1984 media interview. "We know they have elders in many of these cities giving them advice and using them for protection and as go-betweens." While the Red Eagles, the Lotus Family, and other gangs that emerged during the 1980s earned money from extortion, prostitution, and theft, the real money was in drugs. The "elder brothers" in a gang, often working with members of triads and other Asian crime groups in Canada, the United States, or Hong Kong, would set up heroin deals and then have a junior member courier the drugs from Hong Kong to Canada where it would be sold by gang members or wholesaled to other drug dealers (*Vancouver Sun*, June 28, 1984).

While most of the ethnic Chinese that were active in Canada's triads and street gangs came from Hong Kong, Taiwan, or Vietnam, a new Asian criminal force, made up of immigrants originally from mainland China, was making its mark in Canada. Known in Asia as the *Dai Huen Jai* (Big Circle Boys), this loose association of professional criminals and localized crime groups would be responsible for a dramatic upsurge in the scope and sophistication of organized crimes in the country, which included commercial theft, heroin trafficking, marijuana production, immigrant smuggling, currency counterfeiting, as well as cheque and credit card fraud.

The original Big Circle Boys were Chinese nationals, mostly former soldiers and officers who had been purged from the Peoples' Liberation Army and the elite Red Guards during Mao's Great Proletarian Cultural Revolution of the late 1960s. For years, they were confined to prison camps around the provincial capital of Guangzhou, where, along with millions of others, they were "re-educated" in a bid to rid China of its anti-revolutionary bourgeois elements. The prison camps were outlined with big red circles on Chinese government maps of the time, which inspired the name *Dai Huen* or "Big Circle." Between 1969 and 1975, several of the imprisoned soldiers were released from the prison camps, while others escaped. Most headed to Hong Kong where approximately 25 of them formed a loosely knit gang of criminals. "With the military training they received as Red Guards and the brutality they had suffered in the camps, the BCBs settled comfortably into a life of crime, specializing in armed raids; their trademarks were their extreme violence, their propensity for carrying and using guns, and their well-planned operations, aiming for high-dollar targets. Jewelry firms, cash-transit companies, casinos, and payroll offices were their regular targets" (Lamothe & Nicaso, 1994: 83–84). Intelligence information gathered by the Royal Hong Kong Police on those behind the rash of crimes revealed the shared origins of the perpetrators, which led them to coin the name *Dai Huen Jai*.

During the early to mid-1980s, dozens of the former Red Guard officers, soldiers, as well as other hardened criminals left China and Hong Kong for Europe, mainly the Netherlands and Britain, while others went to North America, in particular Canada. Some were smuggled into the country illegally and most claimed refugee status upon arrival. By the late 1980s, they had already made their mark in Vancouver and Toronto, where they became known for their violent kidnappings, armed robberies, and home invasions. While some tenets of the triad hierarchy were applied by the original Big Circle Boys to their own gangs in Canada, they were not a triad, let alone a unified criminal organization. They were devoid of the structure, initiation ceremony, formal membership, or rituals. Instead, the Big Circle Boys was made of numerous small autonomous groups, consisting of between 10 and 30 people at any one time, that were scattered throughout Canada (and the world) but which frequently co-operated on joint criminal ventures. The organizational strength of the Big Circle Boys is their vast networking, which means that criminal conspiracies are planned and carried out between different cells (and other willing partners) located in different cities or countries, while individual offenders may drift in and out of one or more cell or specific criminal ventures. For example, Toronto-based Big Circle criminals may operate an immigrant smuggling operation with a Big Circle Boys group in New York City, while simultaneously importing heroin in partnership with a Hong Kong–based faction. The Big Circle Boys were also known to work with a variety of other criminal syndicates, including Chinese triads, Vietnamese gangs, Eastern European crime groups, outlaw motorcycle gangs, and Aboriginal smuggling rings (Canadian Association of Chiefs of Police, 1992: 25–26; Dubro, 1992: 12–13; Gould, 2004: 37–38; Lintner, 2003: 375; Nicaso & Lamothe, 2005: 83).

Organized groups of criminals from mainland China first came to the attention of Vancouver police in the late 1980s following a number of armed robberies committed within the city's Asian community between November 1986 and January 1987. Police gathered evidence indicating that the robberies were being committed by new Chinese immigrants with assistance from senior members of the Vancouver-based Lotus family, whose job was to identify potential victims and supply the firearms. The author of a 1987 Vancouver police intelligence report did not refer to this new criminal element as a gang. "They are more a loose association of people who have a number of things in common. They have committed crimes but so far they are not organized like some of the other gangs we have in the city" (*Vancouver Sun*, August 19, 1987). A 1989 report prepared by Constable Bill Chu of the Asian Organized Crime Unit in Vancouver stated there were approximately 30 members of this emerging crime network in the city, "with numbers increasing steadily." Most were identified as former Red Army soldiers who were in their twenties or thirties (Chu, 1989: 1). Police in Vancouver also began to associate the local BCB with a new form of violent robbery in the Chinese community—home invasions. One of the first that police became aware of occurred in 1990 when a group of men forcibly entered the residence of a 94-year-old Chinese man. He was tied up, threatened with a gun, and then robbed of hundreds of dollars in cash. The same year, Chinese social clubs were held up by masked Asian men armed with automatic revolvers who made off with jewellery and money (Canadian Association of Chiefs of Police, 1991: 44).

The arrival of the Big Circle Boys on the west coast constitutes one of the most significant developments in British Columbia's modern criminal underworld. Within a few years of their initial appearance in Vancouver in the late 1980s, the local group was so powerful it not only put an end to the fighting among rival Asian gangs but brought them all into the Big Circle Boys network in a subordinate capacity. "What we found is that the gangs had been organized into a sort of super gang," Detective Bill Lean of the Vancouver police major crime squad told the media in 1991. Police intelligence suggests that around this time the major gangs in the city were carrying out specific criminal tasks for Big Circle Boys' members. The Viet Ching conducted robberies, break-ins, extortions, and helped manufacture and circulate fake credit cards. Members of the Gum Wah helped in the importation and trafficking of heroin, while the Lotus family recruited teenaged criminals to carry out break-ins, home invasions, and other thefts while also running errands for Big Circle Boys' members. A lower-echelon member of the Big Circle Boys—what the police called a "Street-Gang Captain"—planned specific crimes with gang leaders. He also funnelled the proceeds of their crimes to his superior and was responsible for paying the young gang members.

Within the local Big Circle Boys group, the Street-Gang Captain reported to the Road Boss who was responsible for planning the criminal activities to be carried out by the subordinate gangs. The Road Boss reported to a Lieutenant of the group, who along with a group leader identified criminal opportunities, worked with other criminal organizations, negotiated international drug deals, and along with the Road Boss "sub-contracted" the dirty work to the subsidiary gangs. Evidence of this new coordinated effort came to light when police arrested 11 people following a jewellery store robbery in

August 1991. In a raid on one safe house in Vancouver, police found members of the Big Circle Boys, the Lotus family, the Gum Wah, the Viet Ching, and the Taiwanese triad, United Bamboo (*The Province*, August 4, 1991, August 18, 1991).

Around 1988, some of these mainland Chinese criminals migrated to Toronto from Vancouver or arrived in the city directly from Hong Kong. They came to the attention of Toronto police later that year following a wave of pickpocketing in Chinatown stores and on subways and streetcars. Thousands of dollars in cash were stolen, along with hundreds of credit cards that were doctored and then used to buy $400,000 in luxury goods for resale. Stolen Bell Canada calling cards were also used to contact criminal triad members in Hong Kong, who were working with them to smuggle immigrants and drugs into Canada. Bell Canada estimated that they were defrauded out of long distance charges worth $10,000 a month. The Toronto-based BCB was also behind an armed robbery in February 1990 that stole $32,000 in cash, jewellery, and fur coats from an upscale down-town Chinese beauty salon. On April 4, 1990, they were blamed for an armed robbery of a Chinese travel agency and, a day later, a Chinese electronics store was robbed by two armed men who fit the description of those who had victimized the travel agency. Earlier that year, Toronto police busted a number of brothels in Chinatown and Scarborough that were linked to local Big Circle Boys members. The prostitutes were from Malaysia and had been brought into the country under the pretence of legitimate jobs as maids. Police discovered that Toronto was part of an international human-trafficking ring that moved the women between Amsterdam, Copenhagen, New York, Los Angeles, Toronto, and Vancouver. There were also at least a dozen kidnappings in Scarborough during 1990 that were attributed to the Big Circle Boys. By the early 1990s, police believed there were some 300 people connected to the Big Circle Boys in Metro Toronto (Lavigne, 1991, 152–54; *Toronto Star*, February 4, 1990, January 13, 1991).

Big Circle Boys groups in Hong Kong, Toronto, and New York were also behind one of the single biggest heroin smuggling conspiracies ever investigated by Canadian police. From 1988 to 1990, up to 545 kilograms (1200 pounds) of nearly pure heroin was shipped from Thailand to eastern Canada. From there it was taken to Toronto and Montreal, where it was broken down into smaller lots and then smuggled to New York City. An undercover investigation was initiated in March 1990, five months after half a kilogram of 99-percent pure heroin was seized in Scarborough. The investigation, involving law enforcement in Canada, the United States, and Hong Kong, ended in February 1991 when seven people in Toronto and six in New York City were arrested. Police seized 11 kilograms of heroin and $8.6 million in American cash from two homes in Brooklyn. They also found a submachine gun, several handguns, body armour, heroin presses, and cloth cylinders used to smuggle the heroin from Thailand (Lavigne, 1991: 125; *Toronto Star*, February 6, 1991).

According to a 1992 report on organized crime by the Canadian Association of Chiefs of Police (CACP), immigrant criminals from the mainland quickly took over Chinese gambling operations in Calgary and used members of the Vietnamese gang the

Young Dragons as security and collectors for gambling debts. They were also involved in prostitution and cocaine trafficking in Alberta. The CACP concluded, "members of the Big Circle Boys are responsible for a tremendous increase in criminal activity committed in Asian communities throughout Canada's major urban centres." As the Big Circle Boys matured, their criminal activities became more sophisticated. In its 1992 annual report, the CACP observed that "infractions against the credit card industry are increasing at an alarming rate" and blamed "criminals of Asian descent, particularly from Hong Kong" for a "large percentage of crimes again the credit card industry" (Canadian Association of Chiefs of Police, 1992: 23, 25, 55). In April 1994, a seven-month undercover investigation by police in Ontario led to the arrest of 17 people on fraud charges over a counterfeit credit card operation. The bogus cards, embossed with valid credit card numbers, were manufactured in Scarborough and sold on the street in Toronto for $300 to $500 each. During the investigation, police discovered that some of the men were also trying to smuggle stolen luxury cars from North America to Vietnam via Singapore (*Globe and Mail*, April 29, 1994; *Toronto Star*, April 29, 1994).

By the late 1990s, it was estimated that there were between 300 and 500 people connected to the Big Circle Boys in the Toronto area and between 250 and 400 in Vancouver. By the end of the decade, the BCB was made up of two generations: the remaining ex–Red Guard soldiers and criminals who came to Canada via Hong Kong in the late 1980s and early 1990s, and younger gang members who were mostly immigrants from China, Hong Kong, and Taiwan. Today, if the term is ever used, *Big Circle Boys* has come to refer generally to ethnic Chinese gangs of criminals from mainland China who frequently work together in a fluid network of localized groups, some of which only have a tenuous connection to the original generation of immigrant mainland Chinese gangsters.

Drug Trafficking in the 1970s and Beyond

The smuggling and trafficking in heroin by the BCB was indicative of the growing influence of Chinese criminal groups in the drug trade—and the heroin trade in particular—in North America.

This can be traced to the start of the 1970s when the Golden Triangle of Southeast Asia began displacing Turkey as Canada's biggest heroin supplier west of Montreal. Accordingly, Chinese syndicates were also surpassing the French Corsicans and the Italian Mafia as the world's biggest heroin producers and suppliers. The shift in supply also meant that Vancouver's role as a port of entry for heroin would increase considerably in subsequent years. A classified intelligence report by the American Bureau of Narcotics and Dangerous Drugs that was leaked to the *Washington Post* in 1973 stated, "concomitant with the influx of Chinese, a steady flow of Southeast Asian heroin enters the Vancouver drug trade" (as cited in the *Washington Post*, May 13, 1973).

In 1974, indictments handed down in New York City detailed an intricate international trafficking network that had smuggled close to 136 kilograms (300 pounds) of pure heroin and 45 kilograms of gum opium into North America between 1970 and 1972. The drugs were smuggled from Bangkok, Singapore, and Hong Kong by Scandinavian merchant seamen and handed over to Chinese distributors in Canada and the United States. Along with San Francisco, Vancouver was a key destination point, and nine people were arrested in the two cities (Coordinated Law Enforcement Unit, 1975, 70; *New York Times*, November 21, 1974). By the mid-1970s, Canada Customs was intercepting numerous shipments of heroin sent through the mail, airports, and marine ports, and the quantity of heroin captured in British Columbia continued to increase in the years to follow. This was partially the result of greater drug interdiction efforts in Vancouver. It was also due to the escalating supply of "China White," which was the product of recent bumper crops in the Golden Triangle and a far greater level of organization and sophistication in the smuggling and distribution of Southeast Asian heroin. The former Chinese Kuomintang army officers and soldiers that controlled the opium fields in the Golden Triangle were expanding production while establishing heroin-processing labs throughout Burma and Thailand. Working closely with them were members of Hong Kong and Taiwanese triads who were ramping up the smuggling end of the partnership.

In January 1977, the *Toronto Star* reported that an international investigation begun 17 months earlier had dismantled a Hong Kong-based heroin-trafficking ring that was believed to have shipped over 1500 kilograms (around 3300 pounds) of the drug to North America through Vancouver, Toronto, and New York. The street value of the heroin was about $3 billion, police estimated. Fourteen people were arrested in six countries. Eight of those were named in an indictment sworn out in Vancouver, seven were residents of Hong Kong, and all were alleged to belong to what police described as "one of the world's most influential heroin trafficking rings" (*Toronto Star*, January 22, 1977). By the end of the decade, CISC was reporting there were "six major heroin trafficking organizations in existence in the Vancouver area, all of which are involved at the 'importing' level" (Criminal Intelligence Service Canada, 1979: 12). A 1985 RCMP drug intelligence report estimated that the Golden Triangle of Thailand, Burma, and Laos was supplying 66 percent of the illicit heroin market in Canada, while Southwest Asian heroin (produced in Pakistan, Afghanistan, and Iran) made up 34 percent of the market (most of it entering the country through Montreal) (Royal Canadian Mounted Police, 1985: 4). During the 1970s, Southeast Asian traffickers controlled a meagre five percent of the heroin market on the US east coast. By 1989, they were estimated to be supplying 80 percent of the market (*Globe and Mail*, May 22, 1989). Canada was not only the destination for the Southeast Asian heroin; it also became an important transit country for the United States, and New York City in particular. Behind the shipments were Hong Kong–based criminal groups, the 14K triad, and the Big Circle Boys.

Illegal Immigration, Human Smuggling, and Human Trafficking

By the early 1990s, the only transnational criminal trade that rivalled drug trafficking in terms of revenue was the smuggling of people from Asia to North America. With the impending handover of Hong Kong to China in 1997, the small smuggling syndicates that moved hundreds of illegal immigrants were blossoming into sophisticated multi-country operations that were now moving thousands of illegal migrants from Hong Kong and mainland China.

In 1984, CISC had predicted that migrant smuggling from Asia would "escalate at a higher rate as the end of the British lease over Hong Kong draws nearer. Several organized smuggling rings now bring people to Canada from Hong Kong. Some of these people had made their way to Hong Kong from the People's Republic of China" (Criminal Intelligence Service Canada, 1984: 19). As inferred by CISC, Hong Kong had already been established as a major transit point for illegal immigrants being smuggled from Communist China. In late 1991, Hong Kong police uncovered 15 different immigrant smuggling syndicates that were moving people from mainland China to North America. A 1993 classified Canadian intelligence report documented the heavy involvement of members of some Chinese triads in this smuggling activity. One Sun Yee On triad enforcer was the director of a travel agency that was a "front organization for Sun Yee On," which arranged documentation and flights that moved bogus refugee claimants on board leased planes from southern China to North America via Belize.

In December 1990, another migrant smuggling ring operated by members of the Big Circle Boys gang in Vancouver was identified. Only 30 to 40 people from China were successfully smuggled into Vancouver before the operation was shut down, but most of these had "criminal histories and/or Asian gang affiliations," according to a 1992 report by CACP. "Passports were purchased in Vancouver, photo-substituted and sent to the P.R.C. where a fraudulent entry stamp was affixed. These passports were then given to individuals who planned to claim refugee status upon arrival in Canada." The fee for the service was between $12,000 and $20,000. Four men said to be behind the smuggling operation were arrested. Police linked these men to other offences in Canada, ranging from credit card fraud to an attempted contract killing of a witness in a Toronto court case (Canadian Association of Chiefs of Police, 1992: 43–44). This latest people smuggling case raised fears among Canadian law enforcement officials that dozens and perhaps even hundreds of immigrants being brought into the country illegally since the mid-1980s were hardened criminals, including members of the Big Circle Boys and Hong Kong–based triads. The larger fear was that the Hong Kong's triads and the BCB were transferring their centre of operations to Canada in advance of 1997. Intelligence assessments from the early 1990s reported that some triads had already begun expanding their networks worldwide, focusing on countries with large Chinese immigrant populations, such as the United States, Canada, Australia, and the Netherlands. Many believed Canada was also the preferred spot for triad members and other criminals seeking to resettle themselves, given its strong trade ties to

Case Study: Operation Overflight

The first public glimpse of this new era of people smuggling occurred in August 1990 when Operation Overflight—an undercover investigation jointly conducted by the RCMP, Metro Toronto Police, Ontario Provincial Police, and federal immigration officials—busted a group that had reportedly transported more than 4000 people from mainland China into Canada over the previous five years. Seized documents showed the smuggling organization was soliciting clients in China while offering the same service to people in Canada who wanted to bring relatives to this country. Between 30 and 40 people from China were smuggled into Canada on a monthly basis, and each was charged up to $15,000 to get into the country. They were levied an extra $4500 if they wanted to enter the United States. In one excursion that was typical of the smuggling operation, a chartered aircraft arrived at Mirabel airport in Montreal in April 1990 with 47 Chinese nationals on board. After being smuggled out of China to Hong Kong, they boarded a plane to Panama. There, they received new travel documents and were then flown to Haiti. While in Haiti, they were given Hong Kong passports and flown to Canada, via the Dominion Republic, on board the chartered aircraft.

Operation Overflight led to the arrest of six people in Canada and eight in Hong Kong, as well as the seizure of forged passports and other travel documents. Among those arrested were Chiu Sing Tsang, who was described in court as the "CEO" of the smuggling network, and his wife King Fon Yue. Tsang was based in Toronto and had entered Canada with forged immigration documents in 1988. He had escorts and other key operatives stationed in more than a dozen cities around the world and had ties with Chinese criminal groups in various cities, including the Kung Lok in Toronto, the 14K in New York and Hong Kong, and other mainland Chinese gangsters in New York and China. The operation made a profit estimated at between $8000 and $10,000 for each person smuggled into the country, while overall profit was conservatively estimated at $10 to $15 million. All the while, King Fon Yue was collecting welfare while living in Toronto (Dubro, 1992: 260; *Toronto Star*, August 8, 1990, August 11, 1990).

Asian countries, the large existing Chinese communities into which they could blend, the port systems through which drugs could be smuggled, and the country's proximity to the United States. An additional incentive, according to the Taiwanese *Chinese Times*, was that "Hong Kong triads prey on businessmen. So if their targets are moving overseas, they will follow their prey, especially to Canada" (as cited in Walsh, 1993: 37–41).

As early as 1986, Toronto police reports were suggesting that some Chinese triad leaders in Asia had already moved themselves and their money to Toronto. Three triads, in particular, were said to be "funnelling millions of illegally earned dollars into Toronto real estate and businesses to form a power base from which to direct their worldwide crime operations" (*Globe and Mail*, December 16, 1986). A classified federal intelligence report on Asian organized crime from 1993, however, estimated that only "13 identified triad members have applied to immigrate to Canada—as well as members of other organized crime groups based in Hong Kong." Notwithstanding this small number, the report raised the concern that "These organized crime groups are seeking footholds in Canada by legal and illegal means, often with the intention of continuing their criminal activities in Canada ... We believe Canada has become a significant international base for Hong Kong-based criminal organizations."

CHINESE ORGANIZED CRIME IN CANADA IN THE 1990S AND BEYOND

Even the best law enforcement intelligence information could not confirm whether Canada became home to large numbers of triad members or headquarters for their international operations. What is clear is that the scope and sophistication of Asian organized crime in Canada expanded dramatically throughout the 1990s and into the new millennium. Not only did Chinese criminal groups elevate Canada's role as a destination and transit country for heroin and illegal immigrants, it helped establish the country as an international centre for currency counterfeiting, credit card fraud, product piracy, and the production and export of high-grade marijuana and chemical drugs.

Chinese criminal networks continue to be the largest suppliers of heroin in Canada and have become involved in the trafficking of cocaine as well as the production and distribution of marijuana and synthetic drugs. In December 1998, 70 kilograms of 99-percent pure heroin were seized from a storage locker in the Vancouver suburb of Richmond. The investigation focused on major heroin importation operations by a transnational network made up of Chinese nationals from the mainland. The amount of heroin seized led the RCMP to speculate that much, if not all, was destined for the United States. Members of this syndicate were also producing counterfeit documents and credit cards and were smuggling illegal migrants into Canada (Criminal Intelligence Service Canada, 1999: 4–5; *The Province*, December 11, 1998). This heroin seizure was eclipsed less than a year later when the RCMP and Canada Customs in Toronto hauled in 156 kilograms—originally arriving in Vancouver from Guangdong province in China and hidden in 1700 fake duck eggs—in the fall of 2000 in two related cases. Also seized by Canadian officials was 17 kilograms of ecstasy pills and $1.2 million in Canadian and American cash. The two shipments of heroin were estimated to have a street value of at least $250 million. Among those arrested were 50-year-old Wei Hong Sun and her son Zhi Yong (Chris) Huang who operated the food wholesale business where the eggs were delivered. Police told the media that the mother was at the "top of the echelon" in the criminal organization and was behind the importation of both shipments. She later received a 17-year sentence and was forced to forfeit $2.5 million in cash and other assets (*Edmonton Journal*, June 1, 2002; *Globe and Mail*, September 6, 2000; *National Post*, September 6, 2000).

The large profits and low risks involved in growing marijuana in Canada have also attracted Chinese criminal groups. In the summer of 2005, large marijuana farms discovered on rural properties in various provinces were linked to Hong Kong–based triads as well as criminals with roots in mainland China. In late July, the Ontario Provincial Police arrested and charged Zhi Ji Chu after discovering more than 21,000 plants on a farm near Iroquois Falls east of Timmins. The crop was planted in mounds to make them look like potatoes and was meticulously cared for. "There wasn't a weed in the field," a police spokesperson told reporters (apparently with no pun intended). During that summer, police raided two other large outdoor marijuana grow operations in Ontario, containing 15,000 and 7000 plants respectively. Both fields were being tended by Chinese immigrants, some of whom were in the country illegally (*Globe and Mail*, August 1, 2005; *Toronto Star*, July 16, 2005). In October 2009, police in Alberta said one marijuana grow-op they discovered, which was producing pot estimated to be worth $2.4 million annually, had ties to a Chinese criminal group (*Calgary Herald*, October 1, 2009).

The quantity of the marijuana discovered on the farms, and in Canada generally, was far greater than the domestic market could absorb, which suggests that a great deal of the pot produced in Canada is shipped to the United States. In its 2006 *National Drug Threat Assessment Report*, the US Justice Department wrote, "increasing distribution of high potency marijuana by Asian criminal groups as well as expansion of domestic high potency marijuana production appears to be significantly raising the average potency of marijuana in U.S. drug markets, elevating the threat posed by the drug." The report goes on to blame the "sharp rise in marijuana smuggling from Canada via the U.S.–Canada border" on Asian criminal groups, which are "increasing their position as wholesale distributors of Canada-produced marijuana" in the United States (*Ottawa Citizen*, March 15, 2006; United States Department of Justice, 2006: 16).

Chinese crime groups in Canada have also become dominant in the production and distribution of synthetic drugs, in particular MDMA (otherwise known as ecstasy). In September 2005, the RCMP raided a home in Richmond, British Columbia, that housed an ecstasy lab containing 200 kilograms of the illicit drug worth an estimated $15 million. Police were tipped off after Transport Canada officials found a package addressed to the Richmond residence from Shanghai that contained 600 kilograms of sodium borohydride, a precursor chemical for ecstasy. In combination with other chemicals, it was enough to produce 15 million ecstasy pills with a street value of $300 million, police said. Four men of Chinese descent, including two Richmond residents and two Hong Kong residents, were arrested. A day later, the RCMP found another clandestine ecstasy lab in Richmond in a home owned by Alfred Luk, prompting the Vancouver RCMP Drug Section to conclude that the two sophisticated labs were linked to one Chinese organized crime group (*The Province*, September 26, 2005; *Vancouver Sun*, September 16, 2005,

September 27, 2005). Chinese criminal syndicates are also known to import large quantities of finished ecstasy into Canada, which along with the Canadian-produced pills, are exported to the United States. According to the 2006 US *National Drug Threat Assessment Report*, "Canada-based Asian criminal groups with access to MDMA from Canada and Europe have surpassed Russian-Israeli drug-trafficking organizations as the primary suppliers of MDMA to U.S. drug markets" (*Ottawa Citizen*, March 15, 2006; United States Department of Justice, 2006).

Much of the chemicals used by Chinese criminal groups in the production of BC-based synthetic drugs is imported into the country (illegally, because most do not have the proper licences) through the province's marine ports. In October 2012, the Canada Border Services Agency at the Prince Rupert Marine Container Examination Facility announced the seizure of 14 tonnes of four different kinds of precursor chemicals for the production of drugs like methamphetamine, MDMA, and GHB. The chemicals originated in China and, according to the CBSA, this was the third seizure of precursor chemicals at the Prince Rupert port in the last two years (Canada Border Services Agency News Release, October 24, 2012).

Along with drugs, immigrant smuggling continues to be a major source of revenue for Asian crime groups. Some intelligence reports even maintain that drug traffickers are leaving the heroin trade to concentrate on people smuggling full-time. Most of the illegal immigrants are from Communist China and enter Canada using forged passports and other travel documents or have no paperwork and claim refugee status once in the country. The majority of those who arrive are smuggled into the United States. One Canadian immigration official estimated that 70 percent of all refugee claimants from the Chinese province of Fujian, the biggest source of illegal immigrants to Canada, disappear once they arrive in the country and never show up for their immigration hearing (*Edmonton Journal*, August 13, 1999).

In December 1998, two Chinese people-smuggling networks were dismantled and 47 people were arrested by Canadian and American authorities. Over a period of at least two years, these groups reportedly brought as many as 3600 people from the Fujian province to New York State through Vancouver, Toronto, and ultimately the Akwesasne reserve, which straddles the Ontario–New York state border. Most had been provided with fake passports and other travel documents to get into Canada and had passed through one or more intermediary countries before arriving by plane in Vancouver or Toronto. Once in Canada, they were instructed to claim refugee status. The fee was as much as $50,000 per person and all of the passengers had to pay a deposit before leaving China. Once in New York City, many were held until they worked off their debts in restaurants, sweatshops, and brothels (Criminal Intelligence Service Canada, 1999: 8; *Montreal Gazette*, December 11, 1998; *Ottawa Citizen*, December 10, 1998; *The Province*, December 10, 1998).

Asian migrant smuggling has also become critically interconnected with the sex trade in Canada and the United States. According to a 1993 classified Canadian intelligence report on Asian organized crime in Canada,

With the growing involvement of Asian crime syndicates, the Asian sex trade has become big business. Many of the women, wanting to escape poverty or menial jobs at home, are lured to Canada with promises of waitressing or office employment. Upon arrival here, however, many are kept virtually as slaves, their passports and papers confiscated. They undertake to repay their fare from their earnings while their employers contrive that they remain in debt for as long as they continue to attract punters. The women are often sent to other syndicate-owned brothels in major urban communities and, during the transit may be used as narcotics couriers.

In September 1997, police and immigration officials in Canada and the United States arrested around 40 people involved in a prostitution ring that smuggled women from Thailand and Malaysia into North America through Vancouver. They were then forced to work in brothels and massage parlours in Vancouver, Toronto, and Los Angeles. The women, who ranged in age from 16 to 30, were recruited by brokers working for Hong Kong–based syndicates. They were made to work off debts that were as much as $40,000. The prostitution ring was estimated to have made between $2 and $3 million a year (Criminal Intelligence Service Canada, 1998: 3). In April 2015, police charged seven people they alleged were members of an Asia-based organized crime syndicate that exploited at least 500 women hailing mostly from China and Korea. The women were smuggled into Canada illegally and then were forced into the sex trade, working in bawdy houses in Halifax, Montreal, Ottawa, Toronto, Winnipeg, Calgary, Edmonton, and Vancouver (Associated Press, April 12, 2015; Canadian Press, April 4, 2015).

Asian crime groups still have a hand in illegal gaming in Canada, including professional-grade underground mahjong clubs, casinos, lotteries, and sports betting. Some of these gambling operations come with their own "credit" department, while Chinese loansharking operations have also been popping up at legal casinos that attract Asian gamblers. In 2001, the Ontario Provincial Police wrapped up a two-year investigation into a group of Chinese men who had been running a loansharking operation inside Casino Rama in Orillia. The group typically charged borrowers 10 percent interest for a three-day loan—the equivalent of 1200 percent annually (Stock, 2001: 26–27). In December 2015, police in Toronto said 28 illegal gaming houses and 5 illegal casinos linked to Chinese organized crime were operating in the Kennedy Road and Finch Avenue area in Scarborough. Three of the casinos were shut down by police and three suspects of Chinese heritage were arrested and charged with keeping a common gaming house. As part of the raids, police said they seized cash, drugs, firearms, baccarat and mahjong tables, slot machines, and other gaming equipment. The size and sophistication of the illegal gaming houses identified by Toronto police varied; the smallest ones accommodate between 15 and 20 people at a few tables, while the larger ones resemble fully operational casinos with 8 to 10 large tables and a number of slot machines. Most of the illegal gaming houses were located in commercial properties and leased out under the guise of being a social club. "These aren't your little mom-and-pop operations and these aren't a couple of guys in garage gambling. These are miniature versions of casinos," the police spokesperson told the media (*CityNews*, October 9, 2015; CP24.com, October 9, 2015; *CTV News*, October 9, 2015a).

In 2013, Detective James Fisher, an expert on Chinese organized crime with the Vancouver Police Department, testified at a 2013 Canadian deportation hearing for Lai Tong Sang, a Chinese national who was eventually deported to China due to his alleged ties to the Wo On Lok Triad in Macau. Fisher said the triads based in China and its two administrative regions, Hong Kong and Macau, continue to have influence in Canada. These include the Lotus Gang, 14K, and the Wo On Lok. "Most of the triads that we have encountered in Canada have an origin in Hong Kong but they operate independently in Canada," Fisher said. "For example, 14K in Vancouver would have a leader here that controls a number of people. He would be related to Hong Kong through a brotherhood, but would not necessarily have to follow orders handed down by Hong Kong" (Canadian Press, February 28, 2013). British Columbia and Ontario continue to be the main bases of operation for Chinese criminal groups and networks, although they have established a presence in almost every province. No longer do they confine their activities to large cities, but are also moving into smaller towns and rural areas where they set up credit card or cigarette counterfeiting plants, operate marijuana farms, or sell heroin at the retail level.

ANALYZING CHINESE ORGANIZED CRIME

The preceding historical description provides some indication of the characteristics of COC in Canada. Using the taxonomy of a criminal organization created in chapter 3, this section examines in more detail the salient characteristics of COC in this country, with emphasis on the Chinese triads (and to a lesser extent, the Big Circle Boys and the criminal network that subsequently grew out of it).

Organizational

Multiple Offenders
Like other dominant organized crime genres, the groups and networks that constitute COC are made up of multiple offenders. Given the secretive and loose structure of triads in Asia and in Canada, it is difficult to determine the exact number of members of individual societies. Even the triad leaders themselves are uncertain of the total number of their followers given their loose structure today (Royal Canadian Mounted Police, 1997: 29–31). In some cases, the larger triad groups in Canada are estimated to have between 80 and 100 members. Others, such as Toronto's Kung Lok, may only have between 25 and 30 members at any one time. Most of the large estimates of the

memberships of triads—especially those that claim membership to be in the tens of thousands—likely include a vast array of individuals associated with the triads, but who are not necessarily members. Regardless, the network of career and some-time offenders that make up COC in Canada today is in the hundreds and perhaps the thousands. And as the previous sections have documented, even within one particular criminal conspiracy, there are multiple people involved.

A Systematic Pattern to the Relationship among the Offenders/Specialization and Division of Labour

As far as an infrastructure for criminal activity is concerned, Chinese triads include both those that traditionally operate as fraternal societies (which may include members involved in criminal activities) as well as those established expressly for criminal purposes and whose membership is made up almost exclusively of professional criminals. Regardless, Chinese triads have traditionally been viewed as self-contained hierarchical associations. A traditional triad society has been referred to as a lodge, and historically, most lodges have a similar organizational structure that determines the level of power and specific responsibilities assigned to each position. Not all modern triads use a formal ranking system, although many still adhere to the traditional triad hierarchy. Traditionally, the titles of the officers of the triad are highly ritualistic and influenced by numerology. The **Dragon Head** (*Shan Chu* or *Chu Chi*) is the leader or head of the society. In some triads that also operate openly as a fraternal club, he may be known informally as the president; in other, less structured triad lodges he is the *Dai Lo* or **Elder Brother**. Below him are three positions of equal rank. The first is the deputy leader (the *Fu Chan Chu*), also known as the Second Route Marshall or the Assistant Mountain Lord, who serves as a key advisor for the Dragon Head and may make decisions in his absence. At the same level in the hierarchy are two other officials: the Ceremony Master or Incense Master (*Heung Chu*) and the Vanguard (*Sin Fung*), both of whom are responsible for administering the triad rituals and ceremonies and may have the power to discipline members. At the next level of the hierarchy are three positions. The **White Paper Fan** (*Pak Tze Sin*) acts as a general administrator and advisor and in criminal circumstances may be responsible for paying off police and gathering intelligence information. The **Red Pole** (*Hung Kwan*) functions as the triad's enforcer and is responsible for carrying out internal discipline and ensuring external security. The **Straw Sandal** (*Chou Hai*) is responsible for internal communications and may also collect extorted money. Finally, there are the rank-and-file members, or soldiers, known as *Say Gou Zai* (Hamilton, 1987: 6; Main, 1991: 159). At the lowest level of the triad are the **49** members (ordinary members or soldiers) and the **Blue Lanterns** (new recruits who have yet to be inducted into the society).

In more recent years, according to Chu (2007: 87), the organizational structure of triad societies has become flexible and decentralized. The traditional rank system has been largely reduced to three: Red Pole (society leader), 49 (ordinary members), and Blue Lanterns (new recruits).

```
┌─────────────────────┐
│    Dragon Head /     │
│  Mountain Master /   │
│      Shan Chai       │
└─────────────────────┘
```

┌──────────────────┐ ┌──────────────────────┐ ┌──────────────────────┐
│ The Vanguard /   │ │   The Deputy /   │ │ The Ceremony Master / │
│   Sin Fung   │ │ Deputy Mountain Master / │ │   Incense Master /   │
│   │ │   Fu Shan Chai   │ │   Heung Chu   │
└──────────────────┘ └──────────────────────┘ └──────────────────────┘

┌──────────────────┐ ┌──────────────────────┐ ┌──────────────────────┐
│   The Advisor /   │ │   The Fighter /   │ │ The Liason Officer / │
│ White Paper Fan / │ │   Red Pole /   │ │   Straw Sandal /   │
│   Pak Tze Sin   │ │   Hung Kwan   │ │   Chou Hai   │
└──────────────────┘ └──────────────────────┘ └──────────────────────┘

┌──────────────────┐ ┌──────────────────────┐
│ Ordinary Member / │ │ Temporary Member /   │
│   49 /   │ │   Blue Lantern /   │
│   Say Gou Zai   │ │   Lan Tang Lung   │
└──────────────────┘ └──────────────────────┘

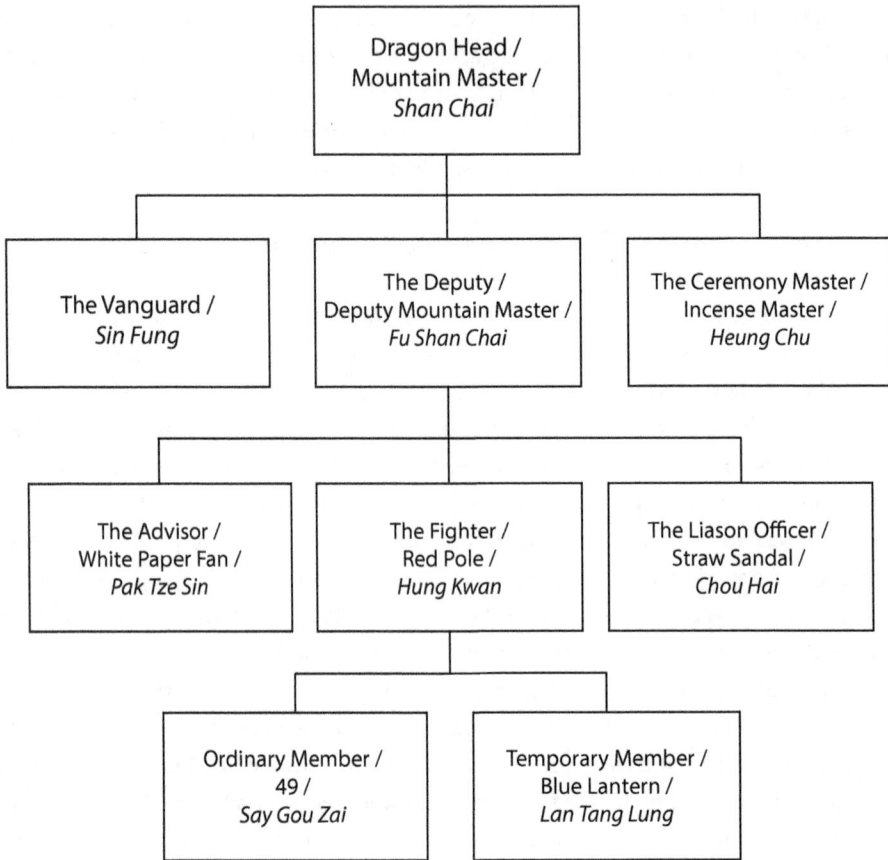

Figure 6.1: Traditional organizational structure of a triad

Triad members and subgroups usually operate with great autonomy from the senior officers of a society and frequently branch out into their own criminal enterprises. The head of a traditional triad society, who may not even be involved in criminal activities, refrains from telling members what criminal activities they should get involved in, nor does he receive any share of the profits from his member's activities (Chu, 2000: 27). In practice, the leadership of a triad lodge is generally only in charge of rituals and maintaining the image of the Triad as a whole (Black, 1991). As such, a former superintendent of the Royal Hong Kong Police argues a triad society is not by definition an organized crime syndicate (Main, 1991).

In this respect, a contemporary triad society may or may not function as the infrastructure for a criminal operation, and the hierarchy may or may not be representative of each member's responsibilities in a criminal enterprise. While the infrastructure of a triad may not itself be used for criminal purposes, they do house members who are professional or occasional criminals. Triad membership is a valuable asset because it facilitates a member's criminal activities. Members of the same triad will often work together in legitimate and illegitimate business undertakings while those from different triad societies (as well as non-members) will also come together to work on a joint criminal venture (Main, 1991: 149–51). As one chief inspector of the Royal Hong Kong Police put it, triad membership is a "lubricant" that "facilitates personal contacts and co-operation between different Triad groups or individuals" (Fuk, 1999). Adds a former member of the 14K triad who testified before a 1992 US Senate subcommittee on Asian organized crime, "Triad members do favours for each other, provide introductions and assistance to each other, engage in criminal schemes with one another ... " (United States Congress, 1992: 5).

Even those triads that have been established expressly for criminal purposes, such as Toronto's Kung Lok, blend a traditional triad hierarchy with a network approach to carrying out crimes. Under the original Dragon Head, each of the elder brothers had his own network of criminal underlings who mostly carried out extortions against Chinese immigrants and businesses. A Toronto-based federal immigration analyst wrote in a 1980 report that that one elder brother, Danny Mo, "may have as many as 50 young followers of his own. Whether these followers have been initiated into the Kung Lok or are so far simply followers of Mo is unknown" (National Archives of Canada, RG 76: Files of the Department of Immigration and Citizenship, Vol. 1447). Today, most criminal groups in Canada purporting to be a triad are a triad in name only; their structure is not based on the traditional hierarchy and most do not practise the elaborate initiation ceremonies. Those who claim to be a representative of a criminal triad do so primarily to gain respect and to instill fear in their victims and the public.

While the traditional structure of a triad society can be well organized, nowadays triads are only a collection of loose-knit groups or gangs. As Chin (2014: 224) writes, "most of the Hong Kong–based triads are made up of many subgroups that function more or less [as] independent entities with their own name, turf, leadership structure, and niches in the legitimate and illegitimate markets." Given the loosely networked structure of COC, today much of their illegal activities are perpetrated by small cells that come together to carry out specific criminal conspiracies in conjunction with other associates and criminal groups. As depicted in the graphic below, a triad-associated criminal activity is a complex interaction of the triad itself, autonomous criminal associates, and networks linked to a triad member (which may include a criminal triad subgroup headed by an elder brother, a youth gang, or another associated criminal organization) (Main, 1991: 150).

In short, contemporary COC in Canada is very much fluid in that most criminal conspiracies are structured as a loose network of offenders (some of whom may be a member of a triad). This is also true of Chinese triads themselves: while the fraternal organization may be hierarchical in nature, members who are involved in crime do so through a networked

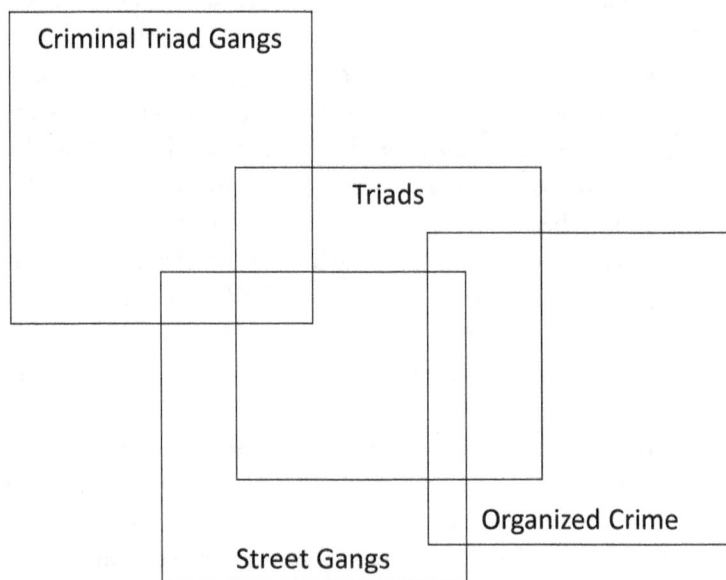

Figure 6.2: Networked structure of Chinese organized crime

Source: Main, 1991: 150

approach. Today, organized, transnational criminal activities based out of Asia, such as human trafficking or drug trafficking, are not carried out by well-structured hierarchical organizations. Nor is the relationship among offenders based on what Ianni (1974) calls the entrepreneurial model. Instead the relationships are more characteristic of what he terms "associational." According to Chin, "contrary to widely held conceptions about Chinese organized crime, individuals who are engaged in human smuggling are predominantly ordinary citizens whose familial networks and fortuitous social contacts have enabled them to pool resources to transport human cargo around the world. They come from diverse backgrounds and form temporary alliances to carry out smuggling operations" (Chin, 2014: 223). This observation is reflected in some of the more recent case studies of drug trafficking and human smuggling affecting Canada in which those involved were associated with one another through kinship.

Insulation against Law Enforcement

Like other organized crime genres, COC groups have utilized a number of measures to insulate themselves from law enforcement. The hierarchical structure of Toronto's Kung Lok, in which lower-level "49" members and their associates carried out much of the hands-on criminal activities, was meant to protect their elder brothers in the triad. In its 2001 annual report, CISC charged that Asian crime groups in the Lower Mainland were targeting high schools with large English-as-a-second-language populations "as a

Case Study: Chinese Nationals Arrested at Large Marijuana Grow Operations in Canada

In the summer of 2005, the RCMP in Manitoba discovered five large grow operations, all located on farmland. In total, 41,700 pot plants were seized, with the largest boasting 13,200 plants. In at least three of the sites, migrant Chinese labourers were found tending to the crops (*Winnipeg Free Press*, September 9, 2005, September 17, 2005). In September 2011, police in Ontario announced the results of Project *Chun Tsao* (Chinese for "Spring Weed"), which resulted in the seizure of more than 20,000 marijuana plants, worth an estimated $15 million, from three grow operations in Pelham, Waterford, and Pickering. Police said all of the eight suspects arrested were Chinese nationals from Fukien province in China (*Simcoe Reformer*, December 10, 2012, September 16, 2013; *Toronto Sun*, September 14, 2011).

labour pool for a variety of lower-level criminal activities, as a source of recruits and as insulation to shield senior members from the attentions of rival gangs or law enforcement" (Criminal Intelligence Service Canada, 2001: 19).

The more common networked approach of COC also helps protect the conspirators from law enforcement because individual members, associates, and cells operate relatively autonomously, thereby making it more difficult to penetrate the entire network. Chinese criminal syndicates in Canada also insulate themselves through the use of Chinese nationals who undertake a particular criminal activity— they are illegally brought into the country, do not speak English, and have little awareness of the broader criminal conspiracy or higher-level organizers. This helps stymie the ability of police to work their way up to the top level of a particular criminal conspiracy. This tactic has been used frequently with respect to marijuana grow-ops or synthetic drug labs operated by Chinese crime groups.

Insulation is also fortified by a strict code of secrecy. Kung Lok triad members, for example, were required to take an oath of secrecy. This oath was fortified by members' mutual pledge of an allegiance to one another as "brothers in blood" (which is reflected in the use of such terms of *elder brother* and *little brother* among triad members).

Specialized Channels and Modes of Communication

Members of Chinese criminal groups and gangs have been known to use sign language and secret signals to communicate. A certain way of holding or placing chopsticks or the number of fingers used to grasp a glass can be of great significance. A complicated system of hand signals may be interpreted only by members of a particular triad or criminal gang, thereby helping them to recognize their "blood brothers." Drug deals have also been known to be negotiated through non-verbal sign language to insulate members from audio surveillance by law enforcement. Given that the meanings of hand signals and code phrases have been published in a number of public sources, it is doubtful that any of the original codes are valid any longer.

Limited or Exclusive Membership

Triad membership is a valuable asset because it facilitates criminal activities similar to the way membership in a business association facilitates the activities of a legitimate businessperson: "While triad leadership does not always initiate and direct the activities of all the triad members, triad clearly serve as international networking associations that facilitate such activity" (United States Congress, 1992: 36). One of the prime factors that limit membership or sustained involvement in COC is ethnicity. While Chinese criminal groups have worked with other criminal professionals and groups outside their ethnicity, membership in a triad is generally restricted to ethnic Chinese. With that said, the Kung Lok triad did open its membership to those whose origins lie in other Asian countries, such as Vietnam (although preference was given to Vietnamese men with Chinese lineage).

Regardless of ethnicity, membership in a traditional triad is a lifelong commitment and absolute loyalty is demanded and expected. To become a member of a triad, certain rites must be followed by the recruit. Initiates into a triad society are required to pay an entrance fee. They must also obtain a sponsor, to whom a further fee is payable—often far in excess of the entrance fee. Sponsorship is a private arrangement and is only reached after the initiate's credentials have been thoroughly checked.

For criminal triads, the intricate initiation ceremony is not simply an opportunity to pay homage to the history and traditions of the Hong Men society, it is meant to instill awe, respect, fear, loyalty, and discipline among new recruits. Toronto's Kung Lok was believed to have used a variation of this traditional ceremony when it initiated many of its members during the 1970s and early 1980s. One teenaged inductee of a Kung Lok initiation ceremony held in Ottawa told police it included the beheading of a live chicken and the ritual drinking of blood from each prospect. Eyewitnesses also described an extravagant altar in the makeshift lodge that was adorned with the name of the Canadian Kung Lok founder, Lau Wing Kui. These elaborate ceremonies are rarely performed by present-day triads (the AIDS scare in the 1980s put an end to drinking of human blood).

Recruitment

During the 1950s, the Chinese organizers of illegal immigrant schemes into Canada were known to recruit prospective members from Hong Kong, who were then smuggled into the country. Using his restaurant in Toronto's Chinatown as a front, the original Dragon Head of the Kung Lok actively recruited and initiated the society's elder brothers from a pool of young immigrant Chinese men. A 1979 intelligence report prepared by the Toronto office of the federal immigration department described how members of the Kung Lok were trying to recruit from the city's secondary schools as well as the Erindale campus of

Case Study: Traditional Triad Initiation Ceremony

A traditional triad membership ceremony is overseen by the Incense Master and the Vanguard and can take up to eight hours to complete. The ceremony is held in a triad "lodge," which can be any place as long as it is properly decorated with the appropriate flags, banners, and name of the Dragon Head. Upon entering the designated lodge, the initiate passes through three "gates" (the various offshoots of the original secret societies were often referred to as "Hong Gates"). Before passing through the first gate (which contains a written warning that reads: "On entering the door, do not proceed further if you are not loyal"), the recruit does a ritual dance. He then passes through an archway made up of crossed swords, a process called "Passing the Mountain of Knives." The second gate is named the "Loyalty and Righteousness Hall," and a sign on the arch announces: "Before the gate of loyalty and righteousness all men are equal." After passing through this gate, the recruit pays his fee, which is handed over to the Vanguard in a red envelope (extortion victims have also been known to hand over money to triad members in red envelopes). The sign on the third arch states, "Through the Heaven and Earth Circle Are Born the Hong Heroes." Beyond this arch is the third gate, the "Heaven and Earth Circle," which is often a bamboo hoop. Passing through the hoop is meant to represent the initiate's rebirth into the world of the triad society. On the other side of the circle is the main hall. The prospective member stands before an altar at the end of the hall and listens to triad poetry read by senior society members. When the recital is over, the recruit washes his face, removes his clothes, and is given white robes and straw sandals to wear. Again, this symbolizes that his old life has been washed away and he is now prepared for his rebirth as a triad member. He then stands in front of the altar and swears 36 oaths (most of which pledge loyalty to the triad and the recruit's fellow members upon threat of such lethal consequences as being struck by five thunderbolts or being killed by a myriad of swords).

All those present at the ceremony then drink a mixture of blood from the recruit and others present (pricked from their fingers), as well as blood from a dead chicken (the decapitation of a live chicken symbolizes the fate of any member who betrays the triad). A little wine is added for flavour and after the mixture has been consumed, the bowl is broken to represent the fate of those who might betray the brotherhood. The ceremony concludes with the burning of a piece of paper, which has the names of those at the ceremony written on it, along with a statement that describes the purpose of their relationship. This final ritual is meant to signify the bonds of brotherhood among the participants. When the initiation is complete, the recruit is now officially a "49" and the ceremony ends with a celebratory feast (Dubro, 1992: 6–7; Lintner, 2003: 388–91; Main, 1991: 148; Murray & Biaoqi, 1994: 31; President's Commission on Organized Crime, 1984b: 51).

the University of Toronto (National Archives of Canada, RG 76: Files of the Department of Immigration and Citizenship, Vol. 1447). When Danny Mo took over the reins of the Kung Lok in Canada, he embarked on an expansion drive through the forced recruitment of Chinese visa students and by importing gang members from New York and Boston.

Forced recruitment is a hallmark of Chinese criminal groups and gangs in Canada. A sizable majority of the new immigrants from Hong Kong and later China are young people, many of whom were sent to be educated in Canada while their parents remained behind. This creates a population highly vulnerable to criminal triads and youth gangs, either as new recruits or as victims of extortion. Some are forced to join as either active members or as an excuse to extort from them money in the form of membership fees.

Recruitment has also been geared toward attracting members with specific skill sets. In 1980, the analysts with the Department of Immigration and Citizenship documented "reliable information" it had received "to the effect that the Kung Lok are considering the recruiting of Vietnamese refugees of Chinese descent into their midst." The fact that many young Vietnamese males had received some military training was considered an asset to the Kung Lok recruiters; "they are all fighters, willing to bully around and have no respect [for] authority." A month later, the Toronto office reported, "that 10 Vietnamese youth (presumably of Chinese ethnic origin) have been inducted into the Kung Lok" (National Archives of Canada, RG 76: Files of the Department of Immigration and Citizenship, Vol. 1447). While most of the recruits for the Kung Lok, 14K, and Ghost Shadows were already living in Canada, the 14K was known to have imported men who have already been initiated as triad members in Hong Kong.

Continuity/Continuing Enterprise

While few of the existing triads can trace their direct roots back before the twentieth century, some of those that are currently dominant have been around for decades. The 14K triad, which is still active in numerous countries, was founded around 1915 in southern China (Black, 1991). Toronto's Kung Lok triad survived over a number of years, beginning in the mid-1970s, despite a change in leadership. The fluid syndicated approach that now predominates in COC means that there is no over-arching organizational structure or centralized command that is sustained over a long period of time—different offenders may join together depending on the criminal conspiracy. But there is no doubt that professional Chinese criminals work together to sustain criminal activities over a period time.

Multi-jurisdictional/Transnational in Scope

A historical overview of some Chinese triads shows that they are international in their scope and activities. The larger triads based in Hong Kong and Taiwan have been known to have cells or and associates located in numerous countries throughout Asia, Europe, North America, and Australia, and work together across national borders for specific criminal conspiracies. The international spread of the triads and Chinese organized

Case Study: Transnational Co-operation among Criminal Triads

A summit that allegedly took place at the Miramar Hotel in Hong Kong in January 1983 is one indication of the transnational networking and coordination within Chinese organized crime and the triads in particular. It was at this meeting that various leaders and representatives of triads and other Chinese criminal groups from Hong Kong, the United States, and Canada met to discuss a possible detente. This subject was part of a broader agenda, set by the host of the meeting, Lau Wing Kui, the former leader of Toronto's Kung Lok. His goal was to formalize co-operation between the Hong Kong triads, the American tongs, and other Chinese gangs in Canada and the United States in order to coordinate criminal activities among the different gangs, divide up territories, and minimize gang wars. Ostensibly, triad leaders in Hong Kong wanted to gain a foothold in and exert control over the Chinese underworld in North America in anticipation of their exodus from the British colony before it was annexed by China in 1997. Among those attending the meeting were Kis Jai (a.k.a. Peter Chin), leader of the New York Ghost Shadows; Vincent Chu (a.k.a. Vincent Jew), the head of the Wah Ching in San Francisco; Tony Young, the Wah Ching leader in Toronto; and Danny Mo, the Canadian Dragon Head for the Kung Lok. In his testimony before the 1984 President's Commission on Organized Crime, Sergeant Barry Hill, at the time a Chinese gang specialist with the Metro Toronto Police, stated that Lau Wing Kui delegated responsibility to Danny Mo to bring the different North American criminal factions together into one cohesive, continent-wide network. Mo was apparently selected as the peace broker and deal maker, not only because he belonged to the same triad as Lau Wing Kui, but because he was already actively criss-crossing the country to form partnerships and pacts with other triad leaders. The meeting also resulted in a realignment of territories, which purportedly included "officially" granting San Francisco's Wah Ching jurisdiction over Vancouver, giving it the rights to control local gangs in the city. The meeting allegedly concluded with the ritual burning of paper with their names on it to symbolize the participants' bonds of brotherhood at the start of their new joint venture (Gould, 2004: 35–36; Hamilton, 1987: 3; Lavigne, 1991: 105; President's Commission on Organized Crime, 1984b: 52–55; *Toronto Star*, September 18, 1983).

crime in general into North America began in earnest during the 1950s and 1960s as Chinese immigration to the United States and Canada exploded. The uncertainty surrounding the transfer of Hong Kong from Great Britain to China purportedly also drove triad members along with thousands of other residents from Hong Kong to Canada and other countries. Among the triads that have or had a presence in Canada are the 14K, the Sun Yee On, and the Taiwanese United Bamboo. The 14K is based in Toronto, maintains a chapter in New York, and operates in other US cities. Sun Yee On members have settled in Toronto, Edmonton, Alberta, and Vancouver, and also operate in the United States. These triads also apparently maintain links with their parent societies in Hong Kong or Taiwan, although for the most part they operate autonomously.

Chin and Zhang (2003) argue that triads were in a steep decline outside of Asia by the turn of the twenty-first century, and they express skepticism of the existence of any triads that are truly international in scope. This is because of a "structural deficiency" in the culture, tradition, and organization of triad societies that may be conducive to effectively enforcing control in local neighbourhoods, but is incompatible with the nature of transnational crimes and limits their capacity to develop strong transnational networks. Broadhurst and Farrelly (2014: 639) appear to agree: "For Chinese law enforcement agencies, organizations with the 'character of black society' are a special type of crime group, and they can be distinguished by their attachment to a particular locality ..." Thus, while a Hong Kong–based triad may have members or subgroups located in Canada, they are largely autonomous from one another and will primarily focus on local profit-oriented criminal activities.

While individual triads may no longer be transnational in scope, organized criminal activities carried out by COC are often transnational in nature. According to Chin (2014: 231), "the existence of a rapidly expanding global Chinese business network, the ease in traveling back and forth between China and the various host societies, and the trust and secrecy based on a common dialect or hometown allow the Chinese in the global village to circumvent the laws and regulations of the host communities." The internationalization of Asian organized crimes was fostered by the escalation of the heroin smuggling from the opium-producing countries of Laos, Myanmar, and Thailand into North America. Other transnational COC activities include migrant smuggling, as well as the importation of contraband cigarettes, other counterfeit goods, and precursor chemicals exported from China to other countries to produce synthetic drugs. Most of these cross-border criminal activities are not carried out by one transnational crime group or triad society that controls operations from start to finish. Instead, it is carried out by loosely organized networks of individuals and gangs active along various smuggling routes from China to North America. Zhang and Chin (2002) characterize Chinese criminal groups and international criminal activities as "temporary business alliances." Chin (2014: 231) refers to "the emergence of a new generation of Chinese who are involved in transnational crimes such as drug trafficking, human smuggling, sex trafficking, and money laundering" that are carried out by a "vertically structured, fluid, and opportunistic" network of Chinese nationals "very often with the help of, or in cooperation with, non-Chinese local people in the host countries."

Within Canada, most Chinese criminal networks are multi-jurisdictional in scope; while their geographic strongholds are the Lower Mainland of British Columbia and the GTA in Ontario, their criminal operations have extended into other provinces. Chinese criminal groups take advantage of their national and international networks to produce drugs or counterfeit goods in one part of the country and then have the goods distributed by cells in other parts of the country. These networks also facilitate the sharing of personnel, expertise, and resources. In 1998, for example, a Big Circle Boys group in Toronto produced over $1 million in counterfeit currency, which was then moved to Vancouver, where another cell wholesaled the notes to smaller criminal groups in the province (Criminal Intelligence Service Canada, 1999, 6).

Commercial

Chinese criminal groups and networks epitomize organized crime in terms of their commercial endeavours: they are extensively involved in multiple types of profit-oriented serious consensual and predatory criminal enterprises that include both illegal or highly regulated goods and services. The illegal activities undertaken by COC in Canada are numerous and include drug production, importing, exporting and trafficking (marijuana, synthetic drugs, cocaine, heroin), human smuggling and trafficking, the sex trade, extortion, kidnapping, home invasions, counterfeiting (currency, bank cards, cigarettes, fashions and other consumer goods), illegal gambling and bookmaking, loansharking, the trade in endangered species, fraud, identity theft, corruption, money laundering, as well as computer hacking and other cybercrimes.

One of the money-making activities of criminal triads is extorting "protection money" from businesses and families within the Chinese community. Triad members are reputed to have control over large parts of the Chinese entertainment industry. Hong Kong entertainers wishing to perform in Canada and abroad are said to have to pay extortion money to avoid having their bookings disrupted or cancelled.

Bookmaking and the control of gaming establishments is another major source of revenue for COC. Its activities in this area include operating mahjong clubs, illegal casinos, card games, and bookmaking, while loansharking has been linked to triad-affiliated underground gambling establishments. COC is also a major player in the international drug trade, and in Canada it is involved in the importation of heroin and the precursor chemicals used to produce synthetic drugs. It includes some of the country's biggest producers and exporters of crystal meth and ecstasy and has also been linked to large marijuana grow operations.

Illegal immigration schemes have become almost as lucrative for COC as narcotics trafficking. In the face of restrictive immigration laws in Canada and the United States, the smuggling of Chinese nationals into North America goes back as far as the late nineteenth century and gained steam during the first half of the twentieth century. More sophisticated human-smuggling operations were detected during the post-war years and were characterized by the forging of travel documents and arranged marriages to Canadian citizens. Today, Chinese crime groups and networks are behind some of the biggest migrant smuggling and human-trafficking conspiracies affecting Canada, which frequently serves as a transit point for illegal immigrants wishing to enter the United States. Migrant smuggling from Asia is also strongly linked to the sex trade, which itself has become big business in Canada. Many of the women, wanting to escape poverty or menial jobs at home, are lured to Canada with promises of legitimate employment. Upon arrival here, however, many are forced into the sex trade.

Chinese criminal organizations and networks are also active in the area of white-collar crime. The syndicates' criminal activities in this area are diverse but are best known for counterfeiting (currency, company paycheques, bank cards, digital products, as well as high-end fashions). Counterfeiting by COC has burgeoned in Canada to the point that Toronto is now known as one of the world's capitals for counterfeiting of bank cards and digital consumer products.

Monopolistic Ambitions

While he was running the Kung Lok triad in Toronto, Danny Mo tried to garner a monopoly on the booking of Chinese entertainers from Hong Kong and Taiwan in Canada and the United States. The companies he formed with other triad leaders in Canada and the United States, such as the Toronto-based Oriental Arts Promotion Company, were incorporated legally. However, Mo used intimidation and violence to force out competing promoters and wrest protection fees from Hong Kong entertainers wishing to perform in Canada. (*Toronto Star*, July 15, 1977). This example is indicative of the efforts the Kung Lok made to monopolize certain illicit activities in the GTA. It resisted, often violently, the intrusion on their territory by competing criminal gangs (but was eventually displaced in the lucrative extortion racket in Toronto's Chinatown by even more violent Vietnamese gangs).

Notwithstanding the example of the Kung Lok, the syndicated approach that characterizes COC today places much more emphasis on networking among like-minded criminals as opposed to aggressive efforts to maintain a monopoly over a particular territory or criminal market in Canada. This is particularly true of the original Big Circle Boys in British Columbia, which set a precedent when it brought together different gangs warring over territory and markets under their umbrella. There is no indication that COC has attempted to monopolize particular criminal activities or markets in Canada—such as drug trafficking or counterfeiting—but are dominant simply by the sheer size of their operations, both domestically and internationally.

Tactical Support Criminal Activities

To support and shield their criminal activities, COC syndicates rely on corrupting government officials, especially in Hong Kong, Taiwan, and the People's Republic of China. In Hong Kong, triad members have infiltrated a number of government agencies, including the Royal Hong Kong Police, which were paid to protect gambling dens, opium dens, and houses of prostitution (United States Congress, 1992: 6). There is also evidence of links between Chinese criminal syndicate and corrupt officials in the government of the People's Republic of China and its administrative centre of Macau, which is also a triad stronghold.

When Danny Mo was leading the Kung Lok in Toronto, he was arrested for his alleged role in an illegal immigration scheme that brought Chinese citizens into Canada. Others implicated in the conspiracy and charged by police included a personnel officer with the Canadian Immigration Department (who was charged with conspiracy, breach of trust, and accepting secret commissions) and a Toronto lawyer (who was charged with conspiracy and offering a secret commission). Revelations from informants that Chinese citizens wishing to relocate to Canada were paying thousands of dollars to have their immigration status "looked after" by Canadian immigration officials and lawyers sparked a joint investigation between the RCMP and Metro Toronto Police in 1982. The following year, the task force confiscated hundreds of counterfeit Canadian immigration forms from a printing shop located in the heart of Toronto's Chinatown (*Toronto Star*, March 24, 1983).

Like other dominant criminal genres, the use of intimidation and violence are central to the operations of COC. Intimidation is a critical factor in undertaking such criminal activities as extortion and protection rackets and is used to ensure victims and other community members do not co-operate with police. COC in North America has been characterized by inter-group violence, as different groups compete for dominance within the same markets—in particular, heroin trafficking or extortion within the entertainment industry. Toronto, Vancouver, and Calgary have all witnessed significant violence among competing Asia gangs from the 1970s to the 1990s. However, this violence tends to be carried out by more rudimentary, street level gangs fighting for dominance in the retail drug trade. Relative to these street gangs and other dominant organized crime genres in Canada, such as outlaw motorcycle gangs, COC has relied less on violence as a tactical imperative in recent years. The more sophisticated Chinese criminal groups have sought to replace inter-gang competitive and violence with inter-gang networking and co-operation. As such, networking can be viewed as a tactic to maximize criminal opportunities and revenues while minimizing violence among competing groups.

With the massive amounts of money generated by their criminal activities, combined with their experience with the extensive commercial and financial markets of Hong Kong's free market economy, Chinese criminal organizations have become adept at money laundering. Triad members and associates have significant investments in legitimate businesses in Hong Kong and in other locales where they have become situated. The triads tend to favour those business and ventures that generate a large cash base as fronts for their criminal activity. Fish markets, restaurants, seafood distribution warehouses, nightclubs, billiard halls, gambling dens, film and video distribution outlets, interior decorating venues, sports and gym clubs, and martial arts and massage parlours are typical of their preferred business ventures. The income earned by criminal societies is invested in legitimate businesses and real estate in North America, Australia, and Europe. In June 2000, police in France arrested 27 people suspected of running a money laundering operation, through two foreign exchange offices in Paris that were connected with Chinese criminal organizations. The value of the funds laundered by this group was estimated at 1.7 billion francs (US $247 million). Some of the laundered money was connected with the illegal smuggling of Chinese immigrants into France (*Agence France Presse*, June 30, 2000).

More recently, there has been widespread speculation that millions of dollars in illicit proceeds of crime are being laundered through Vancouver's housing market primarily by Chinese citizens. "A lot of the illicit money coming into Canada from Chinese citizens is laundered through real estate in Vancouver," Hayley Labbé, a senior forensic investigator with the firm MNP LLP, was quoted as saying in one media report. In August 2015, Postmedia News wrote, "Over the past 10 years, newly rich Chinese have increasingly sent cash abroad by a variety of legal and illegal means. According to U.S. anti-money laundering organization Global Financial Integrity, China leads the world in illicit cash outflows with a staggering $1.25 trillion US leaving the country in the past decade." It is believed that Vancouver's real estate market is the ultimate destination of much of the cash and financial instruments smuggled into the country (Postmedia News, August 4, 2015).

Behavioural

Chronic and Serious Offenders (Career Criminals)
While some of the triads have been around for years, it is unlikely that all members are in fact career criminals. As discussed, triads are a mix of both legitimate and illegitimate entrepreneurs. Some triad members may not be engaged or even aware of the illegal activities of other members. However, it would be naïve to believe that the triads are simply Masonic lodges made up of legitimate businesspeople; while the infrastructure of the triad may not itself be used for criminal purposes, some members are most certainly professional criminals. Canada's first known criminal triad, the Kung Lok, as well as the Big Circle Boys were made up of career criminals. Other individuals associated with COC may be legitimate businesspeople who are only sporadically involved (at the behest of a family member, business associate, or triad associate). In reference to Chinese criminal networks operating internationally, Chin (2014: 231) writes, "Most of these networks are based on family or district, and, while they are not set up to commit crime, the existing networks can be used by individuals to occasionally become involved in crime whenever and wherever an opportunity arises. Most people who are involved in transnational crime are not professional criminals with prior criminal records; rather, they are otherwise legitimate businesspeople who are also opportunists and risk takers."

Rationality/Non-ideological

Like other dominant organized crime genres, contemporary COC is made up of rational offenders in the sense that their activities are geared purely toward profit-oriented illegal and legal activities. Their consensual crimes have long exploited the vices within Canada, from those of the first-generation Chinese immigrant labourer to those of today's consumers who are involved in drug use, gambling, prostitution, or illegal immigration. Despite the historically overt political and revolutionary agenda of the triads, over time their varying ideological beliefs gave way to a purely economic agenda, which focused on profit-oriented criminal activities. And while some triad members have reportedly been used to help disrupt pro-democracy demonstrations in Hong Kong, COC in Canada today has no political or ideological agenda.

Subcultural Norms

There is no doubt that Chinese criminal groups and networks exist within a subculture of organized criminality, underground markets, and violence. The secret societies and their initiation rites and ceremonies are meant to inculcate these subcultural norms within individual members and the triad as a whole. However, it can be argued that instead of rejecting dominant cultural norms and values of Chinese culture, triads and other Chinese criminal groups and networks have integrated mainstream Chinese cultural norms and social dynamics. Some argue that the syndicated structure of Chinese organized crime in Canada and internationally flows from the "traditional Chinese practices of networking" (United States National Security Council, 2000). The importance of networking is of central importance to members of Chinese triads in both their legitimate business endeavours and their criminal endeavours. The importance of networking as a norm within Chinese culture and society may itself be a reflection of another significant Chinese cultural trait, known as *guanxi*—reciprocal obligations between people in personal and social networks (loyalty, especially to family and friends)—which forms a basis for contemporary Chinese organized crime (Broadhurst, 2012: 161). Any member of the Chinese community is part of a "latent organization" because of the existence of *guanxi*. In this cultural setting, formal laws are marginalized and are less important when compared to informal mediating mechanisms within the traditional Chinese family and ethnic community. In turn, these cultural norms facilitate organized crime through a "crucial expression of relationships that helps maintain trust among disparate groups and individuals" (Broadhurst, 2012: 161).

Sophistication

Chinese organized crime constitutes the most widespread, diverse, and sophisticated criminal conspiracy in Canada today. They have long been involved in the importation of multi-kilograms of heroin, cocaine, and precursor chemicals for the domestic production of synthetic drugs. They have also been behind the smuggling of thousands of illegal migrants, sometimes hundreds at a time, which involves a high level of co-ordination. The sophistication of the Chinese criminal conspiracies is also reflected in their ever-expanding use of technology. Triad members have been on the forefront of intricate counterfeiting operations that produce near-exact replicas of bank cards (including the security holograms), government identification (driver's licences and passports), digital products, cigarettes, high-end fashions, and numerous other consumer products. Raids conducted in relation to these counterfeiting operations have discovered an elaborate array of high-tech equipment. In a 1998 interview, Sergeant Jim Fisher, an Asian organized crime expert with the Vancouver police, described Chinese criminal networks as highly mobile, sophisticated offenders who treat their activities like a business, network incessantly, and learn from mistakes. Fisher recounts one raid where he found a member of a local Big Circle Boys gang studying a Crown counsel report on a previous credit card counterfeiting case, trying to determine how the accused was caught (*Vancouver Sun*, July 9, 1998).

Rules, Regulations, and Codes of Conduct/Discipline

Both traditional and criminal triad societies incorporate rules, regulations, and codes of conduct. The original fraternal associations had numerous rules to guide the moral conduct of their members. The criminal triads, such as the Kung Lok in Canada, also adapted the traditional rules, rituals, and symbols as a binding force for their members, to help impose secrecy, discipline, and—above all—loyalty. Ritual initiation, which includes an elaborate ceremony of reciting 36 oaths and drinking blood, has been used to bind triad members. The 36 oaths date back to the seventeenth century, and many of the oaths repeat the message "Be loyal or be killed." The 36 oaths sworn by new members are not solely a reflection of mythology; they are meant to promote the practical realities of ensuring the association's operations remain secret through a code of honour and discipline that is used to control members (Main, 1991: 148). Triad survival depends on the loyalty of members, and strict measures are pursued to ensure such loyalty endures. Discipline is also an important organizational norm embedded in the triads: disloyalty to a triad may result in death. Modern Chinese organized criminal networks, however, have all but abandoned the rules, regulations, rituals, and symbols of the traditional or criminal triad groups.

Chinese numerology has much to do with the rituals and organizational structure of triads. Of special significance is the number three. Each of the three elements of the triad symbol has its own secret number, which is generally in a multiple of three. In particular, the number 36 is used for Heaven, 108 is used for man, and 72 for Earth. These numbers are still respected within the triads to a point where even the entrance fees paid by new members are $1.80, $3.60, $7.20, or $10.80. The sum of money requested in a kidnapping or extortion scheme may also be a specific numerological triad quantity (Hamilton, 1987: 2). The Kung Lok, Toronto's first known triad, often demanded $36.30 as part of their extortions carried out against immigrant Chinese high school students. Others were required to pay $72 (the numerical designation for Earth), while at least one waiter in a Chinese restaurant in Toronto filed a complaint with police that he was paid a visit by two local triad members who demanded $1080. While these monetary figures have ritualistic significance to the members of the Toronto-based triad, they are also used to intimidate victims, mostly Chinese immigrants, who are cognizant of the secret criminal societies and the significant of its numerical sacraments.

KEY TERMS

14K	Kuomintang
49	Red Pole
Big Circle Boys	Straw Sandal
Blue Lanterns	Sun Yee On
Dai Lo (Elder Brother)	*Tong*
Dragon Head	Triad
Golden Triangle	United Bamboo
Hong Men	White Paper Fan
Kung Lok	

REVIEW QUESTIONS

1. What are the origins of Chinese triads in Asia?
2. Should the traditional Chinese triads be considered organized crime? Why or why not? What, if any, is the distinction between a triad as a fraternal organization and as a criminal organization?
3. What are the origins of COC in Canada? What are some of the seminal milestones in the history of COC in Canada?
4. What factors can be attributed to the rise of COC in North America? What etiological theories presented in chapter 4 can be used to explain the origins and spread of COC in Canada?
5. In general, how are COC associations in North America structured? What organizational models presented in chapter 4 are most applicable to explain how COC is structured?
6. What criminal activities is COC involved in?
7. What are the characteristics of COC based on the application of theoretical models from chapter 3?
8. What is the significance of COC when examining organized crime in Canada?

FURTHER READINGS

Broadhurst, R. (2012). Black societies and Triad-like organized crime in China, in F. Allum & S. Gilmour (Eds.), *Routledge Handbook of Transnational Organized Crime* (pp. 157–70). London, New York: Routledge.

Chin, K.-L. (2014). Chinese organized crime, in L. Paoli (Ed.), *The Oxford Handbook of Organized Crime* (pp. 219–34). Oxford, New York: Oxford University Press.

Dubro, J. (1992). *Dragons of Crime: Inside the Asian Underworld*. Toronto: Octopus Books.

Lintner, B. (2003). *Blood Brothers: The Criminal Underworld of Asia*. New York: Palgrave Macmillan.

Main, J. (1991). The truth about triads, *Policing*, 7(2): 144–63.

7 ENGLISH- AND FRENCH-CANADIAN OUTLAW MOTORCYCLE GANGS

CHAPTER OUTLINE

- Introduction and Overview
- The Origins and History of Outlaw Motorcycle Gangs (OMGs) in North America
- Analyzing Outlaw Motorcycle Gangs as Organized Crime: The Case of the Hells Angels

LEARNING OUTCOMES

After reading this chapter, you should have a thorough understanding of the following:

- The origins and history of OMGs in the United States and Canada, including the social, political, legal, and economic factors that helped ferment their genesis and proliferation
- The dominant OMGs in the United States and Canada
- The characteristics of the Hells Angels, based on the application of theoretical models from chapter 1
- The significance of OMGs—and the Hells Angels, in particular—when examining organized crime in Canada

INTRODUCTION AND OVERVIEW

The origins of outlaw motorcycle gangs can be traced to California immediately following World War II. Originally formed for the purposes of camaraderie, excitement, and hell-raising, some of the earliest of the **one-percenter** motorcycle clubs—in particular the Hells Angels and the Outlaws—gradually moved into criminal pursuits. As Daniel Wolf argues, outlaw biker clubs are in many ways "pre-adapted as vehicles of organized crime."

> Para-military organization lies at the core of their tight knit secret society. It is a society capable of enforcing internal discipline; including an iron-clad code of silence which ensures that information about club operations never goes beyond the walls of the clubhouse. Uncompromising commitments of brotherhood generate cohesion, mutual dependence, and a sense of a shared common fate. The lengthy socialization required to become a legitimate "biker" and the two years of proving oneself as a striker in order to become a member make the infiltration of a club by the police a virtual impossibility. The political structure of the club, the anti-establishment attitudes and high-risk nature of the individuals involved, and the marginal social environment in which they operate have the potential to produce a clubhouse of crime. (Wolf, 1991: 265–66)

The criminal one-percenter biker gang is epitomized by the **Hells Angels Motorcycle Club** (HAMC), one of the largest and most powerful OC groups in Canada. In fact, the HAMC was one of the first major groups to be deemed a criminal organization by a Canadian court of law. The Hells Angels are unprecedented in the annals of Canadian organized crime in that they are the first truly national criminal organization; they have a presence in every province in Canada, either through their own chapters or through **puppet clubs** (motorcycle clubs that are separate from but subservient to the HAMC). Canada has become somewhat of an international stronghold for the motorcycle club; there are more Hells Angels chapters and members per capita in Canada than any other country in the world, including the United States. Although Canada has about one-tenth the population of the United States, the Angels have approximately 400 full-patch members in this country, compared to about 700 south of the border. With some 2000 members and prospects in 22 countries, this means that almost one in five Hells Angels worldwide resides in Canada. With approximately 180 of these Canadian members belonging to HAMC chapters in Ontario, Canada's largest province can also boast one of the highest concentrations of Hells Angels internationally, establishing a power base not just for Canada but for the world.

While a significant source of income for OMGs in Canada continues to be from drug trafficking (cocaine, marijuana, and hashish), they are also involved in the sex trade, fraud, extortion, theft, and the fencing of stolen motor vehicle parts.

To facilitate their criminal activities, the Hells Angels rely on corruption and internal conspiracies at marine ports of entry and within labour unions and government agencies. OMGs also readily use violence, especially in protecting or expanding their criminal rackets.

Allen McMillan argues that most of the major outlaw motorcycle groups move through four stages of development toward becoming a criminal organization: (1) the club shows rebellious and anti-social activity that is random and non-utilitarian; (2) a police response causes less-committed members to drop out, while members of weaker clubs either disperse or join stronger clubs; (3) the remaining clubs are better able to exercise discipline and control over their membership, particularly control over violence, which now changes from random and non-utilitarian to instrumental; and (4) the leadership uses organizational skills and intimidation in utilitarian criminal pursuits and the group becomes a fully committed criminal organization (as cited in Abadinsky, 2013: 232).

This theoretical framework is somewhat applicable to Canada. Experts on outlaw motorcycle gangs have argued that the growth of the Canadian Hells Angels in numbers, power, and criminal stature is partially the result of the lack of attention, various miscues, and even a systemic ineptitude by Canada's criminal justice system and law enforcement branches in particular. In his 1999 book, Yves Lavigne writes that law enforcement has "failed to predict the movements of the Hells Angels for twenty years" or to "halt or even slow their growth ... The police allowed biker gangs to take the country and gave us a play-by-play description as each province fell" (Lavigne, 1999: 451–58).

Ostensibly, however, it is not the police or government that should take the blame for the birth of outlaw biker gangs in Canada and the spectacular rise of the Hells Angels as a powerful criminal organization. The HAMC proliferated because of its drive for a monopoly in the one-percenter biker world, in the criminal underworld of various provinces, and in certain illicit markets—in particular, the cocaine market. It also emerged, proliferated, and grew wealthy and powerful in this country because Canadian society provided all the necessary preconditions, including a large consumer market for the goods and services marketed by the HAMC. As such, the Hells Angels and other motorcycle gangs that thrive in this country are mostly a product of Canadian society.

CRITICAL THINKING EXERCISE

As you read through this chapter—and the history of OMGs in Canada specifically—identify and critically analyze etiological theories that can account for the founding and proliferation of biker gangs, and the Hells Angels in particular, in Canada. Also determine if MacMillan's analysis on the four stages of development of OMGs is applicable to the Hells Angels in this country.

THE ORIGINS AND HISTORY OF OUTLAW MOTORCYCLE GANGS (OMGS) IN NORTH AMERICA

The history of OMGs in North America can be broken down into five periods:

- 1946 to 1960: The birth of one-percenter motorcycle club subculture
- 1960 to the 1970s: The shift of one-percenter motorcycle clubs to criminal organizations
- The mid-1970s to 1990: Proliferation, expansion, internationalization, consolidation
- The 1990s: Toward a Hells Angels hegemony in Canada
- 2000 to present: The resiliency of the Hells Angels as a criminal organization

1946 to 1960: The Birth of One-Percenter Motorcycle Club Subculture

The first known motorcycle club to be formed in North America was the McCook Outlaws, which was established in 1935 out of Matilda's Bar on the legendary Route 66 just outside of Chicago. The origins of contemporary OMGs, however, are generally traced to the period immediately following World War II as tens of thousands of American soldiers drifted back from overseas. Although home, some began to reject the values of post-war America. War to them had meant exhilaration and excitement, while America in the late 1940s and 1950s had become boring, repressed, and conformist. One way to reproduce the adrenaline rush of combat was to ride a high-powered motorcycle, and soon the US west coast became the Mecca for ex-soldiers and other young men who roamed the highways looking for excitement and adventure. As Abadinsky (2013: 228) writes, the ex-combat soldiers found a release for "feelings of hostility and alienation" by riding motorcycles and "associating with others in motorcycle clubs," which "became a means of continued quasi-military camaraderie. At the same time, the motorcycle became a symbol of freedom from social responsibilities and restraints."

The first post-war biker group dedicated to "mocking social values and conventional society through acts of vandalism and general lawlessness" (Abadinsky, 2003: 5) was started by a group of army veterans from California that called themselves the POBOBs (Pissed-Off Bastards of Bloomington). A seminal event in the early history of motorcycle gangs took place in a small town called Hollister, located outside of Oakland, California. On July 4, 1947, an annual hill-climb race grew unmanageable and violent. Following the arrest of a POBOB member for fighting, a reported 750 motorcyclists congregated to demand his release. When local authorities refused, the bikers rioted and tore up the town. The Hollister riot was later depicted in the 1953 film of rebellion *The Wild One*, starring Marlon Brando, which would help fuel the outlaw biker phenomenon.

According to Wolf (1991: 37), the term *outlaw* was first applied to deviant and rowdy bikers by the sheriff of Riverside, California, which hosted a biker rally on the Labour Day weekend of 1947 that was also marred by drunken lawlessness. The American Motorcycle Association was so repulsed by the black eye that gangs like the POBOBs were giving to mainstream motorcyclists that it publicly denounced them as only a tiny fraction of motorcycle enthusiasts. To draw a distinction between its members and these rebellious gangs, the AMA characterized the 99 percent of the country's motorcyclists as clean-living motorcycle enthusiasts, "while condemning the other one percent as anti-social barbarians" (Wethern & Colnett, 1978: 54). Revelling in their image as social outcasts, the rebel bikers adopted the "one-percenter" moniker to distinguish themselves from the majority of motorcycle riders and, eventually, the rest of society. This label would signal the start of a concerted effort by some bikers to cultivate a lifestyle and image that would give rise to a subculture dedicated to challenging the accepted norms and values of mainstream American society.

Perhaps the single most important date in the history of one-percenter biker gangs is March 17, 1948. It was on this day that the first official chapter of the Hells Angels Motorcycle Club was founded in San Bernardino, California, by members of the POBOBs. The name "Hells Angel's" (the apostrophe on the copyrighted name was eventually removed) came from one favoured by American World War II fighter pilots. According to the HAMC website, its copyrighted death head insignia "can also be traced to two variant insignia designs, the 85th Fighter Squadron and the 552nd Medium Bomber Squadron."

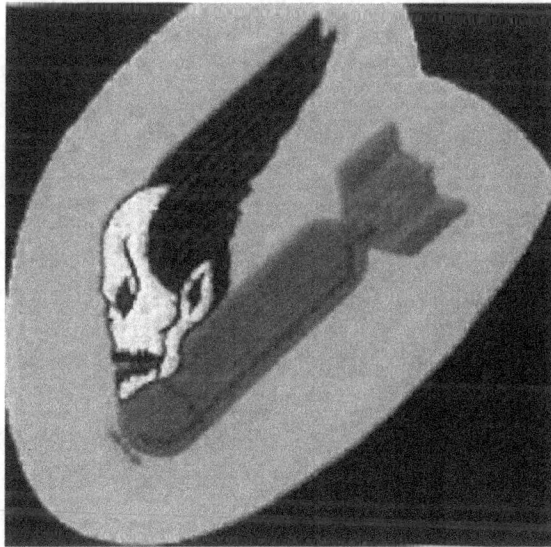

Photo 7.1: Emblem of the US 552nd Fighter-Bomber Squadron

Source: United States Army Airforce, via Wikimedia Commons

By the mid-1950s, the HAMC had chapters and affiliate clubs in other towns and cities throughout California, including Oakland, which would later become the unofficial headquarters of the club. Around the same time, the McCook Outlaws changed its name to the Chicago Outlaws and eventually became the **Outlaws Motorcycle Club Nation**. For years to come, the Outlaws MC was second only in size and power to the Hells Angels MC in North America and the two would grow to become bitter enemies. During the initial years, the HAMC, the Outlaws, and other one-percenter clubs existed simply to seek adventure and to raise hell. There was no intent on becoming a criminal gang *per se*; the bikers just saw themselves as the last bastion of freedom in American society. By the 1960s, members of the Hells Angels began adorning their jackets with the club's official symbol: the grinning, winged, death skull. Also affixed to their **"colours"** was a diamond shaped patch with "1%er" in the middle, an overt expression of their self-nurtured counter-culture existence.

1960 to the 1970s: The Shift of One-Percenter Motorcycle Clubs to Criminal Organizations

By the early 1960s, there were three Hells Angels chapters, all in California, with a fourth being established in (of all places) Auckland, New Zealand. The 1960s was a formative period for the Hells Angels as they began their evolution toward a true criminal enterprise. This road was paved ironically by increased police attention that thinned the ranks of the Hells Angels to fewer than 100. The original San Bernardino chapter was reduced to only a handful of die-hard members, and police enforcement and legal fees left the club on the brink of extinction (Thompson, 1967). Their demise was averted, however, when HAMC members began their descent into the organized criminal underworld through their involvement in minor drug trafficking, which was meant to help pay down their debts. During the 1960s, HAMC members were exposed to the drug subculture through their tenuous relationship with America's other burgeoning anti-establishment culture: the hippies. Needing money to survive, some members began selling methamphetamine (otherwise known as "speed" or "crank"). Quickly realizing the profits that could be made by satisfying the growing demand for hallucinogenics, many of the HAMC Californian chapters began to deal in ever larger quantities. It was not long before members of both the Hells Angels and the Outlaws began manufacturing chemical drugs.

For the next 25 years, the Hells Angels, the Outlaws, and other OMGs practically monopolized the production and trafficking of methamphetamines and phencyclidine (PCP or "angel dust"). The growing popularity of rock concerts also shaped the reputation and future criminal activities of the Angels: not only were concerts an ideal place to sell drugs, but the Hells Angels began hiring themselves out as security. Their penchant for violence (they were often armed with knives, pool cues, and motorcycle chains) was publicized to a national audience after they stabbed to death an audience

Photo 7.2: HAMC death head logo

Source: Lee Brimelow, via Wikimedia Commons

member at the infamous Rolling Stones concert at the Altamont Speedway in 1969 (an event that some say symbolized the end of the hippie-generated peace and love era of the 1960s).

With revenue pouring in from drug sales and their reputation and infamy spiralling due to increased publicity, America's premier biker gang spread across the United States. By the early 1970s, there were ten HAMC chapters in California, eight chapters in other states, and three international chapters with approximately 500 members worldwide (although the majority were still in California) (Royal Canadian Mounted Police, 1980: 10). It was also during this period that the HAMC started becoming much more organized and formalized. In 1966, they became incorporated; in 1970, they registered their notorious horn-winged, helmeted death head logo as a registered trademark. A charter was drawn up that set out rigid rules and regulations for chapters and members to follow.

The Outlaws MC was also expanding in an effort to challenge the Hells Angels for supremacy in the outlaw biker fiefdom. Like their rivals, the Outlaws were transformed into a criminal organization through the involvement in the production and distribution of chemical drugs. As noted in a 1986 report from the President's Commission on Organized Crime, they also "became involved in extortion, armed robbery, rape, mail fraud, auto theft, and witness intimidation." In addition, the Outlaws diversified into semi-legitimate businesses including "pornographic bookstores, massage parlors, marine sales and storage, and the Basic Bible Church … an apparent money-laundering front" (President's Commission on Organized Crime, 1987: 69).

The Mid-1970s to 1990: Proliferation, Expansion, Internationalization, Consolidation

During the late 1960s and early 1970s, interest and membership in OMGs swelled in the United States because of the increasingly high profile of the HAMC and other one-percenter clubs and the return of veterans from the Vietnam War (Lavigne, 1987). Like the United States, Canada witnessed a significant proliferation of one-percenter motorcycle clubs; by the end of the 1970s, there were more than 100 in the country, some of which had multiple chapters. In Nova Scotia, the Thirteenth Tribe was the dominant biker gang. Founded in Halifax in 1968, it was originally made up of former Navy personnel. According to Carrigan (1991: 190–91), the Tribe quickly attracted a large number of rowdy and unmanageable characters. By 1971, the criminal element had taken over, and many of its members had been arrested for violence or weapon offences. Following a police crackdown, the remnants of Tribe toned down their wanton violence and focused on dealing speed (Carrigan, 1991: 190–91). The club was eventually **patched over** to the Hells Angels.

The Popeyes was one of the first outlaw biker clubs in Quebec, with roots stretching back to the 1950s. With chapters in Montreal, Quebec City, Sherbrooke, Sorel, Trois Rivières, Gatineau, and Drummondville, they were known for the prostitutes and strippers they handled, but also provided muscle for other criminal groups in the province, including the Italian Mafia and the Dubois Brothers (Sher & Marsden, 2003: 14). By 1977, the Popeyes had between 250 and 350 members, which made them the largest biker gang in Quebec and the country's second largest after their arch-rival, Satan's Choice. While Satan's Choice had only one chapter in Quebec, located in Montreal, it could count on other chapters in Ontario to support it its conflict with the Popeyes (Appleton & Clark, 1990: 84; Auger, 2002: 146; Lavigne, 1987: 237–38). In Sherbrooke, the Gitans and the Atoms were battling it out, which resulted in six murders in 1973 and 1974. A 1980 report from the Quebec Police Commission described how other more rudimentary French-Canadian biker gangs terrorized local communities, such as the Black Spiders, which demanded that townsfolk pay a toll to use local streets, and the Flambeurs, which gathered "in groups of 15 or 20, or sometimes more" and "spent their evening loitering, driving their motorcycles at excessive speeds by holding impromptu bike races on the streets, insulting passers-by, and committing all kinds of illegal acts" (Commission de police du Québec, 1980: 6–7, 36, 49, 57, 62–63).

There was an estimated 18 one-percenter biker gangs in Ontario by the end of the 1980s, with chapters in a dozen cities and a membership exceeding one thousand. The biggest was the Satan's Choice MC, with nine chapters in that province. There were also the Outlaws, Black Diamond Riders, the Iron Hawks, the Last Chance, the Para Dice Riders, the Vagabonds, the Wild Ones, the Red Devils, the Lobos, the Chosen Few, the Queensmen, the Henchmen, the Bad News, Crazy Horse, Crossbreeds, and the Coffin Wheelers. Unlike Satan's Choice, most clubs just had a single chapter (Criminal Intelligence Service Canada, 1979: 22–23; Lavigne, 1987: 173). At its peak in the mid-1970s, the Satan's Choice MC had 220 active members, almost all of them in Ontario (Kirby & Renner, 1986: 14–15). By the early 1970s, they were smuggling and selling chemical drugs provided by the Outlaws. Satan's Choice then graduated into production and was reportedly the first biker gang in Canada to set up its own laboratories and employ its own chemists. It was at this time that the Outlaws and Satan's Choice helped established Canada as a major source of chemical drugs. The most popular drug produced was a sedative made up of diazepam, commonly referred to by the brand name Valium. Satan's Choice continued to work closely with American chapters of the Outlaws; they provided the chemicals to make the illicit drugs, which were then smuggled across the border to the Outlaws' illicit markets primarily in the American midwest. Marketed in the United States as "Canadian Blue," the drug was so popular that a pound of it fetched $12,000 across the border compared to only $8000 in Canada (President's Commission on Organized Crime, 1986: 67; Schenk & Kesser, 1977: 30).

Satan's Choice members were producing other drugs as well, which became evident in 1975 when police raided a secret laboratory in a remote corner of Ontario and found 9 pounds of PCP tablets and 236 pounds of its chemical ingredients (Royal Canadian Mounted Police and Drug Enforcement Administration, 1986: 19–20). While much was exported to the United States, some stayed in Ontario to satisfy local demand. In Toronto, Satan's Choice co-operated with the Vagabonds and the Para Dice Riders, and the city was divided into three zones for drug trafficking (Wolf, 1991: 321). In August 1977, police in Ontario arrested more than 40 members and associates of Satan's Choice and the Vagabonds and seized over $800,000 worth of drugs, $100,000 in stolen property, as well as nine handguns and eight rifles. Police laid 191 charges including drug trafficking, breaking and entering, possession of stolen property, possession of counterfeit money, and possession of restricted guns, knives, and swords (Criminal Intelligence Service Canada, 1979: 23–24; *Toronto Star*, June 24, 1979). The arrests decimated Satan's Choice, and they lost their supremacy in the province for good when the club split up in 1977 and half their members went over to the Outlaws. The expansion of the Outlaws in Canada resulted in skyrocketing drug production. In a 1986 publication, the RCMP and the US DEA reported that the St. Catharines chapter of the Outlaws was "capable of supplying kilogram quantities of cocaine and methamphetamine as well as 100,000 dosage unit consignments of counterfeit methaqualone (diazepam) on a regular basis" (Royal Canadian Mounted Police and Drug Enforcement Administration, 1986: 19–20).

In British Columbia, the largest and most powerful one-percenter motorcycle club was Satan's Angels. By the early 1980s, they had chapters in Vancouver, White Rock, Nanaimo, Powell River, and Victoria. Satan's Angels were major players in British

Columbia's synthetic drug trade and did not tolerate competition from other biker gangs. As Yves Lavigne puts it, Satan's Angels "strip colors off other bikers like scalps" and run roughshod over the L'il Devils in Vancouver, the Devil's Escorts in Kamloops and the Gypsy Jokers in Oregon. On the wall of their clubhouse, they reportedly had a collection of stolen colours hanging right next to the coats of arms of the Vancouver City Police and the RCMP (Lavigne, 1987: 32–35).

The increase in the number of one-percenter clubs was accompanied by the expansion of some of the dominant clubs, in particular the Hells Angels, in terms of the number of chapters they operated as well as the number of countries and territories they expanded into. A process of consolidation was also in effect whereby many of the larger biker gangs (HAMC, Outlaws, **Bandidos**) either began patching over smaller motorcycle clubs or turning them into their allies, affiliates, or subservient puppet clubs. In 1977, the HAMC made their first inroads into Canada, patching over the Popeyes MC in Montreal (although only a fraction of the Popeyes' members was considered suitable to wear the colours of the Hells Angels). The urgency of issuing a charter for a Hells Angels chapter in Canada was partly driven by the Outlaws' takeover of three Satan's Choice chapters in Ontario in March 1977. In response to the new HAMC "Sorel" chapter in Quebec, the Outlaws established its presence in that province when it patched over the Rockers MC of Montreal in February 1978. A pact was also forged between the Outlaws and several other remaining Satan's Choice chapters in Ontario that formally recognized the members of each club as equals, assuring them of mutual hospitality on biker runs and assistance in the event of territorial intrusions and attacks by the Hells Angels (Kirby & Renner, 1986: 52; Lavigne, 1987: 171–72; Schenk & Kesser, 1977: 32; *Toronto Sun*, November 5, 1979).

The HAMC and the Outlaws had been battling in the United States since 1974, and while the conflict began in America, it quickly crossed over to Canada where it was energized by the determined efforts of both clubs to expand in the country and gain control over the synthetic drug market. Gang warfare spread across Montreal, punctuated by car bombings, attacks on clubhouses, woundings, and murder. On March 21, 1978, Gilles Cadorette, the 27-year-old president of the Outlaws' Montreal chapter, was killed after a bomb planted in his car exploded (Lavigne, 1987, 239–41; Royal Canadian Mounted Police, 1980: 24; *Toronto Star*, October 11, 1978; *Toronto Sun*, November 16, 1979). For the

CRITICAL THINKING EXERCISE

To what extent do you believe the founding of outlaw motorcycle gangs in Canada can be explained by alien conspiracy theory (see chapter 4)? Consider applying both aspects of this theory to the OMGs in Canada: their foreign (American) source and the eventual national presence of the Hells Angels in this country. How would you critique the application of this theory to OMGs in Canada?

remainder of the 1970s, both the Hells Angels and the Outlaws vigorously canvassed other biker gangs in Ontario and Quebec in an attempt to set up more chapters and selectively recruit what Criminal Intelligence Service Canada called "hard-core criminal-type members." While the HAMC was winning the war in Quebec, the Outlaws were expanding in Ontario; by the end of 1979, they had chapters in Windsor, St. Catharines, Hamilton, Toronto, Kingston, and Ottawa (Criminal Intelligence Service Canada, 1979: 20). Unable to make any headway in Ontario, the HAMC focused on fortifying their strength in Quebec, and in September 1979 a second chapter in the province was established. Based in the Montreal suburb of Laval, the "North Chapter" was created when the existing Sorel chapter, which was now overflowing with members, was divided into two. By the end of 1980, more than 20 people belonging to or associated with the two rival gangs had been murdered in Quebec, while another 13 had been wounded. Between 1981 and 1984, CISC linked another 42 murders in Quebec to the Hells Angels–Outlaws conflict, as well as battles between other motorcycle clubs (Carrigan, 1991: 191; Criminal Intelligence Service Canada, 1983: 9, 1984: 1).

Despite the carnage in Quebec, the rivalry between the Hells Angels and the Outlaws had yet to seriously impact Ontario. This was due largely to the ongoing efforts of the Outlaws to thwart the prospect of the Angels' patching over existing one-percenter clubs in the province, combined with the unwillingness of these clubs to get sucked into the war. Despite an intensive recruitment drive, the advances of the Angels were rebuffed by most of the province's established biker gangs, who vowed to remain neutral in the conflict. It would be another 25 years until the HAMC would establish a chapter in Ontario. In the intervening time, the Angels fought a proxy war against the Outlaws in Ontario. From 1979 to 1984, Hamilton became a battleground for a conflict that pitted the Angels-backed Wild Ones against the Hamilton chapter of the Outlaws, which had absorbed the city's Satan's Choice chapter in 1977 (*Hamilton Spectator*, September 5, 1979, September 22, 1980).

Following its conquest of Quebec, and frustrated by its inability to expand into Ontario, the Hells Angels set their sights on other provinces. At the top of their list were two cities strategically placed for the Hells Angels' ambitious national plans: Vancouver and Halifax. Like Montreal, both are port cities and thus fit neatly into the Hells Angels' international smuggling ventures. Vancouver was also attractive because the Lower Mainland has one of the country's largest addict populations, providing a lucrative new drug market for the HAMC (Royal Canadian Mounted Police and Drug Enforcement Administration, 1986: 18–19, 21). The Halifax port was eyed as an important entry point for cocaine coming from South America and Florida. A presence in both provinces also allowed the Angels to establish the outermost flanks in their planned coast-to-coast network of chapters and a national drug pipeline.

As was its strategy in most provinces, the HAMC focused on taking over existing motorcycle clubs, as opposed to starting chapters from scratch. On July 23, 1983, after almost a year of meetings with senior officers of the Quebec Hells Angels, the

Case Study: Yves Buteau

Among the casualties in the Hells Angels–Outlaws war was 32-year-old Yves (Le Boss) Buteau, who was murdered on September 9, 1983. His killer was Gino Goudreau, a small-time drug trafficker who had been repeatedly warned by Buteau to stop selling in Montreal parks located within Angels' territory. Goudreau, whose brother was a member of the Quebec Outlaws, shot Buteau twice in the chest outside Le Petit Bourg bar, a Hells Angels hangout in Montreal.

A former president of the Popeyes, Buteau played a significant role in establishing the HAMC as a major criminal force in Quebec. While he was president of the Popeyes, Buteau was personally courted by Ralph (Sonny) Barger, at the time the unofficial leader of the HAMC in the United States, to persuade his motorcycle club to join the Angels. Barger had such respect for Buteau that he personally awarded him his new colours upon joining the HAMC, backed him as president of the new Sorel chapter, and even anointed him as the only Canadian to wear the "Hells Angels International" rocker on the bottom of his colours. As the first Hells Angels' chapter president in Canada, the savvy, strategically minded, and business-like Buteau was responsible for carrying out Barger's vision of the "new" Hells Angels by transforming the remnants of the Popeyes into a well-oiled, disciplined, money-making criminal machine.

Photo 7.3: Yves Buteau

Source: Illustration by Ben Firsch

Buteau demanded that the HAMC members in Quebec keep a low profile and to refrain from violence directed at ordinary citizens. He also criss-crossed the province and the country, contacting other biker gangs in an effort to establish new HAMC chapters while setting up connections with drug distributors. By the end of the decade, the Sorel chapter had become a major source of chemical drugs for Quebec and other provinces (Kirby & Renner, 1986: 52; Lavigne, 1987: 171–72; Schenk & Kesser, 1977: 32; *Toronto Sun*, November 5, 1979).

Vancouver, White Rock, and Nanaimo chapters of Satan's Angels were patched over. Later that year, a fourth Hells Angels chapter, located in East Vancouver, was formed, and would eventually become the dominant HAMC chapter in the province. For Wolf, the instantaneous and simultaneous emergence of four BC chapters "was a major international coup for the Hell's Angels MC conglomerate. It virtually locked up the Canadian west coast and made the Hell's Angels' position in British Columbia unassailable." By the mid-1980s, the HAMC was in control of "all outlaw motorcycle gang activity in British Columbia," a joint RCMP and DEA report concluded. "The Hells Angels West Coast criminal activity includes trafficking in illicit drugs as well as business interests believed to be fronts for illegal activities" (Royal Canadian Mounted Police and Drug Enforcement Administration, 1986: 21).

On December 5, 1984, the Hells Angels officially spread its wings to the other coast when it patched over the Thirteenth Tribe of Halifax, a move made "to consolidate control of drug trafficking on Canada's East Coast" (Royal Canadian Mounted Police and Drug Enforcement Administration, 1986: 19). On the very same day, the Gitans motorcycle club in Sherbrooke became the third Hells Angels chapter in Quebec. By the end of the year, the HAMC had chapters or affiliate clubs in nine out of ten provinces. They had four chapters and about 72 members in British Columbia, three chapters with 69 members in Quebec, and one chapter with eight members in Halifax. They had also set up partnerships with clubs in Alberta, Saskatchewan, and Manitoba. Around this time, the Outlaws dominated Ontario with about 85 members in eight chapters, although their 38 members in Quebec were greatly outnumbered by their foe (Royal Canadian Mounted Police, 1987a).

By the late 1980s, four groups would come to dominate the one-percenter biker world in the United States and internationally: the Hells Angels, the Outlaws, the Pagans, and the Bandidos. The four had a combined strength of around two thousand members internationally, although it was the HAMC that was clearly on top with more than 60 chapters compared to approximately 35 for the Outlaws, 40 for the Pagans, and 30 for the Bandidos. What truly distinguished the Hells Angels from the other clubs was that almost a third of its chapters were outside the United States (Lavigne, 1987: 160; Royal Canadian Mounted Police, 1987a: 9–10; Wolf, 1991: 332).

Throughout the late 1980s and 1990s, the Hells Angels continued to expand throughout Canada. Not only was its main rival on the ropes, but it was rebuilding existing chapters and adding new ones. By 1992, the province was home to four Hells Angels chapters, located in Sorel, Sherbrooke, Quebec City, and Trois Rivières. They also exerted control over other numerous other one-percenter clubs in the province (Canadian Association of Chiefs of Police, 1992: 14). In contrast, the Outlaws still had only one chapter in Montreal with a membership of just eight and no allies among other biker gangs in the province.

The Hells Angels continued to reign supreme in British Columbia as well. They had an estimated 65 full-patch members in five chapters—located in Nanaimo, White Rock, East Vancouver, Coquitlam, and Haney—and could count on support from puppet clubs in the province. By the mid-1990s, Criminal Intelligence Service Canada was calling the BC Hells Angels "one of the wealthiest outlaw motorcycle gangs in the world" (Criminal Intelligence Service Canada, 1996: 15). The HAMC also exerted significant influence in other western provinces through their ties with other OMGs: the Rebels and Grim Reapers in Alberta, the Rebels in Saskatchewan, and the Los Brovos in Manitoba.

With 69 chapters spread out over 13 countries and four continents, the HAMC had clearly established themselves as the world's most powerful outlaw motorcycle group. As their illegal drug empire expanded, they were also emerging as one of the world's largest criminal networks. Yet despite their growing national and international prominence, they had still not cracked the most prized jewel in the Canadian crown: Ontario. By the early 1990s, there were 14 motorcycle gangs in the province with more than 480 members. And while recent enforcement actions against them took its toll, the Outlaws were still the most powerful and influential gang in Ontario (Canadian Association of Chiefs of Police, 1992: 13).

The 1980s were also marked by the transition of the Hells Angels and other biker gangs in Canada into cocaine trafficking, which had skyrocketed in popularity in recent years. The substantial revenues generated from drug trafficking helped transform the Hells Angels and other one-percenter biker clubs during this period; there was less emphasis on the original hell-raising adventurous, shocking, counter-culture ways, and a greater preoccupation with (criminal) entrepreneurship and maximizing profits. This evolution can be traced to the mid-1960s when Hells Angels' legend Sonny Barger became president of the Oakland chapter. Influenced by his stint in the US army, Barger began promoting a paramilitary organizational structure and rigid internal discipline that extended beyond the one chapter and eventually would influence the HAMC throughout North America. While one-percenter clubs once offered members a hedonistic freedom from society's restraints, by the 1980s, they had become very structured, highly regimented, and thoroughly rule-bound. By this time, the HAMC was no different than other criminal organizations in that their members were focused on profit-oriented criminal pursuits. As Lavigne notes, some of the values that were long held dear to outlaw bikers soon took a back seat to making money:

> Some Hells Angels made big money in the drug business, and suddenly they had something to lose, something to protect. Their bank accounts came first and the brotherhood second. When a member threatened their income, they beat or killed him. The Hells Angels Motorcycle Club was no longer an organization that sheltered social misfits. It became an enclave for some of the underworld's most cunning drug manufacturers and dealers. (Lavigne, 2004: 34)

The 1990s: Toward a Hells Angels hegemony in Canada

The 1990s saw a continuation of consolidation in the outlaw biker world as the three largest clubs—the Hells Angels, the Outlaws, and the Bandidos—expanded in terms of chapters and members by swallowing up smaller clubs and setting up new chapters and puppet clubs throughout the world. Biker gangs were also indefatigable in diversifying their criminal activities during the 1990s; in addition to drug trafficking, they had their hand in large-scale theft, telemarketing fraud, counterfeiting, loansharking, extortion, human trafficking, and the smuggling of and trafficking in illegal weapons, stolen goods, and cigarettes. Their largest source of revenue, however, continued to be drugs and, in addition to synthetic drugs and cocaine, the Hells Angels became heavily involved in Canada's burgeoning home-grown marijuana industry. It was also in the 1990s that the Hells Angels in Canada truly evolved into the most powerful criminal groups in the country. The profits made from illegal activities were reinvested into real estate and legitimate businesses, which generated ever more revenue. Members of the HAMC increasingly distanced themselves from their criminal activities by delegating to **prospects**, "hangers-on," puppet clubs, and other associates. Efforts were even made to polish their image and members became high-profile benefactors of different charities, such as the annual Toys-for-Tots motorcycle parade or charity golf tournaments that raise money for cancer research.

As in the past, the monopolistic tendencies of the HAMC in Canada invariably invited violence. This was on full display in the so-called Quebec biker war that lasted from the mid-1990s to the early 2000s. The conflict between the Hells Angels motorcycle club and its rivals—in particular, the newly formed Rock Machine—was over dominance in Quebec's wholesale cocaine market. For CISC analyst Jean-Pierre Levesque, 1997 proved to be "the year outlaw bikers went from waging a turf war to a total war" (Canadian Press, December 17, 1997). At least 28 deaths were attributed to the conflict that year, which meant by year's end, it had claimed at least 86 lives. In addition, there were "71 attempted murders, 81 bombings, and 93 cases of arson against gang-related businesses and bars, for a total of 313 violent incidents" since the conflict began (Criminal Intelligence Service Canada, 1998: 13). In 2000, more than 30 people with suspected ties to both sides were killed, including 11 Hells Angels associates. By the end of 2000, while sporadic violence continued, the worst of the conflict appeared to be over. On September 26, the leader of the Hells Angels powerful Nomads chapter in Quebec, Maurice Boucher, met with the new Rock Machine leader Frédéric Faucher to negotiate a truce. On October 8, at a restaurant in downtown Montreal, Boucher and Faucher announced that a ceasefire had been reached (Canadian Press, October 10, 2000; *Globe and Mail*, October 10, 2000). By that time, more than 150 deaths had been attributed to the conflict.

In addition to this tenuous armistice, other developments intervened to help put an end to the bloodshed. The first was the arrest of Maurice Boucher on murder charges. The second was a massive police operation launched against the Hells Angels in Quebec that culminated on March 28, 2001, when more than 2000 police officers raided the

Case Study: Maurice (Mom) Boucher

It is Maurice (Mom) Boucher who—more than any other person—has been held responsible for the bloodiest gang war ever fought on Canadian streets. The eldest of eight siblings, Boucher was born on June 21, 1953, to a working-class family in Causapscal, a small town on Quebec's Gaspé Peninsula. At the age of two, his father moved the family to Montreal where he worked in construction and settled his family in Hochelaga-Maisonneuve, one of Montreal's poorest neighbourhoods. While he was close to his mother, Boucher had a strained relationship with his father, who was an alcoholic and abusive. He quit school in grade nine and, a year later, had developed a serious drug problem. Unable to find work and needing cash to support his habit, Boucher resorted to petty crime. He served his first jail time in 1976, when he received a 40-month sentence after he and an accomplice burst into a butcher's shop and robbed the 71-year-old proprietor of $138.39 after threatening him with a sawed-off shotgun and a meat cleaver (*Globe and Mail*, May 6, 2002). When he was released, Boucher reverted to his old ways, committing numerous thefts and before the end of the decade, he had been charged with extortion and possession of a stolen credit card.

His foray into the world of one-percenters began in 1978 when he joined the "SS," a white supremacist biker gang named after Adolf Hitler's feared secret police. The gang folded in 1984, the same year Boucher was handed a 23-month

Photo 7.4: Maurice (Mom) Boucher flashes the peace sign to photographers outside a Montreal funeral home in April 2000

Source: John Mahoney, The Gazette (Montreal)

sentence for sexually assaulting a 16-year-old girl. After being set free in 1986, Boucher was given prospect status in the Montreal chapter of the Hells Angels. By the spring of 1987, he had become a full-patch member.

Even when the ambitious Boucher was establishing the foundation for his future career as a drug baron in the late 1980s, he was still carrying out violent thefts. In 1988, he was arrested for hijacking a truck in Ontario, using nothing more than a board with a nail as his weapon. After he was released from jail in 1990, Boucher kicked his drug habit and soon his ambitious nature and natural leadership abilities earned him the presidency of the Montreal chapter (Cherry, 2005: 62–67; *Montreal Gazette*, May 6, 1987). While barely literate, Boucher was a calculating criminal and had a singular drive to monopolize Quebec's cocaine market. To help achieve this goal, Boucher founded and became president of the Nomads chapter in Quebec, which would become the Hells Angels' central cocaine-trafficking clearing house for the province, as well as its most powerful chapter.

The Nomads purchased the drug in massive quantities (as much as 1000 kilograms at a time), and individual chapters and puppet clubs were then required to purchase the cocaine for resale from the Nomads (*Globe and Mail*, August 12, 2002; *Montreal Gazette*, July 18, 2002). Despite the Hells Angels' growing control over Quebec's drug trade, it still was not enough for Boucher, whose intolerance for any competition set the Angels on a crash course with an upstart competitor in the province: the Rock Machine. Lavigne (1999) argues that Boucher committed a tactical error when he began going after independent drug-trafficking groups, which only galvanized his enemies. "The Rock Machine, independent drug gangs, and a group of bar owners called the Dark Circle, who allowed the sale of narcotics in their establishments, banded together to create the Alliance to fight off the Hells Angels and even take back from the biker gang drug territory they felt was theirs" (Lavigne, 1999: 23). The formation of the powerful "Alliance" led to a battle of attrition with the world's biggest biker gang, which explains the longevity of the biker war and its unprecedented death toll.

The violence escalated even more in 1997 when Boucher embarked on a new strategy to escalate his reign of terror. He began plotting a campaign to destabilize the criminal justice system in Quebec by intimidating and even assassinating police officers, prison guards, and high-ranking members of the provincial government. Hells Angels' informants would later reveal the existence of a hit list, created by Boucher, which included the names of Quebec Public Security Minister Serge Ménard and Montreal police chief Jacques Duchesneau. In June 1997, on Boucher's orders, members of the Rockers gunned down two prison guards. Later that year, Boucher was arrested by police and charged with two counts of first-degree murder. Boucher was pronounced innocent of all charges but was re-tried and convicted in 2002. He was sentenced to life in prison with no chance of parole for 25 years.

CRITICAL THINKING EXERCISE

Boucher's attempts to destabilize the criminal justice system through violence and intimidation muddies the distinction between organized crime and terrorism. Apply what you learned from chapter 2 (comparing and contrasting criminal organizations with terrorist groups) to the Quebec Hells Angels under Boucher to determine whether it should be considered a terrorist organization. What traits of the HAMC and its (violent) history in North America support its characterization as a terrorist group? What are some opposing arguments against characterizing the HAMC as a terrorist organization?

clubhouses, homes, and businesses of the Hells Angels and its affiliates in the province. Dubbed Operation Springtime, the immense police investigation involved 288 police searches in 27 locations and ended up seizing 120 kilograms of hashish, 10 kilograms of cocaine, $12.5 million in Canadian cash, and $2.6 million in American cash. In total, 142 people were arrested, including 80 of Quebec's 106 full-patch Hells Angels members, the entire Nomads chapter, as well as every member in the Hells Angels' affiliate clubs the Rockers and the Evil Ones. When the dust settled, 42 members of the Hells Angels (including all the Nomads) and the Rockers were each charged with 13 counts of first-degree murder, three counts of attempted murder, various drug-trafficking offences, and the new offence of participating in a criminal organization. Of the Hells Angels and Rockers named in the arrest warrants, 14 were already behind bars on previous convictions or awaiting trial on other charges (Cherry, 2005; Royal Canadian Mounted Police, 2002b: 7–9; Sher & Marsden, 2003: 255). Perhaps the most fitting symbol of the war's end occurred on May 6, 2002, when Maurice Boucher was found guilty of first-degree murder in the death of two prison guards and was sentenced to life imprisonment, with no chance of parole for at least 25 years.

2000 to Present: The Resilience of the Hells Angels as a Criminal Organization

The jailing of Boucher and Rock Machine leader Frédéric Faucher signalled the beginning of the end to Quebec's most vicious biker war, but by no means did this end the expansion plans for either group. Before Faucher was sent away, he was instrumental in reinventing the Rock Machine. On June 2, 1999, the gang negotiated hangaround status with the Bandidos Motorcycle Club and officially became its own motorcycle club, complete with red and gold Rock Machine colours and the use of "MC" at the end of their name. More surprising, the club announced it was expanding into Ontario, setting up two new chapters in Kingston and Toronto. All nine of the new Toronto chapter

Photo 7.5: Prospective Canadian members of the Bandidos MC

Source: Courtesy of the RCMP

members were former Outlaws. The developments were particularly troubling for the Hells Angels, who still did not have any chapters in Ontario and watched as their international nemesis, the Bandidos, gained a foothold in Canada.

To counter the growth of the Rock Machine and the subsequent entry of the Bandidos into Canada, the Hells Angels ramped up their own expansion plans. In July 1997, the Grim Reapers of Alberta patched over to join forces with the Hells Angels. As the 1999 CISC annual report notes, the arrival of the Angels in Alberta "brought a noticeable increase in violent crime, as they coerced independent drug dealers into their distribution network. The disbandment of the Kings Crew of Calgary placed the Hells Angels in full control of biker-related criminal activities in Alberta" (Criminal Intelligence Service Canada, 1999: 22). By 2002, the Angels had chapters in Calgary, Edmonton, and Red Deer. In Saskatchewan, the Saskatoon-based Rebels Motorcycle Club received their red and white colours in September 1998. Another chapter was added in Regina at the end of 2001. In 2000, the HAMC established their long-coveted Winnipeg chapter when it patched over the Los Brovos, and over the next seven months, ten people were shot, including members of the new Hells Angels chapter and the rival Spartans club. Twenty people linked to the two biker groups in Manitoba were arrested and charged with more than one hundred weapons offences after police seized 20 kilograms of explosives, 486 rounds of ammunition, and dozens of weapons (*National Post*, June 29, 2001; Sher & Marsden, 2003: 158).

In 1998, the British Columbia Hells Angels added a Nomads chapter in Burnaby. It was their seventh chapter in that province and the tenth Nomads chapter internationally. Unlike their counterparts in Quebec, the Hells Angels in British Columbia were able to fly below police radar for many years and the few attempts to prosecute members were generally unsuccessful. In the fall of 2004, the *Vancouver Sun* reported that more than 30 criminal prosecutions launched against BC Hells Angels members over the past decade had failed (*The Province*, January 25, 2005; *Vancouver Sun*, January 25, 2005).

The most significant expansion of the HAMC in Canada was still to come as their intense efforts to establish chapters in Ontario finally paid off. On December 29, 2000, the Hells Angels' clubhouse in Sorel played host to an extraordinary patch-over ceremony: more than 160 members of four Ontario motorcycle gangs—Satan's Choice, Para-Dice Riders, Last Chance, and Lobos—received full-fledged membership in the Hells Angels. It was the single largest patch-over in the history of the Canadian Hells Angels and one of the largest in the club's international history. Provincial police from Ontario and Quebec watched as industrial-sized sewing machines were lugged into the Sorel clubhouse with newly crested Hells Angels members sauntering out afterward (Cherry, 2005: 25; *Toronto Star*, December 31, 2000). In a move motivated by the recent arrival of the Bandidos on Canadian soil, all of the Hells Angels' newest members were allowed to bypass the probationary stages and become full-patch members of the motorcycle club. By 2002, there were 16 Hells Angels chapters in Ontario, including a Nomads chapter located in Ottawa, with more than 250 full-patch members, prospects, and hangarounds.

By June 2004, the majority of the Quebec Hells Angels and Rockers MC charged as part of Operation Springtime were found guilty. Most were convicted of or pleaded guilty to charges of drug trafficking, conspiracy to murder, and participation in a criminal organization. At least eight members of the Nomads were handed sentences of 20 years or more. While Operation Springtime hit the Quebec Hells Angels hard, the resilient motorcycle club quickly bounced back and even saw its membership increase in the province. Before the raids were conducted, the gang had 106 full-patch members in Quebec. By 2002, police estimated the number had rose to 124 (although this figure includes incarcerated members). And while the Nomads chapter in the province was wiped out, the five remaining chapters in Quebec survived unscathed. Another chapter was added that year when the Sherbrooke chapter split in two with half its two dozen members forming the new Estrie chapter, located not too far from Sherbrooke in Quebec's Eastern Townships. In addition, the Hells Angels still controlled a number of puppet clubs in the province. Their drug-trafficking network also rebounded when the Trois Rivières chapter took over the Nomads' coordinating role in the club's cocaine-trafficking business (Criminal Intelligence Service Canada, 2002: 22; *Montreal Gazette*, March 25, 2006; *National Post*, June 28, 2002).

By 2002, Canada was home to 34 Hells Angels chapters with around 450 members and another 150 prospects and hangarounds (CBC News, April 21, 2009; *National Post*, June 28, 2002). Internationally, the Hells Angels had 217 chapters with approximately 3000 members in 27 countries, and the Outlaws had a membership of 1200 spread over 128 chapters in 10 countries, while the Bandidos had 140 chapters and approximately 2500 members in 12 countries (Royal Canadian Mounted Police, 2002a: 4). The only weak point in the Hells Angels national network was on the east coast, where the Halifax chapter was shut down after a series of arrests and convictions in 2001 and 2002 reduced the chapter to just three full-patch members. Michael McCrea, the president of the Halifax chapter, was allegedly ordered by senior HAMC members in Quebec to rebuild the chapter by recruiting enough people to satisfy the six-member minimum requirement (*Charlottetown Guardian*, January 30, 2003; *Halifax Daily News*, August 25, 2003; Royal Canadian Mounted Police, 2002b: 8). To date, however, the Hells Angels have not been able to resurrect their Halifax chapter.

With the expansion of the Hells Angels, and the elimination of much of their competition, police throughout the country dedicated increased resources to targeting Canada's most powerful and only national outlaw biker group. In almost every province where the HAMC had a presence, members and associates were arrested and convicted, primarily on drug-trafficking charges, but also extortion, theft, fraud, manslaughter, murder, and participating in criminal organization. The situation appeared so dire for the one-percenter motorcycle club that some chapters were "frozen" (meaning they had less than the minimum six members required of an HAMC chapter) and were even forced to forfeit their cherished clubhouses to the government (*Vancouver Sun*, February 25, 2014). In one major police investigation in British Columbia, six full-patch members of the Kelowna chapter of the HAMC were arrested in 2012 as part of an alleged conspiracy in which the sale of marijuana from British Columbia's Okanagan region was used to fund the importation of 500 kilograms of cocaine into Canada (*Kelowna Daily Courier*, August 29, 2012; *The Province*, August 27, 2012; *Vancouver Sun*, August 28, 2012). Among those eventually convicted on drug charges was the chapter vice-president, David Giles, and the sergeant at arms, Bryan Oldham.

Despite these setbacks, the HAMC continued to be the only criminal organization in Canada that was truly national in scope. By 2015, according to Detective Sergeant Len Isnor of the Ontario Provincial Police Biker Enforcement Unit, there were 31 active chapters in Canada and five that were frozen (personal communication, September 14, 2015). In addition, the HAMC continued to expand its network of puppet motorcycle clubs. In British Columbia, for example, in addition to the nine HAMC chapters, they control or at the very least are affiliated with numerous other motorcycle clubs in the province (*Vancouver Sun*, September 24, 2009).

In a 2011 interview, a spokesperson with the Edmonton Integrated Intelligence Unit said that during the previous two years, Alberta had seen the largest growth in outlaw motorcycle gangs compared to anywhere else in the country. In 2009, there were just three outlaw motorcycle gangs in Alberta. By 2014, there were 23, most of which were either chapters of the Hells Angels or one of its affiliated clubs. Membership in one-percenter biker clubs in Alberta grew from approximately 90 in 2010 to around 360 by 2014, according to police sources (*Edmonton Sun*, February 7, 2014).

In Saskatchewan, the Hells Angels currently have two chapters: in Regina and Saskatoon. In addition, they also are said to control numerous puppet clubs in the province that have been established in recent years to capitalize on the prosperous economy there and to cater to the growing drug markets fed by the influx of oil patch workers. One of the biggest drug busts in Saskatchewan's history occurred in January 2015 when charges were laid by police against 14 people, including members of Hells Angels and its puppet club the Fallen Saints. Police raids resulted in the seizure of methamphetamine, cocaine, fentanyl and dilaudid pills, heroin, marijuana, and hashish that had an estimated street value of more than $8 million (CBC News, January 15, 2015; Globalnews.ca, January 26, 2015; *StarPhoenix*, January 15, 2015, January 16, 2015). In Manitoba, the Hells Angels remained the most powerful motorcycle club in the province, despite having only one chapter there. But as in other provinces, its influence within the criminal underworld was extended through its subordinates, including one-percenter motorcycle clubs like the Zig Zag Crew and the Redlined Support Crew, as well as street gangs such as the Indian Posse and Native Syndicate, which also sport the colour red.

In 2015, according to the Hells Angels website, there were 13 chapters in Ontario, some of which were responsible for ensuring the presence and viability of the HAMC in Quebec, where the motorcycle club was hit hard by law enforcement actions in recent years (Langton, 2015; *Toronto Star*, March 5, 2015). Operation SharQc, in particular, led to the arrest of more than 150 people in Quebec, including an unprecedented number of full-patch members—111 in total (CBC News, April 16, 2009; *Sherbrooke Record*, July 24, 2009). By 2015, 24 full patch members of the HAMC in that province had pleaded guilty to charges of murder and conspiracy to commit murder. Despite the impact of Operation SharQc on the Hells Angels in Quebec, they appeared to have regrouped and even assembled enough members to allow the Montreal chapter to restart (the chapter had to shut down temporarily after its "active" membership fell below the minimum number of six active members required of a chapter) (*Montreal Gazette*, March 16, 2015). The HAMC also slowly rebuilt in Quebec by establishing several support clubs in the province, including the Red Devils. In May 2014, the Hells Angels and the Red Devils were targeted in 49 police raids, which resulted in the arrest of 65 suspects in Quebec (see Case Study: Operation Macaque).

In Atlantic Canada, the Bacchus MC has emerged as the most powerful one-percenter motorcycle club. According to its website, the Bacchus was originally formed in 1972 in New Brunswick and has seven chapters in Atlantic Canada: three

Photo 7.6: Patch of the Bacchus MC and Red Devils MC, in commemoration of their "brotherhood"

Source: BacchusMC, via Wikimedia Commons

in New Brunswick, one in Nova Scotia, one in PEI, and two in Newfoundland. In response, the HAMC established its own puppet clubs in the Maritimes, including the Gate Keepers, which is aligned with the London, Ontario, Hells Angels' chapter (CBC News, April 10, 2013; *Chronicle Herald*, September 18, 2014). In late 2016, the Hells Angels founded a chapter in Charlottetown, Prince Edward Island, the first in that province and the only HAMC chapter in Atlantic Canada. In a move that surprised many observers, the Bacchus MC expanded into Hells Angels territory west of Atlantic Canada when they added three new Ontario chapters in Hamilton, Chatham, and Sudbury in 2014. The audacious expansion, which marked the first time the Bacchus has had chapters west of New Brunswick, meant they now had a total of 10 chapters in Canada, with an estimated membership of around 110 (*Chronicle Herald*, November 11, 2014; *Hamilton Spectator*, November 10, 2014; *Toronto Star*, November 10, 2014). Despite their constant entreaties that they are not a criminal organization, in 2014 the Bacchus MC faced a legal attempt by the province of Nova Scotia to have them declared a criminal organization after charges were laid against three members accused of extortion. Police said the charges were in relation to their "aggressive" attempts to dissuade a Halifax-area man who was trying to set up a local chapter of the Brotherhood, an American one-percenter motorcycle club that had already established a chapter in Montreal in 2007 (CBC News, January 4, 2013; *Chronicle Herald*, January 4, 2013).

ANALYZING OUTLAW MOTORCYCLE GANGS AS ORGANIZED CRIME: THE CASE OF THE HELLS ANGELS

The preceding chronology provides some indication of the characteristics of OMGs in North America. Using the theoretical taxonomy of a criminal organization created in chapter 3, this section examines in more detail the salient characteristics of one-percenter motorcycle clubs in Canada, with particular emphasis on the Hells Angels.

Organizational

Multiple Offenders/A Systematic Pattern to the Relationship among the Offenders/Specialization and Division of Labour

At any one time, the number of members of the HAMC in Canada is upwards of hundreds of people (and thousands worldwide). In addition, the HAMC relies on hundreds of associates, including those who are members of affiliated (puppet) clubs, to help carry out criminal activities. There is also a systematic pattern to the relationships among the offenders, which can be discerned at three levels: (1) the relationships among the full-patch members of a particular chapter, (2) the relationships between a particular HAMC chapter member and his associates, and (3) the relationships between different HAMC chapters (and members therein).

The relationships among members of a particular HAMC chapter is influenced by its organizational structure. An HAMC chapter is hierarchical, complete with a division of labour, which is consistent with their founders' military background. (As described later in this chapter, the hierarchical structure of an OMG chapter is not necessarily the same as the organizational structure used to carry out criminal activities.) The structure of a chapter is relatively consistent among most OMGs, as depicted in Figure 7.1.

The chapter president has final say over the business of the club. In many clubs, the power of the chapter president is virtually unlimited and he may receive a cut from the revenue-generating activities of other chapter members. The treasurer is responsible for collecting cash on behalf of the chapter, acts as bookkeeper, and keeps track of who owes what and to whom. The chapter secretary keeps the minutes of a meeting (in some motorcycle clubs these two positions are combined). The **sergeant-at-arms** maintains order at meetings, on the chapter's periodic biker runs, and other at functions and has the power to discipline a club member (Lyman & Potter, 2011: 218). The **road captain** organizes the logistics and security for the time-honoured biker runs (Abadinsky, 2013: 226).

Full-patch members are those who are allowed to wear the colours of the OMG. In general, a chapter will have no less than 6 and no more than 25 members. Each chapter also has prospective members (called "strikers" or "prospects") who spend from one month to one year on probationary status. In addition to official positions within a chapter, the larger OMGs have developed an even more intricate division of labour among full-patch and prospective members to carry out other important functions,

```
                          President
                              |
                              |
                       Vice President
        _____|_____
       |                      |                      |
   Secretary              Treasurer             Sgt.-at-arms
                              |
                              |
                         Road Captain
                              |
                              |
                         Club Members
                              |
                              |
                          Prospects
                              |
                              |
                          Hangers-On
```

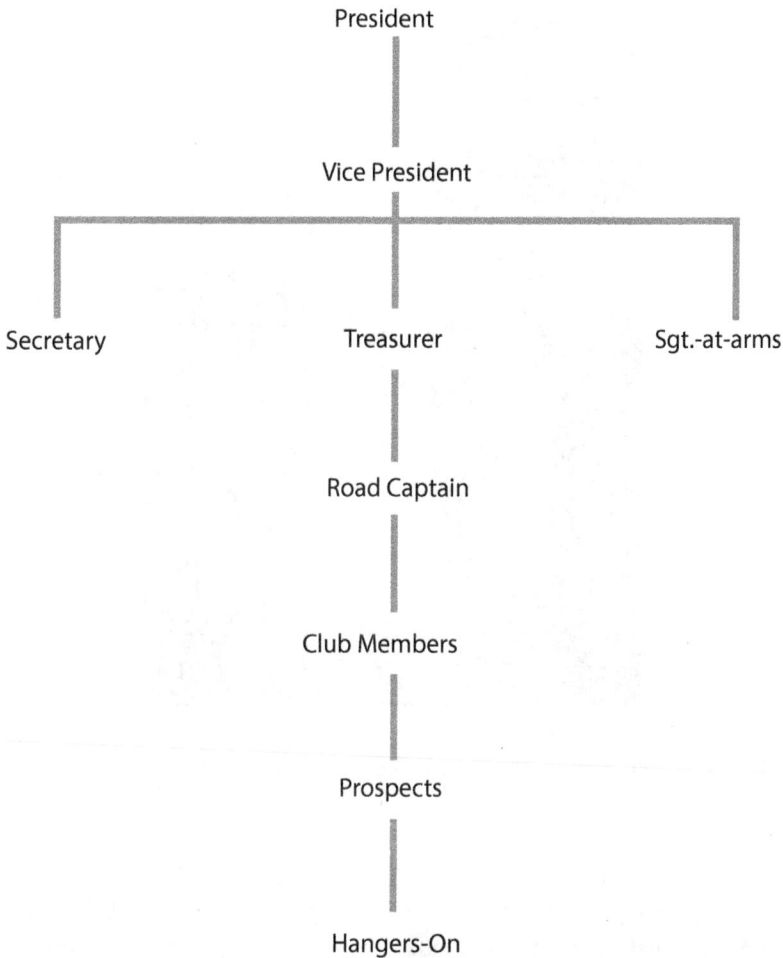

Figure 7.1: Typical structure of an OMG chapter

such as enforcement (i.e., violence). Some Hells Angels enforcers are adorned with Nazi stormtrooper-like lightning bolts tattooed underneath the words "Filthy Few"; the Outlaws have their "SS Death Squad," while the Pagans have the "Black T-shirt Squad." During the 1990s, the Hells Angels affiliate gang in Quebec Rockers MC had a special assassination squad, called the "football team" as well as a "baseball team," which was responsible for carrying out beatings of rivals (Canadian Press, July 9, 2002). Some chapters of an OMG may have an intelligence officer, whose job is to coordinate intelligence gathering against competitors and counter-intelligence against police.

In addition to their connections dictated by their respective positions within a chapter, members of a particular OMG chapter will collaborate when carrying out criminal activities.

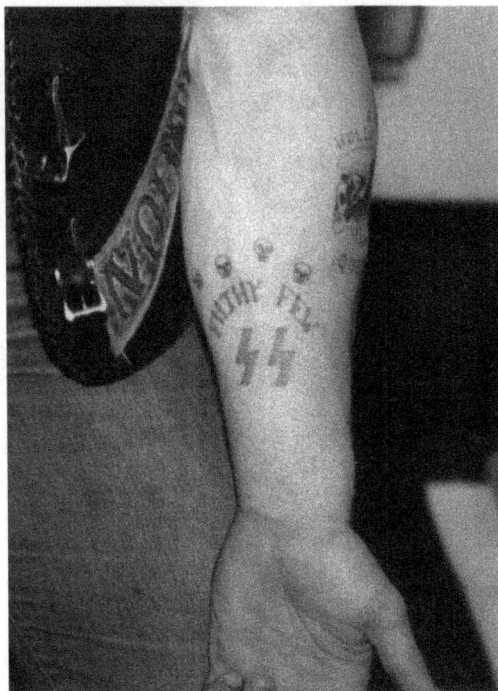

Photo 7.7: The "Filthy Few" tattoo signifies the bearer has killed for the HAMC

Source: Courtesy of the RCMP

The second type of relationship that is evident when examining OMGs as criminal organizations is that between a particular chapter member and his associates. While a chapter of an OMG exhibits a formal organizational structure, individual members will undertake revenue-generating activities in tandem with associates outside of the motorcycle club. For business purposes, each member of the HAMC is at the centre of a network that operates independently of the club, so most members have a number of associates through which they carry out their own criminal rackets. To some extent, the criminal networks operated by individual members of an OMG chapter can be viewed as a reflection of Albini's patron–client model of a criminal organizational structure, which he originally applied to Italian organized crime (see chapter 3).

These associates may be members of a puppet club affiliated with a HAMC chapter and are often directed by one member of that chapter. When he was the president of the Nomads chapter in Quebec during the 1990s, Maurice Boucher established the subservient Rockers MC to facilitate cocaine trafficking in Montreal and to insulate Nomad members from enforcement actions. A more recent example is the Gate Keepers MC, which has chapters in at least two provinces in Canada (Ontario and Nova Scotia) and is affiliated with the London, Ontario, chapter of the HAMC. The Nova Scotia chapter

Case Study: Puppet Motorcycle Clubs as HAMC Criminal Associates in Manitoba

Following raids on numerous homes and businesses in March 2012, police arrested members and associates of the Manitoba chapter of the Hells Angels and laid a number of drug- and gang-related charges. By the end of April, 25 people had been arrested as part of Project Flatlined, an undercover operation that relied on wiretaps and surveillance to gather intelligence information and evidence. The "Flatlined" codename is a reference to the Redlined Support Crew, a puppet club of the Hells Angels that was created in 2010 to counter competing drug-trafficking networks that tried to take over from the HAMC after many of their members were arrested and jailed in the other police operations.

Court documents relating to Project Flatlined revealed that two cell phones used in a dial-a-dealer cocaine network run by the two groups rang an average of 530 times a day over a 10-month period. Winnipeg police allege the phone calls helped generate more than $1.5 million in drug sales. Among these arrested and charged were a full-patch HAMC member and two high-ranking Redlined members. According to the *Winnipeg Sun*, court documents filed by police states the HAMC member was "at the pinnacle of the drug network and supplied cocaine to underlings for the purpose of the drug being cut and broken down into .17 gram rocks for sale on the street." One of the members of Redlined MC acted as the "reloader and street boss" for the dial-a-dealer operation and took instructions from the other on how many rocks should be portioned out. Several other members of the HAMC and Redlined Support Crew were arrested then released after agreeing to the terms of peace bonds section of the *Criminal Code*, which stipulates that they are prohibited from having contact with any Hells Angels member or associate in the province. Part of the aim of the peace bond was to cripple communications between various HAMC members and associates. The result of the arrests was that, at the time, almost every patch-wearing member of the Manitoba Hells Angels were either in custody or barred from having contact with any other member or associate (CTV News, April 21, 2012; *Winnipeg Free Press*, April 10, 2012; *Winnipeg Sun*, April 24, 2012, June 8, 2012a, July 25, 2012).

of the Gate Keepers was established expressly to represent the Hells Angels interests in that province. The nine HAMC chapters in British Columbia are supported by numerous other motorcycle clubs in the province, most if not all of which are one-percenters, according to police. This includes the Jesters MC and Shadow MC in Surrey, the Devil's Army in Campbell River, the Handsome Bastards in Fort St. John, the Renegades in Prince George, the Throttle Lockers out of 100 Mile House, and the Lost Souls in Ashcroft (*Vancouver Sun*, September 24, 2009).

The third type of relationship evident when examining the HAMC as a criminal group is that between different chapters, and by extension, among the members of the different chapters. There is no official national president, headquarters, or lead chapter for the HAMC in Canada. Within each Canadian province, however, there is often one dominant chapter that has influence over other chapters. As discussed earlier, during the 1990s, Maurice Boucher, as well as other senior members of the HAMC from Montreal, Trois Rivières, and Halifax chapters, formed the Nomads chapter. With Boucher taking the lead, the Quebec Nomads was created with four goals in mind: (1) to provide an over-arching leadership for the growing number of Hells Angels in Quebec, (2) to coordinate drug trafficking in the province, (3) to help promote the expansion of the biker club into Ontario and beyond, and (4) to oversee the war against the Rock Machine and other rivals.

The structure and relationship among the different chapters of the HAMC (and its puppet clubs) in Canada is reportedly meant to form a national criminal organization in which different chapters form different roles particularly in forming a national drug pipeline.

In sum, it can be said that OMGs incorporate three operational structures in Canada. The first is the chapter, which entails a hierarchy that includes well-defined positions and functions specific to the operations of both a motorcycle enthusiast club and a criminal organization. The second operational structure involves a fluid network of criminal enterprises that revolve around members of an OMG chapter. The third is the network of chapters provincially or nationally that collectively form a criminal organization. The formal organizational structure of an OMG chapter is not necessarily the same as the structure used to carry out criminal activities. While there is a relatively clear hierarchy within each chapter, "income-generating activities involve several smaller operationally independent units" (Abadinsky, 2000: 238). Lavigne (1997: 246) adds, "The Hells Angels are truthful when they say they are not a criminal organization. Rather, they are an organization of criminals. They go out of their way to maintain a barrier between the Hells Angels as a club and the Hells Angels as a business." As Nicaso (2001b) puts it, "belonging to the Hell's Angels guarantees to each member the possibility of running an illicit activity." Gottschalk (2015: 159) refers to the HAMC as a "criminal matrix organization." In this sense, "the vertical axis of the organization is characterized by a legal men's club of individuals interested in a brotherhood linked to Harley-Davidson motorcycles. The horizontal axis of the organization is characterized by illegal activities organized by individuals in the club."

Notwithstanding the three aforementioned organizational structures inherent in an OMG, the Hells Angels had been deemed a criminal organization by a Canadian court of law. In July 2005, Madam Justice Michele Fuerst found Steven (Tiger) Lindsay and Ray Bonner, both members of the Woodbridge, Ontario, chapter of the HAMC, guilty of extortion and of committing that crime "in association" with a criminal organization. The case stemmed from an altercation on January 23, 2002, between Lindsay and Bonner and a Barrie, Ontario, businessman who had sold them faulty equipment that was supposed to steal satellite television signals. Both HAMC members were wearing their colours when they arrived at the home of the businessman to demand that he pay them $75,000 in compensation; otherwise he would "end up in hospital." By wearing their colours, the two men "presented themselves not as individuals, but as members of a group with a reputation for violence and intimidation," Justice Fuerst wrote in her decision. Lindsay and Bonner deliberately evoked their membership in the Hells Angels "with intent to inspire fear in their victim," according to Justice Fuerst (*Toronto Star*, July 1, 2005).

Insulation against Law Enforcement/Specialized Channels and Modes of Communication

A number of measures have been put in place by OMGs to insulate their chapters, their members, and the broader organization from law enforcement actions. First, the chapter and its leader are insulated through the organizational hierarchy of the chapter as well as associates who are outside the formal organization. Lower-echelon members as well as prospective members of a HAMC chapter are expected to take the fall for more senior members, while associates external to the chapter (hangarounds, puppet clubs, street gang members, and others) are expected to take the fall for a particular crime that may involve a full-patch HAMC member. Second, each chapter is governed by strict rules and regulations, including those demanding utmost loyalty and secrecy, which are meant to keep OMG members in line and to protect the chapter itself from law enforcement actions. Third, like other criminal organizations, members of the HAMC often communicate using codes so as not to provide information that could be picked up through electronic surveillance. Finally, the clubhouses of biker gangs literally protect members through a myriad of both physical and technological fortifications, including bulletproof glass, steel plates in the walls, reinforced doors, barbed wire fences, motion detector sensors, and video surveillance cameras. These fortifications are often there to protect those inside from attacks from rival gangs, but are also meant to delay the quick penetration of police executing search warrants.

Limited or Exclusive Membership/Recruitment

Most OMGs place restrictions on who can become a member. Women are not allowed to be members, and few, if any, of the dominant OMGs allow racial minorities as members (the Bandidos is one exception as they do have Hispanic members). With respect to the HAMC, only a full-patch member is allowed to wear the complete four-piece crest which includes (1) the death head logo, (2) the top **rocker** (which states "Hells Angels"), (3) the bottom rocker (usually the state or territory of the member's chapter or simply "Nomad"), and (4) the rectangular "MC" patch below the wing of the death head. In Canada, prospective members of the HAMC are allowed to wear only a bottom rocker with the province or territory name along with the rectangular "MC" patch. (It should also be noted that only members of the HAMC can wear anything on their person, including clothes or tattoos, with the "Hells Angels" name or death head logo).

Traditionally, prospective members to be recruited to the HAMC were those who fit its original anti-social mould. As the Hells Angels and other biker gangs evolved into criminal fraternities, greater emphasis was placed on recruiting "hard-core criminal-type members" (Criminal Intelligence Service Canada, 1979: 20). In more recent years, recruitment drives have focused on individuals who have skills valued by the HAMC (which includes soliciting military personnel with expertise in explosives). In addition to recruiting individuals to become members, the HAMC also recruit existing biker gangs to patch over to their motorcycle club or at the very least to become puppet clubs.

To become a member of the HAMC, one must first be sponsored by an existing member, who in turn is responsible for his prospect. Prospects must receive a unanimous vote for acceptance into provisional status (and subsequently full-patch membership) by members of a chapter. During his probationary period, the prospect must prove himself worthy of membership by following orders and even committing serious crimes (a practice that helps keep law enforcement agents from posing as prospective members). Carrying out a murder or assaulting a rival is also one way a prospect can become a member or move up through the hierarchy of a chapter. After two men were severely beaten by low-level members of a Quebec Hells Angels chapter in 2002, a member of the Rockers puppet club later told police "the guys all want to get promoted" (*Globe and Mail*, August 12, 2002).

Initiation rituals vary by club and by chapter. Legend has it that during the 1960s and 1970s, prospects with the Hells Angels had to endure a bizarre and often horrific initiation ritual that involved dirtying the prospect by physically soiling his colours—a symbol of the mangy look promoted by OMGs as part of their rebellion against mainstream society. Today, there is less emphasis on these initiation rituals, although a prospect is still expected to commit one or more crimes as part of his probationary period.

Continuity/Continuing Enterprise

The HAMC is clearly a continuing enterprise, having existed since the late 1940s. In Canada, the motorcycle club can trace its roots to 1977, when it established its first chapter in Quebec. Despite the passage of time and the numerous members who have come and gone (some through violent deaths), the original Sorel chapter continues to exist to this day as do most of the other HAMC chapters founded in Canada throughout the years.

Multi-jurisdictional/Transnational in Scope

The world's largest one-percenter biker gangs are multi-jurisdictional and international in scope. By the late 1960s, the HAMC and the Outlaws had chapters in numerous US states and had already established chapters in other countries. The largest one-percenter motorcycle club in the world is truly transnational in scope, as its own website proudly exclaims, "Today the Hells Angels Motorcycle Club has spread its wings all over the World," and has chapters in "North America, Central America, South America, Europe,

Australia, Africa and Asia." The multi-jurisdictional nature of OMGs is deliberate and instrumental to the execution of their criminal activities (which themselves are often inherently multi-jurisdictional and transnational in scope). In his 1978 book *Wayward Angel*, George Wethern, a former senior member of the Oakland chapter of the Hells Angels, notes that the club's carefully controlled expansion was highly strategic. "We didn't believe in granting charters just for the sake of growth, nor to provide us with a place to stay when we were on vacation. The additions were designed to contribute to our image and business concerns, by providing a drug route link, manufacturing a drug, supplying chemicals or distributing drugs in an untapped area" (Wethern & Colnett, 1978: 102). In its annual report on organized crime for 1979, CISC stated that expansion of the Outlaws and the Hells Angels into Canada gave them "the capability of harbouring fugitives in other jurisdictions," and when "violence from Canadian gang rivalry" erupted "American bikers of both the Outlaws and the Hells Angels could be summoned to participate" (Criminal Intelligence Service Canada, 1979: 21–22).

Within Canada, the HAMC has a presence in every province, either through a chapter (or chapters) or via an affiliated puppet club, which is meant to establish a truly national network to facilitate its criminal activities, and drug trafficking specifically. Much of the credit for the Hells Angels' growth across Canada has been given to a HAMC member, Nomad Wolodumyr Stadnick, whose goal was to form a Hells Angels empire in Canada that stretched from coast to coast. During the late 1980s, he paid special attention to establishing a presence in Central Canada. "Stadnick realized that if the Hells Angels stood any chance of becoming a truly national empire, they had to fill the huge gap in Central Canada—and that meant Manitoba and Ontario," Sher and Marsden wrote. Manitoba was important "because it was the axis of distribution for any drugs moving east and west in the country," while Ontario was critical because it was "the Golden Horseshoe for drugs, prostitution and all other proceeds of crime" (Sher & Marsden, 2003: 23, 28–29). Stadnick's hard work paid off when the Los Brovos in Winnipeg became a HAMC chapter and when more than 160 bikers in Ontario patched over to the club.

When the HAMC and the Outlaws began to establish chapters in Canada, one of their goals was to facilitate cross-border transactions. The Outlaws were active in producing chemical drugs in Canada that were then shipped to the United States, while the HAMC has been active in importing cocaine and later become a major exporter of Canadian-produced marijuana to the United States. It was no coincidence that the first three HAMC chapters in Canada were established in port cities—Montreal, Vancouver, and Halifax—which was necessary to facilitate their drug importation activities (and later to export stolen cars). According to a 1986 report by the RCMP and the DEA, Vancouver was a "fertile springboard" and "an important transit point for drugs, weapons, and other contraband. As a result of their meetings with Canadian motorcycle gangs, it became possible for the Hells Angels to set up a pipeline from the United States through British Columbia and across Canada to Quebec" (Royal Canadian Mounted Police and Drug Enforcement Administration, 1986: 18–19, 21).

Photo 7.8: Walter Stadnick (facing the camera) as he leaves a Winnipeg funeral in the early 1990s

Source: Canadian Press photo / Winnipeg Free Press. Used by Permission.

Commercial

Profit-oriented Criminal Activities/Serious Illegal Acts/Multiple Enterprises

The HAMC epitomizes organized crime in terms of its commercial endeavours: it engages in multiple types of profit-oriented, serious consensual and predatory criminal enterprise that deal in both illegal and highly regulated goods and services. The criminal activity of the Hells Angels in Canada has expanded from street-level narcotics distribution and hired muscle to a worldwide network that trafficks in drugs, women, counterfeit currency, weapons, contraband cigarettes, stolen motorcycles, and motorcycle parts. They are also reportedly involved in frauds (telemarketing and mortgage fraud), gambling, loansharking, kidnapping, theft (including truck hijackings), and extortion.

Drugs have long been and continue to be a major revenue source for one-percenter motorcycle gangs. The Hells Angels began in the 1960s as street-level dealers of various drugs and by the 1970s began producing such synthetic drugs as methamphetamines and counterfeit Quaaludes. By the 1980s, they had branched out into cocaine, marijuana, hashish, and prescription drugs, as well as other synthetic

---

Case Study: Operation Macaque

In 2013, members of the Hells Angels and the Red Devils motorcycle clubs were targeted in 49 police raids in Quebec. Some 650 police officers were involved in the raids, which arrested 65 suspects in Saguenay, the Laurentians, and Laval. The Red Devils are a puppet club for the Hells Angels in Quebec and elsewhere, including Ottawa and South Carolina. The raids were part of Operation Macaque, a multi-agency police operation targeting drug networks in Saguenay, Montreal, and the North Shore. Police said one of the cells of this network was suspected of producing marijuana for the Quebec market, while another was believed to have been exporting marijuana to the United States at a rate of 20 kilograms a week, generating a revenue of about $1.2 million. Operation Macaque led to the seizure of 20,000 marijuana plants, 260 kilograms of dried marijuana, 180,000 tablets of methamphetamine, 19.7 kilograms of methamphetamine powder, 1.7 kilograms of hashish, and 3 kilograms of cocaine. In addition, police reported that they seized 27 firearms, more than $500,000 in Canadian cash and $20,000 in American cash, 20 vehicles, a boat, and a tablet press capable of producing 1400 tablets per minute (CTV News, May 7, 2014; *La Presse*, May 8, 2014; Sûreté du Québec Communiqué, May 7, 2014).

---

drugs, including steroids, LSD, PCP, and MDMA. The only drug that HAMC members do no traffick in is heroin, which stems from the ban the club has on using (or selling) any drug that involves a needle. George Wethern, a former ranking member of the Hells Angels Oakland chapter, states that a biker club structure is easily adapted to drug trafficking. All essential jobs could be filled with club members—distributors, dealers, enforcers, and transporters. Because of their reputation for violence and anti-establishment attitudes, they are also ideally suited for this line of work (Wethern & Colnett, 1978).

Today, the HAMC in Canada are involved in the importation and wholesaling of cocaine and hashish as well as the domestic production, wholesaling, and export of synthetic drugs and marijuana. Numerous members and associates of the HAMC have been convicted for cocaine-trafficking-related offences. The Hells Angels are dominant players in the cocaine trade in Canada and have been known to work with Italian and Colombian groups at the importation and wholesale level. In recent years, Canadian HMAC members and associates have been linked to the production of MDMA (commonly known as ecstasy) and fentanyl. A number of police raids targeting HAMC members and their associates have resulted in the seizure of illegal pills as well as pill presses. The penchant that OMGs in Canada have for producing and selling domestically produced synthetic drugs is based on the large market for such drugs, the huge profits that result, and their ability to control it from its manufacture to its

Case Study: Platinum Sports Books

In February 2013, the Combined Forces Special Enforcement Unit of Greater Toronto announced it had arrested six men for numerous offences related to illegal gaming. According to a CFSEU press release, "the lengthy, joint-forces investigation revealed that large-scale illegal gaming was taking place on an off-shore website called Platinum Sports Book.com. The website, allegedly being run by organized crime, is host to thousands of gamblers whose wagers result in millions of dollars in profit for organized crime." As part of the raids, more than $2.5 million in cash was seized as well as computers, cell phones, and business records. A month later, the CFSEU issued another news release indicating that 13 further search warrants had been served and an additional 18 people arrested as part of the ongoing illegal gaming investigation. Approximately $1.5 million in cash was also seized.

CFSEU officials told the media that the latest arrests targeted the "management team" of the alleged illegal gambling operation. Police further alleged that the group running the off-shore betting site, Platinum Sports Book, was a joint enterprise between the Hells Angels and Italian organized crime. Among those arrested was a member (and ex-president) of the London chapter of the Hells Angels and two associates. Each of the accused was charged with numerous offences, including participating or engaging in a criminal organization, bookmaking, and conspiracy to commit a criminal offence. The HAMC did little to hide their connection with Platinum Sports Book; both their web page and an advertisement for a Super Bowl party include a graphic of a skull with wings that closely resembled the Hells Angels' winged death head insignia. On February 3, 2013, police raided the invite-only Super Bowl party, held in Markham, Ontario. The gambling operation was also linked to loansharking. The investigation actually began as a result of a complaint from a person who said he was being extorted for money he allegedly owed to a HAMC member. Police allege that if money borrowed from this organization could not be repaid, exorbitant interest rates were imposed and violence was used to recoup money owed (Combined Forces Special Enforcement Unit—Ontario Press Release, February 4, 2013, March 5, 2013, March 6, 2013; *London Free Press*, February 5, 2013; *National Post*, March 5, 2013; *Toronto Star*, March 7, 2013).

distribution. There is also evidence that HAMC members are heavily into financing and coordinating large-scale marijuana grow operations in Canada. Like other criminal groups in Canada, the Hells Angels are known to export marijuana to the United States in exchange for cocaine, which is then imported into Canada.

Police also allege that the Hells Angels are extensively involved in the trafficking of women for both prostitution and exotic dancing. They are reportedly prominent in the exotic dancer circuits in Montreal, Toronto, and Vancouver through agencies that represent prostitutes and exotic dancers as well as investments in hundreds of strip bars, massage parlours, and escort agencies. Police have also linked the Hells Angels to street gangs that run prostitution rings (Canadian Press, May 15, 2003).

One of the other early criminal activities carried out by OMGs was the theft of automobiles and motorcycles. Stealing motorcycles was long used by prospects to earn membership in a club. Bikers would often gather information from motorcycle dealership salesmen on the names and addresses of recent customers. Once stolen, the motorcycle is taken to a "chop shop" where it is "cannibalized for parts and rebuilt again interchanging the parts from ten or fifteen other stolen bikes, to make a completely different looking bike" (Royal Canadian Mounted Police, 1987: 13). The "new" motorcycle is then privately sold. Members of the Hells Angels have also been involved in the theft of automobiles in Canada, which are then exported for sale in other countries (and facilitated by the influence of the HAMC at commercial marine ports in Vancouver, Montreal, and Halifax). In 2004, Paul Porter, the president of the Nomads chapter in Ontario at the time, was arrested by Quebec Provincial Police for masterminding a car theft ring that stole luxury SUVs, which were then smuggled out of the country and sold around the world (*Globe and Mail*, April 4, 2004; *Ottawa Citizen*, December 13, 2005).

Monopolistic Ambitions

OMGs have been known to monopolize particular criminal markets in the United States and Canada. During the late 1960s and 1970s, they reportedly gained a virtual monopoly over the production and distribution of chemical drugs in some parts of North America. In 1977, the San Francisco police department estimated that the Hells Angels controlled 90 percent of the methamphetamine trade in Northern California, while the same year the RCMP estimated that biker gangs controlled 75 percent of the methamphetamine market in Ontario (as cited in Wolf, 1991: 334). The Hells Angels, in particular, are notorious for trying to monopolize a particular territory or criminal market. The most egregious example of the monopolistic tendencies of the HAMC was in Quebec during the 1990s when, under the leadership of the despotic Maurice Boucher, they tried to control cocaine trafficking in Montreal.

Efforts to monopolize territories may be pursued through less violent politicking. If the Hells Angels want to make in-roads into an area where another biker gang already exists, they will ask that gang to join them as an affiliate or a puppet group. If the gang agrees, they may eventually be patched over to the Hells Angels. This peaceful approach was epitomized in 2001 when the HAMC patched over dozens of smaller one-percenter clubs in Ontario in order to gain a monopoly over all one-percenter biker gangs in the province. This all-encompassing presence also represented a major step toward their efforts to monopolize the cocaine trade in that province.

Police in British Columbia have said that no motorcycle club in that province can wear a four-piece MC patch without the approval of the Hells Angels. As Inspector Gary Shinkaruk of the RCMP's Outlaw Motorcycle Gang unit put it in 2009, British Columbia "is primarily a Hells Angels province when it comes to outlaw motorcycle gangs." The Hells Angels have denied the club operates any puppet or support groups in the province (*Vancouver Sun*, September 24, 2009).

Tactical Support Activities

INTELLIGENCE GATHERING

As part of their tactical toolkit, the more sophisticated biker gangs have become well known for their intelligence gathering and counter-surveillance, which is directed against both rival gangs and law enforcement agencies. Police raids of OMG clubhouses have netted confidential police radio frequency lists as well as scanners tuned to over-hear police messages (Royal Canadian Mounted Police, 1980: 20). After searching a Hells Angels chapter in Alberta, the Edmonton Police Service discovered scanning equipment hooked up to personal computers that were monitoring transmissions used by police (*Edmonton Journal*, February 11, 2002). In one Ontario city, a motorcycle repair shop owned by members of a biker gang was set up across the street from a gas station where police cars, as well as private vehicles belonging to peace officers, regularly filled up. From this observation post, licence plate numbers and descriptions of cars and their occupants were recorded (Royal Canadian Mounted Police, 1980: 20).

During the 1990s, police searches of the clubhouses and homes of the Quebec Hells Angels and its puppet clubs turned up photos as well as a list of names and home addresses of provincial police officers and civilians working for a special outlaw biker task force. Other documents found include police and Crown reports on undercover officers, informants, and witnesses. According to the Union of Canadian Correctional Officers, during the 1990s members of biker gangs were actively compiling information on prison guards across the country (Sher & Marsden, 2003: 218).

Surveillance and intelligence gathering by the HAMC in Quebec was also directed at other criminal gangs. Stéphane Gagné, a former member of the Rockers MC, testified in court in 2002 that his boss, Maurice Boucher, ordered him to video-tape attendants at the funeral of Frank Cotroni. The video, which was shot through a small camera hidden in a tissue box, was meant to keep tabs on associates of the Montreal Mafioso and long-time drug trafficker. The assignment was part of a surveil-lance campaign against those who dared to stop the Hells Angels from taking control over Quebec's drug trade. Gagné said similar surveillance was also undertaken on members of rival biker gangs to assist Hells Angels hitmen in identifying their targets (Canadian Press, July 9, 2002).

It has been reported that some OMG chapters have a designated intelligence officer, whose job is to coordinate intelligence gathering against competitors and counter-intelligence against police. He often travels under a variety of names, does not wear his colours, and is rarely if ever seen near the clubhouse, according to David (1988). Some OMGs will actively recruit individuals who have intelligence skills gleaned from time spent in the military. Women have also played an intelligence gathering role for biker gangs and some have been planted in law enforcement agencies, courtrooms, and government licensing bureaus, where they have access to vital information. According to former Ontario Satan's Choice member Cecil Kirby, his club utilized the service of a woman employed in the Ontario Provincial Police who had access to classified databases:

> Club members carried her number around in their wallets. If a member was worried about the cops, all he had to do was call her number, and she'd access the police computer to see if there were any warrants on him. When we spotted a rival gang member, we'd also use her to see if there were outstanding fugitive warrants on him. If there were, we'd have someone in the club call the cops and tip them off to where that rival was and who was with him. It was a good way of avoiding trouble and getting rid of rival gang members. We could also check out anyone's criminal record through that computer. This helped us spot people trying to infiltrate us from rival gangs or from the cops.

For Kirby, Satan's Choice had "the upper hand in Toronto because we had the best intelligence network around. We were able to move on the other gangs faster than they could move on us because we had such good sources and good information on the habits of the other gangs" (Kirby & Renner, 1986: 45, 52).

CORRUPTION

Corruption of politicians is not typically associated with outlaw motorcycle gangs in Canada. However, OMGs have relied on an alternative form of illicit influence: the infiltration of public- and private-sector organizations, which is used both as a means to facilitate their criminal activities (e.g., smuggling) and to gather intelligence on their enemies. As discussed above, OMGs use corrupt employees within government agencies, such as licensing bureaus, to collect vital information on prospects and competitors. There are even cases where OMGs have corrupted civilian members of criminal justice agencies. In 2002, Tony Cannavino, head of the Quebec Provincial Police Association, accused the Hells Angels of recruiting civilians working in law enforcement agencies to steal information from police computers. Cannavino said at least four people with access to police databases in Quebec were charged that year for selling information to the members of the club. The Angels reportedly paid up to $10,000 to workers who helped steal data, targeting secretaries and security and maintenance staff (*Montreal Gazette*, February 21, 2002).

The infiltration of police agencies by outlaw biker gangs is not restricted to civilian employees; some police officers have been discovered to have relationships with Hells Angels' members. A 1988 investigation by the Ontario Provincial Police accused

Niagara Regional Police members of links with members of motorcycle gangs (*Toronto Star*, October 20, 1988). In April 2013, a patrol officer in Quebec's Sherbrooke Police Force was arrested after he allegedly leaked sensitive information from a Quebec law enforcement database to a crime group associated with the Hells Angels (Canoe.ca, June 11, 2013; *Toronto Sun*, April 5, 2013). That same year, the issue of police corruption in Quebec became national news when in October, Benoît Roberge, a recently retired Montreal police investigator, was criminally charged based on allegations he sold information from ongoing police investigations to the Hells Angels. Roberge, who reportedly was paid at least $125,000 by the HAMC for information, was arrested at his home in Montreal in the company of a man described by police as a member of the Hells Angels. The allegations were particularly alarming because Roberge was a long-time, high-profile member of police enforcement units dedicated to combatting outlaw motorcycle gangs. This gave him privileged access to sensitive police intelligence on the Hells Angels and other one-percenter biker clubs. His police colleagues became suspicious when it became clear that members of the Hells Angels were being tipped off about ongoing police investigations (Canadian Press, October 7, 2013; CBC News, October 7, 2013; *Montreal Gazette*, October 7, 2013).

Government agencies are not the only targets of outlaw biker infiltration and corruption. In February 2002, a Canadian Senate Committee studying Canada's security noted that the Hells Angels have infiltrated companies and unions that operate on Canada's marine ports to expedite the import and export of illegal drugs and other contraband. Customs officials reported to the committee that the Hells Angels is the dominant criminal influence within the Port of Vancouver and that a security company that had operated at the Port of Montreal had links to the Angels (Standing Senate Committee on National Security and Defence, 2002: 43, 45). Other organized crime groups, such as the West End Gang and the Italian Mafia, have penetrated the waterfront in Montreal. On a national level, however, "the most significant criminal influences within the marine ports are linked to the Hells Angels," according to the 2004 CISC annual report (Criminal Intelligence Service Canada, 2004: 11). In their 2003 book on the Hells Angels, Sher and Marsden allege that beginning in the 1980s, the motorcycle club created "a patchwork of full-patch members and associates to infiltrate the ports of Vancouver, Montreal and Halifax" placing them in "key positions to facilitate a 'tailgate operation,' so called because the bikers can organize the movement of drugs from a container right onto one of their waiting vehicles with exquisite precision" (Sher & Marsden, 2003: 180–83). A 2010 report by the Canada Border Services Agency (CBSA) said that the Mafia and Hells Angels "have exerted the most significant criminal influence at major Canadian marine ports ... " The CBSA linked the smuggling to the Hells Angels and other gangsters working at the port "in key positions—longshoremen, equipment operators, foremen and truck drivers" (as cited in *National Post*, May 9, 2015). Journalist Kim Bolan reported in 2015 that there are at least six full-patch Hells Angels from BC chapters who are members of the International Longshore and Warehouse Union and work on commercial marine ports in Vancouver. Detective Sergeant Isnor of the OPP Biker Enforcement Unit is quoted as saying that the Hells Angels have had a presence in Canada's three largest ports for the past 30 years (*National Post*, May 9, 2015).

VIOLENCE

From the very beginning, violence has been an integral part of the outlaw motorcycle subculture, and the history of OMGs in North America is replete with violence. While violence was originally used indiscriminately as an extension of the one-percenters' deviant and hell-raising lifestyle, it has increasingly been deployed for strategic purposes as groups evolved into criminal organizations. Violence is now used by OMGs not as an end in itself but as a means to an end: to facilitate their profit-oriented illegal and legal activities. Violence and intimidation are strategically used by OMGs to help them move into and monopolize markets, legitimate or illegitimate businesses, or specific geographic territories. As the Hells Angels evolved from a rag-tag group of enforcers to an organized crime syndicate, so has their arsenal of weapons evolved. They may have started using pool cues, motorcycle chains, knives and guns, but now use automatic weapons, explosives, remote control detonators, and even rocket launchers and anti-tank weapons.

Violence between the Hells Angels and the Outlaws erupted in 1974, according to a 1986 report from the US President's Commission on Organized Crime. The report pointed out that despite the Hell Angels' well-founded penchant for violence, the Outlaws were no shrinking violets. "Their reputation for violence is strong. According to the Broward County Sheriff's Office in Ft. Lauderdale, Florida, the Outlaws were responsible for as many as 77 murders between 1966 and 1979; another 15 murders in North Carolina have been attributed to the gang. Friction between the Outlaws and the Hell's Angels has resulted in massacres on both sides" (President's Commission on Organized Crime, 1987: 68). The Outlaw insignia once boasted the initials "GFOD" (God forgives; Outlaws don't) and "AHAMD" (All Hells Angels must die). The violence that has permeated the conflict between the Hells Angels and the Outlaws carried over into Canada and resulted in the deaths of dozens on either side. Yet, the bloodiest example of inter-gang violence in Canada is the so-called Quebec biker war, which resulted in more than 150 violent deaths during the 1990s and early part of the 2000s.

As mentioned earlier in this chapter, the larger one-percenter clubs even have specialized units that are tasked with carrying out violence and other enforcement functions, thereby institutionalizing violence within the clubs. The Hells Angels also turn to their puppet clubs to carry out violence. Jean-Guy Bourgoin—a founding member of the Quebec Hells Angels puppet club called the Rockers that was active in the war against the Rock Machine during the 1990s—was once heard telling another member of the club that the financial remuneration for eliminating rival Rock Machine members and associates was $100,000 for a full-patch member, $50,000 for a prospect, and $25,000 for a hangaround (*Montreal Gazette*, July 19, 2002).

Photo 7.9: North (Laval) chapter. The six murdered members of the chapter were Laurent Viau, Jean-Guy Geoffrion, Guy-Louis Adam, Michel Mayrand, Jean-Pierre Mathieu, and Regis Asselin.

Source: Courtesy of the RCMP

Outlaw bikers have been implicated in violence targeting police and other criminal justice officials. In the most infamous Canadian example, Maurice Boucher, the leader of Hells Angels in Quebec during the 1990s, was convicted for ordering the assassination of two federal corrections officers. This was on top of numerous bombs that he ordered to be placed around police stations. Even civilians are not immune to the wrath of the HMAC; in Canada, an attempt on the life of a Montreal reporter who wrote extensively on OMGs was strongly suspected of being ordered by outlaw bikers. On September 13, 2000, veteran crime reporter Michel Auger was ambushed in the parking lot of *Le Journal de Montreal* and shot five times in the back. Despite the multiple wounds, he remained conscious, and after being rushed to the hospital, he survived. A few blocks from the crime scene police found what had become a tell-tale sign of a biker gang attack, a burning minivan that had been used by the assailants to escape (*National Post*, September 14, 2000).

Violence and intimidation are also routinely used internally within one-percenter biker clubs to ensure members are loyal and stay in line and as a form of discipline. One of the most notorious examples of the use of violence as a means of internal discipline occurred in 1985 when five full-patch members of Quebec's Laval chapter of the Hells Angels were murdered by their "brothers" from other chapters because they were deemed too out-of-control. The murders have been cited as a pivotal point in the transition of the HAMC in Quebec to a criminal organization. The HAMC members that were killed reflected the traditional one-percenter bikers who, according to Paul Cherry, "were constantly partying and consuming cocaine they were supposed to sell" and, as such, "didn't fit into the plans the gang had for the future." By this time, the Hells Angels had begun working with more sophisticated drug-trafficking criminal organizations, including the West End Gang and the Mafia. "Those groups were more businesslike and expected the same from their associates." The members who were murdered "weren't considered future elite drug traffickers" (*National Post*, March 24, 2015).

MONEY LAUNDERING

Due to the amount of cash money generated through drugs and other trades, laundering the proceeds of crime has become a necessity for the HAMC in Canada. While there is not a lot of public information on the various ways members of the HAMC launder their drug money, there is evidence that they have made substantial investments in local businesses, real estate, hotels, entertainment complexes, apartment houses, auto repair shops, and bars. A 1986 report by the RCMP and the DEA counted more than 40 registered companies in British Columbia controlled by or under the influence of members of the Hells Angels (Royal Canadian Mounted Police and Drug Enforcement Administration, 1986: 21). Gottschalk (2015: 159) notes that money laundering vehicles in the United States include tattoo studios and construction companies owned by HAMC members.

Behavioural

Chronic and Serious Offenders (Career Criminals)

To become a member of the Hells Angels, one must be ready and willing to commit to a life of crime. A court case that took place in London, Ontario—concerning the refusal of the province to grant a liquor licence for a strip club owned by a member of the local HAMC—shed some light on the criminal careers of HAMC members in that chapter. A written ruling by the court contains an agreed statement of facts showing that as of 2014, a dozen full-patch members of the London HAMC chapter and three "hangarounds" had 105 criminal convictions among them. Three of the 12 full-patch members and one of the three hangarounds had outstanding charges at the time of the court case. In addition, four members of the local Gate Keepers MC, a Hells Angels puppet club, had 17 criminal convictions among them (QMI Agency, October 22, 2014; *Toronto Star*, October 16, 2014). Following a 2002 raid on the Trois Rivières chapter of the HAMC and its affiliate club, the Jokers, three members of the Hells Angels and the entire membership of the puppet gang were arrested. Following the arrests, police in Quebec announced that more than 70 known Hells Angels members in the province were behind bars or awaiting trial on criminal charges (Canadian Press, November 6, 2002; *Montreal Gazette*, November 7, 2002).

Subcultural Norms/Contempt for Society

Originally, OMGs cultivated and conformed to a distinct subculture that set them apart from the rest of society and symbolized by their one-percenter moniker. Within this subculture, there were certain universal traits that the outlaw biker had to live up to: toughness, violence, sexual prowess, transience, and risk taking. Like the Mafioso, outlaw bikers embrace a real sense of bravado; they accentuate the importance of being a man and embrace quintessential masculine characteristics. Toughness is flaunted in many ways. Traditionally, preferred members are tall, muscular, strong, and/or obese. The desired image of the full-patch member was also reflected in the attire that began to emerge in the mid-1960s: the dirty and tattered leather jacket (cut-off at the sleeves); grease-encrusted jeans; steel-toed boots; long, unkempt hair and beards; and skull-and-cross-bone jewellery. By gilding their jackets with such defiant and repulsive patches as "1 %er," Nazi swastikas, "FTW" (Fuck the World), "69" (as in the sexual position), and "coke" (as in the drug, not the soft drink), outlaw bikers put their self-nurtured subculture on display to signal to the world that they had purposely cut themselves off from the majority culture.

Of course, the outlaw biker bravado is also symbolized by the motorcycle, which had to be a big, loud Harley-Davidson (foreign-made motorcycles, especially Japanese bikes, are looked upon with great derision by OMG members). The motorcycle traditionally ridden by the outlaw biker could not be straight out of the factory; it had to be highly modified, a reflection of one-percenter status as well as each member's individuality and quest for non-conformity. By-law 11 of the Hells Angels MC rules states that no member can wear their colours when riding on a standard Harley-Davidson (Royal Canadian Mounted Police, 1987a: 13). As Hunter S. Thompson wrote in his classic 1967 book on the Hells Angels, "The outlaws tend to see their bikes as personal monuments, created in their own image, however abstract, and they develop an affection for them that is hard for outsiders to understand" (Thompson, 1967: 123). The modified Harley-Davidson motorcycle reflects the sacred principles of the outlaw biker: large, manly, non-conformist, individualistic, fast, adventurous, rebellious, phallic, and loud, yet staunchly patriotic (hence the American-made Harley).

The image and lifestyle cultivated by the one-percenter biker was meant to be the antithesis of those in mainstream society. The counter-culture image that was being formed in the 1950s and 1960s took place amidst the growth of the middle class and its conformist values system, personified by a stable job, the nuclear family, and the house in the suburbs. Outlaw bikers rejected these values and sought to live a lifestyle that was

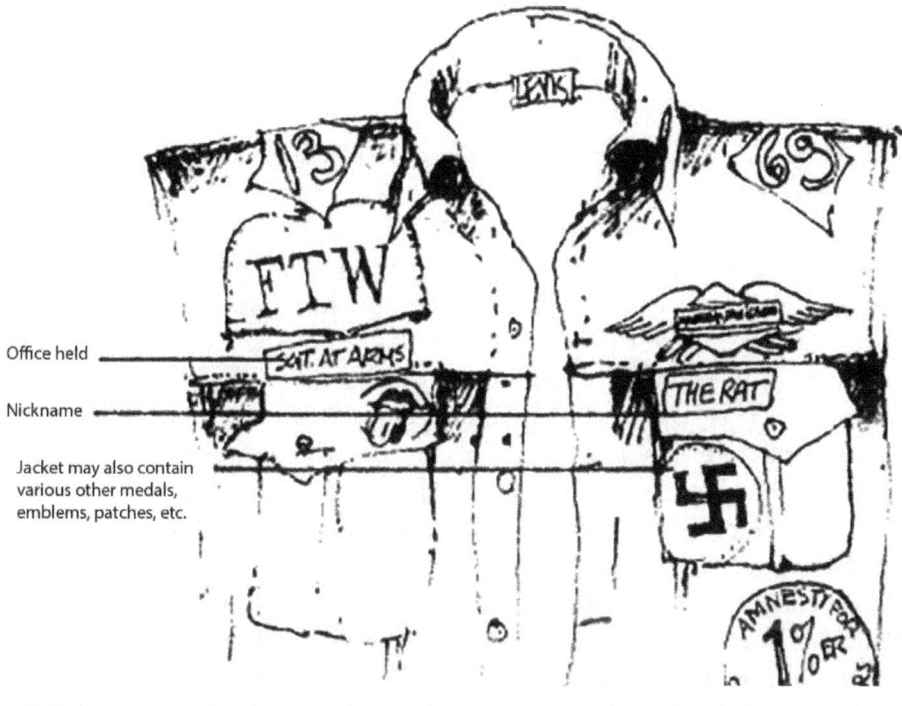

Photo 7.10: Front of a one-percenter vest, circa 1970s. OMGs adorn their jackets with labels—such as 1%er and FTW—to signify their disdain for mainstream society

Source: Courtesy of the RCMP

in direct opposition. It was their motorcycle that not only symbolized this ethos but literally provided them with the vehicle to express their counter-culture nomadic freedom that departed from the staid, stationary mainstream society. As Daniel Wolf writes,

> Outlaw bikers view themselves as nothing less than frontier heroes, living out the "freedom ethic" that they feel the rest of society has largely abandoned. They acknowledge that they are antisocial, but only to the extent that they seek to gain their own unique experiences and express their individuality through their motorcycles. Their "hogs" become personal charms against the regimented world of the "citizen." They view their club as collective leverage that they can use against an establishment that threatens to crush those who find conventional society inhibiting and destructive of individual character. (Wolf, 1991: 9)

The original anti-social dress code and aberrant behaviour of one-percenter motorcycle club members was a conscious expression of their contempt for civil society. This is best reflected in a comment made by Jean-Guy Bourgoin, a member of the Quebec

Rockers MC, a Hells Angels' puppet club. When asked what he thought of regular "citizens," he replied, "I look at people who get up at seven, stuck in traffic for 10 bucks an hour, then come back at night ... They're the fools, we're the ones who are sensible" (*Globe and Mail*, August 12, 2002).

As the HAMC in Canada evolved from a group of motorcycle-riding rowdies to sophisticated criminals, its counter-culture underpinnings faded into the background and was supplanted by efforts to promote an image of respectability. Members were seen less on their motorcycles wearing their traditional colours, and more frequently spotted driving around in luxury cars (and minivans) in everyday street clothes. When their colours are worn, they are clean and pressed, in stark contrast to the past preference for dirt and grime. The Harley-Davidson motorcycles they ride no longer need to be highly modified. Today, members and associates of Canadian chapters of the HAMC are chosen not because of their physical proportions or anti-social predispositions but for their intellect, cunning, criminal expertise, or connections.

In essence, the HAMC has revised its subculture; members still live in an underworld culture of deviance and violence, their erratic, anti-social, nomadic, rabble-rousing ways have been replaced by a subculture of rational, instrumental organized criminality. While still considered sociologically deviant, this lifestyle is much more focused on revenue-generating criminal activities. This transition was recognized in 1986 by the President's Commission on Organized Crime (1986: 65). By this time, the HAMC had completed an "evolution that has been under way for more than 20 years, a period during which the Hells Angels developed from a collection of rowdy rebels into a genuine organized crime group." As Quebec HAMC Nomad member David (Wolf) Carroll once said to his biker protégé Dany Kane, "The Nomads judge you by the size of your portfolio. If you don't have money, you're no good. Our club is no longer really a real biker gang. There are some members who have told me they don't even like biking" (Sher & Marsden, 2003: 217). Thus, it can be said that many of the one-percenter clubs have now bought into at least one dominant institution of Western societies: capitalism.

Sophistication

The Hells Angels are one of the most sophisticated criminal organizations in Canada. This sophistication is exemplified by their national and international infrastructure, the scope of their illegal pursuits, and the tactical activities (corruption, surveillance, intelligence gathering) used to support their drug-trafficking network. The drug-trafficking activities of the HAMC in Canada are immense, requiring an elaborate international and national network of contacts, physical infrastructure, and communications. These include connections with drug suppliers in foreign countries as well as internal conspiracies at marine ports to expedite illegal imports. One of the largest drug-trafficking conspiracies was orchestrated by the Nomads chapter in Quebec during the 1990s and early 2000s. As part of their investigation, police observed couriers carrying bags of drug cash to nondescript apartments used by the Nomads to be counted, stored in safes, and meticulously recorded on computer spreadsheets. The day that police stopped the banking operation, they seized $5.5 million in cash as well as accounting spreadsheets that indicated that the Nomads had supplied 2000 kilograms of cocaine and another 2000 kilograms of hash in one eight-month period in 2000. That year, the Quebec Hells Angels pulled in an estimated $900 million from drug sales (Cherry, 2005: 141–42, 153, 194; *Globe and Mail*, August 12, 2002; *Montreal Gazette*, July 18, 2002; Sher & Marsden, 2003: 247–48).

The large-scale, sophisticated drug trafficking of the HAMC in Canada also extends to marijuana production. In May 2013, the Combined Forces Special Enforcement Unit of British Columbia executed search warrants on four rural properties in Mission and a home in Langley that were the sites of marijuana grow-ops they said were linked to the Hells Angels. "The grow-ops are linked to the outlaw motorcycle gang and show a level of sophistication—both in terms of technology, construction, and security measures—that officers with decades of experience busting grow-ops have not seen," CFSEU-BC spokesman Sergeant Lindsey Houghton was quoted as saying in a press release. "We are talking about large, highly sophisticated grows that are using the latest technology to boost the growing cycle as well as extremely high levels of security to keep the grow operation concealed from police." At one of the sites, the marijuana was being grown in five shipping containers that were buried far underground. According to Houghton, "From trucking the containers in on flatbed trailers, to excavating massive holes, to needing a crane to lower the containers into the ground, and then having people get the grow-op up and running, this was a complex operation that required a great deal of planning and equipment." About 10,000 plants and 200 pounds of dried marijuana were seized from the four grow-ops. Police estimated the crop had a value of between $5 and $10 million, while "the equipment used to produce the marijuana is estimated to be valued at $1 million," the CFSEU press release read. "Of note, each property was operated by a natural gas generator capable of providing power to a small town. Worth an estimated $100,000 each, the generators had to be removed by a large crane" (Combined Forces Special Enforcement Unit—British Columbia Press Release, May 6, 2013; *The Province*, May 7, 2013; *Vancouver Sun*, June 4, 2013).

The HAMC is known to use technology to facilitate their operations, whether it is computer and smartphone technology in their gambling and bookmaking operations, elaborate security systems on their clubhouses, or surveillance technology they employ to keep tabs on their enemies or the police. The vast amounts of revenue produced by members also require the use of a phalanx of professionals, including lawyers and accountants, to keep track of, invest, and launder the proceeds of crime.

Rules, Regulations, and Codes of Conduct

Ironically, while the OMGs originally stressed wild, anarchistic behaviour, most of the clubs are governed by a rigid set of rules, regulations, and codes, all of which stress the primacy of the club. For any member, the club must come first, with the motorcycle second, and family and friends a distant third. Stemming from the importance placed on the outlaw biker club are two other fundamental codes of the OMG: secrecy and loyalty. A member must never reveal anything about the club, its members, or its activities. The primary loyalty of the member is to the club, with secondary loyalty to other members in the club. Adherence to these codes is ensured through strict discipline, which may mean death if they are contravened.

In addition to the unwritten rules of secrecy and loyalty, many OMGs have strict by-laws that must be followed by members. Among the more common by-laws include how a prospect becomes a full-patch member, the payment of dues by club members, who receives a patch and how they are to be worn, prohibition on the use of drugs involving needles (i.e., heroin), the type of motorcycle members must ride (Harley-Davidson), mandatory attendance at club meetings and voting rights, the duties of chapter officers, and the necessary number of members to sustain a chapter. Separate rules and by-laws are also known to exist for the time-honoured ritual of biker runs. Funerals are also big ritualistic events for outlaw bikers and club members come from all over the continent to honour a fallen brother. By-laws are very strict with respect to clothing, including the wearing of colours, patches, and tattoos. The colours worn by any motorcycle gang member is his most prized possession, as the RCMP detail in a 1980 article:

> No one may touch them, not even in a friendly pat-on-the-back gesture. Stealing colours amongst rival gangs is a most serious offence, and killing those responsible is a fact of death readily accepted amongst motorcycle gang brotherhoods. The Hells Angels who first set down the codes for bikers to follow everywhere stated that the crest or patch should never touch the ground. The symbolic emblem with which bikers adorn their backs has today truly acquired the symbolism of a holy relic. Colours are the only single rally "flag" for which bikers will fight to the death ... Policemen have told stories of bikers sitting down and crying unabashedly when stripped of their colours after a raid. Clubs are quick to impose heavy fines, ranging from one hundred dollars to expulsion from the club for losing crests. When worn at a club function the crest furnishes protection from attack by other club members. A biker without his colours is fair game in internal club rivalry in-fighting. (Royal Canadian Mounted Police, 1980: 14–15)

Discipline

Discipline is regularly meted out to members (and associates) of one-percenter biker clubs who break the rules. Discipline can range from paying a fine, the assignment of menial tasks (e.g., cleaning a clubhouse), to expulsion from the club. Violence is also used for internal disciplinary reasons and full-patch members, prospects, and associates have been killed for such transgressions as disobeying rules, co-operating with rival gangs, or turning state witness. On June 22, 2000, Louis Roy, a member of the Quebec HAMC Nomads and a former president of the Trois Rivières chapter, disappeared. Despite his longstanding stature within the Hells Angels in Quebec, police speculated that he was another victim of Maurice Boucher's internal housecleaning because of his refusal to join in with the Nomads' centralized cocaine cartel. Elias Lekkas, the former drug-dealing partner of West End Gang leader Gerald Matticks, testified in court that Roy had been called to a meeting in a meat-processing plant belonging to Matticks and was ground like hamburger meat. His cocaine markets and personal assets were divided among his Hells Angels "brothers" (*Le Journal de Montréal*, December 5, 2002; *National Post*, April 4, 2001; Sher & Marsden, 2003: 228).

Non-ideological/Rationality

Despite the use of violence and intimidation—including that directed toward government agencies and communities—OMGs are non-ideological in the political sense. By the 1960s, perhaps the most discernible ideology among one-percenter clubs was that of fervent patriotism. Even today, however, this patriotism takes a back seat to the one ideology that truly guides the HAMC: making money. Violence or intimidation is not used as terrorists would for social or political change, but to further their revenue-generating (and monopolistic) goals. In short, OMGs, in particular the HAMC in Canada, have evolved from a group of unpredictable, erratic motorcycle-riding rowdies to rationally minded, sophisticated criminals.

KEY TERMS

Bandidos

Colours

Hells Angels Motorcycle Club

One-percenter

Outlaws Motorcycle Club Nation

Patched over

Prospects

Puppet clubs

Rocker

Road captain

Sergeant-at-arms

REVIEW QUESTIONS

1. What are the origins of OMGs in the United States? What are some of the seminal milestones in the history of OMGs, and the HAMC in particular?
2. What are the origins of OMGs in Canada? What are some of the seminal milestones in the history of OMGs, and the HAMC in particular, in Canada?
3. What factors attributed to the rise of OMGs in North America? What etiological theories presented in chapter 4 can be used to explain the origins and spread of COC in Canada?

4. Who are the dominant OMGs in the United States and Canada? What criminal activities are they involved in?
5. In general, how are OMGs in North America structured? What organizational models are most applicable to explain how COC is structured? What, if any, is the distinction between an OMG as a fraternal organization and as a criminal organization?
6. What are the characteristics of the Hells Angels, based on the application of theoretical models from chapter 3?
7. What is the significance of OMGs, and the Hells Angels in particular, when examining organized crime in Canada?

FURTHER READINGS

Barker, T. (2015). *Biker Gangs and Transnational Organized Crime* (2nd Ed.). Amsterdam: Anderson.

Lavigne, Y. (1996). *Hells Angels: Into the Abyss*. Toronto: HarperCollins.

Montgomery, R. (October 1976/1977). The Outlaw motorcycle subculture, *Canadian Journal of Criminology and Corrections*, 18 & 19(4): 332–42, 356–61.

Sher, J., & Marsden, W. (2003). *The Road to Hell: How the Biker Gangs Conquered Canada*. Toronto: Knopf Canada.

Thompson, H.S. (1967). *Hell's Angels: A Strange and Terrible Saga*. New York: Random House.

Wethern, G., & Colnett, V. (1978). *A Wayward Angel*. New York: R. Marek Publishers.

8 OTHER ORGANIZED CRIME GENRES IN CANADA

CHAPTER OUTLINE

- Introduction and Overview
- Indigenous Organized Crime
- Organized Street Gangs
- South Asian Organized Crime
- Vietnamese Organized Crime
- Middle Eastern Organized Crime
- Nigerian Criminal Enterprises
- Conclusion to Part II

LEARNING OUTCOMES

After reading this chapter, you should have a thorough understanding of the following:

- The organized crime genres and groups presented in this chapter
- Basic characteristics of these different genres
- How they compare to Tier I criminal organizations in Canada
- Their origins and history outside of and within Canada
- The etiological theories specific to (organized) criminality by Indigenous peoples in Canada

INTRODUCTION AND OVERVIEW

The preceding chapters discussed what the RCMP consider "Tier I" organized crime threats in Canada—in particular, Italian organized crime (the Sicilian Mafia and the Calabrian 'Ndrangheta), outlaw motorcycle gangs, and Chinese organized crime. This chapter explores other significant organized crime genres in this country, which, while ranked at a lower level on a threat assessment scale (i.e., they are less powerful and widespread), are still considered significant organized criminal associations. The genres that are the focus of this chapter are categorized as Indigenous, South Asian, Vietnamese, Middle Eastern, and Nigerian organized crime, as well as organized street gangs. In addition to a lower threat assessment level, the genres and groups examined in this chapter, for the most part, are more representative of a networked approach to organized crime: they eschew a traditional hierarchical structure and a restricted membership, the ties that bind members are less associational and more entrepreneurial, there is less organizational continuity, and there are no initiation rituals or rules and regulations.

As with the previous chapters, the OC genres presented in this chapter have largely been grouped by ethnicity or nationality. This is even true of the category of "organized street gangs," which are disproportionately made up of young men of African lineage in cities like Halifax, Montreal, Toronto, and Ottawa or of First Nations heritage in the prairie provinces. As described in the preface, categorizing organized crime genres based on ethnicity or nationality does not suggest that there is a causal relationship between ethnicity and organized criminality. As this book has demonstrated throughout, almost every ethnic community in Canada is represented by some form of organized criminal element. Readers should also be reminded that ethnicity may mask other factors that bring offenders together in an organized criminal conspiracy, even if they all share the same ethnicity or nationality.

Some of the organized crime genres and groups examined in this chapter include offenders from other countries (including legal and illegal immigrants). Some may be part of a transnational criminal network that is based in a foreign country, most notably the Nigerian criminal enterprises. As in the Sicilian Mafia or Chinese triads, the rise of some of the criminal associations examined in this chapter can be attributed to root causes in their source countries (e.g., poverty, marginalization, government corruption,

CRITICAL THINKING EXERCISE

Compare and contrast the history and characteristics of the different organized genres and specific groups covered in this chapter as well as with those presented in the previous three chapters. Reflect on the inherent difficulties in generalizing about organized crime associations or neatly categorizing different genres given their inherent complexity and pliability.

and conflict in countries like Vietnam, Nigeria, and Iran). Globalization is also a factor that has contributed to the rise and proliferation of genres and groups that have a trans-national component, such as South Asian Vietnamese, Middle Eastern, and Nigerian organized crime. With that said, theories and explanations as to why these organized crime genres and groups flourish in Canada can also be found in factors indigenous to this country. This includes structural forces and institutions that help create the precon-ditions for organized criminality within racialized (immigrant) communities.

An examination of the structural forces and institutions that marginalize, racialize, and criminalize certain groups of people in Canada is particularly important when ex-ploring the causes of organized criminality within First Nations and other Aboriginal communities in Canada. It can be argued that a history of colonialism, racism, margin-alization, and oppression have all contributed to the high rate of (organized) crime and violence within Canada's Indigenous population. Similar theories may also be applied to explain the over-representation of young men of African lineage in organized crime groups and street gangs in Canada, a group that has also met with widespread discrim-ination and racism in Canadian society.

INDIGENOUS ORGANIZED CRIME

Indigenous organized crime in Canada can be divided into two broad categories: (1) criminal groups and activities in Central Canada (Ontario and Quebec) that revolve around smuggling and the contraband cigarette trade, and (2) gangs located in the prai-rie provinces. The term *Indigenous* is used rather loosely in this chapter to refer to those who are First Nations, Inuit, or Métis.

Indigenous Organized Crime in Central Canada

Indigenous crime groups in Central Canada are active in the smuggling of cigarettes and tobacco leaves, alcohol, drugs, firearms, and people. Overwhelmingly, the smuggling occurs between the United States and Canada through the **Akwesasne** reserve of the **Mohawk Nation**, which straddles the border between the two countries (and which is referred to as the St. Regis Reservation on the American side). Criminal groups and in-dividuals on the reserve are also involved in unregulated manufacturing and distribution

CRITICAL THINKING EXERCISE

As you read through this chapter, refer back to chapter 4 to identify the theories that may (or may not) be applicable to explain the existence of OC genres dis-cussed in this chapter.

of tobacco products at the wholesale and retail levels. Cigarette-manufacturing plants and retail outlets have been established on the Akwesasne reserve outside of Cornwall, Ontario, as well as the Kahnawake reserve south of Montreal, the Kanesatake reserve in southwestern Quebec, and the Six Nations reserve near Brantford, Ontario. Police allege these factories are operating illegally and even have links to criminal entrepreneurs and organized crime groups from on and off the reserves. Together, the factories and the smuggling operations have been blamed for a deluge of cigarettes on the streets of Quebec, Ontario, the Maritimes, and other parts of Canada.

Police contend that at the centre of the smuggling activity on the Akwesasne reserve is the Mohawk Warrior Society. The society was founded in 1972 as a paramilitary organization that seeks to assert Mohawk authority over their traditional lands and is best known for its militant actions in the name of the Mohawk people. It gained national attention in Canada during the Oka Crisis of 1990 when it led a 67-day armed standoff with Canadian police and the military over a local land dispute in Quebec (and which resulted in the death of a Quebec provincial police officer). The Mohawk Warrior Society is a reflection and outgrowth of the longstanding animosity between the Mohawk people and governments in Canada and the United States (Dickson-Gilmore & Whitehead, 2003: 16).

Like a Chinese triad, it would be inaccurate to label the Mohawk Warrior Society a criminal organization; instead certain members and leaders of the group have been accused of being involved in criminal activity and have manipulated the society for this purpose. Since its founding, members of the Mohawk Warrior Society have been accused of subverting its advocacy of nationalist causes "for the mere purpose of making money for themselves" (Caledoniawakeupcall.com, n.d.). In the 1970s, the society began to gain more power on the reserves, including policing, and in doing so they were blamed for allowing smuggling and legalized gambling to flourish. The alleged appropriation of the Warrior Society for criminal purposes purportedly intensified when some of its members started providing security for the Mohawk criminal entrepreneurs involved in smuggling. The money generated from smuggling helped the society purchase weapons while convincing some members to become directly involved in smuggling activities themselves.

Individuals and groups from the Mohawk Nation play a central role in smuggling due primarily to geo-political factors that facilitate the movement of contraband across the Canada–US border. The 14,000-acre Akwesasne reserve straddles this border; in fact, the reserve's territory traverses five jurisdictions—Canada, the United States, Ontario, Quebec, and New York state—and agreements have been negotiated with federal, state, and provincial governments in both countries that uphold the right of the Mohawk people to freely cross the international border that cuts through the reserve. The Mohawk people believe they are responsible for the land of Akwesasne and because they have never signed a treaty of subjugation with Canadian, American, British, or French governments, they have the unconditional right of sovereignty over the land and it is people. The contention

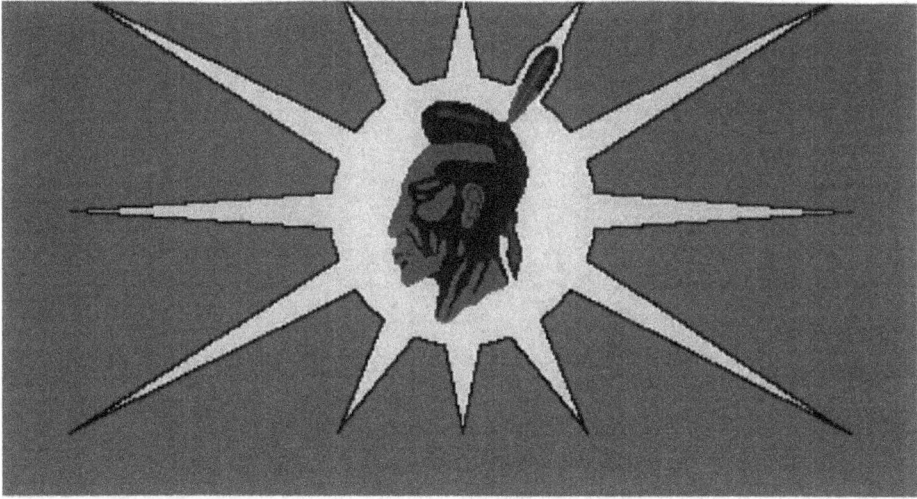

Photo 8.1: Flag of the Mohawk Warrior Society

Source: Xasartha, via Wikimedia Commons

of the Mohawk people that status Indians are not subject to any form of taxation on tribal land and are entitled to unfettered access across the international border, combined with their view of tobacco as a spiritual substance, has helped some rationalize their entry into the cigarette-smuggling trade. A portion of the St. Lawrence River also runs through the reserve, and divides the United States from Canada, which greatly facilitates the smuggling of contraband and people between the two nations.

These factors, combined with an increasingly well-honed smuggling infrastructure, have meant that a variety of contraband, drugs, and weapons cross through the reserve, with resident smugglers constantly shifting products based on demand and profitability (although tobacco products are a mainstay). As Dickson-Gilmore and Whitehead (2003: 13) write, the presence of the border that runs through the two countries "not only contributes to the fervent nationalism which is a large part of modern Mohawk political culture, but also to internal economic prosperity. While they rail against the borders, those boundaries have provided a significant source of illicit economic activity and relative prosperity in a context where legitimate options are often blocked and sometimes non-existent."

The Akwesasne reserve is used by organized crime groups from both on and off the reserve to smuggle bulk tobacco, cigarettes, firearms, and cocaine into Canada, while marijuana and synthetic drugs produced in Canada—as well as illegal migrants from outside of Canada—are smuggled through to the American side. Because they are primarily in the business of smuggling, criminal entrepreneurs and groups that draw from the Mohawk population partner extensively with other non-Indigenous criminal

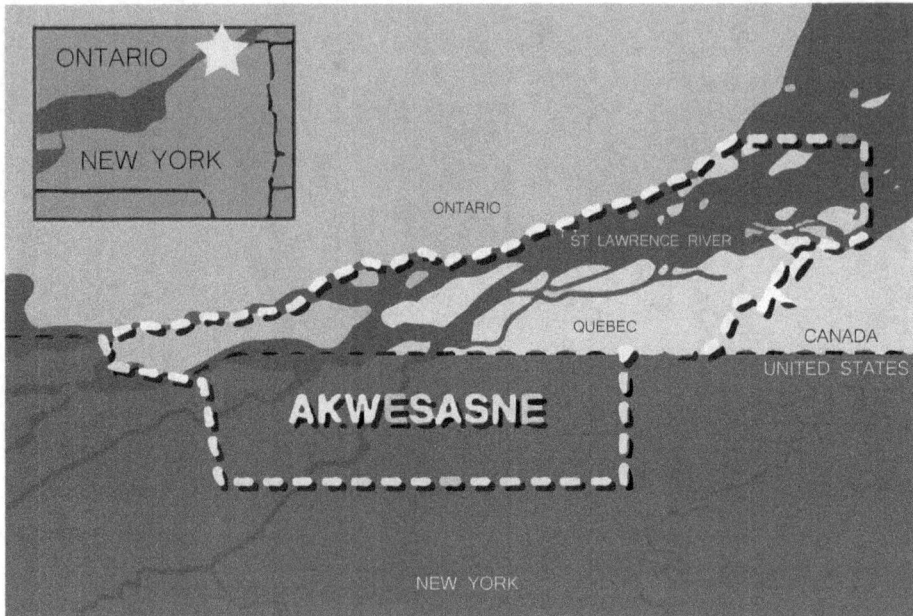

Figure 8.1: Map showing the boundaries of the Akwesasne/St. Regis Mohawk reserve

Source: Map by Devon Rogers

offenders and groups. Police say the Akwesasne reserve has attracted the attention of numerous criminal organizations intent on exploiting its geo-political circumstances and smuggling infrastructure, turning it into what the Mackenzie Institute (1996) calls the "Klondike of Organized Crime." These external groups are mostly responsible for supplying the goods (and people) that are smuggled across the border, and include the Hells Angels, the Italian Mafia in Montreal and New York City, Chinese criminal syndicates, Vietnamese crime groups, and Russian organized crime groups. As a Mohawk Grand Chief once opined, "On their maps, the gangsters put a pin at Akwesasne, and said, 'This is where it's easiest to cross'" (Fennel, 1999: 18).

Tobacco smuggling through First Nation territories (and into Canada generally) increased exponentially in the 1990s when the Canadian government dramatically increased the excise tax on the domestic sale of cigarettes. This was followed by a number of provincial tax hikes. However, no similar tax hikes were imposed on Canadian tobacco products that were destined for export. This resulted in a substantial difference between the price of exported Canadian cigarettes and those sold domestically. This price difference initiated a smuggling maelstrom that typically began with the lawful export of tax-exempt Canadian cigarettes to the United States and the illegal repatriation of these exports into Canada. Large volumes of exported Canadian cigarettes would be purchased in the United States and then smuggled into Canada where they were distributed to wholesalers, retailers, and street vendors who in turn sell them at a rate discounted far below the legitimate market price.

In 1994, RCMP Commissioner Norman Inkster said that as much as 70 percent of the contraband tobacco entering Canada was coming through the Akwesasne reserve. Between 1991 and 1997, a massive cigarette-smuggling conspiracy organized by the RJ Reynolds tobacco company illegally transported an estimated $687 million worth of cigarettes and alcohol into Canada through Akwesasne. Nearly two dozen people were convicted, including several Mohawk businessmen, a former tribal chief, and a top to-bacco executive with Northern Brands, a subsidiary of RJ Reynolds (*Globe and Mail*, July 21, 1997). Federal customs and excise tax policy changes and intensified border enforce-ment in the late 1990s helped to reduce the profitability and extent of the cross-border cigarette-smuggling trade, but it never was completely eradicated. Since this time, the scope of cigarette smuggling through Central Canada has steadily increased, due in part to the legal manufacture of cigarettes on the American side of the reserve. In August 2004, the RCMP said police in Cornwall (located close to the Akwesasne reserve) seized 53,510 cartons in the first half of that year, compared with 40,368 for all of 2003. Most of these brands were produced legally on the American side of the reserve and then smuggled into Canada. Prices of Indigenous-brand cigarettes were as low as $23 for 200—less than a third of the regular price in Canada at the time (*Halifax Daily News*, August 17, 2004; *Montreal Gazette*, August 26, 2004). By 2005, the RCMP estimated that 20,000 cartons of cigarettes crossed the Canadian border every day (*Edmonton Journal*, March 10, 2005). One police investigation in March 2009 resulted in the arrest of 22 people, who were charged with trafficking in cigarettes as well as drug offences. Among the arrested were two members of the Quebec City Hells Angels and two people from the Mohawk Nation in Kahnawake. They were accused of buying cigarettes on the reserve, selling them in towns and cities outside the reserve, and then investing the profits in methamphetamine production. At the time, police seized an array of drugs including crystal meth, cocaine, and marijuana (*Montreal Gazette*, March 26, 2009; *National Post*, September 21, 2010).

An increase in the smuggling of raw tobacco into Canada in recent years has cast a spotlight on another significant development that has transpired in the contraband cigarette trade in Canada in recent years. There is now a vibrant industry in unregulated cigarette manufacturing for the Canadian market on Mohawk reserves on both sides of the border. This has led to the smuggling of massive amounts of tobacco leaves from the United States into Canada.

By 2009, according to the *Montreal Gazette*, there were at least "20 native-owned manufacturers that produce millions of untaxed and unregulated cigarettes a day out of small and medium-size factories at Indian reserves in Ontario, Quebec and across the border in New York State" (*Montreal Gazette*, March 26, 2009). Some of these pro-duction facilitates "operate in clandestine warehouses and garages or makeshift shacks located along back roads on reserves" while "others work out of sophisticated plants sporting reconditioned British-made cigarette machines known as Mark-9s, each capable of producing 3,500 to 5,000 cigarettes a minute" (*Montreal Gazette*, March 26, 2009). The cigarettes produced from the factories are sold on or near the reserves for a fraction of what a regular pack of cigarettes cost in Canada, due to the absence of any provincial or federal sales tax. The cigarettes are also transported outside Ontario and Quebec and are sold as far away as British Columbia. By 2015, the RCMP estimated there were as many as 50 illegal factories in Ontario and Quebec, operating outside of any government regulation, which were able to produce up to 10,000 cigarettes each minute (The National Coalition Against Contraband Tobacco Press Release, November 19, 2015). Police allege that some of the capital used to set up the factory has come from established crime groups from outside the reserve (for more details, see the section on tobacco smuggling in chapter 10). Because the federal government contends the manufacturing plants are illegal, police have undertaken numerous enforcement actions to shut them down.

Case Study: The "Largest Investigation of Contraband Tobacco Ever Undertaken in North America"

At the end of April 2014, an inter-agency task force involving the Sûreté du Québec, the RCMP, and Canadian and US border enforcement agencies arrested 28 people as part of an investigation into a $30-million contraband tobacco conspiracy linked to the Italian Mafia in Montreal and Indigenous criminal groups. It was the "largest investigation of contraband tobacco ever undertaken in North America," a Sûreté du Québec official told the media.

Four hundred police officers executed search warrants and made arrests on the island of Montreal and in Dundee near the border of the Akwesasne reserve. Police seized 40,000 kilograms of tobacco worth around $7 million on the Canadian black market, as well as $450,000 in cash and more than 1300 marijuana plants. Police allege members of the Montreal Mafia purchased bulk tobacco in North Carolina and then smuggled it into Canada illegally in tractor trailers through the St-Bernard-de-Lacolle border crossing or the Akwesasne reserve. According to police, members of Indigenous crime groups helped import the tobacco, which included hiding the trucks in a warehouse on the Akwesasne reserve. The tobacco was then sold to illegal factories where contraband cigarettes were made.

Inspector Michel Pelletier of the Sûreté du Québec told a news conference that there was "a sharing of profits which was done in the order of 60–40 that is 60 per cent of profits went to the Italian Mafia and 40 per cent to aboriginal organized crime." Among those arrested were two Montreal men who police identified as the main organizers of the smuggling conspiracy and who are members of the Rizzuto Mafia family (Canadian Press, April 30, 2014; CBC News, April 30, 2014; Global News, April 30, 2013; Infozine.com, May 1, 2014; Postmedia News, May 14, 2014).

In 2002, Rowena General, then the chief-of-staff at the Akwesasne tribal council, argued that the cigarette manufacturing taking place on the reserve is perfectly legal. "Two manufacturing facilities are fully licensed by the tribal government, fully regulated, they pay all their fees." What they don't pay is the federal excise tax paid by other cigarette manufacturers, which according to Canada Customs and Revenue Agency and RCMP makes the Mohawk cigarettes illegal (*CBC News*, August 7, 2002). Others who defend the on-reserve cigarette manufacturing say that federal governments in either the United States or Canada do not have the legal right to regulate tobacco production on sovereign Mohawk land. Further, the manufacturing plants have become a vital part of the local economy, and thousands of Indigenous and non-Indigenous people are employed in the manufacturing, wholesaling, and retailing of the cigarettes.

Akwesasne has also become what one district attorney with New York's northern office called, "the most significant source of alien smuggling across the northeast border" (United States Congress, House of Representatives, 2000, 158). Officials with the US Border Patrol Agency estimated that in 1999, between 300 and 500 illegal migrants a month were being smuggled from Canada into the United States through the reserve (*Montreal Gazette*, October 5, 1996). In December 1998, US Attorney General Janet Reno announced that Canadian and American law enforcement agencies had broken up the largest immigrant-smuggling conspiracy ever uncovered on America's northern border up to that point. "Operation Over the Rainbow II" targeted a migrant smuggling scheme jointly undertaken by Chinese and Mohawk criminal groups that ferried as many as 150 people a month from mainland China to Canada, and then through the reserve, before ending up in New York City. The price of a one-way ticket was as much as $47,000, and the smuggling enterprise raked in an estimated $170 million (*Montreal Gazette*, December 11, 1998). In August 2015, federal authorities in the United States arrested three Chinese nationals who were on US soil illegally as part of an investigation into a people-smuggling network that was moving Chinese nationals from Toronto to New York City through Akwesasne. Among those arrested was a Chinese national who admitted to having already transported seven people in three previous trips from Akwesasne to New York City. The smuggled individuals "are usually hidden in a home in the community after they are taken by boat across the St. Lawrence River. They are then spirited to a spot on the outskirts of the reserve for the final leg of the trip to New York City or other points. In one case last year, an Akwesasne resident bought bus tickets for two Chinese nationals for the trip to New York City" (APTN National News, November 3, 2015).

Organized Indigenous Gangs in the Prairie Provinces

Indigenous crime groups in the prairie provinces mostly operate as street gangs; however, while they "are generally involved in opportunistic, spontaneous and disorganized street-level criminal activities" (Criminal Intelligence Service Canada, 2004: 20–21), they are also behind more serious crimes, including drug trafficking, prostitution, firearms offences, and witness intimidation (Criminal Intelligence Service of Saskatchewan, 2005). Indigenous street gangs include both older teens and young adults and have been linked to some dominant organized crime groups in the Prairies, including the Hells Angels.

In its 2003 annual report on organized crime, CISC says, "the primary gangs nationally are the Indian Posse, Redd Alert, Warriors and Native Syndicate." These groups are especially active in Prairie cities with a high Indigenous population such as Edmonton, Regina, and Winnipeg. The 2003 report called Indigenous gangs "a low-level organized criminal threat," but then provides a long list of their criminal activities, some of which are well organized: cocaine, crack, and methamphetamine trafficking; prostitution; contraband tobacco sales; break-and-enter, home invasions, and robberies; vehicle theft; illegal gambling; and debt collection and enforcement for other organized crime groups such as the Hells Angels (Criminal Intelligence Service Canada, 2003; *National Post*, October 28, 2003).

In its 2004 annual report, Criminal Intelligence Service Alberta said that at that time there were a "total of 153 federal or provincial inmates with aboriginal gang affiliations" in the province (as cited in the *Edmonton Sun*, January 4, 2004). A 2005 report from Criminal Intelligence Service of Saskatchewan on Indigenous gang activity states, "gang-related crimes and recruitment will continue to escalate throughout the province given our demographic trends" (as cited in Indianz.Com, March 15, 2005). These demographic trends include the large number of Indigenous youth under the age of 25. This is exacerbated by the deplorable social conditions that many on and off reserves have to endure, which contributes to gang involvement and the onset of criminal and delinquent behaviour. The report concludes that Indigenous gangs

Case Study: The Wolfe Brothers, the Indian Posse, and Factors that Put Indigenous Youth at Risk of Gang Involvement and Chronic Offending

The origins of the "Indian Posse" (IP) can be traced to 1988 when it was founded by Daniel Wolfe and his brother Richard in Winnipeg. Born to a mother and father who were both **residential school** survivors, the brothers grew up in poverty as both their parents struggled with addictions. Their father was also abusive and "one moment that left an indelible mark was the day the Wolfe brothers saw their mother in hospital, beaten black and blue by their father," according to a *Globe and Mail* profile of Daniel Wolfe. Both brothers spent time in foster homes, but were often unsupervised, stayed out late many nights, and frequently ran away. Before they were even teenagers, they stole a van and drove from Winnipeg to Regina. They had been gone a week by the time police were able to locate them. Both brothers had been arrested on numerous occasions before they even went through puberty.

The IP was born in the Wolfe family home in the summer of 1988. There were seven founding members, all of them Indigenous and all from poor families from Winnipeg. Daniel was just 12 at the time. "They hit on the name 'Posse' while flipping through the pages of a hip-hop magazine," the *Globe and Mail* article recounts. "They chose Indian, rather than native, much the way black rap groups often defiantly labelled themselves with the N-word."

"It was about us Indians sticking together at the time. Because we were looked down on," Richard says in a *Globe and Mail* interview.

At the age of 13, Richard bought his first handgun, which he took to school tucked in to the back of his pants. It was not long thereafter that he had an AK-47 hidden in a heating vent at his house. The brothers dropped out of school and fully immersed themselves in a life of crime. Before long, they were involved in armed robberies.

"Even back then, they were very violent, as far as street gangs went," Winnipeg Police Constable Nick Leone is quoted as saying.

By 1991, the IP gang began started selling drugs, which helped fuel their expansion across Winnipeg. They then moved onto Indigenous reserves in Manitoba where they not only sold drugs but recruited young people for the gang. "With almost universal unemployment and widespread despair, the market was insatiable. And as the Posse's brand grew, kids eagerly joined up," according to the *Globe and Mail*.

By the time the brothers were in their late teens, each was making $15,000 to $30,000 a week. Much of that revenue was from drug sales and the lower-echelon IP soldiers were expected to "kick up" 35 percent of what they made selling drugs to the gang's leadership. Richard was also running the gang's prostitution business. "The gang muscled out the existing pimps, improved the women's take from 25 per cent to 40 per cent and made $3,000 to $5,000 a night running 10 girls."

Because both brothers were frequently in and out of prison, they were able to recruit more members to the IP. By the late 1990s, the Indian Posse reportedly had more than 1000 members and some estimated it was as high as 3000. As the gang grew in size it included non-Indigenous peoples, such as Ron Taylor, an African-Canadian who was personally recruited by the Wolfe brothers.

In November 2009, Daniel Wolfe was convicted of two counts of first-degree murder and three counts of attempted murder and was sentenced to life with no parole for at least 25 years. The conviction followed his involvement in a deadly home invasion that targeted members of the rival Native Syndicate in Saskatchewan. In January 2010, the 33-year-old Wolfe was stabbed to death during a brawl at the Saskatchewan Penitentiary. His brother Richard died in 2016 as he was serving time at Prince Albert Penitentiary for a sexual offence. Despite the deaths of Daniel and Richard, the IP is still considered one of Winnipeg's biggest gangs and also has a presence in Alberta and Saskatchewan (*Globe and Mail*, June 18, 2011, *Winnipeg Free Press*, January 6, 2010, June 6, 2017).

Photo 8.2: Manitoba Warriors vest

Source: Courtesy of Winnipeg Police Department

have grown to the extent that Saskatchewan now has more young gang members per capita than any other province. The report said that at the time, there were 12 known adult and youth gangs operating in Saskatchewan. Some of the adult-oriented gangs include Native Syndicate, Indian Posse, Redd Alert, Saskatchewan Warriors, Crazy Cree, Mixed Blood, Tribal Warriors, and West Side Soldiers. Among the youth gangs are the Crips, Junior Mixed Blood, Indian Mafia Crips, and North Central Rough Riderz. Of Saskatchewan's 1315 gang members, about 500 operate out of three cities: Regina, Saskatoon, and Prince Albert. Gangs are also expanding their age range—about 70 percent of those involved in gangs in Saskatoon are 18 years or older, while in Regina, the average age of a gang member is around 24 (CBC News, March 14, 2005;

Criminal Intelligence Service of Saskatchewan, 2005; Indianz.Com, March 15, 2005; *Regina Leader Post*, March 16, 2005, March 17, 2005).

One of the main IP rivals is the Manitoba Warriors, which was founded in 1993 and over time claimed between 300 and 400 members, most of them adults. The Warriors distinguish themselves from other Indigenous gangs by adopting an organizational structure similar to outlaw motorcycle gangs. They are identified by the colours black and white and are heavily involved in drug trafficking and prostitution. According to the Winnipeg-based *Police Insider* e-magazine, "The Manitoba Warriors evolved into a highly lucrative drug trafficking organization running dial a dealer crack lines and crack shacks to maximize earning potential. They became a force on the streets and participated in violent confrontations in their fight to control 'turf' with rival street gangs like the Indian Posse" (Jewell, 2014).

In 1998, Winnipeg police arrested 35 members and associates of the Warriors and charged them with a variety of drug trafficking and related offences (Jewell, 2014). In 2012, two men with links to the Manitoba Warriors were arrested following a drug raid by police in Winnipeg. Three other suspects were arrested inside a nearby vehicle, which also contained 21 ounces of cocaine, along with a cutting agent and other drug paraphernalia. Police caught another suspect with a hydraulic pill press, packaging material, a large quantity of cash, and a loaded Cobra .38-calibre handgun. All faced drug and weapons charges (*Winnipeg Sun*, June 8, 2012b). Throughout their existence, the Warriors have been engaged in violent running battles with its rivals. This violence was particularly endemic in 2008 when members of the gang were behind numerous shootouts. In June 2008, four members were arrested after 30 shots were fired into a Winnipeg home. On November 20, 2008, a 26-year-old man police said was an associate of the Warriors associate was shot and killed in Winnipeg (Jewell, 2014).

Discussion and Analysis: Theories to Explain Indigenous (Organized) Crime and Gangs

A significant issue facing Canadian society is the disproportionate contact that Indigenous people have with the criminal justice system. This includes their vast over-representation within the correctional system.

"The disturbing reality of Aboriginal over-representation in Canadian correctional populations is well-known," the website of the federal Office of the Correctional Investigator reads. "Aboriginal people—First Nations, Métis and Inuit—comprise 3.8% of the Canadian population but now account for 23.2% of the total inmate population." Between 2001 and 2012, "the incarcerated Aboriginal population has increased 37.3%, while incarcerated Aboriginal women have increased by 109%. Aboriginal women offenders comprise 33% of the total inmate population under federal jurisdiction" (Office of the Correctional Investigator, 2014).

The factors that contribute to this over-representation, and to the involvement of Indigenous people in gangs and organized crime, are complex, multi-faceted, and historically rooted. Regardless of what theories are applied to explain this unyielding problem, the root causes are most frequently situated in broad structural forces and immediate environmental conditions. This includes the immediate deleterious social environment (dysfunctional family conditions, poor communities, and negative peer networks) that contributes to the onset of criminal behaviour among Indigenous youth all the way to the structural forces and institutions within Canadian society that encourage particular racism, discrimination, marginalization, and colonialization.

Sociological theories already discussed in chapter 4 are somewhat applicable. Strain theory suggests that Indigenous people turn to crime because the ladder for their social mobility is closed within a highly affluent society due to racism, discrimination, and marginalization. Social disorganization theory is also applicable given the often deplorable conditions that characterize First Nations communities as well as the disadvantaged neighbourhoods in urban centres that many off-reserve Indigenous families live. In both cases, these families live in communities that can be considered "socially disorganized," which undermines the ability of the family and entire communities to positively socialize young people.

In this respect, dominant social and cultural institutions of Indigenous communities have been weakened; but the question remains how and why have they been weakened? Structuralist criminological theories, which are oriented toward identifying the root causes of crime and criminality within dominant social, political, economic, and cultural forces and institutions, have been developed that are specific to Indigenous people (in Canada) to answer this question. One structural theory is referred to as the **colonial model**, which argues that the Indigenous population and culture has been colonized by Euro-Canadians, which has devastating psychological and social consequences. The alienation among Indigenous people that results from being colonized may manifest itself in crime, criminal behaviour, and a high rate of violence. The "colonization and conquest" of Indigenous people in Canada has been instrumental in "the destruction of Aboriginal culture, communities and lifeways," Silverman, Teevan, and Sacco write. Furthermore, "the marginalization of Aboriginal peoples in Canadian society" is "reflected in high rates of unemployment, low levels of formal education, poverty and substandard living conditions. Taken together, the condition of Aboriginal peoples is seen to contribute to high rates of criminal behavior" (Silverman, Teevan, & Sacco, 2000: 258).

The **historic trauma transmission model** argues that the acculturation of Indigenous peoples that accompanies colonialization produces a "learned helplessness" or fatalism. This can lead to self-blame, passivity, hostile behaviours, and decreased sense of self, which manifest in suicide, violence, and chronic criminal behaviour (Oriola, 2015: 138–39).

Critical race theory purports that the criminal justice system reflects the norms and values of society's dominant ethnocultural group and, therefore, favours that group. As a result, law enforcement and the interpretation of the law are subjective

Case Study: Burton Rice and Cigarette Manufacturing on First Nations Land

In a 2010 article, the *National Post* describes how Burton Rice, a Mohawk businessman on the Kahnawake reserve in Quebec, faced tax fraud charges in relation to an illicit cigarette-manufacturing operation his company owned on the reserve. He was also accused of having ties to a senior member of the Hells Angels in the province, Salvatore Cazetta, and it was alleged that the Hells Angels provided capital for the operation.

Rice vehemently denied the allegations, saying his family owns the plant that was raided by law enforcement and tax authorities. He acknowledged that Rice Mohawk Industries (RMI) did have an association with Cazetta, but that only involved using his legitimate beverage distribution company to distribute a legal product totally unrelated to manufactured cigarettes. Rice said that when the tobacco-manufacturing plant was first established, it was completely legitimate, with all the appropriate taxes being paid. However, facing opposition and roadblocks from Mohawk and provincial governments, he said RMI eventually had no choice but to operate outside the strict limits of non-Indigenous law.

"There's nothing we've done that is illegal. There's nothing in there that I'm ashamed of," Rice was quoted as saying in the article. "I want justice, I want truth to come out. I'm not going to have my name, my family's name dragged through the mud based on lies."

According to the *National Post*, "Mr. Rice said police wanted to clamp down on Kahnawake cigarette factories earlier, but Mohawk leaders had refused to acquiesce—until police came up with what he calls bogus allegations of links between his company, bikers and narcotics."

In his interview with the newspaper, the private-school-educated Rice said his status as an Indigenous person immersed in white society—where schoolmates taunted him with names like "savage"—helps him identify with the one-percenter bikers. Although he said he does not condone their criminal behaviour, "I've always been viewed as an outsider ... Natives, guys like me, are able ... to say 'I know how you feel'" (*National Post*, September 21, 2010).

At least three of the aforementioned theories may be applicable to this case, and to cigarette manufacturing on First Nations land generally. Strain theory would suggest that Indigenous people turn to illicit manufacturing of cigarettes because legitimate opportunities have been closed to them to do so through stringent government licensing requirements (which benefit large tobacco companies). The colonial model would argue that the colonialization of the Mohawk peoples and the imposition of Canadian laws have undermined their relationship with tobacco as a spiritual substance and their sovereign rights to produce tobacco products on

Continued

their own land, especially since they have not signed any treaties that subjugate their own laws, rights, and beliefs to the Canadian government. While American and Canadian governments view smuggling through the reserve as a crime, many on the reserve do not view it as criminal at all, given the sovereign rights of the Mohawk people to cross the international border freely (with no imposition of taxes or duties). Thus, Indigenous organized crime, at least on the Mohawk reserves, is what Silverman and colleagues call "a perfect example of a 'manufactured' organized crime problem" (Silverman, Teevan, & Sacco, 2000: 296).

Critical race theory would suggest that cigarette-manufacturing laws reflect the norms and values of society's dominant Euro-Canadian population (including the large tobacco companies, which the elites of this population control) and, therefore, favours that group.

CRITICAL THINKING EXERCISE

What other etiological theories do you believe are applicable to explaining Indigenous organized crime in Canada? How is organized criminality by Indigenous people representative of deeper social problems both on and off reserves? To what extent do you accept theories (for instance, from administrative criminology) that reject sociological and structuralist explanations and instead places the blame for organized criminality on Indigenous peoples and cultures?

and lead to conditions in the criminal justice system where racism is normative. Indigenous people are over-represented in the criminal justice system in part because of racism within the criminal justice system itself (Oriola, 2015: 139–40).

Notwithstanding these general theories, Dickson-Gilmore and Whitehead (2003: 13) remind us that the factors that contribute to criminality are highly individualized: "... like all human beings, aboriginal people who participate in antisocial activities come from a range of backgrounds and cultures, and that participation is informed by a range of motivations, aspirations and contexts."

ORGANIZED STREET GANGS

Any discussion of street gangs in a book on Canadian organized crime should begin by making a few salient points. First, as described in chapter 2, street gangs are different from organized crime both conceptually and in real life. Among the differences: they have fewer members, they tend to be spatially concentrated (on one street, a block, a neighbourhood, or a city), their criminal activities don't necessarily revolve around profit-oriented offences (they may form to protect members or to mark out a particular area as their turf), and they are generally less sophisticated.

Second, street gangs in Canada have increasingly been used by criminal organizations—such as the Hells Angels, the Montreal Mafia, and Chinese criminal networks—to undertake certain criminal activities for them (for instance, drug trafficking, human trafficking, extortion, enforcement). By extension, the use of street gangs by criminal organizations is meant to help insulate the latter from law enforcement actions. While some gangs are connected to larger crime groups, others remain stubbornly independent and may actually compete against established criminal organizations, which has led to violent clashes.

Third, street gangs in larger urban centres tend to be disproportionately made up of young men from racial minority groups—those who suffer from the most endemic discrimination in Canadian society. This includes men of African lineage in Halifax, Montreal, Ottawa, and Toronto, as well as those from Indigenous communities in the Prairies.

Fourth, some street gangs have evolved into criminal organizations to the extent that they satisfy many of the definitions and characteristics outlined in chapters 2 and 3. Indeed, a recent history of street gangs in Canada show that they have become more organized, more entrepreneurial, more sophisticated, better armed, and more violent. Membership in these emergent gangs is increasingly multi-ethnic, especially in British Columbia. Many gangs are now also multi-generational; some have been in existence since the 1980s and 1990s, which means their remaining original members, now in their thirties and forties, have been joined by new recruits in their teens and twenties. Involvement in street gangs is fluid (as is the case of organized crime networks) in that members frequently come and go and an individual's allegiance can quickly shift between gangs. The reach of the once-localized gangs has also expanded beyond their neighbourhood and their city, and they even are involved in criminal activities such as drug and human trafficking that cross provincial boundaries. Gun-related violence also continues to be a hallmark of street gangs; the number of gang-related killings has grown as a proportion of the overall murder rate in Canada, which has been steadily declining.

In a 2010 report, Criminal Intelligence Service Canada stated that law enforcement agencies across the country have witnessed an increase in the number of street gangs in urban centres: "This increase may be due to new gangs forming but it may also be attributable to a combination of other factors. Some of these include higher-level organized crime groups being identified as street gangs, cells from larger gangs being identified as new entities, street gangs splintering into smaller criminal groups, or gangs changing names" (Criminal Intelligence Service Canada, 2010: 18). Much media and police attention in recent years has been riveted on the fall of the Rizzuto Mafia family and how this has destabilized the criminal underworld in Montreal. Similar power struggles are occurring in the criminal underground in other major cities in Canada as competition in illegal drug markets has intensified and as "shifting alliances and new power blocks" form among individual criminal offenders and groups, according to Sergeant Lindsey Houghton, spokesman for BC's Combined Forces Special Enforcement Unit (QMI Agency, November 2, 2012). For CISC (Criminal Intelligence Service Canada, 2010: 18), "Gang-related violence is often attributed to street gang expansion or territorial conflict and can also be opportunistic and appear to be spontaneous."

Nova Scotia

A 2008 report from the Halifax Mayor's Roundtable on Violence states that the Halifax Regional Municipality (HRM) is "home to small gangs centered in the drug trade and accountable for a number of retaliatory murders and public-frightening drive-by shootings ... " (Clairmont, 2008: 22). In 2012, an integrated enforcement team involving the Halifax Regional Police and the RCMP was formed to focus on gangs and gang-related gun violence in Greater Halifax. According to one media article, the team's head, Staff Sergeant Jim Butler, indicated police are "watching six to eight gangs, ranging in size from four members up to dozens. Most have six to eight members and most of them are young, some only 15." He went on to say "all of the gangs are in the drug business and have firearms," which are used "to intimidate rivals and protect their own drug-dealing turf and to expand their territory" (*Chronicle Herald*, March 5, 2012).

Gangs identified by police in the greater Halifax area sport such names as Greystone Gangsters, YMOB (Young mob), Spryfield MOB, Downie Town Boys, Hali Soldiers Society, the Murda Squad, and North Preston's Finest (*Chronicle Herald*, August 1, 2011, August 6, 2011; *Metro Halifax*, February 14, 2012). According to a 2007 federal Justice Department report examining urban gangs across Canada, those in Metro Halifax "appear to have started on a small scale but the nature and violence of the offences they are involved (in) seems to have increased." The report identifies five urban gangs in the city with the most prevalent being the Murda Squad, which has said to have between 10 and 15 formal members as well as numerous associates. "They often wear specific coloured bandanas and T-shirts or sweatshirts. They also tend to use hand signs for communication" and are into "robberies, trafficking, weapons, offences, threats and assaults" (as cited in the *Chronicle Herald*, August 6, 2011).

Another gang operating in the HRM is the Hali Soldiers Society, which has approximately 10 members and, according to an RCMP member who monitors outlaw biker gangs for the provincial intelligence unit, has ties to the Hells Angels. However, they are not a one-percenter motorcycle club, the RCMP official stressed. "I consider the Hali Soldiers Society a street gang ... This group consists of a number of members that are well-known as drug dealers. We know that some of their members have been involved in violent incidents recently" (*Chronicle Herald*, August 1, 2011).

One of the longest-lasting and more organized criminal gangs in the province is North Preston's Finest (NPF). Formed in the mid- to late 1980s, the gang's base is the African–Nova Scotian community of North Preston, located in Dartmouth, northeast of Halifax. Estimates on the size of the gang range from 50 to 80 people with ages of between 18 and 28 (Perrin, 2010; *Windsor Star*, October 26, 2007). The gang is best known for human trafficking and prostitution and has been implicated in several police cases in which girls and women have been lured from Nova Scotia and then transported to Ontario to work in the sex trade. NPF members are also alleged to have been involved in murders in Nova Scotia and Ontario's Niagara region (Canada.com, October 25, 2007; CBC News, October 25, 2007; *Niagara Falls Review*, October 7, 2009).

Detective Thai Truong of York Regional Police in Ontario said in a 2014 media interview that it's not uncommon for police in the GTA to run into pimps from North Preston or women who've been moved from the Maritimes to the GTA. "Once the girls are recruited, the Scotian or the pimp is generally, or typically, not going to be pimping her out from where she's from," Truong said. "He's going to be taking her out of her own jurisdiction, out of her comfort zone, where her family is, her friends are. Any social supports she may have. He's going to move her west and essentially they find their way ... a lot of the time in Ontario and the Greater Toronto Area" (CBC News, October 8, 2014). Once in Ontario, the women may be forced to work in strip clubs and are not allowed to leave the clubs until they've met their quota of $1000, which often means they have to resort to prostitution. Violence is used to enforce this quota and to keep the women from leaving; in addition to brutal beatings, members of the women's families have been subject to intimidation and violence. In 2010, a 24-year-old "East Coast pimp" believed to be part of the NPF's sex-trafficking ring in Ontario was sentenced to three years for assault, forcible confinement, resisting arrest, possession of ammunition contrary to a prohibition order, breach of probation, and breach of recognizance (*Toronto Sun*, June 11, 2010).

Montreal

In Montreal, young men of Haitian descent make up a disproportionate number of gangs, such as the Crips, the Bloods, the Bo-Gars, the Syndicate, and the 67s. Black street gangs in Montreal have been known to work for the Hells Angels and the Rizzuto Mafia family. At the same time, the weakening of Quebec's two dominant crime groups in recent years has helped create an unstable underworld in Montreal, and there is evidence that black street gangs have attempted to fill this void.

In 2014, Ducarme Joseph, whom police once described as Montreal's most powerful street gang leader, was murdered in the neighbourhood of St-Michel. The 46-year-old Joseph led the 67 gang—so-named for a bus route that runs through the neighbourhood. Some believe Joseph was trying to fill the aforementioned power vacuum in Montreal's criminal underworld. Joseph is also believed to be linked to the 2009 shooting of Nick Rizzuto, the son of deceased Montreal Mafia leader Vito Rizzuto. *La Presse* reported that police accuse Joseph of driving the getaway car. In their book, *Mafia Inc.*, André Cédilot and André Noel speculate the Rizzuto clan had put a $200,000 price on Joseph's head. According to the *Globe and Mail*, "The high-profile murder may finally be the execution of an old vendetta from the Montreal Mafia, or may be the Hells Angels sending a message to street gangs that the bikers are back after several years on their heels." Montreal police took the unusual step of publicly warning Joseph that a contract had been put out on his life. In 2010, Joseph was the target of a shooting in a store he owned in Montreal. He wasn't injured and was able to escape through the back door. His bodyguard and store manager, however, were both shot and killed in the attack (Cédilot & Noël, 2011: 470–71; *Globe and Mail*, August 4, 2014; *La Presse*, August 2, 2014).

The Bo-Gars is another of the high-profile gangs in the city and a dominant player in drug trafficking and prostitution in north-end Montreal. In August 2012, the QMI

Case Study: Street Gangs and Organized Crime in Montreal

In November 2015, police in Quebec arrested and charged 48 people, including a number of high-ranking figures allegedly linked to the Montreal Mafia and the Hells Angels. The Sûreté du Québec said the raids targeted an alliance among the Hells Angels, the Mafia, and street gangs in the city. Charges against those arrested include drug trafficking, conspiracy to commit murder, and criminal organization offences. The arrests were part of a drug-trafficking investigation, codenamed Project Magot and Mastiff, which began in 2013. Those charged are alleged to have taken part in two different conspiracies to traffic cocaine between January 1, 2013, and November 16, 2015. During the investigation, police seized $1.2 million in cash, 41 guns, 122 cell phones, one Harley-Davidson motorcycle, and 7 kilograms of cocaine.

One of the central figures arrested was Gregory Woolley. "In recent years, police sources have described him as someone who appears to act as a go-between for the Hells Angels, the Mafia and many street gang members," according to the *Montreal Gazette*. "He was a cornerstone of the alliance," Lieutenant-Detective Dubé of the Sûreté du Québec was quoted in the media as saying.

Those arrested "are all key figures in the volatile underworld power struggles that followed the 2013 death of Vito Rizzuto," contends a *Globe and Mail* article. In the wake of Rizzuto's death, the Mafia, Hells Angels, and street gangs formed an alliance to control the drug trade in Montreal and split the revenue among them, according to police. The groups purportedly co-operated to import cocaine and launder the millions of dollars in revenues (CBC News, November 19, 2015; *Globe and Mail*, November 19, 2015; *Montreal Gazette*, November 19, 2015, November 25, 2015).

news agency reported that 37-year-old Chénier Dupuy, who police say was the long-time leader of the Bo-Gars, was murdered just a month after he had supposedly rejected a partnership offer from the Hells Angels. According to QMI, Dupuy "had slapped a rival gang leader in the face during a Hells-sponsored summit north of Montreal aimed at uniting several street gangs under the Hells banner." He then "reportedly stormed out of the meeting" and vowed "never to work with the Hells." As a result, Dupuy was marked for death, QMI reported based on police sources (CBC News, August 13, 2012; *Montreal Gazette*, August 11, 2012; QMI Agency, August 16, 2012).

The aforementioned summit was organized by Gregory Woolley, a former member of the Rockers, the Montreal-based motorcycle gang that was under the control of the Nomads chapter of the Hells Angels in Quebec during the 1990s (he could never had become a member of the Hells Angels because he is black). He was also the reputed leader of the Syndicate, a street gang formed by the Hells Angels in the 1990s at the height of its war with the Rock Machine. Woolley gained notoriety after he was acquitted in two different murder cases.

Southern Ontario

The Galloway Boys are believed to be one of Toronto's larger and better-organized gangs. Police say their territory is centred in the intersection of Kingston and Galloway Roads, a poor neighbourhood of low-rent apartment buildings and government-subsidized housing in Scarborough. However, police investigations show that their criminal activities, such as drug and gun trafficking and prostitution, stretch beyond this neighbourhood to various parts of Toronto and even other cities outside of Ontario. In July 2014, 11 people were charged in connection with an alleged human-trafficking and prostitution ring that stretched from Toronto to Montreal. Police alleged that the teen girls were forced to work as prostitutes out of hotels and motels in the GTA and Montreal by associates of the Galloway Boys gang. Victims were typically recruited in their neighbourhood, police allege (*Scarborough Mirror*, July 7, 2014).

The Galloway Boys began to gain a public profile in the late 1990s and early 2000s, in part due to their violent rivalry with another gang called the Malvern Crew. After a string of shootings in the early 2000s, police laid hundreds of charges on suspected Galloway members, ranging from robbery to first-degree murder. In 2009, three members were convicted of first-degree murder, attempted murder, and committing murder for the benefit of a criminal organization. A jury concluded they were responsible for the drive-by shooting death of a young man whose SUV they mistakenly thought belonged to a Malvern gang member (*Globe and Mail*, September 11, 2012).

Police have linked a number of shootings and homicides in recent years in Toronto to gang activity and the Galloway boys specifically. According to the *Globe and Mail*, the more recent shootings and murders are being committed by a "new generation"

CRITICAL THINKING EXERCISE

What etiological theories do you believe are applicable to explaining the disproportionate number of young males of African descent involved in organized street
gangs in Canada? How is organized criminality by African-Canadians representative of deeper social problems in this country?

of Galloway Boys. "Tutored by older criminals released from jail, a new core of street
criminals are vying for leadership of the Galloway Boys gang in Scarborough, resulting in some of the worst violence ever seen in Toronto ... " Detective Sergeant Brett
Nicol of the Toronto Police was quoted as saying. "We have some information that the
shooters in these incidents are vying for leadership within the Galloway Boys group."
He said the shootings involved a group of four or five gang members counselled by
older members who were convicted during a 2004 crackdown on the gang. Disputes
over turf, the Galloway Boys' propensity for violence, their ability to obtain guns "and
their willingness to seek revenge," was behind the latest wave of violence, Nicol told
the media (*Globe and Mail*, September 11, 2012). In October 2013, Toronto police
announced they had laid charges against more than 40 people, including 25 alleged
members of the Galloway Boys.

Street gangs are also active in Ontario outside of Toronto and some have become so
brazen they are even challenging the local hegemony of the Hells Angels. This became
evident in London, Ontario, on September 9, 2015, when Steve Sinclair, a member of
the Hells Angels puppet club the Gate Keepers was shot and killed. He was murdered
outside a social club frequented by members of the local chapters of the Gate Keepers
MC and the HAMC. Police quickly arrested five people for the murder of the 49-year-
old. One of those charged with first-degree murder was a 15-year-old boy. Before the
arrests were made, police issued a description of the suspect: a slim black man, 18 to
22 years old, and between 5'8" and 5'11" tall. The Hells Angels chapter in London had
already been the target of violence and arson in January 2012 as a result of what police
called a turf war with rival street gangs over the city's illegal drug trade. Five businesses
(some with connections to members of the HAMC) were set ablaze, and two people
(one of them a full-patch member) were shot (CFPL AM 980, September 18, 2015;
London Free Press, September 8, 2015).

Saskatchewan

In 2011, police estimated there were 59 criminal gangs in Saskatchewan, most of which
were made up of Indigenous teenagers and men (this number also includes more sophisticated gangs like the Hells Angels) (*Vancouver Sun*, March 24, 2011). The province has
one of the highest rates of gang-related homicides in the country; according to Statistics

Canada, the rate of murders connected to criminal gangs in the province is three times the national average. Saskatoon is home to numerous gangs, most of which are made up of Indigenous youth. According to a 2011 article in the *StarPhoenix*, "These aboriginal gangs, largely imported from Winnipeg, take advantage of poor or damaged inner-city youth by promising big money, a family and respect, according to various police investigations over the years. Some of them claim a racial or cultural pride motivation, but most victims of their drug dealing, prostitution and violence are aboriginal ... Most mimic the dress, slang and graffiti of African-American inner city gangs of the 1980s and attempt to structure their organizations in the image of the Mafia, Hells Angels or other organized crime groups." Among the dominant gangs in Regina and Saskatoon are the Indian Posse, Crazy Cree, the Native Syndicate, and what may be the largest gang: the Terror Squad. The *StarPhoenix* reports the drug-dealing Terror Squad has "recently established itself as the top street gang" in Regina (*StarPhoenix*, June 23, 2011).

Alberta

In Calgary, the FOB gang and its rivals the FOB Killers were for many years the major cocaine distributors in the city. Both groups are largely made up of youth and adults of Asian descent, including Vietnamese, Chinese, Cambodian, Filipino, and Indo-Canadian members. They are also two of the most violent gangs in the province—between 2002 and 2009, they were responsible for at least 25 homicides (*Calgary Herald*, January 5, 2015). In July 2013, Calgary police laid murder and criminal organization charges on five men associated with the FOB gang in connection with six gang-related killings (two of whom were innocent bystanders), which took place at the height of the gang war in 2008 and 2009. The *Calgary Herald* called this a "milestone in a long-running war between two criminal factions ... police have now laid charges or secured convictions in eight of the 25 homicides with known connections to the conflict between FOB and the FOB Killers." The violence between the two rival gangs stretches back to 2002 and flared as recently as April 2013 when FOB member Nicholas Chan was stabbed and nearly killed. The 35-year-old Chan, who is considered the leader of the FOB gang, was himself charged in connection with three homicide cases (*Calgary Herald*, July 19, 2013, August 31, 2013; CTV News, July 19, 2013).

More recently, CBC News in Calgary reported that "turf battles over drugs in Calgary's northeast have escalated into a gang war," all of which are taking place amid a criminal landscape that's different from any the city has seen before, police warn (CBC News, December 14, 2015, December 16, 2015).

In 2015, the Calgary Police Service identified six to seven gangs and singled out 59 men who are considered "high level" participants in the gangs. These individuals are mostly young men of Middle Eastern descent who were born in Calgary and grew up together in the northeast part of the city. As the CBC describes, like the Asian street gangs of the early 2000s, the current gangs are not exclusively of one ethnicity: "Though gang members are often linked by ethnicity, their connection has far more to do with geography. For the most part, they were born and raised in Calgary and attended high school together in the northeast.... And unlike some of the more rigid hierarchies in previous gangs, these gangsters are more fluid, sometimes moving among the six to seven groups." The gangs in Calgary's northeast are also distinguished by the degree to which the senior members are related through family ties. Among the 59 people believed to be "high level" participants in the gangs are several groups of between 2 and 12 people who share a surname. According to the CBC, "Many of those young men grew up with older siblings and cousins who are involved in the drug trade—which has escalated to retaliatory violence—and know no other lifestyle."

Staff Sergeant Quinn Jacques of the Calgary police guns and gangs unit believes the "fentanyl phenomenon" has helped the gangs to thrive in Calgary. While the FOB and FOB Killers gangs dealt in large quantities of cocaine, now many of the local gangs are dealing in small quantities of the highly addictive fentanyl. The proliferation of guns is also contributing to the violence. Calgary police estimate that around 60 percent of the firearms used in the nearly 100 shootings in 2015 were stolen in break-and-enters. The rest are mostly smuggled into the country from the United States (CBC News, December 14, 2015, December 16, 2015).

Both Alberta and Saskatchewan are also dealing with the emergence of the ultra-violent **White Boy Posse**. According to the *Edmonton Journal*, "The White Boy Posse first hit headlines in a 2004 scuffle with the Crazy Dragon Killers, when Posse members began ramming cars of rival dial-a-dopers to disrupt their cocaine-trafficking operation." The Killers retaliated by kidnapping and beating three White Boy Posse members. Eight members of the Crazy Dragon Killers were later convicted for the assaults. Mark Totten, a researcher who specializes in Canadian gangs, characterizes the White Boy Posse as "incredibly violent." It also stands out among criminal gangs because of its racist ideology. Yet, he argues, there is no evidence the White Boy Posse is linked to other white supremacy groups and their racist ideology may take a back seat to their revenue-generating goals. The *Edmonton Journal* notes that police in that city have linked the White Boy Posse there to street-level drug dealing and the Hells Angels. Given its chaotic leadership structure, Totten concedes that the gang may not fit the typical mould of an organized crime group (*Edmonton Journal*, December 9, 2012).

In March 2008, as part of Project Goliath, 17 members of the White Boy Posse, between the ages of 17 and 33, were arrested by the RCMP's Organized Crime Unit in Alberta. At that time, the RCMP said they had "crippled" the gang. In January 2009, police in Edmonton charged a dozen members of the group with nearly 100 crimes and as part of their raids seized 28 firearms, about $500,000 worth of cocaine, more than $300,000 in cash, 3000 ecstasy pills, and a cache of stolen goods. "The group of individuals that we have arrested and charged, to this point in time, are pretty significant players in the organized crime gang community in Edmonton," RCMP Inspector Bob Simmonds, the officer in charge of the Integrated Response to Organized Crime unit in Alberta told the *Edmonton Sun* at the time. In 2012, four members of the White Boy Posse were charged in three separate murders in Alberta and Saskatchewan, including one in which a severed head was found in an alley in Edmonton (*Edmonton Sun,* January 30, 2009: *Edmonton Journal*, December 9, 2012; *Moose Jaw Times-Herald*, December 5, 2012; Vice.com, December 5, 2012).

British Columbia

A provincial government brief prepared in December 2004 reported that in British Columbia, "a number of hybrid gangs are emerging that include members from multiple ethnic groups including Asian, Aboriginal, Hispanic, Caucasian and Indo-Canadian." The document also warned that violence was increasing among street gangs as they battled over the drug trade. This includes numerous drug rip-offs where rival gangs steal from one another, which includes breaking into marijuana grow-ops. The report also notes that street gangs in British Columbia are becoming more entwined with organized criminal groups involved in drug trafficking, prostitution, debt collection, and credit card fraud. "These street gangs may operate on a 'for hire' basis doing a variety of jobs …" the report says (as cited in *Vancouver Sun*, September 8, 2005).

Criminal groups such as the Independent Soldiers, the Dhak-Duhre gang, the Bacon Brothers, Red Scorpions, and the United Nations Gang gained notoriety in the province during the 2000s. Membership in these criminal groups is fluid and often multi-ethnic, a fact not lost on one group of offenders whose racial diversity led them to adopt the name the United Nations gang. The principal source of revenue for these criminal groups is drug trafficking. This includes operating marijuana grow-ops, smuggling pot and ecstasy into the United States, and wholesale and street-level cocaine distribution.

The gangs have also clashed repeatedly, the result of which is ongoing violence and bloodshed. One deadly rivalry was between the so-called Red Scorpions, led by the three Bacon Brothers, and the United Nations Gang. The Bacons and their Red Scorpion associates stole drugs from the UN gang in its stronghold of the Fraser Valley, and the conflict escalated in 2007 when UN gang leader Clay Roueche was targeted by the Bacons and shot at by one of their associates. In response, Roueche put a contract out on all three Bacon Brothers, with a cascading payout based on each brother's respective importance in the gang—as much as $300,000 for Jamie, the youngest brother; $200,000 for Jonathon; and $100,000 for Jarrod. On August 14, 2011, Jonathon Bacon, the eldest brother, was gunned down as he drove away in a Porsche Cayenne SUV from the Delta Grand hotel in Kelowna. One of the other two men in the vehicle who escaped injury was Larry Amero, a full-patch member of the BC Hells Angels.

The violence reached its apogee on October 19, 2007, when six people were murdered in a Surrey apartment. In a subsequent trial of the hitmen, the court heard they had been sent there by the leadership of the Red Scorpions gang to kill a rival drug dealer named Corey Lal. Three of the other victims were associates of Lal and were in his apartment at the time. Two of the victims—Christopher Mohan and Ed Schellenberg—were innocent bystanders who just happened to be in the proximity of the apartment at the time (*Vancouver Sun*, May 21, 2009).

SOUTH ASIAN ORGANIZED CRIME

The gang violence that occurred in Greater Vancouver between 2007 and 2011 was pre-dated by a bloody war between feuding Indo-Canadian drug-dealing gangs that began in the 1990s and continues to this day. The **Indo-Canadian gangs** or "**East Indian Mafia**" are mostly involved in retail cocaine sales and the smuggling of marijuana and chemical drugs into the United States. The profiles of the original Indo-Canadian criminals are varied. Some are from immigrant families originating in India or Fiji while others are second- or even third- generation Canadians. Some are from well-off families, while others are from the middle-class neighbourhood of South Vancouver. There was little formal hierarchy in the earliest of the Indo-Canadian drug-trafficking groups and, as the police and the public found out over the years, there was also little loyalty to one another—allegiances constantly shifted and friends turned against friends over drug deals gone wrong or for revenge.

This set in motion a wave of violence among Indo-Canadian drug dealers that would cost more than 100 deaths by the end of 2006. Despite the murders, Indo-Canadian gangs continued to be dominant in the drug trade in the BC Lower Mainland and have even expanded to other provinces. The Independent Soldiers gang was formed by Indo-Canadian men from southeast Vancouver (although the gang's membership would be multi-ethnic). The Independent Soldiers were reportedly linked with the now-defunct Red Scorpions and the Hells Angels (along with Hells Angels member Larry Amero, a reputed member of the Independent Soldiers named James Riach was in the Porsche Cayenne when Red Scorpion member Jonathan Bacon was shot in Kelowna). For years, the Independent Soldiers were engaged in a violent battle with its main rivals, the so-called Dhak-Duhre group. Originally from North Vancouver, the Independent Soldiers became so dominant that in 2010 police said they controlled the drug trade in Abbotsford (*The Province*, February 26, 2013). They were busy expanding their drug-dealing operations across Greater Vancouver when, in October 2010, their chief rival Gurmit Dhak was gunned down outside a mall in Burnaby. Some have speculated that Dhak's murder was ordered by the Bacon Brothers under the direction of the Hells Angels (Combined Forces Special Enforcement Unit—British Columbia Press Release, January 22, 2014). It was the murder of Dhak that precipitated the retaliatory shooting of Jonathon Bacon in 2011.

In October 2012, eight Indo-Canadian men were arrested and faced more than 100 criminal charges in relation to a Calgary-based drug-trafficking ring with connections to BC's Independent Soldiers. As part of the investigation, police seized 2.7 kilograms of cocaine, 1 kilogram of marijuana, guns, $166,000 in cash, 7 vehicles, and jewellery worth more than $18,000. In addition, a $1.5-million home in Alberta was seized under proceeds of crime laws (CBC News, October 24, 2012). Indo-Canadian gangs have also been identified as major smugglers of synthetic drugs. On May 9, 2005, two Indo-Canadian men from Abbotsford smuggling 48,000 ecstasy pills across the border were arrested by US Border Patrol agents. A US Border Patrol spokesman told the media he suspected the pills were likely produced in Asia and smuggled to Canada. "Most of the actual movement of the goods is done by Indo-Canadian organizations, either on their own as little freelancers or as subsidiaries to either the [Hells] Angels or some of the more structured Indo-Canadian groups," according to the spokesperson (*Abbotsford Times*, May 13, 2005; *The Province*, May 12, 2005).

In a federally funded study entitled *South Asian-Based Group Crime in British Columbia: 1993–2003*, the gang-related activities, drug dealing, and violence of young Indo-Canadian men were blamed on a combination of cultural issues and the lure of Vancouver's lucrative drug trade. The Indo-Canadian men are treated like spoiled "princes" at home by parents who are too busy earning a living and trying to get ahead to spend time with their children, the report said. In turn, this has "contributed to a breakdown in family communication, especially between father and son." The study contends there is a "consistent pattern where Indo-Canadian criminals are from families who provided their sons with money, freedom, favouritism and a discipline inconsistent with their siblings (primarily female), coupled with the culture's distrust of the police and an emphasis on preserving face or honour." The study also acknowledges that the allure of Vancouver's "explosion of lucrative criminal opportunities in the illicit drug smuggling trade" compounds these underlying cultural causes (as cited in *Vancouver Sun*, May 3, 2004).

CRITICAL THINKING EXERCISE

The conclusions of the aforementioned report on the causes of criminality among Indo-Canadian men in Greater Vancouver is quite different from those of dominant sociological family-based theories of criminality. While the latter emphasizes an impoverished and dysfunctional home environment, complete with deviant, neglectful and/or abusive parents, in many fundamental ways this report argues the exact opposite. Critically analyze the conclusions of this report and try to reconcile them with more dominant etiological theories discussed in chapter 4 (in particular, social disorganization theory and social learning theory). What, if anything, do these two apparently opposing arguments have in common as far as creating a home environment conducive to promoting (violent) criminal behaviour?

The other South Asian criminal entity that has gained notoriety in Canada is the Liberation Tigers of Tamil Eelam (LTTE). The LTTE is the principal force behind the insurgency and civil war in Sri Lanka and has as its objective the establishment of a separate state for its Tamil Hindu minority. In support of this cause, the LTTE reportedly raises large sums of money in Canada. Home to one of the world's largest Sri Lankan Tamil diaspora populations, Canada hosts a number of expatriate political and charitable organizations that allegedly raise millions of dollars for the militant Tamil Tigers. A report on the LTTE in Canada by Rohan Gunaratna estimates that the LTTE raised more than $22 million in 1999 alone (as cited in the *National Post*, June 8, 2000). The Mackenzie Institute claims that the LTTE fundraising machine in Canada is "arguably the most sophisticated of any terrorist organization being undertaken on Canadian soil." Donations to LTEE charitable organizations are voluntary, but may also be the result of coercion, via extortions and intimidation (Mackenzie Institute, 2003).

The Tigers have also been accused of active involvement in criminal activities as part of their separatist fundraising cause. A 2000 criminal intelligence report prepared by the RCMP states, "Tamil criminal groups are involved in a variety of criminal activities including extortion, home invasion, thefts, sales of contraband cigarettes, the importation and trafficking of brown heroin, trafficking of other drugs, arms trafficking, fraud, production and sale of counterfeit passports, illegal migrant smuggling and attempted murders, bank and casino frauds and money laundering" (as cited in the *National Post*, May 18, 2000). On May 10, 2004, two Sri Lankans of Tamil origin residing in Montreal and Toronto, along with a Lebanese immigrant, were arrested by the RCMP for their alleged involvement in counterfeiting Canadian money, credit cards, and passports. The investigation led to the seizure of $284,000 in counterfeit bills, 92 counterfeit travel documents, and more than 9000 plastic cards that were to be used to make forged credit cards, social insurance cards, health insurance cards, and driver's licences. The two Sri Lankan men were alleged to be close associates of the World Tamil Organization, which raises funds for LTTE operations in Sri Lanka under the guise of humanitarian assistance (*Asian Tribune*, May 12, 2005).

In 1987, a Sri Lankan national named Veluppillai Pushpanathan was among eight people arrested in Toronto and accused of selling millions of dollars' worth of heroin. Pushpanathan, who came to Canada in 1985 and became a permanent resident under a special humanitarian program, pleaded guilty and was sentenced to eight years in prison. At a deportation hearing held before the Immigration Review Board in 1993, police officials testified that Pushpanathan was involved in a drug-trafficking organization controlled by the Tamil Tigers. The board eventually ruled that he was "closely associated in criminal activities with members of the LTTE in Canada" (*National Post*, October 5, 2002; Office of the Commissioner for Federal Judicial Affairs, 1999).

VIETNAMESE ORGANIZED CRIME

In Canada, groups made up of Vietnamese criminals first made their mark in Toronto's Chinatown beginning in the late 1970s and eventually became so overpowering they managed to take over the extortion of Asian merchants from the Kung Lok criminal triad. Many of the original gang members were refugees escaping the new Communist regime in Vietnam or had come from refugee camps in Hong Kong. The Vietnamese gang members who emerged in Canada in the 1980s had grown up surrounded by the horrors of war. Following the cessation of hostilities, many were sent to brutal communist re-education gulags and/or escaped to Hong Kong only to be imprisoned in grim, overcrowded refugee camps where they were exposed to crime, drugs, gangs, weapons, violence, and numerous other adversities. Some arrived in Canada already hard-boiled criminals and members of gangs formed in the refugee camps. Others were highly susceptible to gang life in their new country: they had no grasp of English, little education, few meaningful career prospects, no family to support them, difficulty in adjusting to Canadian society, and a well-founded aversion to police and government authority.

The earliest of the Vietnamese gangs in Toronto averaged around 20 members between the ages of 15 and 25. The gangs had little in the way of a hierarchy and most had a transient membership. While the original Vietnamese gangs in Canada were less structured than their Chinese counterparts, they followed the precedent set by Toronto's Kung Lok triad and concentrated their criminal activities in Chinatown, extorting business owners and robbing Chinese-run gambling halls and Asian stores. "These gangs know little fear," a 1987 article in the RCMP *Gazette* stated when discussing one violent robbery (Hamilton, 1987: 3). Around 1983, the Vietnamese gangs in Toronto began to challenge the local supremacy of the Kung Lok by robbing the underground gambling dens controlled by the triad group (*Toronto Star*, September 16, 1983). Sergeant Barry Hill of the Metro Toronto Police's Asian crime unit told the media that there had been three armed robberies of Chinese gambling houses in one three-day period in 1983. "Only one was officially reported," he said, "but it appears the Vietnamese were responsible." Hill also noted that intensified police enforcement "has diluted the power of the Kung Lok and that has enabled the Vietnamese to take liberties they couldn't have taken a year or two ago." He added that the Vietnamese gang members were feared more in Chinatown than the Chinese gangs due to their indiscriminate use of violence (*Toronto Star*, September 17, 1983). Among those beaten or murdered were senior members of the Kung Lok.

Young Vietnamese men were used by the Kung Lok triad as lookouts for their gambling operations, but also so the triad members could to learn more about the Vietnamese gangs. The strategy backfired as the Vietnamese enforcers tipped off other Vietnamese criminals as to where the games of chance were being held, and many were robbed. By

Case Study: Asau Tran

Asau Tran came to Canada as a refugee from Vietnam in 1979. He served in the South Vietnamese army during his youth, and when the war ended, he fled to Hong Kong, where he was placed in a refugee camp. It was there that Tran began his life of crime and soon he had assembled his own coterie of young criminals. Once in Toronto, he quickly made a name for himself in Chinatown's underworld. Because he was an ethnic Chinese, he obtained work as an enforcer for the Kung Lok, collecting protection payments from gambling houses. He gained his first taste of notoriety when he was arrested for the murder of Hong Trieu Thai, which was part of a conflict between different Vietnamese gangsters. Tran and his two accomplices were arrested but later acquitted after a key witness disappeared.

The acquittal contributed to Tran's reputation and, before long, he had started his own gang. Through equal measures of brutal violence, charisma, strong leadership skills, and ties to Vietnamese gangs in Boston, New York, and California, Tran attracted a loyal following. By the mid-1980s, Tran reportedly expanded his criminal gang to more than 100 people through active recruitment and the absorption of other gangs—and for a time, he became the most powerful gang leader in Chinatown. He ran his own gambling, extortion, and prostitution rackets and organized a band of armed thieves that specialized in knocking over jewellery stores. Most of the robberies were undertaken by youths under 18, a tactic used by Tran, who knew they would receive lenient sentences under the *Young Offenders Act* if caught (Dubro, 1992: 222–24; Lavigne, 1991: 101; *Toronto Star*, October 18, 1992).

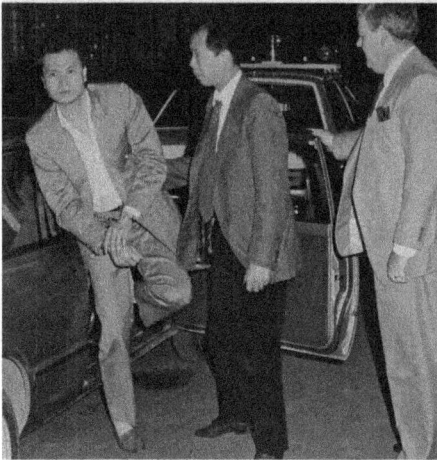

Photo 8.3: Asau Tran is taken into custody by Toronto Police Sergeant Benny Eng

Source: Dubro, J. (1992). *Dragons of Crime: Inside the Asian Underworld*. Toronto: Octopus Books. Used by permission of Benny Eng.

Asau Tran was killed on August 16, 1991, after being ambushed by two assassins as he was leaving a Chinatown restaurant in Toronto. They first shot at his knees with automatic handguns and, as he lay helpless on the ground, 30 more bullets were pumped into his head. A fellow gang member and a waitress also died after being caught in the barrage. Tran's murder has never been solved.

the mid-1980s, Vietnamese gangs were as powerful as—if not more powerful than—the local triad. They extorted Vietnamese merchants and restaurants and had taken over from the Kung Lok in providing protection to the Chinese-run gambling halls. A September 6, 1986, article in the *Toronto Star* declared the "viciousness of Vietnamese gangs in Toronto has created an unprecedented crime wave and climate of terror that are forcing businessmen to flee the downtown for the relatively safer streets of Scarborough." In 1986, the Asian crime squad laid 88 charges against Asau Tran and 27 other gang members, following an 11-month investigation into Vietnamese-run protection rackets, including one that extorted Chinese entertainers performing in Toronto. The investigation also uncovered a juvenile prostitution ring run by Tran and other Vietnamese gang members (Dubro, 1992: 225; *Globe and Mail*, December 17, 1986; *Toronto Star*, September 6, 1986).

An all-out war between the Kung Lok and its Vietnamese nemeses never did occur in Toronto; the Vietnamese gangs prevailed after taking control of most of the Asian gaming houses and pushing the Kung Lok out of Chinatown by the mid-1980s. In his 1987 article, R.B. Hamilton wrote that Toronto was home to two Vietnamese gangs: "One gang is estimated to have approximately 150 members, and the second, 120 members. Both have connections in Montreal, Ottawa, Kitchener, Winnipeg, Edmonton, Calgary, Vancouver, New York, Washington, San Francisco, and Los Angeles." In the article, Hamilton discussed another emerging characteristic of the evolving Vietnamese gangs:

> These criminals are transient. Borders mean nothing. Gang members travel extensively, committing criminal acts as they go from city to city. Having committed a crime in one city, members will then go as far away geographically as possible, to another city, to avoid detection and arrest. They then continue their criminal acts in the new location. Once they believe the heat's off and that they are safe from repercussions, gang members will usually return to their original city. (Hamilton, 1987: 3)

The connections between Vietnamese criminal groups in different cities in Canada and the United States meant that one local gang would organize a local robbery, which would then be carried out by Vietnamese gang members imported from another city. In December 1986, for example, two Vietnamese-run jewellery stores in Toronto were robbed by seven men who were later arrested in Lowell, Massachusetts. Police gathered evidence that they were responsible for similar robberies in Montreal, Calgary, Chicago, and Seattle. In June 1987, two Vietnamese gang members from San Francisco were arrested in Toronto after robbing an illegal gaming house just five hours after their flight touched down in the city (*Calgary Herald*, March 18, 1991; Canadian Association of Chiefs of Police, 1992: 26; Lavigne, 1991: 146; *Toronto Star*, September 6, 1986).

Over time the Vietnamese gangs operating in Canadian cities expanded their territory beyond the Asian communities while branching out into a wider range of criminal activities. By the 1990s, police in Toronto, Montreal, Vancouver, Calgary, Edmonton, and Ottawa were all reporting the presence of Vietnamese gangs, including the Born to Kill and the Flying Dragons, which had links to Vietnamese gangs in New York City. According to a classified 1993 federal intelligence report on Asian organized crime, these two new criminal groups "have challenged the traditional gang and criminal structures in place in the major centers. This development has resulted in a dramatic increase in criminal activity with a corresponding higher rate of violence."

In more recent years, organized Vietnamese criminality in Canada is primarily associated with illegal marijuana cultivation and distribution. In their initial years, during the early 1990s, the Vietnamese-run **marijuana grow operations** were linked to more sophisticated Chinese criminal organizations with Vietnamese nationals tending to the illicit crops. The produce generated from the grow-ops was then passed along to Chinese groups for wholesale distribution or smuggling into the United States (Canadian Press, July 3, 2002). Vietnamese groups eventually began their own grow operations and subsequently have become highly organized around this trade "with extensive interprovincial networks and drug distribution networks to the U.S." (Criminal Intelligence Service Canada, 2003: 7). In its 1999 annual report on organized crime, CISC estimated that "Vietnamese criminals in Vancouver now are responsible for approximately 80 percent of the hydroponic marihuana grow operations that are investigated by the police" (Criminal Intelligence Service Canada, 1999: 5). In 2005, a study conducted into marijuana grow-ops in British Columbia concluded that between 1997 and 2003 the dramatic rise in the number of marijuana grow operations in British Columbia correlates with "a significant increase in the number of suspects of Vietnamese origin" (Plecas, Malm, & Kinney, 2005: 2). Vietnamese groups are known to restrict their grow operations to residences, usually homes in the suburbs.

Before long, intelligence information and law enforcement investigations were turning up Vietnamese-run grow operations in various provinces. In its 2004 report, CISC noted, "Across the country, Vietnamese-based groups remain extensively involved in multiple residential marihuana grow operations with distribution within Canada and to the U.S. These operations are widespread throughout the B.C. Lower Mainland, Alberta and southern Ontario and will continue to increase in Saskatchewan, Manitoba, Quebec and Atlantic Canada. Profits from marihuana cultivation are often reinvested in other criminal activities, such as in the importation of ecstasy and cocaine" (Criminal Intelligence Service Canada, 2004: 6).

Vietnamese crime groups are actively involved in exporting both their product and their expertise abroad. A 2004 report jointly prepared by Canadian and American agencies on marijuana production states, "Over the last five years, organized criminal groups based in Canada have emerged as suppliers of marijuana to the United States, exercising control over production, transportation and financing." Vietnamese and other Asian

Case Study: Vietnamese-run Grow-Ops across the Country

A dramatic rise in the number of Winnipeg's grow operations in 2003 was linked to a Vietnamese organized crime group, which was reportedly behind at least six separate ones in the city. In January 2003, three of them were raided by police who seized more than $3 million worth of pot. The grow operations were all found in residential homes in quiet neighbourhoods. Some of the houses had been purchased and some were rented. All had elaborated electrical work that bypassed the hydro meter to avoid detection as the grow operations required an inordinate amount of heat and light (*Winnipeg Free Press*, February 17, 2003).

In March 2004, police raided homes and businesses in 3 Canadian and 15 US cities, saying they had "decimated" an Ottawa-based Vietnamese drug ring that was generating US $5 million a month in marijuana sales in both countries. Officials said 170 suspects were arrested in both countries, including 29 in Ottawa, 2 in Montreal, and 1 in Toronto. The network also reached into Vietnam and other parts of Southeast Asia, police said. But the heart of the criminal operation was in Ottawa. The alleged ring leader, a 38-year-old women of Vietnamese heritage, was arrested at her Ottawa home. Along with several siblings, she was charged with possession of marijuana for the purpose of trafficking, money laundering, and other related offences. Police raided 32 locations in the capital—some residences, some businesses—and found at least eight marijuana grow operations with crops that were collectively worth millions of dollars. At one middle-class, two-storey house in southwest Ottawa, police removed 300 marijuana plants worth around $300,000 (Canadian Press, March 31, 2004, RCMP Press Release, March 31, 2004).

In 2004, police found thousands of marijuana plants in five posh homes in the Saint John area of New Brunswick. They also found sophisticated grow operations in the homes, located in quiet residential neighbourhoods scattered throughout the city. Seven people were charged with various drug-related offences, including possessing illegal drugs for the purpose of trafficking and producing a controlled substance. In a news conference, police said all seven were of Vietnamese descent and had been in Canada illegally for between 2 and 12 years (*Telegraph-Journal*, January 20, 2004).

criminal organizations have supplanted outlaw motorcycle gangs as the number-one smuggling threat at the border. "These groups are highly organized and transport large quantities of marijuana across the border into the United States" (Canadian Press, February 1, 2005; CanWest News, January 11, 2005).

In supplying the US market, there is some indication that the country' two largest suppliers of marijuana—Vietnamese groups and the Hells Angels—are in fact working together. "Through the use of marijuana brokers, the Hells Angels and Vietnamese-based crime groups control approximately 85 per cent of the marijuana production and distribution in B.C.," according to the 2002 Criminal Intelligence Service Canada annual report (p. 11). A 2003 article in the *Winnipeg Sun* reported that police intelligence "suggest that the Hells Angels in B.C. have made peace" with Vietnamese gangs in order "to do business without interruption." The "Vietnamese gangs are adept at growing dope and the bikers have a strong, almost impenetrable distribution network across Canada and into the United States" (*Winnipeg Free Press*, February 17, 2003). Police have also discovered links between Vietnamese criminal groups in British Columbia and marijuana grow operations in Australia, New Zealand, Great Britain, and some Eastern European countries.

MIDDLE EASTERN ORGANIZED CRIME

Much of the Middle Eastern organized crime in Canada can be broken into two broad groups: Iranian (Persian) groups that traffic in drugs (opium, heroin, and hashish) and Lebanese groups that are involved in organized auto theft as well as tobacco smuggling and drug trafficking in the United States. Iranian gangs came to the attention of law enforcement in Central Canada during the mid- to late-1980s. Many of the Persian dealers had come to Canada claiming refugee status along with thousands of others fleeing the country following the Islamic revolution. They were said to be behind Quebec's glut of Southwest Asian heroin, which was produced from opium grown in the **Golden Crescent** (Afghanistan, Iran, and Pakistan). According to Montreal police, Persian gangs were responsible for around 40 percent of the heroin traffic in Montreal and Toronto areas. In his 1989 book *Merchants of Misery*, Victor Malarek cites Montreal police officials who linked at least 300 Iranian immigrants to various drug rings in the city. "The gangs are generally made up of young men from the same village, town or region in Iran, and many of them have links to Southwest Asia's infamous 'Golden Crescent' area," he writes. The Iranian dealers were able "to avoid a deadly and costly bloodbath with the established mobs which dominated the city's heroin trade" by creating a new market, which involved selling low-priced heroin through bars in Montreal (Malarek, 1989: 40–42).

Malarek credits Shahrokh Amadzadegam with organizing Iranian heroin-smuggling and trafficking groups in Montreal. Also known as "the Shah," Amadzadegam arrived in Canada at the age of 31 in 1980, with a student visa in hand, and immediately asked for refugee status. He already had connections to opium, heroin, and hashish suppliers in the Golden Crescent, and by the mid-1980s he had organized a small band of Iranian nationals who sold heroin and hashish mostly in the downtown core of Montreal. On March 24, 1984, he was arrested and charged with kidnapping, extortion, and conspiracy after he had held hostage the courier of a drug wholesaler whom Amadzadegam accused of supplying substandard hash. Four months later, the Shah was sentenced to two years after being arrested in possession of 18 kilograms of hashish. Upon his release from jail, he began arranging for the import of large quantities of heroin into Canada, smuggled by couriers through Montreal's Mirabel airport. After two couriers were apprehended in 1988, they led police to Amadzadegam who was arrested and subsequently convicted on various drug charges. In 1989, another Iranian national named Mohsen Goldadanishtiani was sentenced to 12 years for importing heroin into Canada. Goldadanishtiani, who had fled Iran in 1986 and applied for refugee status in Canada upon arrival, was described by the sentencing judge as the head of an international gang of smugglers responsible for bringing in millions of dollars of heroin into Canada (Appleton & Clark, 1990: 102; Malarek, 1989: 32–33; *Toronto Star*, March 30, 1989).

In its 2006 report on drug trafficking, the RCMP describes criminal groups of Middle Eastern origins as "among the few groups in Canada that specialize in the importation and trafficking of opium. Some independent criminal networks have also been linked to this market." The report goes on to list some "major seizures" of opium and hashish being trafficked by Persian criminal groups. This includes one in October 2006 that was made up of "10 kilograms of opium and 61 kilograms of hashish from a commercial shipment that arrived via air cargo at Toronto Pearson International Airport. The shipment, declared as lighting fixtures, originated in Iran and was destined for Toronto, Ontario." The next month, 35 kilograms of opium was seized from an air cargo container that originated in Iran and was concealed in a hidden compartment under the floorboards of a crate of furniture. The report goes on to say that much of the opium smuggled into Canada and trafficked by Middle Eastern groups is consumed within the same ethnic community as the smugglers. "The usage of opium is quite common in various segments of Middle Eastern communities, primarily older, middle to upper class males. The majority of the opium imported to Canada is to satisfy the demand of such groups" (Royal Canadian Mounted Police, 2006: 18).

Crime groups in Canada in which the majority of their members are ethnic Lebanese are perhaps best known for their involvement in organized auto theft. These crime groups also maintain affiliations with other Middle Eastern crime groups and terrorist cells in the United States.

An RCMP classified intelligence report from 1999 alleged that a Lebanese auto-theft group operating in Quebec funnelled hundreds of thousands of dollars to a terrorist organization. A series of police raids in June of that year led to the dismantling of the group, which stole millions of dollars' worth of luxury cars for shipment overseas. The RCMP report claims the group made a profit of $3 million within a period of three months, 10 percent of which was funnelled to a terrorist organization the RCMP did not name. As part of the investigation, police seized 55 luxury cars (as cited in *Montreal Gazette*, March 2, 1999; *National Post*, February 13, 2002). A February 2001 RCMP intelligence report entitled *Narcoterrorism and Canada* stated there was a connection between auto-theft rings in Canada and the Lebanese group Hezbollah, which Canada classifies as a terrorist organization (as cited in *Vancouver Sun*, February 16, 2002). A 2012 classified threat assessment report prepared by Canadian Security Intelligence Service

> ### Case Study: Lebanese Auto Theft Ring
>
> In 2001, the Ontario Provincial Police announced that along with other law enforcement agencies in Canada and the United States it had arrested members of a multi-million-dollar auto theft ring that stretched from Ontario into Michigan. In total, more than 270 charges were laid against 25 people, the majority of whom were from Lebanese communities in Ontario and Michigan. Police also said they recovered $7.9 million in Canadian cash as well as hundreds of stolen vehicles worth millions of dollars. The group stole vehicles from dealers' lots, private residences, and public parking lots. The VINs were changed in Ontario, and in some cases, the autos were registered with new plates that were issued in the United States. The plates were brought back across the border and placed on vehicles that were then driven into the United States. Also obtained during the two-year investigation was a quantity of illicit drugs. This included more than 4000 tablets of ecstasy with a street value of approximately $120,000, along with fraudulent and stolen credit cards (Ontario Provincial Police News Release, April 5, 2001).

claims that Hezbollah "has had a presence in Canada" and that its supporters "conduct fundraising, procurement and intelligence activities in Canada, and are involved in organized crime, including fraud" (as cited in QMI News Agency, June 3, 2014).

NIGERIAN CRIMINAL ENTERPRISES

While based primarily in Lagos, **Nigerian criminal enterprises** (NCEs) are known to operate throughout North and South America, Europe, Australia, Africa, and Asia in the pursuit of their criminal activities. NCEs are best known for a wide variety of frauds that mainly target wealthy North American and European countries. Since the mid-1980s, Nigerian drug-trafficking networks have been active in smuggling Southeast Asian heroin and South American cocaine into the United States and Canada. In recent years, they have also been active in organized auto theft rings. Notwithstanding these criminal activities, NCEs are best known for their involvement in fraud—in particular, what is known as **advance fee fraud**. As Williams (2014: 254) writes, "Nigerian criminal organizations and networks are unique in both their ubiquity and the diverse nature of their activities. Drug trafficking in Indonesia, extensive fraudulent activities in the countries of the European Union, trafficking of women to Europe for prostitution, and advance fee fraud in the United States and Australia are just a few manifestations of the Nigerian global criminal presence. Criminals from Nigeria and to a lesser degree elsewhere in West Africa are active in every country with criminal opportunities to be exploited."

Nigeria is a republic located in western Africa and is the most populous country on the continent with a number of different ethnic groups. The economy is dominated by the production of oil, which lies in large reserves below the Niger Delta. While oil wealth has financed major investments in the country's infrastructure, Nigeria remains among the world's 20 poorest countries in terms of per capita income. Without coincidence, Nigeria is also consistently ranked as one of the most corrupt countries in the world. For Williams (2014: 254), Nigeria is an example of the thesis that in certain countries the onset of organized crime is attributed to a fragile, inadequate, and/or corrupt state: "Nigeria is a post-colonial state characterized by weak institutions, a weak civil society, multiple tribal groups and power centers, and high levels of corruption." However, the state-induced factors that have given rise to crime transcend mere corruption of the political elite. "Indeed, in Nigeria it appears that some members of the political elite are not simply the protectors of organized crime; they also provide much of the leadership." Citing other research, Williams claims that the country's political elite "control much of the higher-level prostitution in the country," while politicians and civil servants provide passports and other official government documents to organized offenders to help expedite transnational criminal activities (Williams, 2014: 256). Ellis (2012) agrees, writing that the scope of organized crime within the country is so endemic, it "raises the question whether the Nigerian state is not in fact the main locus of organized crime in the country."

Other factors that Williams cite as contributing to the rise and spread of organized crime in Nigeria include a high rate of youth unemployment and poverty, vast inequality between the haves and have-nots, a stagnant post-colonial economy, and poor state management of the economy (Williams, 2014: 256). At the same time, there are many factors that have helped propel the transnational nature of Nigerian organized crime. The Nigerian elite "has traditionally been very well educated, English-speaking, and cosmopolitan in outlook. This provided an important set of resources for drug trafficking, financial fraud, and other criminal activities." In addition, the country has long been integrated into the global economy which means that "many Nigerians have been comfortable doing business—whether licit or criminal— in other countries" (Williams, 2014: 258). The widespread migration of Nigerian nationals to numerous countries around the world (fuelled in part by the large size of the Nigerian population, widespread poverty, government repression, and brutal civil wars) "has provided an extensive overseas presence or transnational émigré network. The Nigerian diaspora—like many others—has contained significant criminal components which feed off the expatriate communities, seeking recruits, cover and support, and using language and dialect as defensive mechanisms against law enforcement. These factors ensured that, from the early 1980s onward, Nigerian criminal organizations became one of the country's major exports" (Williams, 2014: 258).

The Nigerian criminal group operating in Canada is believed to have connections to a "notorious organized crime group" known as the Black Axe. "There is absolutely no doubt that organized crime enterprises, such as the Black Axe, use the proceeds

Case Study: Auto Theft in Canada Organized by a Nigerian Criminal Enterprise

In December 2015, police in Toronto announced they had arrested and laid 640 criminal charges against 18 people from across the GTA in connection with an alleged organized vehicle theft ring. Project CBG targeted an alleged Nigerian criminal organization, which was accused of stealing high-end vehicles in Canada and exporting them to parts of Africa for resale. The investigation began in April 2015, following a rash of car thefts in affluent areas of Toronto, Acting Deputy Chief Jim Ramer told the media.

He said a number of high-end vehicles worth between $60,000 and $80,000 were disappearing from driveways in the middle of the night, sometimes only a few days after the cars had been purchased. Some homes were targeted multiple times. Speaking with reporters, Toronto Police Staff Inspector Mike Earl said in some cases, the vehicles were targeted for theft before being sold; they were delivered to dealerships, but one of the car's two keys would be missing.

Earl told the media that early on in the investigation police identified two "notorious thieves" that had been previously arrested for similar crimes and appeared to be largely responsible for this operation: 63-year-old Joseph Mensah and 26-year-old Wael Hussein. The investigation eventually revealed the involvement of numerous others in the conspiracy, including those who stole the vehicles, tractor-trailer drivers, shipping company employees, blacksmiths, and an employee of Service Ontario.

Police believe that three employees at two local automobile shipyards would photograph vehicle identification number (VIN) cards and key codes for select new vehicles (rather than stealing the actual car keys). The photos were then sold to the car thieves for approximately $200 each. A locksmith would make copies of the keys and the organization allegedly used two experts with computers to reprogram blank electronic keys for the vehicles that were to be stolen. Once the VIN was obtained, a corrupt employee at a Durham Region Service Ontario office was paid to provide home addresses of the registered owners of the vehicles after they were purchased. With that information, the two men leading the theft ring would then give a team of thieves a list complete with addresses and key codes they could use to enter the vehicles without setting off their security systems. These thieves were then to use laptops to hack into the vehicles' operating system and program a blank key to start the ignition.

After the vehicles were stolen, they were concealed in shipping containers and transported to marine ports in Halifax or Montreal, where they were loaded onto cargo ships and sent to Nigeria. Other stolen vehicles were either disassembled into parts at a chop shop in the west end of Toronto or given new VIN numbers and then either used by members of the criminal enterprise or sold to unsuspecting buyers. Police estimate that this group was responsible for stealing approximately 500 SUVs in the GTA. Ramer said the theft ring was responsible for approximately 10 to 15 percent of all vehicles stolen in Toronto in 2015.

"The value of the vehicles stolen by this group amounts to a staggering $30 million," Ramer is quoted as saying.

Among the 18 people arrested were a locksmith, a Service Ontario employee, and a number of shipping yard workers and car dealership owners. Police also arrested a man who Staff Inspector Earl referred to as "the prince of thieves" and the alleged leader of the group. That man, Joseph Mensah, a Nigerian national, faces 102 charges, including committing an offence for a criminal organization. At the time of the arrests, police continued to search for six other suspects believed to be involved in the ring, including the other alleged leader, Wael Hussein, who is subject to 112 charges in total.

"I truly believe this is the biggest operation that we have seen taken out in Canada. I have never seen anything like this," Earl told reporters (CP24.com, December 11, 2015; CTV News, December 11, 2015; *Globe and Mail*, November 13, 2015; Toronto Police Service News Release, December 11, 2015).

---

of these types of property crimes to further fund and grow their illegal enterprises," Acting Deputy Chief Jim Ramer told a news conference. "And in this case, those illegal enterprises are often offshore" (*Guelph Mercury*, December 12, 2015). The Nigeria-based group is best known for engaging in international fraud operations. In October 2015, six alleged members of the group were charged following an investigation into a so-called romance scam in Toronto and the United States where women were lured into online relationships and then defrauded of money. Toronto police began their investigation in August 2014 when a 63-year-old Toronto widow reported she had been defrauded of $609,000. During their subsequent investigation, Toronto police discovered the case had connections to a larger operation that was under investigation by the US Postal Inspection Service and the FBI. Police said conspirators attempted to defraud victims of more than $5 billion in total. Three Nigerian nationals in the GTA were arrested and charged in connection with the romance scam. All three were also implicated in the US investigation. One of the men, 41-year-old Akohomen Ighedoise of Toronto—alleged to be a member of the Black Axe—was also charged with participating in a criminal organization by police in Canada. "It's come to our attention that persons who have identified themselves with The Black Axe organization in Toronto are attempting to exert influence in the community here, particularly in the ex-patriot Nigerian community," Detective Sergeant Ian Nichol of the Toronto Police Service told the media (CP24.com, December 11, 2015; CTV News, December 11, 2015; *Globe and Mail*, November 13, 2015; Toronto Police Services News Release, December 11, 2015).

Photo 8.4: The Neo Black Movement claims to be unrelated to Black Axe in public statements, but not according to their banners.

Source: Assopre, via Wikimedia Commons

According to Ellis (2012), "Some of the most accomplished criminal operators remain members in secret societies such as the Black Axe, the Buccaneers and many others, enabling them to organize themselves for criminal purposes, their networks extending to the state bureaucracy." As Selena Ross writes in the *Globe and Mail*, the Black Axe is feared in Nigeria, where it originated. Once an idealistic university fraternity, the group has been linked to decades of murders and rapes, although internationally their principal criminal activity is fraud. The "Axemen," as they call themselves, have established chapters around the world, including in Canada, where there is an estimated 200 members. The group is said to be hierarchical in structure and its members must swear a blood oath. According to the *Globe and Mail*, the group tries to maintain a public image of philanthropy and volunteerism. It has been registered as a corporation in Ontario since 2012 under the name "Neo Black Movement of Africa North America," with Toronto's Akohomen Ighedoise being listed as an administrator along with several people. The Black Axe appears to be a splinter group of the NBM.

In general, NCEs are well organized, although "Nigerian criminals are not wedded to any particular organizational form," and as such their operations are highly fluid and adaptable in terms of structure, personnel, methods, and criminal activities. This flexibility is considered one factor that insulates NCEs from law enforcement

(Williams, 2014: 258–59). According to the Federal Bureau of Investigation (1995), individual NCEs are organized along tribal lines. While there may be upwards of 500 small, compartmentalized NCE cells operating around the world, it is not known to what extent these cells are centrally controlled or operate autonomously. "Often these groups operate within a larger network that resembles trade associations rather than traditional mafia hierarchies."

There is much overlap and coordination among these different groups and cells, including frequent exchanges of personnel, knowledge, strategies, smuggling routes, equipment, and email address lists (used for the millions of advance fraud fee emails distributed throughout the world). NCE members are not bound to one particular cell and generally conduct criminal activities for many different cells in order to support themselves. Through mutual relationships, these cells form an intricate network that enables an NCE to engage in criminal activity throughout the world. NCE cells in various cities are in close contact with each other and due to this overlap, it is difficult to estimate the exact number of individuals in each cell. However, various sources indicate that the average cell appears to consist of 10 to 40 individuals (Federal Bureau of Investigation, 1995: 48). The fluid network provides support, structure, and potential connections that can be activated when it is convenient or beneficial to those involved. Some have discerned a form of organization that is project-based in which individuals come together for a particular criminal venture and then disband when it is completed (Williams, 2014: 259).

Although the offenders in the inner circle of an NCE cell are Nigerians, there are no specific requirements for membership in the outer circle of an NCE cell. While leaders of NCE cells prefer to work with their own family members, tribesman, and fellow citizens, they have been known to utilize non-Nigerians to facilitate criminal activities. Generally, these non-Nigerians are used in low-level capacities, such as drug mules.

The heads of NCEs are often referred to as "**Barons**," and they are responsible for directing the international operations of various cells from Nigeria. Barons invest the initial funds needed to establish the NCE and oversee the operations of the cells. These Barons are mostly based in Lagos and "are often among the elite and include people in government, who benefit from the criminal activities that they coordinate or support" (Williams, 2014: 259). While much of the power is concentred in the Baron, a limited number of assistants, sometimes referred to as "Sub-Barons" or "Lieutenants," will also assume important roles. These individuals are often family members who supervise the NCE's daily operations, including drug trafficking, corrupting government officials, and money laundering. Their assorted responsibilities periodically require them to travel outside of Nigeria in order to handle any problems that may arise.

The lieutenants will hire or establish connections with individuals and other cells to carry out responsibilities critical to the functioning of their criminal conspiracies, such as arranging for the purchase of drugs, recruiting and training drug couriers, laundering the proceeds of their crimes, coordinating travel plans for NCE members, setting up front businesses, compiling databases of possible targets of fraud schemes, coordinating the

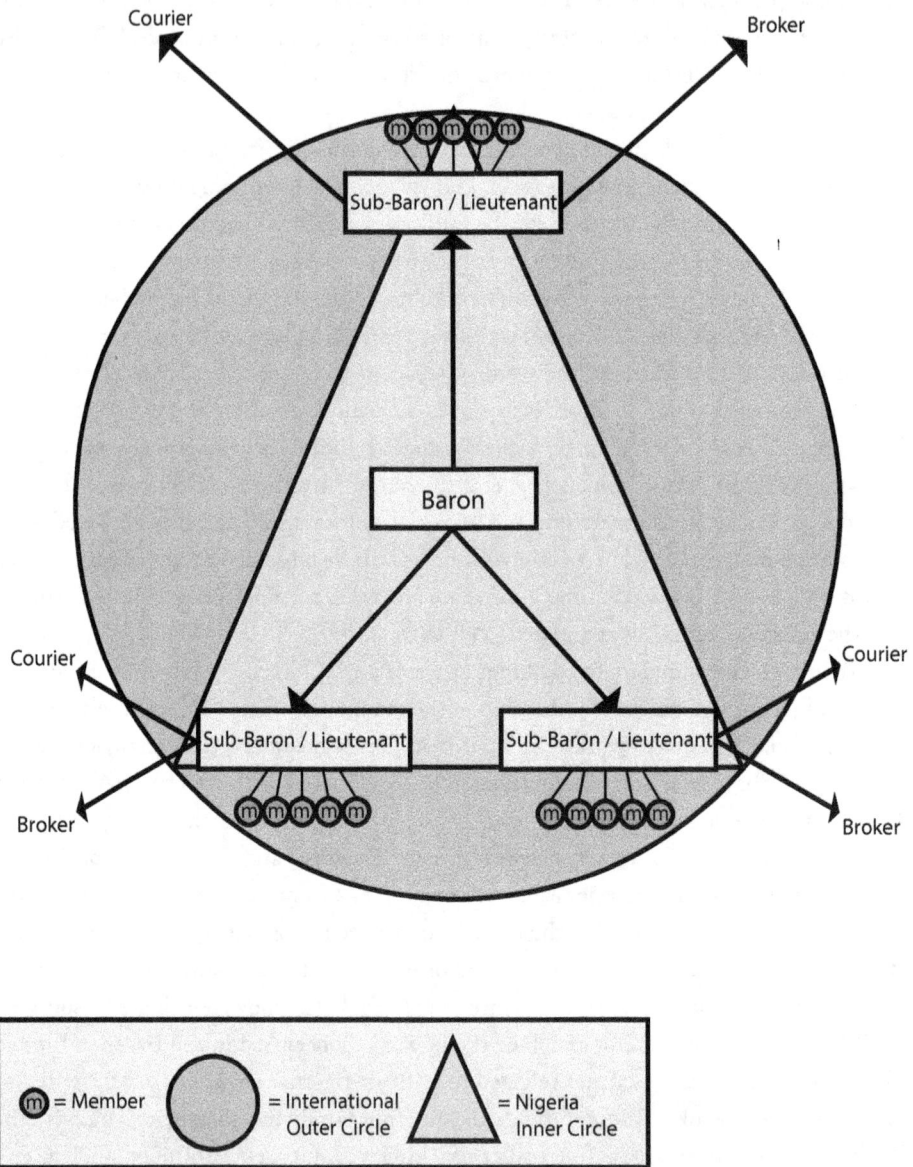

Figure 8.2: Alleged structure of a cell of a Nigerian criminal enterprise

execution of financial schemes, and arranging for operatives to be placed in government or private sector organizations abroad. There is no strict specialization within NCEs; the roles and responsibilities of many NCE members constantly change depending on the current needs of the organization. Most of those involved in the NCE have experience in numerous criminal facets, can easily switch roles, and are required to perform any task, no matter how menial, in order to help the organization make money (Federal Bureau of Investigation, 1995: 49). There are other individuals who are not necessarily members of NCEs, but assist them with their criminal activities, such as "brokers" and "couriers." Brokers are individuals who are acquainted with different NCE members and associates. They function as intermediaries and collect a commission for setting up introductions. Brokers may also buy heroin or other illegal merchandise from one party and sell it to another in return for a commission. They frequently work with several different NCEs.

In sum, NCEs are characterized by their "great flexibility" and they can form and re-form according to operational needs rather than to consist of structured corporations. They form as loose, fluid networks, driven by specific criminal projects, although the associations between various offenders will persist over time and can be drawn upon at any time. "In the final analysis, perhaps the best way to think about Nigerian criminal organizations is in terms of multiple levels of organization and activity, with a capacity to switch structures, activities and even membership easily and seamlessly. For law enforcement this makes Nigerian criminal organizations a very elusive target. Moreover, the high-level organizers—often based in Nigeria itself—are very difficult to link to the low-level operatives. Typically, couriers know little about their employers, as there is no sustained relationship apart from some kind tribal, ethnic, or geographic affiliation" (Williams, 2014: 260).

Like other dominant organized crime groups, NCEs exist exclusively to undertake profit-oriented criminal activities. They are engaged in multiple illegal enterprises, including consensual (drug trafficking) and predatory (fraud, theft) criminal activities, which in turn are supported by corruption and the use of internal conspiracies within government and private sector organizations. "In some instances, Nigerian criminal organizations appear to be highly specialized, whether in financial fraud, drug trafficking or human trafficking; in other instances they combine several criminal activities at one time. They also have a capacity to move easily and seamlessly from one type of criminal activity to another, according to available opportunities and the expertise they can bring to bear." This seems to be consistent with organized crime in West Africa where specialization in a particular field or commodity over the long term is rare (Williams, 2014: 260).

Reports of Nigerian nationals working as drug mules emerged around the mid-1960s. The drug of choice was cannabis and most of the smuggling was conducted through the airlines in relatively small amounts, hidden in suitcases, taped around someone's body, or secreted in cargo containers among legitimate foodstuffs or consumer products. The most frequent destination was the United Kingdom (Ellis, 2009: 175). By the 1980s, Nigerian nationals began smuggling more lucrative drugs, in particular, heroin, "which enterprising Nigerians were buying at source in Asia and Latin America for transport to Europe and

North America" (Ellis, 2012). Once the heroin reached Nigeria, it was repackaged and transported to their overseas markets, primarily in North America and Europe. According to the Federal Bureau of Investigation (1995: 51), NCEs transported heroin to the United States in large quantities and were most active in cities with well-established Nigerian populations. During the 1980s, NCEs also became involved in cocaine smuggling and trafficking. Through their ties with suppliers in South America, the NCEs obtained cocaine in Peru and Colombia and arranged for it to be transported to Brazil, where it was then smuggled by couriers to Lagos and to a lesser extent, South Africa and Europe, for distribution. NCEs utilized their pre-established heroin-trafficking routes to distribute cocaine (Federal Bureau of Investigation, 1995: 51).

Williams (1995) notes that the involvement of Nigerians in drug importation and trafficking is unique relative to other dominant drug trafficking groups because Nigeria is neither a drug-producing nation nor is it located close to any significant drug-producing countries. The rampant corruption among government and military officials in Nigeria helps to explain why this country became a major transit point for international drug trafficking. The growing involvement of Nigerians in the drug trade was facilitated and even encouraged by corrupt government and military officials.

Notwithstanding their drug-trafficking activities, NCEs are probably best known for the vast array of fraudulent activities they carry out internationally, which have resulted in hundreds of millions of dollars of financial losses to consumers, governments, and businesses. Some examples of the fraud, counterfeiting, and theft schemes carried out by Nigerian criminal enterprises are advance fee fraud, credit card fraud, bank fraud, cheque kiting, insurance fraud, entitlement fraud, passport and visa fraud, marriage fraud to obtain US citizenship, student loan fraud, vehicle thefts, counterfeiting of US currency, and counterfeiting of corporate cheques.

In carrying out their fraud schemes, NCEs can be quite sophisticated. They are characterized by careful planning, precise execution, internal conspiracies, and a focus on financial systems designed to be customer friendly. They also take advantage of human greed. Nigerian criminal cells research financial systems and identify weaknesses that allow them access to large sums of money. Glenny (2008: 202) reports that Nigerian nationals working in New York City as night-time cleaners in financial services firms would photocopy confidential details of clients' files that they found on desks or in unlocked filing cabinets. They would then use the information to target potential victims. There is evidence of underground schools in Nigeria that train students to successfully carry out their various fraudulent activities. Police officials in Alabama seized publications that instructed NCE members on how to obtain fake identification cards, social security cards, and birth certificates, and how to commit credit card and bank fraud. Other similar publications have been seized by law enforcement officials throughout the world (Federal Bureau of Investigation, 1995: 52).

One specific type of fraud that has become synonymous with Nigerian criminal enterprises is popularly referred to as "advance fee fraud" (also called "419 Fraud" after the relevant section of the Nigerian *Criminal Code*). **Advance fee fraud** is a variation of the "confidence swindle," which preys on peoples' greed and naïveté. It targets individuals and businesses offering huge sums of money purportedly from government officials or businesspeople in African countries. The targets of the fraud receive a solicitation (by letter, fax, and more recently email) from an alleged businessperson or ex-government official in an African country, promising that a large sum of money (often in the tens of millions of dollars) will be deposited into the target's bank account. In return, the recipient of the letter is offered a percentage of the total amount that purportedly will be wire-transferred from Nigeria (or another African country). The funds that are purportedly to be deposited in a target's account are frequently described as money that must be quickly and surreptitiously transferred out of an African country due to a civil war, bankruptcy fraud, an unclaimed bank account or inheritance, or the embezzlement of money from a government or business. Regardless of the specific claim, the source of the funds is frequently held out as illegally derived. This tactic is used to increase the credibility of the offer (relying on widely held awareness of corruption in African countries) and to deter any victims who accept the offer from going to police due to their own perceived complicity in an illegal action. The solicitation will ask the prospective victim to respond to the correspondence, including name, address, phone number, and banking information. Subsequent correspondence will ask for a processing fee from the target before the money can be transferred. This fee is often in the tens of thousands of dollars and the letter will provide specific directions on how this fee should be paid (usually a wire transfer to an overseas bank account). Once the processing fee is deposited, the funds are quickly withdrawn, and the perpetrators either disappear or attempt to coax even more money from the victim. Some schemes have gone so far as to have victims fly to an African country, where even more money is extorted through intimidation and violence.

CONCLUSION TO PART II

In the attempt to try to fashion a distinctively Canadian conceptualization of organized crime, this section of the book has been more concerned with the common or distinguishing features of Canadian OC groups and networks and what this might reveal about Canada. The overall conclusion is that while the nature and characteristics of organized crime in Canada can be seen as a product and reflective of the Canadian environment, there are few characteristics of Canadian OC groups or networks that are wholly unique when compared to that of other countries. As such, there is little about organized criminal groups and networks in this country that is characteristically and distinctively Canadian.

As discussed in chapter 4, the origins of different organized crime genres and specific groups in Canada are complex and highly individualized. However, the origins of the many OC groups and networks in Canada are really no different from that of other developed countries. Broadly speaking, chapter 4 situates the origins and causes of OC in factors that are both external and indigenous to Canada (including the country's history as well as a broad range of social, political, and economic factors). Organized crime groups with roots outside of Canada have a presence in this country, while numerous criminal groups and networks have been founded in this country with few, if any, links to transnational criminal organizations. In either case, the founding and proliferation of crime groups and black markets would not have been realized without factors indigenous to Canada playing a role. This is not unlike the experiences of other developed countries, including the United States.

The diversity and complexity of OC groups and networks in Canada is both reflective and a product of the highly diverse, complex Canadian society. Yet, the diversity of OC groups in Canada—in terms of their origins, history, structure, membership, and criminal activities—is no different than the diversity of OC groups and networks in other countries. Thus, this element of diversity does not distinguish organized criminal associations in Canadian from those of other countries.

One may be tempted to draw a causal link between Canada's distinctive multicultural policies and resulting multicultural society and the ethnically diverse range of criminal groups and offenders in this country. To do so, however, would be to ignore the fact that all developed countries are multi-ethnic in nature and all of these countries experience some level of ethnic diversity among organized criminal groups and offenders. In other words, there is little evidence to suggest that Canada's unique policy of multiculturalism encourages some form of ethnic-based criminality (let alone multi-ethnic criminal groups).

The different organizational structures of OC conspiracies reflect the varying structures of different social, political, cultural, and economic entities in this country. At the same time, these organizational structures are no different than those seen in other developed countries (or the theoretical models covered in chapter 4). Despite the diversity in how organized criminal associations are structured, a common feature of Canadian organized crime is its networked approach, whether this is the fluid ephemeral nature of Chinese or Nigerian criminal networks or the co-operation that exists between well-established criminal groups. This networked, inter-group co-operation has long been a dominant characteristic of organized crime and international drug trafficking in particular. It may also be seen as a reflection on the Canadian polity, which has been characterized as being less of a unified, coherent nation-state and more of a highly decentralized federation of different governments (provincial governments have significant powers in this country) or as former Prime Minister Joe Clark put it, a "community of communities." However, once again the networked approach to organized criminal conspiracies appears to be a global phenomenon and not one restricted to Canada.

The transnational nature of criminal groups operating in this country is reflective and a product of Canada's reliance on international trade and integration into the global economy. But again, most developed countries have to contend with cells of organized criminal groups and networks that have their origins and tentacles elsewhere as well.

KEY TERMS

Advance fee fraud

Akwesasne

Baron

Colonial model

Critical race theory

East Indian Mafia

Golden Crescent

Historic trauma transmission model

Indo-Canadian gangs

Marijuana grow operation

Mohawk Nation

Nigerian criminal enterprises

Residential school

Tobacco smuggling

White Boy Posse

REVIEW QUESTIONS

1. Identify and describe some of the common characteristics of the organized crime genres presented in this chapter.
2. Using the theoretical framework developed in chapter 3, describe the basic characteristics of the OC genres covered in this chapter.
3. What are the origins and history of these genres both outside of and within Canada?
4. Compare and contrast these different OC genres and specific groups to the Tier I genres covered in the previous chapters.
5. What etiological theories specific to (organized) criminality (covered in chapter 4) are applicable to the different OC genres covered in this chapter?
6. What criminology theories can be applied to Indigenous peoples in Canada to help explain the onset of (organized) criminal behaviour and activities?

FURTHER READINGS

Criminal Intelligence Service Canada. (2010). *Annual Report on Organized Crime in Canada*. Ottawa: Criminal Intelligence Service Canada.

Edwards, P., & Auger, M. (2012). *The Encyclopedia of Canadian Organized Crime: From Captain Kidd to Mom Boucher*. Toronto: McClelland & Stewart.

Schneider, S. (2016). *Iced: The Story of Organized Crime in Canada*. Toronto: HarperCollins.

Williams, P. (2014). Nigerian criminal organizations, in L. Paoli (Ed.), *The Oxford Handbook of Organized Crime* (pp. 254–69). Oxford, New York: Oxford University Press.

PART III

ORGANIZED CRIMINAL ACTIVITIES

As described in chapter 2, in addition to conceptualizing organized crime as an association of criminal offenders, OC can be viewed as a set of serious criminal activities mostly carried out for monetary gain. Some scholars have "suggested getting rid altogether of the expression organized crime and focusing instead on the organization of crime for gain" (Paoli & Vander Beken, 2014: 20). Organized crime has long been equated with the provision of goods and services that are in demand, but which have been made illegal or heavily regulated by the state. As van Duyne indicates, organized crime is inextricably intertwined with illegal markets. "What is organized crime without organizing some kind of criminal trade; without selling and buying of forbidden goods and services in an organizational context? The answer is simply nothing" (van Duyne, 1996: 203). One cannot forget, however, that predatory crimes—such as theft, fraud, and human trafficking—are also common organized crimes.

This part of the book examines organized crimes or organized criminal activity (terms that will be used interchangeably). Chapter 9 begins by examining how crimes become organized and then discusses the various ways organized crimes can be conceptualized. The remainder of this chapter discusses and examines a range of predatory organized crimes, including extortion, theft, human trafficking, business racketeering, labour racketeering, counterfeiting, and fraud. Chapter 10 explores common organized consensual crimes, focusing on gambling, smuggling, and loansharking. The final chapter in this part, chapter 11, examines the one criminal activity that has become synonymous with organized crime: drug trafficking.

9 PREDATORY CRIMES

CHAPTER OUTLINE

- Introduction and Overview
- Conceptualizing Organized Crime Activities
- Organized Predatory Crimes

LEARNING OUTCOMES

After reading this chapter, you should have a thorough understanding of the following:

- What makes organized crimes unique compared to more rudimentary or "disorganized" crimes
- Ways that organized crimes can be conceptualized
- Factors that give rise to profit-oriented criminal opportunities
- Common denominators among the different organized crimes
- Different predatory activities that are carried out by organized crime groups and networks
- How a criminal activity can be both predatory and consensual at the same time

INTRODUCTION AND OVERVIEW

Organized criminal activities are both consensual and predatory in nature. The main business of criminal groups and networks has been described as providing goods and services that satisfy certain vices, especially those that are prohibited or heavily regulated by the state, such as gambling, smoking, sex, drinking, and drug use. Criminal syndicates also engage in an array of predatory crimes that victimize individuals and entire communities. This chapter focuses on some of the common predatory crimes carried out by criminal syndicates in Canada: extortion/protection rackets, theft, fraud, counterfeiting, business and labour racketeering, human trafficking, and stock market offences.

The earliest incarnations of organized crimes were mostly predatory in nature and included theft, extortion, and human trafficking (e.g., the "white slave trade"). This changed during Prohibition and the years to follow, as criminal syndicates organized around highly profitable illicit businesses that satisfied the public's demand for illegal booze, cigarettes, gambling, drugs, and counterfeit consumer goods. Beginning in the 1990s, well-organized predatory crimes seem to have come back into vogue, as witnessed by the increase in frauds (e.g., deceitful mass marketing fraud), counterfeiting (bank cards and consumer products, in particular), theft (vehicle theft, cargo theft, and even identity theft), and cybercrimes (hacking, phishing, etc.).

CONCEPTUALIZING ORGANIZED CRIME ACTIVITIES

Before examining the diverse range of OC activities (both predatory and consensual), it is important to conceptualize some of the unique aspects of organized crimes. This analysis begins by delineating organized from disorganized crimes and then examines the following binaries that help conceptualize and characterize the diverse nature of organized criminal activity: (1) consensual vs. predatory crimes, (2) revenue-generating vs. tactical support activities, (3) goods vs. services, and (4) legal vs. illegal activities.

Organized versus Disorganized Crimes

Drug trafficking, smuggling, bookmaking, and counterfeiting can be carried out by individuals working alone, albeit in a rudimentary fashion. Such illegal enterprises existed long before the dawn of modern organized crime in the twentieth century. Even with the rise of OC during the twentieth century, many revenue-generating illegal enterprises continued to operate independently of OC groups, usually on a small scale. Throughout North America, there continues to be self-employed street-level drug dealers, freelance prostitutes, independent cigarette smugglers, and small-time neighbourhood bookmakers. Conversely, predatory offences typically associated with rudimentary criminals, such as burglary or auto theft, can also be carried out by criminal groups. The point is that the type of crime itself does not inherently dictate whether it will be organized or not. What separates an "organized crime" from a "disorganized crime" is the former are largely distinguished by a greater level of organization necessary to effectively carry them out. This elevated level of organization is characterized by a heightened degree of planning; coordination among multiple offenders, tasks, and resources; rationality; sophistication; the period of time involved in the execution of a particular crime or crimes; and the extent to which tactical support activities (bribery, violence, money laundering) are used to support the revenue-generating crimes.

Thus, **organized crimes** "follow a rational plan, involve the combination of different tasks, and extend over long periods of time" (von Lampe, 2016: 31). These different tasks are not random, but "entail a number of interlocking criminal acts that are carried out repetitively and in a sequential order." This alone sets organized crimes "apart from the mass of ordinary crimes that are typically committed in a hit-and-run fashion" (von Lampe, 2016: 69). Organized crimes are contrasted with **disorganized crimes** or **unorganized crimes**, which are characterized by "spontaneous, impulsive, isolated acts" that are carried out by individuals acting alone or in small, unorganized groups (von Lampe, 2016: 31).

Generally speaking, the larger the scope of the particular illegal enterprise, the greater the need for some level of organization among the participating offenders. Someone selling small amounts of cocaine on a street corner does not require a significant level of organization or sophistication. However, the smuggling of thousands of kilograms of cocaine (hundreds of kilograms at a time) and its subsequent wholesale distribution (without getting caught) will inevitably require some level of organization. This is particularly true if the large-scale criminal activity crosses multiple borders.

Consensual versus Predatory Criminal Activities

Organized crimes include those that are **consensual** and those that are **predatory** in nature, and most of the major organized crime genres examined in this book include both in their revenue-generating repertoire. A consensual crime is one where two or more individuals willingly engage in a (illegal) commercial transaction so that no identifiable victim exists. Like any legitimate business transaction, one of the individuals involved is consuming the good or service without coercion while the other is supplying it. Many have argued that the core business of organized crime is the supply of goods and services that have been made illegal by the state or at least heavily regulated and controlled because they are deemed immoral or destructive to the individual and society. Naylor (2003b: 85) uses the term **market-based crimes** because they "involve the voluntary transfer of illegal goods and services based on some notion of a fair market value." Thus, it is not only the supplier that benefits from this exchange (by making money) but the consumer also benefits (by receiving a product or service he or she demands). This is why consensual crimes or market-based crimes are also referred to as **victimless crimes**.

Satisfying certain vices is a major reason why organized crime exists; it fills the void created by the state's criminalization of specific goods and services. As such, organized crime could not be as profitable and as widespread without the consuming public. As history has clearly shown, laws and their enforcement, no matter how punitive, are largely ineffectual in controlling what some might deem to be immoral or destructive vices; it merely pushes such behaviour into the underground where it can be satisfied by black market (criminal) entrepreneurs. Consensual crimes present a particular challenge to law enforcement because they generally do not leave behind victims to complain to police.

The business of organized crime also includes activities that are not geared toward satisfying demands of the public but that prey on the public. The latter category includes such predatory crimes as extortion (protection rackets), theft, muscle-for-hire, kidnapping, human trafficking, and various types of fraud. Naylor (2003b: 84) characterizes predatory crimes as the coercive or deceptive "redistribution of existing legally owned wealth." von Lampe (2016: 75–76) writes that predatory crimes "are characterized by a conflict, an antagonistic relationship between offender and victim. The confrontational nature of this relationship may manifest itself openly with the use or threat of force in the case of such crimes as robbery and extortion." More simply put, predatory crimes as those in which "perpetrators obtain a benefit at someone else's expense" (von Lampe, 2016: 75).

While criminal activities can be delineated between those that are consensual and those that are predatory in nature, this distinction is not always so clear-cut. Certain so-called consensual crimes do leave victims, in the sense that consumers are negatively impacted by the goods or service they use and are being preyed upon by predacious criminals looking to take advantage of people's weaknesses, vulnerabilities, and addictions. The most cogent examples of these non-traditional victims are drug addicts and compulsive gamblers. The question is: Should compulsive gamblers or heroin addicts be considered victims? von Lampe thinks so when he writes that a prevailing view (especially among policy makers and law enforcement) is that "demand for illegal goods and services is not seen as resulting from autonomous decisions of consumers … Instead, demand appears as something that is purposefully created by aggressive entrepreneurs who exploit human weaknesses. For example, drug use is seen as the result of ruthless dealers enticing weak-minded consumers to use drugs" (von Lampe, 2016: 223). Regardless of whether a drug user sees himself or herself as a victim, consensual crimes carried out by criminal syndicates, such as drug trafficking or illegal gambling, victimize entire communities and society as a whole, which bears a huge cost from drug addictions and problem gambling.

Other so-called consensual crimes can also include a predatory angle. Migrant smuggling may be considered a consensual crime because many migrants yearn to emigrate and are willing to pay the costs and incur the risks. Yet, the migrant may be forced into sexual servitude by the organizers to pay off her debt. (In addition to being forced into the business by pimps, women may be engaged in the sex trade against their wishes due to drug addictions, abusive childhoods, poverty, or all of the above). Moreover, migrant smuggling victimizes those individuals who are trying to immigrate legally, as enforcement and red tape are increased or immigration quotas for destination countries are reduced.

There are also profit-oriented organized criminal activities in which there is both a consumer and a victim. The best example may be product counterfeiting (copyright infringement). While a consumer may benefit from purchasing a cheap knock-off of a

Table 9.1: Consensual versus Predatory Organized Criminal Activities

Consensual	Hybrid Predatory/ Consensual (includes both a victim and a consumer)	Predatory
Drug smuggling and trafficking	Automobile theft	Extortion ("protection rackets")
Smuggling of legal products (tobacco, liquor, other consumer goods)	Human trafficking (indentured slavery and forced prostitution)	Business and labour racketeering
Gambling	Environmental crimes (illegal dumping of waste)	Murder, grievous bodily injury
Migrant smuggling		Kidnapping
Loansharking	Counterfeiting and product piracy (bank cards, government documents, currency, consumer products)	Consumer fraud (advance fee, Ponzi scheme, telemarketing)
Prostitution		Government fraud (tax, health care, employment insurance, social insurance and assistance)
Money laundering	Corruption (of government officials, labour racketeering)	
	Illegal trade in wildlife	
	Illegal trade in organs and tissue (human and animal)	Corporate fraud (credit card, insurance, mortgage)
		Stock market manipulation
	Illegal trafficking in arms, ammunition, and explosives	Theft (robbery, burglary, hijacking)
	Trafficking in nuclear and radioactive substances	Cybercrime
	Illegal trade in stolen artefacts, art, jewellery, precious gems, and other valuables	Identify theft and fraud
	Trafficking in endangered plant species	

high-end handbag, the company that legitimately manufactures and sells these handbags is victimized. The same could be said of smuggling and black market sale of contraband to avoid taxes; while a consumer may be able to buy contraband cigarettes or liquor cheaper in the black market, governments and societies are victimized due to the loss of tax revenue. Labour racketeering is another crime that is both consensual and predatory. Corrupt union officials who do business with organized criminals benefit financially, often by receiving a cut of union funds that are stolen. However, the actual rank-and-file members of the union are ultimately victimized.

In short, there is a considerable debate over whether to label certain organized crimes as predatory, consensual, or a **hybrid** of both. This is related to a parallel debate over whether organized crime (criminal groups and illegal markets) creates the demand for illicit goods and services or whether "on the contrary, it is a widespread demand for these things that stimulates and nourishes the illegal activities of organized crime groups" (Albanese, 2015: 94). The broader philosophical issue at stake here is whether consumers exercise free will in choosing to consume goods or services that can be personally harmful and even life-threatening. This book argues that even when a particular crime can be considered as consensual, it is ultimately predatory. When their addiction goes untreated, addicts often cannot exercise free will. Whether it takes advantage of people's vices and addictions by supplying outlawed goods or services or by preying upon individuals and communities through theft or extortion, organized crime maintains a largely parasitic relationship with society. With the above analysis in mind, Table 9.1 summarizes the wide range of illegal activities with which organized crime is involved and how they transcend a simple binary distinction between predatory and consensual activities.

Revenue-generating versus Tactical Support Activities

Another way to conceptualize organized crimes is to categorize them based on (1) those that directly generate revenue, and (2) those **tactical support activities** that are often necessary to carry out the revenue-generating function of criminal syndicates. In making this distinction, von Lampe (2016: 73) refers to "primary" criminal activities, which are about making money, and "secondary" activities that enable, facilitate, or "aid in the commission of profit-making crimes and in the safeguarding of offenders and illicit proceeds."

As should be clear by now, the majority of the commercial activities associated with organized crime are **profit-motivated offences**. In a survey of 16 police services in Canada carried out by Statistics Canada, the most common organized crimes committed in Canada are drug trafficking, extortion, firearms trafficking, prostitution, motor vehicle theft, counterfeiting, fraud, and money laundering (Sauvé, 1999). The revenue-generating, profit-oriented nature of organized crime distinguishes it from vandalism, crimes of passion, crimes committed for excitement, or terrorist acts committed for the sake of political or social change. Many predatory crimes—break-and-enter, shoplifting, theft of vehicles, theft from vehicles, and arm robberies—are carried out for material gain. The same can be said of "street-level" consensual crimes: drug trafficking (in small amounts), bookmaking, loansharking, and prostitution. However, as Albanese (2015: 41) emphasizes, "The huge interest and participation in consensual criminal activities—gambling, migration, drugs, prostitution, etc.—resulted in the 'commercialization of these enterprises.'" In other words, widespread demand for illegal goods and services invariably leads to profit-oriented underground commercial markets, which in turn are supplied by both independent retailers as well as larger, more organized wholesalers of illicit goods and services.

What often separates organized crime from disorganized crime is the use of certain tactics that are meant to enable, facilitate, and protect revenue streams and the group of individuals carrying out the illicit activities. Organized criminal activities that generate revenue can be distinguished from those activities that are meant to support the former. In other words, unlike the profit-oriented activities, these tactical support activities do not directly generate revenue. In fact, they are treated as necessary expenses by the criminal entrepreneur. Tactical imperatives such as corruption, violence and intimidation, and money laundering have become synonymous with organized crime. Other tactical criminal activities undertaken by more sophisticated groups include intelligence gathering and counter-surveillance, both of which are directed at rival groups and law enforcement agencies. Closely related to corruption and intelligence gathering is "internal conspiracies," which involves placing associates of criminal groups in private sector, union, or government agencies to facilitate criminal activities (e.g., criminal operatives at marine ports to expedite the importation of drugs) and the collection of information. The forgery of documents can also be viewed as a tactical support activity, whether it is the forgery of financial statements to help carry out a mortgage fraud or the use of forged passports to help with illegal immigration schemes or to expedite the international travel of a criminal offender.

Goods versus Services

Consensual illegal enterprises include trafficking in both **goods** and **services**. Criminal goods include drugs, contraband (such as cigarettes or liquor), stolen ("fenced") goods, weapons, counterfeit consumer goods, and even human or animal organs. Illegal services include gambling, prostitution, migrant smuggling, money laundering, muscle-for-hire, and loansharking. In some circumstances, a particular criminal activity can be considered providing both a good and a service; this is particularly true of human trafficking, where people are bought and sold for indentured labour or sexual purposes. This is why human trafficking is often referred to as the "modern slave trade."

For some scholars, the classification of organized crimes goes beyond this simple binary. For Albanese (2015: 7), there are "three primary categories of illicit behavior." These are the "provision of illicit services, provision of illicit goods, and the infiltration of legitimate business or government." The last category is defined as the "coercive use of legal businesses or government agencies (from the inside or from the outside) for purposes of exploitation" (Albanese, 2015: 9).

Legal versus Illegal

Naturally, organized crimes are most often equated with illegal goods and services, whether consensual or predatory. However, criminal groups and networks are also in the business of supplying goods and services that may be legal, but are regulated and controlled in such a way by the state that any unauthorized distribution is illegal. While cigarettes, liquor, computer software, computer parts, and gasoline are legal in most countries, black markets have long supplied them to customers, often at prices below that of legitimate markets.

Underground markets in legal products arise from one of three circumstances. First, the products are traded without payment of necessary government taxes. For example, taxes on liquor in the United States are significantly lower than in Canada, creating a substantial price differential between the two countries. The comparatively lower price has meant that hundreds of thousands of bottles of spirits are smuggled into Canada annually, where they are distributed illegally. Second, the goods or services are strictly controlled by the state, which means access to them for purchase is limited. Prescription drugs may be the best example of this scenario; because legal prescription drugs are heavily regulated by the state and because there is such a large demand for these drugs, there is an extensive illegal traffic in them. Black markets for prescription drugs include legitimate products that have been diverted from legal markets and users for illegal recreational use, as well as counterfeit prescription drugs that cater to demand from consumers with legitimate medical needs (and which are also abused for recreational purposes). The third category of legal goods that are supplied by criminal syndicates are those that have been stolen.

ORGANIZED PREDATORY CRIMES

Predatory crimes involve a victim who has been deprived—either forcibly or through deceit or a betrayal of trust—of some asset that has some monetary value. Thus, theft is really at the essence of all predatory crimes. Extortion is theft because it involves the use of intimidation (and actual violence) to force someone to hand over money. Fraud is a form of theft in which money is stolen through an act of deceit or the betrayal of trust.

Some predatory crimes encompass both theft and fraud. The term *identity theft* is often used interchangeably with "identity fraud." Why? Because there are two steps in a crime involving someone's personal identity: first, important information relating to an individual's identity is stolen (e.g., social insurance, driver's licence, or passport number); and, second, this information is used to defraud others (e.g., the information is used to take out a credit card, loan, or mortgage, which victimizes a financial institution). Organized crimes involving bank cards generally assume three basic steps: (1) steal the victim's personal identification from the encoded strip on their credit or debit card, (2) encode this data onto a counterfeit bank card, and (3) use the counterfeit credit card fraudulently to make purchases or to withdraw cash, thereby stealing money from the financial institution that is responsible for the data on the issued bank card. When certain criminal activities involve multiple (illegal) acts or phases, it naturally follows that such crimes are more organized. The remainder of this chapter discusses and examines the following dominant predatory organized criminal activities: extortion/protection rackets, theft, human trafficking, business racketeering, labour racketeering, counterfeiting, and fraud.

Extortion/Protection Rackets

An **extortion** or **protection racket** is a common organized crime, albeit a less sophisticated form. Section 346 of the *Criminal Code of Canada* defines extortion as "causing someone, without reasonable justification or excuse, to do anything or cause anything to be done by means of threat, accusation, menace or violence." Extortion is essentially the theft of money from an individual or entity through the use of intimidation, violence, or the threat of a calamity that may befall the victim if payments are not forthcoming. Extortion is heavily reliant upon and intertwined with two characteristics that

Case Study: Business Racketeering in the Trucking Industry in Ontario

In September 1978, four men, including a trucking association president, were charged in an extortion ring operating in the independent trucking industry in southern Ontario. Senior police officials told a news conference that many owners of small businesses in southern Ontario had become the targets of Mafia figures trying to extort money or goods. Police said Rocco Luppino and Dominic Musitano, both of Hamilton, along with Angelo Natale of Toronto, were charged with conspiracy to commit extortion. Natale, at the time, was president of the haulers association, while Musitano was the owner and operator of a Hamilton haulage company. Both Musitano and Luppino were made members of Italian Mafia groups in Ontario. Police officials said the investigation revealed numerous incidents of extortion of independent truck drivers and construction companies operating in the Hamilton area. In an attempt to win government garbage pick-up and snow removal contracts, the men reportedly threatened legitimate companies with personal violence and vandalism to dissuade them from bidding on these contracts. The extortion ring was also involved in an attempt to influence the issuing of public commercial vehicle licences in order to gain control of the dump truck industry in southern Ontario (*Ottawa Citizen*, September 7, 1978).

are fundamental to organized crime: intimidation and violence. While extortion can be carried out by individuals working alone, it is most effective and convincing when perpetrated a group—particularly a group that has a reputation for violence. Extortion is carried out under a number of guises, as summarized below.

- Society membership fees—Early Italian secret societies as well as Chinese triads extorted money from individuals by forcing them to pay fees to become a member of the society.
- Protection fees—Businesses or individuals are required to pay a certain sum in order to operate in a territory or market under the control of criminal group. In return, the business receives certain insurance from the crime group, such as protection from arson, violence, robbery, police harassment, union troubles, or the non-delivery of essential supplies. A protection racket is ostensibly extortion in that those who are selling the "protection" services are the same ones who threaten to and actually carrying out the aforementioned problems.
- Human smuggling and trafficking—People who have been smuggled into a country are highly susceptible to being extorted because their "illegal status renders them unable to turn to the police of the host country." In this context, the extortion may include forcing the migrant into slave labour or to commit money-making crimes (in particular, prostitution), the revenue of which is turned over to the extorter (Hobbs, 2010: 733).
- Business racketeering—What makes **business racketeering** unique within the context of extortion is that companies and entrepreneurs are coerced into doing business with criminal offenders (through intimidation, violence, and blackmail), which sometimes means accepting them as partners in their business. Extortion, violence, and intimidation are first used to leverage the entry of criminal offenders into the business or industry and then are employed again against workers, competing businesses, or labour unions to maximize profits and market share for the criminally connected companies.

Organized protection rackets can be traced back as far as the pirates who stationed themselves at the mouths of rivers and forced ships to pay a fee for safe passage. In Sicily, before the twentieth century, the protective service offered by the Mafioso to his beneficiaries soon became an excuse to extort money from peasants and shopkeepers. These practices were carried over to North America, where immigrants of Italian origin were victims of the so-called Black Hand. Mafia families in North America are legendary for their influence with certain labour unions. As a business-racketeering technique, this influence is used to "shake down" money from businesses that do not want to have their commerce disrupted by labour problems. Some of the earliest crimes carried out by the Kung Lok criminal triad in Toronto were the extortion of Chinese businesses. Chinese triads and other crime groups have long run extortion and protection rackets in Hong

CRITICAL THINKING EXERCISE

The term *protection racket* implies a legitimate service is being delivered to those coerced into making a payment. Varese (2014: 343–44) argues that there is "compelling evidence" suggesting that Mafia groups actually provide "a genuine service, not just protection against a threat they themselves create." This is true even when the service is forced upon the victim. Critically analyze the so-called protection racket within the broader cultural context of the Mafia-style organizations (the Sicilian Mafia, Chinese triads, the Russian Mafiya) and their relationship with their constituents. Cite examples of cases where the protection racket actually delivers a needed service to a constituent as well as cases in which it is nothing more than extortion. Discuss how the protection racket is at the same time a consensual and a predatory crime.

Kong. Today, triads reportedly control large parts of the entertainment industry in Hong Kong, and some Chinese entertainers wishing to perform in Toronto during the 1970s and 1980s were required to pay protection money to the Kung Lok to avoid having their bookings disrupted or cancelled. Russian crime groups are also a purveyor of extortion and protection rackets. In Moscow, it is difficult to operate a business without having to pay some sort of protection money (*krysha*) to at least one crime group in the city. Russian organized crime figures have also targeted millionaire Russian hockey players in the NHL with extortion (for more details, see the web-based chapter on Russian organized crime).

Theft, Robbery, Hijacking, and Fencing

Traditionally, **theft**, **burglary**, and **robbery** are not major revenue sources for most organized crime groups in Canada. There are, of course, exceptions to this rule, including the theft of cargo vehicles, and personal identities, home invasions, organized shoplifting, and cybercrimes.

Cargo Theft

Cargo theft is a problem at marine ports and is a growing cause of concern for those in the trucking industry. While cargo theft can be attributed to a wide range of individuals—including port employees and truckers who steal for personal benefit—criminal organizations have also perpetrated large-scale hijackings in Canada.

Vehicle Theft

One form of theft that has become increasingly organized over the years is the theft of automobiles and trucks. Beginning in the mid-1980s, **vehicle theft** in Canada began to rise, which according to a 1998 RCMP intelligence report entitled Project

Case Study: The Bandidos and Cargo Theft

In 2001, police announced they had broken a sophisticated crime ring that stole truckloads of everything from diapers and children's books to satellite dishes and riding lawnmowers. The group of thieves, whose ranks included members of the Bandidos one-percenter motorcycle club, was involved in the theft and distribution of a massive amount of cargo stolen from tractor-trailers, police said. Gang members hijacked tractor-trailers and didn't even know what they contained until they opened them, said Inspector Len Favreau of the Peel Regional Police.

"It was very organized," added Detective Joanna Beaven of the Toronto Police Service, noting that stolen property was stored in warehouses. "They were very aware of all of the trucking companies in the GTA." Those involved had wide-ranging connections including a distribution network to repackage and market products they obtained.

After two waves of arrests in July and September, some 149 charges were laid against 27 people, including several charges of possession of property obtained by crime over $5000. Approximately $3 million in stolen property was recovered, with an unspecified quantity of illegal drugs and weapons, including an Uzi submachine gun. Police learned items were being sold at small independently operated stores in strip malls or at flea markets (*Toronto Star*, October 4, 2001).

Sparkplug, is "largely attributable to the fact that increasingly sophisticated organized crime groups have flooded the stolen car market" (Mogck & Therrien, 1998: i). A 2002 study by Statistics Canada indicated that approximately 20 percent of all cars stolen in Canada can be traced to organized crime groups (Wallace, 2002). One of the main factors that distinguishes organized vehicle theft from the traditional variety is that in the former the vehicles are frequently exported to overseas markets for resale or use. In 2010, *Canadian Underwriter* magazine reported there was a 50 percent recovery rate for stolen vehicles in Ontario, compared to a 90 percent recovery rate in 1990—one indication that the involvement of organized crime in vehicle theft had increased during the intervening years (Canadianunderwriter.ca, May 13, 2010). An Insurance Bureau of Canada news release stated that in 2014, more than $8 million in stolen vehicles intended for export were seized, most of which were discovered in containers at the ports of Montreal and Halifax (Insurance Bureau of Canada Press Release, December 16, 2014).

Criminal organizations in Canada are involved in the theft of mostly new luxury cars, which are exported to foreign markets where profits are high and the chances of being detected are low. As the RCMP note, "organized crime groups are involved in every process of auto theft for export, from placing orders for specific makes/models/years, commissioning the thefts, counterfeiting the identity of the cars, and accompanying

Case Study: Russian Organized Crime and Automobile Theft in Montreal

In 1995, policed blamed Russian crime syndicates, working closely with local auto theft rings, for the theft of hundreds of luxury cars from Montreal streets. The operation was dismantled following the seizure of 11 stolen cars found in a marine container on the waterfront, just before they were to be shipped to Europe. Police also located five more marine containers full of stolen cars that had already reached Belgium. Members of the Russian gang would place orders with Montreal-based car thieves for up to 100 vehicles at a time that were then shipped overseas to intermediary countries like Belgium, Germany, and Finland before ending up in Russia (*Montreal Gazette*, January 6, 1995).

In 2001, two men linked to Russian crime groups, Igor Stepanchikov and Rotislav Serniak, were charged with 39 counts of theft, conspiracy, fraud, and counterfeiting related to the theft of more than 120 cars from around the Greater Toronto Area. Most of these cars were transported to marine containers, taken to various ports, including Halifax, loaded on to ships, and then delivered to Eastern Europe. As part of the investigation, police raided a storage facility in Greater Toronto where they discovered duplicated keys for stolen vehicles, blank counterfeit vehicle identification number plates, blank provincial motor vehicles permits, government-issued identification, counterfeit money and credit cards, equipment used to produce counterfeit credit cards, and more than $70,000 in Canadian and US cash. Stepanchikov was charged in 1998 along with nine other people linked to Russian and Chinese crime groups after the RCMP broke up a currency and credit card counterfeiting conspiracy (*Montreal Gazette*, December 12, 1998; *Toronto Star*, August 2, 2001; *Toronto Sun*, July 29, 2001).

paperwork, transporting the cars out of province, as well as arranging for their illegal export out of the country." Auto theft for export includes several stages, which may occur in different parts of the country. A car stolen in Manitoba, for example, may be driven to Ontario where it will be given a counterfeit vehicle identification number, licence plates, and ownership information and then taken to a port in Montreal where it will be transported via marine containers for shipment overseas. Organized auto theft is perpetrated by outlaw motorcycle gangs and Eastern European crime groups, as well as other networks of criminals that have come together specifically to steal and export cars. This includes a network of Middle Eastern thieves operating in Central Canada that police allege are funnelling their profits to terrorist groups. Montreal has become the "auto theft capital" in Canada partly because of the presence of a number of criminal groups that take advantage of the city's ports to ship stolen vehicles abroad (Canadian Press, August 13, 2001; Mogck & Therrien, 1998: i; Wallace, 2002: 5, 9, 14).

Photo 9.1: Marine containers have become an essential conveyance for exporting stolen cars from Canada

Source: Gazouya-japan, via Wikimedia Commons

Organized auto theft often works on a network basis with a specialized division of labour: established crime groups work through intermediaries who delegate the theft to street gangs or criminals who specialize in auto theft. These specialists include young offenders who have been recruited expressly to protect the upper levels of the theft ring by hiding behind the more lenient youth criminal justice penalties if they are caught. The network may also include people who are responsible for dismantling the vehicle, altering the vehicle identification number, or exporting the vehicle overseas. In April 2014, police in Alberta dismantled an organized automobile theft conspiracy that was allegedly responsible for stealing more than 100 high-end trucks, SUVs, and luxury sedans from Quebec motorists. After the vehicles were stolen in Quebec, the legitimate vehicle identification numbers would be replaced with fake ones. Using the counterfeit VINs, the vehicles were registered in Alberta and other provinces under the ownership of numbered companies using fraudulent bills of sale. The auto theft ring was well organized, with a distinct division of labour; some of the offenders were assigned to stealing certain makes of vehicles, others were tasked with manufacturing the counterfeit vehicle identification papers, and still others others were responsible for registering the vehicles (CBC News, March 13, 2014).

Home Invasions and Armed Robberies

While criminal groups largely stay clear of such petty crimes as break-and-enters, beginning in the late 1980s, a rash of **home invasions** was being reported in Vancouver and Toronto. Unlike break-and-enters, which generally occur when the occupants of homes are away, home invasions are deliberately timed when residents are home and are meant to frighten them into handing over cash and other valuables. The deliberate and malicious infliction of fear, pain, and suffering on residents is what distinguishes a home invasion from a break-and-enter. The underlying terror element of home invasions is used much the same way that violence and intimidation are used by criminal gangs generally: to establish their power and dissuade victims and others from going to police. The origins of home invasions in Canada can be traced to Chinese criminal offenders associated with the Big Circle Boys. Similarly, Vietnamese crime groups were behind the armed robberies of jewellery and electronics stores during the 1970s and 1980s, while Frank Cotroni, a member of Montreal's Cotroni Mafia organization, was involved in bank robberies during the 1960s and 1970s.

Organized Shoplifting

In recent years, shoplifting in Canada has become increasingly organized. In January 2015, the *Toronto Star* reported, "Shoplifting is big business in the criminal underworld, with organized gangs systematically stripping stores." The article cites one case caught on surveillance video of a backroom at a convenience store in Parry Sound, Ontario, in which "a woman in a head scarf, sweater and floor-length skirt" sneaks into the backroom, steals more than $30,000 in tobacco products in under five minutes, and whose escape is concealed by her co-conspirators.

> The store's walk-in safe is open and the woman heads straight for it. She stuffs merchandise into laundry-sized bags concealed beneath her skirt. The bags are latched onto a belt around her waist. There is a name for her garment: It's called a booster skirt. After stuffing the bags to capacity, she hobbles out of the backroom. She is no longer slim. Her skirt has ballooned out and she knocks merchandise onto the floor in her wake. Stepping out of the back room, she is engulfed by accomplices who shield her from view of the lone clerk as they exit. At the counter, the clerk is distracted by two more gang members asking about products hanging on the wall behind her. They make a small purchase and leave.

Sean Sportun, manager of security and loss prevention for the convenience store chain victimized by this group, says that the gang was at work the next day in the GTA, this time at a Winners store in another Ontario town, where they were arrested by police. "They work off the highways. They're very transient. They will jump from place to place, from province to province, wherever they feel they can get the biggest bang for their buck," Sportun was quoted as saying. "For the most part, these folks are really good at what they do. They train for it" (Diamonds.net, October 8, 2014; *Toronto Star*, January 5, 2015).

In February 2014, police in Calgary and Vancouver wrapped up a joint investigation into **organized shoplifting**, saying that it is becoming more common in those cities. On display in Calgary for the media was $230,000 worth of high-end clothing, wallets, purses, coats, sunglasses, and baby items that were stolen from retailers in the Calgary area and recovered in a Vancouver apartment. In total, there were 1570 items stolen. Two Vancouver women were arrested for possession of stolen property worth more than $5000. They were not the only ones involved in the thefts, however. Police acknowledge several other people were involved on the "fringes," some of whom were responsible for organizing the thefts. According to the *Calgary Herald*, the organizers

> ... hire small-time crooks to fill orders of goods—high-end clothing, purses, food—that they want stolen from retailers. They pay the low-level thieves with cash, usually 30 cents on the dollar, or with drugs. Teams of shoplifters raid stores during the day, distracting staff, grabbing jackets worth maybe $3,000 and escaping undetected, the items concealed in bags rigged to evade censors. Once their underlings have stolen enough loot over a period of days or months, the organized retail crime rings approach an intermediary, a fence, to sell the products. It could be through online auction sites, including eBay and Kijiji, or some other means, such as shipping the goods to other jurisdictions for sale. (*Calgary Herald*, February 19, 2014)

Cybercrime

The Internet, and the interconnectivity of the digital world, has helped to create a colossal new forum for organized criminal offenders. As Albanese (2015: 198) writes, "In the same way that the invention of the automobile early in the twentieth century nearly doubled the number of offenses in the criminal codes of the United States, the invention of the computer [and the Internet] will have the same impact in the twenty first century." Williams (2010b: 194) summarizes how the Internet expedites both traditional and new types of criminal offences:

> First, technology has provided a vehicle for the further facilitation of existing criminal activities. Computer networks have become a communications vehicle which facilitates the commission of "traditional" criminal activities. A typical example might be the use of the Internet to appropriate restricted information to facilitate a terrestrial crime, such as gaining access to sensitive company records to facilitate extortion. The second category of computer-related crime involves the creation of new opportunities for criminal activity that are currently recognised by existing criminal or civil law. Everyday crimes have then migrated

or have been re-engineered to function online. Examples would be the use of the Internet by fraudsters to trick victims into divulging their online bank password, username and security information (known as phishing and pharming). Third, entirely new forms of harmful activities that are of dubious legal status have emerged with the increased use of the Internet. Essentially the Internet has allowed for the creation of a new environment within which novel forms of misbehaviour are engineered. Examples include forms on online violence, virtual vandalism and creation of bot networks.

Police cases suggest that during the early years of the Internet, most **cybercrimes** were committed by individuals for fun or excitement or for personal gratification (e.g., child pornography). "Other computer criminals were motivated by the intellectual challenge, by adventure, or by rebellious spirit rather than by mercenary considerations. Practitioners of digital piracy gave products away rather than selling them. Virus writers regarded their activity as an art form rather than as a way to make a living" (Choo & Grabosky, 2014: 490). Today, cybercrime has become more organized, more

Case Study: Bank Robberies through Cyberspace

In February 2015, the world woke up to a report from the Russian internet security firm Kaspersky Lab that an international hacking ring had stolen up to US $1 billion from banks around the globe in what is most likely the largest breach of online banking security to date. The hackers had reportedly been active since at least the end of 2013 and infiltrated more than 100 banks, e-payment systems, and other financial institutions in 30 countries. The criminals infected bank employees' computers with malware, which then spread throughout the banks' internal networks and even enabled video surveillance of staff. That allowed the hackers to learn and mimic employee activity to transfer and steal money. The "Carbanak Gang" also used access to banks' networks to program ATMs to dispense cash at certain times to individuals associated with the gang. Most of the targets of this "unprecedented cyber-robbery" were in Russia and Eastern Europe, although Kaspersky says banks in the United States, Asia, and elsewhere in Europe were also targeted (Associated Press, February 15, 2015; Bloomberg.com, February 15, 2015). The Carbanak Gang theft follows on the heels of other high-profile attacks on large corporations in recent years in the United States, including JP Morgan Chase & Co., health care giant Anthem Inc., and Home Depot. Unlike the aforementioned case, these attacks did not steal money—they stole the personal data of the clients of these companies. These data may be even more valuable than money because it can be used to steal identities, which in turn can be used to commit further crimes related to identity theft (e.g., obtaining a credit card or a home mortgage).

sophisticated, more widespread, and more profitable. Different types of cybercrimes have been committed by well-organized groups and networks, although the ultimate goal of organized cybercrime is theft (including fraud and extortion).

Cybercrimes are the latest episode in how organized offenders have continued their long tradition of opportunistically exploiting information and communication technology to enable their revenue-generating criminal activities, starting with the wire service in the early part of the twentieth century for their gambling and book-making operations, to pagers and cell phones beginning in the 1980s, which became crucial to drug traffickers, to the use of electronic wire transfers to facilitate international money laundering in the 1990s, and the use of the Internet today. For Choo and Grabosky (2014: 495),

> Digital technology has empowered traditional criminal organizations, dramatically increasing the ease with which they can commit offenses such as fraud and extortion. It has also enabled the emergence of entirely new crime groups and entirely new crime types, such as online piracy and vandalism. It is likely that, as digital technology becomes more pervasive, its use as an instrument and as a target of organized crime will become increasingly common. Every new technology, and every new application, will be potentially vulnerable to criminal exploitation.

As with other traditional criminal activities, cybercrimes committed by crime groups are structured as revenue-generating ventures. (This is contrasted with government or corporate cyberespionage, the purpose of which is to steal information, or cyberterrorism, which is meant to inflict harm on a particular facility or population.) According to Smith (2014: 121, 125), "At the intersection of transnational crime, cybercrime, and fraud lies the activities of organized crime groups" which "have found that cyberspace provides a rich and lucrative source of income with far fewer risks of violence, prosecution, or punishment."

Choo and Grabosky (2014: 482) state that there are three types of organized criminal offenders that exploit "information and communications technology" (ICT) for illegal purposes: "(1) traditional organized crime groups, which make use of ICT to enhance their terrestrial criminal activities; (2) organized cybercrime groups, which operate exclusively online; and (3) organized groups of ideologically and politically motivated individuals, who make use of ICT to facilitate their criminal conduct." Specifically, organized crime groups have exploited ICT to "facilitate drug trafficking; to traffic in corporate secrets and identity information; to commit extortion, frauds, and scams online; to launder money using online payment systems; and to distribute illegal materials over the Internet" (Choo & Grabosky, 2014: 485). Among the traditional OC groups involved in cybercrime are "the highly structured and global criminal syndicates such as the Asian triads and Japanese Yakuza, whose criminal activities include computer software piracy and credit card forgery and fraud." Outlaw motorcycle gangs have been known to use social networking sites to perform background checks on prospective members (Choo & Grabosky, 2014: 485), while Italian Mafia groups in Canada have undertaken extensive gambling and bookmaking operations through the Internet and smartphone apps. Chinese and Russian crime groups, some of which are linked to the government of these countries, are known to be involved in hacking into both government and private-sector organizations worldwide to steal information and money. The for-profit cybercrimes mostly carried out by criminal groups are **hacking**, **phishing**, **spamming**, **skimming**, and trafficking. Arntfield (2015: 501–2) defines each of these cybercrimes as follows:

- Hacking—The attempt to remotely circumvent the security or privacy measures initiated by an Internet website, server, or database, for the purposes of either stealing information or interfering with operations and compromising data through distributed denial-of-service attacks, deployment of viruses, or other malicious actions.

- Phishing—The use of misleading or counterfeit electronic transmissions, such as emails purportedly from credit card companies or other financial institutions, requesting sensitive personal information or password data with the intention of compromising the victim's banking or credit accounts.

- Spamming—The use of one or more computer networks and servers to send unsolicited and unwanted bulk messages to other users, often consisting of vexatious advertisements or pornographic content delivered either by email or by pop-up windows in Internet browsers.

- Skimming—The use of specific software *and* hardware to intercept e-transmissions containing sensitive financial data, usually related to credit card purchases. The stolen data enable the cloning or counterfeiting of specific financial instruments (credit cards, bank cards, etc.) for the purposes of theft and fraud.

- Trafficking—Any use of a computer network to move illicit images (or other media), controlled substances, or people. In the context of cybercrime, trafficking can include distributing child pornography; selling or distributing drugs via the "Deep Web"; or making contact with victims to "groom" them for human-trafficking operations—essentially another version of luring but with different objectives and victims.

Statistics Canada reported that in 2012, 9084 incidents of cybercrime were reported by Canadian police services, although this figure greatly underestimates the number of attempted and successful cybercrimes committed in this country. Fraud accounted for 54 percent of all cybercrimes coming to the attention of police (Statistics Canada, 2014). Also in 2012, the San Diego–based information technology security company Websense Inc. released figures suggesting that the number of Canadian servers being targeted by hackers has increased sharply in recent years. A growing number of malicious sites are also being hosted on Canada's Internet service providers. These sites are a base from which criminals carry out cyberattacks on Canadian and international users. "The bad guys are looking to host their malicious content in countries that have good reputations," according to Patrik Runald, the director of security research for Websense (CBC News, May 9, 2012). In a letter and briefing note sent from the RCMP Commissioner Bob Paulson to the Public Safety Minister Steven Blaney in July 2013, he argued that there had been an increase in the use of technology by organized crime in Canada as well as a growth in well-organized, Internet-based mass marketing fraud, copyright infringement, identity theft, money laundering, drug trafficking, and other illegal goods trafficking (Canadian Press, January 16, 2014).

In 2014, the RCMP published a report on cybercrime and concluded that the problem was expanding in Canada due in part to an increased involvement of criminal organizations. "Once considered the domain of criminals with specialized skills, cybercrime activities have expanded to other offenders as the requisite know-how becomes more accessible." In a section entitled "Organized Crime and the Internet," the RCMP write, "The Internet and related technologies have created new opportunities, new markets, and new delivery methods for criminal transactions that are not possible in the 'real' world. For drugs, contrabands and other types of criminal trafficking, these technologies have created a virtual storefront presence where criminal networks can efficiently and anonymously buy, sell and exchange criminal products and services on an unprecedented scale." The report also indicates that criminal groups are using the Internet to launder the proceeds of crime (Royal Canadian Mounted Police, 2014: 11).

Human Trafficking

The United Nations defines **human trafficking** as follows:

> The recruitment, transportation, transfer, harbouring or receipt of persons, by means of the threat or use of force or other forms of coercion, of abduction, of fraud, of deception, of the abuse of power or of a position of vulnerability or of the giving or receiving of payments or benefits to achieve the consent of a person having control over another person, for the purpose of exploitation. Exploitation shall include, at a minimum, the exploitation of the prostitution of others or other forms of sexual exploitation, forced labour or services, slavery or practices similar to slavery, servitude or the removal of organs. (United Nations, 1999: 3)

Albanese (2015: 196) summarizes the three basic elements of human trafficking as such: (1) "exploitive labor (sex, manual labor, servitude)," (2) "the harboring of victims (through recruitment, transport, or receipt)," and (3) "coercion (accomplished through deception, force, or threats)." For Aronowitz (2012: 218), human trafficking comprises three constituent parts: (1) an action (recruitment, transportation, transfer of an individual or individuals); (2) that uses some illegal means (threat, use of force, coercion, abduction, fraud, etc.), (3) to accomplish a particular goal (exploitation). For Kleemans and Smit (2014: 386), there are "three main phases in the trafficking process: recruitment of the victim, transportation, and actual exploitation." One of the common elements in all of the above descriptions is the forced exploitation of people for profit "in the shadow economy of the sex market, but also in more visible and legitimate markets such as the agricultural, fishing, construction, domestic service and the hotel industry" (Aronowitz, 2012: 219).

The diversity inherent in human-trafficking operations makes difficult any attempt to generalize about its level of organization or sophistication. As Aronowitz (2012: 221) notes,

> Trafficking operations can be as simplistic as the smuggling and subsequent exploitation of an individual by a single trafficker within the source country or over a border with or without proper documentation. Alternatively, more sophisticated operations may be involved in large scale recruitment, using forged documents, moving large numbers of persons, distributing them across brothels, farms or constructions sites around the country, and generating huge profits which must subsequently be laundered. Large scale international trafficking operations are, by default, transnational organized crime.

Notwithstanding this diversity, human trafficking tends to be carried out by loosely organized networks of numerous individuals (Aronowitz, 2012: 221).

While the two are conceptually distinct, human trafficking has long been linked to human smuggling. This appears to be particularly the case in regards to Canada, which is both a destination and transit country for thousands of people who are lured from overseas with the promise of jobs and an escape from poverty. Once in the country, they toil in slave-like conditions, while young women may be forced to work as domestic servants or in strip clubs or brothels. "Canada is a destination for persons trafficked into prostitution, and, to a lesser extent, forced labour, with victims coming primarily from China, Thailand, Cambodia, Philippines, Russia, Korea, and Eastern Europe," a 2003 US Department of State report on human trafficking observed. "Traffickers also use Canada as a transit point for moving victims from these countries to the United States" (United States Department of State, 2003). The report estimates that between 1994 and 2003, at least 15,000 Chinese entered Canada illegally, "many of them paying thousands to smugglers only to end up working as indentured servants or prostitutes." Vancouver and Toronto are seen as hubs for organized crime groups that traffic in people (United States Department of State, 2003).

Another study, released in 2014, contends that Toronto is "a hub for a number of human trafficking routes" in North America as victims of sexual exploitation, forced labour, and forced marriage are moved between provinces or brought into and out of

Canada. The report, released at the annual Alliance Against Modern Slavery conference, examined 551 human trafficking cases in Ontario between 2011 and 2013. Of these cases, people were legally and illegally brought into Canada from 18 different countries including Afghanistan, the United States, Ukraine, the Philippines, and India. People were also trafficked out of Canada to Afghanistan, England, and the United States. Sixty-three percent of the victims were between the ages of 15 and 24, and 90 percent were female. The victims were trafficked for the following reasons: sexual exploitation (68.5 percent), forced labour (24.5 percent), forced marriage (7.7 per cent), and petty crimes (6.3 per cent) (as cited in CBC News, June 14, 2014).

Human trafficking is inextricably linked to the sex trade, and thousands of foreign girls and women are recruited or forced by criminal groups to work as prostitutes in Canada. The *2014 Trafficking in Persons Report* from the US Department of State describes Canada as a "source, transit and destination country" for the trafficking of men, women, and children in the sex trade. Roughly half of sex-trafficking victims worked as exotic dancers or in clubs when recruited. Women from Asia and Eastern Europe are also targeted by human traffickers and are often brought to Canada to work in brothels and massage parlours (Canada.com, June 19, 2014; United States Department of State, 2014: 125). In April 2000, when police raided Toronto-area strip clubs, they brought 650 criminal charges against more than 200 men accused of pimping hundreds of women from Eastern Europe, Latin America, and Asia (*National Post*, April 14, 2000). Just a month earlier, the RCMP infiltrated a multi-million-dollar prostitution ring in southern Ontario that, over a four-month period, smuggled as many as 280 Korean women into the United States, where they were forced to work in massage parlours in Los Angeles and New York (Canadian Broadcasting Corporation, March 5, 2002; McClelland, 2001: 20–25). In 2001, an undercover operation in Vancouver uncovered a criminal group that was importing Malaysian women into the city to work in the sex trade. Police found 11 women, ranging in age from 17 to 30, living and working in two apartments furnished only with mattresses in the living and bedrooms and bathrooms containing nothing but toilet paper, mouthwash, and condoms. Some of the women told Vancouver police that their boyfriends in Malaysia had brought them to Canada on the promise of a vacation. The boyfriends turned out to be recruiters for an international network of human traffickers. Once in the country, the women had their passports taken from them and each were sold for an estimated $15,000 to a local prostitution ring. The women were then locked in the primeval brothels and forced to service as many as 15 men a day (McClelland, 2001: 20–25).

The coupling of migrant smuggling and human trafficking points to the broader role of organized crime in the sex trade in Canada. It is crucial to note, however, that human trafficking can be separate and distinct from migrant smuggling; hundreds if not thousands of women and girls are recruited on Canadian soil by domestic pimps and criminal organizations and then forced into the sex trade. The aforementioned 2014 study estimated that 63 percent of the victims of the human trafficking cases in Ontario were Canadian citizens (CBC News, June 14, 2014). The 2014 US Department of State report on human trafficking also notes that "Canadian women and girls are exploited in sex trafficking across the country, and women and girls from Aboriginal communities and minors in the child welfare system are especially vulnerable" (United States Department of State, 2014: 125). Indigenous women and girls are particularly vulnerable to predatory human traffickers because they are more likely to suffer from poverty, drug addictions, and mental-health problems, according to a 2014 study commissioned by Public Safety Canada. The report asserts, "the trafficking of aboriginal women and girls was part of a wider Canadian crisis ... This crisis was a continuum of related phenomena involving the criminal victimization of aboriginal women and girls." This broader criminal victimization is "evident by the large numbers of aboriginal women and girls who are subjected to physical and sexual violence, are trafficked, and who go missing or are murdered" (as cited in Canadian Press, September 18, 2014).

According to CISC (Criminal Intelligence Service Canada, 2008: 1), organized crime networks are "significant suppliers of females to the sex trade in Canada" and include "several long-standing family-based networks in the prostitution criminal market." These criminal networks "use direct force (abductions, rape, forcible confinement, assault) and indirect forms of coercion, such as controlling where they live, work, with whom they associate, and threatening of family members" (Criminal Intelligence Service Canada, 2008: 2). Police have investigated province-wide and even national networks of pimps that transfer women between different cities and provinces. "Most of these networks tend to be highly organized, however, display low levels of sophistication. Several operate inter-provincially, placing members in key locales in several provinces that enable networks to maintain operations in multiple cities, evade law enforcement pressure, and target a larger number of potential recruits in several locations" (Criminal Intelligence Service Canada, 2008: 3). This transfer of sex trade workers across provincial boundaries is quite purposeful— it is "designed to isolate females, facilitate the creation and adherence to new loyalties (typically replacing the traditional family), as well as enable pimps to meet the customer demand for 'new faces.'" The inter-provincial transfer of women also allows the "organized crime networks" to stay a few steps ahead of police (Criminal Intelligence Service Canada, 2008: 1). Some organized crime syndicates have been involved in the illicit sex trade for decades, and "have evolved from individuals involved in street-level pimping (characteristic of the mid-'90s) to well-organized networks that have shifted toward less visible environments, such as strip bars, massage parlours, hotel/motels, the Internet, and private residences. These networks operate within cell-based structures that allow degrees of independence for individual members to have control of their own prostitutes. Most of these networks maintain tight bonds between members, making law enforcement access difficult" (Criminal Intelligence Service Canada, 2008: 2).

CISC reports that the "majority" of human-trafficking networks in Canada are comprised of "street gangs, particularly located in Ontario, Quebec, Nova Scotia, and New Brunswick." The influence of "the street gang ethos and its links to hip hop music, clothing, and prostitution are popularized by several identified networks to facilitate recruitment through social networking (including online), thereby making the sex trade culturally attractive for potential recruits" (Criminal Intelligence Service Canada, 2008: 2). A CIA report released in 2000 identified a gang in British Columbia called the West Coast Players that specialized in prostituting Canadian teenagers locally and in southern California (*National Post*, April 14, 2000; *Victoria News*, November 10, 2006).

On May 15, 2003, police in Quebec announced the arrest of 44 people following a widespread investigation into teenaged prostitution that was allegedly controlled by a street gang called the Wolf Pack. Police said the gang had links to members of the Hells Angels, who took a cut of the profits. Police arrested 17 suspected gang members, 17 suspected clients, and 10 others. According to a Canadian Press report:

> Gang members allegedly recruited young girls at teen hangouts like video arcades, malls, and high-school dances. The girls were lavished with praise, jewellery and other gifts until they fell in love, police say. They eventually had sex—some of them for the first time—with the gang members, who then slowly lured them into sleeping with other men, police said. The teens earned up to $100,000 a year and all of it often went to their pimps, authorities allege. Once they turned 18, they were booted out of the prostitution ring, police say. The gang was believed to have 20 girls working for them at any given time. (Canadian Press, May 15, 2003)

The Hells Angels and other motorcycle gangs have long been involved in the trafficking of women as prostitutes and exotic dancers. Members and associates of the HAMC are known to control agencies that represent strippers and have investments in strip bars, massage parlours, and escort agencies. In major cities like Toronto, Montreal, and Vancouver, there are hundreds of escort agencies that advertise their services online, in the Yellow Pages, or at the back of newspapers. As described by a 2003 *Montreal Gazette* article, the escort industry in that city is made up of a closed circle of operators, some of whom have ties to organized crime groups, and who employ "an ever-changing cast of characters, with the call girls themselves acting essentially as freelancers who move easily from one agency to another." A typical rate for an "escort" in Montreal is $125 to $200 an hour, with the agency collecting about from 40 to 60 percent. The ownership structure of some agencies "is a bewildering maze of shell companies, fronts of varying sophistication, and short-lived businesses." Many of the companies are registered to nominees, who are used because they have no criminal past and addresses provided in incorporation documents are invariably fake (*Montreal Gazette*, January 13, 2003).

CRITICAL THINKING EXERCISE

Traditionally, the sex trade, and prostitution in particular, has been seen as a consensual crime (two people voluntarily participating in a criminal act). This chapter situates prostitution as a predatory crime within the context of human trafficking. Do you think this book has placed too much emphasis on women who are forced into the sex trade? To what extent is (organized) prostitution made up of women who enter the trade on their own volition? As far as the sex trade being either a consensual or predatory criminal activity, is there a difference between women who enter the trade independently versus those who work as prostitutes as part of a more organized syndicate?

Business Racketeering

While the majority of the organized commercial enterprises exist exclusively within the underground economy, criminal entrepreneurs and organizations have long been active in the legitimate business world as well. For Lyman and Potter (2014: 74), "legitimate businesses offer concealment opportunities for illegal activities," such as gambling or drug trafficking, can help launder the proceeds of crime, provide sources of reportable and legitimate income, and helps the criminal entrepreneur integrate into the local community. In some cases, the infiltration of criminal groups in legitimate companies is unaccompanied by illegal activities; they simply invest or own a business to produce another source of income. However, in the quest to maximize revenues, the entry of organized criminals in the legitimate business world is frequently accompanied by illegal acts (extortion, corruption, intimidation, violence) that are meant to help them infiltrate, control, and maximize revenue from a particular legal business venture. This is essentially what business racketeering entails: using illegal means to infiltrate a legitimate business and/or market and to subsequently maximize revenues in said business or marketplace. In its goal of profit maximization, business racketeering may entail an attempt to dominate a legitimate industry or marketplace. As Lyman and Potter (2014: 163) put it, a particular concern stemming from business racketeering "is that organized criminals, by combining their illicit and licit businesses, will make it difficult if not impossible for legitimate businesspersons to compete with them."

The victimization of legitimate businesses by criminal groups is not a recent phenomenon. Beginning in the nineteenth century, local Sicilian Mafiosi captured a monopoly on artichokes, olive oil, wine grapes, and other necessities of Italian life. In the early part of the twentieth century, the Black Hand extorted protection money from businesses. Prohibition provided the foundation for organized crime's influence in such

---

Case Study: Business Racketeering in Hamilton

In 1981, three made members of the Hamilton wing of Buffalo's Magaddino family—Antonio (Tony) Luppino, his brother Johnny, and Geraldo (Gerry) Fumo—were all convicted in connection with the fraudulent takeover of Tops Continental Meats of Hamilton. Tops was a small, family-run meat packing and pasta plant owned by an Italian immigrant named Domenic Returra. As part of his testimony in court, Returra said the accused first offered their services to collect money from delinquent accounts and eventually ended up controlling 60 percent of the company.

Returra's troubles began when he mentioned to a salesman that he was having problems collecting money from his customers. Before long, he was paid a visit by the three men. Returra offered them ten cents on each dollar collected, but the men had grander ideas. Demanding to see his books, they told Returra that they were interested in buying the company and wanted a glimpse into its financial state. Afterward, they forced Returra to sign a contract that handed over shares in the company. Among the tactics used to persuade Returra to sign was a visit by Luppino's brother-in-law, Paulo Violi, at the time the head of the Montreal Mafia.

At the end of their 6-month criminal trial, Tony Luppino received a 15-month sentence while his brother Johnny was handed 12 months and Gerry Fumo, 18 months. The trial received extensive publicity in the local and national media, not only because of the high-profile nature of the defendants, but because of the precedent set in the case of *Regina vs. Fumo and Luppino and Luppino* whereby Judge McWilliams recognized the existence of a secret criminal organization known as the 'Ndrangheta (*Hamilton Spectator*, December 10, 1981, December 19, 1981, May 17, 1982, August 28, 1982).

---

legitimate industries as distilling, transportation, and the hospitality sector. Soon thereafter, bars, restaurants, and retail stores quickly became popular investments for crime groups due to their utility as headquarters, meeting places, gambling halls, and businesses to launder the proceeds of their illegal activities. Through their contacts with organized labour, Mafia families in North America were able to influence, extort, and control numerous business and in some cases entire industries. A 1986 CISC report summarizing the results of a conference on Italian organized crime in Canada stated, "The infiltration of legitimate business enterprises has increasingly been the objective of the Mafia. By buying into a business and applying illegal or strong arm methods to increase profit and inhibit competition; by forcing a loan shark victim to turn over part or all of his business in repayment of a loan; by using the strength of an infiltrated labour union to force business owners into a compromise; or by monopolizing a particular industry with the view of controlling price. All are techniques common to the Mafia" (Criminal Intelligence Service Canada, 1986: 3).

Particularly vulnerable to penetration by Italian organized crime in Central Canada is the construction industry. Much of the construction in Toronto's post-war housing and commercial building boom was carried out by firms owned by Italian-Canadians with the labour chiefly provided by Italian immigrants. For opportunistic Italian Mafiosi, like Paul Volpe and Natale Luppino, this presented an opening to extort unions and construction firms. The result, according to a 1974 report by Justice Harold Waisberg (who was appointed to head a royal commission that investigated violence and corruption in Toronto's construction sector), was that between 1968 and 1974, "a sinister array of characters was introduced to this industry."

In the late 1960s, Cesido Romanelli, the owner of several Toronto-area construction, drywall, and lathing firms, agreed to hire Natale Luppino as an "escort" for $150 a week. Luppino was used by Romanelli to intimidate the unions representing the tradesmen working for him, not only to ensure union peace but also to help Luppino gain control over the unions (*Globe and Mail*, April 5, 1971; Royal Commission into Certain Sectors of the Construction Industry, 1974). Luppino and Volpe terrorized independent contractors and union leaders. According to Toronto police records, between 1968 and 1972 there were 234 acts of willful damage, 23 acts of arson, 15 assaults, and 5 explosions, as well as numerous thefts and break-ins at Ontario construction sites (Royal Canadian Mounted Police, 1975: 7). Among the many acts of violence was the bombing of two lathing companies in 1972 and the shooting of Bruno Zanini, a union organizer and former labour reporter for the *Toronto Telegram* who was conducting a freelance investigation into labour racketeering (*Toronto Star*, August 24, 1972, August 25, 1972).

More recently, Montreal's Rizzuto Mafia family infiltrated and helped to corrupt private-sector construction firms in that city by coercing them to participate in a price-fixing scheme involving government-tendered construction contracts. Members of the Rizzuto family were alleged to have facilitated the process and Vito Rizzuto himself would sometimes choose which construction firm would be the winning bidder on a particular government contract. In return, the family would receive a cut of between two and five percent of the contract. Construction companies that resisted these overtures were threatened with violence.

Labour Racketeering

Labour racketeering is the use of a labour union for personal benefit through fraudulent, illegal, and sometimes violent means. von Lampe (2016: 77) describes labour racketeering as "the creation or infiltration of labor unions and labor union locals for the purpose of diverting union funds and also for using labor union power to extort legal businesses and to help enforce cartel agreements in legal markets." Jacobs and Peters (2003: 230) make the distinction between "labor corruption," which is "the misuse of union office and authority for unlawful personal gain," and "labor racketeering," which refers "to labor corruption committed by, in alliance with, or under the auspices of organized crime groups."

The three core elements of labour racketeering are (1) criminal influence over the supply of union labour, (2) the corruption of union management, and (3) the misuse of union funds (including pension funds). In gaining influence with unions, organized crime groups combine two principal weapons: corruption (mostly of union management) and the capacity to intimidate by threats of violence. For Ronald Goldstock, the "sometimes bewildering array of labor rackets" ultimately assumes three basic forms: the sale of "strike insurance," the "sweetheart deal," and fund raiding (President's Commission on Organized Crime, 1985: 658).

Strike insurance is a means of extortion used by criminal offenders and corrupt union management to steal money from businesses with unionized employees through the threat of strikes or labour slowdowns. In effect, the offenders and union leaders are "selling labour peace" to the business based on their power to prevent or settle a strike or work slow-down. A **sweetheart deal** is the outcome of a negotiation (in bad faith) between corrupt labour leaders and employers, who create a labour agreement that is wholly beneficial to the employer (i.e., is detrimental to the union members—the employees). The result is that the employer receives favourable conditions (stagnant labour costs, less safety measures, etc.) while the corrupt labour leader receives a kickback from the employer. The involvement of criminal groups in sweetheart contracts most frequently derive from their control over labour unions, and they may also receive a payment from the union, the management, or both. Some members of crime groups have been known to dictate the terms of a labour contract. Organized crime groups and corrupt union leaders are also involved in **fund raiding** (stealing from union funds, such as pension plans). Pension payouts to bogus retired union members (often a member of a criminal group) is one fund-raiding technique. Large payments from pension funds may also be made to consultants, lawyers, and insurance carriers for non-existent services (President's Commission on Organized Crime, 1985).

Jacobs and Peters (2003: 229) write that in North America, "the labor movement and its members have long suffered from extortion, thievery, and fraud" and "labor racketeering has been a major source of the *Cosa Nostra* crime families' power and wealth since the 1930s." The Montreal Mafia's influence over labour unions in that city can be traced to the arrival of New York's Bonanno family captain Carmine Galante in the early 1950s. By 1954, Galante had extended his influence to Montreal's legitimate businesses by investing in nightclubs, bars, and restaurants. He also brought in from New York City an ex-burglar named Earl Carluzzi to set up Local 382 of the Hotel, Restaurant and Club Employees' Union, which allowed Galante to control the hirings and firings of all staff in these businesses while raiding union funds. While he headed the Montreal Mafia, Vic Cotroni's revenues from his investments in hotels, restaurants, and bars were bolstered by his influence over the same union (later renamed Hotel and Restaurant Employees International). Officials with the union could be relied upon to keep labour peace within the family's hotel and restaurant businesses and to stir up union troubles among the competition. In the early 1980s, Local 31 of the Hotel and Restaurant Employees International was barred from the Quebec Federation of Labour due to unethical conduct, which included ties to the Montreal Mafia (*Toronto Star*, June 18, 1989).

In October 2013, the Charbonneau Commission, a public inquiry investigating corruption in Montreal's construction sector, turned its attention to trade unions in the province. The construction division of the Fédération des travailleurs et travailleuses du Québec (FTQ), the province's largest and most powerful labour union, became a particular target of allegations of corruption and ties to organized crime. Ken Pereira, the head of a union local who has been described in the media as both a "co-operative witness" and a "whistleblower," told the commission that the men associated with the Hells Angels and the Rizzuto crime family had infiltrated the FTQ through its construction wing. According to the Canadian Press, "Pereira testified that union brass were aware that the former head of the construction wing, Jocelyn Dupuis, had ties to Raynald Desjardins, a close associate of Vito Rizzuto." Pereira also accused Dupuis of being close to Normand (Casper) Ouimet, a Hells Angels member who has been accused of involvement in 22 murders, among other criminal activities. "The Hells are with us. The Hells are part of FTQ-(Construction)," Pereira quoted a colleague as saying. Dupuis made little effort to hide his ties to both the Hells Angels and the Montreal Mafia, according to Pereira, and the FTQ president Michel Arsenault was well aware that Dupuis was close with Desjardins.

Pereira testified about the 2008 election of executives to the FTQ Construction division, which he claimed were fixed in favour of a candidate backed by Dupuis—Richard Goyette. Jacques Émond, a senior member of the Quebec Hells Angels was brought in to force one candidate, Dominique Bérubé, to bow out of the race. Members and associates of the Hells Angels were even seen hanging around outside the convention centre where the vote was held (Canadian Press, October 2, 2013; CBC News, October 21, 2013; *Montreal Gazette*, October 2, 2013, October 31, 2013).

Fraud

The Merriam-Webster dictionary defines **fraud** as the "intentional perversion of truth in order to induce another to part with something of value or to surrender a legal right; an act of deceiving or misrepresenting." For Mackenzie (2010: 137), the essence of a classic fraud is encouraging victims "to take up an offer that presents itself as loaded in their favour when it is in fact loaded against. A slightly more diluted definition of a scam might be an operation that makes a rip-off seem like legitimate business. Scams therefore involve orchestrated deception in the service of profit-taking." Simply put, fraud entails "the obtaining of goods and/or money by deception" (Levi, 2009: 224).

Beginning in the 1950s, organized crime groups in North America started to become involved in different fraud schemes that targeted businesses, consumers, and government agencies. Today, organized fraud costs Canadian companies, governments, and consumers billions of dollars a year. Frauds that target the unprotected, the trusting, the naïve, and the greedy have become increasingly organized and sophisticated. The range of fraud activities carried out by organized crime (as well as independent white-collar offenders) includes bank card fraud (theft and counterfeiting of credit and debit cards); deceitful mass marketing; stock market manipulation; fake lotteries and sweepstakes; tax fraud; insurance fraud; bankruptcy fraud; mortgage fraud; marriage fraud; advance fee fraud; pyramid, Ponzi, and other deceptive "get rich quick" schemes; and identity fraud.

In April 2013, the US Federal Trade Commission released the results of a survey suggesting that nearly 25.6 million Americans were victims of some type of fraud (Anderson, 2013). In their 2015/16 annual global fraud survey conducted among executives of large corporations, the private security firm Kroll reported that 75 percent of all companies surveyed "had fallen victim to a fraud incident within the past year, an increase of 15 percentage points from just three years ago" (Kroll, 2016: 7). Among the Canadian companies responding to this survey, 65 percent indicated their company was a victim of fraud (Kroll, 2016: 32). According to the Association of Certified Fraud Examiners, fraud and abuse cost American organizations more than US $400 billion annually (Young, 2003: 3). While comparable figures are not available for Canada, industry groups and government agencies like the Canadian Bankers Association and the Competition Bureau of Canada have all gathered statistics indicating the rise in numerous forms of fraud in this country.

One reason accounting for this increase is the more organized nature of contemporary fraud scams. Police cases have shown that well-established criminal groups, including Italian, Chinese, Russian, Nigerian, and one-percenter motorcycle gangs, carry out various types of frauds in Canada. The targets of such frauds include corporations, governments, and consumers. Canada has also gained a reputation as an enclave for organized fraud and counterfeiting schemes perpetrated in other countries leading one organized crime expert to proclaim, "international gangs and cosmopolitan criminals have turned Canada into a billion-dollar stage for sophisticated scams" (*Edmonton Journal*, June 28, 1998). Some of the dominant fraud schemes that have been undertaken by criminal organizations in Canada are summarized below.

Bank Card Fraud

Bank card fraud encompasses both credit and debit cards and accounts for some of the largest financial losses to card issuers and banks. The number of Canadian credit cards used fraudulently has risen steadily since statistics were first kept by the Canadian Bankers Association in 1983. From a low of 19,200 that year to 32,851 in 1990, the total number of "fraudulently used" credit cards escalated to 146,310 in 2003 (Canadian Bankers Association, 2004). The rapid growth in the fraudulent use of and financial losses associated with credit cards during this period is attributed to an increase in credit card counterfeiting operations orchestrated by established criminal networks—in particular, Chinese and Russian criminal syndicates.

Case Study: Credit Card Counterfeiting

Police announced in February 2002 that they cracked a North American–wide credit card counterfeiting organization after a joint 15-month investigation by the Calgary Police Service and 13 other law enforcement agencies. They stated that Calgary was a centre of a sophisticated international crime ring involving millions of dollars in credit card fraud. Of the 478 criminal charges laid against 63 people, police said 124 charges involved 18 individuals based in Calgary. The accused, which included members of the Chinese criminal network known as the Big Circle Boys, were involved in the production of counterfeit cards and skimming. It was the Calgary faction that had special expertise in manufacturing the counterfeit cards, police stated. Gang members would make a duplicate card—perfect in every way with built-in holograms, embossing, micro-printing, and every anti-theft security device—and sell it for $500 to $1000. The buyer would then run up huge sums on the card.

Electronic data stolen from thousands of legitimate credit card users at 116 retail merchants across North America were used to manufacture the fake cards, which were then used for purchases in 34 countries. As part of the investigation, eight counterfeit credit card facilities in Calgary, Edmonton, Toronto, and Greater Vancouver were searched and their equipment seized. Thermal printers, embossers, host stamp presses, as well as other sophisticated equipment, were found. Police also seized $879,500 in cash and property from related crimes. Police estimated the investigation prevented $23 million in credit card fraud in Canada alone (*Calgary Herald*, February 1, 2002; Canadian Press, January 31, 2002).

As stated in a 1992 report by the Canadian Association of Chiefs of Police, organized crime groups involved in **credit card counterfeiting** "are highly sophisticated organizations with worldwide networking in place. Credit cards produced in Toronto may be embossed with information received form one part of the world then forwarded to another part of the world for illegal purposes." Chinese criminal organizations are at "the centre of activity for most credit card related offences" and are the biggest players in producing and distributing forged and altered credit cards. In addition, fake credit cards produced abroad are taken to Toronto where they are sold in lots (Canadian Association of Chiefs of Police, 1992: 55–57).

Forged credit cards include both counterfeit and altered cards. An altered card is a genuine credit card manufactured by a certified printer that has one or more features unlawfully changed by mechanical or electronic means. While enhanced security features such as hologram pictures have reduced the incidence of counterfeiting, Canadian police have seized fake bank cards that include almost perfect replicas of these security features. Counterfeit cards are those that are illegally manufactured and are usually encoded with personal and banking information from victims who have had that information stolen from their own cards. A common method of obtaining this information

Case Study: Debit Card Skimming and Counterfeiting

In December 2002, police disrupted a debit card fraud that stretched from Vancouver to Kamloops to Denmark. For months, banks were fielding complaints from distraught customers, many of whom only learned their money had been stolen when bank machines refused to process their cash withdrawal requests. The thefts ranged from a few hundred dollars to $2000. The total losses to consumers and banks were $1.2 million, which at the time was the single largest loss attributed to debit card fraud in Canadian history.

The RCMP in Kamloops arrested Dmitri Brezinev on December 2 as he walked out of a Royal Bank branch after inserting a fake debit card into ATM to withdraw $500. As the request was being denied, Royal Bank staff called police. (Banks in the area had already been hit hard by the fraud scheme activity and were watching transactions at the automated teller machines closely.) Police said Brezinov was carrying 77 counterfeit bank cards. Four others (two men and two women) were arrested in Toronto and Sudbury respectively. Police also seized $280,000 in Canadian cash—all in $20 bills—and 3500 fake bank cards.

The ATM fraud began in March 2002 when one of the conspirators, posing as a legitimate businessman, purchased five ATM machines from a manufacturer. These privately owned "white label" ATMs, worth about $10,000 each, were installed in different locations in the Vancouver area: a pizza restaurant, a few convenience stores, and a tobacco shop. Every time a customer withdrew cash, the machine captured all the information needed to reproduce fully functional debit cards. The ATMs were eventually removed from their locations and the card information stored inside was downloaded on to a computer. With that information, the fraudsters began manufacturing bank cards. Brezinev and the other four arrested were recruited to take the phony cards and make as many withdrawals as possible. In return, they could keep 4 percent of the cash. In August 2003, Brezinev and four other Russian nationals (two men and two women), pleaded guilty. The 35-year-old Brezinev had entered Canada using a counterfeit passport (*Globe and Mail*, December 5, 2002; *Toronto Star*, August 23, 2003).

is called "skimming"—the theft of account and information (including passwords) from the magnetic strip on the back of a victim's credit card. Skimming begins when a customer's legitimate card is swiped through the card reader at a retail store. The person behind the counter, who is complicit in the theft, then swipes the card again through a small computerized reader under the counter and out of the customer's view (alternatively, the point-of-sale card reader may be tampered with to illegally record the banking information). The data is downloaded onto a computer and is later retrieved and encoded on to a counterfeit credit or debit card, produced by the thousands by legally purchased bank card embossing machines.

Debit cards have also proven to be highly susceptible to counterfeiting and fraud by criminal organizations. Eastern European crime groups are most closely associated with debit card fraud, although the problem is much more widespread. Skimming is again the most frequently used technique to steal customer's personal identification numbers from bank-issued debit cards, which is then transferred to a fraudulently produced card. Other techniques used to steal PINs include in-ceiling cameras to watch shoppers when they key in their codes or passwords at ATMs or cash registers. Eastern European crime groups have even purchased ATMs and placed them in public spaces to steal relevant information.

In sum, criminal groups have helped transform the nature of bank card fraud, and by doing so have contributed to the rise in the number of victims and financial losses. Traditionally, the largest financial loss related to credit card fraud was the theft of cards. Today, the greatest losses stem from the counterfeiting of credit and debit cards. This is of even greater concern to issuers and banks because counterfeiting results in much higher dollar losses compared to thefts, because consumers may not find out about the unauthorized charges until they check their monthly statements.

Advance Fee Fraud

Most get-rich-quick scams—including chain letters, investment frauds, and pyramid schemes—have advanced with the technological age and moved online. One particular scheme that is frequently reported to police across Canada relates to a well-established fraud popularized by Nigerian crime groups. Advance fee fraud involves enticing potential investors with enormous rewards in return for an advance fee, which will release frozen funds, allegedly, from Nigeria or another West African country. Originally, this scheme was distributed by mail and then through fax machines. Increasingly, victims are contacted by email. While the scam is most closely associated with Nigerian criminal enterprises, it has been replicated by groups and individuals all over the world (see chapter 8 for more on advance fee fraud).

Identity Theft and Fraud

Identity theft and fraud can be defined as the unauthorized collection of personal information (theft) and the subsequent unauthorized use of that information (fraud). One of the fastest growing forms of identity fraud is where a criminal offender pieces together someone's personal information to impersonate him or her or to create a non-existent person for fraudulent purposes. Personal information that is stolen (including someone's name, date of birth, address, credit card information, social insurance number, and other personal identification) can then be used to open credit card and bank accounts; obtain mortgages and loans; acquire driver's licences, passports, and other government documents; rent or purchase vehicles; and even secure employment. Thus, while identify fraud is itself a serious crime, it is particularly harmful because it facilitates other types of crimes. Misrepresenting one's identity with false documents is frequently used to perpetrate credit card fraud (obtaining a credit card in someone else's name) as well as bank loan or mortgage fraud (obtaining a loan or mortgage in someone else's name). One RCMP official quoted in the media estimated that just one falsified identity can generate between $30,000 and $100,000 in revenue (*Guelph Mercury*, May 28, 2014). In short, identity theft can be broken down into two sequential parts: (1) the (illegal) acquisition of someone's identity, and (2) the subsequent fraudulent use of the identity (Semmens, 2010: 172).

One's identity can be stolen in any number of ways; it is simply a matter of obtaining pertinent and often confidential information on that individual (e.g., social insurance number, bank account number, or credit card number). This may entail the actual theft of one's personal identification documents, such as a driver's licence or passport, or a financial instrument, such as a credit card or cheque. Confidential information can also be obtained from discarded bank account or credit card statements (often stolen from someone's garbage or recycling bin). A victim may also be duped into providing confidential information to fraudsters. For example, in March 2006, more than 100 people in the Ottawa area were victimized by an identity theft ring that used an online employment advertisement to lure people into submitting resumes. Those who responded to the ad received official-looking letters and emails indicating they had been selected as candidates for a $70,000-a-year job as a "programmer analyst" and that they should submit an application form with a $20 processing fee. The application forms asked for the full name, social insurance number, driver's licence number, and a mailing address. Those behind the fraud used this personal information to obtain more than 60 credit cards, driver's licences, and social insurance cards in other people's names. At least $500,000 in charges was made on the phoney credit cards issued in the victims' names (*Calgary Herald*, March 19, 2006; *Ottawa Citizen*, March 9, 2006).

More sophisticated techniques to steal people's identities involve the use of technology. As discussed earlier, skimming entails stealing personal identification information from the magnetic strip on a credit or debit card through ATMs or retail point-of-purchase devices that have been tampered with. Another high-tech approach is phishing, in which potential victims are contacted (via email or text message) by an offender posing as a legitimate organization, such as the victim's bank. The victim is directed to a malicious website, posing as the bank's website, and then asked to input confidential information, such as account numbers and passwords. Identity thieves have also used spyware, "a type of software which takes control of the victim's computer and provides the thieves with access to important personal information stored on the hard drive" (Semmens, 2010: 179).

The danger of identity fraud is not just that it can bilk unsuspecting victims of thousands of dollars. The stolen information can also be used to obtain driver's licences, passports, or other official government documents that can facilitate the travel of criminal offenders and even terrorists.

In Canada, since the start of the 1990s, there has been a substantial escalation in the theft and unauthorized use of names, birth dates, addresses, credit card information, social insurance numbers, and other personal information. In May 2014, a delegation from Equifax Canada estimated that identity fraud schemes potentially cost Canadians $1 billion a year in losses. Between 1998 and 2003, Canada experienced a 500 percent growth in identity theft reports where applications were submitted and damage incurred to a legitimate consumer. The number of Canadian identity theft victims increased 14 percent in 2013, according to the Canadian Anti-Fraud Centre. Government privacy breaches alone almost doubled in 2013 from 109 to 209 incidents, putting personally identifiable information and records of millions of Canadian potentially at risk of identity theft and identity fraud (Equifax Canada Press Release, May 27, 2014). Identify theft has become so prevalent that some insurance companies are now offering policies that will pay the costs that victims incur as they try to fix credit histories ruined by impostors (*Wall Street Journal*, September 29, 1999).

Deceitful Mass Marketing

Deceitful mass marketing is another pervasive form of organized fraud in Canada. It entails the use of mass communication instruments—the telephone, fax machines, email, the Internet, and more recently smartphone apps—to fleece victims of money or property through deceit, high pressure sales tactics, and falsehoods. Traditionally, the term used was "telemarketing fraud," but with the advent of the digital world, the telephone is no longer the exclusive way that fraudsters reach out to unsuspecting victims. The US National Consumer League, which operates a fraud-reporting hotline, breaks down reported frauds into "telemarketing scams" and "Internet scams." Some of the "Overall Top Ten Scams" for North America, as measured by the number of reports the National Consumer League receives through the hotline, are summarized below.

- Fake cheque scams—Companies or private sellers are paid with phony cheques for work or for items they are trying to sell.
- Internet: General merchandise sales (not auctions)—Goods purchased are either never delivered or misrepresented.
- Prizes/sweepstakes—Phoney prize awards that require the "winner" to pay a fee before he or she can claim the prize first (while the prize never materializes).
- Phishing/spoofing—Emails pretending to be from a well-known source ask consumers to enter or confirm personal information, which is then stolen.
- Recovery/refund companies—Scammers contact victims who have already been defrauded claiming to be able to help recover lost funds, for a fee.
- Friendship and sweetheart swindles—As part of "romance frauds," con artist nurture an online relationship with someone (usually a single elderly woman), builds trust with them, and then convinces the victim to send money (National Consumer League, 2014).

Deceitful mass marketing is nothing new, although up until the 1980s it was mostly restricted to pushing shares in speculative stock through high-pressure sales tactics and deception. While some of these "**boiler room** operations" were legally licensed brokerages, they clearly existed on the wrong side of the business ethics divide. In a 1937 article entitled "Swindlers on Rampage," the *Financial Post* cites examples of "some of the high-pressure selling being conducted from Toronto." In their attempt to capitalize on the mining boom at the time, the shady brokerage operations were run by "men whose reputations are so notorious, that they dare not let their presence in Toronto be publically known" (*Financial Post*, January 9, 1937). By the 1940s, Toronto had become infamous as the new North American capital for boiler room operations. "That Ontario has become the hangout and happy hunting ground for the stock shyster and racketeer is clearly the opinion held by many Securities Commissioners in the United States," the *Financial Post* reported in a 1944 article. "Ontario is now regarded as the main plague spot of North America so far as securities selling is concerned" (*Financial Post*, December 23, 1944).

The problem continued after the war, as Alan Phillips summarized in a 1963 *Maclean's* article: "Canada's postwar mining boom had spawned a species of con men who trade on U.S. interest in our new strikes. These stockateers sell shares in worthless bushland known as moose pasture by telephone campaigns so high-pressured the offices they originate in are called boiler shops." The "elite among these gentry," Phillips wrote, are "the promoters, men who put up the capital, set up the company structure, and manipulate the price of shares on the market. These are men of sharp intelligence, sound financial training, and a clear perception of human cupidity." By the early 1950s, the Ontario Securities Commission was successful in cracking down on the shady brokerage firms, but many just fled to Montreal. The result, according to Philips, was that, by 1955, "Montreal had become a haven for sixteen boiler shops, each paying ten percent of their take to the syndicate, who had provincial authorities on their payroll" (Phillips, 1963b: 66).

That "syndicate" was the Cotroni Mafia group, which had its hand in numerous boiler room operations in Quebec. Some were set up by Vic Cotroni's associate Willie Obront and his partner, Harry Workman, who gained a foothold in the fly-by-night brokerage industry by taking over existing firms that were floundering and receptive to new partners. On the front lines of these boiler rooms were "qualifiers," men who phoned potential clients (most of whom were chosen from telephone books), promising innocuous information on the stock market. Those who agreed to receive more information were sent two or three letters that appeared to be unbiased, but actually pushed highly speculative stocks of companies that were giving kickbacks to Workman. The "qualifiers" were responsible for collecting information about those potential clients who expressed interest. The information was then forwarded to salesmen who called the potential client and tried to sell a small number of shares. If an initial sale was made, a more experienced salesman or "loader" called the client to unload even more shares through high-pressure sales tactics. After reviewing the files of 177 clients of one of Workman's loaders, the Commission concluded that 57 had purchased 32,675 shares after refusing to buy more. Some were forced to purchase even

Case Study: Canadian-based Cross-border Telemarketing Fraud

In March 2014, 23 individuals were arrested in relation to a suspected mass telemarketing fraud network that dated back to 2009. The RCMP alleged that they dismantled two boiler room operations that defrauded several thousand victims in the United States out of at least $16 million. Based largely out of Montreal, the operation made cold calls to tens of thousands of American seniors claiming to sell them a card that would provide discounts on prescription drugs and medical services. The card, which was sold for approximately $300 to the victims, was, in fact, free for American citizens. The alleged fraudsters also sold services that would provide protection for personal information. In fact, the victims received no protection at all while money was debited from their bank accounts. These costs of the services ranged from $187 to $397.

According to the National Consumers League (2014), "The defendants are said to have targeted senior citizens who were given false information and were compelled to reveal their bank account information. The scammers used scare tactics and sometimes even went so far as to impersonate bankers and government officials." The account information provided by victims was then used by the fraudsters to illegally withdraw money from the victim's accounts. One victim in Nebraska, for example, complained that after agreeing to purchase a discount card for $398, a total of $1993 was withdrawn from her bank account. The misappropriated funds were then deposited into a network of corporate bank accounts established in the United States and subsequently transferred money to Canadian bank accounts.

The investigation, led by the Centre of Operations Linked to Telemarketing Fraud (COLT), was initiated in June 2013 after the United States Federal Trade Commission received complaints from a number of American victims. COLT is a multi-agency task force that includes Canadian and American government agencies including the RCMP, Quebec Provincial Police, Montreal Police, the US Secret Service, the US Postal Inspection Services, and the FTC (Marvelli & Finckenauer, 2012: 516–17; National Consumers League Press Release, April 2014; RCMP Press Release, March 20, 2014).

after they made repeated requests to sell and to have their accounts closed (Quebec Police Commission Inquiry on Organized Crime, 1977b: 167–83).

By the end of the 1990s, Toronto police estimated there were about 150 telemarketing boiler rooms in the city. The RCMP in Montreal stated that at least 50 were located there, collectively generating around $60 million in revenue annually (Canadian Press, February 16, 2002). In May 2001, Steven Baker, an official with the US Federal Trade Commission in Chicago, told the media that Canada was the source of more than one-quarter of telemarketing fraud in the United States (*Globe and Mail*, May 11, 2001). Cross-border telemarketing fraud had become so widespread that in 1997, Canadian

CRITICAL THINKING EXERCISE

In 2014, Bank of America paid US $772 million in fines and consumer refunds for misleading customers who bought extra credit card products and illegally charged others for credit monitoring and reporting services they didn't receive. Also in 2014, the financial services firm JP Morgan Chase agreed to pay $80 million in fines and about $309 million in refunds for billing customers for ID theft protection they never received. Conduct your own research into these cases and determine for yourself whether the sales and marketing practices associated with the products and services sold to clients constitute deceitful or fraudulent mass marketing. Do you believe these companies should be criminally charged and prosecuted like the criminal groups described in the case studies presented earlier? Why are these companies and their practices treated differently than the criminal organizations described in the case studies in this chapter?

Prime Minister Jean Chretien and US President Bill Clinton agreed to establish a bi-national working group to study the problem. The result of the study was the establishment of a multi-agency task force and the secondment of an FBI agent to the RCMP's commercial crime section in Toronto. In 2003, the Competition Bureau of Canada said deceptive telemarketing is "spreading like a plague." In the same year, PhoneBusters, an Ontario-based call centre for suspected telemarketing fraud (now known as the Canadian Anti-Fraud Centre), estimated that "on any given day, there are 500 to 1,000 boiler rooms operating in Canada" grossing between $1 billion to $5 billion annually (Solicitor General of Canada News Release, May 21, 2003; Young, 2003: 3).

Counterfeiting

According to Kangaspunta and Musumeci (2014: 102), "The interest and involvement of organized crime is probably the most important factor causing the expansion of counterfeiting activities around the globe and making it an example of transnational crime. This element mixed with other favorable factors played a very important part in the process of rendering counterfeiting a global phenomenon in modern times." Below are some examples of organized **counterfeiting**, including those involving currency, international travel documentation, consumer products, and prescription drugs.

Currency Counterfeiting
Currency counterfeiting in Canada can be traced as far back as the 1840s, continued on into the next century, and picked up steam in the post-war years as advances in offset printing, copying, and graphic arts attracted the attention of the organized criminal element. In 1963, RCMP Commissioner C.W. Harvison told journalist Alan

Phillips that counterfeiting has increased tremendously. "Ten years ago we investigated about twenty cases a year. Today it's about two thousand." The larger counterfeiting networks of the day employed dozens of people, each of whom specialized in a particular function, such as developing the plate, obtaining the proper paper, printing the currency, or "pushing" the fake product.

Since the late nineteenth century, currency counterfeiting has been centred in Montreal. By the early 1960s, according to Phillips, there were three large counterfeiting groups located in the city, "one in the east end; one in the west and one downtown." The west-end Montreal group specialized in American $20, $50, and $100 bills, while the east-end group specialized in American $20 bills and was known to send their pushers to Winnipeg and Vancouver, as well as Ohio and as far away as Switzerland. The downtown Montreal group turned out ten-dollar bills and used freelance distributors. Once it left the printers, the forged cash was provided to distributors who in turn passed it along to their "pushers" or "passers" who put the bills into circulation, mostly by purchasing small ticket items. The pushers, Phillips wrote, "all begin at the same hour, work a weekend, perhaps only two hours, then leave town." To protect the counterfeiting organization, each participant was isolated from the other; the pushers did not know the printer, or vice versa, making it difficult to trace the fake currency back to its source (Ontario Police Commission, 1964: 151–52; Phillips, 1963b: 74–75).

In addition to currency, during the 1960s and 1970s counterfeiters were also busy producing forged travellers' cheques, stock certificates, bond coupons, racetrack betting slips, company cheques, birth certificates, driver's licences, registration blanks, and licence plates. In a 1969 classified memo entitled "Mafia (Cosa Nostra) U.S.A.," the RCMP documented a connection between Italian crime groups "in Windsor, Detroit, Michigan, and Sicily in the transporting of counterfeit currency." Among those under investigation were Sicilian crime boss Caesar Joseph Badalamenti and New York Mafioso Joseph Bonanno, as well as Pietro DiLorenzo and Vincenzo Mazzola (the latter two were convicted in Detroit for possession of counterfeit currency). The memo states that Italian tourists brought over to Canada were used to smuggle Canadian-produced counterfeit American currency to the United States and Italy. DiLorenzo and Mazzola smuggled $1 million in fake US bills to Sicily in May 1962 in the trunk of Mazzola's Buick (National Archives of Canada, RG 76: Records of the Department of Immigration and Citizenship, Series D-7, Vol. 14451).

Currency counterfeiting began to escalate further in the 1990s, due in part to the widespread availability of personal computers, desktop publishing systems, digital imaging devices, colour printers, as well as the newfound ability of more sophisticated counterfeiters to replicate currency security features. By 2001, a rash of counterfeit money was in circulation in Canada, prompting several large Canadian retailers to stop accepting $100 bills. Five people were arrested in Windsor on counterfeiting charges in July 2001, and as part of the investigation the RCMP seized personal computers, printers, chemicals, and paints for placing the optical security devices on the bills, as well as heat stamping machines for embossing the notes to give the impression of raised printing (*National Post*, August 9, 2001).

In May 2006, Peel Regional Police shut down a major counterfeiting ring that churned out more than $2.4 million in fake Canadian money. After raiding a small warehouse located inside a Mississauga industrial park, police found a 1960s-vintage German printing press that had been adapted to place the silver foil strips down one side of the fake $20, $50 and $100 bills, and which was capable of producing thousands of pages of counterfeit bank notes a day. Police also seized five guns, including a sawed-off shotgun used to rob a Canadian Imperial Bank of Commerce (CIBC) branch in 2005, ammunition, bulletproof vests, computers, inks, papers, a hot stamp press, dies, foils, 13 point-of-sale terminals, pinhole cameras, DVD recorders, credit and debit card readers, and forged credit cards. More than 10,000 debit and credit card numbers were also found stored in seized computers. Thirty people were arrested and charged with 469 criminal counts. Among those arrested were five men and an 18-year-old woman police alleged were behind the CIBC bank robbery. Also arrested were a number of young women who were hired to push the fake money by purchasing merchandise from major retail stores, which would then be returned for a refund (*Brampton Guardian*, May 19, 2006).

International Travel Document Counterfeiting

Unlike other types of identity fraud or counterfeiting, the primary goal of **international travel document (passport) counterfeiting** is not direct financial gain, but to facilitate illegal immigration. Counterfeit passports are often used as part of organized immigrant-smuggling operations and the illegal entry of crime figures into the United States and Canada. Trafficking organizations have shown increasing sophistication and variety in the ways in which they obtain travel documents, including photo substitution, visa transposing, and forged visas. Investigations have also found that passports are stolen or illegal obtained from corrupt passport-issuing authorities, tourists, and travel agencies.

Counterfeiting of Consumer Products (Copyright Infringement)

In recent years, consumer products—including designer clothing and accessories, electronic equipment, DVDs, digital entertainment products, and computer software—have become the a lucrative target of well-organized forgers. The **counterfeiting of consumer products** also entails **copyright infringement**, which Kangaspunta and Musumeci (2014: 101) define as "the activity dedicated to reproducing the result of someone else's work or inventive and artistic creativity without authorization and with the aim to obtain an undue profit." Wall and Large (2010: 1095) identify three groups of victims of copyright infringement: (1) consumers who purchase fake goods believing them to be authentic and who can be exposed to health and safety risks from counterfeit goods, (2) the copyright owners of the goods or brands being counterfeited, and (3) the general public that is indirectly affected by copyright infringement, such as

Case Study: Identity Fraud and Passport Counterfeiting by and for Criminal Offenders

In May 2014, the RCMP said it dismantled a passport fraud scheme in which purchased identities were used to obtain passports for cocaine traffickers as well as one murder suspect. Harbi Mohamoud (Dave) Gabad was arrested and charged with a number of passport and identity fraud offences after the RCMP searched his apartment in Gatineau, Quebec. The RCMP alleged that Gabad provided fake passports to the Alkhalil brothers, the core of a major drug-trafficking syndicate, one of whom was also wanted for two murders in Toronto and Vancouver. Robby Alkhalil was captured in Greece with a genuine Canadian passport under an assumed identity according to police. The RCMP said that two passport photos of another brother, Hisham Alkhalil, were found on a compact disc at Gabad's home in Gatineau, but they have no evidence Alkhalil obtained a passport. Gabad "was facilitating the obtaining of Canadian passports in exchange for money," said RCMP Inspector Costa Dimopoulos. He told the media that criminal offenders are willing to spend $5000 to $20,000 for a genuine document issued under an assumed name. "Canadian passports are coveted by people in the criminal underworld," Dimopoulos said. "It's allowing you to move freely internationally without fear of being captured. It allows you the ability to hide, essentially, from police." CBC News reported that "to date the RCMP have linked Gabad to 13 fraudulent passport applications, including eight that were actually issued by Passport Canada under assumed identities, according to search warrant documents filed in court." Gabad allegedly paid drug addicts, the homeless, and mentally ill individuals to provide their government-issued identity documents to be used as a basis for the fraudulent passports (CBC News, May 15, 2014).

through increased prices of authentic goods to offset losses due to counterfeiting and taxes that go toward enforcing counterfeiting laws.

In a 2003 report, the International Anti-Counterfeiting Coalition wrote that the "low risk of prosecution and enormous profit potential" has attracted organized crime to the product counterfeiting industry (as cited in the *National Post*, December 12, 2003). Albanese (2015: 232) expands on this, writing, "there are organized crime groups that endeavor to profit from the theft of intellectual property. These groups manufacture optical disks that contain pirated music, movies, software, and video games that are distributed around the world. This form of digital piracy occurs primarily in Asia and parts of the former Soviet Union, with distribution networks through Central and South America into North America, Europe, and Australia." At the 6th Global Congress on Combating Counterfeiting and Piracy in 2011, Microsoft Associate General Counsel David Finn discussed how criminal organizations were increasingly turning to software piracy as a low-risk venture that is profitable in and of itself but was also used to help fund their other criminal activities, including drug and arms trafficking. By way of example, Finn showed a seized counterfeit copy of Microsoft's Office 2007 disc, which was stamped with the logo of the Mexican *La Familia* drug cartel (Hexus.net, January 7, 2011).

In addition to credit cards, Chinese criminal networks are extensively involved in pirating computer software and digital entertainment products. These are either produced in Canada or produced in China and then smuggled into North America. Chinese crime groups have also flooded Canada and other countries with counterfeit cigarettes. In December 2003, police in Toronto raided a warehouse and found cheap cigarettes from China that had been placed in forged packages of popular Canadian brands. Police estimated the street value of the cigarettes at $2.6 million. Also found in the warehouse were a small amount of ecstasy and approximately 500 pieces of counterfeit designer clothing (*National Post*, December 12, 2003).

The International Anti-Counterfeiting Coalition claims that the Canadian market in forged products is worth between $20 billion and $30 billion annually. In 2003, the United States Trade Representative put Canada on its "Special 301 Watch List," which designates countries deemed by the United States as failing to provide adequate protection or enforcement of intellectual property rights. The Congressional International Anti-Piracy Caucus, a bi-partisan committee of US legislators formed to address product counterfeiting, also placed Canada on a list of nations that are the world's top sources of pirated copies of movies, CDs, and software (other countries on the list include China, Russia, Mexico, India, and Malaysia). In its 2006 Country Watch List, the congressional committee concluded, "Canada has become a source of camcorder piracy," which involves sneaking digital camcorders into movie theatres to illegal record first-run movies and then transferring the movies onto DVDs to be sold illegally (The Congressional International Anti-Piracy Caucus, 2006: 3; *Montreal Gazette*, September 6, 2005; Office of the United States Trade Representative, 2005).

In 2011, the International Intellectual Property Alliance (IIPA), which describes itself as "a private sector coalition of trade associations representing U.S. copyright-based industries," placed Canada on its "Priority Watch" list. The list is made up of countries that have a high rate of piracy and copyright infringement, which is due in part to a weak legislative and enforcement regime. "Overall the piracy picture in Canada is at least as bleak as it was a year ago, and it is cementing its reputation as a haven where technologically sophisticated international piracy organizations can operate with virtual impunity," the 2011 report asserts. "The biggest void in Canada's enforcement effort is online. Canada has gained a regrettable but well-deserved reputation as a safe haven for Internet pirates" and "some of the world's most popular illegitimate Internet sites, including illegitimate P2P download and streaming sites" (*Toronto Star*, March 8, 2011). In its 2015 report on Canada, the IIPA was a tad more lenient on Canada, but not much. "Canada's intent to change the country's reputation as a haven for technologically sophisticated international piracy operations has not been fully realized; notorious pirate websites hosted in Canada remain in full operation, undermining the growth of legitimate digital services around the world" (International Intellectual Property Alliance, 2015).

Designer fashions are also the target of a worldwide counterfeiting industry that involves well-established criminal organizations. This includes sophisticated Chinese criminal networks based out of Toronto and in Asia. At a news conference on December 1, 2015, Toronto police officials said an 18-month investigation, conducted in conjunction with other law enforcement agencies and private partners, resulted in the confiscation of $12 million worth of counterfeit items. As the CBC reported, "some of the fake items include Toronto Blue Jays post-season tickets and fake sports jerseys. Other illegitimate products include knock-offs of Coach, Gucci, Hermes, Louis Vuitton, Prada, Chanel, Kate Spade, Tiffany & Co., Michael Kors and Ugg." Acting Staff Superintendent Bryce Evans told reporters, "Public bulletins, documents, and literature by national and international law enforcement groups indicate that the sales of counterfeit goods financially supports organized crime and terrorist groups."

The operation, codenamed Project Pace II (Partners Against Counterfeit Everywhere), targeted people and groups selling pirated products, including a number of retailers from across the GTA as well as Montreal that were active in selling counterfeit products. Toronto police estimated the retail value of pirated goods seized from vendors at the Canadian National Exhibition in Toronto during the summer of 2015 was $1 million. "Fakes of Luxury brands like Tory Burch, Michael Kors, Gucci, Prada, and Rolex were found for sale" by vendors at the CNE, according to CBC News. Project Pace II resulted in a number of people being charged with *Criminal Code* offences.

Project Pace I was concluded in 2013 and resulted in the seizure of goods valued at approximately $6.5 million and more than 100 charges being laid against 21 people. The counterfeit goods, which police said were "substandard and potentially hazardous" included fake versions of Viagra and Cialis as well as makeup, contact lenses, even ice wine and TTC tokens (police said the fake TTC tokens were smuggled to Canada from China inside shower curtain rods). During the investigation, which involved the US Department of Homeland Security and police forces from multiple jurisdictions in Ontario, police executed search warrants on retailers at the CNE, and at stores such as Wireless Wave (CBC News, November 29, 2013, August 30, 2015, December 1, 2015; *York Guardian*, December 1, 2015).

CRITICAL THINKING EXERCISE

What are the factors that have contributed to Canada's reputation as a source of counterfeit consumer products? Are there any causal factors that are unique to Canada, relative to other countries?

Counterfeiting of Prescription Drugs

According to the World Health Organization (2006), a counterfeit drug is a pharmaceutical product "which is deliberately and fraudulently mislabeled with respect to identity and/or source." A 2011 article on counterfeit drugs in the online edition of the *USA Today* indicates that organized crime groups are heavily involved in the production, smuggling, and trafficking of counterfeit prescription drugs:

> Groups that have been associated with counterfeit drugs or online pharmacies include the Russian Mafia, the Chinese triads, the Japanese Yakuza, and the Neapolitan Camorra, among others, who also engage in a range of counterfeiting activities ... There have been numerous cases of counterfeit drug labs operating with complex international frameworks—experts often link the production of counterfeit pharmaceuticals to organized crime. In one case that led to an investigation and seizures, counterfeit drugs produced in China were transported by road to Hong Kong, sent by air to Dubai, passing through London Heathrow on the way to the Bahamas, where the organization kept a warehouse fulfillment center. From there, the drugs were sent to another organization in the U.K., which eventually sent the packages to the U.S. (*USA Today*, October 7, 2011)

In 2012, the Canada Border Service Agency (CBSA) reminded Canadians that they are not immune to the worldwide deluge of counterfeit prescription drugs. In October, CBSA officials held a news conference in Vancouver where they displayed samples of some of the thousands of counterfeit pills that entered Canada by mail and were subsequently seized by border enforcement officials. The presentation followed the culminated of Operation Pangea V, an international investigation, coordinated by Interpol, which included 100 countries and ran between September 25 and October 2, 2012. According to Interpol's website, "Operation Pangea is an international week of action tackling the online sale of counterfeit and illicit medicines and highlighting the dangers of buying medicines online." The international enforcement results from Operation Pangea V, according to Interpol included the confiscation of 3.75 million illicit and counterfeit pills worth approximately US $10.5 million.

An RCMP spokesperson told the media that as part of this international operation, enforcement officials in Canada inspected almost 4000 packages containing prescription drugs mailed into the country and seized 2000 of these packages on suspicion they contained fake drugs. In total, 140,000 fake pills worth an estimated $1 million were seized. Many of the parcels contained thousands of dosages; the largest package intercepted contained 8000 doses.

The fake medications seized included those marketed as anti-depressants, sedatives, prescription weight-loss products, heart medications, hormone-replacement therapies, and erectile dysfunction drugs. The RCMP spokesperson emphasized that fake drugs can endanger lives because the ingredients in many of the products include undisclosed pharmaceutical medicines and dangerous chemicals.

The risk of purchasing counterfeit drugs escalates dramatically when one is attempting to order them online. Purchasing medications through the Internet also increases the chance of customers becoming victims of identity theft and credit card fraud. This is because the suppliers are often connected to organized crime groups that also operate identity theft and credit card counterfeiting operations. China is the primary source of the fake medications, which is not surprising given its reputation as the counterfeit capital of the world (Canadian Press, October 4, 2012; Interpol website, n.d.a; *USA Today*, October 7, 2011).

Organized Crime and the Securities Market

The securities market represents one sector of the legitimate economy that has been targeted for theft, fraud, and manipulation by organized crime (this should be contrasted with cases where criminal offenders pose as legitimate brokers and try to fleece investors through boiler room operations). In the immediate post-war period, organized crime groups were involved in the rudimentary theft of stock certificates. From the 1950s to the early 1970s, traditional crime groups in Canada masterminded schemes to steal millions of dollars' worth of securities certificates (Walter, 1971). During the 1950s, Hamilton's John Papalia used intimidation tactics to extort money and insider information from securities brokers (*Toronto Star*, April 17, 1961). In the 1970s, William Obront, the financial brains behind the Cotroni Mafia group in Montreal, was charged with more than 400 counts of fraudulently manipulating stock market shares over a 15-year period (Quebec Police Commission Inquiry on Organized Crime, 1977b: 148).

In 1997, police began investigating the possible role of outlaw motorcycle gang members in manipulating the publicly traded stock of Montreal-based BioChem Pharma. This investigation was intensified after four bombs exploded outside the company's Quebec headquarters on November 24 and 25 of that year (*Financial Post*, November 28, 1997). One media article reported that over those two days an unusually large number of BioChem "put options" was purchased through the Montreal Exchange. The intent of the bombings may have been to destabilize the stock, causing it to drop rapidly and allowing speculators to make a substantial profit. In April of that year, Claude Duboc, who was arrested and convicted in Florida for his part in masterminding one of the world's largest hashish-trafficking empires, agreed to pay his lawyer F. Lee Bailey in BioChem stock, then worth $5.8 million (soon after making the transfer, the stock shot up in value to over $20 million). When US authorities tried to claim the stock as the proceeds of crime, Bailey refused to give it up. He relented only after a judge jailed him for contempt (*Vancouver Sun*, April 27, 1997).

In November 2002, the Ontario Securities Commission (OSC) acknowledged that organized crime is active in the capital markets across Canada, through money laundering, manipulating share prices, and conducting insider trades. "Organized crime has realized that in a marketplace where hundreds of millions of dollars are trading everyday it would be lucrative if they could get their tentacles into it," according to Michael Watson, director of enforcement at the OSC (*National Post*, November 13, 2002). The OSC's recognition of the involvement of criminal groups in Canada's stock markets is not new; in 1999, it called for a formal partnership between itself and the RCMP in part to crack down on "a disturbing growth in crime in the securities industry, crimes to which a very large degree have been committed by organized syndication" (*Globe and Mail*, October 27, 1999).

Organized crime is also interested in the capital markets to launder the profits of other criminal activities—in particular, drug trafficking. The web-based chapter on Russian organized crime describes in more detail how the proceeds of crime are laundered by taking a private company (previously injected with criminal proceeds) public and offering shares in the company (through a listing on the Toronto Stock Exchange). This technique allows a criminal organization the opportunity to raise capital and thus a seemingly legitimate source of funds. Police cases in Canada also show that drug traffickers have invested money in the markets as a way to launder their illicit funds.

In a 2012 study for Public Safety Canada, Hicks and colleagues summarize the various ways that securities markets are vulnerable to organized crime:

> The securities sector may be a site for the laundering of proceeds of crime generated outside of the industry, for instance, drug money, or a site for fraud and related laundering of proceeds generated to varying degrees within or alongside the sector. Criminal organizations can establish real or paper-based companies and sell real or fictitious stocks outside the regulated market, or attempt to secure the cooperation of industry insiders through the threat of violence or in repayment of gambling debts. It is also possible that criminal organizations or their members may establish partial or direct beneficial ownership of brokerage houses and engage a broader and deeper exploitation of victims. Some schemes that occur in Canada include fraudulent high-yield investments, pyramid or Ponzi schemes, and illicit 'tax-free' investments. (Hicks et. al., 2012: iv)

KEY TERMS

Bank card fraud	Counterfeiting of consumer products
Boiler room	Credit card counterfeiting
Burglary	Currency counterfeiting
Business racketeering	Cybercrime
Cargo theft	Deceitful mass marketing
Consensual	Disorganized crimes
Copyright infringement	Extortion
Counterfeiting	Fraud

Fund raiding
Goods
Hacking
Home invasion
Human trafficking
Hybrid
Identity theft and fraud
International travel document
  counterfeiting
Labour racketeering
Market-based crimes
Organized crimes
Organized shoplifting
Phishing

Predatory
Profit-motivated offences
Protection racket
Robbery
Services
Skimming
Spamming
Strike insurance
Sweetheart deal
Tactical support activities
Theft
Unorganized crimes
Vehicle theft
Victimless crimes

REVIEW QUESTIONS

1. What makes organized crimes unique compared to more rudimentary or "disorganized" crimes?
2. What are some of the different ways that organized crimes can be conceptualized?
3. What are the factors that give rise to these profit-oriented criminal opportunities?
4. What are the common denominators among different organized criminal activities?
5. What are the different predatory activities carried out by organized crime?
6. How can a criminal activity be considered both predatory and consensual?

FURTHER READINGS

Allum, F., & Gilmour, S. (Eds.). (2012). *Routledge Handbook of Transnational Organized Crime.* London, New York: Routledge.

Bouchard, M., & Wilkins, C. (Eds.). (2010). *Illegal Markets and the Economics of Organized Crime.* New York: Routledge.

Brookman, F., Maguire, M., Pierpoint, H., & Bennett, T. (Eds.). (2010). *Handbook on Crime.* Portland, OR: Willan Publishing.

Paoli, L. (Ed.). (2014). *The Oxford Handbook of Organized Crime.* Oxford, New York: Oxford University Press.

10 CONSENSUAL CRIMES

CHAPTER OUTLINE

- Introduction and Overview
- Illegal Gambling
- Loansharking
- Smuggling

LEARNING OUTCOMES

After reading this chapter, you should have a thorough understanding of the following:

- The nature of consensual criminal activities undertaken by organized crime groups (excluding drug trafficking) and how they differ from predatory criminal activities
- Different consensual crimes carried out by criminal organizations
- What makes consensual illegal activities associated with organized crime unique compared to more rudimentary predatory crimes
- Factors that give rise to consensual criminal opportunities
- Common denominators among different consensual criminal activities

INTRODUCTION AND OVERVIEW

Technically speaking, a consensual crime is one where no victim exists; that is, two or more individuals willingly engage in a (illegal) commercial transaction. Like any legitimate business transaction, one of the individuals involved is consuming the good or service without coercion while the other is supplying it. A distinguishing characteristic of organized crime is that it is in the business of providing goods and services to a consuming public primarily through underground "black" markets. Traditionally, these black markets satisfy the demand for goods and services that have been prohibited or heavily regulated by the state because they are deemed immoral or destructive to the individual and society. In other words, satisfying people's vices is a major reason why organized crime exists. By extension, significant interest and participation in consensual criminal activities by both suppliers and consumers has resulted in the "commercialization of these enterprises" (Albanese, 2015: 41). Indeed, illegal markets and consensual criminal activities have been simultaneously fuelled by both demand (for illegal drugs, cheap cigarettes, off-track betting, games of chance, fast loans, and sex) and supply (OC groups and networks have been involved in drug trafficking, cigarette smuggling, bookmaking, gambling, loansharking, and the sex trade).

The goods and services provided by organized criminal offenders, however, is not restricted to the vice industry. They also provide a wide range of other goods and services that are in demand but for one reason or another have been driven into the underground economy. Two such examples are migrant smuggling (based on the demand for illegal immigration) and counterfeit consumer products (based on the demand for goods at a discount). Thus, the goods and services provided in underground markets include those that have either been made illegal by the state (e.g., drugs, bookmaking, the sex trade) or are heavily regulated and controlled by the state (e.g., cigarettes, liquor, prescription drugs, immigration). This chapter examines three broad categories consensual criminal activities that are commonly associated with organized crime in Canada: illegal gaming, loansharking, and smuggling.

ILLEGAL GAMBLING

Albanese (2015: 40) defines **gambling** as "as games of chance, where luck determines the outcome more than skill." While there are numerous forms of legal gambling in North America (bingo, lotteries, fantasy sports leagues), according to Spapens (2014), the state has always had reasons to control this vice "stemming either from practical concerns—such as curbing gambling addiction and maintaining public order—or from religious and ideological principles." Prohibiting or restricting gambling and sports betting, however, inevitably creates illegal markets "that organized crime groups have at times been able to dominate" (Spapens, 2014: 402) partially because operating "a large-scale gambling operation for a prolonged period requires a stable and significant level of organization" (Spapens, 2014: 406). Illegal gambling has been one of the most widespread and profitable organized crimes and can be divided into two broad categories: (1) games of chance, from floating card games to underground casinos, all the way to organized crime's influence in legalized gambling in Las Vegas, Atlantic City, or Macau; and (2) bookmaking, in which bets are taken on horse racing and other sporting events.

Illegal gambling has existed in North America for centuries, and over the years, it has become increasingly organized (both legally and illegally). During the 1890s, the *Toronto Daily Star* ran a number of stories on the illegal gambling parlours in the city. In a May 1894 article entitled "On the Throw of Dice," the newspaper described the "gambling halls in full operation where many men lose most of their earnings and where a few make very comfortable livings without working." The most popular destinations for gamblers in Toronto during this time were the "poker joints," which were "frequent at the present time and have been for many years" (*Toronto Star*, May 21, 1894). By 1901, professional gambling operations in Toronto were perceived to be so widespread and the police response so lax, the city's Board of Police Commissioners was compelled to hold a public inquiry.

In addition to gambling dens, **bookmaking** was becoming a growing source of revenue for underground entrepreneurs in Toronto. Local **horse-books** became widespread with the opening of the Woodbine racetrack in 1874 and its decision to license individuals to take bets on site. It was not long after that hordes of unlicensed bookmakers began showing up at the track, offering better odds than their legitimate counterparts. Off-track betting operations or "bucket shops" were also popping up throughout the city to accommodate those who were unable to attend Woodbine or other racetracks in person (*Toronto Star*, April 4, 1903). Testimony at the 1901 police commission suggests that bookmaking operations in Toronto had already become organized in that some bookies there were part of a larger gambling syndicate based in Buffalo. This relationship allowed residents of upstate New York to place bets on horse races at Woodbine while Toronto residents could bet on races at various tracks in New York state through their local **bookie**.

This long distance relationship among bettors and bookies was greatly facilitated by the telegraph system, which could quickly relay up-to-the-minute information on races and other sporting events between cities. The **wire service** became so vital to off-track betting that any self-respecting bookmaking operation had to have a "wire room," complete with a large blackboard where the odds and results from race tracks all over North America were tallied. The wire service also bolstered the cross-border network of bookmakers by facilitating the transfer of money, whether it was to place a bet, to pay out, or to settle an account (City of Toronto Archives, Fonds 15: Toronto Board of Commissioners of Police Fonds, pp. 65–68).

As gambling operations became better organized, a division of labour began to emerge. This included such specialized positions as runners (those who took bets), collectors (those who collected money), enforcers (those who ensured bets were paid), controllers (mid-level managers who hired and supervised the bookies), bankers (those who controlled the money, paid winners, and bribed police), technicians (to install the wire service), and operators (to decode the information sent over telegraph system). By the 1920s, large-scale bookmaking consortiums were now operating in Canada's major cities, most of which had ties to American gambling syndicates. In December 1923, under the headline "Toronto Is Biggest Betting Place in North America," *Toronto Daily Star* correspondent Ernest Hemingway wrote that bettors could place a wager in Toronto for horse racing or sports events in cities across Canada and the United States. He estimated there were ten thousand bettors in Toronto generating profits for gambling organizations that were as much as $100,000 a day. "It has been estimated that more men are employed in illegal betting in North America than work in the steel business," Hemingway wrote. "And it all goes on under the surface" (*Toronto Daily Star*, December 18, 1923).

Vancouver's Chinatown was also a hotspot for gamblers of all races and ethnicities, and during the 1920s, it came under the microscope of police and the city's judicial inquiry into vice. In 1918, the *Globe* newspaper estimated "there are over forty gambling dens in Chinatown today, and that many of these have advertisements in their windows for 'fantan' as above stated" (*The Globe*, May 23, 1918).

It was with the end of Prohibition that gambling became the most profitable activity for criminal groups in North America. Gambling (except on horse racing) was illegal throughout much of North America, although it was clear that it enjoyed enormous popularity, cutting across social class and ethnic groups. Realizing the demand for gambling outlets, crime groups began to branch out into bookmaking, private card games, and most ambitiously, casino gambling. The enormous profits made from gambling were often lent back to gamblers at usurious rates, making loansharking second only to gambling in terms of profit during the 1930 and 1940s (Hammer, 1975).

To understand the widespread nature of underground gambling and how it became such a lucrative criminal racket, one must appreciate the extent to which illegal gambling operators were protected by law enforcement and politicians in return for generous compensation. Gambling was often viewed as an innocent vice by police and other government officials, thus they could rationalize accepting bribes to look the other way. As such, along with bootlegging, illegal gambling became a significant factor in furthering government corruption and the graft-filled mutually conducive relationship between gangsters and public officials.

While much of *la Cosa Nostra*'s (LCN) involvement in gambling in North America was confined to illegal operations, in 1946, Benjamin (Bugsy) Siegel, with financing from the east coast Mafia families, was instrumental in opening the Flamingo Hotel in Las Vegas, which until then was a non-descript town that served as rest stop for those travelling through the desert to and from Los Angeles. Soon thereafter, Siegel was killed by the very individuals who bankrolled his vision. Despite his death, the major crime families of New York, as well as other parts of the country, continued to invest in, and ultimately controlled, the casinos of Las Vegas, helping to situate the city as the gambling capital of the world.

The post-war years also witnessed an unprecedented expansion of illegal gambling in Ontario and Quebec, due in part to the increased role by well-organized groups. During the late 1940s and early 1950s, Montreal had become a North American Mecca for gambling, which was gradually controlled by the Canadian crews of the American LCN. Tepperman (1976) notes that it was the tightening of gambling laws in the United States following the Kefauver Crime Commission hearings of 1951 that precipitated the expansion of (organized) gambling in Quebec. "In an effort to evade these laws, it is said, the American Mafia figures decided to set up gambling activities in Montreal, connecting them to much of the American network by wire. It is said that at least three New York Families—Profaci, Genovese, and Bonanno—were involved in this operation, and that Carmine Galante, a Bonanno Family lieutenant was sent to Montreal to supervise the gambling and dope-smuggling activities of these families" (Tepperman, 1976: 144). Carmine Galante and his Canadian partner Vic Cotroni began by extorting independent gambling operations and then moved to take direct control over them.

By the mid-1940s, a gambler could lay a bet in one of over 200 underground establishments in greater Montreal, which collectively generated an estimated $100 million annually in revenue (Weintraub, 2004: 61, 85). A 1946 *Time* magazine article

Case Study: Harry Ship, the "King of the Montreal Gamblers"

Harry Ship possessed a number of attributes that propelled him to prominence among professional gamblers in Montreal during the 1940s: he had a great mind for business, was well respected among his peers, was highly innovative when it came to using new technology, and was a brilliant mathematician. Born in 1915, Ship was a mathematics student at Queen's University before dropping out and beginning a career as a bookmaker's clerk. In 1940, he started Montreal's largest bookmaking enterprise when he converted several apartments in a St. Catherine Street residential building. Ship equipped each apartment with five telephone lines and several blackboards. Adapting the headsets worn by Bell telephone operators with long extension cords, each bookie was now free to take calls while writing bets on the blackboards, an innovation that allowed Ship to cut personnel costs by combining two jobs into one. Business became so brisk that Ship used partitions to subdivide apartments into halves and then quarters. Each cubicle housed a slip writer, five telephones, and one or more blackboards. The partitioned apartments became so stuffy that the bookies were often found working in their underwear. Ship was supplied with racing forms from a nearby printing office, and by 1943 he was contracting the telegram service of the Canadian National Railway to receive the results of horse races and sports scores from across the continent. He also had a sports ticker service installed in the hall of the building, which in 1946 was hooked up to a Trans-Lux projector that illuminated onto a large screen the racing information coming in over the ticker service.

Continued

His long distance bills were so large that the Bell Telephone Company required him to make a monthly deposit of $500 (which was raised to $1000 as the number of telephones multiplied). His bookmaking operations covered so many events and his slip writers took so many wagers that blackboards had to be replaced on a monthly basis. When he appeared before a public inquiry into organized gambling and graft in 1952, Ship admitted that between 1940 and 1946 he grossed more than $1 million annually from his bookmaking business, most of which was deposited into a bank account registered in the name of the Victory Cigar Store.

During the same period, Ship's St. Catherine Street operations was raided 34 times by police, leading to 37 convictions against his bookies, the padlocking of various apartments in the building, and thousands of dollars in fines. "The fines we paid took care of the police department's salaries, or a large part of them, and the city coffers were getting fat," he said. "I think that's why we were tolerated." Despite his substantial revenue, Ship cried poverty when he was arrested on gambling charges in 1946. "The horses forgot to win," he laconically explained to Justice Caron. On January 8, 1948, the 33-year-old was convicted on three counts of operating an illegal gaming house and was sentenced to six months in prison (*Montreal Gazette*, January 10, 1948; *Montreal Star*, July 23, 1952; Phillips, 1963a: 11–12; Weintraub, 2004: 74–75).

Photo 10.1: One of Harry Ship's slipwriters working in a partitioned cubicle

Source: Reprinted with permission from the Library and Archives Canada and Southam Inc. / *Montreal Gazette*, PA 144557

describes how gambling at the luxurious Mount Royal Bridge Club, located in a small municipality just beyond the westernmost limits of the city, often took in as much as $100,000 on weekends through its craps games and roulette wheels (*Time*, August 5, 1946). A series of *Montreal Gazette* articles published in the summer of 1945 reported that during their peak periods between 9 p.m. and 4 a.m., the city's *barbotte* houses —so-named after a dice game similar to craps—employed close to 400 people who collected $75,000 in bets every hour (*Montreal Gazette*, July 12, 1945, July 21, 1945).

Harry Ship's assertion that he was broke may very well have been true. He was an inveterate gambler who had no qualms about betting thousands of dollars on a single horse race or sporting event. Because of his chronic gambling, Ship became indebted to Frank Erikson, one of the biggest and wealthiest bookmakers on the American eastern seaboard. By taking **lay-off bets** from other bookies across the United States and Canada, Erickson reportedly made bank deposits that totalled more than $6 million over a period of just four years (Woodiwiss, 2002: 209). Erikson had numerous silent partners in his gambling and bookmaking operations. Among these were some of America's most powerful mobsters: Meyer Lansky, Lucky Luciano, and Frank Costello. Whether or not he knew it at the time, Harry Ship was now indebted to *la Cosa Nostra*. With the backing of Costello and Luciano, Erikson pressured Ship to take on local Mafiosi as partners in his gambling operations. Before long, Costello and other American crime bosses began instructing their bookies and other hired help to pack up and relocate to Montreal. By the spring of 1953, the groundwork had been laid for a radical realignment of the city's criminal world. This included the arrival of some of the largest criminal combines from the United States, the establishment of Montreal as one of the biggest bookmaking centres on the continent, the eventual consolidation of local rackets under New York's Mafia families, and the transformation of organized crime in Quebec into a branch of *la Cosa Nostra*.

During the 1940s and early 1950s, most of the numerous gambling operations in Ontario were largely independent, although the largest operator in the province, Max Bluestein, reportedly had more than 200 people working for him (Freeman & Hewitt, 1979: 79–81). In testimony before Justice Roach, Bluestein stated that 90 percent of the bets taken by him and his associates were on sporting events. In July 1960, betting slips seized by police during a raid on one of Bluestein's gaming parlours showed that the daily average revenue over a nine-day period was $37,700 (Roach, 1962: 358). As in Quebec, however, the days of the independent gambling operator in Ontario were numbered as the emerging provincial Mafia chief, John Papalia, began to consolidate his grip on a number of criminal rackets in that province. His first order of business was to order each of the independent gambling operators to provide him with a cut of their profits. Eventually, all the major gambling operations in the Toronto–Hamilton area, with the exception of Bluestein, were paying protection to Papalia. Along with Danny Gasbarrini, Papalia set up his own gambling hall called the Porcupine Mines Social Club in Hamilton, just a block away from the city's Central Police Station.

Photo 10.2: Max Bluestein

Source: Illustration by Ben Firsch

Years later, Gasbarrini told the press, "For two years the police never bothered with us although they knew it was going on. But we never paid anyone off. It was just that we ran an honest game and had some of the best people in town coming to it" (*Hamilton Spectator*, October 18, 1963, as cited in Freeman & Hewitt, 1979: 80).

By the late 1950s, Papalia had moved into Hamilton gambling operations in a big way. In July of that year, a raid uncovered a large sports betting operation run by Red LeBarrie, Joe and Dominic Papalia (John's brothers), and Tony Pugliese, a brother-in-law. By the end of the 1950s, Papalia was the most powerful organized crime figure in Ontario. When all the other professional gamblers in the province had capitulated to Papalia, Bluestein continued to resist. He would pay for his defiance in April 1961 as he was brutally beaten by Papalia and six of his men as he leaving a Toronto restaurant (Freeman & Hewitt, 1979: 79–81; *Toronto Star*, April 7, 1961).

During the 1960s, a number of structural transformations in gambling began to occur that diminished the mob's powerful control over gambling in the United States and Canada. As governments searched for new sources of revenue, the popularity and profitability of legalized gambling was too hard to resist. Government-run lotteries became the norm throughout the United States and Canada. Other forms of gambling, including off-track and casino betting, were also made legal in a number of jurisdictions. The legalization of various forms of gambling did not eliminate organized crime involvement, however; bookmaking operations in particular continued to flourish. The ongoing legalization and state sponsorship of gambling did eat into the revenues of underground operators, and to compete, professional gamblers and bookmakers began offering their clients better odds, more convenience and selection,

CRITICAL THINKING EXERCISE

Compare and contrast state-run gambling operations in Canada (e.g., Lotto 649) with those run illegally. Critically analyze whether the legalization of some forms of gambling in Canada has resulted in any reduction in illegal gambling and bookmaking.

as well as credit and on-the-spot loans. Criminal groups also branched out into new lucrative forms of gambling that were outlawed or difficult to regulate, such as video lottery terminals and Internet-based casinos and card games.

Today, organized crime groups have little influence over legalized gambling in the United States and Canada, although illegal gambling and bookmaking is still a major source of revenue for some criminal organizations. In their 1992 report on organized crime, the CACP revealed that bookmaking activity in Metropolitan Toronto "is dominated by several established bookmakers who are in the 60- to 70-year age group. These individuals are financially established and very active in sports betting action. They rely on younger individuals to generate new action and to act as a shield between themselves and law enforcement" (Canadian Association of Chiefs of Police, 1992: 78). A 1996 classified report by the Criminal Service of Ontario states that the many types of illegal gambling in the province were taking in an estimated $10 billion a year (*Ottawa Citizen*, March 14, 1996). Three years later, the provincial government established the Illegal Gaming Enforcement Unit, and that year 941 gambling-related charges were laid against 623 people (Criminal Intelligence Service Canada, 2000: 19). Betting on single sporting events with a bookmaker is still prohibited in Canada, although the *Criminal Code* allows Canadians to make what are called "**parlay bets**" (wagering on the outcome of three or more events). Because betting on single sporting events continue to be popular, illegal bookmaking operations take in an estimated $1 billion annually in Ontario alone (Canadian Press, March 9, 2002). In 2012, the Canadian Gaming Association stated Canadians illegally bet more than $10 billion annually on single sporting events (Canadian Gaming Association Press Release, December 5, 2012).

Today, most illegal wagers are placed on professional team sporting events (not horse racing), and bets are made through the Internet and smartphone apps. Montreal's Rizzuto family helped usher in a new era of high-tech bookmaking and police cases

CRITICAL THINKING EXERCISE

While betting on individual sports games is illegal in Canada, fantasy sports leagues are completely legal. Companies like Draft Kings (www.draftkings.com) take in millions of dollars in revenue every month from individuals that build their own fantasy teams in leagues such as the NFL, NBA, NHL, and Major League Baseball, and then compete against other fantasy teams for cash prizes. Conduct your own research into these fantasy leagues and analyze them in the context of sports betting and bookmaking operations. Why do you think fantasy sports leagues are legal but betting on individual sporting events is not? If bookmaking is illegal, do you believe fantasy sports leagues should be illegal as well? Conversely, if fantasy sports leagues are legal, should betting on single games be legal as well?

Case Study: High-tech Bookmaking and the Rizzuto Mafia Family

In November 2002, an Ontario court levied fines and ordered forfeitures totalling $300,000 against Dario Zanetti, who was in charge of a vast inter-provincial book-making ring that police believed was being run by the Montreal Mafia. "He's working for the Rizzuto crime family, and he took the rap for his bosses back in Quebec," one police officer told the press. The financial penalties were the culmination of a police operation codenamed Project Juice, in which more than three dozen people in Toronto, Montreal, and Ottawa were arrested in April 2001 following a seven-month investigation. As part of a plea bargain, charges were dropped against nine other men, including made members and associates of the Rizzuto family. Police said that over a five-month period, the inter-provincial bookmaking ring took in more than $20 million in wagers on professional and college sports, using a website, Blackberry pagers, and Palm Pilots to take bets (*Globe and Mail*, November 9, 2002; *Montreal Gazette*, November 9, 2002; *Toronto Star*, November 10, 2002).

In November 2012, the RCMP in Ottawa announced the results of an inter-agency police investigation called Project Amethyst, which culminated with the arrest of 21 people linked to the Rizzuto family, who were allegedly behind a sophisticated sports bookmaking operation in Ontario and Quebec. The RCMP said that bets of several million dollars were placed over a one-year period, mostly related to the NHL, NFL, and the Olympics. The group allegedly ran an illegal gambling website used to place bets on sport events and over the course of one year, the website took in approximately $5 million in bets that generated nearly $1.2 million in profits. Among those arrested were four people who police said were the main organizers of the bookmaking operation: Gary Saikaley, Benedetto Manasseri, Stephen Parrish, and Domenic Arrechi. All four pleaded guilty in 2014 to a variety of gambling-related charges (CBC News, November 9, 2012; *Ottawa Citizen*, November 9, 2012, April 29, 2014, May 15, 2014; *Ottawa Sun*, May 16, 2014; RCMP Press Release, November 9, 2012).

show it has been linked to a number of sophisticated and highly profitable bookmaking operations in Canada over the years.

In addition to bookmaking, illegal gambling has been revolutionized by the Internet. In 1997, there were around 15 websites that offered online gambling, according to the FBI. One year later, there were at least 140 sites hosted around the world. Today, the number of websites offering professional gaming services is in the thousands. Gambling websites can be broken down into two categories: those that offer casino games such as blackjack, roulette, and poker, and those that take bets on racing and sporting events. Internet gambling sites provide numerous features that are ideally suited for organized crime. The Internet offers a distinct advantage over conventional gambling operations in the sheer volume of

CRITICAL THINKING EXERCISE

A private member's bill to legalize betting on individual sporting events has been introduced in Canadian Parliament on a number of occasions, yet it has never become law. Joe Comartin, a Member of Parliament with the New Democratic Party, first introduced Bill C-290 in 2011. The bill would allow for wagering on the outcome of a single sporting event by repealing a section of the *Criminal Code* that prohibits such betting. Comartin was quoted by the CBC saying, "It's a great method to fight organized crime ... It's just a great tool to take away a huge chunk of money from that type of criminal activity" (CBC News, July 2, 2015). Some professional sports leagues—in particular, the NHL—have come out in opposition to this legislation, while the Canadian Gaming Association firmly supports it. Conduct research into the bill as well as who supports legalizing single sports event betting and who does not. Do you support the legalization of individual event sports betting? What are the pros and cons of legalizing betting on individual sporting events? Do you believe this bill will help eliminate or minimize illegal sports betting and the involvement of criminal groups in bookmaking?

bettors and bets that can be accommodated. An investment of as little as $100,000 can purchase the hardware and software required to establish a gambling website capable of reaching millions of prospective bettors, which can take in tens of millions of dollars in wagers 24 hours a day (Federal Bureau of Investigation, 1998). Most are hosted outside of North America, which effectively puts them beyond the reach of the legal systems of Canada and the United States. In addition, the off-shore location and faceless technology of websites provides shady operators the opportunity to rig games. While most web-based gambling operations are located outside of North America, Spapens (2014: 411) notes that according to 2007 figures, 401 gambling websites could be traced to the Kahnawake Mohawk reserve in Canada. Jurisdictions that host a comparable number of gambling websites include Antigua (537), Costa Rica (474), and Curacao (343).

Video gaming machines have also become a source of illegal revenue for criminal groups in Canada. The Hells Angels, Chinese crime groups, the Italian Mafia, and the Russian Mafiya are all said to be involved in the illegal operation of video lottery terminals. In 1993, the head of the organized crime squad for the Montreal police claimed that illegal video gambling machines in the city were tightly controlled by the Rizzuto family and were second only to drugs as a revenue generator. Francesco Cotroni, the son of long-time Montreal mobster Frank Cotroni, began working in the video poker business after he was released from prison in 1990 on charges of conspiracy to murder, while his brother Santos was charged in 2000 after 50 unlicensed video lottery terminals were seized by police. The charges were later dropped as part of a plea bargain (*Montreal Gazette*, June 15, 2004; *Toronto Star*, July 6, 1993).

In 1996, the Criminal Intelligence Service Ontario estimated there were some 25,000 illegal video gambling machines in the province, "most of them distributed and controlled by a southern Ontario crime family and motorcycle gangs." The machines were estimated to generate around $500 million a year in revenue (as cited in the *Ottawa Citizen*, March 14, 1996). The 2000 annual report for CISC stated that in Western Canada, "video gaming and lottery machines are the newest, and possibly the largest, illicit source of gambling income available to organized crime groups. The machines can earn up to $2000 per machine, per week, making this an extremely lucrative business. The cost of the machines ranges between $2500 and $5000 and is quickly paid off" (Criminal Intelligence Service Canada, 2000: 19).

LOANSHARKING

Usury—the lending of money at interest rates that exceed legal limits (Albanese, 2015: 47)—has long been a source of revenue in the criminal underworld. Prior to the 1960s, it was believed that **loansharking** was second only to gambling as a source of revenue for organized crime. Loansharking operates on two principles: "the assessment of exorbitant interest rates in extending credit and the use of threats and violence in collecting debts" (Goldstock & Coenen 1980: 2). Interest rates levied by loansharks could run anywhere from 100 to 2000 percent annually (the *Criminal Code of Canada* makes it illegal to charge more than 60 percent of the credit advanced). While the threat of violence is viewed as a fundamental premise of loansharking, according to Reuter and Rubinstein (1978: Appendix 3-4), loansharks are not in the "muscle" business; they are in the credit business, and thus "they lend money to customers whom they expect will pay off and eventually re-turn as customers again." Repeat business is the key to success of loansharking operations studied by Reuter and Rubinstein (1978) and, as such, the loanshark tends not to carry out the implicit threat of force. In this respect, loansharks view themselves as businesspeople and operate very much like a traditional bank. They will run credit checks on prospective borrowers and will often secure collateral for the loan. Alternatives to violence are also pursued; the debtor has assets seized, is forced to work off the loan, or takes in a loanshark as a partner in his legitimate business in lieu of repayment or as partial payment.

Loansharking is an illegal activity that is tailor-made for criminal organizations. Access to large amounts of capital allows them to pour substantial cash into the underground credit market. The strength and violent reputation of organized crime groups lends credence to potential reprisals, thus augmenting the aura of fear and intimidation that is critical to success in the loansharking business (Goldstock & Coenen, 1980: 4). Loansharking is also closely tied to gambling, and criminal organizations that have a hand in both can expect their clients who both borrow and gamble to pay them twice for the privilege of losing their money (borrowed money is lost at games of chance, but still must be repaid to the lender).

Photo 10.3: Shakespeare's Jewish character Shylock, the grotesque and comic villain in *The Merchant of Venice*, provided an anti-Semitic stereotypical euphemism for loansharking, just as his demand for a "pound of flesh" has become a metaphor for cruel and relentless greed.

Source: Lamb, C., & Lamb, M. (1901). *Tales from Shakespeare*. Philadelphia: Henry Altemus Company.

Case Study: Loansharking Outside a Casino in Ontario

In March 2001, three Toronto-based members of a Chinese criminal group pleaded guilty to lending money at usurious rates. Police alleged that they operated a loansharking ring in Casino Rama, located about 110 kilometres outside of Toronto. "Most of the victims willingly went to these people just to get money to gamble," according to an official with the Casino Intelligence Unit of the Ontario Provincial Police. The loans averaged about $5000, with 10 percent being taken off the top right away (so a borrower would only receive $4500 cash on a $5000 loan). The borrower then had to repay the entire $5000 within an agreed upon time, usually three days. If the amount was not paid within the specified period, another $500 would be tacked on to the principal (*National Post*, March 14, 2001).

CRITICAL THINKING EXERCISE

The last few years have witnessed the meteoric rise of the so-called **payday loan** industry, which provides short-term, high-interest loans (often advertised as "advances on paycheques") to its customers. This legal industry has been under considerable criticism for its predatory lending practices of charging mostly poor, desperate people annual interest rates that can be as high as 650 percent for cash loans. If a lender is unable to make payments, he or she may be charged additional fees (Financial Consumer Agency of Canada, 2016). Conduct some research into these companies and the controversy that surrounds them. In your opinion, are these payday loan companies simply loansharks masquerading as legitimate businesses? What is the difference between these legal companies and illegal loansharking? Why do they continue to be legal in Canada when the interest rates on their loans are so usurious?

SMUGGLING

Smuggling is one criminal activity that is inexplicably tied to (transnational) organized crime and to underground markets in Canada that deal in a wide variety of drugs and other **contraband**. As Kleemans (2014: 47) writes, "many profitable criminal activities boil down to international smuggling activities—drug trafficking, smuggling illegal immigrants, human trafficking for sexual exploitation, arms trafficking, trafficking in stolen vehicles, and other transnational illegal activities such as money laundering and evasion of taxes ... " As an ubiquitous criminal process, smuggling is central to the trafficking of a range of goods in Canada—both illegal and legal—by criminal groups. Chapter 1 details Canada's long history with smuggling, which dates to its colonial days when tariffs imposed by Britain promoted widespread contraband markets for tea and other necessities. Government taxes on opium and cigarettes continued to fuel smuggling into Canada during the nineteenth century. In 1887, the Commissioner of the North-West Mounted Police alluded to the smuggling of 25 horses purchased in the United States to Canada to avoid paying excise taxes. "These horses had been purchased at Sun River, Montana, and driven into the country by an unfrequented trail, crossing the Canadian Pacific Railway west of Swift Current, and then following down the north of the boundary" (Commissioner of the North-West Mounted Police, 1887: 53).

Since the turn of the twentieth century, organized criminals have been involved in the illegal international movement of a wide range of illicit drugs and other contraband, including motor fuels, automobiles, computer parts, humans, wildlife, artifacts, jewellery, and gems. In the post-war era, the smuggling of and trafficking in drugs has been the principal preoccupation of many transnational crime syndicates, given the high level of demand and profit potential. As detailed in previous chapters, cigarettes and raw tobacco are also one of the most frequently smuggled commodities across the Canadian border. According to a 1994 report prepared for the Organized Crime Committee of the CACP:

> All major facets of organized crime are involved in the smuggling trade. These include traditional organized crime groups, outlaw motorcycle gangs, the aboriginal criminal element, criminals of Asian descent and a variety of other criminally active ethnic groups. Over the past several years, new organized smuggling groups have evolved for the sole purpose of smuggling various products into Canada. These organizations distribute the smuggling goods through extensive underground networks. (Canadian Association of Chiefs of Police, 1994, 7)

A number of factors contribute to Canada's smuggling problems. Public demand for certain legal and illegal goods is arguably a significant underlying factor. The high price of certain goods in Canada relative to the United States, which is often a function of higher taxes in the former, frequently results in underground markets for these products in Canada, which are smuggled in from the United States. In addition to tax policies, the extent of inbound smuggling into and out of Canada is greatly affected by its proximity to the United States, which is a major supplier or transit country for drugs, cigarettes, liquor, and firearms smuggled into Canada. The United States is also the destination for outbound smuggling from Canada as it represents the largest market for marijuana and synthetic drugs produced in this country. In addition, Canada is a transit country for illegal migrants (mostly from Asia) secretly entering the United States and for drugs smuggled out of the United States and then illegally transported to other countries. The fact that the two countries share the world's longest, undefended border—not to mention Canada's thousands of kilometres of poorly enforced coastline—creates an incentive for smugglers who feel that they can easily evade interdiction. Canada also has a large concentration of its population living within a short distance of the border with the US, thereby providing a convenient marketplace for inbound smuggled goods as well as a sympathetic and skilled labour pool from which to draw smugglers. Smuggling routes are well established along the Canada–United States border with some dating back to the nineteenth century. As discussed earlier in this book, a major conduit for smuggling between the United States and Canada is the Akwesasne reserve, which straddles the international border.

China's role as the world's largest producer of counterfeit goods, the presence of well-established Chinese criminal networks in Canada, and the difficulty of effective interdiction along the west coast have only worsened Canada's smuggling problems. China is now a major supplier of illegal drugs (heroin, fentanyl, and precursor chemicals for synthetic drugs, such as methamphetamine, to be manufactured in Canada) and a broad array of counterfeit consumer goods. Illegal drugs are also smuggled into

Canada from other parts of the world, including Southeast Asia (heroin), Southwest Asia (heroin and hashish), Colombia and Mexico (cocaine), and the West Indies (marijuana and cocaine).

Globalization is frequently cited as a factor that has greatly facilitated contemporary smuggling. Numerous studies and police cases have chronicled the global networking capacity of organized crime groups, which have taken advantage of advanced communication, transportation, and financial services technology, as well as the easing of international trade restrictions to facilitate the movement of contraband and prohibited goods. Transnational criminal operations have also capitalized on the primacy of the sovereign nation-state and the resulting limitations this brings to international law enforcement, such as differing legal systems, the lack of an international criminal justice system, and obstacles to co-operation and coordination among law enforcement in different countries. In contrast, the increasing level of international networking and co-operation among organized crime groups and autonomous offenders has greatly augmented smuggling.

Essentially all methods of transportation are used to smuggle contraband into and out of Canada. The largest payloads of drugs and contraband are brought into the country via marine containers (through marine ports) and tractor-trailer trucks (through official land border crossings). Heroin is frequently brought in via the airlines, either through air cargo or hidden in the suitcases of passengers on commercial flights. Smuggling occurs through both official ports of entry (guarded by customs agencies) and "unofficial" ports of entries. As von Lampe (2012: 194) puts it, when authorized border crossings are used, the smuggler and the conveyance (vehicle) blends "into the flow of licit cross-border traffic and trade," but the contraband is hidden. Alternatively, smuggling takes place over the "green border" (in particular, those that are "remote, poorly monitored or difficult to monitor") in which the smuggler, the smuggling conveyance, and the contraband are all meant to be hidden from official scrutiny.

Tobacco Smuggling

The current problem of cigarette smuggling is not without historical precedence. By the end of the nineteenth century, tobacco products had become the most popular contraband in Canada. In the 1890s, the Dominion government imposed an import duty to protect domestic cigarette manufacturers from foreign competition. This duty raised the cost of a small package of cigarettes imported into Canada to 10 cents; in the United States, they could be purchased at half that price. The result, according to an 1895 *Toronto Star* article titled "Smuggle the Vile Cigarette," was that tobacco smugglers were now "doing business on a tremendously large scale, bringing the goods both to Toronto and to Montreal" (*Toronto Star*, August 2, 1895). In 1898, Dominion officials broke up one of the biggest **tobacco-smuggling** operations to date, involving the illegal transport of thousands of cigars from Puerto Rico into Canada, via Halifax. The contraband cigars were delivered to a Halifax grocery store and from there distributed throughout Nova Scotia, New Brunswick, Quebec, and Ontario. "So well and systematically was the enterprise organized," the *Toronto Star* wrote, "that the goods were distributed by express and freight over the Intercolonial and other railways, and the payments collected by draft through the banks." Canadian Revenue officers were dispatched to search tobacconists, grocers, and the barrooms of hotels throughout the Maritimes, Ontario, and Quebec for the contraband cigars. The result was "the biggest seizures of smuggled tobacco ever brought into Canada" (*Toronto Star*, September 6, 1898).

While cigarettes have entered Canada illegally since then, it was in the 1990s that the scope of contraband smuggling into and out of the country exceeded any previous period in its history due to a steep hike in taxes on Canadian cigarettes. The substantial growth in cigarette smuggling into Canada was due to a significant increase the Canadian government tax on the domestic sale of cigarettes (while no similar tax was applied to exports to the United States, which meant they were much cheaper to purchase there). Between 1991 and 1993 alone, cigarette exports to the United States rose 824 percent (Canadian Tobacco Manufacturers Council, n.d.). The vast majority of these cigarettes were then smuggled back to Canada and distributed through networks of wholesalers, legitimate retail outlets, and street vendors, who sold them for far below their legitimate market price. In 1990, the estimated retail value of contraband tobacco products seized by law enforcement agencies in Canada was $17.2 million. By 1993, this had climbed to $53.4 million (*Montreal Gazette*, February 12, 1994). The illegal transport of contraband tobacco products into Canada was so great that by 1993 there were an estimated 90 to 100 million cartons of contraband cigarettes in the country, representing 40 percent of the $12.4 billion Canadian cigarette market (Chretien, 1994: 6). Research conducted in 1998 by the consulting firm KPMG indicated that a case of a thousand cigarettes smuggled into Canada across the New York–Ontario border had a landed cost of $636. When transported to British Columbia, the same case could potentially sell for up to $1750 (KPMG, 1998: 22). The profit potential attracted a diverse range of individuals and groups to a smuggling trade that steadily became more organized, sophisticated, and voluminous.

Throughout the 2000s, as federal and provincial governments once again hiked tobacco taxes as a strategy to curb smoking and raise tax revenues, the smuggling business once again grew exponentially. In 2009, the size of this black market in Canada was conservatively estimated at $1.3 billion (*Montreal Gazette*, March 26, 2009). The National Coalition Against Contraband Tobacco estimated that the sale of contraband cigarettes cost the Canadian government $2.1 billion in lost tax revenue in 2011 alone (CBC News, September 13, 2012). The Ontario Convenience Store Association said in 2015 that contraband tobacco accounts for approximately 33 percent of all cigarettes purchased in Ontario (Postmedia News, May 30, 2015). In comparison, contraband makes up an estimated 10.7 to 11.6 percent of cigarettes consumed worldwide (*Toronto Star*, December 10, 2014).

Photo 10.4: Cigarette smuggling is a global problem. In this photo, the UK Border Agency discovered one million Chinese-made cigarettes hidden inside concrete blocks during a search on October 27, 2010.

Source: U.K. Home Office, via Wikimedia Commons

Not only are name-brand cigarettes smuggled into the country, but loose tobacco is also brought in illegally to be manufactured into cigarettes in the many plants located on Indigenous reserves in Ontario and Quebec (see chapter 8). For example, on January 10, 2013, the CBSA seized more than 13,700 kilograms of loose tobacco from a commercial truck entering Canada from the United States at the Ambassador Bridge border crossing at Windsor, Ontario (Canada Border Services Agency News Release, March 16, 2013). Less than a week later, a tractor-trailer transporting a marine container was referred for secondary examination at the Peace Bridge commercial border crossing, which connects Buffalo, New York, and Fort Erie, Ontario. The goods were declared as herbal leaf formulation. Upon examination of the contents of the shipment, border services officers discovered 99 boxes with 13,464 kilograms of loose tobacco with an estimated value of $1.7 million (Canada Border Services Agency News Release, March 23, 2013).

In 2008, an RCMP threat assessment on contraband tobacco in Canada estimated that "105 organized crime groups of varying levels of sophistication are currently known to be involved in the illicit tobacco trade" (Royal Canadian Mounted Police, 2008: 5). Nearly half of the criminal groups active in the smuggling of tobacco products are based in Central Canada and take advantage of the unique smuggling opportunities presented by the Akwesasne reserve (National Coalition Against Contraband Tobacco Press Release, November 19, 2015). The smuggling trade is attractive to both non-traditional, fledgling groups as well as established criminal organizations. Many smuggling groups and networks were established exclusively around cigarette smuggling due to the profits, ease of entry, low risk, and relatively minor penalties. For existing criminal groups, the contraband cigarette trade represents yet another profitable trade that takes advantage of existing smuggling routes, distribution networks, and internal conspiracies at ports of entry. As the RCMP note in their 2008 report, 69 percent of the criminal groups involved in tobacco smuggling are "also involved in drug trafficking, mainly marihuana and cocaine, and/or weapons trafficking. Furthermore, 30% of these groups are known to have violent tendencies" (Royal Canadian Mounted Police, 2008: 5). Canadian police cases and research demonstrate that most tobacco smuggling and distribution operations are carried out by a network of individuals and small groups, many of who specialize in specific aspects of the smuggling pipeline, such as arranging financing, purchasing the cigarettes in the United States, brokering transportation, physically transporting the goods, storing, wholesaling, and retailing.

Migrant Smuggling

In addition to legal and illegal merchandise, people are also a highly profitable "commodity" smuggled across national borders. Illegal or **undocumented migration** is when someone enters a country (that is not their country of origin) without the proper authority. For as long as history has been recorded, people have yearned to migrate, for a variety of reasons, including economic betterment or escape from persecution and terror. As a result, thousands of people every year are willing to migrate to other countries outside of official channels. The profits to be made from responding to such demand have given rise to the development of a massive, global trade in **migrant smuggling**.

According to the United Nations Global Program Against Trafficking in Human Beings, migrant smuggling is the procurement of illegal entry of a person into a country of which the person is not a citizen with the objective of making a profit. Human smuggling may be contrasted with the related and somewhat more complex concept of human trafficking (examined in chapter 9). Migrant smuggling can be considered a consensual crime when the migrants willingly consent (and even initiate) their unauthorized transport to and entry into another country. When individuals are coerced or forced to migrate to another country, this is more apt to be considered human trafficking. As Di Nicola (2014: 151) points out, "People smuggling divides into at least three phases: recruitment, transfer, and entrance into the destination country. Human trafficking involves a further stage—exploitation … "

Migrant smuggling has increased throughout the world, owing to a number of factors: the surge in international migration, more efficient transportation systems, well-established smuggling routes, an illegal infrastructure to move migrants internationally, and the involvement of well-organized criminal groups and networks. According to Di Nicola (2014: 143), "During the past three decades, immigration has become a profitable area for organized criminals, who have started to provide migration services for people from less developed regions of the world seeking to reach richer countries. The intervening variable in (illegal) migratory processes world-wide is therefore organized crime." As Kleemans and Smit (2014: 384) note, most international human smuggling operations are not dominated or centrally coordinated by Mafia-style, hierarchical, transnational criminal organizations. Instead, "smuggling is harmonized by looser organizations through social networks." The organizers often have social ties with both the countries of origin and destination. Human-smuggling syndicates have been known to charge their clients anywhere from $500 to $50,000, depending on the destination, the distance, and the range of services offered.

Case Study: Smuggling Illegal Migrants from India and Pakistan

In 2012, American federal investigators dismantled a human-smuggling ring that brought dozens of illegal immigrants, including children travelling alone, over the Canadian border. The smuggling operation ran from at least November 2010 until authorities intervened in October 2011. According to the *Seattle Post-Intelligencer*, "Having indicted 16 suspects in recent months, federal prosecutors in Seattle contend the loosely knit group brought more than 70 people into the United States from India and Pakistan. Eleven of the 12 defendants arrested pleaded guilty to conspiracy to smuggle illegal immigrants." Among those were two of the group's purported leaders, Rajendrabhai Patel of Tennessee and British Columbia resident Manjit Dhugga, who admitted to receiving the illegal immigrants in BC and lodging them before they crossed into the United States at uninhabited areas on the border.

Another conspirator, 57-year-old Karnail Singh, who owned a Seattle-area hotel, was sentenced to 15 months in federal custody. Singh admitted to housing the illegal immigrants in his hotel before they were transferred elsewhere in the United States. Singh also hired drivers to take immigrants who crossed into Washington through uninhabited areas along the Canadian border to his hotel, the SeaTac Crest Motor Inn. Those with forged passports were then flown to their destinations; those who did not have proper identification were driven to the east coast. Federal prosecutors in the United States described Singh's hotel as a hub for illegal immigrants passing through the Seattle area on their way around the United States. In addition to charging $1000 per person for transportation from the border to his SeaTac hotel, Karnail Singh charged his guests $3000 for a forged Washington driver's licence, and $20,000 for a fraudulent marriage licence (*Seattle Post Intelligencer*, June 8, 2012).

For years, Canada has been seen a sanctuary for illegal immigrants, in part because most anyone who lands here can immediately claim refugee status and then access the country's health care and social welfare services. Those who are smuggled into the country are often instructed to claim refugee status upon arrival. While Canada may be a destination country for some entering the country illegally, it is mostly used as a transit point for those who wish to enter the United States. Smuggled migrants are brought to Canada aboard airliners, passenger ships, and even in cargo containers, while most of those choosing to go on to the United States are taken across unmanned land border crossings. The source countries for illegal migrants entering Canada are located in every corner of the world, from Asia to Eastern Europe, the West Indies, Africa, and the Middle East. However, the vast majority entering Canada come from the southern provinces of China. Since at least the early 1990s, the largest human-smuggling operations affecting Canada have been carried out by organized Chinese syndicates. As discussed in chapter 8, the Akwesasne reserve, which straddles the Ontario, Quebec, and New York borders, is considered one of the most porous points for migrants being illegally transported into the United States, especially for those from China. An elaborate criminal infrastructure on the reserve now facilitates this illegal entry, which includes safe houses for the migrants to hide in as well as the physical transport of the migrants across the border (usually across the St. Lawrence River).

Beginning around 1983, immigrant and law enforcement agencies in Canada began noticing a sharp increase in organized migrant smuggling into the country. According to that year's annual report from CISC, the groups carrying out people smuggling into Canada and the United States "vary from small, informally organized networks that smuggle a few people each year to large, well-structured organizations which operate at the international level and are involved in smuggling hundreds of people annually" (Criminal Intelligence Service Canada, 1985: 38). By 1992, the agency reported, "organized crime groups have a wide and varied base of operations in Canada and abroad which are utilized for the smuggling of illegal immigrants. Many of these groups are international, ethnic based crime groups who use their connections in foreign countries to relocate their associates to Canada." Around this time, police and immigration officials in British Columbia were investigating at least three illegal alien-smuggling operations in the province, each of which catered to a different ethnic group. Among them was a smuggling ring that was responsible for the movement of between 80 and 100 Indian and Trinidadian nationals into Canada and then the United States.

A 2005 federal study, entitled *Illegal Migrant Smuggling to Canada*, notes that the country has "emerged as a preferred destination in the human smuggling marketplace." The study indicated it is not uncommon for the smuggling groups to provide fake passports, as well as other Canadian immigration documents and Canadian citizenship certificates to those being smuggled. The report estimated that 12 percent of people who arrived in Canada without proper documents between 1997 and 2002 were directly linked to an "escort" or "facilitator"—someone who provided services including a travel

Photo 10.5: An immigrant smuggling ship is towed to Esperanza Inlet on the west coast of Vancouver Island

Source: Nick Didlick / *Vancouver Sun*. Used by permission.

document, air ticket, safe house, or referral to people-smuggling contacts (as cited in Canadian Press, May 1, 2005).

In August 2010, the freighter *MV Sun Sea* arrived at Victoria, British Columbia, carrying 492 undocumented Sri Lankan nationals. A year earlier the *MV Ocean Lady* sailed into BC waters carrying 76 Tamil asylum seekers. In 2012, the RCMP announced they had laid charges against six for organizing the migrants' illegal entry into Canada (CBC News, May 15, 2012; *Globe and Mail*, June 6, 2012; *National Post*, May 25, 2012; *Vancouver Sun*, August 14, 2010).

Weapons Smuggling and Trafficking

Weapons and firearms in particular are used as instruments of crime and their unauthorized movement across national borders constitutes a crime in its own right. Firearms and other weapons are smuggled into Canada by both organized crime groups and individuals acting alone. The market for many of the smuggled weapons is collectors as well as criminal offenders. Firearms that pose the greatest smuggling threat are those that are easily concealable and less detectable. The types of weapons smuggled into Canada for sale in the underground markets include increasingly powerful weapons such as automatic guns, military assault weapons, and even surface-to-air missile launchers.

By far, the greatest source of guns smuggled into Canada is the United States. Many firearms that are restricted or prohibited in Canada, such as handguns and automatic weapons, are readily available throughout the United States. The ridiculously lax US firearm controls contribute to the smuggling of firearms into Canada and most of the smuggled guns are first purchased in the United States from legally registered dealers. Canadians can cross into the United States and attend gun shows, where dealers sell weapons at cut-rate prices with few or no questions asked and without even having to conduct a background check on the buyer. The origins of the majority of guns smuggled into Ontario are Michigan, Florida, Ohio, Georgia, and New York. Many guns are smuggled into Canada in private vehicles through official land border crossings. One Vermont firearms retailer claims to have sold most of his weapons to smugglers who would use the same routes to transport contraband cigarette and liquor into Canada (Canadian Press, January 7, 1995; *Toronto Star*, January 21, 1995). A 1995 report from the Mackenzie Institute estimated that 15 to 20 percent of the smuggled arms from the United States come through reserves in Quebec and eastern Ontario (*Western Report*, May 29, 1995: 7).

According to more recent data from the Ontario Provincial Police, foreign-sourced guns continue to make up the majority of **crime guns** seized by police (a crime gun is any gun that is illegally possessed, has an obliterated serial number, or is seized in relation to a criminal act, such as a shooting). For 2011, the OPP reported that 60 percent of guns used in crimes in Ontario were smuggled across the US border. Twenty percent were locally sourced (usually stolen from homes), while the remaining 20 percent could not be traced (*Ottawa Citizen*, December 29, 2014). "Firearms are one of the most significant threats facing border security today," according to a 2010 internal report by the Canadian Border Services Agency. The report says that 109 "suspected crime guns" were seized at the border from 2006 through 2009—approximately 27 a year. The report notes this total is just a fraction of what is getting through. "Hundreds of firearms are smuggled into Canada yearly destined for the criminal market," according to the CBSA (as cited in *Windsor Star*, December 17, 2013). In 2009, Toronto police seized 861 crime guns in the city. At least 70 percent of these guns were smuggled in from the United States. In the same year, border services in Ontario seized just nine crime guns they believed were headed for the criminal market (*Toronto Star*, April 13, 2013). By the end of October 2012, the number of guns seized at the Canadian border had reached 500 nationwide. This number had already surpassed the total seized in 2011 (473), 2010 (452), and 2009 (474), according to the CBSA. While southern Ontario has historically been the main entry point for guns smuggled into Canada from the United States, the Pacific region now appears to be most vulnerable based on the quantity of guns smuggled into the country (Postmedia News, November 2, 2012).

Smuggling firearms into Canada is attractive due to the profit potential; a handgun purchased for $100 in Detroit can be resold for more than $500 north of the border. A 2013 *Toronto Star* exposé on gun smuggling and trafficking details the US–Toronto handgun pipeline and how it affects pricing (and profit potential) the further the gun travels into Canada:

With a driver's licence, or sometimes without any ID at all, a supplier buys a cheap $150 handgun on the Internet, as Star reporters recently did in Atlanta, or at a store or gun show in Michigan or Georgia, typically anywhere along the Interstate 75 corridor. A smuggler transports the gun across the border. In Windsor, that $150 handgun will sell for $800 to $1,000. Another courier (or the initial smuggler who crossed the border) takes the pistol farther, along Highway 401 to Toronto, where the money doubles, the gun selling for $2,000 or more. Alternatively, smugglers barter guns for cocaine, ecstasy, and other drugs more cheaply available in Toronto than in the U.S. The guns—often stored in a shoebox tucked away in the buyer's closet—are then ready for use in Toronto. Though the pipeline, in some cases, does not end there. *The Star* has found cases where handguns are then rented to the street, in one instance for as much as $600 per night. (*Toronto Star*, April 18, 2013)

Case Study: Gun Smuggling by Canadian Brokers and American Suppliers

In October 2012, four men and one woman from British Columbia were arrested and 80 firearms were seized following an investigation into gun smuggling from the United States into Canada. The only person charged at the time was 32-year-old Riley Stewart Kotz of Vernon, BC. According to Kim Bolan of the *Vancouver Sun*, "corporate records show he ran a company called Hycaps International Outfitters, which appears to be the website through which the guns and parts purchases were being made." Among some of the guns seized were Mach 9s and 10s, AK-47 knock-offs, and hunting rifles, along with silencers and DVDs on how to assemble assault rifles. Dan Malo, Chief Officer of the BC Combined Forces Special Enforcement Unit (CFSEU), said the firearms being smuggled into Canada were illegally modified, including some that were made into fully automatic firearms "capable of firing dozens of rounds per second."

The CFSEU investigation, dubbed E-Nimbus, began when police received a tip in February 2013, and "eventually resulted in undercover officers purchasing numerous guns and accessories that are illegal in Canada," Malo told the media. "These guns and accessories, had we not intercepted them, in all likelihood would have made their way into the hands of gangsters and those looking to commit violent crimes in our communities."

While Kotz was being arrested in Canada, a warrant was executed in Florida by the Bureau of Alcohol, Tobacco, Firearms and Explosives. Ten firearms were seized and a woman was taken into custody. Malo told the media that Kotz was already known to police and while being arrested, "he tried to pull out a handgun he had hidden in his clothing and then allegedly tried to disarm two of our arresting officers before he was able to be handcuffed" (*Vancouver Sun*, October 25, 2012).

Police intelligence indicates that a number of traditional crime groups, including the Mohawk Warrior Society, outlaw motorcycle gangs, and Eastern European crime groups, are active in weapons smuggling through the Akwesasne reserve. At the same time, there are hundreds of independent brokers and smugglers involved. The *Toronto Star* chronicles the efforts of Detroit resident Terrance "Dougie" Coles who was looking for easy money and decided to sell guns to drug dealers in Toronto. "Coles calculated it this way: buy a pistol in Michigan for a couple hundred dollars and feed it to Toronto, where supply cannot pace demand, for 10 times as much. There was a complication: with prior convictions for gun and drug crimes, Coles was unlikely to get across the border." Coles apparently found a way to "quarterback his business plan while floating above the grimy details and the law. He used four young women—including two cash-strapped cousins, one of them eight months pregnant—to mule the guns across the border at the Detroit-Windsor Tunnel crossing" (*Toronto Star*, April 18, 2013). Like other forms of (cross-border) organized criminal activity, gun smuggling and trafficking is structured as a network with numerous individuals performing distinct roles: American suppliers, individuals who broker the sales, individuals who physically smuggle the weapons across the border, and brokers in Canada who traffic or even rent firearms in the black market.

CRITICAL THINKING EXERCISE

This chapter documents police cases and intelligence information indicating that the majority of the "crime guns" used in Canada are smuggled in from the United States. Critically analyze this claim. Is there evidence to contradict this argument? To what extent do guns stolen from legitimate gun owners in Canada become "crime guns" in this country?

KEY TERMS

Bookie

Bookmaking

Contraband

Crime guns

Gambling

Horse-books

Lay-off bets

Loansharking

Migrant smuggling

Parlay bets

Payday loan

Smuggling

Tobacco smuggling

Undocumented migration

Wire service

REVIEW QUESTIONS

1. Describe consensual criminal activities undertaken by organized crime groups (excluding drug trafficking). How they differ from predatory criminal activities?
2. What are some of the consensual crimes carried out by criminal organizations?
3. What are some of the common denominators among different consensual criminal activities?
4. Describe gambling as an organized crime.
5. How does bookmaking fit into the overall pantheon of illegal gambling?
6. Why are some of the factors that contributed to organized smuggling into Canada?
7. How are firearms smuggled into the country? What is a "crime gun?"

FURTHER READINGS

Allum, F., & Gilmour, S. (Eds.). (2012). *Routledge Handbook of Transnational Organized Crime*. London, New York: Routledge.

Bouchard, M., & Chris, W. (Ed.). (2010). *Illegal Markets and the Economics of Organized Crime*. New York: Routledge.

Brookman, F., Maguire, M., Pierpoint, H., & Bennett, T. (Eds.). (2010). *Handbook on Crime*. Portland, OR: Willan Publishing.

Paoli, L. (Ed.). (2014). *The Oxford Handbook of Organized Crime*. Oxford, New York: Oxford University Press.

11 DRUG TRAFFICKING

CHAPTER OUTLINE

- Introduction and Overview
- A Brief History of Drugs and Drug Trafficking in North America
- Heroin
- Fentanyl
- Cocaine
- Marijuana
- Hashish
- Synthetic (Chemical) Drugs
- Conclusion to Part III

LEARNING OUTCOMES

After reading this chapter, you should have a thorough understanding of the following:

- The significance of drug trafficking in the revenue-generating repertoire of organized crime
- The history of illegal drug smuggling and trafficking affecting Canada
- Organized crime genres involved in drug trafficking
- Recent trends and developments concerning drug trafficking in Canada
- Which illegal drugs are dominant in Canada's black market
- Source countries for illegal drugs imported into Canada
- The rise in the domestic production of illegal drugs and Canada's role as an international source country for marijuana and synthetic drugs

Photo 11.1: "But I don't want to go among mad people," Alice remarked.

"Oh, you can't help that," said the Cat. "We're all mad here. I'm mad, you're mad."

Source: Caroll, L. (1866). *Alice in Wonderland.*

INTRODUCTION AND OVERVIEW

The steep escalation of illegal drug use and trafficking that began in the 1960s constitutes one of the most significant developments in the history and study of organized crime. Drug trafficking has transformed OC irrevocably by inciting the following:

- A proliferation of organized crime genres and groups and an increase in their scope and power
- Increased cross-border criminal activity
- Increased co-operation and networking among the many (independent) actors in an international drug-production/smuggling/trafficking conspiracy
- The rise of multi-millionaire and billionaire "drug lords"
- Innovations in product development and marketing by criminal organizations
- An unprecedented level of corruption in drug source and drug-consuming countries
- A level of harm inflicted on drug-consuming societies that is unparalleled among organized crimes
- The unprecedented mobilization of enforcement resources to combat the illegal drug problem

- A meteoric spike in the correctional population (especially in the United States but also in Canada) and the disproportionate incarceration of members of visible minority groups
- An unrelenting debate over the effectiveness of the so-called war on drugs and the broader issue of whether drugs and other human vices should be legal or illegal to minimize their negative impact on society and to control organized crime

Paoli, Spapens, and Fijnaut (2010: 626) write, "Nowadays, the trafficking of illegal narcotics and other psychoactive drugs is considered one of the prototypical activities of organised crime and is a matter of serious concern worldwide." The very logistics of large-scale (transnational) drug trafficking necessitates some level of organization. The illegal production, transportation, and trafficking of drugs involve many phases, processes, and activities—cultivation, refinement, transportation, storage, wholesaling, retail distribution, corruption, security, and money laundering—which potentially involve a large number of autonomous actors, and require a great deal of planning, co-operation, and coordination (Canadian Association of Chiefs of Police, 1994: 63). Due to the logistical complexities of international drug trafficking, it can best be explained through the network model of organized crime; that is, few criminal organizations handle all aspects from cultivation to street-level trafficking. Moreover, as Reuter (2014: 359) notes, it is difficult to generalize about the characteristics of domestic drug markets and how transnational drug trafficking is structured and carried out. "In fact, the nature of the enterprises in drug markets varies greatly across countries, drugs, and levels of distribution in terms of their size, durability, and relationship to other criminal activities. Thus, considerable variability exists in the relationship of these criminal enterprises to organized crime."

Criminal groups produce and sell a wide range of psychoactive drugs in the underground market. A psychoactive drug is a substance that acts primarily upon the central nervous system where it alters brain function, resulting in temporary changes in perception,

CRITICAL THINKING EXERCISE

The extent to which well-organized crime groups dominate transnational drug trafficking and domestic illegal drug markets has produced a highly charged debate. As you read through this chapter, critically analyze claims that transnational criminal groups are responsible for international drug trafficking and similar arguments that large organized crime groups monopolize smuggling, domestic trafficking, and illicit drug markets in Canada. Conduct your own research into specific cases of international drug trafficking to discern for yourself the extent to which they are dominated by large criminal organizations (or are more characteristic of the network model). Also determine whether illicit drug markets in Canada are monopolized by large OC groups (or conversely are highly competitive involving numerous suppliers).

mood, consciousness, and behaviour. While most psychoactive drugs are developed for legitimate medicinal reasons, they are used recreationally as well. Since the recreational use of most psychoactive drugs has been criminalized in Canada, a large black market has emerged, which is ultimately supplied by well-organized criminal syndicates.

The consumption of intoxicating and/or addictive substances for both recreational and medicinal purposes reaches as far back as the origins of civilization. By the turn of the twentieth century, drugs such as opium (and its derivatives morphine and heroin), cocaine, and marijuana were all legal in North America and even used for medicinal purposes. The outlawing of opium and heroin and later marijuana, cocaine, and liquor was the result of temperance movements and prohibitionist forces that swept through North America in the first quarter of the twentieth century. By the beginning of the 1930s, liquor was once again legal in Canada, while the importation, manufacture, distribution, and recreational consumption of opium, heroin, cocaine, and marijuana were thoroughly criminalized in both Canada and the United States. This drove these drugs into the underground market where they are produced and marketed by a wide range of criminal groups and autonomous offenders.

In its 2007 annual report, CISC estimated that 80 percent of the criminal organizations operating in Canada were involved in the illegal drug market (Criminal Intelligence Service Canada, 2007: 24). The Italian Mafia in Montreal is involved in upper-echelon importation and distribution of cocaine, hashish, and heroin. Asian-based groups have maintained their role in heroin trafficking, have continued their expansion into the cocaine trade, and have made considerable inroads into synthetic drug trafficking and marijuana cultivation. Outlaw motorcycle gangs play a major role in the importation and large-scale distribution of cannabis, hashish, and cocaine, and are also domestic manufacturers of synthetic drugs. Independent Canadian and foreign entrepreneurs are also important suppliers of drugs to the Canadian market.

As a criminal activity, drug trafficking can be considered as both consensual and predatory in nature; while most drug deals are between two willing parties, the trade is parasitic in that it preys upon the vices and vulnerabilities of people, while helping to create highly destructive personal addictions which contribute to immense social costs.

A BRIEF HISTORY OF DRUGS AND DRUG TRAFFICKING IN NORTH AMERICA

In order to appreciate the relationship between drug trafficking and organized crime, it is necessary to briefly recount the history of drugs in societies. This includes an examination of the factors that led to the criminalization of heroin, cocaine, and cannabis in North America, which in turn paved the way for a criminal monopoly over their production and distribution. The history of intoxicating and psychoactive substances is rooted in the history of humankind.

Alcohol was made, consumed, and abused as far back as oral history and official recordings extend while hemp, opium, coca, and other plants containing mood-altering ingredients have been imbibed almost as long. Concern over **opium** and its derivatives (**morphine** and **heroin**) was largely responsible for the introduction of the first statutes criminalizing these substances in Canada and the United States (and, as such, this historical review will focus primarily on opium and heroin trafficking). The source of opium is the opium poppy, of which there are many species. As a source of vegetable fat, "the seed oil could have been a major factor attracting early human groups to the opium poppy" (Merlin, 1984: 89). The word *opium* is derived from the Greek word *opion*, meaning "juice of the poppy" and is mentioned by Homer in his epic poem *The Odyssey* (circa 700 BC). The Sumerians may have been the first to use opium, around 5000 BC, suggested by the fact that they have an ideogram for it, which has been translated into English as *Hul*, meaning "joy" or "rejoicing" (Lindesmith, 1968: 207). Alexander the Great may have brought the opium poppy plant to Persia and India around 330 BC, while opium was introduced to East Asia roughly 600 years later by Arab merchants. As Islam began to spread in the seventh century, opium became widely used as an alternative to alcohol, which is forbidden by Islamic laws (Snyder 1989: 30). "Its notorious endemic use in the Orient, however, didn't begin until the 1700s, when industrious European mercantilists turned a modest native herb trade into the most profitable big business in the history of commerce up to that time" (Latimer & Goldberg, 1981: 16). British traders, with the backing of their government, forcibly pushed opium into the Chinese market (and traded for Chinese tea leaves), making them some of the world's first large-scale, transnational drug traffickers. Aggressive efforts by Britain to sell the drug in China despite the Emperor's edict forbidding its importation led to the so-called **Opium Wars** between China and Great Britain, which occurred between 1839 and 1860.

During the eighteenth and nineteenth centuries, its recreational use was popularized by English intellectuals, such as Thomas De Quincey (1785–1859). In his book entitled *Confessions of an English Opium Eater*, De Quincey refers to the "divine luxuries" of ingesting the drug, although the novel must ultimately be viewed as a diary of an increasingly desperate addict, whose 30-year habit destroyed an otherwise brilliant mind. A number of authors, poets, and musicians have composed important works while under influence of opium, including Lewis Carroll (1832–98), Edgar Allen Poe (1809–49), Samuel Coleridge (1772–1836), and Elizabeth Barrett Browning (1806–61).

Around 1803, a German pharmacist named Friedrich Sertürner poured liquid ammonia over opium and obtained an alkaloid in the form of a highly potent white powder. Because of its tendency to cause sleep in some of his test patients, he originally named the substance "morphium" after the Greek god of dreams, Morpheus. By 1827, morphine was being marketed commercially for the relief of pain. Opium itself would become the essential ingredient in innumerable prescriptions and over-the-counter elixirs for the treatment of pain and numerous illnesses. As the primary

Photo 11.2: Thomas De Quincey

ingredient in many medicines, opiates were readily and legally available in the United States and Canada without a prescription up until the first quarter of the twentieth century. The addictive nature of the substance became increasingly apparent and the typical American opiate addict during the nineteenth century, notes David Courtwright (2001), was a middle-aged white woman of the middle or upper class who began ingesting opiates for medicinal purposes.

In North America, the smoking of opium for recreational purposes was popularized by Chinese men who brought the custom with them to California and British Columbia during their immigration to the west coast beginning in the mid-nineteenth century. The Chinese were the first to operate commercial opium dens in North American cities, which were perfectly legal and viewed in the same class as saloons (Katcher, 1959: 287).

Opium was legally imported into Canada from the British colony of Hong Kong and the United States. Because the importation, distribution, and ingestion of opium in Canada were legal during the nineteenth century, newspapers were filled with advertisements for raw and processed versions of the narcotic. British Columbia also became a centre for producing the black tar opium that was used for smoking. The opium dens were the principal clients of the opium factories, although Caucasian-operated pharmacies also became lucrative customers as many were now selling smokable opium to white and Chinese smokers alike. The colonial, provincial, and Dominion governments also benefited from the early opium trade in Canada. They received licensing fees from manufacturers and taxes were imposed on the retail sale of opium, although the real government money was made from tariffs imposed on opium imports. In February 1865, a 50 percent tariff on opium imported into the British colony of British Columbia was imposed, far exceeding the usual 12.5 percent applied to most other imports (*The British Colombian*, February 18, 1865). The substantial tariff prompted the widespread smuggling of opium into Canada. In this regard, the tariffs were a significant impetus to modern-day drug trafficking and organized criminality in North America.

British Columbia's role as a manufacturer and exporter of processed opium increased substantially in 1890 when the US Congress imposed its own prohibitive tariffs on opium and morphine imports. The result was that even larger amounts of raw opium were being brought into Canada (legally and covertly), processed through BC-based opium factories, and then smuggled into the United States to avoid the tariffs. On February 8, 1888, federal officials in the United States captured $25,000 worth of opium at Redwood in upstate New York. According to a *New York Times* article, the opium was brought from China via Vancouver and transported by train to Brockville, Ontario. It was then transferred across the St. Lawrence River "by ferries in summer and sleighs in winter which were met by wagons or sleighs on the American side and then shipped to New York as butter, eggs, etc." (*New York Times*, February 9, 1888). In 1891, 141 pounds of opium was confiscated in Swift Current, Saskatchewan, and a saloon in Sweet Grass, Montana, was shut down when the RCMP told their American counterparts that it was a transfer point for opium entering the United Sates (Chan, 1983: 76). In an 1895 dispatch from Montana, American customs officials

Photo 11.3: Advertisement for opium-laced cough drops, circa 1890s

Source: Miami University Libraries, via Wikimedia Commons

there alleged that "large quantities of opium" were smuggled from the Manitoba side of the border "in the stomachs of live cattle, and that a great many of cattle are also smuggled" (*The Manitoba Free Press*, May 22, 1895).

The Genesis of Modern-Day Drug Trafficking

During the first quarter of the twentieth century, opium, morphine, and heroin were increasingly being consumed for recreational purposes. As Abadinsky (2013: 283) writes, the addict population in North America was already changing. "The public mind came to associate heroin with urban vice and crime. Unlike the (often female and) 'respectable' opiate addicts of the nineteenth century, opiate users of the twentieth century were increasingly male habitués of pool halls and bowling alleys, denizens of the underworld. As in the case of minority groups, this marginal population was an easy target of drug laws and drug-law enforcement."

As part of the growing movement to outlaw opium, racist and xenophobic politicians, temperance movement leaders, and other "moral entrepreneurs" blamed the Chinese for selling and using the drug. According to Giffen, Endicott, and Lambert

Photo 11.4: William Lyon Mackenzie King

Source: The World's Work, via Wikimedia Commons

(1991: 45), three converging forces were instrumental in bringing about drug prohibition laws in Canada: (1) a general climate of moral reform, (2) an international movement to stop the opium trade in China, and (3) general hostility toward Chinese immigrants in Canada. In 1908, the Dominion government enacted the *Opium Act*, prohibiting the sale, importation, and manufacture of opium in this country. For the first time in Canadian history, a narcotic substance was now outlawed. In 1911, a more stringent *Opium and Drug Act* made opium smoking and possession a criminal offence and created penalties for using the drug or being present when it was smoked or otherwise ingested. By 1921, amendments to the *Opium and Drug Act* included a maximum seven-year penalty for the importation, manufacture, and sale of opium or any other narcotic drug mentioned in the act. In 1922, Parliament added cocaine to the schedule of prohibited drugs, and the following year marijuana was added to the list of prohibited drugs. In 1929, this whirlwind of legislative action culminated in the *Opium and Narcotic Drug Act*, one of the country's most punitive pieces of criminal legislation, which increased jail sentences for trafficking and possession, broadened the police search and seizure powers, and increased the scope of possession charges. The legislation would be in force until the 1960s.

The driving force behind the criminalization of narcotic drugs in Canada was William Lyon Mackenzie King, which began when he was a federal civil servant, continued during his time as a cabinet minister in Wilfred Laurier's Liberal government, and later as Canada's tenth prime minister. In fact, he used his notoriety as an anti-drug crusader as a springboard to enter politics and eventually became Canada's longest serving prime minister. As Neil Boyd observes in his book *High Times*, King adroitly positioned himself at the leading edge of a new **moral entrepreneurship** in Canada and abroad that "successfully marketed a new morality with respect to drug use" (Boyd, 1991: 10).

While the legal opium manufacturers were put out of business, the original 1908 legislation was a boon to the patent medicine industry and to the pharmacists who legally dispensed opium and opiate-based elixirs. Because opium was still legal for medicinal purposes, doctors and pharmacists became some of the biggest dispensers of opiates

CRITICAL THINKING EXERCISE

Criminal laws may be changed due to numerous factors (and not simply because the target of the legislative amendments posed a particular social problem). Using the Canadian government's criminalization of heroin in 1908 or the criminalization of marijuana in the United States in the 1920s and 1930s, identify, discuss, and analyze the different social and political factors that contributed to changes in the respective criminal law, including the processes, motivations, and powerful entities behind the changes.

in the country. In Ontario, a large number of police investigations and prosecutions were directed at pharmacists based on allegations that they were dispensing raw and processed opium in quantities that far exceeded medicinal demand. Following the new federal drug laws, some pharmacists began purchasing inordinately large amounts of opium and other narcotics from wholesalers. In a memo dated March 5, 1917, an official with the Ontario College of Pharmacy in Woodstock wrote, "A quite of lot of opium has been coming in here lately from Toronto, Montreal, and London. One druggist had 50 pounds in a month as you can easily find by looking up the wholesale of record." The memo also describes a druggist in Woodstock "who professes to furnish the Chinese with laundry sundries and going around amongst them in this way he also deals opium" (Archives of the Province of Ontario, RG 23).

Doctors also became drug traffickers of sort, catering to an exclusive clientele, according to David T. Courtwright in his book on the history of opiate addictions in America. "The upper-class background of many addicts is certainly consistent with the allegation that some doctors courted the wealthy client with a little morphine. Even worse, it was common practice for 'quack cure joints' to offer 10 to 20 percent kick-backs for referring addicted patients. The utterly unscrupulous practitioner could realize a handsome profit by addicting patients and then having them trek from one asylum to another—asylums with which he had an arrangement" (Courtwright, 2001: 50). Between April 1921 and March 1922, the Dominion government prosecuted under the provisions of the *Opium and Drug Act* 23 doctors, 11 pharmacists, and 4 veterinary surgeons (Murphy, 1922b: 18–19). In its annual report for 1925, the RCMP reported that the Quebec City detachment "made a very good clean up of the drug situation" in the city, "apprehending a number of doctors and druggists." In its report for the following year, the RCMP Commissioner extolled the Mounties' ongoing "purification of the medical profession by exposure and conviction of a number of it's [sic] members—few in proportion, I should add—who have sunk into the practice of dispensing these drugs illegally" (Royal Canadian Mounted Police, 1926: 13).

As the 1920s wore on, pharmacies and physicians were less and less a source of legal or illegal opiates, due to increased regulatory control over pharmaceutical drugs and the refusal of retailers to stock opiates because of moral objections or the increased risk of hold-ups and break-ins by addicts. The retreat of these professionals from opium distribution, in conjunction with the ongoing criminalization of narcotics, pushed the drug trade even further underground. The expansion of the black market in opium and morphine was also quickened by a substantial growth in the supply and demand for these illegal drugs in the post-war years. During World War I, government controls severely limited the international distribution and availability of narcotic drugs. When the war ended, supply—both legal and illegal—escalated, in part to meet the heightened demands of the many morphine-addicted soldiers whose return from the battlefields in Europe or whose release from domestic hospitals swelled the addict population in Canada. In 1922, the RCMP was calling attention to "the alarming increase in the use of narcotic drugs in Canada and the growing traffic in the same." Throughout the 1920s and 1930s, drug trafficking became an enforcement priority for the RCMP. Between October 1920 and September 1921, the number of drug cases investigated by the RCMP in Quebec was 167. During the following fiscal year, the number had jumped to 531, and for the rest of the decade the RCMP investigated an average of 250 cases annually in the province (Royal Canadian Mounted Police, 1922: 59, 1923: 57). As the RCMP Commissioner wrote in an annual report for 1922:

> An important and arduous task is the support of the Department of Public Health in enforcing the Opium and Narcotic Drugs Act. Reference was made in the last annual report to the calamitous nature of this traffic; I regret to be obliged to state that the evil persists, and I fear has grown in some parts of the country. To check it will require the united efforts of this force and the provincial and municipal priorities, and also drastic punishment of the agents, such as the peddlers who desperately create addicts.... the figures already given show that we have been active, having arrested over one thousand persons and having secured 800 convictions. (Royal Canadian Mounted Police, 1923: 10)

In 1922, the federal Opium and Narcotic Drug Branch declared that the illegal opium traffic "is controlled almost altogether by large drug rings, which employ numerous agents to distribute the drug. Some of these agents simply act as a medium or distribution, between a dealer with a large stock and the small peddler, and work on a commission basis" (City of Vancouver Archives, MSS. 69). The January 14, 1922, edition of the *Vancouver World* newspaper had this to say about a particular drug ring operating in that city: "Investigations made by the authorities have led them to the conclusions that the most powerful and wealthy criminal organization on the American continent has its headquarters here. Its object is the handling of drugs. Its ramifications extend as far east as Montreal and Chicago. It will undertake to sell $100,000 worth of 'dope,' or it will sell it by the 'deck,' the small package sold by the street vendor for from one to five dollars" (*Vancouver Daily World*, January 14, 1922).

In reality, most of the drug-trafficking groups in Canada had little in the way of a national presence, although drug connections were being forged among groups and individuals in Montreal, Toronto, Winnipeg, and Vancouver. Importantly, smuggling and trafficking linkages began to emerge between Canadian and American cities, the most notable being Montreal and New York. It was during the 1920s that Montreal became established as a central conduit through which opium, morphine, and heroin from Europe or Southwest Asia would be transported to New York. In addition to its marine ports, Montreal was a popular entry point for drug smuggling because it was a terminus for nearly all Canadian and United States railways, was located close to the American border, and was connected to New York and other major American cities along the eastern seaboard through new asphalt highways. Montreal's vibrant red light district and large addict population also helped to ensure a substantial domestic market.

High-profile cases also kept the narcotics trade on the front pages of Montreal newspapers. In 1924, a shipment of cocoa and other legal goods was sent from a firm in Switzerland to a variety of companies in Montreal. All of these companies had the

Case Study: 1920s Narcotics Trafficking in Ontario

One of the largest drug importation rings in Ontario during the 1920s was headed by Rocco Perri, although many believe it was his common-law wife Bessie Starkman who was the driving force behind both their large-scale bootlegging and narcotic-trafficking operations. As early as 1922, RCMP reports were chronicling the "suspected dealing in narcotics on a large scale" by an Italian immigrant in Canada. In a March 12, 1926, letter, a US Narcotics Bureau agent accused "Rocco Perry" of supplying "Italian dope peddling" rings in Pennsylvania. Rocco and Bessie's network of associates were strategically placed in various locations in southern Ontario, mostly along the American border. Some were running booze into the United States and returning with loads of raw opium to be processed into smoking opium or morphine. One RCMP informant alleged that drugs were also brought into Ontario by seaplanes that landed on Lake Ontario near Burlington or by dropping packages by silk parachutes onto old flying fields near Hamilton. "There is no doubt this is the cleverest gang of drug runners in the country," an undercover Mountie wrote of the Perri–Starkman gang in a 1929 memo. "The ring leaders are very shrewd and have deliberately withheld introducing a new customer until they knew more about him." If there were suspicions that police were on to them, they would "rather close down temporarily rather than take any unnecessary risks." The memo also acknowledges that Bessie "is the brains of the whole gang and nothing is being done without her consent" (National Archives of Canada, RG 18, File No: HQ-189-O-1).

same address on St. Peter Street in Montreal, which aroused the suspicion of customs agents. With the assistance of the RCMP, more than 3000 pounds of morphine, heroin, and cocaine were seized *en route* to the Canadian consignees (*The Globe*, April 9, 1926). This would be one of the largest drug seizures ever made in Canada. A 1925 report by Inspector J.W. Phillips of the RCMP's Quebec division reflects the growing organization and sophistication of the underground drug trade in that province. "Slightly better progress has been made against offenders under the Opium and Narcotic Drugs Act, but as time goes on our work becomes more and more difficult … The traffic in drugs in Montreal has now reached such a science and has been driven so far underground that it is only with the greatest difficulty we can obtain any good results" (Royal Canadian Mounted Police, 1925: 36). Vancouver also continued to be a major port of entry for opium from Southeast Asia and a major transhipment point for other markets in the Pacific Northwest of the United States and as far east as Toronto. According to one confidential RCMP report dated May 20, 1922, of the 14,000 tins (114,000 ounces) of opium estimated to have been smuggled through Vancouver's ports, some 9000 tins (72,000 ounces) were sent to the United States and the balance was consumed locally, in the interior of British Columbia, and in Alberta (National Archives of Canada, RG 18, File No: 1922-HQ-189-Q-1).

Post–World War II: The Rise of the French Connection

The illegal heroin trade would expand tremendously following the Second World War due to a substantial spike in demand and supply. By 1947, the number of RCMP drug investigations had jumped by 40 percent over the previous year, and in 1949 they increased by another 28 percent (Royal Canadian Mounted Police, 1947: 24–25, 1949: 28). This was due to a number of factors, including the return of thousands of morphine-addicted veterans and a rise in drug-friendly counter-culture movements such as the beatniks. The end of the war also meant an increase in supply in North America as there were fewer obstacles to opium production in Asia and heroin refining in Europe, as well as the reopening of merchant shipping. Some have also blamed US foreign policy and the CIA in particular for bolstering heroin supply. According to Alfred McCoy (1991: 18, 25), the CIA played a significant role "in sustaining a global narcotics industry that supplied the United States" during the Cold War by partnering with anti-Communist forces in Asia that were involved in growing opium and trafficking heroin. The sheer profitability of the heroin trade also contributed to an abundance in supply; wholesalers paying US $3500 for a kilogram of heroin in Europe were generating revenues as high as $40,000 a kilogram once it was diluted and sold on Canadian streets. A final reason the heroin supply increased in the post-war years was because production, smuggling, and wholesale distribution became increasingly concentrated in the hands of a confederation of drug-trafficking syndicates—the French **L'Union Corse**, the Sicilian Mafia, as well as the American *Cosa Nostra* and its Canadian subsidiaries. Together, they constituted what would become known as the **French Connection**, one of the largest and longest ongoing heroin-trafficking conspiracies of all time.

At the start of the 1940s, Italian Mafia families in the United States and Canada became the largest illegal dispensers of opiates, and for the next 40 years they held an almost complete monopoly over the wholesale distribution of Turkish heroin in both countries. Their main suppliers were French Corsicans, who had become the world's biggest heroin producers. The criminal syndicate behind the French Connection was *L'Union Corse*, so named because most of its leaders and members hailed from Corsica, an island located southeast of France in the Mediterranean Sea. *L'Union Corse* rivalled the Sicilian Mafia in terms of the scope of its criminal operation and, according to a 1972 edition of *Time* magazine, it "is more tightly knit and more secretive than its Sicilian counterpart" (*Time*, September 4, 1972). Until the mid-1970s, the world capital for heroin production and distribution was the French port city of Marseilles. Located less than an hour's plane ride from Corsica and with direct maritime connections to opium sources in Southwest Asia and to heroin markets in North America, Marseilles became the hub for the conversion of Turkish opium into heroin. From there it would be smuggled to the United States and Canada (Charbonneau, 1976: 45–48; Mann, 1968: 176; The McClellan Committee, 1976: 188–94).

Quebec's cultural, commercial, and linguistic ties to France, the subservience of the Mafia in the province to New York's Bonanno family, as well as Montreal's inviting seaports and close proximity to New York solidified the city's status as entry point for heroin from Europe. According to a 1963 US Senate Committee on organized crime, "The advent of the Corsicans as major traffickers brought changes in the smuggling operations; for years, the main port of entry had been New York but now the French Corsicans supplied the drugs to their French-speaking Canadian confederates for smuggling into the United States" (The McClellan Committee, 1976: 196). Throughout the 1950s, the American *Cosa Nostra* and its Canadian branches were the biggest patrons of the heroin trafficking arm of *L'Union Corse*. By the end of the decade, Sicilian and North American Mafia families agreed to work together to smuggle heroin from Marseilles to Sicily and then to the United States and Canada. Starting in the late 1950s, members of the Bonanno family in New York and Montreal became much more active in organizing the importation and distribution of heroin, which significantly increased the importance of Montreal's marine ports as a North American access point for European-processed heroin (Shawcross & Young, 1987: 44–45). Arrangements were also made to fly heroin into Toronto. Facilitating the importation of the heroin into Canada were the branch plants of the American *Cosa Nostra*—the Cotroni organization in Montreal, which reported to the Bonanno family, and in Ontario, Anthony Sylvestro, the Agueci brothers, and John Papalia, who answered to Stefano Magaddino in Buffalo.

In 1971, the Nixon administration persuaded Turkey to ban the cultivation of opium in exchange for subsidization of alternative crops. That same year, an official agreement was reached with French authorities to crack down on the extensive heroin-processing and trafficking network based in Marseilles. The result of these measures was a major reorganization of heroin trafficking: Turkey was replaced as the chief supplier of opium by the **Golden Triangle** of Thailand, Burma, and Laos and the **Golden Crescent** of Pakistan, Iran, and Afghanistan. The break-up of *L'Union Corse* provided the North American *Cosa Nostra* with an even greater monopoly over the Southwest Asian heroin traffic and Sicily resumed its role as a major heroin processor in the mid-1970s. By the late 1970s, Sicilian Mafia families in partnership with New York's Bonanno family established another massive heroin importation conspiracy, which came to be known as the Pizza Connection because much of the heroin that made it into America was sold through pizza parlours. The disruption of the Pizza Connection by American and Italian law enforcement in the 1980s signalled the end of the Mafia's dominance in the global heroin trade. But the international heroin partnership forged between the French Corsicans, the Sicilian Mafia, and the American *Cosa Nostra* and its Canadian branches not only transformed Italian organized crime but also modernized the international narcotics trade. It gave Canada and Canadian mobsters a pivotal role in the global heroin traffic, while further pulling the country's criminal underworld into the orbit of the American *Cosa Nostra*.

Drugs in the Psychedelic Era and Beyond

As the so-called **psychedelic era** emerged in North America in the 1960s, illegal drug consumption skyrocketed and many endeavoured to cash in on the demand. Like Prohibition, the escalation of recreational drug use would radically transform the criminal underworld in North America, propelling it toward levels of profit and power never before seen. The dramatic escalation of the drug trade also paved the way for the emergence and ascendance of a variety of different crime groups from all over North America and the world. In the 1960s, the Hells Angels began as street-level dealers of speed, and by the 1970s they had branched out into marijuana and other chemical drugs, such as Lysergic acid diethylamide (LSD) and Phencyclidine (PCP). Soon, they began to exert considerable control over the production and distribution of a number of synthetic drugs illegally available in North America. During the 1970s, Chinese criminal traffickers began to dominate the heroin trade, flooding the North American market with what was referred to as **China White**. A significant and deadly trend also began in Canada's drug markets: the rise in heroin's purity and its drop in price, a combination that signalled its overabundance on the street. By the early 1990s, **purity** levels at the wholesale stage were as high as 99 percent, while at the street-level purities were as much as 85 percent. The result was an epidemic of overdoses among addicts who were accustomed to heroin that was only 5 to 8 percent pure. Of the 53 heroin-related deaths in Ontario in 1992, 36 involved heroin that was between 80 and 85 percent pure. The number of overdose deaths in British Columbia increased from 67 in 1989 to 160 in 1992 (*Vancouver Sun*, October 30, 1992).

Another significant change in the drug-trafficking world was the remarkable rise in the demand for and supply of cocaine that began in the mid-1970s. From that time through to the mid-1990s, Colombian groups were some of the biggest cocaine whole-salers in Canada. While the Medellin and Cali cartels were the foremost importers and wholesalers in the country during this time, they were both competing with (and supplying) a number of large cocaine-trafficking groups in Canada, most notably the Hells Angels and the Italian Mafia. As CISC noted in 1985, the year in which cocaine prices were at their highest, the astronomical revenues accruing to traffickers at all levels attracted numerous OC groups to the trade. "Depending upon where it is distributed, a retailer can buy a single kilogram of pure cocaine from a wholesaler for between $60,000 and $95,000. Then the retailer cuts the drug to 50% purity and sells it on the street as a mixture of 50% cocaine and 50% filler. Since one gram of this mixture contains only ½ gram of cocaine and sells for $100 to $300, the actual selling price for cocaine has doubled to between $200,000 and $600,000 for a kilogram of pure cocaine" (Criminal Intelligence Service Canada, 1985: 19).

By the late 1980s, crack cocaine was being marketed in many US cities and then later major Canadian urban centres. Catering to those who could not afford the pricey powdered substance, the emergence of crack cocaine led to a significant expansion of the addict popu-lation and is also blamed for a substantial increase in gang violence in America's inner cities. Around this time, domestic marijuana **grow operations** were being discovered by police in Canada, and in the following years the number of grow-ops and the amount of high-potency pot produced in this country exploded. Not only did Canada become self-sufficient in an illegal product that used to be imported from other countries, it was now exporting large quantities to the United States. By the new millennium, marijuana produc-tion and export would become a stock-in-trade for criminal groups throughout Canada.

The 1990s also heralded a boom in so-called designer drugs—in particular, ecstasy and later the highly addictive crystal meth. Driven in part by Chinese criminal networks and outlaw biker gangs, Canada became a major producer and exporter of both. By 2005, illegal drug labs were being discovered across the country. "Clandestine laborato-ries, particularly those producing methamphetamine, continue to grow rapidly and are being reported in British Columbia, Alberta, Saskatchewan, Manitoba, Ontario, and Quebec," an RCMP press statement read (RCMP Press Release, September 7, 2005). The rebirth of synthetic drug production in Canada in the late 1990s was due to a num-ber of factors: intensified enforcement actions in the United States, restrictions on the sale of precursor chemicals in that country (and the lack of such restrictions in Canada), the ease in which ecstasy and crystal meth can be produced, the high profit potential of both, the country's proximity to the large US market, and the presence of criminal groups with plenty of experience in drug manufacturing and trafficking.

Other notable trends and developments in Canada's drug trade in recent years include an increase in **poly-drug trafficking** (the handling of numerous kinds of illegal drugs by criminal groups and networks), the involvement of Canadian crime groups in both the southbound smuggling of Canadian-produced drugs (ecstasy and marijuana) and the northbound smuggling of cocaine into Canada, and the co-operation among different criminal groups in these illegal ventures. All of these trends are reflected in the case below.

By 2010, a new opioid epidemic was gripping America, a problem that was compounded by the introduction of an even more powerful synthetic opioid: **fentanyl**. This in itself highlighted another worrying trend in North America's drug markets: the

---

Case Study: The Poly-drug Trafficking "Consortium"

In 2012, more than 1000 police officers took part in a series of raids targeting what police called a vast drug-trafficking "consortium" across Quebec, Ontario, and British Columbia. Police alleged the network involved members of the Hells Angels, the Italian Mafia, and the West End Gang. In total, 103 people were arrested in different parts of Canada, according to police. This included two of the of alleged ringleaders: Larry Amero, a full-patch member of the Hells Angels in British Columbia, and Shane Maloney, who police alleged was linked to Montreal's **West End Gang**. As part of this investigation, police seized 158 kilos of cocaine, more than 46,000 methamphetamine pills, and 13 barrels of a solvent, banned in Canada, which is used to produce gamma-hydroxybutyrate (GHB), the so-called date rape drug. Police also confiscated 161 guns, 291 other prohibited weapons, 1486 explosives, and 50 detonators. Thirty-five vehicles, five homes worth about $1.5 million, and $255,000 in cash were also seized as proceeds of crime.

Police said the "consortium," which had been under investigation for about six months, managed to generate an estimated $50 million in drug revenue in that short time. The group had the capacity to import and distribute about 75 kilograms of cocaine per week, according to police, and used an intermediary to obtain the drugs from Mexican drug cartels. The cocaine was imported into Canada via the United States using trucks.

The involvement of offenders from different existing crime groups in this massive drug trafficking conspiracy demonstrates "that the country's criminal underworld is as interconnected as it is unstable," Sûreté du Québec Inspector Michel Forget told the media. "Gang members continue to spread their tentacles from B.C. to other provinces," Dan Malo, the officer in charge of the Combined Forces Special Enforcement Unit in British Columbia, added in a statement. Police say the BC-based leaders—the Hells Angels' Larry Amero in particular—managed to implant themselves in Quebec because of a void that had developed there due to successful police operations in that province against the Hells Angels, the Italian Mafia, and street gangs, all of which were large importers and wholesalers of cocaine in Quebec (Canadian Press, November 1, 2012; CBC News, November 1, 2012; QMI Agency, November 2, 2012; *Vancouver Sun*, November 1, 2012, November 3, 2012).

introduction of more potent and highly addictive (synthetic) narcotic drugs. In the summer of 2016, law enforcement officials in the United States and Canada began warning the public about Carfentanil, a synthetic derivative of opium that is many times more potent (and is normally used as an elephant tranquilizer). Tim Ingram, the health commissioner for Hamilton County in Ohio, told the media, "We may be seeing a whole new shift in street drugs in our culture, moving away from traditional heroin and so forth to the synthetic opioids which are much more potent, faster to market and at less cost" (CBC News, September 10, 2016).

The remainder of this chapter examines those illegal drugs that currently predominate among recreational users and organized suppliers in Canada. This list includes heroin, fentanyl, cocaine, marijuana, hashish, and synthetic drugs.

HEROIN

Heroin is a derivative of morphine, both of which come from the opium poppy. The opium poppy requires a hot, dry climate and very careful cultivation. The poppy matures in three months when the green stem is topped by a brightly coloured flower. Gradually, the flower petals fall off, leaving a seedpod about the size of a small egg. If an incision is made in the pod just after the petals have fallen but before it is fully ripe, a milky-white fluid will ooze out and after 12 hours, will harden into dark brown, gummy opium.

Photo 11.5: Opium Poppy Field in Afghanistan

Source: davric, via Wikimedia Commons

Morphine is produced by dissolving the raw opium in hot water along with lime fertilizer (calcium oxide), which draws out organic wastes and leaves the morphine suspended near the surface. The residual waste is removed, and the morphine is then heated and mixed with concentrated ammonia.

The transformation into heroin begins by treating the raw morphine with water and chloroform until the impurities precipitate out. The result is drained off and sodium carbonate is added until crude heroin particles solidify and drop to the bottom. The particles are filtered out and purified in a solution of alcohol and activated charcoal. This mixture is heated until the alcohol begins to evaporate, leaving almost pure granules of heroin at the bottom. This is known as No.3 heroin. In the final step, the opium poppy granules are dissolved in alcohol and ether, and hydrochloric acid is added to the solution. Tiny white flakes form and are filtered out under pressure and dried. The result is a white crystalline powder of between 80 and 99 percent purity, known as No.4 heroin (McCoy, 1972: 13). For street sale, the crystalline powder is diluted ("stepped on") with any powdery substance that dissolves when heated, such as lactose, quinine, or cornstarch.

Heroin is typically ingested intravenously. Powdered heroin can also be sniffed like cocaine, or smoked by heating the heroin powder and inhaling the fumes through a small tube. The appeal of this method—as opposed to injecting the substance—has helped to spread the use of heroin in the 1990s. Retail heroin prepared for intravenous use traditionally had a purity level of less than 5 percent. In more recent years, purity levels have increased. In 1995 and 1996, the average purity level in Canada was

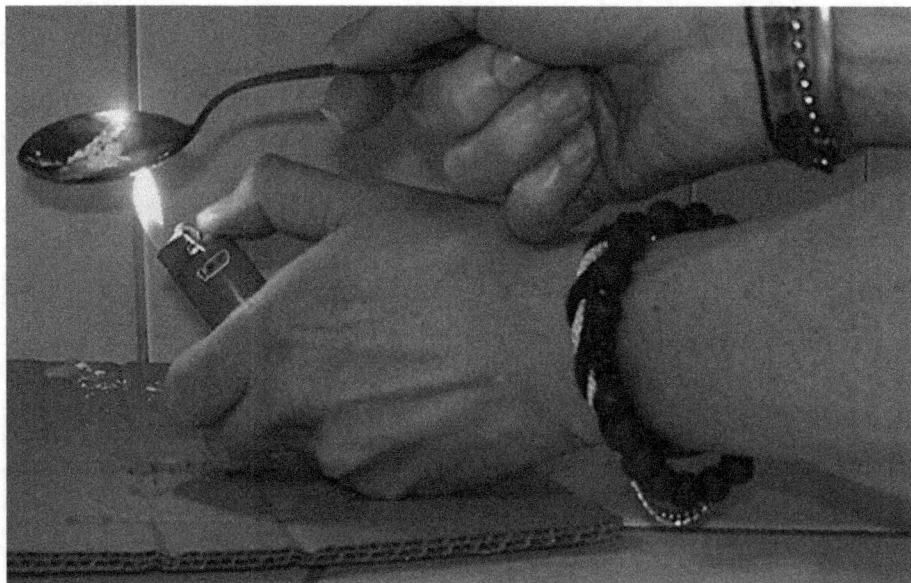

Photo 11.6: Boiling heroin crystals into liquid form for intravenous use

Source: Wikimedia Commons

39.7 percent. On November 26, 1998, 70 kilograms of heroin was seized in Vancouver that was tested at 93 percent pure. Two years later, 43 kilograms of Southeast Asian heroin was seized at the Port of Vancouver that was 99 percent pure (Royal Canadian Mounted Police, 2000a: 5).

Heroin has analgesic and euphoric properties. While sharp, localized pain is poorly relieved by opiates, duller, chronic, and less-localized pain can effectively be ameliorated through morphine and heroin. Heroin appears to reduce anxiety and distress, creating a detachment from psychological and physical pain. The continued use of heroin produces tolerance, "a progressive increase in the ability of the body to adapt to the effects of a drug that is used at regular and frequent intervals." The result of this increased tolerance is twofold: (1) progressively larger doses must be administered to produce the same effects; and (2) eventually as much as ten or more times the original lethal dose can be safely taken (Ausubel, 1978: 14). A very dangerous side effect of heroin is that it depresses the respiratory centres in the brain, so an overdose can result in respiratory arrest, leading to brain damage, physical deterioration, and death.

As discussed, the majority of the world's opiates originate in Southwest Asia and Southeast Asia. According to the United Nations *World Drug Report* Afghanistan is the world's single largest supplier of opium (United Nations Office on Drugs and Crime, 2015). A small percentage of the world's remaining opiate supply is spread among a number of countries, including Mexico and Colombia. There is nothing unique about the soil or environment that makes these locations particularly conducive to opium cultivation. Instead, these areas are fertile producers due to economic reasons. "Because the yield per acre is small and because laborious care is required in collecting the juice, [the opium poppy] can only be grown profitably where both land and labour are cheap" (Ausubel, 1978: 9).

International heroin-smuggling and trafficking conspiracies are usually perpetrated on a networked basis (as illustrated by the French Connection), and the heroin rarely remains under the control of a single organization as it moves from poppy fields and refineries to the streets of the United States and Canada. After the heroin is imported to North America, it is usually sold in quantities of 10 to 50 kilograms to national or regional wholesalers. The wholesaler then arranges for the dilution of the almost pure heroin and when the cutting is complete, it is sold to street wholesalers in quantities of 2 to 5 kilograms. From there it moves to street retailers, and finally to consumers. At each step of the process, the heroin is continuously cut, resulting in street level purities that are far below that at the wholesale level. However, the dilution at each level increases the amount available for sale, thereby maximizing profits for the wholesalers and retailers. Despite fluctuations in opium production, the heroin supply in North America has been quite abundant, as evidenced by its stable or dropping price (the price has been dropping despite the high level of purity that is found on the street).

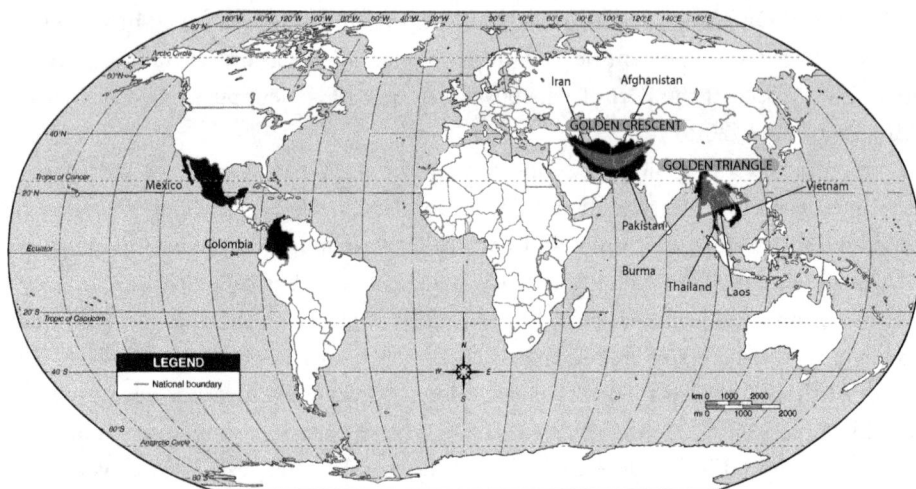

Figure 11.1: Main opium-producing regions of the world

Source: Map by Devon Rogers

The United States receives heroin from four sources: South America (Colombia), Mexico, Southeast Asia (Myanmar), and Southwest Asia (Afghanistan). Since the new millennium, the United States has seen a dramatic shift in its heroin supply; the once-dominant Southeast Asian heroin has been eclipsed in quantity by South American heroin. Mexico is now the single largest supplier of heroin to the United States and the majority of the drug enters the US through the southwestern land border. The Drug Enforcement Administration (DEA) reported that between 2009 and 2013, there was a 324 percent increase in heroin seizures at the US–Mexican border (which also includes heroin produced in Colombia and Guatemala) (United States Department of State, 2015: 9). The 2015 *International Narcotics Control Strategy Report* by the US Department of State notes that over the past several years, there has been an "alarming surge" in the use and abuse of heroin in the United States and between 2006 and 2011 there was a 110 percent increase in deaths linked to heroin overdoses (United States Department of State, 2015: 9).

For years, much of the heroin supply in Canada west of Ontario was from Southeast Asian sources, which connects independent brokers and shippers in Asia to ethnic Chinese criminal wholesalers in Canada. The majority of Southeast Asian heroin imported into Canada enters through the west coast and Vancouver specifically (the city is also a major conduit for Southeast Asia heroin destined for the United States). Seizures are routinely made at marine ports and at Vancouver's international airport.

While heroin is routinely smuggled into Canada via cargo, the most frequent seizures are from passengers and their luggage arriving on commercial flights. This smuggling technique relies on a number of non-descript couriers, usually women, who take

Case Study: Heroin Seizure at Vancouver International Airport

In May 2014, two men were arrested after 35 kilograms of heroin were seized at Vancouver's international airport. They were arrested after an 18-month criminal investigation into the suspected transport of drugs from Southeast Asia into Canada through the airport. One of the men arrested was an airport employee who worked in the air cargo warehouses. A Canada Border Services Agency spokesperson said the investigation began when a shipment of heroin that left Vancouver was seized overseas. The investigation eventually led to one of YVR's air cargo warehouses, and on May 22, investigators witnessed the employee removing an inbound shipment from a secure area of the warehouse without authorization (*24 Hours Vancouver*, June 12, 2014; *MetroNews*, June 11, 2014; *Richmond Review*, June 13, 2014).

circuitous routes to Canada from source countries. The quantities smuggled into the country in this fashion are inevitably small, so the smuggling organizations use a number of different couriers. In recent years, the Calgary International Airport has been the site for a number of significant seizures of Southeast Asian heroin from passengers' luggage. On April 24, 2013, 12 kilograms of heroin were seized from the suitcases of a female traveller arriving from Amsterdam (the largest-ever seizure of heroin in Alberta by the CBSA). Around a week later, a second traveller was arrested for attempting to smuggle 4 kilograms of suspected heroin. In both cases, the drugs were concealed in false-bottom compartments of suitcases. An RCMP inspector said it is not clear if the drugs were destined for Calgary. He estimated that 16 kilograms would be equivalent to at least 800,000 doses of heroin (*Calgary Herald*, May 3, 2013).

Toronto and Montreal international airports are frequent entry points for Southwest Asian heroin smuggled into Canada by couriers travelling on commercial aircraft. West African groups, in particular those from Ghana and Nigeria, as well as trafficking groups organized by Iranian nationals, are major importers and wholesale distributors of Southwest Asian heroin into Canada. Some of the largest seizures from individual passengers have occurred at the Toronto (Pearson) airport. According to the CBSA, during the first four months of 2013 alone, agency officers in the Greater Toronto Area seized over 127 kilograms of suspected heroin (Canada Border Service Agency Press Release, May 27, 2013). The single most frequent country from which passengers carrying heroin arrive into Toronto is Pakistan. In May 2013, for example, the CBSA announced it had made a "significant seizure" of more than 22 kilograms of heroin at Pearson airport off a passenger flight from Pakistan. A single duffle bag missing a luggage tag was selected for further examination. When the duffle bag was opened, officers found multiple rectangular-shaped packets wrapped in a floral-pattern fabric. An X-ray indicated possible organic matter concealed inside the packets, and subsequent narcotics testing proved positive for heroin (Canada Border Service Agency Press Release, May 27, 2013). Heroin is also shipped through Pearson Airport via air cargo. In June 2014, four people from Toronto were arrested after 22.4 kilograms of heroin were discovered at the airport by CBSA officers inspecting a shipment of carpets from Pakistan. The heroin was concealed in several strings and woven within the weave of four area carpets (*Mississauga News*, June 27, 2014; *Toronto Star*, June 27, 2014).

FENTANYL

As mentioned, a new drug sold in underground markets Canada in recent years is fentanyl, a synthetic opioid analgesic that is said to be 80 times more potent than morphine and 15 to 20 times more potent than heroin. The opiate is normally prescribed to treat terminal illnesses or severe pain following surgery. However, like many prescription drugs, it has made its way to the underground economy and is consumed as a recreational drug. In many instances, fentanyl pills are manufactured to resemble OxyContin pills and sold as such (primarily because fentanyl is cheaper to produce). Yet, fentanyl is much more powerful than OxyContin, which is one of the reasons why the drug has been linked to hundreds of overdose deaths in British Columbia, Alberta, and Saskatchewan. Overdoses have also occurred because other types of drugs, such as heroin, have been laced with fentanyl (primarily because it makes a cheaper filler).

Police say the fentanyl illegally distributed in Canada is coming from China or perhaps Mexico in powdered or liquid form. Much of it enters the country through the Port of Vancouver or BC land border crossings. Police cases have also uncovered clandestine labs in Canada that turn the powdered fentanyl into pills.

COCAINE

Cocaine is an alkaloid found only in the leaves of two species of the **coca** shrub. One species grows in the Andes of Ecuador, Peru, and Bolivia; the other is found in the mountainous regions of Colombia and in northeastern Peru. The practice of chewing coca leaves has been part of the culture of Indigenous people in Peru for centuries. When Spanish explorers observed this, they introduced the idea of adding lime (calcium carbonate), which releases the cocaine from the leaves when chewed. The leaves are still used as a poultice for wounds and to brew a tea that is said to cure headaches brought about by the 12,000-foot altitude of the Andes. While many crops raised on the mountain slopes of the Andes require a great deal of care—the nutrient-poor soil needs continuous fertilization—coca is a hardy jungle plant with abundant seeds that needs little or no fertilizer. "Once a coca field is planted, it will yield four to five crops a year for thirty to forty years, needing little in return but seasonal weeding" (Morales, 1989: xvi).

Case Study: Arrests of OMG Members for Drug Trafficking

In January 2015, charges were laid by Saskatoon police against 14 people who were trafficking in cocaine, heroin, methamphetamine, and fentanyl. Nearly 3360 fentanyl pills, which were produced to resemble OxyContin, were seized. The arrests were part of Project Forseti, a joint force investigation that began in November 2013 and targeted the Hells Angels and its puppet club, the Fallen Saints, in Alberta and Saskatchewan.

Police said the investigation resulted in the seizure of the following: 5.4 kilograms of methamphetamine, 2.6 kilograms of cocaine, 3358 fentanyl pills, 107 grams of heroin, 145 pounds of marijuana, 456 dilaudid pills, and 454 grams of hash. In total, the drugs were valued at over $8 million. In addition, police confiscated approximately 200 firearms, including prohibited and restricted firearms, tens of thousands of rounds of ammunition, and four ballistic vests. Approximately $100,000 in cash and seven vehicles were seized as proceeds of crime.

The investigation stretched all the way to Burnaby, British Columbia, where police seized two pill presses and mixtures used for manufacturing the fentanyl and dilaudid pills (police said the presses had previously been used to produce ecstasy and counterfeit OxyContin pills). The investigation originated in Saskatchewan following the deaths of three teenagers who overdosed on fentanyl in September 2014. Police say the pills that killed the Saskatoon teenagers had the same chemical composition as those seized in the drug raid targeting the two Saskatoon biker gangs. However, police would not say if the pills that killed the teens came from the gangs.

Among those arrested and charged were a full-patch member of the Hells Angels in Saskatoon, the local president of the Fallen Saints MC, a full-patch member of the Hells Angels in Calgary, and another member of the Fallen Saints MC in Saskatoon (CBC News, January 15, 2015; Globalnews.ca, January 26, 2015; *StarPhoenix*, January 15, 2015, January 16, 2015).

The coca bush stands one to two metres tall. Each shrub yields at most four ounces of waxy, elliptical leaves that are about one percent cocaine by weight. To process the coca leaves into cocaine, they are first pulverized and then soaked and shaken in a mixture of alcohol and benzol. The liquid is drained, sulphuric acid is added, and the solution is again shaken. Sodium carbonate is added, forming a precipitate, which is washed with kerosene and chilled, leaving behind crystals of crude cocaine known as coca paste. Between 200 and 500 kilograms of leaves produce 1 kilogram of paste; approximately 2.5 kilograms of coca paste are converted into 1 kilogram of cocaine base—a malodorous, grainy, greenish yellow powder, the purity of which is around 66 percent. Cocaine base is converted into cocaine hydrochloride by treating it with ether, acetone, and hydrochloric acid. One kilogram of cocaine base is synthesized into 1 kilogram of cocaine

Photo 11.7: Women gathering leaves from coca plants in Bolivia, wood carving 1870

Source: Courtesy of Wellcomeimages.org

---

hydrochloride, a white crystalline powder that is about 95 percent pure. Once in North America, cocaine hydrochloride is diluted for retail sale by adding sugars such as lactose, inositol, or mannitol; talcum powder, borax, or other neutral substances; and local anesthetics such as procaine hydrochloride (novocaine). After it is cut, cocaine sold at the retail level typically has a purity of less than 20 percent. In recent years, cocaine with purity levels as high as 50 percent has been seized by police.

For most recreational users of cocaine, it is inhaled directly into the nostrils using a straw or rolled paper (usually paper currency) or from a small spoon. When the drug is inhaled, its effects peak in 15 to 20 minutes and disappear in 60 to 90 minutes. Cocaine causes the release of the natural substance adrenaline, which often causes butterflies in the user's stomach. In small doses, cocaine will bring about a sensation of extreme euphoria, along with illusions of increased mental and sensory alertness and physical strength. The drug can also be injected intravenously which results in a results in a more intense rush that crests in three to five minutes and wanes in about 30 to 40 minutes.

In the middle of the nineteenth century, scientists began experimenting with the substance, noting that it showed promise as a local anesthetic. Sigmund Freud was an enthusiastic advocate of cocaine use. By the late 1880s, cocaine was the main active ingredient in many tonics and potions that were sold as a cure for everything from

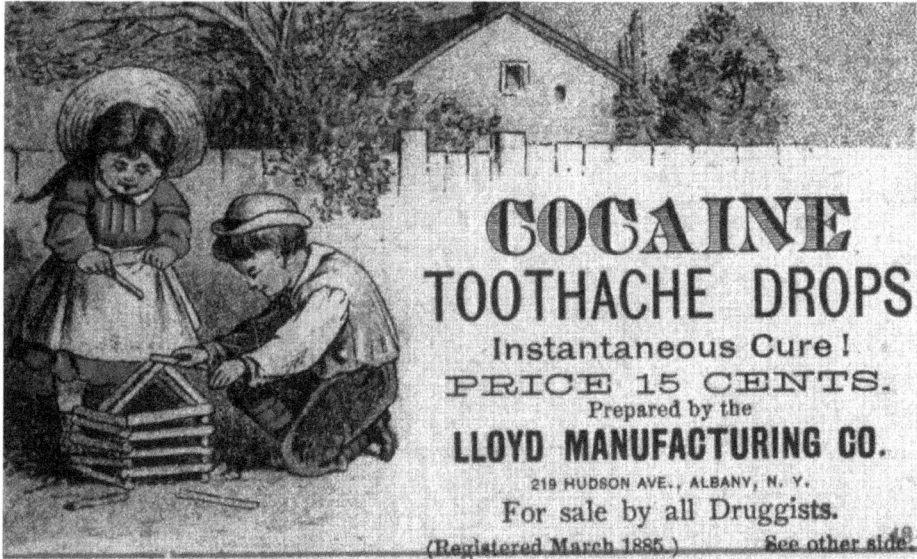

Photo 11.8: Advertisement for cocaine toothache drops circa late nineteenth century

Source: KiloByte, via Wikimedia Commons

toothaches to hysteria. It was also used for flavouring in drinks, the most famous example being Coca-Cola, which was first bottled in 1894. In 1908, a US government report listed over 40 brands of soft drinks containing cocaine (Helmer, 1975).

During the 1920s, cocaine use became associated with the deviant underworld, and by the next decade cocaine was criminalized throughout North America. Up until the 1960s, there was limited demand for the drug, but by the mid-1970s attitudes relaxed and cocaine became associated with the privileged elite and the disco glitterati. As demand escalated across North America and Europe, the cocaine industry changed dramatically. Hundreds of clandestine laboratories sprang up in Peru, Bolivia, and Colombia, and before long the Colombian cartels came to dominate the international distribution of cocaine. Since the implosion of the Colombian cartels, the production, export, and wholesale distribution of cocaine has become much more decentralized, although Mexican drug-trafficking organizations have become the dominant source, especially for the American and European markets.

The 2015 *UN World Drug Report* reaffirms that Colombia, Bolivia, and Peru continue to cultivate virtually the world's entire supply of coca for cocaine (United Nations Office on Drugs and Crime, 2015). The largest cocaine-producing country continues to be Colombia, followed by Bolivia and Peru. US law enforcement agencies estimate that approximately 84 percent of all cocaine entering the United States first passes through Central America and Mexico (United States Department of State, 2015: 10, 28).

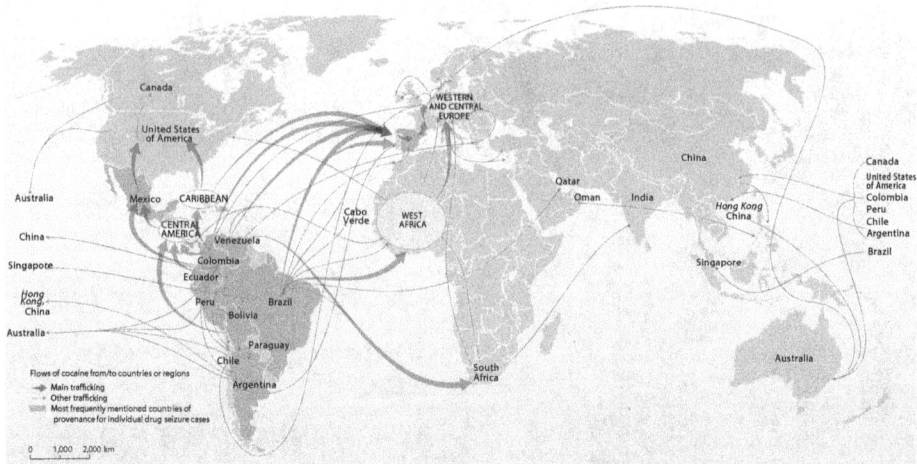

Figure 11.2: Global cocaine smuggling routes

Source: United Nations. (2015). *UN World Drug Report, 2015*, p. xv.

Like heroin, cocaine is attractive to many criminal entrepreneurs because of the enormous profits that can accrue at each level of the industry. In South America, a kilogram of pure cocaine hydrochloride sells for around $5000. Once it is in Canada, the same kilogram can be wholesaled for between $35,000 and $50,000 a kilogram. As discussed in the web-based chapter on the Colombian cartels, cocaine was first smuggled into Canada in small quantities by airline passengers. Beginning in the late 1980s, the Medellin cartel began using small planes to fly in hundreds of kilograms into the country, while the Cali cartel preferred to use large "motherships," which would anchor in international waters off North America and then offload hundreds and sometimes thousands of kilograms of the drug into smaller speedboats. By the start of the new millennium, much of the cocaine was shipped through marine containers that arrive at Canadian ports. Today, it is rare for the cocaine to be shipped in marine containers directly from Colombia. Instead, most seagoing shipments destined for Canada come from transit countries.

While marine containers continue to be a popular method of smuggling cocaine into Canada, the use of tractor-trailers that enter through official land border crossings appears to have increased in recent years. This trend is a reflection of the changing nature of the cocaine trade in North America, most notably the rise of the Mexican cartels as the continent's main supplier of the drug. Most of the cocaine smuggled into the United States from Mexico comes through land border crossings in California and Texas on commercial trucks, which then fan out throughout the United States and Canada to wholesale customers. As the 2013 *International Narcotics Control Strategy Report* from the US Department of State notes, "Although most cocaine destined for

Case Study: Smuggling of Cocaine into Canada through Marine Ports via Transit Countries

In June 2013, the Canada Border Services Agency announced it seized about 170 kilograms of cocaine—with an estimated street value of around $21 million—in two separate incidents at the port of Saint John in New Brunswick. The first seizure of 121 kilograms was made on May 29 after CBSA officials at the port decided to conduct an inspection of a container from Guyana. The marine shipping container was on its way to Mississauga and was filled with sauces, seasonings, and noodles. CBSA inspectors later discovered the cocaine in several plastic bags concealed within hollowed-out wooden pallets. This was the largest cocaine seizure at the Saint John port since 2008, when 270 kilograms of cocaine was discovered in a shipping container. On June 5, another shipping container from Guyana was inspected and found to contain 49 kilograms of cocaine. CBSA officers found the drugs stashed in between corrugated cardboard that separated bottles of hot sauce (*Cape Breton Post*, June 23, 2012; *The Daily Gleaner*, June 23, 2012).

On January 30, 2014, the CBSA announced that its officers had seized 244 kilograms of cocaine at the Port of Montreal. The narcotics were found hidden in a container on a ship coming from Paraguay. The declared goods were scrap metal. However, an X-ray inspection conducted by the CBSA showed the presence of a dense mass at the back of the container. When the contents were searched, border services officers discovered 16 metal boxes containing the cocaine (Government of Canada News Release, February 7, 2014). On October 29, 2014, the CBSA made a "massive" seizure of more than 459 kilograms of cocaine found hidden in a commercial cargo shipment at the Port of Halifax. The seizure took place when border services officers discovered the drugs while searching a container ship from Argentina that arrived via Panama (CBC News, November 3, 2014; Government of Canada News Release, November 5, 2014).

Canada originates in South America, the United States is the predominant transit point for cocaine smuggled into Canada" (United States Department of State, 2013: 113). In 2013, CBC News reported that at least a dozen truckers from the Greater Toronto Area alone had been charged with smuggling drugs, mostly cocaine, in recent years. The payloads vary, but it is not unusual for a single shipment to be hundreds of kilograms in size (CBC News, March 26, 2013; QMI Agency, January 16, 2013). The busiest official land border crossing for cocaine imports appears to be the Ambassador Bridge, connecting Detroit to Windsor, which is not surprising given it is the busiest border crossing for commercial traffic between the two countries. More cocaine is seized there by customs officials than any other land border crossing in Canada (CBC News, March 28, 2013).

Case Study: Canadian-Mexican Mennonites and Cocaine Smuggling

The Mennonites are a Christian sect that settled in the Prairies at the turn of the twentieth century following persecution in Europe and Russia. In the 1920s, several thousand Mennonites from Manitoba and the Swift Current area of Saskatchewan moved to Mexico to form colonies. Of the approximately 100,000 Mennonites living in Mexico, 90,000 are in the northern state of Chihuahua. There are close links between Mennonite communities in the two countries.

In 2012, two men belonging to a Mennonite community in Alberta were charged with importing 16 kilograms of cocaine following a police investigation into a drug-smuggling network that stretched from Chihuahua to a small southern Alberta farming community. The first seizure occurred on July 27, 2011, when 10 kilograms were intercepted by American Border Services agents in Great Falls, Montana. They found the drugs secreted in a truck compartment. Canadian Border Services Agency officials found another six kilograms on March 22, 2012, hidden in a piece of furniture at the land border crossing at Coutts, Alberta (*Calgary Herald*, June 27, 2012; CNews.com, June 26, 2012). In 2013, seven people were charged after US officials seized thousands of kilograms of cocaine headed for the small southern Alberta town of Grassy Lake, a mostly Mennonite community of around 600 people (CBC News, August 30, 2014).

In another case, Jacob Fehr was sentenced to seven years in prison for his role in smuggling cocaine across the Coutts border crossing, also in 2011. At his trial in 2014, Fehr testified that his family and others in Chihuahua's Mennonite community were threatened with death by members of Mexican drug cartels if they did not smuggle the coke into Canada. According to CBC News, "He said it was his third trip to Alberta, which would have completed his commitment to the cartel when he was caught with two kilograms packed into his SUV. His wife and four daughters were in the vehicle at the time." According to DEA agent Jim Schrant, the cocaine smuggled into Alberta was ultimately destined for Calgary where it can be sold at a higher profit compared to the United States (*National Post*, September 25, 2013).

Mennonites from other parts of Canada have been implicated in other cocaine-smuggling cases. In May 2014, eight people from a Mennonite community in Simcoe, Ontario, all with dual Mexican–Canadian citizenship, were charged after being caught with 12 kilograms of cocaine coming into the country from the United States at the Windsor border crossing. Police said the cocaine originated in the state of Chihuahua and was being smuggled into the country by as part of an ongoing conspiracy that also brought in methamphetamines. The cocaine was allegedly transferred to local traffickers in different parts of Ontario, including Toronto. In addition to the cocaine, police seized 3.5 kilograms of methamphetamine, $89,955 in Canadian cash and $38,000 in American cash.

During the summer of 2015, for example, the CBSA made two sizable cocaine seizures from commercial tractor-trailer trucks at the Ambassador Bridge border. The first was on July 27, when it seized 52 kilograms after the driver was referred to a secondary examination by CBSA officers. The second seizure occurred on September 16, when CBSA officers found approximately 24 kilograms of cocaine inside a commercial truck (Government of Canada News Release, August 31, 2015; Oakland Press, September 24, 2015). British Columbia's land border crossings are also the sites of particularly large cocaine seizures, such as the one made in 2009 at the Huntingdon border crossing in Abbotsford, in which customs officials found 114 kilograms of the white powder in a truck belonging to a Vancouver area transportation company (*Abbotsford News*, July 24, 2009; CTV News, July 24, 2009; Vancouverite.com, July 24, 2009). Two years later, CBSA officials found 115 kilograms of cocaine at the Pacific Highway border crossing, also hidden in a commercial tractor-trailer (Canada Border Services Agency News Release, July 11, 2013). Land border crossings into Alberta have also been a frequent crossing point for cocaine into Canada and recent police cases indicate that some within the Mennonite community in Canada and Mexico have been involved in the smuggling.

With the emergence of the Mexican cartels as North American's main suppliers of cocaine, Canadian drug smugglers and traffickers have been travelling to Mexico to cut deals directly with the drug cartels. One indication of the increased direct contact between Canadian drug traffickers and their Mexican suppliers is the rash of killings of suspected Canadian traffickers while in Mexico. According to an internal RCMP report cited by the *Toronto Star*, between 2008 and 2012, at least nine Canadians "with extensive criminal associations" were shot or killed in that country. The victims included three members of the BC-based United Nations gang, which had become a major supplier of cocaine in that province (*Toronto Star*, April 19, 2013).

The increased role of Canada as a cocaine trans-shipment country is another sign that traffickers in this country have solidified their connections with Mexican suppliers (Insight.com, September 12, 2014). A 2013 report by the Australian Crime Commission noted that the Netherlands was the transit country that accounted for the greatest number of "cocaine detections" in Australia, while Canada and Germany are "other prominent embarkment points." In terms of the cumulative weight of cocaine imports detected in Australia, Canada was second only to Chile as a trans-shipment country (Australian Crime Commission, 2013: 105). Cocaine is smuggled out of Canada primarily through marine ports and airports. The Port of Vancouver is the main conduit for cocaine destined for Pacific Rim countries, while Toronto's Pearson Airport has been identified as a departure point for cocaine being smuggled to the United Kingdom (Royal Canadian Mounted Police Press Release, November 15, 2013).

For years, the largest cocaine importers and wholesalers in Canada were the Rizzuto Mafia family, Montreal's West End Gang, the Colombian cartels, and the Hells Angels, although these groups never did have a monopoly individually or collectively. Today, the wholesaling and national distribution of cocaine in Canada is carried out by a diverse range of individuals, groups, and networks. The following summarizes recent cases that entail the involvement of three of dominant criminal organizations in Canada—the Montreal Mafia, the Hells Angels, and Ontario's 'Ndrangheta clans—in cocaine importation and distribution.

Case Studies: Recent Cocaine Smuggling and Trafficking Cases by Tier I Criminal Groups

In June 2012, 45-year-old Giuseppe (Ponytail) De Vito was sentenced to a 15-year prison term for his role in a conspiracy to import cocaine from Haiti through Pierre Elliott Trudeau International Airport in Montreal. De Vito became known to police during Project Colisée, an investigation into the Rizzuto Mafia family in 2005, after a shipment of 218 kilograms of cocaine was seized by the RCMP. He was convicted of conspiracy to smuggle cocaine and committing a crime for the benefit of a criminal organization. According to a story in the *Montreal Gazette*, "wiretaps revealed De Vito was furious, not because the cocaine had been seized but because the people who did the actual smuggling lied to the Mafia about how much they were importing to avoid a so-called tax the organization charged for 'a door' through the airport created by De Vito." According to police evidence, De Vito played a key role in recruiting airport employees to help bring cocaine into Canada (*Montreal Gazette*, June 5, 2012, June 20, 2012).

Five full-patch members of the Hells Angels were arrested in British Columbia in 2012 (and later convicted) following a series of police raids, including one at their Kelowna clubhouse. Among those arrested was David Giles, vice-president of the Kelowna Hells Angels chapter. Police allege that Giles, four other Hells Angels members, and four other associates conspired to import and traffic 500 kilograms of cocaine from September 2011 to August 2012 (*Kelowna Daily Courier*, August 29, 2012; *Vancouver Sun*, August 28, 2012). Also in 2012, two full-patch members of the Hells Angels in Alberta—Alan Knapczyk and John Alcantara—were convicted of conspiring to traffic cocaine for a criminal organization. Justice Sheila Greckol ruled the men conspired with Fort McMurray drug dealer Jeffrey Caines and others to traffic in cocaine by entering into an agreement to enforce and protect the drug gang and solve any problems the organization had with competitors (*Edmonton Sun*, August 17, 2012).

A series of raids executed across Greater Toronto in June 2015 resulted in the arrests of almost 20 people, which police said were connected to two Toronto cells of the 'Ndrangheta. According to police, the cells operated independently of one another but routinely co-operated to import cocaine and marijuana from Caribbean countries including Jamaica, Costa Rica, Guyana, and Dominican Republic, via Toronto and Halifax ports. The raids resulted in a seizure of 8.5 kilograms of cocaine and 7 kilograms of marijuana, as well as cash and three guns. One of the 'Ndrangheta cells was led by Giuseppe Ursino of Bradford, Ontario, who was charged with trafficking in cocaine and conspiracy to import cocaine, among other charges. Speculation has been rampant that the Ontario-based 'Ndrangheta clans were behind the murders of members and associates of the Sicilian Rizzuto family in Montreal in order to gain some influence over the Port of Montreal to facilitate the importation of cocaine and other illegal drugs into Canada. The 'Ndrangheta is one of the biggest cocaine importers in Europe and allegedly obtain their supply directly from Mexican drug cartels (CBC News, June 3, 2015; Combined Forces Special Enforcement Unit—Ontario Press Release, June 3, 2015; CTV News, June 2, 2015; *Toronto Star*, June 3, 2015).

CRITICAL THINKING EXERCISE

Research and critically examine the extent to which Canada's wholesale cocaine importation and wholesaling is dominated by large Tier I criminal organizations. Find case studies and other evidence that supports this argument as well as those that contradict this thesis. Is the retail ("street-level") cocaine market in Canada (or any one province) dominated by a particular criminal group or is it more characterized by what Reuter calls "disorganized crime"?

MARIJUANA

For many years, **marijuana** has been the most widely consumed illegal substance in North America. The source of marijuana is *cannabis sativa*, an annual herbaceous that grows wild throughout most of the tropical and temperate regions of the world. In addition to its psychotropic properties, the *cannabis sativa* plant can be cultivated for several useful products: the fibre can be used to make rope, clothing, paper, and more; the seeds can be eaten or crushed into oil for lighting, soap, cooking, and in the manufacture of varnish, linoleum, and paint; and it is used for medicinal and spiritual purposes.

It has been only in the last 50 years that the use of cannabis as an intoxicant has spread widely in Western societies. Marijuana was never a particularly popular or widespread drug during the nineteenth or early twentieth century. Nonetheless, it was caught up in the temperance movements and drug prohibition laws that swept through North America in the first half of the twentieth century. Like other drugs, prohibitionists (erroneously) equated marijuana with racialized and ethnic minority groups, deviants, crime, psychoses, and violence. In America, laws prohibiting marijuana were not the result of widespread misuse or rigorous scientific or medical evidence proving its negative health

Photo 11.9: Flowering marijuana plant

Source: Wikimedia Commons

impacts or addictive properties. Instead, the criminalization of marijuana was partially the result of the nativist reaction to Mexican immigrants who were accused of bring the "loco weed" into the United States. Very powerful entities in America took up the campaign to criminalize marijuana. Harry J. Anslinger, the first director of the US Bureau of Narcotics, played the race card (he once said "the primary reason to outlaw marijuana is its effect on the degenerate races"), warned against the highly addictive properties of marijuana (although no evidence backed up his claims), and argued simultaneously that marijuana led to both unbridled violence and pacifism (the latter was particularly dangerous because it leads to Communist brainwashing). William Randolf Hearst, the most powerful publisher in the United States during the first half of the twentieth century, used his vast chain of newspapers to rally against marijuana. His opposition stemmed from his own racist views of Mexicans as well as his belief that the hemp plant's role in producing paper would undermine his investments in the timber industry, which was tied to pulp and paper production for his newspapers. The southern cotton growers also reportedly lobbied the US government to outlaw the hemp plant because of its potential to produce fibres for clothes, in direct competition with cotton. Chemical and pharmaceutical companies advocated for outlawing the *cannabis sativa* plant because it represented competition to nylon (newly invented by Dupont Chemicals) and medicines respectively.

The groundswell of opposition to marijuana in the 1920s and 1930s produced an avalanche of hysterical anti-marijuana propaganda. One editorial in Hearst's *San Francisco Chronicle* newspaper warned, "Marihuana is a short cut to the insane asylum. Smoke marihuana cigarettes for a month and what was once your brain will be nothing but a storehouse of horrid specters. Hasheesh makes a murderer who kills for the love of killing out of the mildest mannered man who ever laughed at the idea that any habit could ever get him...." (as cited in drugwarrant.com, n.d.). The most enduring symbol of all the anti-marijuana propaganda was the laughable 1936 film *Reefer Madness*. While the docudrama intends to present a frightening portrait of the marijuana user, much of the film entails

Photo 11.10: Still from the 1936 movie *Reefer Madness*

Source: Wikimedia Commons

unintentional slapstick scenes of high school kids smoking pot, playing "evil" jazz music, experiencing psychosis, and ultimately embarking on a violent murder spree.

Within Canada, laws against the use of marijuana (as well as heroin and cocaine) were greatly influenced by the sensationalized and bigoted writings of Judge Emily Murphy. In one chapter of her 1922 book *The Black Candle*, a Los Angeles County Chief of Police is quoted as saying, " ... persons using this narcotic smoke the dry leaves of the plant, which has the effect of driving them completely insane. The addict loses all sense of moral responsibility. Addicts to this drug, while under its influence are immune to pain. While in this condition they become raving maniacs and are liable to kill or indulge in any forms of violence to other persons, using the most savage methods of cruelty without, as said before, any sense of moral responsibility." When the book was released, its sole purpose was to arouse public opinion and pressure the government into creating stricter drug laws. In 1923, cannabis was made illegal in Canada through the *Opium and Narcotic Drug Act*. In 1937, the US Congress passed the *Marijuana Tax Act*, which put an end to lawful recreational use of the substance.

While marijuana was not a particularly widely abused drug, beginning in the 1960s, its popularity skyrocketed as rebellious youth and counter-cultures asserted their independence from mainstream society. There was a heightened awareness of the rather benign health effects of pot, relative to heroin or cocaine, and people who wanted to experiment or occasionally get high felt that they could indulge without the dangers of serious long-term health damage or physical addiction. These perceptions continue to this day, and marijuana consumption cuts across all social, economic, racial, and age groups.

Marijuana is traditionally smoked through a pipe or rolled in cigarette paper. More recently, devices that vaporize it have become popular as they allow the user to avoid drawing smoke into his or her lungs. The user inhales the smoke or vapours deeply and holds it in the lungs for as long as possible. The psychoactive reaction occurs in one to 10 minutes and peaks in about 10 to 30 minutes, with a duration of up to three to four hours. Cannabis can also be eaten, and although the high is slower to materialize, it tends to last longer compared to smoking it. In general, low doses of pot tend to induce an increasing sense of well-being and gregariousness, followed by a dreamy state of relaxation. Hunger (especially a craving for junk food!) frequently accompanies a marijuana high.

The psychoactive substance of the marijuana plant is (–)3,4-trans-delta-1- tetrahydro-cannabinol, also known as delta-1-THC, delta-9-THC, or simply **THC**. It is most highly concentrated in the resinous flowering (or "buds") of the cannabis plant. The THC level of marijuana varies considerably, based on how it is grown and pollinated. Historically, most of the marijuana grown or imported into North America had less than 0.5 percent THC, since the plants were originally introduced to produce hemp fibre. More recently, some strains exhibit much higher levels of THC, the result of careful cross-breeding. These more potent plants are cultivated expressly to maximize the psychotropic qualities of marijuana. In addition to cross-breeding, the introduction of hydroponic cultivation—a method of growing plants with their roots in nutrient mineral solutions rather than in soil—has also been credited with increasing the THC levels.

Within the global context, Canada has traditionally been a marijuana-consuming country with most of the marijuana sold being imported from tropical climes, such as Jamaica, Colombia, Mexico, Cambodia, Thailand, and California. According to the RCMP, of the foreign marijuana seized in or *en route* to Canada in 1999, at least 5535 kilograms originated from Jamaica, 825 kilograms from South Africa, and 860 kilograms from Mexico. Foreign shipments arrive directly into Canadian ports of entry or transit through the United States before reaching Canada. On June 11, 1999, US Customs intercepted 2464 kilos of Jamaican marijuana and 141 kilos of hash oil at Newark, New Jersey, in a marine container bound for Montreal. On June 20, 1999, 2617 kilos of Jamaican pot destined for Canada were seized in Stuart, Florida (Royal Canadian Mounted Police, 2000a: 6).

No longer is this much pot imported into the country; Canada is now a major producer of marijuana, most of which is grown indoors. These indoor grow operations produce a potent form of marijuana that has become known internationally as "BC Bud" or "Canadian Gold." In addition to providing ideal year-round growing conditions, indoor "grow-ops" avoid the need for large plots of land, which enhances privacy. As

Photo 11.11: Growing marijuana indoors

Source: Wikimedia Commons

importantly, indoor pot producers use specialized horticultural technology and cloning methods that have led to a rise in the potency of the drug.

By the end of the 1990s, there were thousands of marijuana grow operations in the country and the number has only increased in the new millennium. RCMP estimates indicate that from 1994 to 2002, the amount of domestically grown marijuana seized in Canada grew by more than 600 percent (from 6472 to 54,372 kilograms), a statistic that is reflective of both an increase in production and intensified enforcement attention (Royal Canadian Mounted Police, 2002c). In 2003, the RCMP estimated the annual production of marijuana in Canada to be at least 800 metric tonnes, approximately five million plants (Royal Canadian Mounted Police, 2003). According to a 2002 RCMP report entitled *Marihuana Cultivation in Canada Evolution and Current Trend*, "every year, several multi-thousand plant operations are discovered, both indoor and outdoor." Profit is the most obvious attraction. With a "comparatively small initial investment, the grower can potentially reap profits of well over $1,000,000 within the first year for an operation capable of producing a few hundred plants of high quality marijuana about every three months," the report says (*Ottawa Citizen*, April 29, 2003; Royal Canadian Mounted Police, 2002c). In 2009, Canadian law enforcement seized a total of 34,391 kilos of marijuana and 1,845,734 plants (Royal Canadian Mounted Police, 2009: 16).

British Columbia is considered the marijuana grow-op capital of Canada, and in 2001 the province's Organized Crime Agency estimated the marijuana cultivation industry in that province is "a $6 billion annual cash crop" (MacQueen, 2001: 28). In a 2004 study entitled *Marijuana Growth in British Columbia*, Stephen Easton, a professor of economics at Simon Fraser University, wrote that there were as many as 17,500 grow operations in the province in 2000 (Easton, 2004: 3). While Canada's westernmost province is the epicentre of pot production in the country, cannabis cultivation has spread to other provinces in a big way. A study prepared for the Ontario Association of Chiefs of Police suggests that indoor marijuana grow operations in that province increased by more than 250 percent between 2000 and 2002. In 2002, Ontario was home to as many as 15,000 cultivation operations, producing marijuana worth up to $12.7 billion, making it the third most valuable agricultural crop in the province (Ontario Association of Chiefs of Police, 2002: 2; *Toronto Star*, December 18, 2003). Between September 8 and 19, 2003, a police task force in eastern Ontario seized more than 12,000 marijuana plants (RCMP Press Release, September 29, 2003). The underground production of marijuana is now a multi-billion-dollar industry in Canada that employs thousands of people.

The proliferation of marijuana grow operations throughout Canada is due to a number of factors. These include the following:

- The relatively low level of capital required to begin operations
- Advances in cultivation technology and the widespread and legal availability of this technology and other equipment
- A high profit potential
- A large and receptive consumer market—both domestically (Canada ranks fifth in the world in per capita marijuana consumption and first among industrialized nations, according to the 2007 United Nations *World Drug Report*) and internationally
- The internationally recognized quality of Canadian-grown pot
- The relatively lenient penalties for marijuana offences in this country

Like other illegal drug markets, the extent to which the domestic marijuana is controlled by well-organized criminal enterprises is a matter of dispute. There is research to suggest that the industry is a highly competitive market made up of numerous suppliers. A written submission to the federal task force on marijuana legalization in Canada in 2016, co-authored by criminologist Neil Boyd on behalf of Canadian Drug Policy Coalition, cites government data over an eight-year period indicating that just five percent of a random sample of 500 criminal cases involving marijuana production had links to criminal organizations or street gangs. Boyd told the *Globe and Mail* newspaper, "A lot of this comes down to your definition of organized crime. If you think three people acting together and potentially making some kind of profit necessarily means that these are organized criminals, then, of course, everybody in the cannabis industry is an organized criminal. But if you think along the lines of the Justice Canada website, where the focus is on corruption [and] the use of force or violence, you'll find very few people in the marijuana industry are properly defined as organized criminals" (*Globe and Mail*, August 9, 2016).

While Boyd argues that police in Canada have long overestimated the scope of organized crime's involvement in the illegal marijuana business, he does not deny that well-organized criminal groups play a role in production and trafficking of the illicit crop. It can even be argued that the entry of established organized criminal groups into the Canadian marijuana industry helped to bolster the production, distribution, and export of domestically grown pot. In the early 1970s, the Royal Commission on the Non Medical Use of Drugs concluded that the Canadian marijuana market at that time was "loosely organized" and "largely free of professional criminal involvement." More recently, marijuana production in Canada has become what the RCMP calls "a staple for all crime groups" (Royal Canadian Mounted Police, 2003). Police investigations have repeatedly turned up large grow operations controlled by outlaw motorcycle gangs. In 1996, police raided a warehouse in a suburban Montreal industrial park that housed a hydroponic facility with 11,000 plants in full bloom. This installation was traced to the Rockers, a motorcycle gang affiliated with the Hells Angels (Criminal Intelligence Service Canada, 1997: 24). Since this case, police have linked hundreds of marijuana grow operations across the country to the Hells Angels and its associates.

While there is little doubt that the HAMC is involved in this profitable enterprise, they may, in fact, be second to Asian crime groups in terms of the number of grow operations and quantities produced. As discussed in chapter 8, Vietnamese groups have been particularly active in establishing grow operations in urban and suburban residences in British Columbia, Alberta, Manitoba, and Ontario. They are highly organized and control all aspects of the business, including locating, renovating, and equipping homes for cultivation; operating hydroponic stores and nurseries to supply the necessary equipment, seeds, plant clones, and fertilizers; employing crop sitters; and distributing the final product. In more recent years, Chinese criminal syndicates have been linked to some of the largest outdoor grow operations in the country and are seen as a major force behind the escalation of Canadian-grown pot being smuggled into the United States.

The criminal organizations involved in marijuana production in Canada effectively distance themselves from the actual day-to-day production. They will hire or contract out production to others, who may be registered as the owners of homes or farmland used for the crops and who will get a cut of the profits. These "crop sitters" tend to the plants, look after the lighting and watering systems, and may act as security. The RCMP has said that some of those who owe money to crime groups are coerced into becoming crop sitters to pay off their loans, or gambling or drugs debts (Royal Canadian Mounted Police, 2003). Farmers and landowners have been subjected to intimidation tactics by members and associates of outlaw motorcycle gangs that want to use their fields to plant illegal crops. The problem was given intense media coverage during the fall of 1999 in Quebec when a federal MP undertook efforts to seek protection for some of his rural constituents, only to be threatened himself (Royal Canadian Mounted Police, 2000a: 6). One sure sign of the involvement of organized crime groups in marijuana production is the scale of some of the grow operations raided by police. The sheer size of marijuana grow operations had reached "unprecedented levels," the RCMP observed in 2002 (Royal Canadian Mounted Police, 2002c). As the scale of individual grow operations increased, the trend has been to move away from residential homes to industrial spaces that can accommodate larger operations.

Most marijuana grow operations in Canada are located in urban centres, within either homes or industrial facilities. By 2003, police began discovering grow operations in more remote locations in British Columbia and other parts of Canada.

Case Study: Use of Industrial Facilities to House Massive Marijuana Grow Operations

On January 12, 2004, police raided the largest indoor marijuana grow operation found in Canada to date, which was located in a former Molson Brewery in Ontario. Inside, police found approximately 30,000 plants in various stages of production. The pot factory (which one attending officer called "little Saskatchewan") operated 24 hours a day and was capable of producing as many as three or four crops annually that could be worth as much as $100 million. Plants covered more than 60,000 square feet of space, and hundreds of thousands of dollars were spent to convert the old brewery, which included the addition of dormitory-type living quarters for up to 50 workers. Many of the plants were maturing inside 25 beer vats that had been turned into hothouses with the installation of a thousand high-powered lights. Each vat also had a filtration system that pumped fresh air into the vats and then removed the unmistakable skunk-scented air, which was filtered and then sent into a separate self-contained room (*Globe and Mail*, January 12, 2004; *Toronto Star*, January 12, 2004, January 13, 2004).

A month after this discovery, in February 2004, police in Edmonton raided a warehouse where they found a grow operation with more than 5600 plants. The warehouse had an electrical system that regulated 212 grow lamps, supported by two additional electrical transformers. Six people, all from British Columbia and all of Chinese descent, were arrested at the scene (Canadian Press, February 13, 2004). At the end of the year, Winnipeg police uncovered the largest grow-op in that province to date in a warehouse only two blocks from downtown police headquarters. A pre-dawn raid on December 2, 2004, ended with the seizure of more than 10,000 plants (Canadian Press, December 3, 2004; *Winnipeg Sun*, October 22, 2004).

The location of grow-ops on farmland signalled a new trend in which organized criminal groups were buying or leasing big, cheap, vacant farms located in more northerly parts to grow their cannabis crops. In addition to the secrecy that remote properties provide, the warm summer days and cool nights allow for excellent growing conditions. Producers have even enriched the clay soil, while new strains have been tested to determine which ones grow best in the northern climate. Outdoor crops also allow for economies of scale in that a large amount of pot can be harvested from relatively inexpensive farmland, compared to the smaller yields grown indoors in expensive urban and suburban homes.

Canada has not only become self-sufficient in marijuana, it has become an exporter to the United States where Canadian-grown marijuana is highly popular and fetches a high price, due to its quality and relative scarcity in the United States. While the quantity of Canadian pot imported into the United States is estimated at only one-fifth of what comes from Mexico, there has been a steady rise in exports from Canada. This is reflected in an increase in the quantity of Canadian pot seized in the United States: from 2235 kilos in 2000 to 9487 kilos in 2002 (Royal Canadian Mounted Police, 2003). In its 2004 annual report, the White House Office of National Drug Control Policy concluded, the "marijuana Americans smoke comes from three main sources: U.S. outdoor

Case Studies: Large-Scale Marijuana Grow Operations in Rural Canada

On September 19, 2003, Canadian military police showed reporters 783 mature cannabis plants they had seized from a field located midway between Montreal and Quebec City. The land is owned by the Department of National Defence and is used as an ammunition testing ground (*Globe and Mail*, September 20, 2003). In November 2003, RCMP officers seized 3600 marijuana plants and 1.6 kilograms of dried pot from an elaborate grow operation in two underground bunkers, 30 kilometres west of Dawson Creek in British Columbia (*Peace River Block Daily News*, November 8, 2003). In October 2004, 16 people were arrested in connection with a major grow operation in the tiny community of Seymour Arm, at the north end of Shuswap Lake in British Columbia. Police discovered 20,000 marijuana plants located in attics, basements, and bunkers, some of which were capable of holding more than 5000 plants at a time. "We figure that just over half of the residents were involved in this well-organized criminal enterprise," an RCMP spokesperson told the media (CBC News, October 6, 2004, October 8, 2004). Sûreté du Quebec officers carried out one of the largest marijuana seizures in the province's history on June 23, 2005, when they discovered 17,000 plants in a farmer's field. Two men police believe were linked to a Chinese crime group were arrested (*Ottawa Citizen*, June 23, 2005).

and indoor cultivation, Mexican outdoor cultivation, and high-potency indoor cultivation from Canada." The report estimates that on an annual basis, Mexico supplies
approximately 5000 metric tonnes, 2500 metric tonnes are grown domestically in the
United States, with roughly 1000 tonnes coming from Canada (White House Office of
National Drug Control Policy, 2004: 43).

The demand for potent Canadian cannabis in the United States results in a substantial increase in its price as soon as it crosses the border. As a 2000 report by the DEA
states, Canadian-produced cannabis "sells for $1,500 to $2,000 per pound in Vancouver.
Smuggled to Bellingham, Washington, the price increases to about $3,000; if brought
to California, it can sell for as much as $6,000. In New York City, Canadian marijuana
has sold for up to $8,000 per pound. DEA officials in Portland, Maine, report that high
potency Canadian-grown marijuana is sold in the region at up to five times the price of
domestic and Mexican marijuana" (United States Drug Enforcement Administration,
2000). The inflated price fetched in the United States contributes to greater profits for
producers and distributors, which in turn has led to increased production in Canada and
the smuggling of larger amounts across the border.

The involvement of criminal groups in marijuana production has also contributed
to the increase in exports to the United States, and some groups in Canada produce
marijuana exclusively for the US market (Royal Canadian Mounted Police, 2009: 17).
Canadian-produced pot is sometimes used as a currency to purchase cocaine that is
warehoused in the United States. The exchange ratio is about three kilograms of marijuana to one kilogram of cocaine, although exchanges of one to one have been rumoured.
Other Canadian traffickers transport quantities of marijuana to the United States, which
is sold to local buyers, with the proceeds being used to purchase cocaine from American
traffickers, which is then smuggled into Canada.

The passage of years has not slowed the production of marijuana in Canada or its
export to the United States. In 2010, the International Narcotics Control Board maintained that Canada continued to be self-sufficient in illicit cannabis, but also supplies a
"significant amount" of the homegrown product to the United States, some of which is
traded for "cocaine and other contraband, such as firearms and tobacco" (*National Post*,
March 2, 2011). In 2013, the RCMP in British Columbia seized 12,000 marijuana
plants that were just about to be harvested on Crown land in the Pemberton area. A
spokesperson for the RCMP told the media that between August 23 and September 6,
they discovered 25 illegal grow operations in the area. The sizes of the grow-ops ranged
from 150 to 1009 plants, although all of them were located on steep hills (*Vancouver Sun*,
September 12, 2013). Some of the largest grow operations discovered in Canada in the
last few years were in Ontario. This includes one discovered in a warehouse in Greater
Toronto in 2008, which housed 14,000 plants. Police described it as a "very sophisticated"
operation complete with conveyor belts to move plants from one area to another as they
grew. Given the equipment found on the premises, Toronto police estimated that the
operators could have grown crops this size three to four times per year, bringing in

Case Study: Marijuana Smuggling between British Columbia and Washington State

At the end of June 2006, Canadian and American police dismantled one BC-based smuggling network that used remote, mountainous locations as staging points for helicopters and airplanes transporting thousands of kilograms of BC marijuana to Washington State and hundreds of kilograms of cocaine into Canada. Codenamed "Frozen Timber," the two-year investigation ended with the seizure of 3640 kilograms of marijuana, 365 kilograms of cocaine, three aircraft, and $1.5 million in American cash.

Six people were arrested in Canada, while 40 arrests were made in the United States. The key Canadian figure in the smuggling ring was Daryl Desjardins, who, according to police, was subcontracted by several criminal groups (including the Hells Angels, the Montreal Mafia, Indo-Canadian gangs, and Asian crime groups) to ferry the drugs between the two countries. Desjardins was arrested in a Bell Jet Ranger helicopter on May 10 after allegedly transporting 150 kilograms of pot across the border. He was convicted of smuggling and trafficking in a BC court-room and sentenced to 4.5 years (Canada NewsWire, June 29, 2006; *Chilliwack Progress*, August 18, 2006; *Vancouver Sun*, June 29, 2006).

In a somewhat less sophisticated (albeit more labour-intensive) smuggling operation, three men were arrested by DEA agents in the United States who had been monitoring the efforts of the trio as they toiled for eight months digging a 110-metre tunnel that ran from Aldergrove, British Columbia, to Lyndon, Washington. The tunnel was constructed using shovels, a mechanical winch to raise and lower cart-loads of drugs, and a sump pump to drain off water. It was wired for lighting and its walls were reinforced with concrete, steel, and about 1000 two-by-six-inch wood supports spaced two inches apart. The cost involved in building the tunnel and acquiring the property on both sides of the border was in excess of a million dollars, which led police to believe it was funded by at least one well-heeled criminal organization. The men were arrested in Bellingham, Washington, after they had transported 42 kilos of marijuana through the tunnel (*Globe and Mail*, July 22, 2005, July 23, 2005; *Vancouver Sun*, July 22, 2005).

anywhere from $42 million to $56 million annually (*Toronto Sun*, December 1, 2010). The largest marijuana grow-op ever discovered in Canada was located in a cornfield, in eastern Ontario, about 150 kilometres from Ottawa. Police were astounded to find a massive plantation of 40,000 plants (*Toronto Star*, September 22, 2008).

Alongside illegal marijuana production in this country is the medical marijuana industry, in which plants are grown legally with a licence from the federal government. However, even this legitimate industry has been used to supply the underground market, in part because of the infiltration of crime groups. A 2012 intelligence report by the RCMP says, "Criminal groups are currently exploiting Health Canada's medical marijuana program," by producing more than the quantity allowed under a Health Canada permit with the excess being diverted to the black market. According to a RCMP affidavit filed in court, criminal groups have been known to pay terminal cancer patients to obtain a marijuana grow licence (*Vancouver Sun*, February 18, 2014). The findings follow numerous warnings and reports of illegal activity linked to Health Canada's Marijuana Medical Access Regulations (MMAR) initiative. In its 2009 Drug Situation report, the RCMP wrote, the MMAR "is susceptible to exploitation by drug trafficking organizations" (Royal Canadian Mounted Police, 2009: 16). In March 2013, the RCMP and the Niagara Regional Police laid criminal organization charges after it was discovered that one federally licenced marijuana production facility in the region had generated hundreds of thousands of dollars in profits from the "egregious exploitation" of Canada's medical marijuana laws. Police told the media a Hamilton-based criminal group obtained "several dozen" licences to produce marijuana under the guise it was for medical purposes. However, police allege that most of the pot was sold on the black market. In effect, the group was running a highly profitable marijuana grow operation whose distribution network stretched to Newfoundland, police claim. In all, 12 people were charged with a variety of criminal offences (*Hamilton Spectator*, March 8, 2013; Postmedia News, March 7, 2013).

HASHISH

Hashish is a derivative of marijuana and contains the intoxicating resinous secretions of the cannabis plant, which are collected, dried, and then compressed into a variety of forms. Its potency typically exceeds that of marijuana, which helps to explain its popularity. Most hash is imported into Canada from Middle East and Southwest Asian countries—in particular Lebanon, Pakistan, Afghanistan, and Morocco. Hundreds of tonnes of hashish enter Canada every year; according to the 2009 RCMP drug intelligence report, 9907 kilos was seized that year, six times greater than that seized in 2008 (Royal Canadian Mounted Police, 2009: 20). Generally speaking, hash is imported into Canada on a networked basis: the marijuana is grown in one of the aforementioned regions and usually converted to hashish there. Brokers arrange for the shipment, while Canadian groups coordinate their entry into Canada. Much of the hashish imported into the country is shipped via marine containers and enters through Montreal or Halifax, and multi-tonne shipments direct from Pakistan are common. Marine containers are the preferred conveyance for smuggling hashish into Canada, due to the large shipments that are imported into this country. As one RCMP officer observed following a large bust at the port of Montreal, marine containers are essential to hashish smuggling into Canada "because it's hard to hide 4,000 pounds of hash in the trunk of a car" (Canada NewsWire, June 5, 2006; *Montreal Gazette*, August 9, 2002, June 6, 2006, September 26, 2006).

Photo 11.12: Hashish (cannabis resin)

Source: Wikimedia Commons

One Canadian crime group that has dominated the importation and domestic wholesale distribution of hashish in Central Canada is Montreal's West End Gang, a moniker applied by police to a network of offenders, mostly of Irish descent, who grew up in Montreal's West End. Despite its changing leadership and a varying cast of characters since the 1970s, the West End Gang has emerged as the biggest known importer of hashish in the country. The fateful decision to start importing hashish was made in the mid-1970s by Paul Ryan, the original leader of the gang whose criminal background up to that point was largely confined to robberies. Ryan realized that the real money to be made was in drugs and, using his criminal contacts, he began to purchase and sell small quantities of hashish. By the end of the decade, he had made enough money to start importing hash shipments himself. Before long, he was one of the biggest distributors in Montreal. Under Ryan's leadership, hash arrived at the Port of Montreal by the tonne and was then distributed through a network of wholesalers that extended west into Ontario and east into the Maritimes (Burke, 1987: 23–30).

By the late 1980s, the West End Gang was under the leadership of Gerald Matticks, who wholesaled hashish and cocaine to the elite of Quebec's underworld—the Hells Angels, the Rock Machine, and the Rizzuto family, as well as Asian and Russian criminal groups. Matticks was able to move large quantities into Montreal because of the

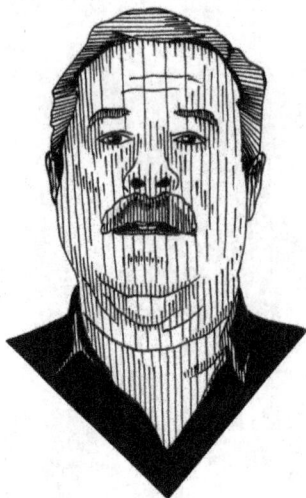

Photo 11.13: Gerald Matticks

Source: Illustration by Ben Firsch

influence he had at the marine ports. He had great sway over the hiring of "checkers," a waterfront job responsible for overseeing the movement of containers off ships and essential to ensuring the safe passage of contraband through the port. Gerald's son Donald even worked on the docks as a checker for 15 years before being caught up in a police dragnet in 2002. Donald Matticks would later tell a parole board that he began working at the port at the age of 24 and used his position to sneak drug-filled containers past the port gates without being inspected (*Le Journal de Montréal*, December 6, 2002; *Montreal Gazette*, December 5, 2002).

Gerald Matticks was arrested on May 26, 1994, when he, his brother Richard, and nine others were charged by the Sûreté du Quebec (SQ) in connection with a 2650-kilogram shipment of hashish found in a shipping container on the Montreal waterfront earlier that month. At the time, it was one of the largest hashish seizures ever in Quebec. The SQ announced that the Matticks would also be charged in connection with another 1000 kilograms discovered in March. When the case came to court, however, allegations began to surface that the provincial police had planted incriminating evidence against Matticks. In June of the following year, all of the charges were dismissed by a Quebec court judge who ruled that the SQ had fabricated evidence, falsified documents, and provided inconsistent testimony in court.

The brush with the law did not deter Matticks. In December 1999, he and a drug-dealing partner, Louis Lekkas, orchestrated a 2363-kilogram shipment of hash that landed at the Montreal port. This was followed a month later by another load of over 20,000 kilograms, although this one was seized by police. In April 2000, they brought in 265 kilograms of cocaine from Panama, some of which was sold to the Hells Angels. Later that year, Matticks and Lekkas imported 4037 kilograms of hash and sold 1500 kilograms to the Angels. Another consignment in October 2000 brought in 5485 kilograms of hash, but this was also seized by police. Their last shipment of 9000 kilograms landed at the Montreal port in February 2001. In a little over a year, Matticks and Lekkas orchestrated eight shipments through the port, which brought more than 44,000 kilograms of hashish and 265 kilograms of cocaine into Montreal. Police estimated that once on the street, the drugs had a value of around $2 billion. On August 6, 2001, Matticks pleaded guilty to drug charges and received a 12-year sentence. While in jail, he was hit with a bill for $2.1 million from the Quebec government for taxes owed on his drug sales (Cherry, 2005: 181–82; *Globe and Mail*, April 23, 2004; *Montreal Gazette*, August 9, 2002; Sher & Marsden, 2003: 336; Sûreté du Quebec Communiqué, December 4, 2002).

Following the conviction of Gerald Matticks, veteran crime reporter Michel Auger wrote that despite the jail term, "his people are still there." Auger was referring to the West End Gang's influence at the Port of Montreal, which was still intact despite the recent convictions. Sure enough, on May 10, 2006, the RCMP seized 989 bales of hashish, weighing around 22,500 kilograms off of a ship that departed from Angola in southern Africa and was destined for the Port of Montreal. The hash had been transported part of the way by an "undercover" ship chartered by the RCMP and crewed by police officers. Once in Montreal, a controlled delivery of the hash was made by police to a home about 50 kilometres southeast of Montreal. Three men were arrested—Peter Toman, his son Andrew, and Sidney Lallouz—all from Montreal and all affiliated with the West End Gang, according to the RCMP. The three men were convicted and sentenced to terms ranging from two years for Andrew Toman to 11 years for his father, who police called the mastermind behind the operation (Canada NewsWire, June 5, 2006; *Montreal Gazette*, August 9, 2002, June 6, 2006, September 26, 2006).

Despite the arrests, the remnants of the West End Gang continue to be involved in importing hashish through Montreal. In April 2012, nine Montreal-area residents were charged in connection with a number of seizures of hashish between March and November 2010 that eventually totalled an astounding 43,000 kilograms (worth an estimated $860 million). The RCMP began their investigation in early 2010 when Canada Border Services agents found tonnes of hash hidden in containers at the ports of Halifax and Montreal. Eight men were charged with conspiracy as well as importing and possessing cannabis resin for the purpose of trafficking. Among those arrested were two men who are listed as members of the International Longshoremen's Association, a union that represents workers at the Port of Montreal. Due to the sheer size of the hash shipments and the collusion of port employees, police allege Montreal's West End Gang was involved. Police say that the members of the West End Gang brought the hash in Pakistan and from there it was hidden in coffee and clothes shipments that were then sent to several European cities before ending up in Montreal. When the hash arrived in Canada, corrupt workers checking containers at the Port of Montreal alerted the West End Gang their shipment was ready. Police believe the cache of drugs was divided up and then shipped throughout North America (Canadian Broadcasting Corporation, April 19, 2012; CBC News, April 19, 2012; *Montreal Gazette*, April 19, 2012).

Since that time, customs agents and police continue to seize huge shipments of hashish imported through marine ports in Quebec and Nova Scotia. In May 2014, the CBSA seized 858 kilograms of hashish at its Port of Montreal container examination facility after having targeted a container arriving from Morocco. In July, the CBSA seized another 209 kilograms of hash, hidden in boxes of chocolate, at the Montreal Trudeau

International Airport (Government of Canada News Release, July 24, 2014, August 15, 2014). On December 10, 2015, Canada Border Services agents at the Port of Montreal seized more than 1300 kilograms of suspected hashish. The drugs were found in a marine container arriving from Malawi filled with floorboards and wooden handcrafted furniture (Canadian Border Services Agency News Release, December 24, 2015).

SYNTHETIC (CHEMICAL) DRUGS

Cocaine, heroin, and cannabis are all derived from naturally occurring plants. The underground drug market is also characterized by an ever-expanding array of **synthetic drugs**, which are wholly made up of chemicals. As discussed in chapter 7, the Outlaws and Satan's Choice motorcycle gangs established Canada as illegal synthetic drug producers in the late 1960s and 1970s, when they began manufacturing "Canadian Blue," a sedative made up of diazepam. Soon the Hells Angels and their puppet clubs also became involved, and subsequent raids on synthetic drug labs in Ontario resulted in the seizure of LSD, PCP, and methamphetamines. In 1982, the RCMP ended a two-year undercover operation with the arrests of 22 people, most of whom were members of the Outlaws or the Hells Angels. Along with the arrests, police seized 51 pounds of phencyclidine powder, 10,787 PCP tablets, and 34,800 tabs of LSD (*Montreal Gazette*, October 9, 1982). When a laboratory in Madoc, Ontario, was busted in 1983, police said they found enough chemicals to make methamphetamines worth $3.6 million. Members of Toronto's Satan's Choice and Para-Dice Riders chapters were arrested in that raid (*Toronto Star*, September 20, 1983). In 1984, Toronto police raided another outlaw biker lab and seized about 2.8 kilograms of methamphetamine with a street value of $4 million, arresting a chemist and his assistant in the process (Criminal Intelligence Service Canada, 1985: 22). In July 1985, Quebec provincial police showed off a laboratory they claim was responsible for producing part of the $8 million worth of synthetic drugs seized at Hells Angels hiding places across Quebec the month before. The lab, which was set up in a Montreal home, was capable of producing 15 pounds of methamphetamines a week, which could have generated an annual revenue of $25 million. Police estimated the cost of the lab equipment and chemicals needed to produce the drug was a mere $3000 (*Montreal Gazette*, July 10, 1985). In its national drug estimates for 1987, the RCMP wrote that outlaw motorcycle gangs in Quebec are "believed to be responsible for much of Canada's PCP production, while the gangs located in Ontario are active in the production of methamphetamine" (Royal Canadian Mounted Police, 1987b: 8).

Beginning in the early 1980s, Willie Obront, once the financial brains of the Cotroni Mafia family, became involved in a network that produced illegal sedatives also made up of diazepam. Most of the drugs were exported to Florida where Obront and other some Quebec mobsters had relocated. In 1987, police raided two secret laboratories that were manufacturing the counterfeit pills in Quebec, resulting in the confiscation of approximately 1 million diazepam tablets, as well as 34 kilograms of diazepam powder, which could have produced several million more tablets. The RCMP estimated that between 1981 and 1986 these two pill factories supplied the United States with approximately 13.5 million illegal pills (Royal Canadian Mounted Police, 1987b: 7). Since these initial forays, clandestine synthetic drug production has increased significantly in Canada. In particular, there has been a surge in the domestic product of MDMA and "crystal meth" as well as a spike in the importation of chemicals used to produce these synthetic drugs.

MDMA

By the early 1990s, Canadian law enforcement agencies began intercepting imports of a new "designer drug" that had already gained widespread popularity in Europe. The pharmacological name of the drug is **methylenedioxymethamphetamine**, but it is commonly referred to by its abbreviation **MDMA** or by its street name **ecstasy**. Ecstasy comes in a pill form and generally contains between 70 and 120 milligrams of MDMA. The profit margin for MDMA is extremely high: during the mid-1990s, one ecstasy pill selling for $35 to $40 cost between 50 cents to $2 to produce. Throughout the decade, most of Canada's supply of MDMA was imported from the Netherlands and Belgium by couriers arriving on commercial air flights. In 1999, for example, seven separate seizures at Pearson Airport in Toronto netted 12,925 pills. In February 2000, two Hamilton teenagers arriving on an Air Canada flight from France were caught at Pearson airport body-packing more than 34,800 pills. Another 73,000 pills were discovered following body searches of five people returning to Canada from France between January 15 and February 1, 2000. On May 4 of the same year, 144,000 ecstasy pills were found at Montreal's Dorval airport stashed inside computers that had arrived on a cargo jet from Belgium. On May 17, 2000, the RCMP at Pearson airport found 170,000 tablets hidden in crude body packs strapped to three passengers who had just flown in from Rotterdam. In December 2000, the RCMP seized another 150,000 MDMA tablets in Toronto that had been shipped via a courier company from Brussels by an Israeli drug-trafficking organization. The shipment was destined for the United States. In May 2001, almost 860,000 tablets were seized from an air cargo shipment to Canada declared as bed sheets (*Globe and Mail*, May 18, 2000; Royal Canadian Mounted Police, 2002c; *Toronto Sun*, May 11, 2000; United States Drug Enforcement Administration, 2001).

In addition to imported ecstasy, Canadian police also had to contend with the domestic production of MDMA. In June 1999, the RCMP dismantled a laboratory in Sainte-Julie, Quebec, that had sufficient chemicals to produce 750,000 ecstasy tablets. In October of that year, police raided a laboratory in Chilliwack, British Columbia, with a potential to produce two million tablets. A month later, two MDMA labs were discovered in Ontario, the first in a rural area near Hawkesbury and the second in a large apartment complex in Mississauga. Eight MDMA labs were discovered by Canadian police in 2000, and between November 2002 and July 2005 police dismantled 17 labs in midwestern Ontario alone. In July 2003, police busted an ecstasy lab in

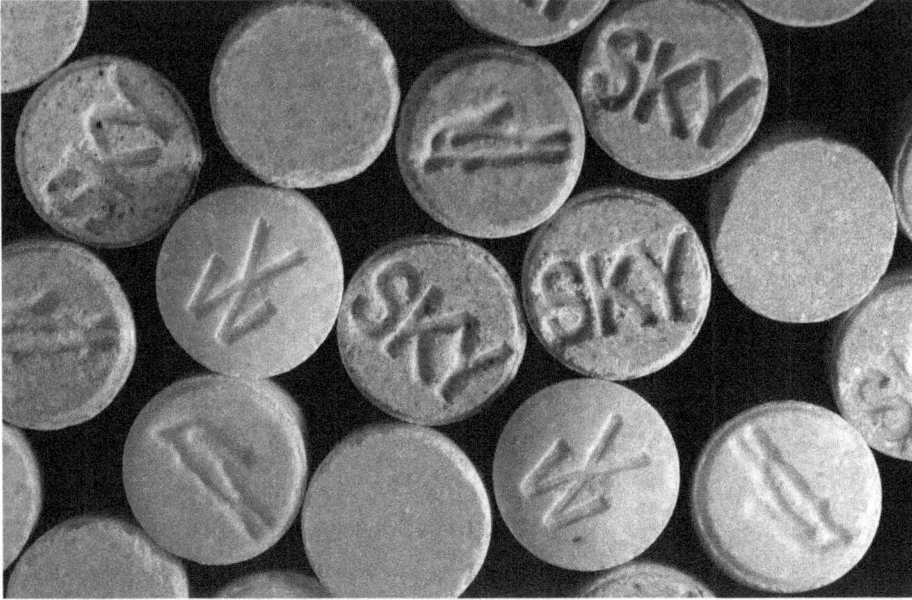

Photo 11.14: Ecstasy tablets

Source: US Drug Enforcement Administration, via Wikimedia Commons

the basement of a middle-class Scarborough home, confiscating 93,000 pills and more than 100 kilograms of powder, which police believe was a combination of ecstasy and methamphetamine that could produce more than 800,000 pills. Later that summer, Canada Customs agents at the port of Montreal found 260 kilograms of MDMA powder, enough to produce 2.6 million pills. The discovery was made aboard a freighter that had originated in Belgium and was ultimately destined for British Columbia, where the powder supposedly would be pressed into pills. A controlled delivery was made to Vancouver by rail and when it arrived on the west coast, police arrested its recipient, Chi Fai Leung of Burnaby, who was charged with possession for the purposes of trafficking (Canada Customs News Release, December 11, 2003; Royal Canadian Mounted Police, 2000a: 9, 2001; *Toronto Star*, July 30, 2003).

On June 27, 2005, Vancouver police removed toxic chemicals from an illegal drug lab housed in a multi-million-dollar home in the affluent neighbourhood of West Point Grey. Inside police found 85 litres of solvents, 40 litres of muriatic acid, 80 kilograms of red phosphorous, along with heating equipment and condenser tubes (*Kitchener-Waterloo Record*, June 25, 2005; *The Province*, June 28, 2005; *St. Mary's Journal*, June 29, 2005; *Vancouver Sun*, June 28, 2005). Also in June of that year, Calgary police made one of the largest ecstasy busts ever in that province, seizing 213,000 tablets worth about $4.25 million during a search of a home. The seizure was the result of an eight-month investigation that was initiated after police learned a shipment of ecstasy was coming to

Calgary by land from Vancouver. The 250-milligram ecstasy tablets were laced with 20 milligrams of methamphetamine, which is supposed to increase the intensity of the high. In addition to the drugs, $25,000 cash, two stun guns, a semi-automatic rifle with a partially loaded clip, and body armour were seized from the residence. One 32-year-old man, Hui Xu (a.k.a. Phillip Tu), was charged (Canadian Press, August 17, 2005; *Globe and Mail*, August 18, 2005).

Secret drug labs have also been discovered in other parts of British Columbia. In September 2014, the RCMP in Mission announced that investigators discovered a total of approximately 60 kilograms of ecstasy—enough for 600,000 individual doses—which would be worth up to $3 million on the street. That month, Mission Fire and Rescue Service crews were called to a building for a suspected structure fire. While smoke was billowing from the structure, the first responders found only a small fire; much of the smoke was being produced from a chemical reaction. After recognizing products commonly used in clandestine drug labs, firefighters evacuated people from the building as well as from several nearby businesses. The RCMP confirmed the existence of the drug lab, saying it may be the biggest one ever found in the province. They also said the lab was storing enough volatile chemicals to level a city block in the event of an explosion. "It's a large-scale operation and it's sophisticated as well," RCMP Staff Sergeant Rob Dixon said. "It looks like it's been established for some time" (CBC News, September 10, 2014; *Mission Record*, September 10, 2014).

Methamphetamine (Crystal Meth)

In addition to ecstasy, Canadian police also have to contend with the domestic production of **crystal meth**, the street name for a popular smokable version of **methamphetamine**. Meth is made by mixing various forms of amphetamine or derivatives with other chemicals to boost its potency. Ephedrine or pseudoephedrine, which is found in many cough medications, is often used as the basis for the production of the drug. The meth "cook" extracts ingredients from those medications and to increase its strength may combine the substance with chemicals such as drain cleaner, battery acid, lantern fuel, or antifreeze.

In a 2000 report on drug trafficking in Canada, the RCMP wrote, "Underground methamphetamine laboratories, which seem to be more prevalent in Western Canada than in the East, are operated primarily by independent entrepreneurs and outlaw motorcycle gang associates. Of the 19 clandestine laboratories investigated in British Columbia in 1999, twelve were manufacturing methamphetamine. American producers of methamphetamine often take advantage of Canada's lack of precursor chemical-related legislation and come here to purchase ingredients. Some even stay to manufacture methamphetamine before returning to the United States" (Royal Canadian Mounted Police, 2000a: 10). Today, Chinese criminal networks are the largest producers, distributors, and exporters of methamphetamine in Canada. Police intelligence indicates that more than half of Canada's production of methamphetamine occurs in British Columbia.

Photo 11.15: Crystal meth rock

Source: Psychonaught, via Wikimedia Commons

Canada as a Synthetic Drug Source Country

As with marijuana, the production of synthetic drugs in Canada is not just for domestic consumption: Canada is now exporter of MDMA and crystal meth. In its 2005 *International Narcotics Control Strategy Report*, the US Department of State declared that the sharp increase in the production of ecstasy north of the border had created conditions "for Canada to become a major U.S. supplier of this dangerous drug." According to the Department of State, criminal groups prefer to locate their ecstasy labs in Canada because, unlike the United States, there is no requirement to register pill presses, which are imported legally from China and the United States into Canada. Federal penalties for ecstasy offences in the United States are also much harsher than Canadian criminal penalties (United States Department of State, 2005). In its 2010 report, the UN-affiliated International Narcotics Control Board stated that Canada supplies a "significant share" of the international market for methamphetamine and is also a "major source" internationally of MDMA (as cited in the *National Post*, March 2, 2011).

The growing frequency of MDMA seizures by American authorities at Canadian border crossings only corroborates these conclusions. Between January and May 2005, American customs agents along the Washington State border seized more than 500,000 doses of ecstasy that were being smuggled in from British Columbia. This amount was nearly double the 258,026 pills seized in 2004 and more than ten times the 2003 total of 47,686. On May 9, two men from Abbotsford were arrested after they attempted to smuggle 48,000 ecstasy pills across the border (*Abbotsford Times*, May 13, 2005; *The Province*, May 12, 2005). On June 12, American border agents in Washington State arrested a man and a woman and seized 167,000 ecstasy pills that were being smuggled in a pickup truck (*Vancouver Sun*, June 17, 2005). On June 23, 2005, two Quebec men were arrested in New York state with 350,000 ecstasy tablets and 15 kilograms of cocaine. According to the US Drug Enforcement Administration, the two men were part of an organization that was "providing ecstasy directly from the source and going to wholesale distributors in the New York City area" (*Montreal Gazette*, June 25, 2005). On August 1, 94,000 ecstasy tablets were discovered in a car driven by a Windsor man that was entering the United States through the Detroit–Windsor Tunnel. On August 12, another 204,000 pills were intercepted entering the United States by ferry from Walpole Island (CBC News, September 6, 2005).

By the end of 2005, approximately 2.4 million MDMA tablets were seized at US border points in New York, Michigan, and Washington. "The continuing rise in domestic Ecstasy production has given Canada an increased role as a source country in both the domestic and international markets," the RCMP wrote in its 2005 drug intelligence report. "This was confirmed in 2005 by escalated cross-border MDMA trafficking from Canada to the United States and overseas smuggling of MDMA and methamphetamine, particularly to Japan and Australia" (Royal Canadian Mounted Police, 2006: 11–12).

In 2009, two Japanese students were arrested at Vancouver International Airport after 47,000 ecstasy pills with the "Chanel" logo were seized from their luggage (*Toronto Sun*, January 28, 2012). They were accused of smuggling the drugs back to Japan. This case provides a glimpse into the emergence of Pacific Rim countries as an emerging destination for Canadian-produced synthetic drugs. In 2013, the Combined Forces Special Enforcement Unit in British Columbia announced they dismantled a drug-trafficking organization that smuggled $35 million worth of methamphetamine and cocaine between Canada and Australia. CFSEU officials said the two people arrested in British Columbia were linked to a warehouse in Port Coquitlam where police seized a kilogram of cocaine and a kilogram of crystal meth. Both are also alleged to be associates of a Hells Angels member. According to a CFSEU spokesperson, "This complex investigation revealed that in addition to the national distribution of drugs, the scope extended beyond Canada's borders and this network was shipping drugs, primarily methamphetamine and cocaine, to Australia, possibly since 2009." Police in Canada began their investigation of the drug-trafficking group and its Canadian operations in May 2012. Based on this investigation, the CFSEU shared information with the Australian Federal Police, which led to their interception of 45.5 kilograms of methamphetamine and 5.2 kilograms of cocaine hidden in furniture imported from Canada in December 2012. Two Canadians were charged in Australia at the time (*Vancouver Sun*, October 21, 2013). One of the reasons Australia and other Pacific Rim countries have become such an attractive destination for Canadian drug smugglers is that the street values of cocaine and synthetic drugs are far higher there, resulting in much greater profits than if the drugs were sold in Canada. Canadian traffickers also have "significant connections" with Australian outlaw biker gangs and other criminal organizations, according to the Australian Crime Commission (as cited in Canadian Press, August 31, 2014).

Border officials not only have to contend with the export of synthetic drugs produced in Canada, but they also have to be on the lookout for the precursor chemicals that are imported into this country. The vast majority of these chemicals are smuggled from China into the country through the Port of Vancouver and even smaller ports along the BC coast. In October 2012, for instance, the CBSA at the Prince Rupert Marine Container Examination Facility in British Columbia announced the seizure of 14 tonnes of four different kinds of precursor chemicals for the production of drugs like methamphetamine and MDMA. The chemicals originated in China, and, according to the CBSA, this was the third seizure of precursor chemicals at Prince Rupert Port in the last two years (Canada Border Services Agency News Release, October 24, 2012). On April 19, 2013, CBSA officers at the Port of Vancouver Container Examination Facility seized over 2000 litres of hypophosphorous acid, a precursor chemical used in the production of methamphetamine (Canada Border Services Agency News Release, April 30, 2013).

CONCLUSION TO PART III

The third part of this book described and analyzed a sample of the profit-oriented organized crimes that are undertaken in Canada. Based upon what was documented in the last three chapters, a number of salient features of these Canadian organized crimes can be identified:

- Organized crimes encompass both predatory and consensual crimes as well as those that can be considered as hybrids (i.e., the crime may take place between two consenting adults, but ultimately one of these parties may be considered a victim).
- The business of organized crime—in particular, those crimes that are considered consensual in nature—includes trafficking in both goods and services.
- The business of organized crime includes transactions in the underground economy and the legitimate economy.
- Extensive underground markets exist for a wide range of illegal goods and services as well as legal contraband that has been diverted there.
- Smuggling has long been connected to a number of dominant organized crimes in this country (e.g., drug trafficking, contraband cigarettes, and human trafficking).

- Organized criminal activities in this country are facilitated by the corruption of public- and private-sector actors, although corruption is not absolutely necessary to carrying out most organized crimes.
- Drug trafficking is a staple of many organized crime groups and networks in this country.
- Criminal groups are extremely opportunistic in developing and marketing new illicit goods, services, and markets.
- Organized crimes in Canada frequently cross provincial borders as well as national borders.

None of the organized crimes described in this part of the book, or the features listed above, are unique to Canada. As such, one cannot really conclude there is a distinctive Canadian take on organized criminal activities. With that said, there is one remaining issue that characterizes organized crimes in Canada that has not been fully addressed: the different roles that Canada plays in the global theatre of transnational organized crimes. These various roles include the following: a consumer of international illegal goods and services; a source of counterfeit consumer products and mass marketing fraud; and a source, destination, and transit country for international migrant smuggling, human trafficking, and illegal drugs.

Canada's role in transnational organized crimes has often been misrepresented as largely a consumer of illegal goods smuggled into the country (in particular, drugs and contraband cigarettes). Yet, Canada has also emerged as an international source of illegal goods. For most of its history, the sole destination of exported, Canadian-made illicit goods was the United States. During the nineteenth century, Canada was a source of counterfeit US currency as well as opium processed in British Columbia. A good portion of both of these illegal goods were smuggled into the United States. During the 1920s, this country was the main supplier of illegal liquor imported into a dry America. Between the 1930s and 1970s, Canada was a major transit country through which heroin entered the United States and also played a central role in transborder bookmaking operations (facilitated through the wire service). Around the 1950s, Canada was again identified as a major source of counterfeit American currency and was also accused of being home to numerous boiler room operations that pressured and bamboozled Canadian and American citizens to purchase worthless stock. During the late 1960s, Canada emerged as a source country for synthetic drugs produced by outlaw motorcycle gangs, and beginning in the 1990s, British Columbia became a significant exporter of high-grade marijuana to the United States. Today, counterfeit consumer products, marijuana, and synthetic drugs (ecstasy and crystal meth) produced in Canada are exported to countries outside of North America.

There are a number of reasons why Canada has become a global player in transnational organized crimes. The first reason may simply be due to this country's proximity to the United States. In this regard, Canada's role in transborder crime is strongly tied to smuggling, which, as indicated above, is central to many organized crimes in this country.

What may make Canada unique among other countries as far as conditions for smuggling is concerned is twofold: first, this country has the world's longest undefended border with the United States (the world's largest national black market for illegal goods), and a population where more than 80 percent live less than 100 kilometres from this border (which provides a pool of labour, resources, and expertise to smuggle goods out of the country).

Another reason Canada has become a global emitter of illegal goods and predatory criminal activities is because transnational organized crime groups have established a presence in this country. Their goal is not simply to supply the domestic market, but to capitalize on Canada's proximity to America's vast underground markets and to obfuscate their smuggling through the extensive legitimate trade between the two countries. This is particularly true of Chinese criminal networks, which are active in smuggling Canadian-produced cannabis and synthetic drugs into the United States, while also using Canada as a transit country for Southeast Asian heroin and migrants illegally transported south of the border. These criminal networks also take advantage of Canada's extensive trading relationship with China, and, concomitantly, the role the Port of Vancouver plays as a North American portal for precursor chemicals (for synthetic drug production), Southeast Asian heroin, counterfeit consumer goods, and contraband cigarettes exported from China.

In sum, similar to the conclusions reached in part II of this book, an analysis of organized crimes in Canada does not reveal anything that may be distinctively Canadian except perhaps for how its long, unguarded border with the United States has contributed to establishing Canada as a major source and transit country for smuggling. Even this conclusion must be tempered by the fact that Canada is not really unique in this regards because the same situation applies to Mexico.

KEY TERMS

Cannabis satvia	Marijuana
China White	MDMA
Coca	Methamphetamine
Cocaine	Methylenedioxymethamphetamine
Crystal meth	Moral entrepreneurship
Ecstasy	Morphine
Fentanyl	Opium
French Connection	Opium Wars
Golden Crescent	Poly-drug trafficking
Golden Triangle	Psychedelic era
Grow operation (grow-op)	Purity
Hashish	Synthetic drugs
Heroin	THC
L'Union Corse	West End Gang

REVIEW QUESTIONS

1. What is the significance of drug trafficking in the study of organized crime in Canada and internationally?
2. What are some of the significant milestones in the history of illegal drug smuggling and trafficking affecting Canada?
3. Which illegal drugs are dominant in Canada's black market?
4. What organized crime genres are involved in drug trafficking? Which illegal drugs are typically trafficked by the different genres?
5. What are some recent trends and developments concerning illegal drugs and trafficking in Canada?
6. What are the source countries for illegal drugs imported into Canada?
7. Explain the history, nature, and scope of domestic illegal drug production in Canada.
8. Explain Canada's role as an international source country for illegal drugs.

FURTHER READINGS

Charbonneau, J.-P. (1976). *The Canadian Connection: An Expose on the Mafia in Canada and Its International Ramifications.* Montreal: Optimum.

Jenner, M. (2014). Drug trafficking as a transnational crime, in P.L. Reichel & J. Albanese (Eds.), *Handbook of Transnational Crime and Justice* (2nd Ed.) (pp. 65–84). Los Angeles: Sage Publications.

Lamothe, L., & Nicaso, A. (2002). *Bloodlines: Project Omerta and the Fall of the Mafia's Royal Family.* Toronto: HarperCollins.

Paoli, L., Spapens, T., & Fijnaut, C. (2010). Drug trafficking, in F. Brookman, M. Maguire, H. Pierpoint, & T. Bennett (Eds.), *Handbook on Crime* (pp. 626–50). Portland, OR: Willan Publishing.

Reuter, P. (2014). Drug markets and organized crime, in L. Paoli (Ed.), *The Oxford Handbook of Organized Crime* (pp. 359–80). Oxford, New York: Oxford University Press.

United Nations Office on Drugs and Crime. (2015). *World Drug Report.* New York: United Nations Office on Drugs and Crime.

PART IV

CONTROLLING ORGANIZED CRIME

The final part of this textbook examines the theory and practice involved in controlling organized crime. Chapter 12 describes and analyzes organized crime control in conceptual terms, focusing on underlying principles, theories, objectives, and strategies. Chapter 13 then explores OC control in Canada with emphasis on criminal justice policies (laws and legislation) as well as the principal state agencies (and the units and programs in these agencies) tasked with combatting this criminal problem. While the focus of both chapters is Canada, information on OC control measures implemented in the United States have also been included for comparative purposes.

A major thesis of this textbook is that the nature and scope of organized crime in Canada is reflective of and offers some insight into Canadian society. The same can be said of efforts to combat this problem; the type of interventions implemented by governments to combat organized crime (and crime in general) provides a glimpse into broader governance issues. This may be especially apparent when comparing Canada's response to serious crimes—which some criticize as wanting in terms of criminal laws—to legislative measures adopted in the United States, which are far more punitive.

As in the other chapters, students are encouraged to critically analyze the theories, concepts, and application of organized crime control measures discussed in the next two chapters. Students should scrutinize the efficacy of OC control initiatives in light of what they have learned thus far in regards to the causes, nature, scope, and impact of OC in Canada. A particularly salient question is whether the scope and nature of the control measures adopted in Canada are commensurate with the causes, complexion, scope, and harm of organized crime in this country. This critical analysis is especially significant in light of the argument that the extent of the problem far exceeds the scope of Canada's resources and laws and that the containment of organized criminality, let alone its eradication, is an unachievable goal.

CRITICAL THINKING EXERCISE

Analyzing traditional approaches to combatting OC is particularly amenable to nurturing one's critical thinking skills. This is because the dominant prohibition and enforcement model—in which certain goods and substances are criminalized and then subject to criminal law enforcement—is so controversial. This traditional enforcement approach is epitomized by the highly contentious war on drugs, which has been roundly criticized as ineffective in combatting both the supply of and demand for illegal drugs (and some say has done more harm than good). As you read through the next two chapters, critically analyze both traditional and alternative approaches to combatting organized crime in Canada, including their assumptions, theoretical groundings, social construction, and actual effectiveness, while also acknowledging the inherent challenges in preventing and controlling organized crime.

12 ORGANIZED CRIME CONTROL IN THEORY: THEORETICAL OVERVIEW, CONCEPTS, OBJECTIVES, AND STRATEGIES

CHAPTER OUTLINE

- Introduction and Overview
- Organized Crime Control Objectives
- Traditional Organized Crime Enforcement: The Prohibition/Enforcement Model
- Enforcement Operational Tactics and Techniques
- Alternative Organized Crime Control Tactics and Techniques
- Best Practices in Organized Crime Control

LEARNING OBJECTIVES

After reading this chapter, you should have a thorough understanding of the following:

- The broad objectives of organized crime control
- The difference between organized crime control and organized crime enforcement
- The traditional organized crime prohibition/enforcement model
- Traditional organized crime enforcement strategies
- Common enforcement (operational) tactics and techniques
- Alternative (non–criminal justice) organized crime control tactics and techniques and how they differ from traditional criminal justice approaches
- Best practices in organized crime control

INTRODUCTION AND OVERVIEW

The purpose of this chapter is to provide a conceptual overview of organized crime control measures. This includes describing and analyzing OC control objectives, strategies, techniques, and tactics that predominate and the assumptions, theories, principles, and concepts that guide them. The term **control** is used instead of the narrower concept of **enforcement** for two reasons. First, while measures to combat the problem of OC are overwhelmingly characterized by criminal law enforcement, there are organizations and strategies that fall outside the criminal justice system. Second, it is almost universally recognized that the goal of eradicating organized crime is unattainable, so the emphasis is now placed on simply controlling it—that is, managing and reducing the harms that OC inflicts on society. Within this context, chapter 12 divides OC control measures into two broad categories: (1) traditional organized crime enforcement, and (2) alternative organized crime control tactics and techniques. The first category can be further divided into two categories: (a) the strategies necessary to achieve the enforcement goals, and (b) enforcement operational tactics and techniques used as part of each broad enforcement strategy. This conceptual breakdown of organized crime control is depicted in Figure 12.1.

In addition to broad control strategies, OC control can be broken down by its different targets. In carrying out an organized crime prevention or enforcement strategy, criminal justice agencies generally target one or more of the following: (1) individual offenders or groups of offenders, (2) criminal activities, (3) the fruits of the criminal activity, (4) consumers, and (5) underground markets.

Efforts to combat OC in North America and around the world are overwhelmingly based on the criminal justice enforcement approach. As Naylor (2003a: 36) notes,

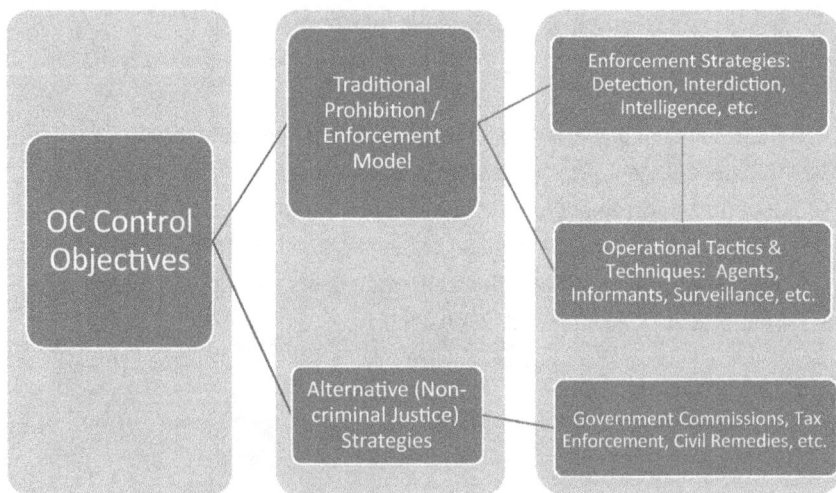

Figure 12.1: An organized crime control conceptual framework

the traditional criminal justice system appears to have fallen short in containing OC and minimizing the harms it imposes on societies. However, the reaction has been to double-down on the traditional enforcement model, which means "there are frequent calls for dramatic new investigatory and prosecutorial powers. These take the form, among others, of increased freedom for police to use illegal means in conducting undercover operations, measures to trace and seize the proceeds of crime, and laws to make membership in a criminal 'organization' a crime per se." Paoli (2014a: 2) adds that there have also been "numerous regional and international initiatives, meant to foster police and justice cooperation in the fight against organized crime, and many of these have had large international support." Paoli and Vander Beken (2014: 15) also acknowledge that "since the 1990s, the majority of governments, at least in the developed world, and many international organizations, including the UN, have adopted bills, decrees, action plans, or international treaties specifically targeting organized crime, often foreseeing extensive new prosecutorial powers to law enforcement agencies—as the United States had already done in the 1960s and 1970s."

The introduction of new punitive laws or international conventions and the expansion of law enforcement resources and powers have been criticized as being premised upon faulty assumptions, a lack of theoretical grounding, and the absence of any proven techniques that actually work to contain organized crime. Moreover, some lawmakers and agencies have been accused of inflating the threat posed by (transnational) organized crime in order to "increase their competencies and powers and/or to harmonize and extend criminal laws and law enforcement procedural powers" across different countries (Paoli & Vander Beken, 2014: 15). The United States and United Nations have been particularly singled out by critics for advocating for the "Americanization" of organized crime enforcement internationally, which includes pressuring countries to adopt criminal laws as punitive as those implemented in the United States while continuing to emphasize prohibition and pursue the war on drugs.

In more recent years, governments in North America and elsewhere have implemented alternative approaches to combatting organized crime, many of which fall outside the criminal justice system. These alternative approaches have arisen largely due to the failures and limitations of the criminal justice-centred approach, although the vast majority of government resources continue to be dedicated to traditional enforcement measures. The specific strategies and tactics used as part of the traditional (criminal justice) enforcement measures and alternative (**extra-judicial**) approaches is summarized in Table 12.1.

ORGANIZED CRIME CONTROL OBJECTIVES

Ideally, the ultimate goal in any overall effort to combat OC is its eradication. This would include incarcerating or otherwise debilitating criminal offenders, dismantling or incapacitating criminal groups and networks, eliminating organized and other serious

Table 12.1: Traditional Criminal Justice Tactics and Alternative Approaches to Organized Crime Control

Traditional Enforcement Strategies and Operational Tactics	Alternative (Non-criminal Justice) Control Approaches
Strategies	Government commissions
Detection/interdiction	Tax enforcement
Investigative function	Currency and suspicious activity reporting
Intelligence function	Government regulatory agencies
Prosecution	Civil remedies (in particular, civil
Punishment	forfeiture)
	The armed forces
Operational Tactics	National and foreign security intelligence
Witnesses, informants, and agents (including immunity and witness protection programs)	agencies
	Citizen-based action
Surveillance	Private-sector initiatives
Undercover operations	
Controlled deliveries	
Search and seizure (obtaining physical evidence)	
Proceeds of crime enforcement	
The urban and highway patrol function	
Multi-agency co-operation and coordination	

crimes, and wiping out the underground markets through which illegal (and legal) goods and services are bought and sold. As should be apparent by now, most countries, including Canada, will never be rid of organized crime, illicit markets, or the demand for prohibited goods and services that help sustain both. Edelhertz, Cole, and Berk (1984: 51–52) argue that OC is not an adversary that can be targeted, attacked, and defeated once and for all. Instead, the best we can hope for is to contain the problem. "It is a form of group behaviour that can be expected to surface again and again in response to new opportunities or to markets for illicit goods or services. Since total victory and perpetual safety are not attainable, states engaged in enforcement programs should strive to create responses and conditions that will minimize the threat to their citizens and maximize the integrity of their persons and property. We call this objective **containment** ..."

One enforcement strategy that is expressly geared toward containment is referred to as **incident reduction**, which consist of rapid responses by law enforcement agencies to the first detected instances of an illegal act so that the offenders do not expand, become more powerful and more organized, or inflict more harm on victims or society-at-large. Incident reduction strategies epitomize the OC containment approach in that they attempt to limit the proliferation, power, criminal activities, violence, and territorial expansion of criminal syndicates. An incident reduction strategy that targets the territorial expansion of an organized crime group may be geared toward restricting its ability to move into the territory or criminal market of a competing criminal group. While this may enhance the monopoly of the criminal group currently in that territory or market, it can help to circumvent any violence associated with turf wars and allows law enforcement to focus on one criminal group, as opposed to multiple criminal groups (Edelhertz, Cole, & Berk, 1984: 58).

Deterring crime and potential offenders is a fundamental goal of the criminal justice system. While deterrence may be seen as a goal in and of itself, deterring offenders and criminal organizations from committing crimes is really a strategy that aims to help society reach a broader goal—the prevention, reduction, and containment of crime. The concept of deterrence as a means to control crime is premised on the rational choice theory of offender decision-making, which argues that criminals make (opportunistic) choices and decisions in the course of planning and carrying out a criminal act, and thus can be deterred (Clarke & Cornish, 1985). Thus, a major goal of the punishment component of the criminal justice system is to make a criminal act less attractive to and less likely for the motivated, rationally thinking offender. In theory, sanctions such as incarceration, fines, and even capital punishment are said to deter those convicted from re-offending while dissuading other would-be offenders from committing similar crimes.

Criminal justice deterrence strategies are usually aimed at decreasing the potential reward from or increasing the potential penalty for specific criminal activities and behaviours. One example of a deterrence strategy specific to organized crime is criminal laws that provide harsher penalties for crimes committed as part of a criminal organization. Proceeds of crime enforcement and asset forfeiture, in which the state confiscates the ill-gotten gains of criminal offenders, is an example of a deterrence strategy that is premised on both punishment and reward-reduction. The appropriation of offenders' assets is meant to punish them but is also meant to serve as a deterrent by reducing the financial rewards of (profit-oriented) crimes. Monetary fines levied by the courts or regulatory agencies are supposed to serve the same deterrent effect.

The deterrent effect of criminal justice strategies and sanctions on organized criminal offenders has been the subject of intense scrutiny as research and critics argue that the prospect of arrest and imprisonment (or even execution) does not serve to deter the most serious and chronic offenders (Nagin, 2013). Some offenders may not be deemed sufficiently rational to be deterred from committing crimes or may suffer from a number of cognitive or behavioural deficits that obstruct them from adapting more pro-social behaviour and desisting from crime. Other serious and chronic offenders are not deterred because they simply do not want to leave this deviant lifestyle or criminal subculture that is to them very exciting and rewarding. Others who may want to adopt a

CRITICAL THINKING EXERCISE

Conduct your own research into the deterrent effect of (punitive) criminal justice laws on organized criminal offenders. First, begin by reviewing the theory of deterrence as well as empirical research that examines whether tough penalties actually serve to deter offenders and control crime. Second, review any theories or research pertaining to the deterrence effect of laws specific to organized crime offenders. Answer such questions as: Do punitive laws serve to deter individuals from becoming involved in profit-oriented organized criminal activities? Do tough sentences, incarceration, or asset forfeiture reduce recidivism by convicted organized criminal offenders? Finally, consider whether the profit-oriented nature of organized crimes plays a role in diluting the deterrence effect of tough criminal laws and punishment.

more pro-social lifestyle could be subject to intense pressure to remain in a particular criminal organization, market, or activity. Many offenders may be so attracted by the profit potential of lucrative organized crimes that they are willing to assume the risk and therefore are not easily deterred by the prospect of arrest and punishment.

Even the less ambitious goals of containment and deterrence appears to have failed given the proliferation of organized crime groups and networks and the ever-expanding repertoire of their illegal activities. The growing realization that the war against organized crime (and drugs) has effectively been lost speaks volumes about society's ability to control crime and to eliminate or even regulate certain vices and underground markets. For Paoli (2014a: 6), a more realistic goal is **harm reduction**— "interventions that can reduce the total harms resulting from both the organized crime phenomena and the policies aiming to control these phenomena, drawing from the realization that both organized crime actors and activities and the related policies cause harms and that bad policies may even inadvertently create opportunities for organized crime." An example of a harm reduction strategy would be to prioritize those criminal activities and groups that inflict the most harm on society (e.g., prioritizing heroin trafficking over marijuana grow-ops) while minimizing the collateral damage inflicted by drug enforcement (e.g., treating instead of jailing addicts or marginalized individuals operating as low-level dealers).

TRADITIONAL ORGANIZED CRIME ENFORCEMENT: THE PROHIBITION/ENFORCEMENT MODEL

The strategies that have traditionally been executed to combat organized crime in North America overwhelmingly fall within what can be called the **prohibition/enforcement model**. As reflected in its title, this expansive approach encompasses two fundamental elements: (1) the prohibition (criminalization) of particular goods and services by the state that are deemed personally and socially harmful, and (2) the enforcement of such laws by the state, exclusively through the criminal justice system (cops, courts, and corrections). Admittedly, the goal of the prohibition/criminalization half of this model is less about combatting organized crime and more about reducing the apparent harms of particular goods and services. Yet, as described in chapter 4, the enactment of prohibition policies by the state—the criminalization of narcotic drugs, gambling, smuggling, etc.—helps to fuel organized crime and underground markets. In this context, there is a symbiotic relationship between prohibition policies and law enforcement; because the state helps create organized crime through criminal laws it must then counteract criminal groups and markets through the one state institution normally used to deal with crime—the criminal justice system. As described in chapter 13, the stark alternative to the prohibition/enforcement model is the **legalization/regulation model**, which proponents argue will lead to a reduction in criminal groups and markets (through legalization) while state regulations and agencies minimize the harms of the now legalized goods and services.

One of the many important debates in OC enforcement is whether to focus on the criminal offenders or criminal activities. According to Marvelli and Finckenauer (2012: 511), "The traditional law enforcement approach has been to identify criminal organizations and individuals with the goal of disruption and/or prosecution." This individual-centred approach targets the leader or leaders of a particular conspiracy or organization, and is often called a **king pin investigation**. This tactic may begin with the arrests of lower-level participants in a crime or criminal group and then pressuring them to become state witnesses. "Flipping is the time-honored practice of arresting a low-level offender on a relatively minor charge with the goal of using his or her testimony against either the boss or another higher-up in the organization. Because conspiracy places a high premium on the arrested person's position in the organized crime hierarchy, the farther up that hierarchy an arrest goes, the more disruptive it is to the business of organized crime" (Lyman & Potter, 2014: 395–97). There are two significant weaknesses of the king pin approach. First, removing the leadership of a particular criminal group does not necessarily mean an end to the group or its illicit activities. As Albanese (2015: 111) puts it:

> Perhaps the biggest problem with the hierarchical model of organized crime is that it leads to the conclusion that prosecution of the "bosses" and others in control will make organized crime less prevalent and less threatening. The successful mob prosecutions of the 1980s and 1990s illustrate that this is not necessarily the case because the demand for drugs, gambling, stolen property, and a weak regulatory system provoke the emergence of illicit entrepreneurs to cater to the illegal markets or to exploit the legal marketplace. Once these entrepreneurs are removed by arrest or incarceration, others emerge because the demand remains, as do the opportunities for criminal exploitation of the legitimate marketplace.

Another weakness of the king pin approach, according to Lyman and Potter (2014: 397) is that it underestimates the adaptability of organized crime:

> Organized crime syndicates long ago learned that to be successful in a threatening legal environment, they must be prepared to adapt their structures and practices. The irony of the situation is that the more successful federal investigators and prosecutors become in incarcerating organized crime leaders, the more the industry responds by decentralizing and maintaining temporary and ephemeral working relationships. Because the headhunting approach never disables more than a small proportion of the total number of organized crime entrepreneurs at any given time, it can actually strengthen some organized crime groups by weeding out their slothful and inefficient competitors.

Alternatively, law enforcement can focus on criminal activities (e.g., interdicting drugs), although sole reliance on this strategy is not recommended because the success of a particular enforcement initiative is only achieved if one or more of the criminal offenders involved are arrested and punished in connection with the criminal activity.

The remainder of this section focuses on specific OC enforcement strategies. Whether the goals of OC enforcement are eradication or containment, a number of strategies have been developed and employed (some more than others) to combat criminal syndicates, underground markets, and serious criminal activities. Adapting a typology first developed by Edelhertz, Cole, and Berk (1984), this section examines five broad strategies used as part of the enforcement model: (1) detection and interdiction, (2) the investigative function, (3) the intelligence function, (4) prosecution, and (5) punishment. These strategies are not mutually exclusive, but interconnected and inter-dependent; the challenge to any comprehensive organized crime control program is to ensure that all of these strategies are in place, are compatible with one another, are coordinated, and are implemented with a high degree of fidelity, justice, and integrity.

Detection and Interdiction

A fundamental part of policing and law enforcement is detecting and then stopping a particular criminal act, which includes seizing illegal goods (e.g., drugs) and the conveyances (e.g., trucks) used in committing the criminal act. **Detection** and **interdiction** play a central role in all levels of policing and can be considered the most frequently used organized crime enforcement strategy in that it cuts across most other strategies and techniques listed in this chapter.

Border control agencies that guard against the illegal importation of drugs, other contraband, and migrants represent the most vivid illustration of the OC enforcement detection and interdiction function. Because it is impossible to subject every vehicle (automobile, marine, and airplane) or individual entering a country to a thorough

Case Studies: Detection and Interdiction Function at Canada's Ports of Entry

Some cases where drugs and other contraband were detected and interdicted by Canadian Border Services Agency agents through the use of intelligence, targeting, and examinations are summarized below.

- A detector dog identified more than 300 kilograms of hash oil concealed in the cradle of a yacht from Jamaica. This yacht was targeted for examination based upon its departure from a high-risk country.
- Almost 400 kilograms of cocaine were seized from a marine container at a Halifax marine port. This container was targeted for examination based upon a number of suspicious indicators: the container departed from a drug source country (Pakistan), the routing was unusual (from Pakistan to Morocco to New York to Halifax), there was no listing for the importer in the telephone directory, and the freight was prepaid in cash.
- A task force investigating drug smuggling by the Mennonite community in southern Ontario issued a number of intelligence alerts to various border points in the region. Based on this information, a primary check of a vehicle's licence plate by Canada Border Services officers resulted in a positive hit. A secondary examination of the vehicle noted the spare tire was unusually heavy. A search by detector dog resulted in a seizure of 44 kilograms of marijuana, with an estimated street value of $220,000.

search, border control agencies use certain techniques that target individuals or conveyances that may be involved in smuggling. For example, officials at border crossing points use computers containing intelligence information about known or suspected smugglers, such as licence plate numbers and names as part of their detection strategies. In addition, certain vehicles or marine vessels will be targeted based on high-risk factors, such as country of origin of the vessel or suspicious inconsistencies in their paperwork. The detection and interdiction of drugs and other contraband are facilitated by the use of technology (such as X-ray machines and ion scanners) and specially trained inspectors and detector dogs.

The detection of organized crimes and groups is much more challenging compared to more rudimentary, street-level crimes for a number of reasons. Since many organized criminal activities are consensual in nature, there is no victim to make a report to police. The violence, intimidation, and corruption tactics employed by crime groups can also be effective in dissuading victims, witnesses, and others from reporting crimes. The increasingly sophisticated techniques used to smuggle drugs and other contraband have made detection and interdiction by law enforcement agencies difficult. The insulation of the upper echelons of an OC group or the different cells of a criminal network also poses challenges for detecting the involvement of these individuals in criminal activities. In short, the unique characteristics of organized crime present inherent challenges to detection and interdiction. Not only must law enforcement agents become as sophisticated as their adversaries in attempting to detect criminal activities and interdict illegal goods or services, they must also be able to identify many individuals and crimes in order to prove the existence of an organized criminal conspiracy.

The Investigative Function

Along with interdiction, the investigative function is the bread-and-butter of organized crime enforcement. **Investigation** is a broad umbrella term that covers a wide range of techniques to identify criminal offenders and offences and to gather information and evidence used to arrest, charge, and convict them (Edelhertz, Cole, & Berk, 1984: 59). Some of the most complex, time-consuming, and resource-intensive investigations a law enforcement agency can undertake are concerned with organized crime. They are often conducted over several months or years; are preceded by intelligence gathering and strategic planning; require a pre-determined budget, which can run into the millions of dollars; integrate multiple functions, areas of expertise, and agencies; and are often multi-jurisdictional in scope. Common techniques used in an OC investigation include electronic eavesdropping, physical surveillance, physical evidence gathering and analysis, undercover operations, interviewing witnesses and suspects, and the use of informants and agents.

Organized crime investigations are presented with unique challenges due to the inherent nature of organized crimes, groups, and offenders. One of the most daunting challenges of OC enforcement is the sheer scope of some of the targeted conspiracies. This challenge is met through large-scale, project-style law enforcement investigations that target a number of offenders involved in multiple criminal acts persisting over time. The goal is to identify and charge as many conspirators as possible, with the ultimate goal of arresting the upper echelons of a criminal organization or the linchpins of a criminal network, while significantly disrupting or ending a particular criminal conspiracy or organization. Lyman (1989: 125–26) details the basic steps in an intelligence-led, project-style investigation of an organized crime conspiracy.

STEP 1:   Review any available intelligence to help determine the organized crime group's membership, structure, and criminal activities.

STEP 2:   Conduct a background check on the suspected members and associates of the criminal group by using agency files, public record checks, and informant information.

STEP 3:   Gather original intelligence data specific to the criminal conspiracy in order to identify other information on the criminal group that will be essential to the investigation, such as meeting places, methods of communication among members, criminal activities conducted, jurisdictions in which they operate, vulnerabilities of the group or individual members, etc.

STEP 4: Decide on the scope of the investigation, as well as specific techniques that will be used. Will it be an overt or covert investigation? Will it be an undercover investigation? If so, will it involve a police undercover operator or will an agent or informant be used? If surveillance is to be used, will it be electronic or physical? Will there be concurrent proceeds of crime investigation? What other organizations (law enforcement and otherwise) should be involved? Will the investigation require the participation of law enforcement agencies in other countries?

STEP 5: Draft an operational plan to address all of the above questions and detail how the investigation will be conducted (including techniques to be used), the resources required, enforcement units and/or agencies to be involved, a work plan, and a timeline.

STEP 6: Approve the operational plan and begin the investigation, emphasizing the collection of information that is to be used for evidentiary and/or intelligence purposes.

STEP 7: Once sufficient evidence has been collected, management decides the next steps in the investigation, including how it is to be concluded (e.g., how arrests are to be made).

STEP 8: Make arrests and collect the remaining physical evidence.

STEP 9: Interview the arrested subjects with a view to obtaining confessions and further evidence. Decisions are made as to providing immunity to lower-echelon members in return for their becoming witnesses for the prosecution.

STEP 10: Prepared appropriate reports for prosecutors. Disclosure is made to defence counsel.

The Intelligence Function

The United States Department of Justice (2003: 54) defines **criminal intelligence** as "information compiled, analyzed, and/or disseminated in an effort to anticipate, prevent, or monitor criminal activity." Criminal intelligence can be divided into two categories: tactical and strategic. **Tactical intelligence** (also called *operational intelligence*) is collected for the short term in support of an immediate law enforcement objective, in particular, an active investigation. **Strategic intelligence** encompasses the collection and analysis of data in support of a law enforcement agency's long-term planning, management, and threat assessments (i.e., to understand the "big picture"). Interpol touches on both when it states that "the central tasks of criminal intelligence analysis are to: help officials—senior law enforcers, policy makers and decision makers—deal more effectively with uncertainty and new challenges; provide timely warning of threats; and support operational activities and complex investigations" (Interpol website, n.d.b).

While applied to a range of criminal problems, the intelligence function is closely associated with organized crime and drug-trafficking enforcement due to the proactive need for tactical intelligence information as part of the planning stage for complex, project-style investigations or interdiction of drugs and other contraband. Strategic intelligence is needed to broadly monitor the landscape of organized criminality and illicit markets within a particular jurisdiction to identify which groups or markets pose the greatest threat and, in turn, to establish operational priorities for a law enforcement agency (or government as a whole).

Prosecution

A **prosecution** entails all the activities surrounding the preparation of a criminal case and its litigation in court. Prosecution strategies only proceed once criminal charges are laid (Edelhertz, Cole, & Berk, 1984: 60). There are unique challenges to prosecuting those involved with organized criminal associations and who commit serious offences. These include the difficulties in linking the upper echelons of criminal organizations to crimes they never physically took part in, prosecuting numerous defendants simultaneously (see mega-trials below), handling vast amounts of evidence and many witnesses (including those who are reluctant to provide testimony against organized crime figures), and having to compete against expensive and astute criminal defence lawyers. Many government justice departments and attorneys often dedicate extra resources and have formed special prosecutorial teams to deal with organized crime prosecutions.

Case Study: Mega-Trials

Reflecting the fact that multiple offenders are involved in organized crime groups and activities, provincial and federal attorneys general in Canada have used the strategy of simultaneously prosecuting several defendants involved in an organized criminal conspiracy in one criminal trial, otherwise known as a **mega-trial**. Because of the complexity of these massive cases, the danger is that they may take too long to get to trial, thereby violating the rights of the defendants to a speedy trial, as enshrined in the *Canadian Charter of Rights and Freedoms*. The collapse of at least two high-profile mega-trial court cases for this reason represents a blow to the viability of mega-trials in Canada.

In 2003, an Edmonton judge threw out charges against 11 people accused of conspiring to traffic in cocaine, saying the lengthy delay in trying the case—chiefly because federal prosecutors and the RCMP were slow in disclosing 38 banker boxes of evidence to the defence—violated the defendants' Charter rights. The men on trial were arrested in 1999 and already had charges related to participating in a criminal organization dropped by the Crown in 2001. The federal government had spent an estimated $20 million in fees for defence lawyers and the Alberta government paid $2 million to build a high-security courtroom for the case. Given the number of defendants and the complexity of the case, the Crown was expected to enter into evidence 281,000 wiretapped conversations and 180,000 pages of documents (*Globe and Mail*, September 10, 2003, September 12, 2003, September 25, 2003).

In 2013, Quebec's appeals court issued a decision that upheld a lower court decision to free 31 Hells Angels members and associates arrested and charged as a result of Operation SharQc because it would have taken too long to put them on trial. The charges were originally laid in 2009 and the defendants were ordered released by Superior Court Justice James Brunton in 2011 after he decided it would take too long for their trial dates to come around. According to the Canadian Press, "He stressed at the time his decision had nothing to do with guilt or innocence— but with the fact the justice system was ill-equipped to deal with the complex file." The released defendants were charged with drug trafficking and participation in a criminal organization (CTV News, April 11, 2013; *Montreal Gazette*, April 5, 2013; *Vancouver Sun*, April 6, 2013).

Following the collapse of the Edmonton case, University of Manitoba law professor Lee Stuesser told the media that mega-trials are too big and complex to work. Given the sheer number of defendants, charges, witnesses, and evidence introduced at a mega-trial, "They are simply too unwieldy," he said. "Prosecutors try to do too much. He said the inability of the police and the crown to disclose evidence to the defence counsel in a full and timely manner is frequently the reason that mega-trials fail" (*Globe and Mail*, September 12, 2003). Critics of mega-trials also worry that a jury may not be able to digest the hundreds of witnesses' testimonies, the tens of thousands of pieces of evidence, and the laborious wiretaps and police surveillance videos presented during a mega-trial.

CRITICAL THINKING EXERCISE

A mega-trial involving multiple defendants would seem to be perfectly suited for individuals accused of involvement in an organized criminal conspiracy. Critically analyze the use of mega-trials to prosecute individuals accused of serious (organized) criminal offences. Do you believe that the provisions of the Charter that guarantee an accused a speedy trial should be relaxed given the time needed to prepare for a complex mega-trial and the seriousness of the charges laid?

Punishment

Punishment is designed to deal with a convicted defendant and results in criminal sanctions that range from probation to incarceration. Criminal sanctions in Canada are dictated primarily by the *Criminal Code* (and other federal legislation, including drug statutes). One form of punishment that is unique to drug trafficking and other serious profit-oriented criminal conspiracies is forcing the convicted defendant to forfeit money and assets deemed to be the proceeds of crime. In Canada, specific laws were introduced beginning in the late 1990s to increase the punishment of offenders who have committed crimes for the furtherance of a criminal organization (see chapter 13 for more details).

ENFORCEMENT OPERATIONAL TACTICS AND TECHNIQUES

The previous section outlines some of the core tenets of a criminal justice–based enforcement regime for organized crime. This section identifies operational tactics that are commonly used as part of enforcement strategies targeting organized criminal offenders and crimes. Most of these tactics are related to law enforcement's investigative function and are summarized in Table 12.1.

Witnesses, Informants, and Agents

The criminal law system in Western societies relies heavily on the direct testimony of witnesses to establish the facts upon which criminal guilt must rest. The term **witness** is used as an umbrella designation referring to any person who can provide evidence (usually testimony) that will further a criminal investigation and can be used in a court of law to prosecute or defend any individual charged with a criminal offence. Witnesses fall into one of two categories: the "good citizen" and the "criminal offender." The former is usually an innocent bystander or a victim of a criminal offence. The latter is often someone involved in the criminal underworld or even a member of the criminal syndicate targeted by law enforcement and who has decided to co-operate with police and prosecutors in exchange for a reduced charge, sentence, or immunity from prosecution. In Canada and the United States, reliance on the "criminal offender" informant in organized crime cases is common. Albanese (2015: 271) writes, "the use of confidential informants is the most cost-effective investigative tool in organized crime cases." However, "The low cost of informants is offset to some degree by problems of reliability and credibility." As witnesses, the greatest problem of using informants with a criminal past is their reliability and credibility, which are inevitably attacked by defence counsel. This is especially true if the informants are to be compensated by the government for their testimony.

    In law enforcement circles, the witness provides evidence either as an informant or an agent. An **informant** supplies information to a police investigation, usually based on prior knowledge of a criminal offence, and does not become actively involved in an investigation. An informant may be either a "good citizen" or "criminal offender" witness. Unlike an informant, an **agent** will become an active participant in a police investigation by gathering evidence upon the direction by police. This evidence is gathered through the agent's immersion in the criminal underworld and even a specific criminal syndicate or illegal activity. An agent often falls in the "criminal offender" category of witnesses and may be indemnified from prosecution if he or she takes part in an illegal offence; however, measures are often taken to preclude agents from doing so as part of an active criminal investigation. In fact, a common provision in a contract between a law enforcement agency and an agent is that he or she not be engaged in anything deemed illegal while working as a police agent.

While there are a number of ethical issues stemming from the use of informants and agents, they have become an extremely important resource to law enforcement in intelligence gathering, initiating cases, gathering evidence, and successfully prosecuting organized crime offenders. A cursory review of the prosecutions of major organized crime figures in Canada in the last 40 years or so demonstrates the frequent use of informants and agents by police and the crucial role they play as a state witness in successful prosecutions.

One of the greatest challenges facing police in encouraging criminal offenders to provide evidence to charge and convict others is to convince them to break the code of silence that is supposedly a sacrosanct principle among offenders. One of the reasons that members of the American *Cosa Nostra* were able to escape prosecution for so many years was that the Mafiosi took their oath of *omerta* so seriously. It took until 1963 for a reputed Mafioso to break this oath. That year, Joseph Valachi, a low-level soldier with New York's Genovese family, testified to a Senate committee that the Mafia did indeed exist in America and stretched all the way into Canada. Valachi's decision to become informant was part of a plea bargain that allowed him to avoid the death penalty for a murder he had committed. He reportedly was also motivated by a well-founded belief that he was to be killed on orders of his boss Vito Genovese.

Because of the inherent challenges in recruiting informants and agents to testify against criminal organizations, police and prosecutors provide incentives to individuals to become a **state witness**. As described above, a common incentive is immunity from prosecution. Immunizing witnesses who have been criminally charged means that some or even all of the charges may be waived by prosecutors. Immunity is often offered to lower-level members of a criminal group (who have been arrested and threatened with prosecution) if they provide evidence that indicts their bosses in a particular criminal conspiracy. Abadinsky (2000: 392) characterizes the "criminal offender" informant or agent (also pejoratively referred to as a "snitch," "fink," or "rat") as someone who has a vested interest in turning state witness. These individuals provide "help to law enforcement in order to further his or her own ends. These include vengeance, an effort to drive competition out of business, financial rewards, and most frequently 'working off a beef'—securing leniency for criminal activities that have become known to the authorities."

Case Study: Dany Kane, Police Agent

One of the more infamous police agents in Canada was Dany Kane. While a member of the Rockers, a Montreal-based puppet club that answered to the Nomads chapter of the Quebec Hells Angels during the 1990s, Kane was working as an agent for the RCMP and later the Sûreté du Quebec. From 1994—the time he began wearing a wire, meeting with police handlers, and providing disks from Hells Angels' computers—to his death in 2000, Kane would become the most productive informant ever to infiltrate the Hells Angels in Canada. His job as a police agent meant that he was living a double life. He was not only a contract killer for the Angels (participating in at least 11 murders between 1994 and 1997), but was a husband and father of four children. He was also the gay lover of fellow hitman Aimé (Ace) Simard, whom he had met through a personal ad.

Kane's life as a police agent began when he contacted the RCMP while serving a sentence for firearms violations. After carrying out various assassinations and other jobs for the Hells Angels, Kane was made a full-fledged Rocker in 1995. In this new position, he often acted as a bodyguard and driver for Nomads' David Carroll and Normand Robitaille, a job that elevated Kane's status as a police agent. In February 1997, Kane and Simard were ordered by Carroll to travel to Nova Scotia and eliminate a drug dealer named Robert MacFarlane who owed them money. The two faithfully carried out the orders. The only problem was that Kane was a police agent at the time. After it was revealed that Kane was involved in MacFarlane's slaying, his contract with the RCMP was terminated, and he was arrested and sent to Halifax where he was charged with murder. These charges were dismissed in November 1998 when the judge declared a mistrial due to the inconsistent evidence and testimony provided by police. Kane returned to the Rockers and was given a new contract by the Sûreté du Quebec. It was in his capacity as a SQ agent that Kane gathered firsthand information that led to the arrest of dozens of members of the Hells Angels and the Rockers.

Kane would never see the fruits of his labour. On August 7, 2000, the 31-year-old was found dead by his son in his garage at home. He was asphyxiated by carbon monoxide poisoning and his death was ruled a suicide. Kane left a suicide note that reflected an identity crisis of existential proportions brought about by his multiple lives. In his rambling note, he scribbled, "Who am I? Am I a biker? Am I a policeman? Am I good or evil? Am I heterosexual or gay? Am I loved or feared? Am I exploited or the exploiter?" Notwithstanding Kane's death, the evidence provided to police was crucial in forcing many of his colleagues with the Rockers to plead guilty to murder, drug trafficking, and participation in a criminal organization in 2002 (*Montreal Gazette*, April 19, 2002, May 17, 2002, May 22, 2002, May 28, 2002; Sher & Marsden, 2003: 235).

Case Study: Role of the State Witness in the Conviction of Maurice Boucher

On June 26, 1997, two members of the Rockers Motorcycle Club, Stéphane Gagné and André Tousignant, gunned down 42-year-old prison guard Diane Lavigne as she drove home following the end of her shift at Montreal's Bordeaux prison. On September 8, Gagné and another Rocker named Paul Fontaine struck again. This time, the victim was Pierre Rondeau, a 49-year-old guard at Rivière des Prairies jail in northeast Montreal, who was shot while sitting behind the wheel of an empty prison transport bus. After receiving a tip from an arrested drug dealer, Gagné was picked up by police on December 5. He confessed to the murders and agreed to provide evidence implicating Hells Angels Quebec Nomad President Maurice Boucher, who had ordered both men to kill correctional officials as part of his campaign to destabilize the criminal justice system in Quebec. Less than two weeks later Boucher was arrested by police.

Gagné eventually pleaded guilty to the first-degree murder of Diane Lavigne and the attempted murder of fellow prison guard Robert Corriveau, who was wounded when Rondeau was killed. The Crown dropped a second murder charge for Rondeau's death in return for Gagné's testimony against Boucher.

Boucher's trial for the murder of the two prison guards began on November 2, 1998. Gagné was the main witness for the Crown; in fact, the informant was all the Crown had to link Boucher to the two murders. Throughout his trial, Boucher's defence team hammered away at the Crown witness to such an extent that Gagné had little credibility in the eyes of the jury. As a result, Boucher was pronounced innocent of all charges. However, Boucher was arrested and charged again with the murders. On May 6, 2002, Boucher was found guilty of first-degree murder in the death of both prison guards and sentenced to life imprisonment, with no chance of parole for at least 25 years. The main prosecution witness in this trial was once again Stéphane Gagné, who by this time was much more polished and credible when he took the stand. He was supported this time by other Hells Angels' associates who had become Crown witnesses (Cherry, 2005: 188; Sher & Marsden, 2003: 351).

Witness Protection Programs

Witness protection programs are also used to encourage the co-operation of informants, agents, innocent bystanders, and victims while providing them with security from those against whom they are testifying. According to former New York District Attorney Rudolph Guiliani (1986: 104), before the US federal government began protecting its witnesses, organized criminals had a history of acquittals that far exceeded acquittal rates for other types of defendants. This was due in part to the ability of organized crime figures to corrupt, intimidate, hurt, or even kill witnesses testifying against them. "Since the advent of the Witness Security Program, established by Title V of the *Organized Crime Control Act of 1970*, almost every major racketeering prosecution has depended, at least in part, on the testimony of one or more protected witnesses. There are repeated instances, for example in New York, of witnesses who refused to talk or lied in connection with state prosecutions, because they feared for their lives, and who later testified truthfully when under federal protection. Because of organized crime's demonstrated use of murder and other acts of violence over the years were it not for the Witness Security Program the Government would have few if any witnesses available for its organized crime prosecutions."

Witness protection may entail escorting a witness to court, giving the witness (and his or her family) a new identity, providing financial compensation, relocating the witness to another jurisdiction, and helping him or her start a new life. Witness protection programs are routinely criticized for providing chronic and violent offenders with a new identity "that may allow them to victimize an unwary public in jurisdictions where they have relocated" (Guiliani, 1986: 115–16). In Canada, providing immunity to criminal offenders is also controversial in that it has allowed some literally to get away with murder. One of the more notorious gangsters who received immunity from prosecution in Canada was Cecil Kirby, a former member of the Satan's Choice Motorcycle Gang. Kirby was implicated in a number of murders as well as other violence in his work as an enforcer for the Commisso brothers, an 'Ndrangheta cell in the GTA during the 1970s and 1980s. But he received immunity from prosecution for his testimony against the Commissos (Kirby & Renner, 1986). Numerous other serious and chronic offenders associated with criminal organizations in Canada, including those linked to multiple murders, have been granted immunity from prosecution for their evidence. While it is highly unpalatable to provide immunity to a career criminal and murderer, police and prosecutors will argue that the greater good is delivered to society when more powerful crime bosses are convicted based on the invaluable evidence provided by credible informants.

In Canada, a national witness protection program is operated by the RCMP, while smaller programs are operated by some of the provincial attorney generals. While each police force in Canada is responsible for ensuring the safety and security of its witnesses, most municipal law enforcement agencies in Canada participate in the RCMP Source Witness Protection Program (SWPP) on a cost-recovery basis. According to a 2013 document prepared by the Canadian Department of Justice for new witness protection legislation, "Recognizing the crucial role of witnesses in criminal investigations and prosecutions, governments and police services in Canada have adopted various measures over time that are designated to protect vulnerable witnesses or witnesses whose safety is in jeopardy because of their cooperation with the justice system" (Casavant & Morrise, 2013: 2).

The RCMP witness protection program is mandated to protect state witnesses by providing everything from short-term protection to permanent relocation and identity changes. According to the RCMP website, the program is meant to ensure the safety of "protectees," address their needs (e.g., counselling, addiction treatment, etc.), and allow for their self-sufficiency and easy reestablishment. "Depending on the case, there is a range of protective measures available. When appropriate, there are immediate, short-term measures available, which allow coordinators to respond quickly to potential threats. Long-term measures may include relocation, accommodation and change of identity. It usually includes counselling and financial support to ensure the protectees' security and facilitate their reestablishment and self-sufficiency (financial support is limited and does eventually expire)" (Royal Canadian Mounted Police, 2016).

While the RCMP has operated the SWPP since 1984, in 1996, the federal government established a statutory foundation for witness protection in Canada by introducing legislation called the *Witness Protection Program Act* (see chapter 13 for more information on this legislation). This legislation was enacted due to controversies over the protection of witnesses by the RCMP, including "the lack of transparency in its management and failure to honour protection agreements. In fact, some protectees who were dissatisfied with their treatment by the RCMP jeopardized their own safety by publicizing their disputes with the RCMP" (Casavant & Morris, 2013: 3). Indeed, witness protection programs at the federal and provincial levels in Canada have been criticized by those who have been enrolled in the programs. Their complaints centre on poor treatment by criminal justice authorities and their allegations include police coercing them into making false statements, not respecting the terms of their agreements, failing to adequately provide them with new identities and failing to protect them while enrolled in the program (*Globe and Mail*, April 14, 2004, May 4, 2004). In 2016, a woman who entered the federal witness protection program after agreeing to provide evidence on drug investigations launched a civil suit against the RCMP for negligence alleging they compromised her identity and stopped providing her with financial support (CBC News, June 13, 2016).

Surveillance

In addition to eyewitness testimony, police frequently undertake **surveillance** of the targets of a criminal investigation to secure evidence that can be used as a basis to lay charges against one or more offender. The goal of police surveillance is the collection of incriminating statements or actions without the consent of the target. The very nature of organized crime and the challenges inherent in securing credible eyewitness testimony or penetrating criminal organizations through agents or police undercover operations often necessitates the use of surveillance.

Broadly speaking, police surveillance can be divided into two categories: **physical surveillance** (in which police follow and watch suspects) and **electronic surveillance** (through audio and video recordings). These two approaches are often used as part of the same criminal investigation in that physical surveillance may also involve video and audio recordings. Physical surveillance may include following suspects or setting up an observation post outside a home, a place of business, or a frequent meeting place. An electronic surveillance scenario (also called *electronic eavesdropping*) may entail one or more of the following: having an undercover police officer or agent wear a recording device, setting up an audio or video recorder in a particular locale, or intercepting telephone conversations. In more recent years, electronic surveillance may entail intercepting a suspect's emails, text messages, or web browsing.

The conversations overheard through electronic eavesdropping may yield not only leads that law enforcement officers can use to obtain other types of evidence, but they may also be admissible during a criminal trial. In Canada, telephone **wiretaps** and other forms of electronic surveillance are referred to as a **Part VI investigation**. This term stems from the part of the *Criminal Code* that details the legal authorization necessary for police to conduct electronic surveillance and the strict provisions they must adhere to after obtaining authorization to do so. These provisions are in the *Criminal Code* to safeguard against privacy concerns and other abuses that may result from the use of such intrusive measures. Police in Canada must go before a provincial or superior court judge to show just cause as to why they believe they need to conduct electronic surveillance.

One of the downsides of surveillance for law enforcement agencies is its costs. "Many law enforcement agencies find lawful authorization of electronic surveillance too expensive to pursue; it is a high-cost method of investigation. Such costs are attributed to (1) the assignment of personnel to supervise the command post and conduct surveillance assignments (which usually pulls officers away from their regular assignments); (2) extensive overtime because most wires are staffed on a 24-hour basis; (3) the acquisition of expensive and highly technical equipment, such as pen registers, computers, and cellular and GPS technologies; (4) training for the use of the equipment; and (5) overtime for clerical and staff support who must type numerous surveillance reports and transcribe recorded conversations" (Lyman & Potter, 2014: 386).

According to Albanese (2015), "The cost and effectiveness of electronic surveillance remain matters of debate. Electronic surveillance has formed the basis for many significant organized crime convictions in recent years, but some have questioned its cost-benefit." Electronic surveillance is often impractical because of the costs, its time- and labour-intensive nature, the many restrictions that are intended to prevent the abuse of such an intrusive method, and the difficulty in recording suspects in multiple locations. The conversations recorded may also be easily dismissed as evidence because they are taken out of context or due to problems of interpretation (words and phrases

Case Studies: Audio and Video Surveillance of the Montreal Mafia

In December 1970, Bob Menard, an undercover police officer posing as an electrician, began renting a flat above Reggio Bar, located on Jean-Talon Street in the St. Leonard district of Montreal. The bar was owned by Paolo Violi, a senior member of the Montreal wing of New York's Bonanno crime family. Menard's new residency allowed police to plant electronic listening devices throughout the bar and Violi's adjoining offices. Along with the telephone surveillance already in place, police now had almost unlimited access to conversations Violi and his colleagues held in his *de facto* headquarters (Charney, 1979: 29, 31).

Beginning in October 1975, the provincial crime commission began to release publicly some transcripts of the recordings. The result, according to journalist Anne Charney, was that "Violi's private conversations, revealed for all the world to hear, made him vulnerable not only to public authority but also the authority of the Mafia. In a world where silence, *omerta*, is a first commandment, the daily serialization of Violi's rule rendered him instantly obsolete" (Charney, 1979: 29, 31). Violi's power and stature within New York's Bonanno family was obliterated by the public release of the police wiretap transcripts; he would never be forgiven for allowing himself to become enmeshed in a police dragnet. On January 22, 1978, Violi was murdered—an assassination sanctioned by his superiors in New York—ironically while at the Reggio Bar playing cards. The public release of the transcripts transgressed a fundamental ethical principle of police surveillance: ensure the investigative technique does not endanger the life of any individual, including those who are subject to the recording.

Years later, police in Montreal installed video surveillance cameras inside the favourite meeting place for members of the Montreal Mafia: the Consenza Social Club, also located in the St. Leonard district. The surveillance was part of Project Colisée, which concluded in 2006 and resulted in successful convictions against numerous members and associates of the Rizzuto crime family. Among other things, the surveillance captured couriers transporting thousands of dollars in tightly packed wads of cash in and out of the club. A description of the tribute system of the Montreal Mafia, and the recipients of the cash tributes, was captured by police surveillance on May 23, 2005, when Rocco Sollecito cryptically told another man, "When they do something—and it doesn't matter when they do it—they always bring something here so that it can be divided up among us five." The five he was referring to were the most senior members of the Rizzuto family at the time: Nicolo Rizzuto, Paolo Renda, Frank Arcadi, Vito Rizzuto, and Sollecito. All five men (except Vito who was in jail at the time) were observed by police cameras at one time or another counting the money in the

Continued

club and then dividing it amongst themselves. The RCMP surveillance video captured the payment of a "tax" levied by the Rizzuto family on construction firms who won municipal government construction contracts. Nick Rizzuto came to the club several times a week to pick up his share of the payments (and that owing to his son Vito). He would place the cash in his socks, pockets, wallet, or any combination of the three, depending on the size of the wad.

The video surveillance was also crucial to the Charbonneau Commission investigating corruption in Montreal's construction industry. On numerous occasions, the cameras captured the corrupt owners of some construction firms in the social club. Nicola Milioto, a construction firm owner who allegedly served as a middleman between the Rizzuto clan and other construction companies, was seen more than 200 times at the Consenza Café. In many recordings he is seen handing over cash to mob leaders (Canadian Press, September 25, 2012; *Montreal Gazette*, March 17, 2007, September 27, 2012).

may be vague and interpreted differently or those heard on the recording may, in fact, be lying or bragging). More astute criminals undermine electronic eavesdropping by speaking in code, taking measures to detect a recording device, or holding conversations in noisy environments.

Undercover Operations

In addition to surveillance, another commonly used approach to surreptitiously gathering intelligence and/or evidentiary information is infiltrating a criminal organization or criminal conspiracy by a police officer or an agent who is co-operating with police. An **undercover operation** may last for just one illegal transaction (e.g., one drug deal) or it may be ongoing, lasting several months, and, in rare cases, several years. It can be an effective enforcement approach because it allows the undercover operator to witness criminal activity firsthand while also facilitating the collection of evidence. When a police officer or an agent acts as a buyer of an illegal substance or service, the undercover work is called a **sting** operation. When police or an agent acts as a seller or a broker of an illegal substance or service, the undercover work is called a **reverse sting** operation.

Controlled Deliveries

A **controlled delivery** is an enforcement technique in which law enforcement authorities allow specific consignments of illicit drugs or other controlled substances they have interdicted to reach their ultimate destination. This allows police the opportunity to collect important evidence and intelligence information that may not be obtained if the shipment were seized at its original point of interdiction. The ultimate goal of a controlled delivery is

Case Study: Money Laundering Reverse Sting Operations in Canada

In the 1990s, the RCMP-led Integrated Anti-Drug Profiteering (IADP) units, which targeted the proceeds of crime and money laundering by drug-trafficking organizations, embarked on ambitious reverse sting operations in Montreal, Toronto, and Vancouver. The Montreal IADP unit initiated Project Compote, which entailed establishing a retail currency exchange business called the Centre International Monétaire de Montréal (CIMM) on de Maisonneuve Boulevard in the downtown core. Based on the Montreal model, the Vancouver IADP unit launched Project Eyespy, which also involved a fake retail currency exchange operation, Pacific Rim International Currency Exchange, staffed by undercover police personnel.

The goals of the undercover operations were to identify and collect sufficient intelligence and evidentiary information on large-scale drug-trafficking organizations by luring them to the currency exchange businesses with the promise of providing a much-needed service: laundering drug money. Police used informants to put the word out that the currency exchange businesses would provide a number of services that would launder large amounts of cash for a nominal fee.

At the culmination of the Montreal undercover operation on August 30, 1994, 57 people were arrested and charged with hundreds of counts of money laundering and drug offences. The undercover operations can be considered a success given the high-level targets that did business with the covert currency exchanges. One of those who used the services of CIMM was a Montreal lawyer named Giuseppe (Joseph) Lagana, who had ties to Vito Rizzuto. Undercover RCMP officers working at the bogus exchange business took in millions of dollars in cash personally delivered by Lagana and other employees of his law firm. All three were actively involved in laundering the proceeds of crime by personally picking up and transporting drug money to CIMM, making arrangements to convert large volumes of small denominations of Canadian currency into larger denominations of Canadian or American currency or bank drafts, arranging for international wire transfers, and opening bank accounts and establishing companies in Switzerland as part of the money transfers. Police were able to prove that the funds provided to CIMM were from criminal organizations active in drug trafficking and that Lagana was personally responsible for laundering more than $15 million in Canadian funds over four years. Based on evidence collected as part of the undercover operation, he was sentenced to 13 years for proceeds of crime and money laundering offences. The undercover investigation also revealed a plot by reputed members of the Montreal Mafia and the Hells Angels to transport 558 kilograms of cocaine from Colombia to Europe. Based on this information, Jorge Luis Cantieri, a Montreal businessman who ran numerous import-export companies, was handed a 15-year prison term for orchestrating the cocaine shipment (*Globe and Mail*, June 30, 1995; *Montreal Gazette*, October 16, 1994, June 30, 1995).

Continued

According to the RCMP, Project Eyespy, which ran from 1993 to 1996, identified 430 people in the Vancouver area who laundered money through the undercover currency exchange business. In the end, 90 people were charged with more than 1000 criminal counts related to the laundering of approximately $40 million in criminal proceeds. Most of the money was revenue from cocaine and marijuana trafficking and, to a lesser extent, contraband liquor and tobacco sales. The exchange was particularly attractive to those selling British Columbia marijuana in the United States, which typically involves converting American dollars smuggled back into Canada into Canadian currency. The undercover operation also led to the seizure of 222 kilograms of marijuana, 815 kilograms of cocaine, $2.5 million in cash, and several handguns, and led to the dismantling of at least three marijuana grow operations in Greater Vancouver (*Edmonton Journal*, January 25, 1996; *Montreal Gazette*, January 25, 1996; *The Province*, January 25, 1996; *Vancouver Sun*, January 26, 1996).

Despite these successes, the RCMP came under fire when the *Ottawa Citizen* published a series of articles in June 1998 accusing CIMM of assisting drug traffickers in laundering millions of dollars in drug proceeds over a four-year period. Because the IADP unit was so overwhelmed with the volume of cash processed through the exchange, it could only seize $16.5 million from the $141.5 million in drug money that passed through the operation. The RCMP was accused of helping to move more than $94.7 million in drug money to Colombia in 1992 and 1993 (*Ottawa Citizen*, June 11, 1998, June 12, 1998, June 13, 1998, June 14, 1998). Citing an internal RCMP report, the *Citizen* accused the undercover operation of facilitating drug purchases—the conversion of Canadian to American currency allowed traffickers to purchase cocaine in the United States while the conversion of American to Canadian cash allowed purchases of high-grade hydroponic marijuana in British Columbia. The *Citizen* articles asserted that the RCMP-led operation was undermined by (1) a chronic shortage of police human and technical resources, such as specialized computers needed to perform wiretap operations; (2) missed drug seizures; and (3) internal security breaches by two or more corrupt RCMP officers (*Ottawa Citizen*, June 11, 1998).

Once police converted Canadian cash into US currency or US dollar bank drafts and handed it over to their drug world "clients," they had no control over what happened to the money as soon as the traffickers walked out the door. Without a sufficient number of surveillance teams and investigators, police often failed to discover where the drug money came from and where it went (*Ottawa Citizen*, June 11, 1998). Police personnel shortages were so bad that two years into the undercover operation one incensed RCMP investigator complained in writing to his superiors that "without the necessary resources and personnel to do proper and complete investigations, it seems like all we are doing is offering a money laundering service for drug traffickers" (*Ottawa Citizen*, June 13, 1998).

to identify and arrest the individuals while in possession of the illegal shipment. Ideally, a controlled delivery can facilitate the arrest of multiple offenders involved in a criminal conspiracy by putting pressure on those in receipt of the illegal goods to become a state witness.

In order to safeguard a controlled delivery operation, police will sometimes remove the drug or other contraband from its conveyance upon detection and replace it with a legal substance (e.g., cocaine will be replaced by sugar). This is to guard against problems that may occur with the transport of illegal substances by police (such as the goods getting lost, the offenders absconding with the illegal goods upon delivery, or even charges that police are abetting an illegal transaction).

Search and Seizure (Obtaining Physical Evidence)

Of great importance to arresting, charging, and successfully prosecuting a criminal offender is the ability of police to secure physical evidence relevant to the criminal offence, such as drugs, illegal gambling equipment, cars or vehicles used to transport drugs, other contraband, and financial records. The legal means of obtaining physical evidence is chiefly accomplished through a judicially authorized search of a specific site or sites, which usually takes place in the later stages of an investigation.

Proceeds of Crime/Money Laundering Enforcement

Along with tax enforcement (see the following section) proceeds of crime enforcement is part of what Kilchling (2014: 657) calls "Finance-Oriented Strategies of Organized Crime Control," which are meant to target the profit-oriented nature of OC. The pre-eminent tool used by law enforcement in North America to take the profit out of crime is to confiscate the illicit revenues and accumulated assets of offenders and criminal organizations. This is often referred to as **asset forfeiture**, in that offenders are forced to forfeit their assets to the state as part of a criminal prosecution (or in some cases, the result of a civil suit). The legal principle behind asset forfeiture is that the state may permanently take property from an individual or organization "without compensation to the owner if the property is acquired or used illegally" (Albanese, 2015: 342).

An underlying assumption of this strategy is that rational criminal offenders involved in profit-oriented illegal activities will desist if they are deprived of the prime motivation of such criminal offending. For Kilchling (2014: 658), "The leading argument is that traditional responses such as imprisonment and fines alone are ineffective; the better alternative is to attack the property (rather than persons)." In fact, asset forfeiture should be seen as a complement to traditional punishment. With that said, proceeds of crime enforcement is not simply about punishing and deterring offenders; it is also said to be a principal technique to disrupt a criminal organization. Like legitimate companies, organized crime syndicates are in business to make money. As such, sustained financial losses may effectively put a criminal organization or an individual offender out of business. In short, "in addition to the purpose of neutralizing the main incentive of crime, i.e., the greed for illegal profit, it has further preventive purposes, aiming at removing the capital for future—illegal and legal (or apparently legal)—investment activities of organized crime groups, as well as at protecting the legitimate economy from corruption and infiltration" (Kilchling, 2014:657–58). Two other benefits of the asset forfeiture strategy are that it can produce revenue for the state (which can be reinvested into policing or distributed to victims) and it can reduce what is seen to be "particularly dangerous about highly lucrative criminality—i.e., the infiltration of dirty money into the legitimate economy" (Beare, 2012: 268).

For Kilchling (2014: 658), proceeds of crime enforcement consists of three major elements: "(1) the tracing of assets, (2) their provisional blocking (freezing, seizing), and (3) their final removal or recovery (forfeiture, confiscation)." In order to force a defendant to forfeit assets through a criminal court in Canada, there first must have been a conviction of a predicate offence that generated the proceeds of crime (e.g., drug trafficking, extortion, fraud, etc.) and proof beyond a reasonable doubt that the seized assets derive from this specified criminal offence. Because asset forfeiture through the criminal courts in Canada requires a predicate criminal offence first be established, proceeds of crime investigations are carried out concurrent with or following the investigation of the revenue-generating offence.

The identification and investigation of proceeds of crime offences by police presents a difficult task from the outset; the *raison d'être* of criminal money laundering is to conceal the source and ownership of illicit wealth. Proceeds of crime investigations are also encumbered by the complexities of conducting investigations in legitimate financial and commercial sectors through which the proceeds of crime are laundered, which requires a detailed knowledge of financial accounting and commerce. The complexities of financial investigations, combined with the challenges in proving beyond a reasonable doubt that an offender's assets were derived from criminal activity, mean that law enforcement agencies must often rely on specialized **forensic accounting** and auditing skills and resources. The use of forensic accountants by law enforcement revolves around three functions. First, they are used in active investigations to analyze the financial documentation uncovered by a police officer, thereby facilitating the building of a case and the laying of charges. Second, the forensic accountant prepares evidence for court, such as a net-worth analysis of the target (which is to provide that money and assets belonging to the target could not have been generated from legitimate means). Third, forensic accountants are used by law enforcement to provide expert testimony during court cases. In addition to the financial analysis, a proceeds of crime investigation must also incorporate aspects of traditional police investigative techniques and resources, including undercover operations, surveillance, search warrants, sophisticated intelligence gathering and analysis, the use of informants and referrals, and criminal as well as financial investigative experience.

The Canadian government has introduced a number of policies and programs in the last 10 years targeting the proceeds of crime and money laundering. This includes (1) legislation that criminalizes the possession of proceeds of crime and money laundering and provides the state with the powers to force an accused to forfeit cash and other assets derived from criminal activity to the government (subsection 462.37(1) or (2.01) or 462.38(2) of the *Criminal Code*); (2) the funding of Integrated Proceeds of Crime (IPOC) units, a joint-force, multi-disciplinary law enforcement initiative led by the RCMP that focuses on the financial aspects of organized crime and terrorist groups; and (3) the adoption of the *Proceeds of Crime (Money Laundering) Act*, which requires certain commercial entities and professionals in the private sector to report large cash and suspicious transactions that may indicate money laundering while also requiring anyone entering or leaving the country with cash over $10,000 to file a report with the CBSA.

Like other new enforcement strategies, proceeds of crime enforcement and asset forfeiture strategies were initially met with great optimism as a way to combat organized crime and serious profit-motivated offences. However, as Beare (2012) argues, "no one has been able to determine with any remote degree of confidence whether or not the proceeds-of-crime approach to crime control has had any discernible impact on the operation of illegal markets or on the amount, distribution and behavior of illegal income and wealth." Moreover, "there is no evidence that anti-laundering works as an effective 'prevention' strategy to significantly reduce the amount of organized crime or terrorism" (Beare, 2012: 269).

The Urban and Highway Patrol Function

Often forgotten in the fight against organized crime and drug trafficking are city and highway patrol officers. Both can serve a number of valuable enforcement functions, including detection, interdiction, intelligence gathering, education, and harm reduction. A 1974 manual on organized crime that was prepared for Canadian patrol officers states, "if a patrol officer is lax in observing violations, overlooks gambling and prostitution, and fails to make reports regarding suspicious actions, he or she is contributing to the success of organized criminal groups" (Securesearch, 1974: 3).

Both the urban and highway patrol officers are the first to arrive on a crime scene that may be part of a broader organized criminal conspiracy, where they can arrest suspects and collect relevant evidence. Another contribution patrol officers can make to organized crime enforcement stems from their ability to gather intelligence information from the "street." Patrol officers are often in a good position to recruit informants for organized crime enforcement if they are well integrated into local communities. Urban patrol officers are especially useful in gathering intelligence and recruiting informants when done so under the auspices of community policing, a defining principle of which is a full partnership between local citizens and the police in identifying and ameliorating local crime and disorder problems (Leighton, 1991: 3).

Highway patrol officers have also gradually been asked to play a proactive role in detecting and interdicting drugs as well as other contraband on North American highways. One pioneering program is Operation Pipeline, which began in 1984, based on the experiences of state police in New Mexico and New Jersey. According to the Drug Enforcement Administration,

> As drug traffickers established their networks within U.S. borders, they began to rely heavily on the highway system to move their wares from entry points to distribution hubs around the country. Beginning in the early 1980s, New Mexico state troopers grew suspicious when they noticed a sharp increase in the number of motor vehicle violations that resulted in drug seizures and arrests. At the same time, and unknown to the troopers in New Mexico, troopers in New Jersey began making similar seizures during highway stops along the Interstate-95 "drug corridor" from Florida to the Northeast. Independently, troopers in New Mexico and New Jersey established their own highway drug interdiction programs. Over time, as their seizures mounted, law enforcement officers found that highway drug couriers shared many characteristics, tendencies, and methods. Highway law enforcement officers began to ask key questions to help determine whether or not motorists they had stopped for traffic violations were also carrying drugs. (United States Drug Enforcement Administration, n.d.a)

The success of the highway interdiction programs in New Jersey and New Mexico led to the creation of Operation Pipeline, which encourages a coordinated response from law enforcement agencies at all levels to deter the flow of drugs that are frequently transported along highways. The original DEA-funded program featured state police and highway patrol officers with expertise in highway interdiction who provided training to other officers throughout the country to detect and interdict drugs or other contraband from passenger vehicles or commercial trucks. Similar programs have been implemented that attempt to detect contraband tobacco transported between the Akwesasne reserve and cities and towns in Ontario and Quebec where they are sold.

This approach is not without controversy. Critics charge that it involves racial profiling—targeting individuals based on their race—which police in Canada and the United States vehemently deny. Other critics charge that the program violates people's constitutional rights through unlawful search and seizure and unreasonable detention. As Gary Webb writes in a 2007 article in *Esquire* magazine, "Over the past thirteen years, Operation Pipeline has been waging an expanding and largely invisible war on the nation's highways against 'mules,' people who haul cash and drugs for dope dealers. In its time, Pipeline has scored some impressive victories. But as with any war, it has left considerable collateral damage in its wake: legions of law-abiding motorists who have been ticketed, interrogated, and searched simply because they looked or acted funny—or happened not to be white" (Webb, 2007).

Multi-Agency Co-operation and Coordination

Historically, efforts to combat crime have been characterized by the unilateral actions of individual law enforcement agencies within their respective jurisdictions. In fact, one of the greatest limitations of traditional OC enforcement has been a lack of inter-agency coordination and co-operation. This problem has been prompted by a number of disjunctive factors, such as geographical boundaries, differing mandates, and rivalries. It is almost universally agreed that combatting criminal syndicates, especially those that are span different regions, demands a coordinated effort among a number of different agencies, both within and outside of the criminal justice sector. This integrated, multi-agency, coordinated approach—and the need to pool resources, share intelligence, and work across jurisdictional boundaries—has been deemed essential given the nature of organized crime, which can be very well-resourced, multi-jurisdictional, multi-layered, and at times quite sophisticated.

There are dozens (perhaps hundreds) of initiatives that have been undertaken in numerous countries to promote (and even legislate) a greater coordination and co-operation among domestic enforcement agencies. Through the creation of the regional crime squads in the early 1960s, Great Britain was one of the first countries to recognize the need to address criminal activity that crossed the boundaries of individual police forces. The units were mandated to combat multi-jurisdictional crime and were comprised of detective officers seconded from different police forces within each designated region (Adamoli et al., 1998: 163). The United States government began to fund and promote inter-agency partnerships in the early 1970s following the 1967 Presidential Commission on Law Enforcement, which criticized the parochial nature of law enforcement in America. As a result of this commission, the US government has provided special program funding to entice greater co-operation and coordination among federal enforcement agencies, as well as among federal, state, and local agencies. Today, the United States boasts a number of inter-agency task forces that focus on different illegal commodities or services (e.g., drugs, fraud, migrant smuggling), different groups (e.g., Mexican drug cartels, Eastern European, Nigerian), and high-risk areas (e.g., cities, border regions, marine ports).

In Canada, there has also been movement toward greater inter-agency coordination. The Canadian government used program funding to create the multi-agency Integrated Proceeds of Crime units. These units are made up of the RCMP as well as provincial and municipal police forces, Crown lawyers, forensic accountants, and even Canada Revenue Agency taxation officials. Federal funding to combat contraband smuggling through the anti-smuggling initiative in the 1990s also promoted increased coordination through the Integrated Border Enforcement Teams (see below). In the face of escalating violence among rival outlaw biker gangs in Quebec in the 1990s, Project Carcajou was formed and consisted of more than 100 members from the municipal, provincial, and federal police (this initiative was weakened by poor relations among the different police forces, and the Montreal police force eventually pulled out citing budget constraints) (Reuters, August 7, 1998). Subsequent multi-agency task forces in Quebec have realized more permanency. The Combined Forces Special Enforcement Units (CFSEU), which are located in Ontario, Quebec, British Columbia, and other provinces, are mandated to undertake large-scale investigations targeting organized crime groups.

Like law enforcement as a whole, the criminal intelligence community has also traditionally been restricted by geographic and other jurisdictional boundaries that have served to hamper the sharing of intelligence information on a regional, national, and international basis. Some countries have confronted the obstacles to inter-agency intelligence sharing by creating new agencies or joint-force operations expressly to coordinate the sharing and dissemination of intelligence information. Criminal Intelligence Service Canada (CISC) is made up of Canadian law enforcement agencies and is mandated to facilitate the exchange of criminal intelligence between enforcement agencies and CISC provincial bureaus. Ostensibly, CISC exists to unite the criminal intelligence units of Canadian law enforcement agencies in the fight against organized crime in Canada (Schramm, 1988).

Finally, there are inter-agency task forces made up of Canadian and American law enforcement agencies. Most notable is the Integrated Border Enforcement Teams

Case Study: Combined Forces Special Enforcement Unit— British Columbia

According to promotional material dated 2013, the CFSEU–BC is "an integrated joint forces operation that draws upon and develops highly specialized officers from federal, provincial and municipal agencies around the province." One of the benefits of this integrated unit is that it "enhances intelligence sharing, co-ordination, and strategic deployment against threats of violence posed by organized crime groups and gangs in B.C." (Combined Forces Special Enforcement Unit—British Columbia website, n.d.a: 2). The integrated nature of the CFSEU is also "a cost-saving measure by reducing duplication of efforts" among the different agencies involved in combatting organized crime in the province (Combined Forces Special Enforcement Unit—British Columbia website, n.d.b). The CFSEU–BC integrates 14 law enforcement agencies in the province, including municipal agencies (e.g., Vancouver police, Abbotsford police, Delta police), federal agencies (the RCMP, Canada Border Services Agency), and one provincial law enforcement agency (Organized Crime Control Agency of British Columbia). Within the CFSEU–BC are more than 400 employees divided among nine investigative teams and six specialty teams. This includes outlaw motorcycle gang coordinators, asset forfeiture investigative teams, uniform gang enforcement teams, and firearms enforcement teams.

(IBET), which targets cross-border criminal activity between the two countries. The agencies involved are the Canada Border Services Agency, the Royal Canadian Mounted Police, US Customs and Border Protection, the US Coast Guard, and the US Immigration and Customs Enforcement. According to Public Safety Canada, "Originally developed in 1996 as an innovative method to address cross-border crime along land and marine borders between British Columbia and Washington State, IBETs have evolved into a major enforcement success. IBETs have effectively disrupted smuggling rings, confiscated illegal drugs, weapons, liquor, tobacco and vehicles, and made numerous arrests. IBETs have also intercepted criminal networks attempting to smuggle illegal migrants across the border" (Public Safety Canada website, 2015a). In its annual performance evaluation report for 2014–15, the RCMP made reference to the "Shiprider program," in which the RCMP and the US Coast Guard "work together to seamlessly enforce the law on both sides of the border in shared waterways." This includes placing Canadian and US "law enforcement officers on a single patrol vessel," combining law enforcement resources, and providing "the operational flexibility required to interdict suspect vessels across jurisdictions, removing the international maritime boundary as a barrier to law enforcement" (Royal Canadian Mounted Police, 2015: 25).

ALTERNATIVE ORGANIZED CRIME CONTROL TACTICS AND TECHNIQUES

In addition to the dominant law enforcement approach to combatting organized crime, there are numerous other alternatives that fall outside the criminal justice system. Many of these initiatives pursue approaches that are preventative in nature, which contrasts with the overwhelmingly reactive tactics that characterize the traditional enforcement paradigm. Organized crime prevention strategies that fall outside the criminal justice system are typically directed at potential victims and encourage measures and activities to make them less susceptible to victimization. Some examples of prevention strategies specific to organized crime are summarized as follows:

- Situational crime prevention initiatives that attempt to reduce the opportunity for certain crimes to be committed, such as "hardening" a target (e.g., increased security at marine ports to prevent cargo theft) or enacting laws that prohibit access to conveyances that are exploited for organized criminal activity (e.g., strict regulatory controls over chemicals and pill presses used in the production of illegal synthetic drugs).
- The creation of agencies and/or policies and procedures that regulate legitimate industries and commercial sectors vulnerable to organized crime (e.g., construction, marine ports, waste removal, transportation, and legalized gambling). Albanese (2015: 346) describes how the Trade Waste Commission was created

in New York City to screen and license every waste service provider after 23 trash-hauling companies and four trade associations were indicted for corruption. Since its creation, the commission has realized some success in preventing criminal groups from further infiltration into waste management in the city.

- More stringent screening of employees of industries vulnerable to organized crime (e.g., banks, marine ports, government agencies, and casinos) to ensure these employees are not connected to criminal offenders or organizations.

- The prevention of corruption within the public sector. According to Lyman and Potter (2014: 397), "At a minimum, increased and more comprehensive reporting of assets and sources of income by public officials in key decision-making positions is required."

- Civil remedies that require residential and commercial landlords to put in place measures to prevent and detect the presence of gangs and criminal groups, drug trafficking, and other criminal activity. In the United States, "civil gang injunctions" rely on public nuisance ordinances to curtail gang activity by restricting certain (legal) activities of particular gang members (e.g., possessing a cell phone, associating with other gang members) or seek to exclude them from certain public or private spaces. Civil remedies can be both proactive and reactive in pursuit of their ultimate purpose. "They may aim to prevent behaviors and situations before they become a problem, or they may aim to reduce or eliminate problems that already exist" (Mazerolle & Roehl, 1998: 7–8).

- Public education campaigns to raise awareness, for example, about consumer fraud schemes to prevent victimization or how consumption of contraband cigarettes helps fund criminal groups. According to Pace and Styles (1975: 89), the "most positive approach for controlling organized crime is to inform the police and citizens of the magnitude and implications of organized crime in a community."

Case Study: Contraband Tobacco Public Education Campaigns

In their 2008 contraband tobacco strategy, the RCMP acknowledges, "raising awareness of the tobacco black market and the consequences of purchasing and possessing contraband tobacco is essential to reducing the demand" (Royal Canadian Mounted Police, 2008: 39). One of the main goals of the National Coalition Against Contraband Tobacco, according to its website, is to "educate people and urge government to take quick action to stop this growing threat." In Ontario as well as other provinces, Crime Stoppers has produced television and radio commercials as well as billboard ads that are meant to educate the public on how the purchase of contraband cigarettes contributes to the coffers of organized crime (Crime Stoppers News Release, September 17, 2015).

Photo 12.1: Crime Stoppers ad depicting the link between contraband cigarettes and organized crime

Source: Used by permission of Ontario Crime Stoppers

A more fundamental preventative approach targets the root causes of criminal behaviour. The topic of **criminality prevention** is vast and it is beyond the scope of this book to adequately delve into the goals, strategies, tactics, and best practices in this field. Suffice to say, social problem-solving measures designed to prevent the onset of criminal and violent behaviour by addressing their root causes—especially among youth at risk of serious and chronic offending—holds great promise. In her report entitled *Youth and Gun Violence: The Outstanding Case for Prevention*, Shaw (2005: 6–7) identifies a range of social problem-solving interventions that collectively forms a comprehensive strategic plan to reduce gun violence by young men:

- Targeted support for high-risk children and youth
- Early intervention home visiting, parental and family support programs
- Targeted and school-based educational and curriculum programs to change attitudes and behaviours to violence
- Conflict resolution, peace building, and peace-making training
- Cross-cultural youth life-skills and leadership training
- Projects around gender and masculinity
- Education, job training, micro-credit, and job creation to provide alternative outlets for young people
- Targeting high-risk areas, local communities, and the general public
- Child and youth recreational and cultural programs
- School-based educational and curriculum programs to change attitudes
- Projects to strengthen community capacity
- Urban renewal projects
- Public education campaigns to change attitudes, behaviour, and social norms using creative media (Internet, film, music, etc.)
- Social, health, and economic support services
- Mentoring programs to provide ongoing supports, and life skills and leadership training (Shaw, 2005: 6–7).

Particularly relevant to organized crime control is prevention-based initiatives that target gangs and gang-involved youth. In the United States and Canada, schools have become central institutions through which gang awareness and prevention interventions are delivered. One of the most widespread school-based programs is Gang Resistance Education and Training (GREAT), a nine-week instructional program taught to secondary school students on a universal basis by trained, uniformed police officers. The goal of the program is to help youth develop positive life skills and social competencies, minimize risky behaviour, resist peer pressure, resolve conflict, and make positive, pro-social choices, while imparting facts about the consequences of gang involvement and drugs (Esbensen, 2004). Other school-based prevention programs have focused specifically on violence and the heightened risk of youth becoming involved in violence through gangs. These programs typically raise awareness of the inherently violent nature of gangs and the detrimental impact of violence on individuals and communities. They also give students an understanding of how and why violence is initiated and how it can be avoided through critical thinking, peaceful problem-solving, learning to understand the perspective of others, and conflict resolution skills.

Gang intervention strategies target gang-involved individuals with the goal of inducing them to leave a gang or at the very least to reduce their gang-related criminal and violent activity (Maher, 2010: 318; Maxson et al., 2014: 441). Broadly speaking, gang exit strategies take one of three forms. First, there is the social problem-solving approach that targets the risk factors that sustains an individual's involvement in a gang (e.g., treatment of mental health or substance abuse disorders, social and life skills training, access to crisis shelters, job training, and education). The second is a criminal justice (suppression) approach that seeks to remove an individual from a gang through incarceration. The third approach is a "deterrence supplemented with social service provisions" (McGarrell et al., 2013: 34) model that persuades gang members to leave through a "stick and carrot" method, combining the threat of criminal justice sanctions (the stick) with the provision of meaningful alternatives to a gang lifestyle (the carrot), such as education and employment, as well as other social developmental initiatives (e.g., substance abuse treatment).

Government Commissions

Various countries have established special governmental commissions to conduct strategic assessments of organized crime and individual organized criminal activities. Often created through legislation and run by elected officials or judges, these committees can be granted extraordinary powers, including compelling testimony from witnesses through subpoenas and invoking prison sentences if this testimony is not forthcoming or involves perjury. The commissions are often highly public affairs, which helps to raise awareness of organized crime issues. Smith and Salerno (1970: 103) argue that the main purpose of these commissions is one of exposure: focusing public attention on the problem. (One of the downsides of these commissions is that due to their highly public nature, they have been hijacked by politicians hoping to promote their own careers and the resulting conclusions may be highly vitriolic and flawed, leading to misguided enforcement policy and programs.) A secondary objective of these commissions is to conduct basic research to understand the causes, scope, nature, and impact of the problem as well as applied research that can be used to inform effective policies and programs. While these commissions have the power to compel witnesses to testify, they are not criminal courts so they do not have the jurisdiction to find individuals guilty of criminal offences.

In the United States, at the federal level, there have been a number of special congressional and presidential commissions that have addressed organized crime, including the Kefauver Committee (1950–51), the McClellan Committee (1963), the President's Commission on Law Enforcement and Administration of Justice (1965–69), and the President's Commission on Organized Crime (1983–86). Government commissions investigating organized crime have also taken place in Canada at the provincial and municipal levels. During the first 30 years of the twentieth century, each of Canada's three largest cities had at least one judicial inquiry into government corruption resulting from organized criminal activities, and gambling, in particular. Toronto's first judicial inquiry was held in 1901 (there would be more municipal and provincial corruption investigation in the years to come) and was charged with investigating underground gambling and government corruption in the city. The inquiry was formed following a series of newspaper articles that claimed the police department was failing to suppress professional gambling and even accused some police officials of being in collusion with gambling operators and bookmakers. While the commission exonerated most senior police officials, the inquiry did find that a number of police officers were placing bets with local bookmakers (City of Toronto Archives, Fonds 15).

A judicial inquiry into vice and its enforcement in Montreal conducted by Justice Louis Coderre in 1924 and 1925 documented the dozens of "houses of ill repute" operating in the city's red light district (*Montreal Star*, March 14, 1925). A judicial inquiry into the local vice industry and resulting police corruption was held in Vancouver in 1928 (City of Vancouver Archives, Vancouver Police Fonds, Series 181, Vols. 5, 6, & 9). Allegations of lackadaisical enforcement, protection of gambling operations, and corruption within the Montreal police force resulted in another public inquiry—the Commission of Inquiry into Gambling and Commercialized Vice in Montreal—which was held between 1950 and 1953 under Justice François Caron. In his final report, Justice Caron concluded that the Montreal police were allowing commercial vice to go largely unenforced. The commission led to a provincial police investigation that resulted in charges being laid against 20 municipal police officers (Archives of the City of Montreal, P43).

In the late 1950s and early 1960s, a number of high-profile police raids of illegal gambling operations in Toronto and accusations that prominent provincial politicians intervened to secure charters for the social clubs used for gambling led to the creation of a Royal Commission in Ontario headed by Justice Wilfred D. Roach. The inquiry, which began public hearings on March 20, 1962, and concluded with the commissioner's report dated March 15, 1963, focused on illegal gambling and the extent to which it was controlled by organized crime (Roach, 1962). In the end, Justice Roach cleared government officials of corruption. He acknowledged that illegal gambling had reached a "staggering" volume in the province, but concluded that little evidence existed suggesting "there was organized crime in the province in any alarming extent except in the field of organized gambling." He also denied the existence of the Mafia in Canada. These findings contradicted recent events, and some observers later said Roach whitewashed the commission's findings in order to take the pressure off the provincial attorney general and the Conservative government, which had been accused of corruption and failing to take sufficient action against organized crime in the province.

The discovery of corruption within the OPP's anti-gambling squad, as well as emerging developments that contradicted Roach's conclusions, led to yet another provincial commission in Ontario, this one headed by Judge Bruce Macdonald, who delivered his report on January 31, 1964. In startling contrast to the conclusions of the Roach Commission, Justice Macdonald asserted, "organized crime has existed in Ontario and in some cases still does, in varying degrees from time to time as conditions change." He also stated there was solid evidence that American criminal syndicates had infiltrated Ontario, although no one group had a monopoly over a particular region or criminal activity (Ontario Police Commission, 1964: 117–18).

Beginning in the late 1960s and continuing in the 1970s, the Quebec government held a number of commissions that targeted organized crime. These commissions were given subpoena power and powerful gangsters in Montreal were forced to appear before the commission, including Vic Cotroni and Paolo Violi. When both refused, they were cited for contempt and incarcerated. More recently, the Quebec government convened a public inquiry into allegations of corruption in the tendering of public construction contracts in Montreal. Otherwise known as the Charbonneau Commission, as it was presided over by Quebec Superior Court Justice France Charbonneau, the inquiry began in May 2012 and heard startling testimony from bureaucrats, engineering executives, union officials, and construction company owners and managers about widespread collusion that hiked the price of government construction contracts. Various witnesses revealed that companies, the Mafia, political parties, and corrupt municipal and provincial bureaucrats all benefited materially from the collusion. In November 2015, the commission submitted its 1741-page report with 60 recommendations for the Quebec government (CBC News, November 24, 2015; *Globe and Mail*, November 24, 2015; Macleans.ca, November 24, 2015; *Montreal Gazette*, November 24, 2015a, November 24, 2015b).

Tax Enforcement

Tax enforcement is a unique tool in the arsenal of governments to prosecute and punish organized crime figures while indirectly confiscating the proceeds of crime. It is unique in that it is one of the few approaches used by the state to convict criminal offenders for violation of laws not directly related to the organization's illegal activities. Tax fraud is a charge that is now routinely applied to criminal entrepreneurs, in addition to or in lieu of asset forfeitures that result from a criminal conviction. This technique provides the government with a broad spectrum of weapons against organized criminals. As taxpayers, they are prosecutable for a wide range of acts and omissions involving tax laws. They are liable if they fail to file required returns or maintain required records. If they do file, but submit a false return or make a false statement in documents relevant to their taxes, they violate any number of tax laws. These various offences are not confined to personal income taxes; they can also apply to various other forms of tax evasion, including customs, excise, and sales taxes.

The objective of a tax assessment into criminal offenders and criminally controlled entities is not to ensure they pay the proper amount of taxes, but to deprive them of their wealth through hefty penalties that result from non-compliance with tax laws. Under most taxation legislation, government authorities only have to prove that unreported revenue received by an individual or entity is taxable to initiate a civil assessment (and this revenue can be both legally or illegally obtained). Once it is proven that a criminal offender has generated certain revenue and has not paid taxes on that revenue, an order can be made forcing the defendant to pay back taxes as well

Case Study: The Tax Assessment of William Obront

During the early to mid-1970s, William Obront maintained at least nine personal accounts at four banks. From 1974 to 1975, 46 people and 14 companies made deposits—ranging from $2500 to $1.7 million—into these accounts. During this two-year period, the deposits that were made up of his own revenue plus that which was laundered for other members and associates of the Cotroni Mafia group totalled over $18 million. Obront's annual declared income during this time was around $38,000. When Quebec's Department of Revenue re-assessed his taxable income for the years 1965 to 1973 to include estimates of his illegal income, the government figured he had undeclared income of $2,197,801, which meant he had an unpaid tax bill of $1,058,102.79 (plus fines and interest). After the assessment, the Quebec government seized Obront's assets and charged him with tax fraud. He was also sentenced to 20 months in jail and was ordered to pay $683,046 in back taxes and fines (*Globe and Mail*, February 1, 1979; Quebec Police Commission Inquiry on Organized Crime, 1977b: 12).

as significant monetary penalties (effectively serving the goal of asset forfeiture). The offender can also be hit with other penalties under tax laws, including the garnishing of future wages or revenues and even incarceration.

Currency and Suspicious Transaction Reporting

A financial transaction-monitoring and reporting system is part of a series of public policies that mandate the private sector to detect and report suspected proceeds of crime and money laundering to government agencies. The private-sector entities are primarily in the financial services sector, but other vulnerable industries are also mandated to report, such as casinos. The significance of transaction reporting is that it represents a fundamental shift in responsibility for detecting a specific OC activity from the state to the private sector. Transaction reporting by the private sector is designed to expose the money laundering process at its most vulnerable choke points, that is, when cash enters the financial system, is transported across national borders, or when funds are transferred between financial intermediaries.

By imposing an obligation to provide information that may reveal organized criminal activity, a transaction-reporting regime can theoretically serve a number of important policing and regulatory functions. It provides government agencies with a greater capacity to uncover evidence of money laundering as well as the criminal sources of the illicit proceeds. It also works to ensure that proper records are in place within private-sector companies to facilitate subsequent money laundering investigations. Transaction reporting is also meant to serve as a deterrent or at the very least an inconvenience, to those attempting to launder the proceeds of crime. Due in part to pressure from the United States and multinational bodies such as the Financial Action Task Force, transaction reporting has been adopted by a growing number of countries throughout the world, including Canada.

Transaction reporting can be demarcated into two general categories: currency transaction reporting (CTR) and suspicious activity reporting (SAR). A CTR system requires that specified financial intermediaries report any currency transaction over a specified threshold ($10,000 in Canada and the United States). A SAR system mandates regulated entities to report transactions that appear to be suspicious, regardless of the amount, and this is meant to provide more discriminate information relative to a CTR system.

To process the reports submitted by private-sector companies and professionals, most countries have created a financial intelligence unit (FIU), a specialized national government agency created to "serve as a national centre for the collection, analysis and dissemination of information regarding potential money-laundering" (United Nations, 2000: Appendix X, Article 7, paragraph 1b). The role of the FIU is to facilitate one of the key issues involved in proceeds of crime enforcement: "ensuring that the critical piece or pieces of information make it to the right people—the investigators and prosecutors charged with putting criminals behind bars and taking their illegally obtained wealth away—in a timely and useful manner" (Egmont Group, 2004: 1). The FIU in Canada is known as the Financial Transactions Reporting Agency (more on this agency, as well as the laws and regulations that it enforces, is described in chapter 13).

Government Regulatory Agencies

It is the government regulatory system that carries much of the burden for monitoring legitimate industries and the commercial and financial transactions that are vulnerable to organized criminal activity. As such, public regulatory agencies have a potentially significant role to play in combatting racketeering in specific sectors of the economy. In the United States, the power and resources of different federal and state regulatory agencies have been adapted to address various OC activities, such as fraud, corruption, labour racketeering, product counterfeiting, gambling, and hazardous waste disposal.

In the United States, the Federal Reserve Board is responsible for supervising federally incorporated banking institutions and is empowered to ensure compliance with the *Bank Secrecy Act*, primarily through its examination, audit, and investigative functions. In addition, the Federal Reserve Board develops and disseminates anti-money laundering guidance procedures for regulated banks, provides advice and support to US law enforcement agencies, and trains foreign central banks and government agencies in money laundering controls (Federal Reserve Board, 1997). At the state level, the New York State Department of Financial Services, which regulates state-chartered financial service providers, uses its mandate to ensure money laundering prevention and compliance programs are in place within state-licensed financial institutions. Its predecessor, the New York State Department of Banking, was involved in joint-force operations with law enforcement agencies, such as the El Dorado Money Laundering Task Force, which also included the US Customs Service, the Internal Revenue Service, and the New York City Police Department. The task force has enjoyed success in identifying and prosecuting money laundering offences that have utilized money transmitters (New York State Department of Banking Press Release, October 31, 1997). According to a December 1, 2015, press release, the department claims, "Over the last four years, the New York State Department of Financial Services (NYDFS) has conducted a series of investigations into terrorist financing, sanctions violations, and anti-money laundering compliance at financial institutions. As a result of these investigations, the Department has uncovered (among other issues) serious shortcomings in the transaction monitoring and filtering programs of these institutions and that a lack of robust governance, oversight, and accountability at senior levels of these institutions has contributed to these shortcomings." The press release goes on to outline new regulations to be implemented by the NYDS that regulated financial services providers must follow to combat money laundering and terrorist financing (New York, Department of Financial Services Press Release, December 1, 2015).

In Canada, the Office of the Superintendent of Financial Institutions (OSFI) is the primary regulator of federally incorporated financial institutions and pension plans in Canada. The mission of this agency is to safeguard policy holders, depositors, and pension plan members from undue loss, and administer a regulatory framework that contributes to public confidence in a competitive financial system. This agency has also taken steps to help address money laundering through its regulatory oversight of the banking sector. The initial focus of OSFI in this area was on encouraging financial institutions under its supervision to "maintain and strengthen internal rules and procedures to detect money laundering and to urge full cooperation with law enforcement agencies investigating money laundering activities" (Mitchell, 1989: 2). In 1990, OSFI issued a best practices document that was intended to guide the financial community in policies that would serve to identify suspicious transactions. Around the same time, its deposit-taking institutions division began initiatives to encourage the development of policies and programs within chartered banks to address money laundering. Since the 1990 study, OSFI has developed more formal polices and directives for the prevention and detection of money laundering through regulated companies. Most significantly, in 1996, a document entitled *Guideline: Deterring and Detecting Money Laundering* was issued by OSFI. This document outlines guidelines that all federally regulated deposit-taking institutions are expected to implement, although these measures are not mandated by law.

Civil Remedies

For criminal convictions, nation-states using common law systems require proof beyond a reasonable doubt, which often translates into a heavy burden for state prosecutors, especially in relation to the prosecution of high-level organized crime offenders who have successfully escaped criminal convictions by insulating themselves from the illegal operations of their organizations. Some governments have enacted legislation that provides the state with the tools to undertake civil action against individuals and entities involved in criminal activity. This includes "civil forfeiture" laws that provide the state with the power to seize property through civil, rather than criminal courts. "A civil forfeiture occurs independently of any criminal proceeding and is directed at the property itself having been used or acquired illegally. Conviction of the property owner is not relevant in a civil forfeiture" (Albanese, 2015: 342). Because the asset forfeiture is now pursued through the civil courts, the burden of proof placed is reduced from "beyond a reasonable doubt" to a "balance of probabilities." In other words, governments can confiscate money or assets where a reasonable suspicion exists that cash or assets constitute the proceeds of crime and the owner is unable to provide a satisfactory explanation of its legitimate origin. Onus of proof is now shared between the state and the defendant; that is, unlike a criminal trial where there is no obligation by the defendant to prove his innocence, in a civil forfeiture process there is now an onus placed on the defendant to prove that the assets in question were derived through legal and legitimate means.

The application of civil sanctions against organized and economic crimes has been most vigorously (and controversially) applied in the United States. The federal *Racketeer Influenced Corrupt Organization* (RICO) *Act* makes it unlawful to acquire, operate, or receive income from an enterprise through criminal means. RICO allows the government or a private citizen to file a civil suit requesting the court to order sanctions or to provide injunctive relief against an individual or organization involved in a "pattern of racketeering" (see chapter 13 for more information on RICO).

While the Canadian government has long resisted the adoption of civil forfeiture laws to combat organized crime and terrorism, a number of provinces have enacted them. Ontario was the first and, in 2002, new legislation was enacted that would allow police in that province to confiscate cash or any other assets suspected of being purchased with the proceeds of crime, without a criminal conviction. When Ontario passed their civil forfeiture legislation, they boasted that the benefit of these powers was that "the government didn't ever need to charge or convict the person." The *Remedies for Organized Crime and Other Unlawful Activities Act* would allow a civil court judge to authorize the seizure of assets once the Crown has proven on a "balance of probabilities" that the assets were obtained with the proceeds of crime. The bill also gave the province the power to file civil suits against two or more people who conspire to commit unlawful activities that harm the public.

The provincial legislation initially met with stiff opposition from the legal community in Canada. The law "presumes guilt," John Rosen, a noted criminal lawyer in Toronto, said in a media interview. "It's contrary to our whole history of criminal justice in our country." The Ontario government argues that the legislation does not intrude on federal jurisdiction because it is made up of civil laws, which is within the jurisdiction of provincial governments. Provincial governments also contend that the legislation focuses on criminally derived property, and property rights are not protected in the Charter of Rights (*National Post*, December 7, 2000).

The Manitoba government followed suit and introduced legislation that would strip individuals of their assets even if they were not convicted of an offence. *The Criminal Property Forfeiture Act* would allow police to seize the homes, cars, cash, and other property of any person, as long as they could convince a judge that the person is a member of a criminal organization. The onus would then be on the individual being sued to prove the assets were earned through a legitimate income and not the proceeds of crime (Canadian Press, November 26, 2003).

Provincial governments have implemented other civil remedies targeting criminal gangs and organizations. Section 69.1 of the provincial *Gaming and Liquor Act* in Alberta grants police discretion to direct people "associated with a gang" to leave licensed premises (such as bars, taverns, pubs, etc.). "The section does not prohibit people who are associated with a gang from being in licensed premises," a background document prepared by a provincial justice official reads. "Instead, it gives police discretion to tell them to leave and charges arise only if they refuse to do so. It enables proactive 'public order' policing, which seeks to prevent criminal activity and to limit its effects. The general purpose of s.69.1 is to eliminate bars as places where gangs congregate" (Wiltshire, 2015).

The Armed Forces

Many countries have engaged their military to support organized crime enforcement. While the emphasis has been on drug interdiction along international borders and in source countries, naval forces have been used by Western governments to combat seaborne drug and migrant smuggling. The deployment of the armed forces is meant to capitalize on its advanced reconnaissance and intelligence-gathering capability, its omnipresence in high-risk regions of the world, and its overwhelming logistical prowess and military might.

In the United States, the Department of Defense (DOD) has been designated the lead agency for detecting and monitoring the aerial and maritime transit of illegal drugs into that country. This responsibility is coordinated through a deputy assistant defence secretary for Drug Enforcement Program and Support. Selected US commands have been directed to execute these responsibilities and joint task forces have been created to assist in the coordination of DOD resources in support of law enforcement agencies. The US Coast Guard, which has primary jurisdiction over American maritime civilian law enforcement, deploys its personnel on US navy vessels (which do not have civilian policing powers) to take advantage of its resources in monitoring high-risk smuggling routes in international waters. The DOD also provides training and technical assistance to foreign governments and army battalions in conjunction with the Department of State.

In Canada, the Department of National Defence is mandated to assist other federal departments in achieving various national goals, including drug interdiction and smuggling enforcement. In February 1994, the RCMP along with Canadian military fighter jets and the navy destroyer *Terra Nova* combined to haul in five metric tonnes of cocaine from the hold of a fishing boat off the coast of Shelburne in southwestern Nova Scotia (Criminal Intelligence Service Canada, 1996: 17). The Canadian navy has also detected Chinese migrant-smuggling ships off the west coast using intelligence information passed along from the US Navy (*Vancouver Sun*, September 24, 1999). More recently, the RCMP has partnered with the Department of National Defence in a domestic marijuana eradication program known as Project Sabot, which uses military helicopters to identify illegal outdoor marijuana farms (Canadian Armed Forces, 2016). The involvement of the Canadian Armed Forces in criminal enforcement operations is sanctioned under subsection 273.6 (1) of the *National Defence Act*, which states the federal government "may authorize the Canadian Forces to perform any duty involving public service."

National and Foreign Security Intelligence Agencies

Combatting crime has traditionally been the domain of law enforcement agencies, while national security issues, in particular terrorism, fall primarily under the mandate of security intelligence agencies. Transnational organized crime blurs the line between the two because of its perceived threats to national and international security, including arms and nuclear material smuggling and trafficking, corrupting democratic governments, and supporting rebel forces. The role of national security agencies in combatting transnational crime is premised on the need to harness the source intelligence, the international networks, as well as the analytical elements of these agencies.

In the United States, national and foreign security intelligence agencies have been given a mandate to gather intelligence information on crime groups and activities that may threaten national security. The objective of the Counter Narcotics and Crime Center of the US Central Intelligence Agency (CIA) is to bring together source intelligence and the analytical and technical elements of the CIA to bear on international crime. The centre also functions to coordinate the actions of law enforcement and national security agencies to address intelligence problems of common concern.

Following a 1993 Canadian Department of Justice legal opinion that affirmed the view that certain types of transnational organized crimes could represent a threat to the security of Canada, a role was identified within the mandate of Canadian Security Intelligence Service (CSIS) to assist domestic law enforcement agencies. This new role for CSIS represented a significant departure from the service's traditional area of responsibility in which criminal activities were generally investigated only in the context of espionage and serious politically motivated violence. Commencing in 1995, CSIS initiated a number of intelligence gathering investigations into transnational criminal activity. From the outset, the role of CSIS was limited to the collection of strategic intelligence, and involvement in criminal enforcement of a tactical nature was avoided. As part of this mandate, CSIS drafted plans to gather intelligence information and conduct national security threat assessments of such criminal activities as fraud, money laundering, drug smuggling, bribery, abuse of the immigration process, corruption, and interference with Canada's foreign policy. CSIS created the Transnational Criminal Activity (TCA) section in January 1996, as part of a government-wide effort to carry out its new mandate. This unit draws on the service's operational and strategic analysis resources in order to collect intelligence related to transnational crime (Canadian Security Intelligence Service, 1998).

A declassified version of a study conducted by the Security Intelligence Review Committee questions whether CSIS should be investigating the criminal underworld. The report reflects the government watchdog's misgivings about the spy service's efforts to gather intelligence about criminal groups and activities. The committee's study concludes that CSIS lacked a clear blueprint to ensure investigators were looking only at activities that posed a threat to Canada's strategic interests. "The result has been the investigation of what have turned out to be street-level crime or crimes already being investigated by police." The study says if CSIS cannot bring "a unique perspective" to an international crime probe, it "should leave the matter in the hands of the appropriate law enforcement agencies" (as cited in the *Ottawa Citizen*, May 20, 2000).

Citizen-based Action

One of the common denominators of both organized and unorganized crime is their negative impact on local communities. As such, it logically follows that preventative approaches should incorporate a community-based emphasis. A central assumption of community crime prevention is that private citizens play a major role in maintaining order in a free society and, therefore, should be encouraged to accept more responsibility for public safety at the local level. Pace and Styles (1975: 89) contend one of the cornerstones of any comprehensive effort to control organized "is an aroused citizenry."

The importance of citizen involvement in the fight against organized crime is reflected in the expanded efforts of law enforcement agencies to disseminate information to, raise awareness of, and educate people on its scope and nature and the challenges of its enforcement. These campaigns have utilized direct mail, public presentations, the media, and the Internet. Law enforcement agencies have also relied on toll-free "tip lines"—traditionally geared toward local property crime and violent offences—to solicit information on organized crimes, such as drug trafficking, fraud, and contraband smuggling. The RCMP has worked with Crime Stoppers to solicit anonymous tips on suspected smuggling operations and local contraband suppliers. This was adapted to cigarette smuggling through the "River Watch Program," which involves an intensive campaign by police to encourage residents living along the St. Lawrence Seaway to be watchful of and report suspicious activity in well-known smuggling routes. Public tip lines have also been dedicated to specific organized crime genres, such as the outlaw biker hotline established by CISC.

A number of tip lines are now dedicated to combat consumer fraud and deceitful telemarketing. Two North American examples include the National Fraud Information

Center, operated by the Washington-based National Consumers League, and the Canadian Anti-Fraud Centre, a joint initiative involving the federal Competition Bureau, the RCMP, and the Ontario Provincial Police. Both agencies operate call centres that take reports and complaints from consumers and provide public education campaigns to alert the public to current fraud schemes targeting the public.

Private-Sector Initiatives

The financial services sector is particularly vulnerable to organized fraud and money laundering schemes and, as a result, companies and associations within this sector have undertaken a number of initiatives to address victimization at the hands of organized crime. As the industry representative for chartered banks in Canada, the Canadian Bankers Association (CBA) has taken a number of steps to address the problem of money laundering within the banking sector. The CBA established a task force to address money laundering–related issues and concerns common to all banks. Composed of the security directors of individual banks, the task force was originally charged with determining the scope of the problem in Canada, monitoring new developments in money laundering schemes at home and abroad, reviewing protective measures already in place along with those contemplated for future implementation, and promoting industry liaison with law enforcement groups, government agencies, and other banking associations and organizations throughout the world. The CBA has also provided input into Canadian proceeds of crime legislation and has worked with federal and local law enforcement in the preparation of educational programs, and compliance protocols for dealing with this legislation (Ballard, 1991; Canadian Bankers Association Press Release, June 2, 1988).

The tremendous growth of private policing in recent years, combined with the decreased capacity of public police forces to unilaterally control commercial crime, has produced a burgeoning forensic accounting industry. In North America, forensic accounting practices provide a number of investigative, risk management, and consulting services to the public and private sectors. While traditionally focused on white-collar crime such as fraud or internal theft, given their expertise and resources, combined with the growing overlap between organized and commercial crime, these firms are increasingly providing services to combat the involvement of criminal groups in the private sector. Such services include conducting risk assessments and forensic audits to identify the nature and scope of organized crime within private-sector industries or individual firms, developing money laundering and fraud prevention and compliance programs, undertaking fraud investigations, tracing assets stolen by criminal organizations, conducting background checks on investors or suppliers to ensure there are no ties to crime groups, and monitoring the activities of a company and its clients to detect suspicious activities (*Dallas Morning News*, July 1, 1998; *Financial Post*, July 4, 1998; Schneider, 1998).

BEST PRACTICES IN ORGANIZED CRIME CONTROL

This chapter has identified a number of approaches to combatting organized crime, including traditional enforcement techniques as well as alternative measures that fall outside the criminal justice system. A number of principles underlying innovative and effective approaches to combatting organized crime can be gleaned from the strategies, tactics, and cases described in this chapter and are summarized below.

- *Inter-agency co-operation and coordination*: Inter-agency co-operation and co-ordination has emerged as the most important development in combatting organized crime in recent years. While most coordination occurs between domestic law enforcement agencies, some have included partnerships between criminal justice agencies and other public-sector bodies (regulatory, policy, security intelligence, military, etc.) as well as multi-sectoral partnerships involving public, private, and non-governmental sectors. Given the transnational character of OC, and the immense challenges confronting international law enforcement, perhaps the most important development is the creation of joint-force operations that involve law enforcement agencies from different countries as well as mutual legal assistance treaties that provide the legal basis for such enforcement.

- *Strategic approach, including a strong intelligence function*: The sophisticated, complex, and transnational nature of organized crime groups and activities demands that a long-term policy and enforcement approach be undertaken. Traditional emphasis on "quick hits" of lower-echelon members or seizures of illegal commodities have been replaced by project-style investigations that target upper-echelon members and seek to dismantle criminal organizations or networks. Law enforcement agencies that have patiently nurtured source intelligence, collected information, developed long-term plans, coordinated with other agencies and then conducted simultaneous operations have been the most successful in targeting large, serious criminal conspiracies. National strategic planning is an essential foundation for a comprehensive approach that relies on the use of different targeting foci (contraband, groups, routes, etc.), approaches (prevention, deterrence, enforcement), sanctions (criminal, regulatory, civil), and key partners (public, private, and NGO sectors).

- *Complement criminal enforcement with regulatory, civil, and administrative sanctions*: Effective strategic OC control efforts have relied on the use of a variety of criminal, civil, regulatory, and administrative sanctions. Regulatory enforcement can play a proactive role by preventing the infiltration of organized crime into a particular industry, while administrative sanctions and civil penalties can be applied in addition to or in lieu of criminal penalties.

- *Combining prevention and enforcement*: Reactive law enforcement approaches need to be on par with measures that are more preventative in nature. A comprehensive, strategic response to organized crime involves complementing traditional enforcement approaches with more preventative measures, especially those that address the root causes.
- *Impact assessment*: Law enforcement policies, procedures, and programs should be constantly assessed—through rigorous research carried out by external researchers—to determine if they are meeting their tactical and strategic objectives. If such objectives are being met, there should be a determination of best practices. If they are not being met, a determination should be made as to why, and then any necessary modifications should be made.
- *Reducing harm inflicted by law enforcement*: As described in chapter 13, some have criticized drug enforcement for doing more harm than good. In this vein, Paoli (2014a: 6) summarizes the importance of ensuring that policies and enforcement agencies take concrete steps to minimize the harm they may inflict. "Policy interventions to control whatever form of organized crime should, in other words, be inspired by the realization of the governments' limits and potential for harm" with special attention being paid to "the policy's unintended consequences … " (Paoli, 2014a: 6).

KEY TERMS

Agent

Asset forfeiture

Containment

Control

Controlled delivery

Criminal intelligence

Criminality prevention

Detection

Electronic surveillance

Enforcement

Extra-judicial

Forensic accounting

Harm reduction

Incident reduction

Informant

Interdiction

Investigation

King pin investigation

Legalization/regulation model

Mega-trial

Part VI investigation

Physical surveillance

Prohibition/enforcement model

Prosecution

Punishment

Reverse sting

State witness

Sting

Strategic intelligence

Surveillance

Tactical intelligence

Undercover operation

Wiretap

Witness

Witness protection program

REVIEW QUESTIONS

1. What are the broad objectives of organized crime control? What is the difference between eradication, deterrence, harm reduction, and containment as objectives?
2. What is the difference between organized crime control and organized crime enforcement?
3. What are the broad parameters and characteristics of the traditional organized crime prohibition/enforcement model?
4. What are common organized crime enforcement strategies?
5. What are common enforcement (operational) tactics and techniques?
6. What are alternative (non–criminal justice) organized crime control tactics and techniques and how do they differ from traditional criminal justice approaches?
7. What are the best practices in organized crime control?

FURTHER READINGS

Beare, M.E., & Martens, F.T. (1998). Policing organized crime: The comparative structures, traditions and policies within the United States and Canada, *Journal of Contemporary Criminal Justice*, 14(4): 398–427.

Camilleri, J.D. (Ed.). (2011). *Organized Crime: Challenges, Trends and Reduction Strategies.* Hauppauge, NY: Nova Science Publishers.

Edelhertz, H., Cole, R., & Berk, B. (1984). *The Containment of Organized Crime.* Lexington: D.C. Heath and Company.

Gottschalk, P. (2009). *Policing Organized Crime: Intelligence Strategy Implementation.* Boca Raton: CRC Press.

Tusikov, N. (2012). Measuring organised crime-related harms: Exploring five policing methods, *Crime, Law and Social Change*, 57(1): 99–115.

13 ORGANIZED CRIME CONTROL IN PRACTICE: CRIMINAL LAW AND ENFORCEMENT AGENCIES IN CANADA

CHAPTER OUTLINE

- Introduction and Overview
- Organized Crime Laws and Legislation
- Organized Crime Enforcement in Canada: Responsibilities, Jurisdictions, and Agencies
- The Theory and Practice of Organized Crime Enforcement: A Critical Analysis
- Future Organized Crime Enforcement Policy Options
- Conclusion to Part IV

LEARNING OUTCOMES

The objective of this chapter is to examine the application of organized crime control principles, strategies, and tactics outlined in the previous chapter to Canada, with emphasis on the criminal laws and criminal justice agencies mandated to combat this problem. Information on American laws will also be described for comparative purposes. More specifically, this chapter is intended to foster a better understanding and critical analysis of the following:

- The role of criminal laws in combatting organized crime
- How the legal concept of conspiracy is central to laws and legislation targeting organized crime
- Laws and legislation in Canada relevant to organized crime control
- Selective laws that have been adopted in the United States to combat organized crime
- How Canadian criminal laws to specific organized crime compare to those of the United States
- The structure of OC enforcement in Canada, including responsibilities, jurisdictions, and agencies involved

- Critiques of the traditional enforcement model as applied in Canada
- Factors that make the goal of containing—let alone eradicating—organized crime in Canadian society so difficult
- The constraints that are placed on traditional enforcement strategies in free, democratic, common-law countries with a strong emphasis on human rights
- Critiques and weaknesses of organized crime enforcement in Canada
- Future organized crime enforcement policy options
- Pros and cons of legalization of recreational drugs and its impact on organized crime

INTRODUCTION AND OVERVIEW

The business of organized crime invariably violates numerous laws in Canada. The two most important statutes that are used as the legislative basis to combat organized crime in Canada are the *Criminal Code of Canada* and the *Controlled Drugs and Substances Act*. An important foundation of organized crime enforcement lies in the legal concept of conspiracy—an agreement between two or more people to commit a criminal act. Legislators have augmented specific criminal offences (such as fraud, extortion, or drug trafficking) and conspiracy laws with statutes specifically targeting organized criminal associations and activities. The legislative focus on organized crime began in the United States through the creation of the *Racketeer Influenced Corrupt Organizations* (RICO) *Act*. There is no equivalent of the RICO statute in Canada, although the *Criminal Code* has been amended to enshrine a definition of a criminal organization and designates three related offences: participation in a criminal organization, committing an indictable offence for a criminal organization, and instructing another person to commit an indictable offence for the benefit of a criminal organization. On top of predicate offences, such as drug trafficking or extortion, offenders can now be convicted of committing a criminal action for a criminal organization and receive a jail sentence to be served consecutively with the sentence handed down for the predicate offence. The additional penalties are meant to reflect the increased harm inflicted on society when crimes are carried out in an organized manner.

These laws are enforced by federal, provincial, and municipal police departments and are prosecuted by provincial attorneys general (in the case of *Criminal Code* violations) or the federal department of justice (in regards to large-scale drug-trafficking offences). Criminal law enforcement, including drug and organized crime enforcement, is a shared responsibility between the federal, provincial, and municipal governments. This chapter will focus primarily on the role of the federal government, including relevant federal criminal laws and agencies.

Historically, the federal government, through the RCMP, has taken the lead in combatting organized crime in this country, and there are a number of units within the force to carry out this mandate. Today, municipal police and provincial governments (through provincial police forces and prosecutors) are also active in organized crime enforcement on their own or as part of integrated, multi-agency task forces.

Organized crime enforcement mandates and objectives in Canada are increasingly being couched in less ambitious (and more realistic) objectives, such as organized crime control, harm reduction, and containment. Yet even these more modest goals have not been achieved. Organized crime has not been contained, and the harm it inflicts on society is as great now as it has ever been. In fact, the scope of organized crime groups and criminal activity has steadily grown since the end of World War II.

There are myriad reasons why organized crime continues to persist in society. Its inherent characteristics, combined with ongoing demand for its products and services, partially account for its resilience. There are also the weaknesses of the traditional enforcement model, unavoidable constraints that limit the effectiveness of criminal law enforcement in free, democratic, common-law countries with a strong emphasis on human rights, as well as a myriad of weaknesses of and mistakes made by government policy makers and criminal justice agencies in their implementation of the traditional enforcement model. One of the most persistent critiques of organized crime enforcement in Canada is that policy makers and enforcement agencies in Canada did not take the scope of and threat posed by organized crime seriously until the problem became too big to control.

The staying power of organized crime should also be placed in the context of the crime in general. Unlike organized crime, no one presumes that crime, in general, will ever be eradicated, so why is there a presumption that traditional enforcement methods will lead to the eradication of organized crime?

Future policy options to boost the effectiveness organized crime enforcement in Canada include the following: (1) increase law enforcement resources; (2) expand the authority and powers of law enforcement, including more powerful laws and legislation; (3) shift resources toward more preventative approaches; and (4) decrease criminal opportunity and illicit markets by decriminalizing or legalizing products and services currently offered exclusively in the underworld.

ORGANIZED CRIME LAWS AND LEGISLATION

The business of organized crime involves multiple offences that violate numerous laws. Historically, offenders have been charged with specific criminal offences regardless of whether the individual acted alone or as part of a criminal organization. This began to change in the late 1960s and early 1970s in the United States when criminal legislation introduced offences targeting organized criminal conspiracies or "racketeering" was enacted. The Canadian government followed suit in the 1990s. Before examining some of the laws that are used specifically to combat organized crime in North America, this chapter shall examine a legal concept that is central to these laws: conspiracy.

Conspiracy Laws

An important foundation of laws and legislation targeting organized crime control lies in the legal concept of **conspiracy**, which is codified in both Canadian and American criminal statutes. In this legal context, conspiracy refers to an agreement between two or more people to commit a criminal act. In Canada, the offence of conspiracy is set out at section 465 of the *Criminal Code of Canada* and states that anyone who conspires with another person to commit an **indictable offence** "is guilty of an indictable offence and liable to the same punishment as that to which an accused who is guilty of that offence would, on conviction, be liable." A conviction for a conspiracy offence requires proof beyond a reasonable doubt that the conspiracy exists and that the accused was one of two or more people who planned to commit or committed an indictable offence (*R. v. Carter*). The conspiracy need not be a formal agreement, but can be implicit (Goode, 1975: 16) as long as there is a "a common plan with a common objective" among the co-conspirators (*R. v. Cotroni*). Other Supreme Court decisions have ruled that the crime of conspiracy is a separate offence from the predicate offence the co-conspirators planned to commit or committed, and the predicate offence need not actually be perpetrated for the offenders to be convicted of conspiracy.

Conspiracy statutes provide valuable tools for prosecuting those involved in an ongoing criminal operation for at least two reasons. First, conspiracy laws target more than one person (and, of course, a fundamental trait of organized crime is the involvement of multiple offenders). Second, conspiracy laws target not just those offenders who are caught physically committing a crime; any other person who conspires to commit the offences is also subject to prosecution. Thus, conspiracy laws can be invaluable in indicting those who occupy the upper echelons of organized crime syndicates and direct the illegal activities of others without being physically involved in committing the predicate offence. Earle Johnson Jr., Special Attorney in the Organized Crime and Racketeering Section of the US Department of Justice, in 1963, wrote: "The conspiracy theory has much to recommend it as a technique for ensnaring the well-insulated leadership of organized crime. The fundamental essence of a conspiracy obviates the necessity of establishing that the organization leader himself committed a physical act amounting to a crime or that he even committed an overt act in furtherance of the object of the conspiracy. It is sufficient if he can be shown to have been a party to the conspiratorial agreement" (Johnson, 1963: 2). In Canada, some of the highest profile organized crime figures, including Frank Cotroni and John Papalia, have been convicted of conspiracy.

Subsequent legislation targeting organized crime in the United States and Canada has built upon conspiracy laws. This explicit statutory focus on organized crime began in the United States through the creation of one of the most powerful (and controversial) criminal laws in the Western world: the *Racketeer Influenced and Corrupt Organizations Act.*

Laws and Legislation in the United States: *Racketeer Influenced and Corrupt Organizations Act*

The *Racketeer Influenced and Corrupt Organizations* (RICO) *Act* may be considered the single most important piece of federal legislation in the United States to combat organized crime in that country. While derided by some as an unfair infringement on such ingrained constitutional rights as due process, it has been used extensively and successfully to prosecute thousands of individuals and organizations in the US. Part of the federal *Organized Crime Control Act of 1970*, RICO makes it unlawful to acquire, operate, or receive income from an enterprise through a pattern of racketeering activity. Specifically geared toward organized criminal conspiracies, the thrust of RICO is to prove a pattern of crimes conducted through an "enterprise," which the statute defines as "any individual, partnership, corporation, association, or other legal entity, and any union or group of individuals associated in fact, although not a legal entity." Under RICO, it is a crime for an individual to belong to an "enterprise" that is involved in a pattern of racketeering, even if the racketeering was committed by other members. In order for an individual or organization to be convicted of racketeering under RICO, there must be proof of a "pattern" of illegal offences, which RICO defines as the commission of at least two identified criminal offences within a 10-year period. Rudolph Giuliani, the former US attorney for the southern district of New York who successfully used RICO in prosecuting organized crime cases, argues,

> The federal prosecutor derives a variety of benefits from the RICO statute's definitions of enterprise and racketeering activity. For example, it is the only criminal statute that enables the Government to present a jury with the whole picture of how an enterprise, such as an organized crime family, operates. Rather than pursuing the leader of a small group or subordinates for a single crime or scheme, the Government is able to indict the entire hierarchy of an organized crime family for the diverse criminal activities in which that "enterprise" engages. Instead of merely proving one criminal act in a defendant's life, it permits proof of a defendant's whole life in crime. (Giuliani, 1986: 106)

RICO defines racketeering as "any act or threat involving murder, kidnapping, gambling, arson, robbery, bribery, extortion, or dealing in narcotic or other dangerous drugs, which is chargeable under State law and punishable by imprisonment for more than one year." In addition, RICO lists numerous federal offences that the statute defines as "racketeering": bribery, sports bribery, counterfeiting, and embezzlement from union funds, loansharking, mail fraud, wire fraud, obstruction of justice, contraband cigarettes, prostitution, human trafficking, bankruptcy fraud, drug violations, and obscenity.

The maximum criminal penalty for violating RICO includes a $250,000 fine and imprisonment for 20 years. These penalties are imposed on top of the penalties incurred by the defendants for the substantive offences committed during a 10-year period. In other words, an offender convicted and handed a prison sentence under the provisions of RICO for loansharking and extortion will also have penalties imposed under different federal or state criminal statutes for the substantive offences of loansharking and extortion. These sentences are often to be served consecutively (e.g., 10 years for RICO violations and then another 10 years for the substantive offences). In addition to the criminal penalties, RICO also proscribes penalties that can be pursued against a defendant in the civil courts. Specifically, RICO allows for the state or a private party victimized by a defendant to sue civilly for damages. If successful, the victim may be able to recoup "treble" damages; that is, the defendant must pay to the plaintiff three times the amount of damages as well as legal expenses that have been determined by a court. RICO also allows the government or a private party to file a civil suit requesting that the court force a defendant to forfeit assets, order sanctions, or provide injunctive relief against an individual or organization involved in a pattern of racketeering.

With respect to asset forfeiture, the government can seize what it deems to be the proceeds of crime through a civil suit launched against a defendant. The government can seize property if it can prove there is a reasonable expectation that the property is associated with criminal activity. In this respect, criminal charges need not be laid against a defendant to set in motion the civil forfeiture proceedings. In contrast to criminal prosecutions, where the burden of proof is beyond a reasonable doubt, only the lesser standard of proof—a balance of probabilities—is required under the civil provisions of RICO. The attraction of this approach is that the onus of proof is shifted to the defendant, who must prove that assets were acquired through legitimate means.

In addition to asset forfeitures, RICO's **civil injunction** provisions can prohibit individuals from owning or becoming involved in certain legitimate or illegitimate organizations or activities. These civil injunctive provisions can even be used to terminate a particular legal entity if it is proven it has been implicated in racketeering (Gardiner, 1998; Giuliani, 1986). For example, under the provisions of RICO, the government can file a petition in a federal district court seeking to have a company set up to facilitate fraud put in receivership. Such a petition could also be used against a corrupt local chapter of a labour union, which may entail removing the leadership of the union and even placing the union in receivership.

While it took some time for federal prosecutors to fully understand and incorporate RICO into their array of prosecutorial tools, the statute has been used extensively and has realized particular success when used against Italian Mafia groups and associated offenders in the United States. "The hierarchies of the five New York LCN [*La Cosa Nostra*] Families have been prosecuted, and similar prosecutions have dented the LCN hierarchies in Boston, Cleveland, Denver, Kansas City, Milwaukee, New

Case Study: The Commission Case

Use of the RICO statute resulted in one of the most important prosecutions ever brought against LCN families in the United States. On November 19, 1986, in what became known at the "Commission Case" (*United States v. Salerno*, 85 CR 139, S.D.N.Y., 1985), a number of New York Mafia bosses were convicted of conducting the affairs of "the Commission of La Cosa Nostra" in a pattern of racketeering that violated the RICO statutes. The government's argument was that the LCN Commission constituted a criminal enterprise and that each defendant had committed two or more racketeering acts in furtherance of the commission's goals. According to the prosecution, the defendants' predicate racketeering acts fell into three categories: first, management of a multi-family bid-rigging and extortion scheme in the New York concrete industry; second, conspiracy to organize loansharking territories in Staten Island; and, third, the murders of Bonanno family boss Carmine Galante and two of his associates in furtherance of the commission's effort to resolve a Bonanno family leadership dispute (Jacobs, Panarella, & Worthington, 1994: 81).

During the trial, defence counsel admitted the existence of the LCN and the commission in New York City. They denied, however, the commission's involvement in criminal activity. The defence was not successful and in 1986 all of the defendants—including Carmine Persico, boss of the Colombo Family; Anthony Salerno, boss of the Genovese Family; and Anthony Corallo, boss of the Lucchese Family—were found guilty.

Jersey, Philadelphia, Pittsburgh and St. Louis," according to the Pennsylvania Crime Commission (1991: 18). Since then the RICO statute has been used to prosecute members of outlaw motorcycle gangs, Chinese gangs in New York, Russian organized crime, and an Armenian criminal syndicate.

RICO has been at the centre of vociferous criticism since it was enacted. Many have argued that the broad wording of the RICO statute (as well as subsequent court decisions) has meant the legislation significantly overreaches, leading to the prosecution of individuals who—although they may have been involved in criminal behaviour—are not remotely connected to organized crime (Abadinsky, 2013: 354). For instance, both the criminal and civil aspects of RICO have been used successfully by abortion clinics to sue anti-abortion protest groups for damages (*Chicago Tribune*, April 21, 1998). Other RICO defendants have included anti-obscenity protesters, video storeowners, adult bookstore owners, major corporations, banks, investment firms, the Chicago Mercantile Exchange, politicians, doctors, local and state law enforcement personnel, and husbands who have been sued by their ex-wives for defrauding them of marital property (Abadinsky, 2000: 403).

CRITICAL THINKING EXERCISE

Conduct further research into the RICO statute, including its provisions, as well as the controversies that have surrounded it. Based on what you know about RICO, organized crime in Canada, and current laws in this country, should similar legislation be enacted in Canada?

Laws and Legislation in Canada

The enactment of criminal law in Canada is the exclusive jurisdiction of the federal Parliament, a responsibility that derives from the *British North America Act* passed in 1867. As such, the federal government is responsible for drafting and introducing the vast majority of legislation concerned with OC in this country. The two most important statutes that are used as the legislative basis to combat OC in this country are the *Criminal Code of Canada* and the *Controlled Drugs and Substances Act*. Other relevant legislation, including the *Customs Act* and the *Immigration Act*, contain provisions that address specific organized crimes. The *Income Tax Act* is also relevant, insofar as it can be used to prosecute and indirectly forfeit the proceeds of crime from professional criminals for contravening income tax laws.

Criminal Code of Canada
In 1892, Canada's Parliament passed legislation called *An Act respecting the criminal law (Criminal Code)*, which consolidated all crimes and criminal law procedure in a single statute. Since its initial enactment, it has been amended on numerous occasions. It is within the *Criminal Code* where most activities traditionally associated with organized crime are made illegal, including the following:

- Travel document offences, including counterfeiting, fraudulent use of passports, etc. (sections 57 and 58)
- Weapons trafficking (sections 99 to 101)
- Corruption of government officials (sections 118 to 125)
- Illegal gaming and betting (sections 201 to 209)
- Prostitution-related offences (sections 210 to 213)
- Theft (sections 322 to 334)
- Extortion (section 346)
- Criminal interest rate (section 347)
- Forgery (sections 366 to 378)
- Fraud (sections 380 to 396)
- Product piracy (sections 406 to 414)

- Counterfeit money (section 448 to 462)
- Possession of the proceeds of crime/money laundering (sections 462.31 to 462.5)
- Conspiracy (section 465)

The *Criminal Code* also proscribes certain intrusive investigative techniques that can be used by police against suspected criminal offenders, such as electronic surveillance or searches of private property.

Unlike the RICO statute, for much of its existence, the *Criminal Code* did not look beyond individual offences when prosecuting offenders. This changed in recent years with amendments to the *Criminal Code*, in particular, the addition of section 467.1 (**Participation in a Criminal Organization**). As Freedman (2006: 172) notes, "Canada and a host of other countries have created new forms of individual criminal liability through targeted organized crime legislation ... These new laws specify culpability for individual conduct but place the act within the context of group activity, rationalizing more onerous individual punishment as deterrence of group-oriented criminality." Beginning in 1997, federal Parliament amended the *Criminal Code*, as well as other relevant federal statutes, to specifically address organized criminal conspiracies. This included amendments that, for the first time, defined a criminal organization, criminalized participation in a criminal organization, and proscribed penalties for such participation or specific crimes committed as part of an ongoing criminal conspiracy. Bill C-95—officially called *An Act to amend the Criminal Code (criminal organizations) and to amend other Acts in consequence*—became law on April 25, 1997. Enacted in the wake of the violent turf war between outlaw biker gangs in Quebec, Bill C-95 introduced the legal concepts of "criminal organization," "criminal organization offence," and "participation in a criminal organization offence" into the *Criminal Code*.

Following the enactment of amendments in 2002, section 467 of the *Criminal Code* now begins by defining a criminal organization as "a group, however organized, that (a) is composed of three or more persons in or outside Canada; and (b) has as one of its main purposes or main activities the facilitation or commission of one or more serious offences that, if committed, would likely result in the direct or indirect receipt of a material benefit, including a financial benefit, by the group or by any of the persons who constitute the group." Section 467 makes a point to exclude "a group of persons that forms randomly for the immediate commission of a single offence" from this definition. This section of the *Criminal Code* then creates offences specific to "participation in activities of a criminal organization." Section 467.11 proclaims, "Every person who, for the purpose of enhancing the ability of a criminal organization to facilitate or commit an indictable offence under this or any other Act of Parliament, knowingly, by act or omission, participates in or contributes to any activity of the criminal organization is guilty of an indictable offence and liable to imprisonment for a term not exceeding five years." As specified in subsection 467.11(1), in order to successfully prosecute an individual or individuals under this section, the Crown does not have to prove "(a) the criminal organization actually facilitated or committed an indictable offence; (b) the participation or contribution of the accused actually enhanced the ability of the criminal organization to facilitate or commit an indictable offence; (c) the accused knew the specific nature of any indictable offence that may have been facilitated or committed by the criminal organization; or (d) the accused knew the identity of any of the persons who constitute the criminal organization."

Case Study: Early Application of Section 467 and Resulting Court Rulings

Since the original enactment of the legislation in 1997, charges under section 467.1 have been laid regularly by police throughout Canada. The first major test of the legislation was not particularly successful, however. In July 2000, the Crown dropped criminal organization charges against 12 alleged members of the Manitoba Warriors gang in exchange for guilty pleas for cocaine trafficking. The original accused were arrested and charged in October 1998 with numerous drug-trafficking offences as well as offences under section 467. Of the 35 originally arrested, only two people—both of whom were deemed minor players in the drug trafficking case—actually pleaded guilty to participating in a criminal organization and received jail time (*Montreal Gazette*, May 17, 2000).

A more successful test of the legislation came in July 2005. That month, Madam Justice Michele Fuerst found two members of an Ontario chapter of the Hells Angels guilty of extortion and of committing that crime in association with a criminal organization. The ruling was viewed as a significant victory for the government, not only because it upheld section 467.12 of the *Criminal Code*, but because Justice Fuerst ruled the Hells Angels to be a criminal organization (*R. v. Lindsay*). (See chapter 5 for more details on the case and the judicial decision).

Later that year another court ruling called into question the constitutionality of section 467.13. The trial involved three BC Hells Angels who were subject to various drug-trafficking and criminal organization charges, including one count under section 467.13 whereby the three were accused of instructing another person to sell cocaine and heroin for the benefit of a criminal organization. BC Supreme Court Justice Heather Holmes struck down the provisions, concluding that the law was too broad. Her rationale was that "Parliament had a constitutional duty to make clear the legal basis" on which a person is deemed to be a member of a criminal organization, and that section 467.13 failed to do that (*R. v. Terezakis*, 2005 BCSC 1727; *Vancouver Sun*, December 13, 2005). Shortly after this decision was made, the federal Crown announced it would appeal the decision, and in 2007 the BC Court of Appeals overturned Holmes's decision (*R. v. Terezakis*, 2007 BCCA 384).

Subsection 467.12(1) creates an offence and corresponding penalties for anyone who commits an indictable offence or offences on behalf of a criminal organization. This subsection reads: "Every person who commits an indictable offence under this or any other Act of Parliament for the benefit of, at the direction of, or in association with, a criminal organization is guilty of an indictable offence and liable to imprisonment for a term not exceeding fourteen years." Subsection 467.13(1) is meant to target the upper echelons of a criminal organization who may provide direction but are not actually involved in physically carrying out a crime. Specifically, this subsection creates an offence and corresponding penalties for anyone who instructs another person or persons to commit a criminal offence for a criminal organization. The subsection reads, "Every person who is one of the persons who constitute a criminal organization and who knowingly instructs, directly or indirectly, any person to commit an offence under this or any other Act of Parliament for the benefit of, at the direction of, or in association with, the criminal organization is guilty of an indictable offence and liable to imprisonment for life."

As can be seen, the penalties proscribed under section 467 can be substantial and include life imprisonment (which generally means a sentence of no more than 25 years). Moreover, section 467.14 states that any sentence handed down for any of the offences listed in section 467.1 shall be served consecutively to any other sentence handed to the defendant for the predicate offences committed in relation to the criminal organization offences. Thus, if a defendant is convicted of a drug-trafficking offence (and receives a 10-year sentence) and is then subsequently convicted under section 467.12 for selling the drugs on behalf of a criminal organization (and receives a 10-year sentence for this offence), the offender's total sentence is 20 years (**consecutive sentencing** is in contrast to a concurrent sentence in which someone convicted of two offences is eligible to serve both sentences at the same time; that is, two 10-year sentences are served in one 10-year period).

Other relevant amendments to the *Criminal Code* include Bill C-14—*An Act to amend the Criminal Code (organized crime and protection of justice system participants)*— which came into force in 2009. Amongst other things, the bill amended the *Criminal Code* "so that any murder committed in connection with a criminal organization is first degree murder, regardless of whether it is planned and deliberate." Section 270 of the *Criminal Code*, which deals with assaults on police officers, was also amended to increase the maximum penalty from 5 to 10 years.

Controlled Drugs and Substances Act

In May 1997, Bill C-8 was enacted, which created the **Controlled Drugs and Substances Act** (CDSA). This act replaced two separate statutes: *The Narcotics Control Act* and the *Foods and Drug Act*. Like its predecessors, the CDSA provides the legal framework for dealing with controlled substances and proscribes offences in relation to the possession, use, manufacture, importation, and trafficking of both prohibited drugs (those that are illegal) and controlled drugs (those that are legal but are subject to restrictions on their distribution and use—in particular, prescription drugs). The legislation also proscribes certain powers to a peace officer in carrying out duties when enforcing the statute, such as search, seizure, and detention. In addition, the CDSA includes proceeds of crime and money laundering offences committed in relation to drug offences and provides police with the powers to seize cash and other assets deemed to be the proceeds of drug trafficking. Courts are also given the power to force a defendant convicted of proceeds of crime offences to forfeit relevant assets. Finally, the statute provides the legislative foundation for police to be protected from prosecution while committing illegal acts as part of their undercover operations (e.g., selling drugs as part of reverse sting operations).

Immigration and Refugee Protection Act

The *Immigration and Refugee Protection Act* (IRPA) came into effect in June 2002 and covers all legal issues pertaining to foreign nationals who are visiting, immigrating, or claiming refugee status in Canada. Part III of the IRPA codifies into law issues related to illegal immigration, including sections on "human smuggling and trafficking" and offences related to official travel documents (e.g., counterfeiting). The IRPA addresses a number of enforcement priorities related to organized immigration offences—in particular, migrant smuggling. The legislation includes a new offence for human trafficking and introduces significant penalties—such as fines of up to $1 million and life in prison— for individuals involved in the smuggling of migrants. It also creates new offences that allow the federal government to seize and forfeit the proceeds of crime derived from specific immigration offences. Other enforcement-related provisions in the IRPA empower government officials to bar from entering Canada anyone accused of "serious criminality" or "organized criminality," people who present security risks, or violators of human rights. According to subsection 37(1) of the legislation, "A permanent resident or a foreign national" is inadmissible to Canada on grounds of organized criminality if it can be proved that said person "is a member of an organization that is believed on reasonable grounds to be or to have been engaged in activity that is part of a pattern of criminal activity planned and organized by a number of persons acting in concert in furtherance of the commission of an offence punishable under an Act of Parliament by way of indictment, or in furtherance of the commission of an offence outside Canada that, if committed in Canada, would constitute such an offence, or engaging in activity that is part of such a pattern ... "

Income Tax Act

As described in chapter 12, income tax legislation can be used to sanction criminal offenders. While there are no provisions specifically targeting organized crime *per se*, the federal *Income Tax Act* can and has been used as a legislative basis to conduct tax assessments of offenders who have not paid taxes on their revenue, regardless of whether the revenue was legally or illegally derived. In effect, the application of the *Income Tax Act* to criminal offenders serves to penalize them by depriving them of their assets (through back taxes and fines). They can also be incarcerated for noncompliance with the *Income Tax Act*. Tax enforcement has often been used in lieu of or in addition to proceeds of crime enforcement due to the use of civil proceedings, which can be more efficient and effective in depriving criminal offenders of their unreported illicit wealth. Under the *Income Tax Act*, the Crown only has to prove that the income of an individual or organization is taxable to raise a civil assessment. Persons or corporations found guilty of an offence on summary conviction are liable for a fine of between 50 and 200 percent of the tax evaded and imprisonment for a maximum of two years. Persons or corporations found guilty of a more serious indictable offence are liable to a fine of between 100 and 200 percent of the tax evaded and imprisonment for a maximum of five years.

Customs Act

The **Customs Act** is the principal piece of legislation that pertains to the smuggling of contraband and drugs into Canada. Part VI of the *Customs Act* details specific enforcement provisions, including customs-related offences and the powers of customs officers to search individuals and vehicles coming into Canada and to seize any items that may contravene the *Customs Act* or any act of Parliament that "prohibits, controls or regulates the importation or exportation of goods" (*Customs Act*, R.S.C., 1985, c. 1 (2nd Supp.), s. 101).

Proceeds of Crime (Money Laundering) & Terrorist Financing Act

The **Proceeds of Crime (Money Laundering) & Terrorist Financing Act** establishes the regime to detect and deter the proceeds of criminal activity or funds that may be related to the financing of terrorist activities. It does so by establishing record-keeping and client identification requirements for private-sector companies and other persons or entities that engage in businesses, professions, or financial or commercial activities that are susceptible to being used for money laundering or the financing of extremist activities. The legislation sets out the obligations of these entities to report suspicious financial transactions and cross-border movements of currency and monetary instruments. It also established the Financial Transactions and Reports Analysis Centre of Canada (FINTRAC), which is the federal agency that receives reports and then disseminates information to relevant law enforcement agencies for possible proceeds of crime or terrorist-financing investigations.

Witness Protection Program Act

The **Witness Protection Program Act**, which came into force in 1996, establishes a formal, national program to protect persons (including providing a new identity) who are involved directly or indirectly in providing assistance and testimony in law enforcement matters. The act outlines admission criteria, reasons for terminating a witness's enrollment in the program, and the range of protective measures offered to witnesses. In 2014, amendments to the act were made to improve the effectiveness of the Federal Witness Protection Program, administered by the RCMP, to better meet the needs of witnesses in the program. These amendments included expanding the types of witnesses permitted to be enrolled in the program, greater coordination with provincial governments, placing further restrictions on the disclosure of information of individuals in the federal witness program, and providing for the extension of emergency assistance to witnesses not enrolled in the protection program (Casavant & Morrise, 2013: 1–2; Government of Canada News Release, November 1, 2014).

Competition Act

In 1999, Bill C-20 amended the *Competition Act* by creating new offences related to "deceptive marketing practices," which it defines as "a representation to the public that is false or misleading in a material respect." Among the type of deceptive marketing covered by the act: bait-and-switch selling, charging above the advertised price, and promotional contests. Maximum penalties for these offences are fines of $15 million for corporations and $1 million for individuals. The government can also issue an injunction that stops an individual or organization from conducting any further business. A further amendment allows the government to seize and forfeit any proceeds from the commission of this offence.

Extradition Act

The *Extradition Act*, along with deportation agreements negotiated with foreign governments, provides the legal framework to deport someone from Canada on the request of another country with which Canada has an extradition treaty (*Extradition Act*, S.C. 1999, c. 18, s. 3(1)). In general, individuals are extradited to face charges or punishment or has escaped justice in another country. One of the conditions that must be met before an individual is extradited is that the criminal offence in respect of which the extradition is requested must be an offence in Canada and is punishable by imprisonment of at least two years.

Mutual Legal Assistance in Criminal Matters Act

A **mutual legal assistance treaty** (MLAT) is an agreement between two or more countries for the purpose of gathering and exchanging information in an effort to enforce public or criminal laws. According to the Department of Justice, "A foreign state may request assistance from Canada in the gathering of evidence or the enforcement of some criminal orders (seizure orders, confiscation orders, fines) through three separate routes: (i) treaty and convention requests, (ii) letters rogatory (court issued non-treaty letter of request) and (iii) non-treaty requests." In Canada, requests made under a treaty or international convention that seek court-ordered assistance are executed under the *Mutual Legal Assistance in Criminal Matters Act*. "The Act gives Canadian courts the power to issue orders to gather evidence for a requesting State, including by search warrant; to locate a person who is suspected of having committed an offence in the requesting State; and to enforce orders of seizure and confiscation. The Act permits assistance to be rendered at any stage of a criminal matter, from investigation to appeal." In most cases, before a court in Canada can issue an order to give effect to a request for assistance, the Canadian court must be satisfied, on reasonable grounds, that a criminal offence has been committed and that the evidence sought from Canada will be found in this country. "Therefore, when seeking assistance that requires the issuance of compulsory measures (e.g., production orders, search warrants, orders compelling statements/ testimony), a requesting country must provide Canada with sufficient and clear information to establish a connection between the foreign investigation/prosecution and the evidence or assistance requested" (Department of Justice Canada, 2013: 2).

Multilateral Conventions and Their Influence on Canadian Laws

As noted in chapter 2, it is not coincidental that the definition of a criminal organization in the *Criminal Code* is a carbon copy of that in the ***United Nations Convention Against Transnational Organized Crime***; as a signatory to the convention, the Canadian government was obligated to provide a similar legal definition. The broader issue is how the many multilateral international treaties addressing (transnational) organized criminal activities that Canada has signed influence domestic criminal laws and policies.

Throughout the years, a number of multilateral conventions covering crime and justice issues have been negotiated through the UN, including ones addressing the treatment of prisoners, the conduct of law enforcement officials, the rights of juveniles, and a ban of torture. One of the main goals of such conventions is to ensure that signatory countries follow certain international standards and norms. As Reichel and Albanese (2014: 281) write, "The efforts of the U.N., as the most globally representative international body, serve to build a common language and consensus on fundamental issues of human rights and justice, and the agreements negotiated there have built a body of work since World War II that guides the development and evaluation of criminal justice and crime prevention in all world regions." With respect to organized crime, a particular goal of the multilateral conventions is the harmonization of laws across different countries. In the context of organized crime, Wheatley (2012: 77) acknowledges the underlying justification behind such transnational harmonization:

> Organized crime groups move across national borders with less difficulty than national law enforcement authorities, which are confined to their domestic jurisdictions and which must cooperate with foreign authorities to investigate crimes occurring beyond their borders. Accordingly, differences in legislation and policies across states may result in uneven progress against a given group in the places where it operates, since a group may move its operations to less risky jurisdictions. It is not essential for legislation and policies to be consistent from state to state. However, greater consistency may facilitate progress against organized crime groups, as governments engaging in cross-border law enforcement would not have to navigate such differences in their investigations and prosecutions. Likewise, organized crime groups would be less able to capitalize on differences in legal systems to limit risks to their groups.

The centrepiece UN treaty that addresses organized crime is the *Convention Against Transnational Organized Crime*, which was finalized in December 2000. The convention lays out a definition of a criminal organization as well as model laws, policies, enforcement techniques, and prevention strategies that signatory countries are expected to follow. Member states that ratify the convention commit themselves to adopt domestic laws that criminalize participation in criminal organizations (Article 5), money laundering (Article 6), corruption (Article 8), and obstruction of justice (Article 23). The convention also directs participating countries to co-operate with one another (through mutual legal assistance treaties, the adoption of extradition frameworks, law enforcement co-operation, as well as aid in training and technical assistance). As of March 2014, 179 of the world's 193 UN member states have ratified this convention (Paoli, 2014a: 2).

The convention is supplemented by three separate protocols that target the related issues of human trafficking (*The Protocol to Prevent, Suppress and Punish Trafficking in Persons, Especially Women and Children*), migrant smuggling (*The Protocol against the Smuggling of Migrants by Land, Sea and Air*), and illegal firearms production and trafficking (*The Protocol against the Illicit Manufacturing of and Trafficking in Firearms, Their Parts and Components and Ammunition*). Similar to the *Convention Against Organized Crime*, these three protocols direct countries to criminalize actions relevant to these issues and take steps to investigate and prosecute suspects, as well as devote resources to training and prevention efforts.

Canada is a signatory to the above convention and the accompanying protocols and has implemented what is required of member states. In turn, this has exposed Canada to what some critics argue are fundamental problems with the convention and how it was arrived at (the critiques are not unlike the social constructionist critiques of how organized crime is conceptualized and defined as described in chapter 1). Paoli and Vander Beken (2014: 24) contend that "the new emphasis on the complexity and borderlessness of transnational organized crime was exploited to foster increased and more effective international cooperation. Countries were called to adopt many of the measures pioneered by the United States and Italy in their fight against mafia-type organized crime, neglecting the fact that this form of organized crime was not present in most UN Member States and was far from controlling illegal markets and exhausting organized crime *qua* enterprise crime even in the two aforementioned countries."

Both the UN and the United States have been accused of using this convention for their own political purposes. "For the UN this consisted of an explicit reconfirmation of its role in criminal matters: taking the initiative in furthering coordination of international criminal law. For the US it was satisfying that its stand on a tough drugs policy was maintained while its anti-money laundering policy became internationally accepted" (van Duyne & Nelemans, 2012: 41). As detailed later in this chapter, the UN convention was seen as another attempt by the United States to export its definition of organized crime, its war on drugs, and its punitive prohibition/enforcement philosophy. Particularly troubling to some critics is the emphasis placed on defining and

CRITICAL THINKING EXERCISE

Do you believe that Canada should be a signatory to multilateral conventions, especially given the above critiques as well as criticisms that it restricts our sovereignty (most enforcement of organized crime is domestic in nature anyway)? Consider this question in light of the current federal Liberal government policy of marijuana legalization, which means Canada will be in defiance of the *UN Convention Against Illicit Traffic in Narcotic Drugs and Psychotropic Substances.*

conceptualizing such a complex issue in generic terms and then promoting global laws that would apply to a disparate range of countries with diverse legal systems and differing experiences with organized crime (Mitsilegas, 2003: 84). This problem is embodied in the rather vague definition of a "criminal organization" specified in the convention (and largely adopted verbatim in Canada's *Criminal Code*).

ORGANIZED CRIME ENFORCEMENT IN CANADA: RESPONSIBILITIES, JURISDICTIONS, AND AGENCIES

Since the early part of the twentieth century, the federal government in Canada, with its federal police force, the **Royal Canadian Mounted Police**, has assumed the lead in combatting organized crime in this country. With that said, municipal and provincial police have long been involved in countering OC and drug trafficking, both on their own and as part of multi-agency task forces.

Royal Canadian Mounted Police

As the problem of drug trafficking intensified beginning in the 1920s, the RCMP became the *de facto* lead agency in investigating organized criminality. During the 1960s, the RCMP was designated as the coordinating body for the collection, analysis, and dissemination of criminal intelligence at the national level. Under the heading "Serious and Organized Crime," the RCMP website states, it "identified the fight against organized crime as a strategic priority in 2001."

> Using an intelligence-led, integrated approach, the RCMP is focusing its activities on reducing the threat and impact of organized crime. In fulfilling its mandate, the RCMP is working closely with domestic and international partners in a sustained effort to dismantle today's criminal groups. To contribute to a successful outcome, the RCMP will:

- reduce the total harmful effects caused by organized crime by disrupting illicit markets
- improve the quality of the criminal intelligence/information process
- share intelligence with partners and cooperate with enforcement units at the municipal, national and international levels
- formulate an up-to-date picture of the threat of organized crime and prioritize investigations
- provide scientific and technical support and new technologies to enhance investigative abilities
- enhance public awareness of the dangers and impacts of organized crime
- reduce demand for illicit products (Royal Canadian Mounted Police website, 2013)

Much of the OC-related enforcement carried out by the RCMP falls under its Federal Enforcement Directorate, which is responsible for investigating "serious and organized crime, economic crime (including corruption) and terrorist criminal activity. It also enforces federal statutes, collects criminal intelligence, conducts criminal investigations, secures Canada's borders and ensures the safety of major events, state officials, dignitaries and foreign missions" (Royal Canadian Mounted Police, 2015: 23). According to the RCMP website, "RCMP Federal Services will work with the community, clients and partners to target organized crime and provide a quality policing service through problem solving, education, prevention and enforcement of Federal

Photo 13.1: The RCMP is Canada's lead police agency in combatting organized crime

Source: Vince Alongi, via Wikimedia Commons

Statutes and Laws of Canada in an effort to provide safe homes and communities." The RCMP programs that fall within this directorate and are involved in OC enforcement are Criminal Intelligence; Border Enforcement; Commercial Crime Enforcement; Drug Enforcement; Immigration, Passport and Citizenship Enforcement; Proceeds of Crime/ Financial Crime Enforcement; Technical Operations; and International Operations. For each program, enforcement is carried out by applicable "sections" that are located at RCMP divisions, subdivisions, and detachments throughout the country. A summary of the mandates of those federal enforcement units are provided below.

- *Criminal Intelligence Directorate*: The Criminal Intelligence Directorate was formed in 1991 to centralize and coordinate the RCMP's criminal intelligence function. According to the RCMP Criminal Intelligence Program Guide, "The mission of the Criminal Intelligence Directorate is to provide a national program for the management of criminal information and intelligence which will permit the RCMP to detect and prevent crime having an organized, serious or national security dimension in Canada, or internationally as it affects Canada" (Royal Canadian Mounted Police, 1998: 11).

- *Border enforcement*: This program is mandated to enforce the country's customs laws and help to secure the border by addressing inbound and outbound criminal threats. This mandate includes "identifying, investigating and interdicting persons, organizations and goods that either threaten the national security of one or both countries or that are involved in organized criminal activity" (Royal Canadian Mounted Police website, 2015). Much of the work that falls within this program is concerned with investigating contraband smuggling. Federal enforcement of contraband and drug smuggling is shared with the Canada Border Services Agency, which is responsible for interdiction at all official ports of entry (see description of the CBSA below). The RCMP has law enforcement jurisdiction over all other locations along Canada's borders as well as inland investigations into contraventions against the *Customs Act*. According to its annual performance report for fiscal year 2014–15, the RCMP's "border integrity" program "supports Canada's ability to manage its borders through leveraging partnerships to implement intelligence-led police operations in the detection and investigation of border breaches between the ports of entry and along Canada's coastlines. While contributing to the secure and effective international movement of people and goods, it also identifies and investigates criminal organizations which threaten the security of Canada's borders within, at or away from its borders" (Royal Canadian Mounted Police, 2015: 25).

- *Commercial crime enforcement*: The Commercial Crime program is responsible for criminal offences in relation to white-collar and corporate crimes such as fraud and false pretences, theft, breach of trust, secret commissions, offences against the Government of Canada, the corruption of public officials, counterfeiting and offences relating to intellectual property rights, crimes involving computer and telecommunications technology (cybercrime), the insolvency process, and securities fraud. Included under this banner is the Integrated Market Enforcement Teams, a joint-force operation with provincial securities regulators and local law enforcement agencies to combat crime in Canada securities markets.

- *Drug enforcement*: This section enforces all applicable drug laws in Canada and is particularly concerned with large-scale organized drug manufacturing, importation, and trafficking. While all RCMP members are responsible for enforcing Canadian drug laws, approximately 1000 are assigned exclusively to this task through the drug enforcement sections located at all RCMP's divisions. The RCMP's performance report for the fiscal year 2014–15 says the drug enforcement section undertakes "intelligence-led police operations in partnership with a variety of domestic and international partners. It also works in partnership with domestic and international agencies to reduce the impact of organized crime activities and substance abuse issues through prevention, education and awareness. It also comprises a research and operational support component to enhance the effectiveness of these investigations and operations" (Royal Canadian Mounted Police, 2015: 24).

- *Immigration, passport, and citizenship enforcement*: This program is responsible for investigating violations of the *Immigration Act*, *Citizenship Act*, and *Criminal Code* relating to immigration offences and government travel document offences (e.g., forged passports). Immigration enforcement priorities include combatting criminal organizations involved in smuggling illegal migrants into Canada, conducting investigations on refugee claimants arriving in Canada, criminal screening to identify OC groups and war criminals who may want entry into Canada, and arresting people who are subject of an *Immigration Act* warrant (e.g., for being in the country illegally or who are subject to deportation hearings).

- *Proceeds of crime/financial crime*: The Proceeds of Crime (POC) program is mandated to identify, assess, and seize cash and other assets accumulated through criminal activities. Since the mid-1990s, the POC sections worked under the auspices of the "Integrated Proceeds of Crime" (IPOC) Units, a multi-agency task force also comprised of provincial and municipal police, Department of Justice lawyers, forensic accountants, and CBSA officers. More recently, proceeds of crime enforcement has morphed into a broader Financial Crime program, which is mandated to "maintain the integrity of the Canadian economy by protecting Canadians, their governments and financial systems from financial crimes committed by criminal organizations and others." Particular emphasis is placed on targeting "threats by individuals and groups involved in money laundering and terrorist financing" (Royal Canadian Mounted Police, 2015: 26).

- *Technical services*: Technical services sections provide support for criminal investigations, primarily through dedicated technical and human resources in such areas as the authorized interception of communications (electronic eavesdropping), physical surveillance (including both ground and aerial surveillance), and "Internet intercepts" (detecting and seizing digital data).
- *International operations*: This branch provides direction, support, and assistance to Canadian law enforcement agencies to detect and prevent international offences that may affect Canada. This mandate is operationalized through the Liaison Officer (LO) program in which RCMP members are located in countries around the world, often working out of Canadian embassies. According to the RCMP website, there are currently 37 LOs deployed to 26 locations around the world. "The primary role of an LO is to maintain a link between law enforcement agencies in Canada and in their countries of accreditation in order to facilitate bilateral cooperation to advance criminal matters that have a Canadian connection. LOs will assist whenever the RCMP engages another country in pursuing major, long-term investigations related for instance to national security, drugs, organized crime, homicide, proceeds of crime, corruption and human smuggling." The LOs do not have police powers in foreign countries and do not conduct investigations overseas. Their role instead is to "facilitate major Canadian investigative inquiries in foreign countries, develop and maintain the exchange of criminal intelligence between the RCMP and foreign authorities, and provide assistance to foreign agencies in investigations that affect Canada" (Royal Canadian Mounted Police website, 2010).

Canada Border Services Agency

On December 12, 2003, the Canadian government announced the creation of the **Canada Border Services Agency** (CBSA), which also falls under the ministerial authority of the Department of Public Safety and Emergency Preparedness. The CBSA incorporates a number of enforcement and intelligence functions formerly carried out by Canada Customs and Revenue Agency, Citizenship and Immigration Canada, and the Canadian Food Inspection Agency. The mandate of the CBSA is to provide "integrated border services that support national security priorities and facilitate the free flow of people and goods, including food, plants, animals and related products across the border" (Canada Border Services Agency, 2015: 7).

The main organized crime enforcement role played by the CBSA is the detection and interdiction of prohibited and restricted goods (drugs, weapons, and other contraband) that are transported across official border entry points (land border crossings, airports, marine ports, and Canada Post international mail sorting centres). The *Proceeds of Crime (Money Laundering) and Terrorist Financing Act* also empowers CBSA agents to identify and seize cash (above $10,000) or other suspicious monetary instruments or

Photo 13.2: Emblem of the Canada Border Services Agency

Source: Ng556, via Wikimedia Commons

assets that may constitute the proceeds of crime or terrorist financing. Key enforcement tactics used by the CBSA to combat drug and contraband smuggling include examinations, risk assessments, intelligence collection and dissemination, security screening, and investigations.

One of the main organized crime enforcement functions played by CBSA is examinations—inspecting inbound traffic to detect drugs or other contraband. As such, the CBSA is on the front lines (literally) in interdicting drugs, contraband, and people being smuggled into the country. "Examinations may be performed with the use of specialized tools (e.g., gamma ray imaging, Vehicle and Cargo Inspection System, ion scanners and detector dogs) and may include a full or partial offload of the goods to detect the presence of prohibited or restricted goods (e.g., narcotics or weapons)" (Canada Border Services Agency, 2015: 33).

Its risk assessment and targeting functions seek to identify high-risk inbound ships, planes, or vehicles that should be subject to an examination once in Canada. "The Risk Assessment Program 'pushes the border out' by seeking to identify high-risk people, goods and conveyances as early possible in the travel trade continuum to prevent inadmissible people and goods from entering Canada" (Canada Border Services Agency, 2015: 19). The CBSA operates "a number of automated advanced information sources from carriers and importers to identify people, goods, and conveyances that may pose a threat to Canada" (Canada Border Services Agency, 2015: 22). This is complemented by a staff of analysts who are trained to identify anomalies and other signs that may indicate suspicious cargo or individuals.

According to its 2014–15 performance report, the intelligence program of the CBSA

> collects, analyzes and distributes actionable intelligence regarding people, goods, shipments or conveyances bound for or leaving Canada to help the CBSA and other law enforcement partners identify people, goods, shipments or conveyances that may be inadmissible or pose a threat to the security of Canada. CBSA officers located within Canada, at ports of embarkation or at posts abroad assess information collected form a wide range of sources. In addition, the CBSA provides timely, accurate, strategic, operational and tactical intelligence advice to government authorities, like-minded counterpart nations and stakeholders related to threats to national security, including information on terrorism, weapons proliferation, war crimes, organized crime, smuggling, immigration fraud and irregular immigration, fraudulent documentation, and border enforcement/intelligence products such as lookouts, alerts, scientific reports, and threat and risk assessments inform, support and enhance the Agency's screening and targeting capabilities and other CBSA programs (such as Admissibility Determination, Criminal Investigations, and Immigration Enforcement). (Canada Border Services Agency, 2015: 20–21)

The CBSA operates its own intelligence systems: the Integrated Criminal Enforcement System (an intelligence database) and the Primary Automated Lookout System (an automated system to identify high-risk travellers at official ports).

The CBSA also plays a role in immigration enforcement through its security screening mandate. The Security Screening Program is responsible for vetting foreign nationals who have been referred to the agency by an official with Citizenship and Immigration Canada (CIC). "The CBSA is responsible for ensuring that there are no security concerns related to the individual seeking entry to Canada (e.g., counter-terrorism, counter-espionage, war crimes, crimes against humanity and organized crime) and, based on a thorough screening exercise (including the review of information and intelligence from a wide variety of internal and external sources), makes a recommendation to CIC on the admissibility of the individual" (Canada Border Services Agency, 2015: 24). The CBSA is also mandated to remove individuals who may pose significant threats to Canada.

Although it does not have the powers to lay criminal charges, the CBSA does operate a criminal investigations program to deal with offences against laws that it is mandated to enforce. "CBSA investigators conduct criminal investigations into suspected cases of evasion or fraud with respect to various pieces of border legislation that regulate the importation and exportation of goods, or the admissibility of persons to Canada" (Canada Border Services website, 2011).

Financial Transactions and Reports Analysis Centre of Canada

In the fall of 2001, new legislation to combat money laundering and terrorist financing came into force that creates a mandatory reporting system for large-volume cash and suspicious transactions as well as the cross-border movement of currency and monetary instruments. This legislation also established an independent government body to receive and analyze reported information about regulated transactions and cross-border currency movements. This new body, called the Financial Transactions and Reports Analysis Centre of Canada (FINTRAC), is the central repository for information about money laundering activities across Canada. FINTRAC also has primary responsibility for monitoring the compliance of private-sector financial intermediaries with the legislation.

As a financial intelligence unit, the mandate of FINTRAC is to receive and analyze cash and suspicious transaction reports filed by private-sector entities (and Canada Customs in the case of cross-border currency reports) with a view to creating useful intelligence information that can be used by law enforcement and national security intelligence agencies to combat organized crime-related money laundering and terrorist financing. In order to facilitate organized crime enforcement, FINTRAC has the authority to disclose information related to suspicious financial transactions in limited circumstances to Canadian law enforcement and security intelligence agencies as part of a proceeds of crime or terrorist financing investigation. Information can also be released to foreign law enforcement agencies if the federal government has entered into an agreement with a foreign state or international organization regarding the exchange of such information.

Department of Justice

The primary responsibilities of the federal Department of Justice in relation to (organized) crime are the development of criminal legislation and the prosecution of cases under federal statutes—in particular drug, immigration, and customs statutes (provincial attorneys general are mandated by the Constitution to prosecute *Criminal Code* infractions). Unlike the Department of Justice in the United States, the Canadian DOJ does not take an active role in coordinating criminal investigations; its role is to prosecute files that are brought to them by law enforcement agencies.

Criminal Intelligence Service Canada

Criminal Intelligence Service Canada (CISC) is not a federal agency, but an organization made up of Canadian law enforcement agencies. The primary purpose of CISC is to provide facilities to enable the exchange of criminal intelligence among enforcement units, intelligence units, and CISC provincial bureaus (CISC is made up

Photo 13.3: Entrance to the Department of Justice headquarters in Ottawa

Source: S. Schneider

of bureaus located in each province). Any Canadian police agency that has one or more staff engaged in full-time criminal intelligence can apply for regular membership. Associate membership is extended to police agencies without a full-time intelligence unit, and affiliate membership to non-police agencies. Its regular membership is nationwide and includes the RCMP, the Ontario Provincial Police, the Quebec Police Force, the Royal Newfoundland Constabulary, and more than 60 municipal and regional police departments.

CISC's principal mechanism for facilitating intelligence information sharing is the Automated Criminal Intelligence Information System (ACIIS), an online system that includes criminal information on all major organized crime groups and their activities. Member agencies wishing to obtain additional information can contact the source agency that entered the information. The source agency will then provide any information that they have. For years, CISC also operated Project Focus, a national database on outlaw motorcycle gangs. While this database has now been incorporated into ACIIS, CISC continues to operate a toll-free hotline for information on outlaw motorcycle gangs.

National Coordinating Committee on Organized Crime/Deputy Ministers Steering Committee on Organized Crime

The National Coordinating Committee (NCC) and its five Regional/Provincial Coordinating Committees (RCCs) are mandated to "create a link between law enforcement agencies and public policy makers to combat organized crime."

Membership in the NCC is limited to federal, provincial, and territorial Assistant Deputy Ministers who have primary responsibility for public safety, policing, and criminal prosecutions in their respective jurisdictions; senior representatives of the policing community in Canada; and senior representatives of other federal and provincial authorities that have responsibilities directly related to the problem of organized crime.

The NCC is responsible for the identification of national public policy issues, developing national strategies and initiatives to combat organized crime, and advising the federal, provincial, and territorial Deputy Ministers Steering Committee on Organized Crime on the nature, scope, and impact of organized crime. It provides a national forum where the interests and concerns of Canada's law enforcement community can be brought to the attention of senior government officials who deal with law, policy, and the administration of justice.

The RCCs work at a more operational level and are tasked with identifying issues and developing strategies to counter organized crime regionally and locally. They advise on the nature, scope, and impact of organized crime, in their respective jurisdictions, as well as liaise with the NCC. The RCCs communicate operational and enforcement needs and concerns to the NCC, acting as a bridge between enforcement agencies and officials and public policy makers (Public Safety Canada website, 2015b).

Organized Crime Enforcement at the Provincial Level

While the federal government has the *de facto* lead for organized crime enforcement in Canada, provincial and municipal law enforcement agencies are also active in specific enforcement areas, both unilaterally and as part of multi-agency, joint-force units and task forces. This section briefly describes some representative examples of organized crime enforcement agencies and units in British Columbia, Ontario, and Quebec.

The Organized Crime Agency of British Columbia (OCABC) was established under the provincial *Police Act* in 1999 and, like municipal police departments, the OCABC is an independent law enforcement agency. It was established following a report of the Independent Review Committee on Organized Crime, which was highly critical of OCABC's predecessor—the Coordinated Law Enforcement Unit (CLEU)—which was viewed as largely ineffective, in part due to a lack of commitment by participating federal, provincial, and municipal law enforcement agencies. The mandate of OCABC, according to its website, is to provide "designated Policing and designated Law Enforcement to reduce and eliminate organized crime and other significant criminal activity in British Columbia." The OCABC, along with the RCMP and more than a dozen law enforcement agencies, are part of the Combined Forces Special Enforcement Unit—British Columbia (CFSEU–BC), an integrated, multi-agency task force that co-ordinates organized crime enforcement in that province (described in chapter 12). The OCABC provides "operational and administrative support" to the CFSEU–BC through its "highly trained and specialized professionals" that includes "subject matter experts in important investigational, technical and analytical disciplines" (Organized Crime Agency of British Columbia, n.d.).

In Ontario, the provincial police is the lead agency with respect to investigating and combatting organized and other serious crimes in that province. "Investigations and Organized Crime" is one of four "senior command areas" within the Ontario Provincial Police and is mandated to conduct investigations "in numerous areas from health care fraud to organized crime." Located within this command area is the **Organized Crime Enforcement Bureau**, the purpose of which is "to disrupt and suppress organized crime." The OPP is also home to the Biker Enforcement Unit (BEU), which is mandated to investigate and disrupt the organized criminal activities of outlaw motorcycle gangs. The BEU is a joint-force operation led by the OPP and includes enforcement officials from federal, provincial, and municipal police agencies. "This multi-agency partnership allows for investigations into OMG activities that cross traditional police jurisdiction boundaries. Investigators gather intelligence and evidence on organizations and individuals. They then use this information to develop strategies to combat criminal activities" (Ontario Provincial Police, n.d.). While the BEU restricts its investigations to Ontario, it has become a national resource for law enforcement agencies in their efforts to combat one-percenter motorcycle clubs. As such, "Members of the BEU are also counted on as experts in this type of organized crime. They routinely train or assist other front-line officers and investigators to combat these specific crimes. They also provide expert testimony in court on specific investigations, and on the gangs themselves" (Ontario Provincial Police, n.d.).

In Quebec, the provincial police, known in French as Sûreté du Québec, is the lead agency for organized crime investigations in that province and is responsible for coordinating joint-force regional squads targeting criminal groups and activities in Quebec. The provincial government also operates the Unité permanente anticorruption (Permanent Anticorruption Unit) whose aim is to fight corruption, collusion, and other economic crimes. Founded in February 2011, the unit is housed in the Ministry of Public Security and serves to coordinate the efforts of various provincial agencies to combat corruption in provincial and municipal government agencies in the province. The unit is supported by a team of provincial Crown investigators and prosecutors. While the unit investigates all forms of corruption within government agencies, it focuses on the infiltration of criminal groups and was formed following allegations that the Rizzuto Mafia family and the Hells Angels had corrupted individuals in government agencies (including police departments), private-sector companies, and trade unions.

The unit operates a toll-free telephone line and web-based reporting form that accepts anonymous information and tips on suspected corruption in government agencies (Unité permanente anticorruption, n.d.).

In addition to the enforcement agencies, provincial attorneys general are responsible for prosecuting all *Criminal Code* offences, including the criminal organization laws. Some provincial justice departments include special units designated to prosecute criminal groups and gangs. As described in chapter 12, many provinces also operate units or agencies mandated to expedite the civil forfeiture of assets from criminal offenders, which means they are responsible for litigating lawsuits against such offenders.

THE THEORY AND PRACTICE OF ORGANIZED CRIME ENFORCEMENT: A CRITICAL ANALYSIS

Governments throughout the world have allocated billions of dollars to fight organized crime. Swelling enforcement budgets have been accompanied by intensified investigative, intelligence, and interdiction efforts and techniques; powerful new laws and legislative tools; and the creation of new agencies and joint-force task forces. Despite this expansion and intensification, however, traditional enforcement approaches continue to fall short of their objectives of containing organized crime, let alone eradicating it. There is considerable evidence of a growing pluralism of organized criminal groups and networks in Canada, which has been accompanied by an ongoing proliferation, diversification, and sophistication of organized crimes.

In his review of the literature on the effectiveness of organized crime control policies, Gabor (2003) found no empirical support for the assertion that the traditional enforcement approach has led to any discernible reduction in organized criminal activity. Lyman and Potter (2014: 396) cite American studies collectively indicating that prosecutions have had "only a negligible impact on the operations of organized crime syndicates." To repeat a tired, but apparently true cliché: the traditional enforcement model has contributed to victory in some battles (it has kept some drugs and contraband off the streets, dismantled a few conspiracies, put a lot of people in jail), but has failed to win the war against organized crime. As Lyman and Potter (2014: 395–97) put it, "Some argue that the idea that vigorous prosecution and stiff criminal penalties will win the war against organized crime is at variance not only with current research on organized crime but also with historic precedent. Literally thousands of cases in which organized crime offenders have been arrested, convicted, and imprisoned in the past five decades could be discussed here. The fundamental question remains—So what? There is little evidence that these prosecutions have negatively affected or altered the activities of organized criminal entrepreneurial groups in illicit markets." In short, "after more than a century of scrutiny by government officials and scholars, no final, workable solution to address organized crime has been found. Whether it will ever be purged from society completely is highly doubtful. Perhaps control of organized crime should be viewed as a perennial task likened to taking out the garbage: Every day you identify it, collect it, and throw it away" (Lyman & Potter, 2014: 400).

Critiques of the traditional enforcement model abound and encompass vigorous denunciations of both its underlying theory and its application. The remainder of this section provides a critical analysis of the theories behind the dominant prohibition/ enforcement model and its real-life application. This includes an analysis of some of the constraints on, obstacles to, and weaknesses of OC enforcement in Canada.

Critiques of the Traditional Criminal Justice Enforcement Model

One critique of the traditional enforcement approach is that it fails to appreciate the inherent nature of organized crime. OC's persistence in many societies stem from one of its more fundamental characteristics—that of continuity—so by definition, many criminal groups and networks are structured to resist permanent damage inflicted by law enforcement. Numerous other inherent characteristics, detailed in chapter 3, contribute to the resilience of specific organized criminal associations. The networked approach that many modern organized criminal conspiracies have assumed has made them less vulnerable to traditional law enforcement actions (through anonymity among different cells and offenders, greater fluidity, lack of centralized control, etc.). Other characteristics that help sustain organized criminal associations and repel law enforcement actions include insulation (e.g., through an increased use of lower-level associates to commit crimes, a code of silence, use of corruption of public officials), sophistication (e.g., the use of counter-surveillance against police), and the profit-oriented nature of organized crimes (which means avaricious offenders are willing to assume the risk of being caught).

Perhaps the one trait intrinsic to organized crime that allows it to persist over time, regardless of law enforcement efforts, is its symbiotic relationship with broader society. OC survives and thrives because it involves consensual crimes that cater to the demands for certain (prohibited) products and services. As long as there continues to be such vices among the consuming public, there will be underground markets, criminal entrepreneurs, and well-organized groups to satisfy demand. In sum, the traditional prohibition/ enforcement model will never truly eradicate organized crime because it erroneously treats it as "a threat to, rather than part of, society" (Woodiwiss, 2003: 4).

In its attempts to reduce the supply of illicit goods and services, the traditional enforcement model itself has been hampered by failed strategies and tactics. One of these is the stratagem of targeting and incarcerating the leaders or coordinators of OC groups or networks, the so-called king pin strategy. In the case of Mafia-style hierarchical criminal groups, history has shown that decapitating the organization by prosecuting and incarcerating its leader poses minimal long-term damage to the organization. The alternative **head-hunting** strategy—in which a maximum number of offenders are arrested, charged, and punished—is also fraught with challenges, the most significant being the number of offenders willing to fill the void in criminal groups created by mass incarceration. As described in chapter 12, the concept of deterrence—a fundamental goal of the criminal justice system—has been criticized in the context of serious and chronic (organized) criminal offenders because they are not easily deterred from committing crimes due to a number reasons (paramount of which may be the highly attractive profit potential of organized crimes).

The lightning rod for discontent over OC enforcement is the much-criticized war on drugs, which is characterized by its aggressive and intensive supply-side focus on interdicting drugs, eliminating illegal drug markets, and incarcerating drug traffickers. Once again it is safe to use the old adage that while drug enforcement has won a few battles, the war on drugs has been lost or, at the very least, is at a "stalemate" (Grayson, 2003: 147). Paoli (2014a: 5) succinctly argues that drug enforcement in the United States "may have helped keep the U.S. drug market relatively 'disorganized' but has failed to reach its main goal of reducing drug availability." More concerning is the growing evidence that the supply of many recreational drugs and their purity levels have increased while prices have dropped (Werb et al., 2013). The uninterrupted introduction of new types of illegal street drugs in recent years (crack cocaine, crystal meth, bath salts, ecstasy, synthetic marijuana, fentanyl, etc.) is another indicator of how a reliance on supply-side enforcement has failed to curtail illegal drug markets.

The failed war on drugs also portends to another criticism of the traditional prohibition/enforcement model: it does more harm than good. Paoli (2014a: 4–5) summarizes the many costs to the state and society that accompany the traditional prohibition/enforcement model. "First, these interventions involve the disbursement of considerable financial and human resources that could have been used elsewhere. Second, they restrict the rights of the defendants, convicts, and sometimes even of the public at large. Third, through the criminalization of specific goods and services, they also create opportunities for corruption and violence, because the criminals involved aim to obtain the covert support of government officials or the control of legitimate businesses, or because they resort to violence or the threat of violence to solve conflicts that obviously cannot be brought to court. Fourth, these policy interventions occasionally prompt the offenders and/or the final customers to engage in very harmful practices."

Domestically, the war on drugs in the United States is partly responsible for the unprecedented surge in correctional inmates in America, with drug convictions accounting for "almost half of American prisoners in federal prisons and 17% of those under state jurisdiction" (Carson & Golinelli, 2013: 3, as cited in Paoli, 2014a: 5). Perhaps the group of people most victimized by the war on drugs are those sent to prison for mere possession offences, which is made worse by the fact that many have untreated drug addictions and mental health disorders. The other low-hanging fruit for law enforcement agencies are the street-level traffickers, who have been jailed by the hundreds of thousands. Many of them are involved in trafficking to support a drug habit.

Grayson (2003: 157) contends that "drug laws and the war on drugs have served as justifications for increasing levels of surveillance on American citizens, particularly those who are members of minority groups." In the United States, black men and those who live in poverty are disproportionately jailed as part of the war on drugs, some of whom have had their civil rights trampled upon in the process. Despite the fact "that it was the demand of 'white' America that fuelled the 'cocaine boom' of the 1980s, minority group members have borne the brunt of the war on drugs, particularly African Americans. While incarceration rates for both whites and African Americans have skyrocketed since the beginning of the war on drugs, the rate for African-American males is 7.0 times that for whites" (Grayson, 2003: 152). Research and statistics also reveal that black men in Canada are incarcerated at a rate that is disproportionate to their population size and, according to a research report prepared for Correctional Service Canada, "A larger proportion of visible minority than Caucasian offenders are incarcerated for drug-related offences" (Trevethan & Rastin, 2004).

At the international level, the American-led interdiction of illegal drugs "has helped spread the problem of drug production and trafficking to a number of Latin American countries, has created endless opportunities for corruption and violence in both the United States and abroad, and has unintentionally contributed to the destabilization of several, already weak Central American and, more recently, West African countries" (Paoli, 2014a: 5).

Organized crime and drug enforcement agencies, as well as policy makers, have been accused of constantly campaigning for increased criminal justice powers and resources. These actors "claim that organized crime has come to represent such an unprecedented level of threat that the only way to protect society and its citizens is to take additional security measures, even if in a different context the latter would not be acceptable." This process "has often been criticized for increasing the power of State and international actors, through the issuing of security discourses arguing in favour of the multiplication of repressive and preventive instruments at the expense of citizens' civil liberties" (Carrapiço, 2012: 27). Few dispute that criminal groups exist, locally, nationally, and internationally, and that their criminal activities do considerable harm. The criticism is that the threats may have been overblown, were based on faulty research or no research at all, advocated by self-serving politicians and law enforcement agencies, and unduly influenced by American interests and hegemony (all the while serious crimes committed by political and economic elites were largely downplayed by state actors and the media).

Constraints on and Weaknesses in Applied Organized Crime Enforcement

In addition to the aforementioned critiques of the theory and practice of organized crime and drug enforcement, numerous factors have undermined efforts to contain OC in Canada. These factors can be grouped into two broad categories: (1) unavoidable constraints that limit the effectiveness of enforcement, and (2) the failures and weaknesses of government efforts to combat the problem.

Unavoidable Constraints that Limit the Effectiveness of Organized Crime Enforcement
The persistence of organized crime in Canada is partially due to the unavoidable constraints that face law enforcement, lawmakers, and the overall societal effort to combat the problem.

CONSTITUTIONAL CONSTRAINTS

One significant constraint on organized crime enforcement that has often been cited (especially by law enforcement personnel) stems from the importance placed on civil and human rights in Western societies (enshrined in Canada through the *Canadian Charter of Rights and Freedoms*). While protections against unwarranted government actions are the cornerstone of freedom, liberty, and rights of individual citizens, the fact remains that criminal offenders often benefit from such protections. The right to remain silent, the right to legal counsel, the right to a speedy trial, the right to confront witnesses, the right to refuse to provide self-incriminating testimony, the right to see all evidence collected by police, and the right to be protected from unreasonable searches and seizures are all entrenched in the Charter. While one does not want to pejoratively characterize human rights as constraints, they have served to place limitations on the powers of law enforcement to combat organized crime.

A number of accusations have been made that criminal offenders and their defence counsel use the *Charter of Rights and Freedoms* to avoid criminal penalties. The guilt of the defendants that pursue Charter challenges is often never in doubt; what is called into question is certain law enforcement tactics that may be interpreted as violations of the Charter. Since the Charter was enacted in the early 1980s, dozens of offenders and their lawyers have challenged law enforcement tactics to avoid or overturn criminal convictions. Some of these challenges have been successful and the resulting case law has had significant (and often negative) implications for organized crime enforcement.

Two Supreme Court decisions resulting from Charter challenges have had particularly significant effects on organized crime enforcement in Canada. The first is *R. v. Campbell*, which resulted in restrictions on the use of undercover operations by police; the second is *R. v. Stinchcombe*, which expanded upon the obligation of police and prosecutors to disclose all evidence they have gathered to defence counsel in a timely manner. As far as the latter decision is concerned, police often complain that, in addition to the burdensome amount of work required to disclose all information to the accused in a timely fashion, this latter decision publicly exposes highly sensitive source intelligence and law enforcement techniques. Lack of disclosure of evidence collected by police in a full and timely manner has led to serious charges being thrown out against members of criminal organizations in Canada by the courts.

Police and prosecutors in Canada often divide law enforcement in Canada into two historical periods: the pre-Charter era and the post-Charter era. While the Charter may make this country the envy of many people throughout the world, some say it has tilted the pendulum toward the rights of offenders and away from the collective safety and security of the public. The implication of Charter decisions on law enforcement in Canada is not that they have necessarily restricted police in their ability to do their jobs. Instead, it has made it more time-consuming and labour intensive to do so. Many

Case Study: Dismissal of Serious Charges against Members of the Quebec Hells Angels

In October 2015, a Superior Court judge in Quebec presiding over a murder trial involving Hells Angels members granted a defence motion for a stay of proceedings, thereby ending their trial. The ruling by Justice James Brunton was in response to the fact the Crown withheld evidence from the defence for years. The defendants, members of the Sherbrooke chapter in Quebec, had all been charged with first-degree murder and conspiracy to commit murder. The charges were laid as part of Operation SharQc, a major police initiative that led to the arrest of more than 150 people in Quebec—including 111 full-patch members of the Hells Angels—as a result of the biker war that took place during the 1990s.

"As a result of Brunton's ruling, they all walked away free men," the *Montreal Gazette* reported. "About 10 prosecutors who were in the room looked stunned by Brunton's criticisms about how they had only disclosed key evidence to the defence a month ago."

Justice Brunton made the decision exactly one month after the jury began hearing evidence. At that time, the Crown told Brunton it was in possession of new evidence concerning two previous investigations into the Hells Angels. Defence lawyers had been demanding the Crown disclose the evidence pertaining to those investigations since April 2011. In December 2011, the Crown responded to the request by saying that they did not have the documents in their possession. According to the *Montreal Gazette*, that evidence was critical to the defence of the Hells Angels members on trial because it contradicted the testimony given by a key informant for the Crown.

Justice Brunton was highly critical of the Crown and police for failing to disclose the evidence and conceded that their refusal to do so in a timely manner made it impossible for a new trial to commence. "No other remedy can make up for the abuse described in this judgment," Justice Brunton said in his decision. "The court doesn't hesitate to conclude that it has before it a serious abuse of process ... This abuse goes beyond negligence or even vexatious actions. It constitutes an attack on the fundamental principles of fairness that all criminal cases should benefit from." Brunton said that the prosecutors had adopted "a desire to win at all costs to the detriment to the fundamental principles that form the foundation of our penal justice system." The Provincial Crown in Quebec said it would not appeal Brunton's decision (Canadian Press, October 16, 2015; CBC News, August 8, 2015; CTV News, October 9, 2015b; *Montreal Gazette*, October 10, 2015).

argue that the added responsibilities for ensuring justice is served that has been placed on policing and prosecutions are reasonable given the importance of protecting human and civil rights in Canada.

As discussed, some organized crime groups in Canada operate across different jurisdictions, including provincial international borders. Law enforcement, however, is largely carried out by local police forces. Even those federal law enforcement agencies that have national jurisdiction—such as the FBI, DEA, RCMP, or CBSA—are limited due to the transnational nature of organized crime groups and activities and the constraints in conducting international investigations. Indeed, it is the transnational aspect of organized crime that most exposes the jurisdictional constraints of laws and law enforcement. Criminal laws do not extend beyond national boundaries, there is no international police force, nor is there an international criminal court dedicated to prosecuting profit-oriented criminal offences. International co-operation and coordination among police forces, while steadily increasing in recent years, pales in comparison to the nature and scope of the international co-operation that exists among criminal entrepreneurs and groups. The legal means that are available to law enforcement to facilitate international enforcement—such as extradition, mutual legal assistance treaties, and letters rogatory—can take months and often years to expedite. Meanwhile, organized crime groups and networks do not require any of this legal apparatus to forge international connections. Some have called for the creation of an international police force that goes beyond the limited information-sharing mandate of Interpol. There is little hope that this will ever reach fruition, however. Resistance to the creation of international police forces and criminal courts stems from the contention that because these institutions would be granted certain investigative and prosecution powers, countries will have to give up some of their sovereignty in criminal law matters.

In Canada, while some law enforcement budgets have increased in recent years, this increase has been offset by the more time- and labour-intensive nature of organized crime investigations. Threat assessment models that help prioritize law enforcement investigations have emerged, in part, due to the limited resources of law enforcement agencies, forcing them to be selective about what groups they will target. It is not unusual for some investigations of criminal groups to be postponed indefinitely due to a lack of law enforcement resources. The lack of enforcement resources often means that investigations have to be cut short, or plea bargains made, to avoid time-consuming and costly litigation. In turn, this may undermine the objective of dismantling criminal organizations.

The resource constraints facing organized crime enforcement have only been heightened as finite government resources have been shifted to national security enforcement in the wake of the 2001 US terrorist attacks and the subsequent increased threat posed by global and homegrown terrorists. Less than a month following the 2001 terrorist attacks in the United States, the Canadian Police Association told a Parliamentary Justice Committee that the RCMP had to shelve important organized crime work across the country to work on terrorism investigations because it has insufficient resources to do both. "Officers previously assigned to organized crime priorities have had to abandon those investigations for their current anti-terrorism assignments," Michael Niedbudek, a CPA vice-president, told MPs (*National Post*, November 2, 2001; *Toronto Star*, November 2, 2001).

In December 2014, this author made a presentation to a group of senior RCMP officers in Halifax. Just two months earlier, two members of the armed forces were killed on Canadian soil by self-styled extremists. Immediately following my presentation, one of the officers took me aside and expressed his concern over how, because of these attacks, federal resources were once again being shifted from organized crime investigations to domestic terrorism enforcement. By February 2015, the RCMP had made it public: 300 investigators had been reassigned from organized crime and financial crimes files to National Security Enforcement Teams across the country. Citing an unnamed RCMP source, the Canadian Press estimated the number of reallocated personnel was closer to 500. The news service went on to quote Pierre-Yves Bourduas, a retired deputy commissioner with the RCMP, who voiced his own concern that if this trend continued, organized crime in Canada would "flourish" and "then there might be consequences for Canadian society writ large." Bourduas added that the greatest threat to safety and security in Canada is organized crime and that the foremost "weapon of mass destruction" is illicit drugs (Canadian Press, February 4, 2015).

Weaknesses and Failures of Organized Crime Enforcement in Canada

The often unavoidable constraints and limitations that confront government and law enforcement efforts against organized crime have been exacerbated by a history of ill-informed and often weak and ineffectual policies, legislation, and enforcement practices and programs in Canada. The genesis of organized crime enforcement failures in Canada can be traced to the head-in-the-sand approach that some politicians and senior police officials took when it came to confronting the existence of the Mafia in this country. Carrigan (1991: 200) succinctly summarizes this problem as such:

> As late as the 1960s police and officials in some jurisdictions were still claiming that organized crime was not a problem in Canada. A 1963 Ontario Royal Commission report found very little evidence of organized crime except in gambling. It also stated there was no evidence "that any of the activities those engaged in organized crime were in any way associated with Mafia." The Attorney-General at the time the commission was established went even further. He confidently stated that any suggestion that the Mafia was operating in Ontario was "ignorance and loose talk." He went on to claim that, even in Italy, the Mafia had been pretty well

eliminated by Mussolini. Subsequent revelations have shown that such statements were rather uninformed and naive.

The same critiques have been applied in more recent years to the failure of government agencies to slow the growth of the Hells Angels in Canada. Sher and Marsden (2003) criticize police agencies and government policy makers for allowing Canada's most powerful outlaw biker gang to expand almost unfettered across the country. They accuse Canadian police of "ignoring the bikers for too long" and allege that they were so "plagued by rivalries, incompetence and a general underestimation of the threat posed by the bikers" that they "did little to take on the Hells Angels until their power made them virtually impregnable" (Sher & Marsden, 2003: 313, 363–64).

One of the chief ongoing criticisms of organized crime enforcement in Canada has been that it is highly fractionalized, epitomized by a lack of co-operation, coordination, and information-sharing among criminal justice agencies at the local and national levels. This lack of coordination and co-operation has been fostered by a number of factors, including jurisdictional boundaries, differing mandates, rivalries, and statistics-driven enforcement. Cecil Kirby, the long-time Satan's Choice member and Mafia enforcer had this to say in his 1986 autobiography:

> Local forces hate the RCMP—and maybe for good reason. On one case, an important mob informer of a local police force was not registered with the RCMP witness protection program because they did not want the RCMP involved in the case, so they threw up every road block possible. It seems to me it was more jealousy than anything else. And the RCMP doesn't trust local forces. They don't like sharing their information with the locals—they want the glory. The RCMP likes to operate on a one-way street. They like to information from other police forces, but they don't give information unless they have to because they don't want to share the credit for a big arrest or don't trust the local force they're supposed to be working with. The result of these rivalries and the mistrust between police forces is that organized crime profits by it. Members of different mobs learn to work together because it means saving their own skins and making big money. That's something police at national levels haven't learned to do yet, and until they do, the mobs will always slip through these cracks of rivalries and mistrust. (Kirby & Renner, 1986)

While the level of co-operation and coordination among law enforcement agencies has greatly improved in recent years—and has been institutionalized in numerous joint-force task forces, not to mention the creation of the CISC—it pales in comparison to that among criminal organizations.

Other criticisms that have been levelled at organized crime enforcement and the broader justice system in Canada can be summarized as follows:

- Inadequate laws and legislation (e.g., some would like to see more powerful legislation similar to the American RICO statute)
- A judiciary that coddles criminals through lenient sentences and an interpretation of the *Charter of Rights and Freedoms* that places undue restrictions on law enforcement
- An overwhelming focus on illegal commodities and services (as well as individuals), at the expense of a focus on criminal organizations
- The absence of a long-term, strategic national plan to combat the problem of organized crime
- Too much emphasis on reactive enforcement approaches, at the expense of more proactive and preventative approaches, especially those that address the root causes of (organized) criminality
- An insufficient emphasis on the use of regulatory, civil, and administrative sanctions
- A preoccupation with reducing the supply of drugs and other contraband, at the expense of attempts to reduce demand
- A lack of basic and applied research which can foster a better understanding of organized crime and identify and anticipate emerging trends and developments

The findings of a study examining the operational effectiveness of the Combined Forces Special Enforcement Unit (CFSEU) in Greater Toronto encapsulated some of the constraints and weaknesses that impinge upon organized crime enforcement operations in Canada. Those involved in the CFSEU and surveyed as part of the research viewed the joint-force operation favourably although "most believe that it simply has insufficient resources to make a significant impact on organized crime, especially in relation to the growing scope and sophisticated nature of the problem. Other survey respondents identified legislative and judicial obstacles to the CFSEU's effectiveness, such as inadequate legislation and the judicial interpretation of existing laws (i.e., lenient sentences)." Research participants identified weaknesses that were more in the control of the units, "such as the low quality of some personnel and a lack of intelligence sharing with member agencies" (Schneider, 2004: 2).

The Americanization of Organized Crime and Drug Enforcement

In different parts of this textbook, accusations have been made that a disproportionate amount of the organized crime control agenda adopted internationally, and in Canada specifically, has been heavily influenced by American definitions, approaches, and policies. Wheatley (2012) writes that the *UN Convention Against Transnational Organized Crime* was most influenced by and reflective of American and Italian experiences with the Mafia. Some see the *UN Convention Against Illicit Traffic in Narcotic Drugs and Psychotropic Substances*, with its unyielding stance on the prohibition and criminal enforcement of recreational drugs, as nothing more than an extension of the US war on drugs (van Duyne & Nelemans, 2012: 40). As Carrapiço (2012: 24) writes, "The US's growing perception of its domestic narcotic situation as a war on drugs gradually established itself as an important element of the country's foreign policy, which in turn rapidly became part of the international agenda."

After the collapse of the Soviet Union, some say that America's attention globally shifted to transnational drug-trafficking organizations, which supplanted the Communists "as the international bogeymen threatening global security" (Roth, 2014: 17). Thus, the Cold War narratives were replaced by (or extended to) the war on drugs. This meant the illicit drug production and trafficking could now be framed as a national security issue. "By invoking these traditional definitions of security in framing responses to the international drug trade, policy makers have led many Americans to believe that the dangers posed are so great that 'war,' traditionally considered the last recourse of political activity, is the only way to address the issues of drug production, trafficking, and consumption" (Grayson, 2003: 146). Policy makers knew that framing drugs and transnational organized crime as a national security issue would lead to a massive mobilization of national and international resources, including military resources, which never could have been realized if drugs were viewed only as a criminal justice issue. "As the war on drugs continued, the process of militarization became more and more pronounced. What had begun under the guise of a law enforcement exercise began to turn into a military campaign" (Grayson, 2003:153).

Canadian laws as well as other policies and programs directed at recreational drugs has been influenced both directly and indirectly by the United States. Indirectly, it has adopted all of the aforementioned UN conventions. In 1993, the US Department of State designated Canada as a "primary concern" for global money laundering activities—part of the pressure placed on Canada to adopt America's more punitive proceeds of crime laws—and this designation exists to this day. "Well aware that they are being monitored for drug-related activities, countries such as Canada are encouraged to turn drugs into a major domestic and international issue." Canada has also "been threatened by the United States for not being proactive in the fight against marijuana cultivation," according to Grayson (2003: 159).

FUTURE ORGANIZED CRIME ENFORCEMENT POLICY OPTIONS

The limitations of and criticisms levelled at OC enforcement have prompted a lively debate over how to move forward in the future. Based loosely on categories developed by Abadinsky (2000), policy options that are routinely put forward to maximize the effectiveness of OC enforcement include the following: (1) increase law enforcement resources; (2) expand the authority of law enforcement, including introducing new laws and regulations; (3) shift resources toward more preventative approaches, such as addressing the root causes of crime or reducing the demand for illicit goods and services; and (4) decrease organized criminal opportunities (through legalization). Each of these policy options is discussed below.

Increase Law Enforcement Resources

One policy option that is constantly touted as a way to heighten the effectiveness of OC enforcement is to increase the amount of resources provided to relevant enforcement units and prosecution bodies. In Canada, hundreds of millions of dollars have been added to existing budgets as well as new initiatives to combat organized crime, including such multi-million-dollar projects as the Integrated Proceeds of Crime Units, the Anti-Smuggling Initiative, and the new Financial Transactions Reports Analysis Centre. At the same time, finite resources have been shifted to other priority areas, particularly national security enforcement. Even if resources are increased, there are no guarantees this would decrease the threats posed by and harms realized from organized crime. History has shown that while increased budgets may lead to short-term victories, it has little impact overall problem of organized crime (as discussed earlier in this chapter).

Expand the Power and Authority of Government and Law Enforcement

In addition to, or in lieu of, allocating more resources, the power and authority of government agencies could be enhanced. This would inevitably involve new legislation and regulations to increase the intrusive powers of law enforcement agencies in conducting electronic surveillance, undercover operations, search and seizure, etc. While these changes may enhance organized crime enforcement by making it more efficient, they could very well be implemented at the expense of privacy and individual liberties. Such measures would also inevitably be faced with Charter challenges in Canada.

In recent years, legislation has been introduced that augments the power of government agencies to combat organized and serious crimes. This includes enhancements meant to address the limitations placed on law enforcement by Supreme Court decisions, such as allowing police to commit crimes in the course of their (undercover) criminal operations. Other recent examples include the *Proceeds of Crime (Money Laundering) and Terrorist Financing Act*, which enhances the power of federal government agencies to collect information from private industries, and civil forfeiture legislation adopted by provincial governments, which allow provincial authorities to seize assets deemed to be the proceeds of crime, without having to lay criminal charges. There has been calls for the federal government to adopt similar civil forfeiture provisions, but it thus far has resisted.

Shift Resources Toward More Preventative Approaches

The vast majority of resources that have been mobilized in the fight against OC have been dedicated to reactive, supply-side enforcement initiatives, such as investigations, interdiction, prosecutions, and punishment. Calls for more preventative resources and interventions have arisen out of the failures of the predominately reactive enforcement approach. The field of crime prevention, in fact, arose as an explicit critique of the ability of the criminal justice system to control crime. The argument is that the traditional "cops, courts and corrections" approach is an insufficient deterrent to acts threatening the public safety and has ultimately failed to control crime. Crime prevention is based upon the assumptions that the criminal justice system has failed to cope with the actual quantity of crime, identify many criminal offenders and bring them to justice, rehabilitate those offenders who are identified by the criminal justice system, and address the underlying factors associated with crime and criminality.

As discussed in chapter 12, crime prevention is antithetical to traditional criminal justice approaches in that it is meant to be more proactive, including addressing the root causes and other factors that give rise to crime. Preventative approaches specific to addressing organized crime would entail greater emphasis on reducing demand for illicit goods and services—drugs, in particular. The argument is that demand reduction approaches would not only diminish the scope and power of organized crime, but it may also reduce other crimes that stem from drug abuse (e.g., property crime, street-level drug trafficking, and prostitution). In this context, there is a need to implement what are known as "drug courts" for offenders with substance abuse problems, which "seek to rehabilitate drug-involved offenders through a combination of community-based treatment and intensive judicial oversight" (Rempel, Green, & Kralstein, 2012: 166).

A preventative approach to organized crime would pay particular attention to youth and young adults that are susceptible to becoming involved in criminal gangs and syndicates. Given the strong correlation between dropping out of school on the one hand, and criminal and violent behaviour and gang involvement on the other, drop-out prevention and recovery initiatives must be considered as significant crime and violence prevention initiatives. The lure of gangs and entrepreneurial crime, like drug trafficking, to high-risk young men can also be reduced by making legitimate economic opportunities more readily available to those at high risk of serious and chronic offending.

Despite its attraction, Peter Andreas and his colleagues (1991–92) acknowledge the weaknesses of prevention as a broad strategic approach to organized crime. "The cons of a more preventative approach is that it does not address the immediate impact of ongoing organized crime conspiracies, which really only can be addressed through supply-side enforcement initiatives. In addition, crime prevention approaches do not guarantee to be able to address all the factors that contribute to criminality; that is, there is no guarantee that preventative approaches will actually reduce crime, let alone organized crime."

Decrease Organized Criminal Opportunities (through Legalization)

One of the most controversial policy options to combat organized crime is to legalize the consensual goods and services that fuel black markets. The most glaring historical example of this legalization approach was when the US government repealed Prohibition laws in the early 1930s, in part because of the role of well-organized criminal groups in illegal bootlegging (and the violence and corruption that accompanied bootlegging). The theory behind **legalization** is that once a product or service is legal, the production and distribution are taken out of the underground markets and placed in legitimate markets, where it can be regulated by governments. As such, the theoretical benefits of this policy are twofold: it removes the sale of goods and services from illegal markets and criminal offenders, while the legal distribution means the state is better able to reduce the harm of such goods and services through regulation.

For every benefit that may be derived from legalizing certain vices, however, there may be an equal number of social costs. Moreover, legalizing a certain vice, such as boozing, gambling, or drug use, does not guarantee the end of the involvement of organized crime in that venture. The debate surrounding the legalization of drugs is particularly contentious. The major point of contention centres around the damage that illegal drugs and substance abuse inflicts on society and whether this damage will increase or decrease if recreational drugs are legalized.

The issue surrounding the debate over legalization that is most germane to this textbook is whether the legalization of drugs will rid society of organized crime and illicit markets or at least reduce their scope and impact. Those who advocate for legalization argue it would greatly diminish criminal control over the manufacture and distribution of drugs and deprive crime groups of a major source of revenue. This in turn would minimize other deleterious effects that illegal drug-trafficking groups have on society, such as gang-related violence and corruption. Legalization may also result in reducing the considerable government resources necessary for drug law enforcement and incarceration. These resources could then be shifted to more productive areas of crime control, to drug treatment and prevention efforts, or to addressing other social problems (including social problem-solving initiatives that address the root causes of crime and criminality).

The pro-legalization argument is also based on the contention that the war on drugs has failed miserably and that governments simply do not have the resources to effectively combat the plethora of organized criminal activities and groups that tower over the comparatively meagre criminal justice resources. The growing scope of organized criminality at the national and international levels, especially in the face of limited and largely ineffectual law enforcement initiatives, requires some prioritization, which may involve legalizing less harmful substances, such as marijuana, which would free up resources to combat far more harmful drugs, whether it is heroin, crystal meth, or cocaine.

580 PART IV CONTROLLING ORGANIZED CRIME

The counter-argument to the above is that the legalization of a product does not guarantee it will no longer be available in the black market, which is substantiated by the vast underground trade in cigarettes and prescription drugs. The laws of supply and demand mean that black markets often offer legalized products at a lower price or a higher quality (or both) compared with legitimate markets. Legal drugs would inevitably be accompanied by a government tax, to help feed the state's voracious appetite for revenue, which could potentially would sustain an underground market in lower-priced products. As with gambling, the legalization of drugs would create yet another instance where government would be in competition with organized criminals for profits and market share.

The legalization of drugs will most certainly not eradicate organized crime. Most criminal groups and networks are engaged in multiple enterprises and if their participation in one enterprise is eliminated, they may simply turn to another. For example, when liquor was legalized in 1933, criminal groups seamlessly shifted their efforts to satisfying other vices, most notably gambling. Moreover, while consensual crimes serve as a major revenue source for organized crime groups, they also make their money from predatory crimes that can never be legalized, such as extortion, theft, fraud, and labour racketeering. If a government drives organized crime from servicing society's vices, this may cause an increase in predatory crimes.

The legalization of drugs as a viable policy option sheds light on the importance of the over-arching goal of harm reduction in the fight against organized crime and drug trafficking. Explicit in the harm reduction approach is the assumption that because eradicating organized crime or illegal drugs is impossible, the focus must be placing on reducing the harm it inflicts on society. At the broad government policy level, this means developing strategies not only geared toward minimizing the harm that organized crimes have on society but also minimizing the amount of harm that a particular control policy may have (especially on the most vulnerable and marginalized communities that often feel the greatest brunt of drug enforcement).

CRITICAL THINKING EXERCISE

Are you in agreement with the federal Liberal government's policy of legalizing marijuana in Canada? What are the pros and cons of this policy? What impact, if any, do you think this policy will have on underground markets in Canada? On organized crime's involvement in the production and trafficking of marijuana? Do you think this policy should be extended to harder drugs, such as heroin, cocaine, or crystal meth?

CONCLUSION TO PART IV

The failure to eradicate or even contain organized crime is a combination of many factors: the continual existence of the root causes of crime in society, the inherent characteristics of organized crime, the unavoidable constraints that limit policing and law enforcement in free democratic societies, as well as the avoidable weaknesses and mistakes of government (organized) crime policies and criminal justice programs.

While there have been notable successes in law enforcement efforts to contain organized crime in North America—including the incarceration of major drug "king pins," the large-scale seizure of drugs, the dismantling of criminal organizations, and the diminution of the once dominating Italian-American Mafia—it is generally acknowledged that the war against organized crime and drug trafficking has effectively been lost. As such, organized crime enforcement mandates and objectives are increasingly being couched in less ambitious (and more realistic) objectives, such as organized crime "control," "harm reduction," or "containment." Yet as detailed throughout this book, it can be argued that even these more modest goals have not been achieved. Organized crime has not been controlled or contained and the harm inflicted on society is as great now as it has ever been. It may even be greater given the illegal opioid epidemic that has been sweeping across North America and claiming thousands of lives in recent years.

Responding to organized crime in Canada—and a realistic assessment of the extent to which this problem can be controlled, let alone eradicated—requires a sense of proportion and an appreciation of Canadian history. As this book has demonstrated, organized criminality can be traced as far back as the sixteenth century. As importantly, a history of organized crime in Canada illuminates the inherent contradictions of organized crime's symbiotic nature with Canadian society and the country's dominant institutions. It is the state that leads that the charge against organized crime, yet it is government legislation that has helped to create the conditions for organized crime to emerge and prosper. To unilaterally place the blame on the state, however, would be unfair; Canadian society's various vices and its rapacious demand for goods and services to satisfy these vices are also instrumental in helping to create these underground markets and keep the illicit suppliers in business.

Over the decades and centuries, organized crime has evolved and proliferated. Traditional criminal justice policies and programs have also evolved and expanded to meet the growing threat of organized crime but lag considerably behind its underworld nemesis. Government efforts must also confront an inherently uneven playing field: while the major criminal syndicates in this country are well resourced and profitable, the state has finite resources; criminal syndicates work almost seamlessly across jurisdictions and borders, while international law enforcement is still mired in legal and bureaucratic obstacles; organized crime is mostly structured around a highly flexible, adaptable, and fluid networked structure, while law enforcement is moribund by rigid hierarchical structures that are anything but flexible. Criminal justice actors must adhere to provisions of the Canadian *Charter of Rights*, which some say favours the criminal offender over the demands of law enforcement and the collective security of society. Whether this is true or not is subject to debate. What is clear is that criminal organizations do not have to adhere to the provisions of the Charter. Indeed, law enforcement efforts to combat organized crime are constrained by the requirements of its democratic system and strong emphasis on human rights, which provides a great deal of legal protection to even its criminal citizens.

Some have argued that the most effective measures implemented to counter organized crime have been the reversal of public policy decisions that have helped spur underground industries in the first place, such as the repeal of liquor prohibition laws, the legalization of gambling, or the lowering of federal taxes on cigarettes. Legalizing illegal recreational substances has been cited as one alternative to the bankrupt "war on drugs," and one of the goals of the marijuana legalization policy proposed by the current federal Liberal government is to remove this highly profitable commercial industry from the clutches of the criminal element and integrate it within the legitimate commercial sectors of mainstream society. The thinking is that once in the legitimate economy, marijuana can be better regulated and its benefits to society can be harnessed (through the socially productive investment of tax revenues from the legal sale of pot).

Notwithstanding the consideration that should be given to this policy option, one would be naïve to think that laws legalizing certain narcotic drugs would eliminate the illegal market in drugs, let alone discard organized crime to the ashbin of history. As Earle Johnson Jr., Special Attorney in the Organized Crime and Racketeering Section of the United States Department of Justice, said back in 1963,

> It would be unrealistic to suggest that organized crime can be overcome merely by new applications of old laws or by enacting some new ones. Organized crime is not merely a legal problem. It is a social-political-economic-legal problem. Various aspects of the problem admit in varying degrees to a legal solution. There are certain aspects for which no change in the law could possibly be of assistance. Certainly one cannot legislate public arousal. On the other hand, just as certainly, there are procedural and substantive legal techniques which can minimize the effects of the size, wealth, and systematic methods of criminal organizations and the political corruption which they have been able to engender. (Johnson, 1963: 1)

Johnson's erudite statement emphasizes the importance of implementing laws and other policy measures that may have a greater impact on organized crime and underground markets. Governments can no longer slavishly pursue failed policies (read: the war on drugs) while ignoring viable alternatives. There is really no scientific basis to the prohibition/enforcement model that currently dominates; policies and programs aimed at controlling organized crime in this country demand a more scientific approach to discerning the costs and benefits of different approaches. Every government policy comes with certain benefits and costs; the goal of any public policy is to maximize the benefits to society with minimizing costs. Given the billions of dollars spent of the criminal justice system every year, governments should discern, through rigorous scientific methods, which approach delivers the greatest net benefit to society (or at the very least results in the smallest net cost to society). This means rigorously and comprehensively calculating and then comparing the costs and benefits of prohibition and enforcement against alternative models, including legalization and regulation. Paoli (2014a: 4) writes, "If the prospects of controlling global illegal market flows are rather bleak, government authorities, even in democratic societies, are not powerless vis-à-vis organized crime activities. In particular, government action can heavily impact the size, organization, and operating methods of the groups—or 'enterprises'—that engage in predatory activities or produce, or trade in, illegal products." This optimism is refreshing, but to ensure it is realized, governments in Canada may have to completely re-think how they deal with organized crime in this country; at the very least this must entail a more scientific approach that includes a comprehensive, empirically informed understanding of the causes, nature, scope, and impact of the problem in this country.

KEY TERMS

Canada Border Services Agency

Civil injunction

Competition Act

Consecutive sentencing

Conspiracy

Controlled Drugs and Substances Act

Criminal Code of Canada

Customs Act

Extradition Act

Head-hunting

Immigration and Refugee Protection Act

Income Tax Act

Indictable offence

Legalization

Mutual Legal Assistance in Criminal
  Matters Act

Mutual legal assistance treaty

Organized Crime Enforcement Bureau

Participation in a criminal organization

Proceeds of Crime (Money Laundering)
  and Terrorist Financing Act

Racketeer Influenced and Corrupt
  Organizations Act

Royal Canadian Mounted Police

United Nations Convention Against
  Transnational Organized Crime

Witness Protection Program Act

REVIEW QUESTIONS

1. What is the role of criminal law in combatting organized crime?
2. How is the legal concept of conspiracy central to laws and legislation targeting organized crime?

3. What is the *Racketeer Influence Corrupt Organizations Act*? Why is it considered so controversial?

4. What are the principal laws and legislation in Canada used to combat organized and serious crime in Canada? Which sections of the *Criminal Code* are most relevant to efforts to combat organized crime?

5. How do Canadian criminal laws specific to organized crime compare to those in the United States?

6. What federal departments and agencies are involved in organized crime control in Canada?

7. What are some of the main critiques of the traditional enforcement model? Why is the goal of controlling, let alone eradicating, organized crime in Canadian society so difficult?

8. What are some of the unavoidable constraints that law enforcement face in combatting organized crime in a free, democratic society with a strong emphasis on human rights?

9. What are some of the critiques that have been levelled at organized crime enforcement in Canada?

10. What are some common policy options as far as improving the effectiveness of organized crime enforcement?

FURTHER READINGS

Allum, F., & Gilmour, S. (Eds.). (2012). *Routledge Handbook of Transnational Organized Crime*. London, New York: Routledge.

Canada Border Services Agency. (2015). *Departmental Performance Report, 2014–15*. Ottawa: Minister of Public Safety and Emergency Preparedness.

Freedman, D. (2006). The new law of criminal organizations in Canada, *Canadian Bar Review*, 85(2): 171–219.

Gabor, T. (2003). *Assessing the Effectiveness of Organized Crime Control Strategies: A Review of the Literature*. Ottawa: Department of Justice Canada.

Mecone, J.M., Shapiro, J.B., & Martin, T.B. (2006). Racketeer influenced and corrupt organizations, *American Criminal Law Review*, 43(2): 869–919.

Royal Canadian Mounted Police. (2015). *Royal Canadian Mounted Police 2014–15 Departmental Performance Report*. Ottawa: Minister of Public Safety and Emergency Preparedness.

CONCLUSION

IS THERE A DISTINCTIVELY CANADIAN VERSION OF ORGANIZED CRIME?

One over-arching conclusion of this book is that there is little to suggest from a description and analysis of the history, causes, nature, scope, and impact of organized crime that there is an appreciable difference between organized criminality in Canada and that of other countries, including the United States. In other words, it would be a misnomer to say there a distinctively Canadian version of organized crime. The characteristics of OC groups, criminal offenders, the type of and methods through which organized crimes are carried out, as well as the illegal markets in this country, are similar to that of other countries. In the same vein, the causes, nature, and scope of the problem are not unlike those of the United States.

While Canadian OC may not be distinct in comparative terms, one goal of this book is to encourage the reader to view organized crime as a product of structural and systemic forces and institutions in Canada. The onset, development, proliferation, and diversification of OC in Canada are the result of the following:

- The many vices of Canadians that are satisfied through illegal goods and services provided by criminal entrepreneurs
- Government policies that have criminalized certain goods and services, thereby facilitating the creation of illicit markets and organized criminal entrepreneurs
- The many social conditions and problems (e.g., poverty, inequality, and family breakup) that contribute to the onset and persistence of criminal behaviour among high-risk individuals and within certain demographic groups (that have been subject to intense discrimination, racialization, and marginalization)
- Canada's historical foreign relations (influenced first by its colonial ties with Great Britain, then its post-colonial ties to America, and more recently its economic and cultural ties to China) as well as its integration into the global economy

In short, organized crime has flourished in Canada (and most other countries) because criminal offenders have exploited opportunities arising from social, economic, and political circumstances. As Allum and Gilmour (2012: 1) write, organized crime is "not an extension of a foreign body to the existing system, country or infrastructure. If anything it is the product of a country's history, its social conditions, its economic system, its political elite and its law enforcement regime. It is a bacterium that lives and is produced in the body and which attacks and contaminates it."

There is no one factor accounting for the rise in organized criminal groups and activities in this country. Some argue that Canada's relatively lax criminal laws are to blame; Canada is said to play an important role in international organized crime, according to a *Globe and Mail* article, because it "has a well-earned reputation for letting drug traffickers off lightly when they get nabbed." Generally speaking, large-scale drug traffickers can count on spending only four to six years in a Canadian federal correctional institution for every ten years served in a federal penitentiary in the United States. This also means that there is considerably less incentive for an operative who is arrested in Canada to roll over and play witness (*Globe and Mail*, April 20, 1996). This line of reasoning, however, is undermined by a similar proliferation of organized crime in other countries with much more punitive criminal justice systems, such as the United States, Russia, or China.

Globalization has certainly increased opportunities for transnational OC in Canada as it has for many other countries. Emerging technologies such as the wire service, fax machine, email, cell phones, and the Internet have broadened the international reach of Canadian mass marketing fraudsters, for example, who often prey on American seniors. The influence that technology has on organized crime is nothing new; as documented earlier, beginning in the 1920s, the wire service became the main technological catalyst for a transcontinental bookmaking operation that drew Canada even closer into the web of American organized crime.

Canada's proximity to and undefended border with the United States has been a major factor in the growth of OC in this country. No doubt the American demand for Canadian illicit products—whether it was for opium during the nineteenth century, liquor during the 1920s, or more recently synthetic drugs, marijuana, and counterfeit consumer products—has contributed to the growth of OC in this country. The United States not only represents a huge market for illicit goods, its large population provides a ready-made pool of potential victims for Canadian-based groups and companies engaged in predatory crimes, such as mass marketing fraud. The influx of sophisticated transnational crime groups into Canada has also increased this country's position as a global epicentre of illegal drug production, currency and credit card counterfeiting, product piracy, and telemarketing fraud.

Government policies have been a catalyst for the creation and persistence of illegal drug and contraband markets, whether they have been the prohibitive taxes imposed by the British government on tea and other necessities of colonial life starting in the eighteenth century, the outlawing of professional gambling and the sex trade in the nineteenth century, the criminalization of drugs beginning in the early part of the twentieth century, temperance laws in Canada and the United States that prohibited liquor in the first quarter of the twentieth century, or hikes in cigarette taxes during the 1990s. Prohibitionist policies help create underground markets, and, regardless of the commodity, there is a common pattern in the criminal organization of these illicit industries. The earliest stages are characterized by pure competition, with a large number of individuals and small groups operating relatively autonomously. Eventually, criminal oligopolies are formed as small operations consolidate under more successful black market entrepreneurs or well-established criminal groups, which capitalize on their existing capacities, networks, and economies of scale while driving out smaller groups through intimidation and violence.

The smuggling trade, which underpins much of organized crimes in this country, also accentuates the realization that OC is an extension of the broader economic, political, and social forces of Canada. Underground markets embody the principles of the free market system and, in fact, are a capitalist's dream: an unfettered market with no government regulation. The massive cross-border traffic in both legal and illegal commodities simply reflects (and takes advantage of) the massive trading relationship between Canada and the United States.

The multi-ethnic character of organized crime is a reflection of the multicultural nature of Canadian society. This is aggravated by historically rooted institutionalized racism in Canada whereby certain ethnic and racialized groups—the Irish, Jews, Chinese, Italians, Hispanics, Jamaicans, Indigenous peoples—have been serially shut out of legitimate economic opportunities *en masse*. Therefore, a disproportionate number of individuals from these groups have had to turn to the underground economy to eke out a living.

Social critics in Canada view organized crime and serious and chronic criminal behaviour generally as a product of social, political, and economic cleavages in Canadian society itself. The post-war political economy helped forge the structural preconditions for spatial concentrations of crime and the root causes of criminality in most larger cities and First Nations by fuelling socioeconomic disparities and the concentration of poverty and other social problems within certain neighbourhoods or groups.

This conclusion accentuates the need to dedicate greater resources to addressing the root causes of serious and chronic criminality in this country. What is required most essentially is a policy that strengthens those institutions that can truly have a deep-seated impact on the root causes of the problem. These institutions include the family, the community, schools, the labour market, the non-profit sector, the healthcare system, faith-based groups, and cultural and recreational organizations. Moreover, support of these institutions must be complemented by a focused approach that targets high-risk communities, families, and individuals and is concerned with preventing criminal predispositions from developing in the first place. Research shows that many chronic criminals come from some type of disadvantaged childhood. A social problem-solving approach to criminality relies on targeted strategies that attempt to reduce, eliminate, or offset a child's deleterious social environment (e.g., by promoting more positive and effective parenting) and the child's personal risk factors (e.g., through remedial education, social competency training, therapy, and mentoring).

The efficacy of a preventative, social problem approach to crime brings to the fore the many limitations and weaknesses of the criminal justice system as the primary institution to control crime in Canadian society: it is almost entirely reactive, it identifies only a fraction of criminal offenders and offences, it only addresses the symptoms of much deeper social problems, it discriminates against people of colour and those in lower socioeconomic circumstances, it is extremely costly, and in some cases it does more harm than good. In other words, the one institution that Canada places at the forefront to combat crime is incapable of preventing, in a proactive manner, the causes of the problem that is the focus of its attention.

Governments can no longer slavishly pursue failed policies, such as the war on drugs, while ignoring viable and proven alternatives. There is no scientific basis to the traditional prohibition/enforcement model that currently dominates in North America and globally. Given the billions of dollars spent on the criminal justice system every year, governments must discern, through rigorous scientific research, those measures that deliver the greatest net benefit to society or, at the very least, results in the smallest net cost to society. This means comprehensively calculating and comparing the costs and benefits of prohibition and enforcement against alternative models, including legalization and regulation.

Legalizing illegal drugs is of course the most oft-cited alternative to the traditional prohibition/enforcement model, but it would be unrealistic to think that this policy would entirely eliminate illegal drug trafficking or organized crime. Resilient and innovative professional criminals would surely find a way to maintain market share by working around the inherent limitations of such government policies. Legal drugs would inevitably be accompanied by a government tax, to help feed the state's voracious appetite for revenue, which would sustain a lower-priced underground market. With that said, policy makers must give at least some consideration to the legalization of certain consensually traded products and services that are in great demand, but are prohibited by the state. The issue of legalization also places a spotlight on the need for the criminal justice system to focus on more predatory organized crimes that cannot be addressed through legalization. It is increasingly difficult for governments to justify allocating vast resources to chasing after pot dealers or bookies, while white-collar fraudsters who wipe out the life savings of retirees receive only a modicum of attention from the criminal justice apparatus.

Organized crime will not be eradicated in Canada any time soon, if ever. Where society can help most is in drying up the recruiting pool. Social developmental approaches to crime and criminality hold out the promise that the factors that lead to an individual's involvement in organized criminality and the chronic abuse of illegal drugs are simultaneously addressed. Governments in Canada must shift resources toward addressing the many social problems that give rise to the widespread demand for illicit drugs and create the root causes of criminal behaviour among those involved in the trafficking of illegal drugs. A just and equitable society that places a premium on helping those who are most in need is the greatest defence that can be mustered in the fight against the social ill of crime and organized crime specifically.

REFERENCES

Abadinsky, H. (1983). *The Criminal Elite: Professional and Organized Crime*. Westport, CT: Greenwood Press.

Abadinsky, H. (1990). *Organized Crime* (3rd Ed.). Chicago: Nelson Hall.

Abadinsky, H. (2000). *Organized Crime* (6th Ed.). New York: Wadsworth Publishing.

Abadinsky, H. (2003). *Organized Crime* (7th Ed.). Belmont, CA: Thomson Wadsworth.

Abadinsky, H. (2013). *Organized Crime* (10th Ed.). Belmont, CA: Wadsworth Publishing.

Adamoli, S., Di Nicola, A., Savona, E., & Zoffi, P. (1998). *Organised Crime around the World*. Helsinki: European Institute for Crime Prevention and Control.

Albanese, J.S. (1985). *Organized Crime in America*. Cincinnati, OH: Anderson Publishing.

Albanese, J.S. (1996). *Organized Crime in America* (3rd Ed.). Cincinnati, OH: Anderson Publishing.

Albanese, J.S. (2014). The Italian-American Mafia, in L. Paoli (Ed.), *The Oxford Handbook of Organized Crime* (pp. 142–58). Oxford, New York: Oxford University Press.

Albanese, J.S. (2015). *Organized Crime in America* (7th Ed.). New York: Routledge.

Albini, J.L. (1971). *American Mafia: Genesis of a Legend*. New York: Appleton-Century-Crofts.

Albini, J.L. (1992). The distribution of drugs: Models of criminal organization and their integration, in T. Meiczkowski (Ed.), *Drugs, Crime and Social Policy: Research Issues and Concerns* (pp. 79–108). Boston: Allyn and Bacon.

Allen, R. (1961). *Ordeal by Fire. Canada, 1910–1945*. Toronto: Doubleday Canada.

Allum, F., & Gilmour, S. (2012). Introduction, in F. Allum & S. Gilmour (Eds.), *Routledge Handbook of Transnational Organized Crime* (pp. 1–16). London, New York: Routledge.

Anderson, A.G. (1979). *The Business of Organized Crime: A Cosa Nostra Family*. Stanford, CA: Hoover Institution Press.

Anderson, K. (2013). *Consumer Fraud in the United States, 2011: The Third FTC Survey Staff Report of the Bureau of Economics*. Washington, DC: Federal Trade Commission.

Andreas, P., Bertram, E.C., Blachman, M.J., & Sharpe, K.E. (1991–92). Dead end drug wars, *Foreign Policy*, (Winter): 106–28.

Appleton, P.L., & Clark, D. (1990). *Billion $$$ High: The Drug Invasion of Canada*. Montreal: McGraw-Hill Ryerson.

Arculus, P. (2003). *Mayhem to Murder: The History of the Markham Gang. Organized Crime in Canada West in the 1840s*. Port Perry, ON: Observer Publisher of Port Perry.

Arlacchi, P. (1987). Effects of the new anti mafia law on the proceeds of crime and on the Italian economy, in S. Alessandrini & B. Dallago (Eds.), *The Unofficial Economy: Consequences and Perspectives in Different Economic Systems* (pp. 247–55). Aldershot: Gower.

Arntfield, M. (2015). Cybercrime and cyberdeviance, in R. Linden (Ed.), *Criminology: A Canadian Perspective* (pp. 500–16). Toronto: Nelson Canada.

Aronowitz, A.A. (2012). The human trafficking-organized crime nexus, in F. Allum & S. Gilmour (Eds.), *Routledge Handbook of Transnational Organized Crime* (pp. 217–33). London, New York: Routledge.

Arsovska, J. (2012). Ethnicity, migration and transnational organized crime, in F. Allum & S. Gilmour (Eds.), *Routledge Handbook of Transnational Organized Crime* (pp. 307–20). London, New York: Routledge.

Atton, H., & Holland, H.H. (1908). *The King's Customs. Vol. 1*. London: E.P. Dutton and Co.

Auger, M. (2002). *The Biker Who Shot Me: Recollections of a Crime Reporter* [J.-P. Murray, trans.]. Toronto: McClellan & Stewart.

Australian Crime Commission. (2013). *Illicit Drug Data Report*. Canberra: ACC.

Ausubel, D.P. (1978). *What Every Well-Informed Person Should Know about Drug Addiction*. Chicago: Nelson-Hall.

Ballard, M. (1991). On the safe side: Money laundering (building our defences), *Canadian Banker*, (2, March): 98.

Bandidos MC website. (n.d.). [Web Page], http://www.bandidosmc.com.

Beare, M.E. (2003a). Introduction, in M. Beare (Ed.), *Critical Reflections on Transnational Organized Crime, Money Laundering, and Corruption* (pp. xi–xxix). Toronto: University of Toronto Press.

Beare, M.E. (2003b). Organized corporate criminality: Corporate complicity in tobacco smuggling, in M. Beare (Ed.), *Critical Reflections on Transnational Organized Crime, Money Laundering, and Corruption*. (pp. 183–206). Toronto: University of Toronto Press.

Beare, M.E. (2012). Responding to transnational organized crimes: "Follow the money," in F. Allum & S. Gilmour (Eds.), *Routledge Handbook of Transnational Organized Crime* (pp. 263–78). London, New York: Routledge.

Bell, D. (1953). Crime as an American way of life, *The Antioch Review*, 13(2): 131–54.

Berry, G.L. (1953). Fort Whoop-Up and the Whiskey Traders, *The Alberta Historical Review*, (July): 32.

Bjelopera, J.P., & Finklea, K.M. (2012). *Organized Crime: An Evolving Challenge for U.S. Law Enforcement*. Washington, DC: Congressional Research Service.

Black, C., Vander Beken, T., & De Ruyver, B. (2000). *Measuring Organised Crime in Belgium: A Risk-based Methodology*. Antwerp: Maklu.

Black, D. (1991). *Triad Takeover: A Terrifying Account of the Spread of Triad Crime in the West*. London: Sidgwick & Jackson.

Block, A.A., & Chambliss, W.J. (1981). *Organizing Crime*. New York: Elsevier.

Blok, A. (1974). *The Mafia of a Sicilian Village, 1860–1960: A Study of Violent Peasant Entrepeneurs*. Oxford: Basil Blackwell.

Bonanno, J., & Lalli, S. (1983). *A Man of Honour: The Autobiography of Joseph Bonanno*. New York: Simon and Schuster.

Booth, M. (1999). *The Dragon Syndicates: The Global Phenomenon of the Triads*. London: Doubleday.

Bouchard, M. (2006). Segmentation et structure des risques d'arrestation dans les marchés de drogues illégales. PhD thesis, Université de Montréal.

Bouchard, M., & Morselli, C. (2014). Opportunistic structures of organized crime, in L. Paoli (Ed.), *The Oxford Handbook of Organized Crime* (pp. 288–302). Oxford, New York: Oxford University Press.

Boyd, N. (1991). *High Society: Legal and Illegal Drugs in Canada*. Toronto: Key Porter Books.

Braithwaite, J. (1989). Criminological theory and crime, *Justice Quarterly*, 6(3): 333–58.

Brantingham, P.L., & Brantingham, P.J. (1981). *Patterns in Crime*. New York: MacMillan.

Brantingham, P.L., & Brantingham, P.J. (1998). Environmental criminology: From theory to urban planning practice, *Studies on Crime and Crime Prevention*, 7(1): 31–60.

Brenner, M. (1990). Prime time godfather, *Vanity Fair* (May): 109–15, 176–81.

Broadhurst, R. (2012). Black societies and triad-like organized crime in China, in F. Allum & S. Gilmour (Eds.), *Routledge Handbook of Transnational Organized Crime* (pp. 157–70). New York: Routledge.

Broadhurst, R., & Farrelly, N. (2014). Organized crime "control" in Asia: Experiences from India, China, and the Golden Triangle, in L. Paoli (Ed.), *The Oxford Handbook of Organized Crime*. (pp. 634–54). Oxford, New York: Oxford University Press.

Burke, D. (1987). An uncommon criminal: Dunie Ryan became king of the West End gang in Montreal, *Saturday Night*, 102(3): 23–30.

Bynum, T.S. (1987). *Organized Crime in America: Concepts and Controversies*. Monsey, NY: Criminal Justice Press.

Caledoniawakeupcall.com. (n.d.). *The Anti-Sovereignty Actions of the Warrior Society* [Web Page]. http://www.caledoniawakeupcall.com/mohawks/intro.html (accessed July 2, 2016).

Canada Border Services Agency. (2015). *2014/15 Departmental Performance Report*. Ottawa: Minister of Public Safety and Emergency Preparedness.

Canada Border Services Agency website. (2011). *Criminal Investigations* [Web Page]. http://www.cbsa-asfc.gc.ca/contact/investigation/menu-eng.html (accessed November 15, 2012).

Canadian Anti-Fraud Centre. (2013). *Canadian Anti-Fraud Centre Criminal Intelligence Analytical Unit Annual Statistical Report 2013*. Ottawa: CAFC.

Canadian Armed Forces. (2016). *Operation SABOT* [Web Page]. http://www.forces.gc.ca/en/operations-canada-north-america-recurring/op-sabot.page (accessed February 12, 2016).

Canadian Association of Chiefs of Police. (1988). *Organized Crime Committee Report, 1988*. Ottawa: CACP.

Canadian Association of Chiefs of Police. (1990). *Organized Crime Committee Report, 1990*. Ottawa: CACP.

Canadian Association of Chiefs of Police. (1991). *Organized Crime Committee Report, 1991*. Ottawa: CACP.

Canadian Association of Chiefs of Police. (1992). *Organized Crime Committee Report, 1992*. Ottawa: CACP.

Canadian Association of Chiefs of Police. (1994). *Organized Crime Committee Report, 1994: Smuggling Activities in Canada*. Ottawa: CACP.

Canadian Bankers Association. (2004). *Credit Card Statistics—VISA and MasterCard* [Web Page]. http://www.cba.ca.

Canadian Security Intelligence Service. (1998). *Transnational Criminal Activity*. Ottawa, ON: Canadian Security Intelligence Service.

Canadian Tobacco Manufacturers Council. (n.d.). *Cigarette Export Statistics*. Ottawa: Canadian Tobacco Manufacturers Council.

Carrapiço, H. (2012). Transnational organized crime as a security concept, in F. Allum & S. Gilmour (Eds.), *Routledge Handbook of Transnational Organized Crime* (pp. 19–35). London, New York: Routledge.

Carrigan, D.O. (1991). *Crime and Punishment in Canada: A History*. Toronto: McClelland & Stewart.

Carson, E.A., & Golinelli, D. (2013). *Prisoners in 2012: Trends in Admissions and Releases, 1991–2012*. Washington, DC: United States Department of Justice, Bureau of Justice Statistics.

Casavant, L., & Morrise, C. (2013). *Legislative Summary. Bill C-51: An Act to amend the Witness Protection Program Act and make a consequential amendment to another Act*. Ottawa: Library of Parliament.

Caulkins, J.P., & Reuter, P. (2010). How drug enforcement affects drug prices, in M. Tonry (Ed.), *Crime and Justice: A Review of Research*, Vol. 39 (pp. 213–71). Chicago: University of Chicago Press.

Cédilot, A., & Noël, A. (2011). *Mafia Inc.: The Long, Bloody Reign of Canada's Sicilian Clan*. Toronto: Random House Canada.

Chambliss, W.J. (1989). State-organized crime, *Criminology*, 27(2): 183–208.

Chambliss, W.J. (2005). Piracy and other crimes of war, *Nathanson Centre for the Study of Organized Crime and Corruption Newsletter* (4, Winter): 12.

Chambliss, W.J., & Williams, E. (2012). Transnational organized crime and social sciences myths, in F. Allum & S. Gilmour (Eds.), *Routledge Handbook of Transnational Organized Crime* (pp. 52–64). London, New York: Routledge.

Chan, A.B. (1983). *Gold Mountain: The Chinese in the New World*. Vancouver: New Star Books.

Charbonneau, J.-P. (1976). *The Canadian Connection: An Expose on the Mafia in Canada and Its International Ramifications*. Montreal: Optimum Pub. Co.

Charney, A. (1979). The life and death of Paolo Violi, *Weekend Magazine*, (January 20): 25–31.

Chepesiuk, R. (2006). The fall of the Cali Cartel, *CrimeMagazine.com*, October 21, www.crimemagazine.com/fall-cali-cartel-0 (accessed October 16, 2017).

Cherry, P. (2005). *The Biker Trials: Bringing Down the Hells Angels*. Montreal: ECW Press.

Chin, K.-L. (2014). Chinese organized crime, in L. Paoli (Ed.), *The Oxford Handbook of Organized Crime* (pp. 219–34). Oxford, New York: Oxford University Press.

Chin, K.-L., & Zhang, S. X. (2003). The declining significance of triad societies in transnational illegal activities: A structural deficiency perspective, *The British Journal of Criminology*, 43(3): 469–88.

Choo, K., & Grabosky, P. (2014). Cybercrime, in L. Paoli (Ed.), *The Oxford Handbook of Organized Crime* (pp. 482–99). Oxford, New York: Oxford University Press.

Chretien, J.T. (1994). *Government Action Plan on Smuggling*. Ottawa: House of Commons, Parliament of Canada.

Chu, B. (1989). *Dai Huen Jai. (Big Circle Boys). A Canadian Perspective*. Unpublished paper. Vancouver: Vancouver Police Department, Asian Organized Crime Section.

Chu, Y.K. (2000). *The Triads as Business*. London: Routledge.

Chu, Y.K. (2007). Hong Kong gangs, Appendix D-3, in J.O. Kinckenauer & K. Chin (Eds.), *Asian Transnational Organized Crime* (pp. 87–95). New York: Nova Science.

Clairmont, D. (2008). *Violence and Public Safety in the Halifax Regional Municipality: A Report to the Mayor as a Result of the Roundtable*. Halifax: Halifax Regional Municipality.

Clark, S.D. (1942). *The Social Development of Canada*. Toronto: University of Toronto Press.

Clarke, R.V., & Cornish, D.B. (1985). Modeling offender's decisions: A framework for policy and research, in M. Tonry & N. Morris (Eds.), *Crime and Justice: An Annual Review of Research*, Vol. 6 (pp. 147–85). Chicago: University of Chicago.

Cohen, L.E., & Felson, M. (1979). Social change and crime rate trends: A routine activity approach, *American Sociological Review*, 44: 588–608.

Combined Forces Special Enforcement Unit—British Columbia website. (n.d.a). *BC's Anti-Gang Police* [Web Page].

Combined Forces Special Enforcement Unit—British Columbia website. (n.d.b). *About OCABC (Organized Crime Agency of British Columbia)* [Web Page]. http://www.cfseu.bc.ca/about-cfseu-bc/about-ocabc/.

Commission de Police du Québec. Enquête sur le Crime Organisé. (1980). *Report on an Inquiry into the Activities of Motorcycle Gangs in Havre Saint Pierre, Sept Îles, Mont Joli, Saint Gédéon, Sherbrooke and Asbestos*. Quebec: Commission de police du Québec.

Commission of the European Communities & EUROPOL. (2001). *General Conclusions of the Forum on Organised Crime Prevention, The Hague, 4th and 5th November 1999*. The Hague: EUROPOL and the European Commission.

Commissioner of the North-West Mounted Police. (1887). *Report of the Commissioner of the North-West Mounted Police Force, 1886*. Ottawa: Maclean, Roger & Company.

Con, H., & Wickberg, E. (1982). *From China to Canada: A History of the Chinese Communities in Canada*. Toronto: McClelland & Stewart.

Congressional International Anti-Piracy Caucus. (2006). *2006 Country Watch List*. Washington: The Caucus.

Conlin, D. (1998). A historiography of private sea war in Nova Scotia, *Journal of the Nova Scotia Historical Society*, 1: 79–92.

Coordinated Law Enforcement Unit. (1975). *Second Report on Organized Crime in British Columbia*. Victoria, BC: Ministry of the Attorney General, Coordinated Law Enforcement Unit.

Coordinated Law Enforcement Unit. (1993). *Lower Mainland Gangs: Review of Criminal History and Country of Origin*. Victoria, BC: Province of British Columbia, Ministry of Attorney General, Coordinated Law Enforcement Unit.

Cornish, D.B. (1994). The procedural analysis of offending and its relevance for situational prevention, in R.V. Clarke (Ed.), *Crime prevention Studies*, Vol. 3 (pp. 151–96). Monsey, NY: Criminal Justice Press.

Courtwright, D.T. (2001). *Dark Paradise: A History of Opiate Addiction in America*. Cambridge, MA: Harvard University Press.

Cressey, D.R. (1967). The functions and structure of criminal syndicates, in *President's Commission on Law Enforcement and Administration of Justice Task Force Report: Organized Crime* (pp. 25–59). Washington, DC: United States Government Printing Office.

Cressey, D.R. (1969). *Theft of a Nation: The Structure and Operations of Organized Crime in America*. New York: Harper and Row.

Cressey, D.R. (1972). *Organized Crime and Criminal Organizations*. New York: Heinemann Educational Books.

Criminal Intelligence Service Canada. (1979). *Annual Report on Organized Crime in Canada, 1979*. Ottawa: CISC.

Criminal Intelligence Service Canada. (1983). *Annual Report on Organized Crime in Canada, 1983*. Ottawa: CISC.

Criminal Intelligence Service Canada. (1984). *Annual Report on Organized Crime in Canada, 1984*. Ottawa: CISC.

Criminal Intelligence Service Canada. (1985). *Annual Report on Organized Crime in Canada, 1985*. Ottawa: CISC.

Criminal Intelligence Service Canada. (1986). *Italian Organized Crime Workshop*. Ottawa: CISC.

Criminal Intelligence Service Canada. (1992). *Annual Report on Organized Crime in Canada, 1992*. Ottawa: CISC.

Criminal Intelligence Service Canada. (1996). *Annual Report on Organized Crime in Canada, 1996*. Ottawa: CISC.

Criminal Intelligence Service Canada. (1997). *Annual Report on Organized Crime in Canada, 1997*. Ottawa: CISC.

Criminal Intelligence Service Canada. (1998). *Annual Report on Organized Crime in Canada, 1998*. Ottawa: CISC.

Criminal Intelligence Service Canada. (1999). *Annual Report on Organized Crime in Canada, 1999*. Ottawa: CISC.

Criminal Intelligence Service Canada. (2000). *Criminal Intelligence Service Canada Annual Report, 2000*. Ottawa: CISC.

Criminal Intelligence Service Canada. (2001). *Annual Report on Organized Crime in Canada, 2001*. Ottawa: CISC.

Criminal Intelligence Service Canada. (2002). *Annual Report on Organized Crime in Canada, 2002*. Ottawa: CISC.

Criminal Intelligence Service Canada. (2003). *Annual Report on Organized Crime in Canada, 2003*. Ottawa: CISC.

Criminal Intelligence Service Canada. (2004). *Annual Report on Organized Crime in Canada, 2004*. Ottawa: CISC.

Criminal Intelligence Service Canada. (2006). *Annual Report on Organized Crime in Canada, 2006*. Ottawa: CISC.

Criminal Intelligence Service Canada. (2007). *Annual Report on Organized Crime in Canada, 2007*. Ottawa: CISC.

Criminal Intelligence Service Canada. (2008). *Organized Crime and Domestic Trafficking in Persons in Canada*. Ottawa: CISC.

Criminal Intelligence Service Canada. (2009). *Annual Report on Organized Crime in Canada, 2009*. Ottawa: CISC.

Criminal Intelligence Service Canada. (2010). *Annual Report on Organized Crime in Canada, 2010*. Ottawa: CISC.

Criminal Intelligence Service Canada. (2014). *Organized Crime in Canada—Backgrounder* [Web Page]. http://www.cisc.gc.ca/media/2014/2014-08-22-eng.htm (accessed July 24, 2016).

Criminal Intelligence Service of Saskatchewan. (2005). *Intelligence Trends: Aboriginal-based Gangs in Saskatchewan*. Regina: Criminal Intelligence Service of Saskatchewan.

Croall, H. (2010). Middle-range business crime: Rogue and respectable businesses, family firms and entrepreneurs, in F. Brookman, M. Maguire, H. Pierpoint, & T. Bennett (Eds.), *Handbook on Crime* (pp. 678–97). Portland, OR: Willan Publishing.

Cruise, D., & Griffiths, A. (1996). *The Great Adventure: How the Mounties Conquered the West*. Toronto: Viking Penguin.

David, J. (1988). Outlaw motorcycle gangs: A transnational problem. Paper presented at the *Conference on International Terrorism and Transnational Organized Crime*, Chicago, August 21.

Decker, S.H., & Curry, G.D. (2000). Addressing a key feature of gang membership: Measuring the involvement of young members, *Journal of Criminal Justice*, 28: 473–82.

Decker, S.H., & Pyrooz, D.C. (2014). Gangs: Another form of organized crime?, in L. Paoli (Ed.), *The Oxford Handbook of Organized Crime* (pp. 270–87). Oxford, New York: Oxford University Press.

de la Rochefoucauld, F. (1799). *Travels through the United States of North America, the Country of the Iroquois, and Upper Canada, in the Years 1795, 1796, and 1797; With an Authentic Account of Lower Canada. Vol. 1*. London: R. Phillips.

Della Porta, D. (2012). Foreword: Political science and transnational organized crime: What is the connection?, in F. Allum & S. Gilmour (Eds.), *Routledge Handbook of Transnational Organized Crime* (pp. xiii–xiv). London, New York: Routledge.

Department of Justice Canada. (2013). *Requesting Mutual Legal Assistance from Canada: A Step-by-Step Guide*. Ottawa: Department of Justice Canada.

DesRoches, F.J. (2005). *The Crime that Pays: Drug Trafficking and Organized Crime in Canada*. Toronto: Canadian Scholars Press.

Diamonds.net. (2014). *Organized Retail Crime Drives Up Instances of Return Fraud* [Web Page]. http://www.diamonds.net (accessed January 28, 2007).

Dickie, P., & Wilson, P. (1993). Defining organized crime: An operational perspective, *Current Issues in Criminology*, 4 (3, March): 215–24.

Dickson-Gilmore, E.J. (2002). *Communities, Contraband and Conflict: Considering Restorative Responses to Repairing the Harms Implicit In Smuggling in the Akwesasne Mohawk Nation*. Ottawa: Royal Canadian Mounted Police.

Di Nicola, A. (2014). Trafficking in persons and smuggling of migrants, in P.L. Reichel & J. Albanese (Eds.), *Handbook of Transnational Crime and Justice* (2nd Ed.) (pp. 143–64). Los Angeles: Sage Publications.

Drugwarrant.com. (n.d.). *Why Is Marijuana Illegal?* [Web Page]. http://www.drugwarrant.com/articles/why-is-marijuana-illegal/ (accessed May 24, 2012).

Dubro, J. (1985). *Mob Rule: Inside the Canadian Mafia*. Toronto: Macmillan of Canada.

Dubro, J. (1986). *Mob Rule: Inside the Canadian Mafia*. Toronto: Macmillan of Canada.

Dubro, J. (1992). *Dragons of Crime: Inside the Asian Underworld*. Toronto: Octopus Books.

Dubro, J., & Rowland, R. (1988). Prohibition: Saint John's connection, *Atlantic Insight* (March): 28–32.

Dubro, J., & Roy, R. (1985). Mountain of skulls, *Hamilton This Month* (May): p. 37.

Easton, S. (2004). *Marijuana Growth in British Columbia*. Vancouver: Fraser Institute.

Edelhertz, H., Cole, R., & Berk, B. (1984). *The Containment of Organized Crime*. Lexington, MA: Lexington Books.

Edwards, P. (1990). *Blood Brothers: How Canada's Most Powerful, Mafia Family Runs Its Business*. Toronto: Key Porter Books.

Edwards, P. (1991). *The Big Sting. The True Story of the Canadian Who Betrayed Colombia's Drug Barons*. Toronto: Key Porter Books.

Edwards, P., & Nicaso, A. (1993). *Deadly Silence: Canadian Mafia Murders*. Toronto: Macmillan Canada.

Edwards, P., & Nicaso, A. (2015). *Business or Blood: Mafia Boss Vito Rizzuto's Last War*. Toronto: Random House Canada.

Egmont Group. (2004). *Information Paper on the Financial Intelligence Units and the Egmont Group*. Brussels: Egmont Group.

Ellis, S. (2009). West Africa's international drug trade, *African Affairs*, 108(431): 171–96.

Ellis, S. (2012). Nigerian organized crime, in F. Allum & S. Gilmour (Eds.), *Routledge Handbook of Transnational Organized Crime*. New York: Routledge.

Esbensen, F.-A. (2004). *Evaluating G.R.E.A.T.: A School-Based Gang Prevention Program*. Washington, DC: National Institute of Justice, Office of Justice Programs, US Department of Justice.

Everest, A.S. (1978). *Rum Across the Border. The Prohibition Era in Northern New York*. Syracuse, NY: Syracuse University Press.

Federal Bureau of Investigation. (n.d.). *Italian Organized Crime* [Web Page]. https://www.fbi.gov/about-us/investigate/organizedcrime/italian_mafia (accessed May 22, 2014).

Federal Bureau of Investigation. (1995). Eurasian criminal enterprises, in Federal Bureau of Investigation (Ed.), *Overview of International Organized Crime* (pp. 13–37). Washington, DC: Federal Bureau of Investigation.

Federal Bureau of Investigation. (1998). *Internet Bookmaking Operations*. Washington, DC: Federal Bureau of Investigation.

Federal Reserve Board. (1997). Board of Governors. *Bank Secrecy Act Examination Manual*. Washington, DC: Federal Reserve Board.

Fennel, T. (1999). The human smugglers, *Maclean's* 47(November 22).

Ferracuti, F., & Wolfgang, M. (1967). *The Subculture of Violence: Toward an Integrated Theory of Criminology*. New York: Routledge.

Fijnaut, C. (2014). Searching for organized crime in history, in L. Paoli (Ed.), *The Oxford Handbook of Organized Crime* (pp. 53–95). Oxford, New York: Oxford University Press.

Financial Consumer Agency of Canada. (2016). Payday loans [Web Page]. https://www.canada.ca/content/dam/fcac-acfc/documents/programs/research-surveys-studies-reports/payday-loans-market-trends.pdf.

Finckenauer, J.O. (2005). Problems of definition: What is organized crime?, *Trends in Organized Crime*, 8(3): 63–83.

Finckenauer, J.O., & Albanese, J.S. (2014). Organized crime in North America, in P.L. Reichel & J. Albanese (Eds.), *Handbook of Transnational Crime and Justice* (2nd Ed.) (pp. 483–500). Los Angeles: Sage Publications.

Fitzgerald, R., Wisener, M., & Savoie, J. (2001). *Neighbourhood Characteristics and the Distribution of Crime in Winnipeg*. Ottawa: Statistics Canada.

Freedman, D. (2006). The new law of criminal organizations in Canada, *Canadian Bar Review*, 85(2): 171–219.

Freeman, B.A., & Hewitt, M. (1979). *Their Town: The Mafia, the Media and the Party Machine*. Toronto: Lorimer.

Fuk, I.P. (1999). Organized crime in Hong Kong. Presentation at the Organized Crime and the 21st Century. June 26, 1999, the Centre for Criminology & SPACE, the University of Hong Kong.

Gabor, T. (2003). *Assessing the Effectiveness of Organized Crime Control Strategies: A Review of the Literature*. Ottawa: Department of Justice Canada.

Galgay, F., & McCarthy, M. (1989). *Buried Treasures of Newfoundland and Labrador*. St. John's, NL: Harry Cuff Publications.

Gambetta, D. (1993). *The Sicilian Mafia: The Business of Private Protection*. Cambridge, London: Harvard University Press.

Gambino, R. (1974). *Blood of My Blood: The Dilemma of the Italian-American*. Garden City, NJ: Doubleday.

Gardiner, M.A. (1988). The enterprise requirement: Getting to the heart of civil RICO, *Wisconsin Law Review*, (July/August).

Gendron, A. (2012). Transnational organized crime and terrorism: Global networks in pursuit of plunder, global alliances in pursuit of plunderers, in F. Allum & S. Gilmour (Eds.), *Routledge Handbook of Transnational Organized Crime* (pp. 403–17). London, New York: Routledge.

Giffen, P.J., Endicott, S., & Lambert, S. (1991). *Panic and Indifference: The Politics of Canada's Drug Laws*. Ottawa: Canadian Centre on Substance Abuse.

Glenny, M. (2008). *McMafia: A Journey through the Global Criminal Underworld*. New York: Knopf Books.

Goldstock, R., & Coenen, D.T. (1980). Controlling the contemporary loanshark: The law of illicit lending and the problem of witness fear, *Cornell Law Review*, 65(January), 127–289.

Goode, M. (1975). *Criminal Conspiracy in Canada*. Toronto: Carswell.

Gosse, P. (1976). *The History of Piracy*. New York: Tudor Publishing Company.

Gottschalk, P. (2015). Hells Angels in the shadow economy, in M. Edelbacher, P.C. Kratcoski, & B. Dobovšek (Eds.), *Corruption, Organized Crime, and the Shadow Economy* (pp. 159–66). Boca Raton: CRC Press.

Gould, T. (2004). *Paper Fan: The Hunt for Triad Gangster Steven Wong*. New York: Thunder's Mouth Press.

Gray, J. (1972). *Booze: The Impact of Whiskey on the Prairie West*. Toronto: Signet.

Grayson, K.G. (2003). Discourse, identity, and the U.S. "war on drugs," in M. Beare (Ed.), *Critical Reflections on Transnational Organized Crime, Money Laundering, and Corruption* (pp. 145–70). Toronto: University of Toronto Press.

Guiliani, R. (1986). Legal remedies for attacking organized crime, in H. Edelhertz (Ed.), *Major Issues in Organized Crime Control* (pp. 103–30). Washington, DC: United States Department of Justice.

Haller, M. (1990). Illegal enterprise: A theoretical and historical interpretation, *Criminology*, 28(2): 207–34.

Hamilton, R.B. (1987). Triad and crime gangs of Vietnamese origin, *Gazette* [Royal Canadian Mounted Police], 49(9): 1–7.

Hammer, R. (1975). *Gangland, U.S.A.: The Making of the Mob*. Chicago: Playboy Press.

Harvison, C. (1967). *The Horsemen*. Toronto: McClelland & Stewart.

Hawkins, G. (1969). God and the Mafia, *Public Interest*, 14(Winter): 24–51.

Helmer, J. (1975). *Drugs and Minority Oppression*. New York: Seabury Press.

Herbert, D.L., & Tritt, H. (1984). *Corporations of Corruption: A Systematic Study of Organized Crime*. Springfield, IL: Thomas.

Hess, H. (1973). *Mafia and Mafiosi: The Structure of Power*. Lexington, MA: Heath Lexington Books.

Hess, H. (1986). Traditional Sicilian Mafia: Organized crime and repressive crime, in R.J. Kelly (Ed.), *Organized Crime: A Global Perspective* (pp. 113–33). Totawa, NJ: Rowman and Littlefield.

Hicks, D., Kiedrowski, D., Gabor, T., Levi, M., Goldstoek, R., & Melchers, R. (2012). *Economic Sectors Vulnerable to Organized Crime: Securities*. Report submitted to Public Safety Canada.

Hignett, K. (2012). Transnational organized crime and the global village, in F. Allum & S. Gilmour (Eds.), *Routledge Handbook of Transnational Organized Crime* (pp. 281–93). London, New York: Routledge.

Hobbs, D. (2010). Extortion, in F. Brookman, M. Maguire, H. Pierpoint, & T. Bennett (Eds.), *Handbook on Crime* (pp. 726–38). Portland, OR: Willan Publishing.

Hobbs, D., & Antonopoulos, G.A. (2014). How to research organized crime, in L. Paoli (Ed.), *The Oxford Handbook of Organized Crime* (pp. 96–118). Oxford, New York: Oxford University Press.

Hobsbawm, E.J. (1976). Mafia, in F. Ianni & E. Reuss-Ianni (Eds.), *The Crime Society* (pp. 90–98). New York: New American Library.

Horwood, H., & Butts, E. (1984). *Pirates and Outlaws of Canada, 1610–1932*. Toronto: Doubleday.

Horwood, H., & Butts, E. (1988). *Bandits and Privateers. Canada in the Age of Gunpowder*. Halifax: Goodread Biographies.

Howell, J.C. (2007). Menacing or mimicking? Realities of youth gangs, *Juvenile and Family Court Journal*, 58(2): 39–50.

Hunt, C.W. (1988). *Booze, Boats and Billions: Smuggling Liquid Gold*. Toronto: McClelland & Stewart.

Hunt, E. (2000). Easton, Peter, in *Dictionary of Canadian Biography Online* [Web Page]. Ottawa: Library and Archives Canada. http://www.biographi.ca.

Ianni, F. (1974). *Black Mafia: Ethnic Succession in Organized Crime*. New York: Simon & Schuster.

Ianni, F., & Reuss-Ianni, E. (1972). *A Family Business: Kinship and Social Control in Organized Crime*. New York: Russell Sage Foundation.

Ianni, F., & Reuss-Ianni, E. (1976). *The Crime Society: Organized Crime and Corruption in America*. New York: New American Library.

Ianni, F., & Reuss-Ianni, E. (1983). Organized crime, in S. Kadish (Ed.), *Encyclopedia of Crime and Social Justice*, Vol. 3 (pp. 1094–106). New York: Free Press.

Inciardi, J.A. (1975). *Careers in Crime*. Chicago: Rand McNally College Publishing.

International Intellectual Property Alliance. (2015). *International Intellectual Property Alliance* [Web Page]. www.iipawebsite.com/rbc/2015/2015SPEC 301CANADA.pdf (accessed October 4, 2017).

International Labour Office. (2012). *ILO Global Estimate of Forced Labour. Results and Methodology*. Geneva: International Labour Office, Special Action Programme to Combat Forced Labour.

Interpol website. (n.d.a). *Operation Pangea* [Web Page]. www.interpol.int/Crime-areas/Pharmaceutical-crime/Operations/Operation-Pangea (accessed March 29, 2013).

Interpol website. (n.d.b). *Criminal Intelligence Analysis* [Web Page]. http://www.interpol.int/INTERPOL-expertise/Criminal-Intelligence-analysis (accessed June 21, 2014).

Jacobs, J., Panarella, C., & Worthington, J. (1994). *Busting the Mob: United States v. Cosa Nostra*. New York: New York University Press.

Jacobs, J.B., & Peters, E. (2003). Labor racketeering: The Mafia and the unions, *Crime and Justice*, 30: 229–82.

Jenner, M. (2014). Drug trafficking as a transnational crime, in P.L. Reichel & J. Albanese (Eds.), *Handbook of Transnational Crime and Justice* (2nd Ed.) (pp. 65–84). Los Angeles: Sage Publications.

Jewell, J. (2014). The Manitoba Warrior: Gangs incorporated, *Police Insider*, (January 16), http://thepoliceinsider.com/?p=2839.

Johnson, E., Jr. (1963). Organized crime: Challenge to the American legal system. Part II: The legal weapon: Their actual and potential usefulness in law enforcement, *Journal of Criminal Law, Criminology, and Police Science*, 54: 1–29.

Kangaspunta, K., & Musumeci, M. (2014). Trafficking in counterfeit goods, in P.L. Reichel & J. Albanese (Eds.), *Handbook of Transnational Crime and Justice* (2nd Ed.) (pp. 101–18). Los Angeles: Sage Publications.

Karstedt, S. (2014). Organizing crime: The state as agent, in L. Paoli (Ed.), *The Oxford Handbook of Organized Crime* (pp. 303–20). Oxford, New York: Oxford University Press.

Katcher, L. (1959). *The Big Bankroll: The Life and Times of Arnold Rothstein*. New York: Harper and Brothers.

Kelly, R. (1987). The nature of organized crime, in H. Edelhertz (Ed.), *Major Issues in Organized Crime Control* (pp. 5–43). Washington, DC: National Institute of Justice.

Kert, F. (1986). *The Fortunes of War: Privateering in Atlantic Canada in the War of 1812*. MA thesis. Ottawa: Carleton University.

Kert, F. (1997). *Prize and Prejudice: Privateering and Naval Prize in Atlantic Canada in the War of 1812*. St. John's: International Maritime Economic History Association.

Kilchling, M. (2014). Finance-oriented strategies of organized crime control, in L. Paoli (Ed.), *The Oxford Handbook of Organized Crime* (pp. 655–73). Oxford, New York: Oxford University Press.

King, R. (n.d.). *Traditional Organized Crime*. Unpublished document.

Kirby, C., & Renner, T.C. (1986). *Mafia Assassin: The Inside Story of a Canadian Biker*. Toronto: Methuen.

Kleemans, E.R. (2014). Theoretical perspectives on organized crime, in L. Paoli (Ed.), *The Oxford Handbook of Organized Crime* (pp. 32–52). Oxford, New York: Oxford University Press.

Kleemans, E.R., & Smit, M. (2014). Human smuggling, human trafficking, and exploitation in the sex industry, in L. Paoli (Ed.), *The Oxford Handbook of Organized Crime* (pp. 381–401). Oxford, New York: Oxford University Press.

Klerks, P. (2000). *Groot in de Hasj: Theorie en Praktijk de Georganiseerde Criminaliteit. (Big in Hash: Theory and Practice of Organised Crime.)* Doctoral Dissertation, Eramus University Rotterdam. Unpublished.

Kobayashi, C. (1978). Sexual slavery in Canada: Our herstory, *Asianadian: A Journal of Current Writing by Asian-Canadians*, 2(Fall).

Konkel, K.G.E. (2009). Canada makes its mark—or its bones, *Globe and Mail*, July 11.

KPMG. (1998). *Study of Contraband Tobacco in Canada. Report submitted to the Canadian Tobacco Manufacturers Council*. Ottawa: KPMG.

Kroll. (2016). *Global Fraud Report: Vulnerabilities on the Rise*. New York: Kroll.

Lamothe, L., & Humphreys, A. (2006). *The Sixth Family: The Collapse of the New York Mafia and the Rise of Vito Rizzuto*. Toronto: Wiley & Sons Canada.

Lamothe, L., & Nicaso, A. (1994). *Global Mafia: The New World Order of Organized Crime*. Toronto: MacMillan Canada.

Langton, J. (2015). *Cold War: How Organized Crime Works in Canada and Why It's Just About to Get More Violent*. Toronto: HarperCollins Canada.

Latimer, D., & Goldberg, J. (1981). *Flowers in the Blood: The Story of Opium*. New York: Franklin Watts.

Lavigne, Y. (1987). *Hell's Angels: Taking Care of Business*. Toronto: Deneau and Wayne.

Lavigne, Y. (1991). *Good Guy, Bad Guy: Drugs and the Changing Face of Organized Crime*. Toronto: Random House of Canada.

Lavigne, Y. (1997). *Hells Angels: Into the Abyss*. Toronto: HarperCollins.

Lavigne, Y. (1999). *Hells Angels at War*. Toronto: HarperCollins.

Lavigne, Y. (2004). *Hells Angels: Into the Abyss* (2nd Ed.). Toronto: HarperCollins.

Leighton, B. (1991). Visions of community policing: Rhetoric and reality in Canada, *Canadian Journal of Criminology*, 33(3–4): 485–522.

Lennon, M. (2015). Hackers hit 100 banks in "unprecedented" $1 billion cyber heist: Kaspersky lab, *Security Week*, February 15, www.securityweek.com.

Levi, M. (2002). The organization of serious crimes, in M.M.R. Maguire & R. Reiner (Eds.), *The Oxford Handbook of Criminology*. Oxford: Oxford University Press.

Levi, M. (2009). Financial crime, in M. Tonry (Ed.), *Oxford Handbook of Crime and Public Policy* (pp. 223–46). New York: Oxford University Press.

Liberal Party of Canada. *Real Change: A New Plan for a Strong Middle Class*. Ottawa: Liberal Party of Canada.

Lindesmith, A.R. (1968). *Addiction and Opiates*. Chicago: Aldine Pub. Co.

Lintner, B. (2003). *Blood Brothers: The Criminal Underworld of Asia*. New York: Palgrave Macmillan.

Lombardo, R. (1979). *Organized Crime and the Concept of Community*. Unpublished paper, Department of Sociology, University of Illinois at Chicago.

Lotz, R., & Gillespie, D.F. (1975). Prolegomenon to research on organized crime. Paper presented at the Annual Meetings of the Pacific Sociological Association. Victoria, BC, March 1975.

Lupsha, P.A. (1981). Individual choice, material culture, and organized crime, *Criminology: An Interdisciplinary Journal*, 19(May): 3–24.

Lupsha, P.A. (1986). Organized crime in the United States, in R.J. Kelly (Ed.), *Organized Crime: A Global Perspective* (pp. 58–77). Totowa, NJ: Rowman and Littlefield.

Lyman, M.D. (1989). *Gangland: Drug Trafficking by Organized Criminals*. Springfield, IL: Charles Thomas.

Lyman, M.D., & Potter, G.W. (2011). *Organized Crime* (5th Ed.). Upper Saddle River, NJ: Pearson Prentice Hall.

Lyman, M.D., & Potter, G.W. (2014). *Organized Crime* (6th Ed.). Boston: Pearson.

Lyman, S.M., Willmott, W.E., & Ho, B. (1964). Rules of a Chinese secret society in British Columbia, *Bulletin of the School of Oriental and African Studies*, 27(3): 530–39.

Maas, P. (1968). *The Valachi Papers*. New York: Putnam.

Mackenzie, S. (2010). Scams, in F. Brookman, M. Maguire, H. Pierpoint, & T. Bennett (Eds.),

Handbook on Crime (pp. 137–52). Portland, OR: Willan Publishing.

Mackenzie Institute. (1996). *The Long Fall of the Mohawk Warriors* [Web Page]. http://www.mackenzieinstitute.com (accessed May 14, 2012).

Mackenzie Institute. (2003). *Other People's Wars: A Review of Overseas Terrorism in Canada.* Toronto: Mackenzie Institute.

MacQueen, K. (2001). Blowing smoke in Vansterdam, *MacLean's*, 114(32, August 6): 28–29.

Maher, J. (2010). Youth gang crime, in F. Brookman, M. Macguire, H. Pierpoint, & T. Bennett (Eds.), *Handbook on Crime* (pp. 308–30). Portland, OR: Willan Publishing.

Main, J. (1991). The truth about triads, *Policing*, 7(2): 144–63.

Makarenko, T. (2012). Foundations and evolution of the crime-terror nexus, in F. Allum & S. Gilmour (Eds.), *Routledge Handbook of Transnational Organized Crime* (pp. 234–49). London, New York: Routledge.

Malarek, V. (1989). *Merchants of Misery.* Toronto: Macmillan of Canada.

Maltz, M. (1976). On defining organized crime: The development of a definition and typology, *Crime and Delinquency*, 22(3, July): 338–46.

Mann, W.E. (1968). *Some Aspects of Organized Crime in Canada: A Preliminary Review.* Toronto: Social Science Publishers.

Manwaring, G.E. (Ed). (1920). *The Life and Works of Sir Henry Mainwaring*, Vol. 1. London: Navy Records Society.

Marrus, M. (1991). *Mr. Sam. The Life and Times of Sam Bronfman.* Viking Press: Toronto.

Marsters, R. (2004). *Bold Privateers: Terror, Plunder and Profit on Canada's Atlantic Coast.* Halifax: Formac.

Martens, F.T., & Miller-Longfellow, C. (1982). Shadows of substance: Organized crime reconsidered, *Federal Probation*, 46(December): 3–9.

Martin, G.B. (1996). *The Shanghai Green Gang: Politics and Organized Crime, 1919–1937.* Berkeley: University of California Press.

Marvelli, D.A., & Finckenauer, J.O. (2012). The threat of harm by transnational organized criminals: A US perspective, in F. Allum & S. Gilmour (Eds.), *Routledge Handbook of Transnational Organized Crime* (pp. 509–21). London, New York: Routledge.

Maxson, C.L., Egley A., Jr., Miller, J., & Klein, M.W. (2014). Section VIII Introduction, in C.L. Maxson, A. Egley Jr., J. Miller, & M.W. Klein (Eds.), *The Modern Gang Reader* (pp. 441–42). New York: Oxford University Press.

Mazerolle, L.G., & Roehl, J. (1998). Civil remedies and crime prevention: An introduction, *Crime Prevention Studies*, 9: 1–20.

McClellan Committee. (1976). Organized crime and illicit traffic in narcotics, in F. Ianni & E. Reuss-Ianni (Eds.), *The Crime Society: Organized Crime and Corruption in America* (pp. 186–200). New York: New American Library.

McClelland, S. (2001). Inside the sex trade, *Maclean's*, 114(49, December 3): 20–25.

McCoy, A. (1972). *The Politics of Heroin in Southeast Asia.* New York: Harper and Row.

McCoy, A.W. (1991). *The Politics of Heroin: CIA Complicity in the Global Drug Trade.* Brooklyn, NY: Lawrence Hill Books.

McGarrell, E.F., Bynum. T., Corsaro, N., & Cobbina, J. (2013). Attempting to reduce firearms violence through a comprehensive anti-gang initiative (CAGI): An evaluation of process and impact, *Journal of Criminal Justice*, 41: 33–43.

McInnis, E. (1929). The political aspect of whisky, *Canadian Forum*, (September).

McIntosh, D. (1984). *The Collectors: A History of Canadian Customs and Excise.* Toronto: NC Press Ltd.

McIntosh, M. (1975). *The Organisation of Crime.* London: Macmillan.

McKenzie, V. (1926). Customs house-cleaning imperative. No matter whose head comes off, *Maclean's* (March 1): 24–26, 42–47.

McKeown, T.W. (2007) *Chinese Freemasons* [Web Page]. http://freemasonry.bcy.ca/history/chinese_freemasons/index.html (accessed April 5, 2008).

McNulty, W. (1923). Smuggling whisky from Canada, in *The New York Times Current History* (pp. 123–25). June.

McSweeney, S.M. (1987). The Sicilian Mafia and its impact on the United States, *FBI Law Enforcement Bulletin*, 56 (February): 1–10.

Merlin, M. (1984). *On the Trail of the American Opium Poppy.* Rutherford, NJ: Fairleigh Dickinson University Press.

Merton, R. (1938). Social structure and anomie, *American Sociological Review*, 3: 672–82.

Merton, R. (1964). Anomie, anomia, and social interaction, in M.B. Clinard (Ed.), *Anomie and Deviant Behavior.* New York: Free Press.

Mitchell, R. (1989). Presentation to representatives of Schedule "B" banks, *Money Laundering and the Law Conference.* Sponsored by the Canadian Bankers Association. Toronto, ON, January 20.

Mitsilegas, V. (2003). From national to global, from empirical to legal: The ambivalent concept of transnational organized crime, in M. Beare (Ed.), *Critical Reflections on Transnational Organized Crime, Money Laundering, and Corruption* (pp. 55–87). Toronto: University of Toronto Press.

Moffitt, T.E. (1993). Adolescence-limited and life-course-persistent antisocial behavior: A developmental taxonomy, *Psychological Review*, 100(4): 674–701.

Mogck, J., & Therrien, J. (1998). *Project Sparkplug.* Ottawa: Royal Canadian Mounted Police, Criminal Intelligence Branch.

Moore, W.H. (1974). *The Kefauver Committee and the Politics of Crime, 1950–1952.* Columbia: University of Missouri Press.

Morales, E. (1989). *Cocaine: White Gold Rush in Peru.* Tuscon: University of Arizona Press.

Mori, C. (1933). *The last struggle with the Mafia.* New York: Putnam.

Morselli, C. (2005). *Contacts, Opportunities, and Criminal Enterprise.* Toronto: University of Toronto Press.

Morselli, C. (2009). Hells Angels in springtime, *Trends in Organized Crime*, 12 (2, June): 145–58.

Morselli, C., & Roy, J. (2008). Brokerage qualifications in ringing operations, *Criminology*, 46(1): 71–98.

Murphy, E. (1922a). *The Black Candle.* Toronto: Thomas Allen.

Murphy, E. (1922b). Curbing illicit vendors of drugs, *Maclean's* (July 15): 18–19.

Murray, D.H., & Biaoqi, Q. (1994). *The Origins of the Tiandihui: The Chinese Triads in Legend and History.* Stanford, CA: Stanford University Press.

Nagin, D. (2013). Deterrence in the 21st century, in M. Tonry (Ed.), *Crime and Justice in America: 1975–2025.* Chicago: University of Chicago Press.

Nash, J.R. (1993). *World Encyclopedia of Organized Crime.* New York: De Capo Press.

National Advisory Committee on Criminal Justice Standards and Goals. (1976). *Report of the Task Force on Organized Crime.* Washington, DC: US Government Printing Office.

National Commission on Law Observance and Enforcement. (1931). *Report on the Enforcement of the Prohibition Laws of the United States.* Washington, DC: The Commission.

National Consumer League. (2014). *Top Scams of 2013, 2104* [Web Page]. http://fraud.org/images/PDF/2014_scams_report.pdf (accessed December 13, 2015).

Naylor, R.T. (2003a). Predators, parasites, or free-market pioneers: Reflections on the nature and analysis of profit-driven crime, in M. Beare (Ed.), *Critical Reflections on Transnational Organized Crime, Money Laundering, and Corruption* (pp. 35–54). Toronto: University of Toronto Press.

Naylor, R.T. (2003b). Towards a general theory of profit-driven crimes, *British Journal of Criminology*, 43(1): 81–101.

Naylor, R.T. (2004). *Hot Money and the Politics of Debt.* Montreal, Kingston: McGill-Queen's University Press.

Nelli, H.S. (1976). *The Business of Crime: Italians and Syndicate Crime in the United States.* New York: Oxford University Press.

Neuberger, R.L. (1953). *Royal Canadian Mounted Police.* New York: Random House.

Newman, P. (1978). *Bronfman Dynasty: The Rothschilds of the New World.* Toronto: McClelland & Stewart.

Newman, P.C. (1985). *Company of Adventurers, Vol. 1.* Toronto: Penguin Books Canada.

Nicaso, A. (2001a). Extortion and racketeering. Part 2—The rise of organized crime in Canada and the hold of Mano Nera [Special Series: Le Mafie]. *Tandem News*, (May), http://tandemnews.com.

Nicaso, A. (2001b). Angels with dirty faces. Part 15—How the world's richest and most ferocious motorcycle gang is expanding its wings in Canada [Special Series: Le Mafie]. *Tandem News* (May 24). http://tandemnews.com.

Nicaso, A., & Lamothe. L. (1995). *The Global Mafia. The New World Order of Organized Crime.* Toronto: Macmillan Canada.

Nicaso, A., & Lamothe, L. (2005). *Angels, Mobsters & Narco-terrorists: The Rising Menace of Global Criminal Empires.* Toronto: John Wiley & Sons Canada.

Nichols, G.E. (1908). Notes on Nova Scotian privateers, *Collections of the Nova Scotia Historical Society*, 13: 111–52.

Office of National Drug Control Policy. (2004). *Technical Report for the Price and Purity of Illicit Drugs: 1981 through the Second Quarter of 2003.* Washington DC: Executive Office of the President.

Office of the Correctional Investigator. (2014). *Aboriginal Issues* [Web Page]. http://www.oci-bec.gc.ca/cnt/priorities-priorites/aboriginals-autochtones-eng.aspx.

Office of the United States Trade Representative. (2005). *Special 301 Report.* Washington, DC: Office of the United States Trade Representative.

Ontario Association of Chiefs of Police. (2002). *Green Tide: Indoor Marijuana Production and Its Impact on Ontario.* Toronto: Ontario Association of Chiefs of Police.

Ontario Police Commission. (1964). *Report to the Attorney General for Ontario on Organized Crime.* Toronto: Ontario Police Commission.

Ontario Provincial Police. (n.d.). *Outlaw Motorcycle Gangs* [Web Page]. http://www.opp.ca/index.php?id=115&lng=en&entryid=576c23208f94ac7035355e0f (accessed October 5, 2016).

Organized Crime Agency of British Columbia. (n.d.). *The Organized Crime Agency of British Columbia (OABC)* [Web Page]. http://www.cfseu.bc.ca/about-cfseu-bc/about-ocabc/ (accessed October 2, 2016).

Oriola, T. (2015). Correlates of criminal, in R. Linden (Ed.), *Criminology: A Canadian Perspective* (pp. 119–54). Toronto: Nelson.

Pace, D.F., & Styles, J.C. (1975). *Organized Crime: Concepts and Control*. Englewood Cliffs, NJ: Prentice-Hall.

Paoli, L. (2014a). Introduction, in L. Paoli (Ed.), *The Oxford Handbook of Organized Crime*. (pp. 1–10). Oxford, New York: Oxford University Press.

Paoli, L. (2014b). The Italian Mafia, in L. Paoli (Ed.), *The Oxford Handbook of Organized Crime* (pp. 121–41). Oxford, New York: Oxford University Press.

Paoli, L., Spapens, T., & Fijnaut, C. (2010). Drug trafficking, in F. Brookman, M. Maguire, H. Pierpoint, & T. Bennett (Eds.), *Handbook on Crime* (pp. 626–50). Portland, OR: Willan Publishing.

Paoli, L., & Vander Beken, T. (2014). Organized crime: A contested concept, in L. Paoli (Ed.), *The Oxford Handbook of Organized Crime* (pp. 13–31). Oxford, New York: Oxford University Press.

Payne, E. (1997). The Chih-Kung T'ang in Barkerville: The history of a Chinese secret society in the Cariboo, *B.C. Historical News*, Fall, 9-13.

Pennsylvania Crime Commission. (1991). *A Decade of Change: 1990 Report*. Conshohocken, PA: Pennsylvania Crime Commission.

Perrin, B. (2010). *Invisible Chains: Canada's Underground World of Human Trafficking*. Toronto: Viking Press.

Peterson, V.W. (1983). *The Mob: 200 Years of Organized Crime in New York*. Ottawa, IL: Green Hill Publishers.

Phillips, A. (1962). The criminal society that dominates the Chinese in Canada, *MacLean's* (April 7): 11–48.

Phillips, A. (1963a). The Mafia in Canada, *MacLean's*, 76(16, August 24): 10–13, 40–44.

Phillips, A. (1963b). The inner workings of the crime cartel, *MacLean's*, 76(19, October 5): 24, 66–75.

Phillips, A. (1964). The Mafia in Canada Part 5: Gambling. The greatest criminal conspiracy of them all, *MacLean's* (March 7).

Pileggi, N. (1985). *Wise Guy: Life in a Mafia Family*. New York: Pocket Books.

Plecas, D., Malm, A., & Kinney, B. (2005). *Marihuana Growing Operations in British Columbia Revisited, 1997–2003*. Abbostsford, BC: Department of Criminology and Criminal Justice and International Centre for Urban Research Studies, University College of the Fraser Valley, March.

Porteous, S. (1998). *Organized Crime Impact Study*. Ottawa: Public Works and Government Services of Canada.

Potter, G.W. (1994). *Criminal Organizations: Vice, Racketeering, and Politics in an American City*. Prospect Heights, IL: Waveland Press.

President's Commission on Law Enforcement and Administration of Justice. (1967). Task Force on Organized Crime. *Task Force Report: Organized Crime*. Washington, DC: United States Government Printing Office.

President's Commission on Organized Crime. (1984a). *Organized Crime and Cocaine Trafficking. Record of Hearing IV, November 27–29, 1984*. Washington, DC: United States Government Printing Office.

President's Commission on Organized Crime. (1984b). *Record of Hearing III, October 23–25, 1984: Organized Crime of Asian Origin*. Washington, DC: United States Government Printing Office.

President's Commission on Organized Crime. (1985). *Organized Crime and Labor Management Racketeering in the United States*. Washington, DC: United States Government Printing Office.

President's Commission on Organized Crime. (1986). *America's Habit. Drug Abuse, Drug Trafficking, & Organized Crime*. Washington, DC: United States Government Printing Office.

President's Commission on Organized Crime. (1987). *The Impact: Organized Crime Today*. Washington, DC: United States Government Printing Office.

Presidia Security Consulting Inc., & Schneider, S. (2011). *A Study of the Vulnerability of Marine Port Operations to Organized Crime*. Report submitted to Public Safety Canada.

Public Safety Canada website. (2015a). *Integrated Border Enforcement Teams* [Web Page]. http://www.publicsafety.gc.ca (accessed December 15, 2015).

Public Safety Canada website. (2015b). *National Coordinating Committee on Organized Crime* [Web Page]. https://www.publicsafety.gc.ca/cnt/cntrng-crm/rgnzd-crm/ntnl-crdntng-cmmtt-en.aspx (accessed September 25, 2017).

Purchas, S. (1907/1625). *His Pilgrimes, Vol. 4* (pp. 417–18). London. Reprinted in David B. Quinn (Ed.), *Newfoundland from Fishery to Colony: Northwest Passage Searches*. New York: Arno Press and H. Bye.

Quebec Police Commission. (1975). *Report of the Quebec Police Commission*. Quebec: Government of Quebec.

Quebec Police Commission Inquiry on Organized Crime. (1977a). *The Fight against Organized Crime in Quebec: Report of the Commission on Organized Crime and Recommendations*. Québec: Editeur officiel du Québec.

Quebec Police Commission Inquiry on Organized Crime. (1977b). *Organized Crime and the World of Business*. Montreal: Government of Quebec.

Raddall, T. (1958). *The Rover: The Story of a Canadian Privateer*. Toronto: Macmillan.

Rawlinson, P. (2012). Transnational organized crime: Media, myths and moralities, in F. Allum & S. Gilmour (Eds.), *Routledge Handbook of Transnational Organized Crime* (pp. 294–306). London: Routledge.

Reichel, P.L., & Albanese, J.S. (2014). *Handbook of Transnational Crime and Justice*. Los Angeles: Sage Publications.

Reid, E. (1952). *Mafia*. New York: Random House.

Rempel, M., Green, M., & Kralstein, D. (2012). The impact of adult drug courts on crime and incarceration: Findings from a multi-site quasi-experimental design, *Journal of Experimental Criminology*, 8: 165–92.

Reppetto, T. (2007). *Bring Down the Mob: The War Against the American Mafia*. New York: Holt Paperbacks.

Reuter, P. (1983). *Disorganized Crime: The Economies of the Visible Hand*. Cambridge, MA: MIT Press.

Reuter, P. (2014). Drug markets and organized crime, in L. Paoli (Ed.), *The Oxford Handbook of Organized Crime* (pp. 359–80). Oxford, New York: Oxford University Press.

Reuter, P., & Rubinstein, J.B. (1978). Fact, fancy, and organized crime, *Public Interest*, 53(Fall): 45–67.

Rhodes, W., Layne, M.J.P., & Hodik, L. (2000). *What America's Users Spend on Illegal Drugs: 1988–1998*. Washington, DC: Office of National Drug Control Policy.

Roach, W. (1962). *Report of the Honourable Mr. Justice Wilfrid D. Roach as a Commissioner Appointed under the Public Inquiries Act by Letters Patent Dated December 11, 1961*. Toronto: Commission of Inquiry.

Robb, P. (1996). *Midnight in Sicily*. Boston: Faber and Faber.

Robinson, J. (1999). *The Merger: How Organized Crime Is Taking Over Canada and the World*. Toronto: McClelland & Stewart.

Ross, J.I. (2000). *Varieties of State Crime and Its Control*. Monsey, NJ: Criminal Justice Press.

Roth, M. (2014). Historical overview of transnational cime, in P.L. Reichel & J. Albanese (Eds.), *Handbook of Transnational Crime and Justice* (2nd Ed.) (pp. 5–22). Los Angeles: Sage Publications.

Royal Canadian Mounted Police. (1922). *Report of the Royal Canadian Mounted Police for the Year Ended September 30, 1921*. Ottawa: F.A. Acland.

Royal Canadian Mounted Police. (1923). *Annual Report for the Year Ended September 30, 1922*. Ottawa: F.A. Acland.

Royal Canadian Mounted Police. (1925). *Report of the Royal Canadian Mounted Police. Year Ended September 30, 1925*. Ottawa: F.A. Acland.

Royal Canadian Mounted Police. (1926). *Report of the Royal Canadian Mounted Police. Year Ended September 30, 1926*. Ottawa: F.A. Acland.

Royal Canadian Mounted Police. (1929). *Report of the Royal Canadian Mounted Police for the Year Ended September 30, 1928*. Ottawa: F.A. Acland.

Royal Canadian Mounted Police. (1947). *Report of the Royal Canadian Mounted Police, Year Ended March 31, 1947*. Ottawa: F.A. Acland.

Royal Canadian Mounted Police. (1949). *Report of the Royal Canadian Mounted Police, Year Ended March 31, 1949*. Ottawa: King's Printer and Controller of Stationary.

Royal Canadian Mounted Police. (1961). *Report of the Royal Canadian Mounted Police, Year Ended September 30, 1961*. Ottawa: F.A. Acland.

Royal Canadian Mounted Police. (1965). *Report of the Royal Canadian Mounted Police, Year Ended March 31, 1965*. Ottawa: F.A. Acland.

Royal Canadian Mounted Police. (1975). Organized crime, *Gazette* [Royal Canadian Mounted Police], 37(10).

Royal Canadian Mounted Police. (1980). Motorcycle gangs, *Gazette* [Royal Canadian Mounted Police], 42(10): 1–40.

Royal Canadian Mounted Police. (1985). *RCMP National Drug Intelligence Estimate 1984/85*. Ottawa: RCMP.

Royal Canadian Mounted Police. (1986). *RCMP National Drug Intelligence Estimate 1985/86*. Ottawa: RCMP.

Royal Canadian Mounted Police. (1987a). Outlaw motorcycle gangs, *Gazette* [Royal Canadian Mounted Police], 49(5).

Royal Canadian Mounted Police. (1987b). *RCMP National Drug Intelligence Estimate 1986/87*. Ottawa: RCMP.

Royal Canadian Mounted Police. (1997). Asian organized crime, *Pony Express*, December: 29–31.

Royal Canadian Mounted Police. (1998). *Criminal Intelligence Program: Roles and Functions.* Ottawa: RCMP Criminal Intelligence Directorate.

Royal Canadian Mounted Police. (2000a). *Drug Situation in Canada 1999.* Ottawa: RCMP, Criminal Analysis Branch, Criminal Intelligence Directorate, Organized Crime Analysis Section.

Royal Canadian Mounted Police. (2000b). *Project Sleipnir: The Long Matrix for Organized Crime.* August. Ottawa: RCMP, Criminal Intelligence Directorate.

Royal Canadian Mounted Police. (2001). *Drug Situation in Canada 2000.* Ottawa: RCMP, Criminal Analysis Branch, Criminal Intelligence Directorate, Organized Crime Analysis Section.

Royal Canadian Mounted Police. (2002a). Bonds of brotherhood, *Gazette* [Royal Canadian Mounted Police], 64(2): 4–5.

Royal Canadian Mounted Police. (2002b). Finding a formula that fits. Partnership spells success in fight against outlaw bikers, *Gazette* [Royal Canadian Mounted Police], 64(2): 7–9.

Royal Canadian Mounted Police. (2002c). *Marihuana Cultivation in Canada: Evolution and Current Trends.* Ottawa: RCMP.

Royal Canadian Mounted Police. (2003). *Drug Situation in Canada 2002.* Ottawa: RCMP, Criminal Analysis Branch, Criminal Intelligence Directorate, Organized Crime Analysis Section.

Royal Canadian Mounted Police. (2006). *Drug Situation Report, 2005.* Ottawa: RCMP, Criminal Analysis Branch, Criminal Intelligence Directorate, Organized Crime Analysis Section.

Royal Canadian Mounted Police. (2007). *Drug Situation Report, 2007.* Ottawa: RCMP, Criminal Intelligence Directorate.

Royal Canadian Mounted Police. (2008). *2008 Contraband Tobacco Strategy.* Ottawa: RCMP.

Royal Canadian Mounted Police. (2009). *Report of the Illicit Drug Situation in Canada—2009.* Ottawa: RCMP, Criminal Analysis Branch, Criminal Intelligence Directorate, Organized Crime Analysis Section.

Royal Canadian Mounted Police. (2014). *Cybercrime: An Overview of Incidents and Issues in Canada.* Ottawa: RCMP.

Royal Canadian Mounted Police. (2015). *2014–15 Departmental Performance Report.* Ottawa: Minister of Public Safety and Emergency Preparedness.

Royal Canadian Mounted Police. (2016). *Witness Protection Program* [Web Page]. http://www.rcmp-grc.gc.ca/fwpp-pfpt/qa-qr-eng.htm (accessed October 15, 2016).

Royal Canadian Mounted Police and Drug Enforcement Administration. (1986). *Outlaw Motorcycle Gangs and the Drug Trade.* Ottawa: RCMP/DEA.

Royal Canadian Mounted Police "E" Division. (2005). *The Scope and Impact of Organized Crime in British Columbia.* Vancouver: Prepared for Criminal Intelligence Service British Columbia/Yukon Provincial Executive Committee and British Columbia Policing Operations Council.

Royal Canadian Mounted Police website. (2010). *International Operations Branch* [Web Page]. http://www.rcmp-grc.gc.ca/ip-pi/iob-soi-eng.htm (accessed August 12, 2013).

Royal Canadian Mounted Police website. (2013). *Serious and Organized Crime* [Web Page]. http://www.rcmp-grc.gc.ca/soc-cgco/index-eng.htm (accessed October 11, 2016).

Royal Canadian Mounted Police website. (2015). *Border Law Enforcement* [Web Page]. http://www.rcmp-grc.gc.ca/bi-if/index-eng.htm (accessed August 4, 2016).

Royal Commission into Certain Sectors of the Construction Industry ("Waisberg Commission"). (1974). *Report of the Royal Commission into Certain Sectors of the Construction Industry.* Toronto: Government of Ontario.

Royal Commission on Chinese Immigration. (1885). *Report on the Royal Commission on Chinese Immigration, in Dominion of Canada. Sessional Papers, Volume II, Third Session of the Fifth Parliament of the Dominion of Canada. 48 Victoria, Volume XVII.* Ottawa: McLean, Roger, & Co.

Royal Commission on Customs and Excise. (1928). *Interim Reports. Nos. 1 to 10.* Ottawa: F.A. Acland.

Royal Commission to Investigate Chinese and Japanese Immigration into British Columbia. (1902). *Report of the Royal Commission to Investigate Chinese and Japanese Immigration into British Columbia, 1900–1902. Sessional Papers, Volume 13, Second Session of the Ninth Parliament of the Dominion of Canada. Vol. XXXVI.* Ottawa: McLean, Roger, & Co.

Salerno, R.F. (1967). Syndicate personnel structure, *Canadian Police Chief,* 55(3, July): 7+.

Sauvé, J. (1999). *Organized Crime Activity in Canada, 1998: Results of a "Pilot" Survey of 16 Police Services.* Ottawa: Statistics Canada, Canadian Centre for Justice Statistics.

Savona, E. (1999). *European Money Trails.* London: Harwood Academic Publishers.

Schelling, T. (1967). Economic analysis of organized crime, in President's Commission on Law Enforcement and the Administration of Justice, *Task Force Report: Organized Crime.* Washington, DC: United States Government Printing Office.

Schenk, J., & Kesser, J. (1977). Born-to-raise-hell Inc., *Maclean's* (August 22): 30–33.

Schneider, J., & Schneider, P. (2012). Civil society and transnational organized crime: The case of the Italian antimafia movement, in F. Allum & S. Gilmour (Eds.), *Routledge Handbook of Transnational Organized Crime*. (pp. 353–65). London, New York: Routledge.

Schneider, S. (1998). Combatting organized crime in (and by) the private sector: A normative role for Canada's forensic investigative firms, *Journal of Contemporary Criminal Justice*, 14(4, November): 351–67.

Schneider, S. (2004). *Partnership Satisfaction Survey: Combined Forces Special Enforcement Unit*. Report Submitted to Chief Superintendent Ben Soave, Officer-in-Charge, CFSEU–GTA.

Schneider, S. (2015a). Unethical and unlawful behaviour by pathological financial institutions: Implications for human rights and social justice. Paper presented at Fifth National Conference Critical Perspectives: Criminology and Social Justice, May 28–29, 2015, University of Ottawa.

Schneider, S. (2015b). Deferred prosecution won't put a dent in corporate crime, *Globe and Mail*, June 2 [online].

Schneider, S. (2016). *Iced: The Story of Organized Crime in Canada*. Toronto: HarperCollins.

Schramm, R.R. (1988). Organized crime: A Canadian approach, *The Police Chief*, 55(1, January): 32–34.

Securesearch. (1974). *A Guidebook for Canadian Law Enforcement Officers on Tactics of Organized Crime*. Ottawa: Securesearch, Crime Prevention Research Bureau.

Semmens, N. (2010). Identity theft and fraud, in F. Brookman, M. Maguire, H. Pierpoint & T. Bennett (Eds.), *Handbook on Crime* (pp. 172–90). Portland, OR: Willan Publishing.

Shaw, C., & McKay, H.D. (1972). *Juvenile Delinquency and Urban Areas*. Chicago: University of Chicago Press.

Shaw, M. (2005). *Youth and Gun Violence: The Outstanding Case for Prevention*. Montreal: International Centre for the Prevention of Crime.

Shawcross, T., & Young, M. (1987). *Men of Honour: The Confessions of Tommaso Buscetta*. London: Collins.

Sheptycki, J. (2003). Against transnational organized crime, in M. Beare (Ed.), *Critical Reflections on Transnational Organized Crime, Money Laundering, and Corruption*. (pp. 120–144). Toronto: University of Toronto Press.

Sher, J., & Marsden, W. (2003). *The Road to Hell: How the Biker Gangs Conquered Canada*. Toronto: Knopf Canada.

Siekman, P. (1966). The Bronfmans: An instinct for dynasty, *Fortune*, 144–210.

Silverman, R.A., Teevan, J.J., & Sacco, V.F. (2000). *Crime in Canadian Society* (6th Ed.). Toronto: Harcourt Brace.

Simard, R., & Vastel, M. (1988). *The Nephew: The Making of a Mafia Hitman*. Scarborough, ON: Prentice-Hall Canada.

Smith, D. (1975). *Mafia Mystique*. New York: Basic Books.

Smith, D. (1980). Paragons, pariahs and pirates: A spectrum based theory of enterprise, *Crime and Delinquency*, 26(3): 358–86.

Smith, D.C. (1994). Illicit enterprise: An organized crime paradigm for the nineties, in R.J. Kelly, K.-L. Chin, & R. Schatzberg (Eds.), *Handbook of Organized Crime in the United States* (pp. 121–50). Westport, CT: Greenwood.

Smith, D., & Salerno, R. (1970). The use of strategies in organized crime control, *Journal of Criminal Law, Criminology, and Police Science*, 61(1): 101–11.

Smith, R. (2014). Transnational cybercrime and fraud, in P.L. Reichel & J. Albanese (Eds.), *Handbook of Transnational Crime and Justice* (2nd Ed.) (pp. 119–42). Los Angeles: Sage Publications.

Snyder, S. (1989). *Brainstorming: The Science of Politics and Opiate Research*. Cambridge, MA: Harvard University Press.

Spapens, T. (2014). Illegal gambling, in L. Paoli (Ed.), *The Oxford Handbook of Organized Crime* (pp. 402–18). Oxford, New York: Oxford University Press.

Standing Senate Committee on National Security and Defence [Canada]. (2002). *Canadian Security and Military Preparedness: Report of the Standing Senate. Committee on National Security and Defence. 37th Parliament—1st Session*. Ottawa: Senate of Canada.

Statistics Canada. (2014). *Police-reported Cybercrime in Canada, 2012*. Ottawa: Statistics Canada.

Stewart, R. (1980). *Identification and Investigation of Organized Criminal Activity*. Houston, TX: National College of District Attorneys.

Stock, P. (2001). Where the easy money is: Slapped on the wrist, loan sharks prove that casino crime can pay, *Report Newsmagazine* [British Columbia Edition] (April 16): 26–27.

Sutherland, E. (1934). *Principles of Criminology*. Chicago: J.B. Lippencott.

Sutherland, E. (1949). *White Collar Crime*. New York: Holt, Rinehart, and Winston.

Sutherland, E. (1973). *Edwin Sutherland: On Analyzing Crime* [K. Schuessler (Ed.)]. Chicago: University of Chicago Press.

Sutton, W., with E. Linn. (1976). *Where the Money Was: The Memoirs of a Bank Robber.* New York: Viking Press.

Talese, G. (1971). *Honor Thy Father.* New York: World Publishers.

Taylor, I., Watson. P., & Young, J. (1973). *The New Criminology.* New York: Harper & Row.

Tepperman, L. (1976). *The Modernization of Crime.* Ottawa: Solicitor General of Canada.

Thompson, H.S. (1967). *Hell's Angels; A Strange and Terrible Saga.* New York: Random House.

Trevethan, S., & Rastin, C.J. (2004). *A Profile of Visible Minority Offenders in the Federal Canadian Correctional System.* Ottawa: Correctional Service of Canada.

Transparency International website. (n.d.). Home page [Web Page]. https://www.transparency.org/ (accessed February 17, 2013).

Turkus, B., & Feder, S. (1951). *Murder, Inc.: The Story of the Syndicate.* New York: Farrar, Straus and Young.

Tyler, G. (1962). The roots of organized crime, *Crime and Delinquency,* 8 (October): 325–38.

United Nations. Ninth United Nations Congress on the Prevention of Crime and the Treatment of Offenders, Cairo, Egypt 29 April to 8 May 1995 (1995). *International Cooperation and Practical Technical Assistance for Strengthening the Rule of Law: Promoting the United Nations Crime Prevention and Criminal Justice Programme Action Against National and Transnational Economic and Organized Crime, and the Role of Criminal Law in the protection of, 'The Environment: National Experiences and International Cooperation. Results of the Supplement to the Fourth United Nations Survey of Crime Trends and Operations of Criminal Justice Systems, on Transnational Crime Interim Report by the Secretariat.* Cairo: United Nations.

United Nations. (1999). *Global Program against Trafficking in Human Beings.* Vienna: United Nations, Centre for International Crime Prevention, United Nations Interregional Crime and Justice Research Institute.

United Nations. (2000). *The United Nations Convention against Transnational Organized Crime.* Palermo, Sicily: United Nations.

United Nations Office on Drugs and Crime. (2002). *Results of a Pilot Survey of Forty Selected Organized Criminal Groups in Sixteen Countries.* Vienna: United Nations Office on Drugs and Crime.

United Nations Office on Drugs and Crime. (2007). *World Drug Report.* Vienna: United Nations.

United Nations Office on Drugs and Crime. (2012a). *World Drug Report.* New York: United Nations Office on Drugs and Crime.

United Nations Office on Drugs and Crime. (2012b). *Global Report on Trafficking in Persons, 2012.* Vienna: United Nations Office on Drugs and Crime.

United Nations Office on Drugs and Crime. (2015). *World Drug Report.* New York: United Nations Office on Drugs and Crime.

United States Congress, House of Representatives, Committee on the Judiciary, Subcommittee on Immigration and Claims. (2000). *Law Enforcement Problems at the Border between the United States and Canada: Drug Smuggling, Illegal Immigration, and Terrorism. One Hundred Sixth Congress, First Session, April 14, 1999.* Washington, DC: United States Government Printing Office.

United States Congress. Senate. Special Committee to Investigate Organized Crime in Interstate Commerce. (1951). *Investigation of Organized Crime in Interstate Commerce: Hearings Before a Special Committee to Investigate Organized Crime in Interstate Commerce, United States Senate, Eighty-first Congress, Second Session, Pursuant to S. Res. 202.* Washington, DC: United States Government Printing Office.

United States Congress. Senate. Permanent Subcommittee on Investigations. Committee on Government Operations. (1965). *Final Report of the McClellan Subcommittee: Organized Crime and Illicit Traffic in Narcotics.* Washington, DC: United States Government Printing Office.

United States Congress. Senate. Committee on Governmental Affairs. Permanent Subcommittee on Investigations. (1992). *The New International Criminal and Asian Organized Crime.* Washington, DC: United States Government Printing Office.

United States Department of Justice. (2003). *The National Criminal Intelligence Sharing Plan.* Washington, DC: United States Department of Justice.

United States Department of Justice. (2006). *National Drug Threat Assessment.* Washington, DC: United States Department of Justice, National Drug Intelligence Center.

United States Department of Justice. (2008). *Overview of the Law Enforcement Strategy to Combat International Organized Crime.* Washington, DC: United States Government Printing Office.

United States Department of State. (2002). *International Narcotics Control Strategy Report.* Washington, DC: United States Department of State.

United States Department of State. (2003). *Trafficking in Persons Report.* Washington, DC: United States Department of State.

United States Department of State. (2005). *International Narcotics Control Strategy Report.* Washington, DC: United States Department of

State, Bureau for International Narcotics and Law Enforcement Affairs.

United States Department of State. (2013). *International Narcotics Control Strategy Report Volume I, Drug and Chemical Control*. Washington, DC: United States Department of State, Bureau for International Narcotics and Law Enforcement Affairs.

United States Department of State. (2014). *2014 Trafficking in Persons Report*. Washington, DC: United States Department of State.

United States Department of State. (2015). *International Narcotics Control Strategy Report Volume I, Drug and Chemical Control*. Washington, DC: United States Department of State, Bureau for International Narcotics and Law Enforcement Affairs.

United States Drug Enforcement Administration. (n.d.a). Operation Pipeline, 1984, in *Drug Enforcement Administration 1980–1985* [Web Page]. http://www.dea.gov/about/history/1980-1985.pdf (accessed February 10, 2014).

United States Drug Enforcement Administration. (n.d.b). *Major Traffickers and Their Organizations*. Washington, DC: United States Drug Enforcement Administration.

United States Drug Enforcement Administration. (n.d.c). *DEA History Book, 1990–1994* [Web Page]. https://www.usdoj.gov/dea/pubs/history/deahistory_05.htm (accessed March 25, 2003).

United States Drug Enforcement Administration. (2000). BC bud: Growth of the Canadian marijuana trade, *Drug Intelligence Brief*. Washington, DC: United States Drug Enforcement Administration.

United States Drug Enforcement Administration. (2001). *United States Drug Enforcement Administration*. Washington, DC: United States Drug Enforcement Administration.

United States National Security Council. (2000). *International Crime Threat Assessment*. Washington, DC: United States National Security Council.

Unité permanente anticorruption. (n.d.) *Mandate* [Web Page]. https://www.upac.gouv.qc.ca/upac/mandat.html (accessed October 11, 2016).

van de Bunt, H., Siegel, D., & Zaitch, D. (2014). The social embeddedness of organized crime, in L. Paoli (Ed.), *The Oxford Handbook of Organized Crime* (pp. 321–40). Oxford, New York: Oxford University Press.

van Dijk, J., & Spapens, T. (2014). Transnational organized crime networks, in P.L. Reichel & J. Albanese (Eds.), *Handbook of Transnational Crime and Justice* (2nd Ed.) (pp. 213–26). Los Angeles: Sage Publications.

van Duyne, P.C. (1996). Organized crime, corruption, and power, *Crime, Law and Social Change*, 26(3): 201–38.

van Duyne, P.C., & Nelemans, M.D.H. (2012). Transnational organized crime: Thinking in and out of Plato's cave, in F. Allum & S. Gilmour (Eds.), *Routledge Handbook of Transnational Organized Crime* (pp. 36–51). London, New York: Routledge.

Vander Beken, T. (2012). The many faces of organized crime in Europe, and its assessment, in F. Allum & S. Gilmour (Eds.), *Routledge Handbook of Transnational Organized Crime* (pp. 83–96). London, New York: Routledge.

Varese, F. (2014). Protection and Extortion, in L. Paoli (Ed.), *The Oxford Handbook of Organized Crime* (pp. 343–58). Oxford, New York: Oxford University Press.

Verizon Business Risk Team. (2009). *Data Breach Investigation Report* [Web Page]. www.verizonbusiness.com/resources/security/reports/2009_databreach_rp.pdf [2011, September 21] (accessed March 9, 2012).

Volkov, V. (2014). The Russian Mafia: Rise and extinction, in L. Paoli (Ed.), *The Oxford Handbook of Organized Crime* (pp. 159–76). Oxford, New York: Oxford University Press.

von Lampe, K. (2012). The practice of transnational organized crime, in F. Allum & S. Gilmour (Eds.), *Routledge Handbook of Transnational Organized Crime* (pp. 186–200). London, New York: Routledge.

von Lampe, K. (2016). *Organized Crime: Analyzing Illegal Activities, Criminal Structures, and Extra-legal Governance*. Los Angeles: Sage Publications.

Wakeman, F., Jr. (1988). Policing modern Shanghai, *China Quarterly*, 115: 408–40.

Wall, D.S., & Large, J. (2010). Jailhouse frocks: Locating the public interest in policing counterfeit luxury fashion goods, *British Journal of Criminology*, 50: 1094–116.

Wallace, M. (2002). *Exploring the Involvement of Organized Crime in Motor Vehicle Theft*. Ottawa: Statistics Canada.

Walsh, J. (1993). Triads go global, *Time*, (February 8): 37–41.

Walter, R. (1971). Organized crime, *Canadian Securities Magazine*, (May): 1–6.

Wasserstein, B. (1999). *Secret War in Shanghai*. New York: Houghton Mifflin Company.

Webb, G. (2007). Driving while black. Tracking unspoken law-enforcement racism, *Esquire*, (January 29).

Weintraub, W. (2004). *City Unique: Montreal Days and Nights in the 1940s and '50s*. Toronto: Robin Bass Studio.

Werb D., Kerr T., Nosyk, B., Strathdee, S., Montaner, J., & Wood, E. (2013). The temporal relationship between drug supply indicators: An audit of international government surveillance systems, *British Medical Journal Open.*

Wethern, G., & Colnett, V. (1978). *A Wayward Angel.* New York: R. Marek Publishers.

Wheatley, J. (2012). Transnational organized crime: A survey of laws, policies and international conventions, in F. Allum & S. Gilmour (Eds.), *Routledge Handbook of Transnational Organized Crime* (pp. 65–80). London, New York: Routledge.

Whitbourne, R. (1870/1622). *Westward Hoe for Avalon in the New-found-land: As described by Captain Richard Whitbourne, of Exmouth, Devon, 1622* [T. Whitburn (Ed.)]. London: S. Low, Son and Marston.

White House Office of National Drug Control Policy. (2004). *National Drug Control Strategy.* Washington, DC: The White House.

Williams, K.S. (2010a). State crime, in F. Brookman, M. Maguire, H. Pierpoint, & T. Bennett (Eds.), *Handbook on Crime* (pp. 741–61). Portland, OR: Willan Publishing.

Williams, M. (2010b). Cybercrime, in F. Brookman, M. Maguire, H. Pierpoint, & T. Bennett (Eds.), *Handbook on Crime* (pp. 191–214). Portland, OR: Willan Publishing.

Williams, P. (1995). The new threat: Transnational criminal organizations and international security, *Criminal Organizations*, 9(3, 4): 3–19.

Williams, P. (2014). Nigerian criminal organizations, in L. Paoli (Ed.), *The Oxford Handbook of Organized Crime* (pp. 254–69). Oxford, New York: Oxford University Press.

Wiltshire, R. (2015). *Barr and Kirkland vs. Alberta.* Unpublished document.

Wolf, D.R. (1991). *The Rebels: A Brotherhood of Outlaw Bikers.* Toronto: University of Toronto Press.

Wolfgang, M., & Ferracuti, F. (1967). *The Subculture of Violence: Toward and Integrated Theory in Criminology.* London: Tavistock.

Woodiwiss, M. (2002). *Organized Crime and American Power: A History.* Toronto: University of Toronto Press.

Woodiwiss, M. (2003). Transnational organized crime: The strange career of an American concept, in M. Beare (Ed.), *Critical Reflections on Transnational Organized Crime, Money Laundering, and Corruption* (pp. 3–34). Toronto: University of Toronto Press.

Woodiwiss, M. (2012). The past and present of transnational organized crime in America, in F. Allum & S. Gilmour (Eds.), *Routledge Handbook of Transnational Organized Crime* (pp. 97–110). London, New York: Routledge.

World Health Organization. (2006). *Factsheet on Counterfeit Medicines* [Web Page]. http://www.who.int/medicines/services/counterfeit/impact/ImpactF_S/en/ (accessed October 1, 2016).

Young, J. (2001). Identity, community and social exclusion, in M. Roger & J. Pitts (Eds.), *Crime, Disorder, and Community Safety: A New Agenda?* (pp. 26–53). London: Routledge.

Young, L. (2003). Canada becomes fraud haven. *Marketing Magazine*, 108(29, September 1).

Zhang, S., & Chin, K. (2002). Enter the dragon: Inside Chinese human smuggling organizations, *Criminology*, 40(4): 737–68.

NEWS MEDIA SOURCES

24 HOURS VANCOUVER
Jun. 12, 2014, "Large 35 kilogram heroin shipment seized at YVR airport."

ABBOTSFORD NEWS
Jul. 24, 2009, "144 kilos of cocaine seized at B.C. border crossing" [online].

ABBOTSFORD TIMES
May 13, 2005, "'E' seized at border."

AGENCE FRANCE PRESSE
Jun. 30, 2000, "French take down Chinese money launderers, arrest 27."

APTN NATIONAL NEWS
Nov. 3, 2015, "US authorities targeting Toronto-New York City Chinese human smuggling network using Akwesasne" [online].

ASIAN TRIBUNE
May 12, 2005, "Canadian police arrest two Tamils of Sri Lankan origin connected with LTTE front group WTO for counterfeiting" [online].

ASSOCIATED PRESS
Feb. 15, 2015, "$1 billion stolen from banks in Cyberheist, Kaspersky Lab says" [online].

Apr. 12, 2015, "Canada police: 7 arrested in massive Asian prostitution ring" [online].

BLOOMBERG.COM

Feb. 15, 2015, "Online bank robbers steal up to $1 billion: Kaspersky" [online].

BRAMPTON GUARDIAN

May 19, 2006, "Counterfeiting plant shut down" [online].

BRITISH COLOMBIAN

Jul. 25, 1863, "Gambling and Sabbath desecration in the Cariboo."

Feb. 18, 1865, "The Customs Amendment Ordinance, 1865."

CALGARY HERALD

Mar. 18, 1991, "Arrest ends fugitive's flight."

Feb. 1, 2002, "Police smash credit card ring: Calgary focus of massive investigation" [online].

Mar. 19, 2006, "The war on credit card fraud race" [online].

Oct. 1, 2009, "Police in Alberta bust $2.4M marijuana grow-op with ties to Chinese organized crime."

Jun. 27, 2012, "Two Alberta men arrested in connection to drug network that stretched from Taber to Mexico" [online].

May 3, 2013, "Border agents make record heroin seizure at Calgary airport" [online].

Jul. 19, 2013, "Gangs remain a threat in Calgary, police chief warns" [online].

Aug. 31, 2013, "Gang threat remains in Calgary, say police."

Jan. 5, 2015, "The face of organized crime in Alberta is changing, says RCMP commander" [online].

CANADA BORDER SERVICES AGENCY NEWS RELEASE [ONLINE, CBSA WEBSITE]

Oct. 24, 2012, "CBSA seizes a record 14 tonnes of precursor chemicals in Prince Rupert."

Mar. 16, 2013, "CBSA seizes tobacco valued at $1.7 million at the Windsor Ambassador Bridge."

Mar. 23, 2013, "CBSA officers seize $3.4 million in loose tobacco."

Apr. 30, 2013, "Large shipment of precursor chemicals seized by CBSA in Vancouver."

May 27, 2013, "CBSA intercepts over 22 kilograms of suspected heroin at the Toronto Pearson International Airport."

Jul. 11, 2013, "CBSA intercepts more than 62 kilos of suspected cocaine at Pacific Highway crossing."

Dec. 24, 2015, "The CBSA seizes over 1.3 ton of suspected hashish in the Port of Montreal."

CANADA.COM

Oct. 25, 2007, "GTA police seeking task force to deal with N.S. pimp problem."

Jun. 19, 2014, "Canada needs to do more to help victims of human trafficking: U.S. report."

CANADA CUSTOMS NEWS RELEASE

Dec. 11, 2003, "CCRA and RCMP seize record amount of ecstasy."

CANADA NEWSWIRE

Jun. 5, 2006, "First ever operation of its kind in Canada."

Jun. 29, 2006, "U.S., Canadian police bust drug smuggling ring."

CANADIAN BANKERS ASSOCIATION PRESS RELEASE

Jun. 2, 1988, "Statement by Robert M. McIntosh, President, Canadian Bankers' Association."

CANADIAN BROADCASTING CORPORATION

Nov. 8, 1983, "Lomo," originally broadcast on *The Fifth Estate*.

Mar. 5, 2002, "How Malaysian women are lured to Canada and forced to prostitute," originally broadcast on *Disclosure*.

Apr. 19, 2012, "The RCMP says that it's played a key role in a major international drug bust," originally broadcast on *The National*.

CANADIAN GAMING ASSOCIATION PRESS RELEASE

Dec. 5, 2012, "Single event sport betting: What the experts think," http://canadiangaming.ca/news-a-articles/112-single-event-sports-betting-what-the-experts-think.html.

CANADIAN PRESS

Jan. 7, 1995, "Guns from one US arms dealer used in dozens of Canadian crimes."

Dec. 17, 1997, "Biker war heated up in 1997."

Oct. 10, 2000, "Dinner is served: Bikers break bread, not heads."

Aug. 13, 2001, "Dorval airport one of worst in North America for car theft."

Jan. 31, 2002, "Police say Calgary headquarters of counterfeit credit card operation."

Feb. 16, 2002, "Canadian laws under scrutiny as phone fraud flourishes in big cities."

Mar. 9, 2002, "Illegal gambling flourishing despite legal casinos, says RCMP expert."

Jul. 3, 2002, "Twelve people charged in major fake credit card, drug smuggling ring."

Jul. 9, 2002, "Montreal trial told Hells Angels video-taped funeral of Cotroni family member."

Nov. 6, 2002, "Quebec police used armoured vehicle in raid on Hells Angels affiliates."

May 15, 2003, "Quebec City police end investigation into alleged juvenile-prostitution ring."

Nov. 26, 2003, "Manitoba law to strip gang members of assets even if not convicted of crime."

Feb. 13, 2004, "Police bust $5.6 M marijuana grow operation in Edmonton."

Mar. 31, 2004, "Police smash North America-wide organized crime network."

Dec. 3, 2004, "Winnipeg police uncover huge mari-juana grow operation near police headquarters."

Feb. 1, 2005, "Canadian pot seizures up 259 per cent."

May 1, 2005, "Study released on human-smuggling market."

Aug. 17, 2005, "Calgary cops announce one of largest ecstasy busts in Alta history."

Oct. 16, 2009, "Report of mob control over infrastruc-ture spending prompts inquiry demand."

Sep. 25, 2012, "Construction bosses were regulars at Montreal Mafia hangout, Quebec inquiry hears."

Sep. 26, 2012, "Mafia 'tax' on construction projects hit 30% at height of Rizzutos' power, Quebec inquiry hears."

Oct. 4, 2012, "Organized crime behind counterfeit prescription drugs: RCMP."

Nov. 1, 2012, "Police arrest 103 from alleged crime 'consortium' in cross-Canada operation."

Feb. 28, 2013, "'A blight on society': Asian gangs responsible for kidnappings, drug smuggling in Canada, immigration hearing told."

Jul. 3, 2013, "Organized crime exploiting medical marijuana program: RCMP."

Oct. 2, 2013, "Quebec union had big ties to organized crime, inquiry hears."

Oct. 7, 2013, "Ex-cop accused of selling info to biker gangs."

Oct. 21, 2013, "Canadian-led crystal meth ring busted in Australia."

Jan. 16, 2014, "Tory slack on cybercrime hurting economy, RCMP boss says."

Apr. 30, 2014, "Quebec tobacco ring allegedly involved Montreal Mafia and native organized crime."

Aug. 31, 2014, "Australian drug trade 'high-reward' for Canadian criminals, B.C. police say."

Sep. 18, 2014, "Aboriginal women, girls targets for human trafficking, says new report."

Feb. 4, 2015, "As RCMP focuses on terrorism, it's a 'great day' to be in organized crime."

Apr. 4, 2015, "RCMP bust Canada-wide human-smuggling, prostitution ring."

Oct. 16, 2015, "Quebec Crown won't appeal decision to end trial of 5 Hells Angels."

CANADIANUNDERWRITER.CA

May 13, 2010, "Recovery rate for stolen vehicles drop, suggesting organized crime involvement: Ontario Provincial Police" [online].

CANOE.CA

Jun. 11, 2013, "De nouvelles accusations contre le policier Alex Therrien" [online].

CANWEST NEWS

Jan. 11, 2005, "B.C. bud makes a run for the border."

CAPE BRETON POST

Jun. 23, 2012, "Eight arrested after 170 kilograms of cocaine seized in New Brunswick."

CBC NEWS [ONLINE]

Oct. 6, 2004, "Big bust in Shuswap community."

Oct. 8, 2004, "Pot grower denies he's part of organized crime."

Mar. 14, 2005, "Gang numbers, violence growing, police say."

Sep. 6, 2005, "Americans seize record amount of ecstasy at Canadian border in Aug."

Oct. 25, 2007, "Police target Nova Scotia pimping ring in Ontario."

Apr. 16, 2009, "Hells Angels raids 'dismantle' biker gang in Quebec: Police."

Apr. 21, 2009, "Biker gangs in Canada."

Apr. 19, 2012, "43 tonnes of hash destined for Canada seized."

May 9, 2012, "Cybercrime in Canada said to be skyrocketing."

May 15, 2012, "Tamil migrant ship smuggling probe leads to more charges."

Aug. 13, 2012, "Gang links examined in trio of Montreal slayings."

Sep. 13, 2012, "Illegal cigarettes cost Ottawa millions in lost tax."

Oct. 24, 2012, "Police arrest 8 in organized crime bust near Calgary."

Nov. 1, 2012, "Quebec police dismantle massive drug network."

Nov. 9, 2012, "Illegal gambling website busted in Ottawa."

Jan. 4, 2013, "Brotherhood chapter at centre of Bacchus gang complaint."

Mar. 26, 2013, "Drugs increasingly being smuggled into Canada by truckers."

Mar. 28, 2013, "Ambassador Bridge leads Canada in cocaine seized."

Apr. 10, 2013, "Biker gang turf war on the horizon, warn police."

Jun. 28, 2013, "Ontario man accused of Mafia links faces prison in Italy."

Oct. 7, 2013, "Ex-Montreal officer arrested for alleged leak to Hells Angels."

Oct. 21, 2013, "FTQ members try to unseat boss Arsenault over Hells links; Arsenault is running for re-election as head of the FTQ labour union."

Nov. 29, 2013, "Fake goods valued at $6.5M seized in Toronto."

Mar. 13, 2014, "International auto theft ring busted in Alberta, Quebec."

Apr. 30, 2014, "Tobacco smuggling between Canada-U.S. results in 25 arrests—Montreal."

May 15, 2014, "RCMP bust passport fraud scheme tied to Canada's 'most wanted.'"

Jun. 14, 2014, "Toronto a 'hub' for human trafficking, report says."

Aug. 30, 2014, "Mennonite ties to Mexican drug cartels years in the making."

Sep. 10, 2014, "'Breaking Bad' drug lab bust: 600K doses of ecstasy found in Mission."

Oct. 8, 2014, "North Preston's Finest gang funnels girls to Ontario for prostitution: Police."

Nov. 3, 2014, "Cocaine wrapped in Louis Vuitton logos seized at Halifax port."

Jan. 15, 2015, "Hells Angels targeted in organized crime busts in Saskatchewan, Alberta Police seize fake OxyContin, guns in raids that also focused on Fallen Saints gang."

May 30, 2015, "Hells Angels biker mega-trial set to begin Aug. 3."

Jun. 3, 2015, "RCMP raids in GTA made 'significant dent' in 'Ndrangheta crime group."

Jul. 2, 2015, "Bill C-290 on single-event sports betting hasn't passed Senate, election looms."

Aug. 8, 2015, "Hells Angels biker mega-trial: Émery Martin sentenced, released."

Aug. 30, 2015, "CNE raid collects $1M worth of counterfeit goods."

Nov. 19, 2015, "'Mom' Boucher, daughter charged with conspiracy to commit murder."

Nov. 24, 2015, "Charbonneau Commission finds corruption widespread in Quebec's construction sector."

Dec. 1, 2015, "Toronto police seize $12M in counterfeit goods."

Dec. 14, 2015, "Calgary faces all-out gang war defined by impulsive gun violence."

Dec. 16, 2015, "Calgary's new gang war marked by close family ties, police say."

Jun. 13, 2016, "Woman in witness protection program sues RCMP for negligence."

Aug. 14, 2016, "What Quebec cops learned at a Hells Angels funeral."

Sep. 10, 2016, "Elephant sedative carfentanil becomes deadly street drug."

CFPL AM 980

Sep. 18, 2015, "15-year-old charged in deadly East London shooting due back in court Oct.16th."

CHARLOTTETOWN GUARDIAN

Jan. 30, 2003, "'Halifax Bikers' clubhouse forfeited to feds."

CHICAGO TRIBUNE

Apr. 21, 1998, "Abortion foes suffer a big setback."

CHILLIWACK PROGRESS

Aug. 18, 2006, "Heli drug smuggler gets four years."

CHRONICLE HERALD [HALIFAX, NOVA SCOTIA]

Oct. 28, 2004, "Regional police, RCMP team up in OxyContin bust; Eight arrested in C.B. operation."

Aug. 1, 2011, "Cops keep eye on new Halifax street gang" [online].

Aug. 6, 2011, "'Murda Squad' gang suspected in Reader killing."

Mar. 5, 2012, "New team takes aim at guns, gangs, unit formed in quest to clamp down on shootings, drug wars" [online].

Jan. 4, 2013, "Mounties lay gang charges against Bacchus members" [online].

Sep. 18, 2014, "Hells Angels building up for return to Halifax" [online].

Nov. 11, 2014, "Bacchus motorcycle gang expands into Ontario" [online].

Nov. 14, 2014, "Quebec corruption inquiry ends after 30 months of public hearings" [online].

CITYNEWS.CA

Oct. 9, 2015, "Police say spike in illegal gaming houses linked to organized crime."

CNEWS.COM

Jun. 26, 2012, "Two Albertans face charges over cocaine from Mexico."

COMBINED FORCES SPECIAL ENFORCEMENT UNIT—BRITISH COLUMBIA PRESS RELEASE [ONLINE]

May 6, 2013, "CFSEU-BC shuts down four sophisticated marijuana grow ops."

Jan. 22, 2014, "Two gang associates arrested and charged following CFSEU-BC investigation."

COMBINED FORCES SPECIAL ENFORCEMENT UNIT—ONTARIO PRESS RELEASE [ONLINE]

Feb. 4, 2013, "CFSEU dismantles illegal gaming enterprise."

Mar. 5, 2013, "More arrests linked to illegal gaming and Platinum Sportsbook."

Mar. 6, 2013, "Update on organized crime charges."

Jun. 3, 2015, "CFSEU dismantles 'Ndrangheta criminal organization."

CP24.COM

Oct. 9, 2015, "Police say illegal gaming houses in Scarborough area may be linked to organized crime."

Dec. 11, 2015, "35 search warrants executed in GTA organized crime bust."

CRIME STOPPERS NEWS RELEASE

Sep. 17, 2015, "Crime Stoppers raising awareness on contraband tobacco and organized crime."

CTV NEWS [ONLINE]

Jul. 24, 2009, "Border agents report record cocaine seizure."

Apr. 21, 2012, "Police issue arrest warrants for four men in connection with Hells Angels bust."

Apr. 11, 2013, "Quebec appeals court upholds ruling freeing 31 Hells Angels due to trial delays."

Jul. 19, 2013, "Arrests made in organized crime murders, one suspect remains at large."

May 7, 2014, "Police arrest 65 in major biker gang drug bust."

Jun. 2, 2015, "19 arrested in GTA bust targeting Italy's 'Ndrangheta crime syndicate."

Oct. 9, 2015a, "Spike in violence linked to illegal gaming houses, casinos in Scarborough: Police."

Oct. 9, 2015b, "Five Hells Angels members freed, trial cut short."

Dec. 11, 2015, "640 charges laid in alleged high-end vehicle theft ring."

DAILY GLEANER [FREDERICTON]

Jun. 23, 2012, "Tip leads to seizure of drugs with a street value of $21-million."

DALLAS MORNING NEWS

Jul. 1, 1998, "High-tech sleuths carving niche in top companies."

DAWSON NEWS

Mar. 22, 1908, "Maker of history."

EDMONTON JOURNAL

Jan. 25, 1996, "Mounties' sting store laundered drug money."

Jun. 28, 1998, "Global swindlers at home in Canada."

Aug. 13, 1999, "Migrants on ships likely headed to U.S."

Jun. 1, 2002, "Woman gets 17 years for smuggling $50M in heroin."

Mar. 10, 2005, "Smuggling increases at Akwesasne."

Dec. 9, 2012, "Money, drugs and violence: The evolution of White Boy Posse" [online].

EDMONTON SUN

Feb. 11, 2002, "Police computers penetrated: Audit reveals Hells Angels pay enforcement personnel for passwords."

Jan. 4, 2004, "Asian gangs deadliest organized crime threat in Alta, says report" [online].

Jan. 30, 2009, "12 charged in major gang bust" [online].

Aug. 17, 2012, "Hells Angels members convicted for cocaine trafficking."

Feb. 7, 2014, "Outlaw biker gangs on the rise in Alberta."

EQUIFAX CANADA PRESS RELEASE [MARKETWIRED NEWS SERVICE]

May 27, 2014, "Equifax Canada warns Parliamentary Committee about identity-related crimes—Synthetic identities hold chilling consequences" [online].

FERNIE FREE PRESS

Jul. 3, 1908, "The Black Hand Society."

FINANCIAL POST

Jan. 9, 1937, "Swindlers on rampage."

Dec. 23, 1944, "Ontario is big stock racket centre, U.S. security sales officials claim."

Nov. 28, 1997, "Caller says BioChem animal rights target, but expert suggests Tuesday's bombings were too sophisticated for Animal Liberation Front."

Jul. 4, 1998, "Private justice: Companies turn to former Mounties for swift, discreet crime-fighting."

GLOBALNEWS.CA

Apr. 30, 2013, "Quebec tobacco ring allegedly involved Montreal Mafia and native organized crime."

Jan. 26, 2015, "Sask. RCMP say danger still exists after 'Project Forseti' drug bust."

THE GLOBE
Dec. 21, 1865, "Smuggling from Canada."

Mar. 25, 1885, "The Anti-Chinese movement."

Aug. 27, 1908, "The yellow peril: Whites may be driven out of the west entirely."

May 23, 1918, "Gambling in Vancouver."

Jun. 21, 1919, "Huge opium shipments to BC since May 20."

Apr. 9, 1926, "Birds of paradise shipped as talcum and opium as cocoa."

Feb. 27, 1928, "Sentence is given in extortion case."

Dec. 20, 1929, "Official was paid to block evidence, Regina court hears."

THE GLOBE AND MAIL
Oct. 17, 1963, "20 Ontario men named in U.S. as Mafia links."

Apr. 5, 1971, "Mafia figure tried to be intermediary, union official says."

Jun. 2, 1972, "Metro police raid turned up copy of Mafia linked society's secret rituals, court is told."

Feb. 1, 1979, "Obront is jailed for 20 months in tax case."

Aug. 18, 1982, "Tapes identify Mafia members, RCMP say."

Jul. 6, 1986, "Tapes allude to Mafia deals; Court is told of organized crime links to United States in 3 Canadian cities."

Dec. 16, 1986, "Hong Kong gangs set up in Toronto."

Dec. 17, 1986, "Street gangs challenge organized crime triads."

May 22, 1989, "Triad societies seeking control of heroin market, police say."

Apr. 29, 1994, "Arrests made in credit-card fraud."

Jun. 30, 1995, "Lawyer handed 13-year prison sentence for overseeing money-laundering scheme."

Apr. 20, 1996, "A drug lord's comedown."

Jul. 21, 1997, "Mounties provide keys to smuggling puzzle."

Oct. 27, 1999, "OSC warns of rising securities crimes: Calls for full-time RCMP fraud squad policing markets."

May 18, 2000, "Five B.C. residents arrested after 170,000 pills arrive on a Paris-to-Toronto charter flight."

Sep. 6, 2000, "Drug haul biggest in Canadian history."

Oct. 10, 2000, "Warring biker chiefs make up over dinner."

May 11, 2001, "Canadian swindlers targeting Americans" [online].

May 6, 2002, "Biker boss flaunted his notoriety" [online].

Aug. 12, 2002, "Compelling tales of crime told at biker trial" [online].

Nov. 9, 2002, "Ontario judge levies record gambling fine" [online].

Dec. 5, 2002, "B.C. is stung as debit card criminals hit hundreds see their bank accounts drained in $1.2-million theft of secret banking data" [online].

Sep. 10, 2003, "Alberta judge quashes charges in mega-trial" [online].

Sep. 12, 2003, "Megatrials don't serve justice, experts say" [online].

Sep. 20, 2003, "Police nab pot grown at military facility" [online].

Sep. 25, 2003, "Government to look at megatrial overhaul" [online].

Jan. 12, 2004, "Pot bust worth $30-million, police say" [online].

Jan. 21, 2004, "Reputed boss of Montreal Mafia arrested in murder case" [online].

Apr. 4, 2004, "Alleged biker leader surrenders to police in car-theft probe" [online].

Apr. 14, 2004, "Jailbirds of a feather flock together" [online].

Apr. 23, 2004, "Quebec to seek sales taxes owed by drug pushers" [online].

May 4, 2004, "Misconduct accusations hit Canadian police on two fronts. Hit man says police ignored drug killing" [online].

Jul. 22, 2005, "B.C. trio had tunnel vision, but police saw through it" [online].

Jul. 23, 2005, "Tunnel crew Hells Angels' rivals" [online].

Aug. 1, 2005 "Lack of a tractor tips Ontario police to pot fields aplenty" [online].

Aug. 18, 2005, "Ecstasy haul the biggest in Alberta, police say" [online].

Jun. 18, 2011, "The ballad of Daniel Wolfe" [online].

Jun. 6, 2012, "RCMP 'pulling out all the stops' with new charges in Tamil smuggling case" [online].

Sep. 11, 2012, "Leadership fight, revenge behind gang-related violence in Toronto: Police" [online].

Aug. 4, 2014, "Montreal gangland killing shatters tenuous underworld peace" [online].

Nov. 13, 2015, "Shadowy Black Axe group leaves trail of tattered lives" [online].

Nov. 19, 2015, "Major police operation targets high-ranking mobsters in Montreal" [online].

Nov. 24, 2015, "Quebec corruption report flags 'culture of impunity' in construction industry" [online].

Aug. 9, 2016, "Most of Canada's marijuana growers are otherwise law-abiding: Advocates" [online].

GOVERNMENT OF CANADA NEWS RELEASE [ONLINE]

Feb. 7, 2014, "CBSA seizes 244 kg of suspected cocaine at the Port of Montréal."

Jul. 4, 2014, "CBSA finds suspected heroin in a cargo shipment at Toronto Pearson International Airport."

Aug. 15, 2014, "CBSA seizes 858 kg of hashish at the Port of Montreal."

Nov. 1, 2014, "Minister Blaney highlights coming-in-to-force of the Safer Witnesses Act."

Nov. 5, 2014, "CBSA makes massive suspected cocaine seizure at Port of Halifax."

Aug. 31, 2015, "Seizure of 52 kg of suspected cocaine leads to arrest at the Ambassador Bridge."

GUARDIAN

Jun. 8, 2006, "Move over, Costa Nostra."

GUELPH MERCURY

May 28, 2014, "Fraudsters creating ID 'out of thin air,' RCMP says."

Dec. 12, 2015, "International car theft ring targeted high-end vehicles."

HALIFAX DAILY NEWS

Aug. 25, 2003, "Halifax Angels ordered back to work."

Aug. 17, 2004, "Spectacular tobacco heists catch the attention of organized crime: RCMP."

HAMILTON SPECTATOR

Sep. 5, 1979, "Car bombing may be gang war: Police."

Sep. 22, 1980, "A chronology of a decade of bombings."

Dec. 10, 1981, "Collectors' took control of firm, ex-owner says."

Dec. 19, 1981, "Three guilty of fraud in meat firm case."

May 17, 1982, "Judge allows witness to describe his fear of trio."

Jul. 6, 1982, "Organized crime had hierarchy: RCMP."

Jul. 7, 1982, "Harsh crime world rules dictate obedience: RCMP."

Jul. 10, 1982, "RCMP officer opens book on world of crime."

Aug. 28, 1982, "Luppinos jailed in fraud but Mafia link unproven."

Aug. 31, 1984, "The Godfather. These years have not been kind to Giaccomo Luppino."

Apr. 12, 2001, "Gambling syndicate smashed."

Oct. 2, 2012, "Inquiry offers insight into power Montreal crime boss held" [online].

Mar. 8, 2013, "André Gravelle, 11 others, charged in medical marijuana bust" [online].

Nov. 10, 2014, "Hamilton-based Red Devils biker gang no more" [online].

HEXUS.NET

Jan. 7, 2011, "Organized crime at the heart of software piracy: Microsoft" [online].

INDIANZ.COM

Mar. 15, 2005, "Report cites increase in Native gang activity."

INFOZINE.COM

May 1, 2014, "Canadian, US authorities shut down cross-border smuggling ring."

INSIGHT.COM [ONLINE]

Sep. 12, 2014, "Canada drug trafficking groups expanding Mexico ties."

INSURANCE BUREAU OF CANADA NEWS RELEASE [CANADA NEWSWIRE]

Dec. 16, 2014, "Joint police forces investigation nabs alleged international car theft ring."

LE JOURNAL DE MONTRÉAL

Dec. 5, 2002, "Le Gang de l'Ouest décimé" [online].

Dec. 6, 2002, "Moyennant une prime de 33%, Matticks assurait les cargaisons de drogue" [online].

KELOWNA DAILY COURIER

Aug. 29, 2012, "Arrests of top Hells Angels leaves rival gangs vying for a bigger cut of the drug trade."

KITCHENER-WATERLOO RECORD

Jun. 25, 2005, "38 charged in drug raids."

LONDON FREE PRESS

Feb. 5, 2013, "Organized crime hits home" [online].

Sep. 8, 2015, "'There will be more violence'" [online].

MACLEANS.CA

Nov. 24, 2015, "No one can deny it now: Quebec is facing a corruption crisis" [online].

MANITOBA FREE PRESS

May 22, 1895, "A novel method: Opium smuggled over the border in live cattle."

METRO HALIFAX

Feb. 14, 2012, "Unorganized gangs emerging in HRM."

METRONEWS [VANCOUVER]

Jun. 11, 2014, "Massive heroin bust at Vancouver airport."

MISSISSAUGA NEWS

Jun. 27, 2014, "Here's one drug bust that won't be swept under the rug...."

MISSION RECORD

Sep. 10, 2014, "Sixty kilograms of suspected ecstasy seized from apparent drug lab."

MONTREAL GAZETTE

Jun. 12, 1918, "Farmhouse raid netted opium and Chinamen: Inspector Belanger seized drug making plant near Back River."

Jul. 12, 1945, "Betting house men are assessed—$100."

Jul. 21, 1945, "$75,000 an hour is played here during 'rush' hours at barbotte."

Jan. 10, 1948, "Ship convicted on gaming counts."

Nov. 29, 1975, "Paolo Violi called new crime 'Godfather.'"

Oct. 9, 1982, "Police arrest 22 in $250,000 illicit drug haul."

Jul. 10, 1985, "Drug lab in Montreal supplied Hells Angels, police say."

May 6, 1987, "Man slain in bar."

Feb. 12, 1994, "Cigarette smuggling has spread like wildfire and taken root."

Oct. 16, 1994, "RCMP traces cash in huge money-laundering case."

Jan. 6, 1995, "Russian mobsters behind luxury-car thefts."

Jun. 30, 1995, "Lawyer jailed for 13 years."

Jan. 25, 1996, "Police sting operation bags 120 for drugs, money-laundering."

Oct. 5, 1996, "Smuggling illegal immigrants increasing, U.S. cop says."

Dec. 11, 1998, "Chinese alien smuggling ring busted in U.S."

Dec. 12, 1998, "7 charged with fraud."

Mar. 2, 1999, "Terrorists netted car-theft cash: RCMP" [online].

May 17, 2000, "Judge splits massive trial based on anti-gang law" [online].

Dec. 7, 2000, "Rock Machine boss busted" [online].

Feb. 21, 2002, "Police fear bikers have pals among guards" [online].

Apr. 19, 2002, "Hells megatrial begins today" [online].

May 17, 2002, "Snitch killed 2 men while on cop payroll" [online].

May 22, 2002, "Biker informant hid killing" [online].

May 28, 2002, "Autopsy photos show dead biker informant" [online].

Jul. 18, 2002, "Hells bought cocaine in bulk" [online].

Jul. 19, 2002, "Angels set bounties on rival bikers, trial told" [online].

Aug. 9, 2002, "Drug dealers as busy as ever" [online].

Nov. 7, 2002, "Cops grab gang that ruled roost in Saint-Jean" [online].

Nov. 9, 2002, "Ring proves bad bet: Montrealer fined $150,000 for bookmaking" [online].

Dec. 5, 2002, "Montreal waterfront supplied bikers, street gangs" [online].

Jan. 13, 2003, "Elusive escort agencies secretive, successful" [online].

Jun. 15, 2004, "Charges against Cotroni's son dropped" [online].

Aug. 26, 2004, "Cigarette smuggling up as smokers seek price relief" [online].

Jun. 25, 2005, "Quebecers arrested in N.Y. ecstasy bust" [online].

Sep. 6, 2005, "Montreal counterfeit items pose real threat to public" [online].

Mar. 25, 2006, "Hells Angels resurface with reinforcements" [online].

Jun. 6, 2006, "High seas sting grabs hash" [online].

Sep. 26, 2006, "Traffickers sentenced" [online].

Mar. 17, 2007, "As police tapes rolled, conversation flowed at café" [online].

May 5, 2007, "Downfall of a Don 'I participated in this'" [online].

Mar. 26, 2009, "Mohawks, gangs and tobacco" [online].

Apr. 19, 2012, "Former alleged Dubois gang member arrested" [online].

Jun. 5, 2012, "15-year term sought for Mafia drug-case fugitive" [online].

Jun. 20, 2012, "15-year sentence for Giuseppe De Vito" [online].

Aug. 11, 2012, "Slayings 'could be the beginning of the revenge" [online].

Sep. 27, 2012, "Charbonneau Commission: Detective lists construction firms linked to Mafia" [online].

Sep. 28, 2012, "Charbonneau Commission: 'Montreal is a closed market,' Lino Zambito says" [online].

Apr. 5, 2013, "Hells Angels convicted, but could be free soon" [online].

Oct. 2, 2013, "FTQ brass fully aware of criminal ties, Charbonneau Commission hears" [online].

Oct. 7, 2013, "Former Montreal police officer charged with gangsterism."

Oct. 31, 2013, "Hells Angels helped fix FTQ elections, inquiry told" [online].

Mar. 16, 2015, "Operation SharQc: Eighteen Hells Angels plead guilty to taking part in general conspiracy to commit murder" [online].

May 7, 2015, "Another group of Hells Angels plead guilty."

May 15, 2015, "90-month prison term for alleged West End Gang associate" [online].

Oct. 10, 2015, "Judge orders end of SharQC Hells Angels trial over Crown's handling of evidence" [online].

Oct. 15, 2015, "Laval mayor files request to expedite former mayor's gangsterism court case" [online].

Nov. 19, 2015, "Leonardo Rizzuto arrested, fingered as Montreal Mafia leader" [online].

Nov. 24, 2015a, "Recap: Charbonneau report finds organized crime has infiltrated several sectors of Quebec's economy" [online].

Nov. 24, 2015b, "Editorial: Lessons from the Charbonneau inquiry" [online].

Nov. 25, 2015, "Major players arrested in Mafia investigation last week will remain behind bars for another week" [online].

MONTREAL STAR

Mar. 14, 1925, "Judge Coderre condemns police in its entirety in Montreal."

Jul. 23, 1952, "Bookie's gross $1 million yearly."

Dec. 3, 1975, "Violi, Cotroni crime branch 'co-directors.'"

MOOSE JAW TIMES-HERALD

Dec. 5, 2012, "Organized crime members charged in multiple murders in Alberta, Saskatchewan."

NATIONAL COALITION AGAINST CONTRABAND TOBACCO PRESS RELEASE

Nov. 19, 2015, "Taking the oxygen out of organized crime: Three-quarters of Ontarians want tougher penalties for illegal tobacco traffickers."

NATIONAL CONSUMERS LEAGUE PRESS RELEASE

Apr. 2014, "FTC crackdown on telemarketing scams is a reminder that the phone is a potent weapon for fraudsters."

NATIONAL POST

Apr. 14, 2000, "650 charges in Canadian sex slave trade."

May 18, 2000, "Tamil street gangs expanding illegal activities, report says."

Jun. 8, 2000, "Canadian cash flow confirmed as Tigers kill 21. Terrorist suicide bomber: Money collected in Canada may pay for Tamil weapons."

Sep. 6, 2000, "Police uncover shipment of hidden heroin."

Sep. 14, 2000, "Crime reporter shot 5 times in back."

Mar. 14, 2001, "Loan sharks worked Casino Rama" [online].

Apr. 4, 2001, "Second man who evaded Hells Angels raid found: 15 still wanted by police" [online].

Jun. 29, 2001, "Winnipeg gang war feared" [online].

Aug. 9, 2001, "Chain stores suspicious of $50 and $100 bills" [online].

Nov. 2, 2001, "War on Terrorism: Anti-Terror Bill" [online].

Feb. 13, 2002, "Supporting Hezbollah [online].

Jun. 28, 2002, "Hells Angels branching out" [online].

Oct. 5, 2002, "Sri Lankan to be extradited for 'narco-terrorism': Sold drugs for Tigers [online].

Nov. 13, 2002, "Dirty funds haunt small exchanges" [online].

Oct. 28, 2003, "Aboriginal crime gangs no longer an RCMP priority. Focusing on bikers, Mafia: Police stretched thin by post-9/11 security concerns" [online].

Dec. 12, 2003, "Easy money, low risk attract organized crime" [online].

Sep. 21, 2010, "'There's nothing we've done that's illegal' Mohawk leaders deny that organized crime is involved in the industry" [online].

Mar. 2, 2011, "Canada trafficking more illicit drugs: UN" [online].

May 25, 2012, "CSIS tip led to bust of alleged human smuggling ring" [online].

Sep. 20, 2012, "Canada's Mafiosi hide in plain sight, detective tells Quebec corruption inquiry" [online].

Mar. 5, 2013, "18 new arrests made in Ontario gambling ring investigation" [online].

May 8, 2013, "Juan Ramon Fernandez allegedly running Italy-to-Canada drug network" [online].

May 9, 2013, "Violent death of Canada mobster in Sicily ambush a sign Montreal's mob war has spread" [online].

May 10, 2013, "Montreal mob boss Vito Rizzuto paid for breaking Mafia rules, Sicily wiretaps show" [online].

Sep. 25, 2013, "Mennonites linked to Mexican cartels established cocaine smuggling pipeline near Alberta border: police" [online].

Mar. 24, 2015, "How the Hells Angels slaughtered five of its own in Quebec 30 years ago only to become more powerful" [online].

May 9, 2015, "How Hells Angels and criminal gangs came to control much of the Vancouver docks" [online].

NETWORKWORLD.COM

May 9, 2007, "Cybercrime update: Is organized crime moving into cybersphere? FBI says malware currently purview of loosely organized criminals."

NEW YORK, DEPARTMENT OF FINANCIAL SERVICES PRESS RELEASE

Dec. 1, 2015, "Governor Cuomo announces anti-terrorism regulation requiring senior financial executives to certify effectiveness of anti-money laundering systems."

NEW YORK STATE DEPARTMENT OF BANKING PRESS RELEASE

Oct. 31, 1997, "Banking department suspends license of money transmitter."

NEW YORK TIMES

Aug. 10, 1854, "Arrest of an extensive band of counterfeiting in Canada."

Sep. 28, 1884, "Smuggling Chinese from Canada."

Feb. 9, 1888, "Opium smuggling: A large consignment brought from China, via Winnipeg, seized near Brockville."

Feb. 29, 1904, "'Black Hand' death threat."

Dec. 12, 1904, "'Black Hand' after baker."

May 23, 1905, "Dynamited by the Black Hand."

Jul. 9, 1905, "'Black Hand' scare."

Dec. 5, 1970, "Crime groups said to smuggle hundreds of Sicilians into U.S."

Nov. 21, 1974, "U.S. indictments here describe global narcotics smuggling ring."

Feb. 20, 1977, "An obscure gangster is emerging as the Mafia chieftain in New York."

Sep. 10, 2012, "Smugglers go under the sea to move drugs" [online].

NIAGARA FALLS REVIEW

Oct. 7, 2009, "Shooting gang-related? Slain man had a lengthy police record."

OAKLAND PRESS

Sep. 24, 2015, "24 kilos of cocaine seized at Ambassador Bridge."

ONTARIO PROVINCIAL POLICE NEWS RELEASE

Apr. 5, 2001, "Multi-million dollar auto theft ring smashed."

OTTAWA CITIZEN

Sep. 7, 1978, "Anti-crime plea follows arrest."

Mar. 14, 1996, "Illegal gambling sucks billions from economy, Ontario police say."

Jun. 11, 1998, "RCMP's sting aided drug lords."

Jun. 12, 1998, "RCMP sting sparks call for inquiry."

Jun. 13, 1998, "Government defies court order to open files on 'illegal' drug sting."

Jun. 14, 1998, "Mounties didn't have government's OK for covert drug sting."

Dec. 10, 1998, "City/Region."

May 20, 2000, "Leave crooks to the police, CSIS told. Watchdog doubts spycatchers' ability to fight organized crime."

Apr. 12, 2001, "Police deal gambling ring a heavy blow."

Apr. 29, 2003, "Illegal raising of marijuana an 'epidemic.'"

Jun. 23, 2005, "Police seize 17,000 marijuana plants" [online].

Dec. 13, 2005, "Ottawa Hells Angels linked to multi-million-dollar heist" [online].

Mar. 9, 2006, "Identity-theft scam catches 100 people in net" [online].

Mar. 15, 2006, "U.S. report warns of Canadian marijuana, drug labs" [online].

Nov. 9, 2012, "21 charged in RCMP-led organized crime investigation" [online].

Apr. 29, 2014, "Ottawa judge jails mob bookie to 18 months in jail" [online].

May 15, 2014, "Ottawa trio admit running illegal gambling website" [online].

Dec. 29, 2014, "Illegal guns in Ottawa smuggled from several U.S. states" [online].

OTTAWA SUN

May 16, 2014, "Gambling ring craps out" [online].

PEACE RIVER BLOCK DAILY NEWS

Nov. 8, 2003, "3,600 plants seized from underground bunker in northern B.C. marijuana bust."

POSTMEDIA NEWS

Nov. 2, 2012, "A look inside gun smuggling, gun trafficking investigations reveals there's 'no typical profile.'"

Mar. 7, 2013, "Abuse of medical marijuana access program forces Health Canada to rethink production licensing."

May 14, 2014, "Police deal blow to tobacco smuggling ring."

May 30, 2015, "World No Tobacco Day shines spotlight on illicit tobacco trade in Ontario."

Aug. 4, 2015, "Vancouver airport acts as major entry port for millions in cash smuggled by mostly Chinese citizens."

LA PRESSE

May 8, 2014, "Opération Macaque: dur coup porté au crime organise" [online].

Aug. 2, 2014, "Ducarme Joseph pourrait avoir été la cible de la mafia" [online].

Aug. 19, 2015, "Gilles Vaillancourt ne conteste plus l'accusation de gangstérisme" [online].

THE PROVINCE [VANCOUVER]

Dec. 13, 1923, "Brought huge opium cargoes."

Aug. 4, 1991, "Police raids bare new gang pacts."

Aug. 18, 1991, "How the gang system works."

Jan. 25, 1996, "Police spring trap in massive drug sting."

Dec. 11, 1998, "Charged in heroin haul."

Dec. 10, 1998, "St. Lawrence smuggling ring broken."

Jan. 25, 2005, "Hells Angels bosses arrested as police swoop down on crime ring" [online].

May 12, 2005, "Pair caught with $1.2m in ecstasy pills" [online].

Jun. 28, 2005, "City's biggest meth lab found in Point Grey" [online].

Sep. 26, 2005, "Huge meth lab, found by chance, shut by police" [online].

Dec. 4, 2005, "Organized crime is on the rise in B.C." [online].

Aug. 27, 2012, "B.C. RCMP arrest several Hells Angels in international drug ring bust" [online].

Nov. 1, 2012, "B.C. organized crime link: 1,000 officers bust nationwide drug ring Thursday" [online].

Feb. 26, 2013, "Duhre gang: Who are they?" [online].

May 7, 2013, "$10M in marijuana seized from sophisticated grow-ops in Fraser Valley" [online].

QMI AGENCY

Aug. 16, 2012, "Dead gang leader rebuffed top biker prior to assassination."

Nov. 2, 2012, "Bust shows connections in criminal underworld in Canada."

Jan. 16, 2013, "Cdn drug rings a scourge for U.S.: Court docs."

Jun. 3, 2014, "Hezbollah tied to organized crime in Canada, says spy agency."

Oct. 22, 2014, "Hells Angels club's criminal records detailed in documents."

REGINA LEADER POST

Mar. 16, 2005, "FSIN says it tried to warn police about gang activity."

Mar. 17, 2005, "Gang problem may grow."

REUTERS

Aug. 7, 1998, "Quebec's Hells Angels terror only to increase."

RICHMOND REVIEW

Jun. 13, 2014, "Big heroin haul for officials at YVR."

RCMP PRESS RELEASE [ONLINE]

Sep. 29, 2003, "Police agency cooperation nets over $12 million worth of marihuana plants in Eastern Ontario."

Mar. 31, 2004, "Project Codi."

Sep. 7, 2005, "Clandestine drug labs grow across Canada - RCMP host two-day conference targeting chemical precursor diversion."

Nov. 9, 2012, "Major RCMP investigation nets 21 individuals with ties to Organized Crime."

Nov. 15, 2013, "RCMP and UK's National Crime Agency collaborate to make further arrests in international cocaine smuggling ring."

Mar. 20, 2014, "Crack down on a mass telemarketing fraud network: 23 arrests."

SCARBOROUGH MIRROR

Jul. 7, 2014, "Police arrest 11th suspect in connection with human trafficking ring linked to Galloway Boys street gang."

SEATTLE POST INTELLIGENCER

Jun. 8, 2012, "Trafficking ring busted smuggling kids over U.S.-Canadian border."

SHERBROOKE RECORD

Jul. 24, 2009, "Quebec prosecutors prepare for trial of 120 Hells Angels and associates."

SIMCOE REFORMER [ONLINE]

Dec. 10, 2012, "Three agree to testify in drug bust trial."

Sep. 16, 2013, "Waterford grow-op trial off the tracks: Judge."

SOLICITOR GENERAL OF CANADA NEWS RELEASE

May 21, 2003, "U.S. Attorney General and Solicitor General of Canada release five-year report on mass-marketing fraud."

STAR PHOENIX [REGINA][ONLINE]

Jun. 23, 2011, "Inside the terror squad: Documents provide window into drug trade."

Jan. 15, 2015, "Project Forseti: Who was charged?"

Jan. 16, 2015, "Biker gangs busted: Police raids link arrests to deadly fentanyl."

ST. MARY'S JOURNAL

Jun. 29, 2005, "Drugs seized in four-county OPP blitz."

SÛRETÉ DU QUÉBEC COMMUNIQUÉ

May 7, 2014, "Projet Macaque—Plus de 60 arrestations."

Dec. 4, 2002, "Démantèlement d'un réseau de drogue relié au gang de l'Ouest."

TELEGRAPH-JOURNAL [NEW BRUNSWICK]

Jan. 20, 2004, "Major marijuana growing ring operation discovered in posh N.B. homes."

TIME

Aug. 5, 1946, "Innocents abroad."

Sep. 4, 1972, "The milieu of the Corsican Godfathers."

TORONTO BRITISH COLONIST

Jun. 13, 1845, [no article title].

Feb. 6, 1846, [no article title].

Feb. 30, 1846, [no article title].

Jul. 9, 1846, Special supplement: "An interesting account of the organization and mode of operations of the celebrated horde of robbers known as the Markham Gang."

TORONTO POLICE SERVICES NEWS RELEASE

Dec. 11, 2015, "Project CBG takedown, 175 police officers execute more than 35 search warrants, High-end GTA vehicles stolen, shipped overseas."

TORONTO STAR

May 21, 1894, "On the throw of dice."

Oct. 13, 1894, "Gambling hells in our midst."

Aug. 2, 1895, "Smuggle the vile cigarette."

Sep. 6, 1898, "Seizing smuggled cigars all over Canada."

Feb. 15, 1902, "The Chinese of the Queen City."

Apr. 4, 1903, "Present law can't stop gambling."

May 4, 1906, "Black Hand again: Italians at Port Colborne said to have been terrorized."

Jan. 9, 1909, "Expose methods of Black Hand."

Dec. 18, 1923, "Toronto is biggest betting place in North America."

Feb. 27, 1948, "Windsor grills Detroit's chief on race data."

Apr. 7, 1961, "An amazing case of mass blindness at the town tavern."

Apr. 17, 1961, "How gangsters move in on Toronto's stock operations."

Oct. 11, 1962, "Our hoods in Canada: JFK."

Aug. 24, 1972, "Zanini was shot as a warning to quit building probe trade."

Aug. 25, 1972, "Special squad to investigate crime in construction unions."

Jan. 21, 1977, "'Banker moved $84 million for underworld."

Jan. 22, 1977, "Global investigation destroys $3 billion heroin conspiracy."

Jul. 15, 1977, "Police fear street gangs moving into Chinatown."

Oct. 11, 1978, "2 die, 4 hurt in Montreal gang shooting."

Jun. 24, 1979, "Rival bike gangs gearing for 'open war' in Ontario."

May 14, 1981, "2 held in Chinese extortion bid."

Jul. 17, 1981, "Police name 2 murder suspects."

Jan. 14, 1982, "Metro Chinese fear secret society."

Jan. 15, 1982, "Extortion gang plays on Chinese traditions."

Jul. 7, 1982, "Gang found killing easy, trial told."

Mar. 24, 1983, "Immigration officer charged with fixing papers for Asians."

Aug. 31, 1983, "Orientals live in fear of gang, officer says."

Sep. 1, 1983, "Man denies trying extortion based on secret society fears."

Sep. 13, 1983, "Extortion attempt gets pair two years."

Sep. 16, 1983, "Chinatown gamblers robbed by gunmen."

Sep. 17, 1983, "Chinatown gang war looms, police say."

Sep. 18, 1983, "Kung Lok."

Sep. 20, 1983, "Bloody war just beginning OPP biker squad warns."

Jun. 4, 1985, "'One of most feared' members of Chinese gang found guilty."

Jun. 7, 1985, "'One of most feared' members of Chinese gang found guilty."

Sep. 6, 1986, "Gangs put Chinatown under siege."

Mar. 23, 1987, "Funeral today for reputed mob 'godfather.'"

Oct. 20, 1988, "Niagara police are linked to crime, documents show."

Mar. 30, 1989, "Iranian gangs linked to heroin trafficking in Metro, Montreal."

Jun. 18, 1989, "Metro's powerful hotel union boss laughs at link with Mafia kingpin."

Feb. 4, 1990, "Impoverished Asian women recruited for Metro brothels."

Aug. 8, 1990, "Chinese criminals smuggled into Metro, police say."

Aug. 11, 1990, "Five detained in illegal aliens case."

Jan. 13, 1991, "Vicious new gangs terrorize Chinatown."

Feb. 6, 1991, "7 from Metro charged in heroin ring."

Oct. 18, 1992, "White glove under body assassins' grim warning."

Jul. 6, 1993, "Mob's casino interests run deep."

Apr. 29, 1994, "Fake credit card rings smashed in Metro."

Jan. 21, 1995, "Guns across the border."

Dec. 31, 2000, "Hells already setting up chapters."

Apr. 12, 2001, "54 face charges in huge gambling bust."

Aug. 2, 2001, "Pile of keys marks end of car scam."

Oct. 4, 2001, "Gang hijacked trucks full of goods: Police 27 people charged after probe lasting six months."

Nov. 2, 2001, "Criminals smile as terror keeps police busy. Police investigations of bikers, Mafia suffer since Sep. 11."

Nov. 10, 2002, "$300,000 fine levied in betting case."

Jul. 30, 2003, "Police find $22 million of ecstasy."

Aug. 23, 2003, "How an ATM scam unravelled. Canada's biggest debit-card fraud netted $1.2 million" [online].

Dec. 18, 2003, "Pot cultivation takes a rising toll" [online].

Jan. 12, 2004, "Pot bust biggest ever" [online].

Jan. 13, 2004, "Police stunned by grow-op's sophistication" [online].

Jul. 1, 2005, "Being Hells Angel is now a crime" [online].

Jul. 16, 2005, "Pot bust called one of biggest in Ontario" [online].

Sep. 22, 2008, "Police seize 40,000 pot plants near Pembroke" [online].

Mar. 8, 2011, "Canada criticized by international body for counterfeiting, copyright infringement" [online].

Sep. 22, 2012, "Is Montreal mobster Vito Rizzuto coming to town?" [online].

Mar. 7, 2013, "Super Bowl Gambling bust: Seven York Region residents charged" [online].

Apr. 13, 2013, "The gun pipeline: Mules who bring firearms across border pay high price for fast money" [online].

Apr. 18, 2013, "Star investigation: How one U.S. gun broker moved firearms across the border" [online].

Apr. 19, 2013, "Mexican drug cartel violence hits Canadian mobsters" [online].

May 9, 2013, "Former Laval mayor Gilles Vaillancourt among 37 arrested in Quebec anti-corruption sweep" [online].

Jun. 27, 2014, "RCMP seize 22.4kg of heroin woven into carpets at Pearson" [online].

Oct. 16, 2014, "Hells Angels' strip club still stripped of liquor licence."

Nov. 10, 2014, "Red Devils of Canada, country's oldest outlaw biker club, gives up ghost" [online].

Dec. 10, 2014, "Canada's contraband problem is about much more than lost revenue" [online].

Jan. 5, 2015, "Organized retail crime taking off in Canada" [online].

Mar. 5, 2015, "Ontario Hells Angels keep riding in Quebec, say police" [online].

Jun. 3, 2015, "19 arrested in GTA raids targeting 'Ndrangheta crime families" [online].

TORONTO SUN

Nov. 5, 1979, "Bikers on the warpath."

Nov. 16, 1979, "Toronto gangs mourn with Outlaws."

May 11, 2000, "Record ecstasy bust at Dorval."

Jul. 29, 2001, "Pair charged in auto thefts."

Jun. 11, 2010, "East Coast 'pimp' Marlo Williams gets three years for exploiting 19-year-old" [online].

Dec. 1, 2010, "Huge pot grow-op bust in T.O." [online].

Sep. 14, 2011, "3 busts seize 20,500 pot plants" [online].

Jan. 28, 2012, "Exclusive: Canada's illicit drug boom" [online].

Apr. 5, 2013, "Cop charged with leaking info to crime syndicate" [online].

TORONTO TELEGRAM

May 6, 1909, "Black Hand gang caught at Duluth."

Oct. 23, 1959, "10,000 Chinese sneak in."

Apr. 24, 1961, "Left Toronto for … Northland Apalachin."

Apr. 28, 1961, "More gambling arrests Ontario farm crime link."

USA TODAY

Oct. 7, 2011, "The dangerous world of counterfeit prescription drugs" [online].

VANCOUVER DAILY WORLD

Jan. 14, 1922, "Drugs pollute city! Are men of high standing in community ringleaders? Officials' lives threatened."

VANCOUVERITE.COM

Jul. 24, 2009, "144 kilos of cocaine was concealed in truck entering B.C."

VANCOUVER SUN

Nov. 24, 1923, "Chinese says police sold opium to him."

Jul. 15, 1927, "$100,000 in dope seized."

May 2, 1928, "Says Taylor told police not to act."

May 16, 1928, "Protection order made cop angry."

May 18, 1928a, "Chinese joints probed."

May 18, 1928b, "Gambler says boss named police recipients of graft."

Jan. 28, 1984, "Killings trigger demand for inquiry into organized crime."

Jun. 28, 1984, "Chinatown crime spreads as armed gangs wage war."

Sep. 6, 1986, "Smith vows crackdown on gang violence."

Aug. 19, 1987, "Police say crime suspects likely Chinese ex-soldiers."

Oct. 30, 1992, "Purer heroin blamed for rash of drug overdose deaths."

Jan. 26, 1996, "Business people laundered cash: Police said the 'main player' for the companies will be arrested shortly."

Apr. 27, 1997, "B.C. bust ended one of world's biggest drug empires."

Jul. 9, 1998, "Home invasion linked to gang with international tentacles."

Dec. 22, 1998, "Gang network spawned Johal."

Sep. 24, 1999, "Interception of migrants thanks to U.S. Navy."

Feb. 16, 2002, "Canada's hashish trade 'funds terrorists': RCMP believe extremists get millions from drugs."

May 3, 2004, "Survey cites culture clash for youth violence."

Jan. 25, 2005, "Top B.C. Hells Angel arrested" [online].

Jun. 17, 2005, "Canada now major maker of ecstasy" [online].

Jun. 28, 2005, "Meth lab found in Point Grey house shocks neighbours" [online].

Jul. 22, 2005, "Tunnel scheme buried" [online].

Sep. 8, 2005, "Street gangs for hire: Ethnically mixed gangs parcel out their services to organized crime groups" [online].

Sep. 16, 2005, "Ecstasy lab chemicals enough to blow up a whole block" [online].

Sep. 27, 2005, "Rural meth lab capable of producing 12 kg of the drug every 48 hours" [online].

Dec. 13, 2005, "Ruling hobbles organized crime battle, police say."

Jun. 29, 2006, "Canada-U.S. drug raid nets 46 arrests" [online].

May 21, 2009, "Gangster convicted in Surrey Six slayings has other charges stayed" [online].

Sep. 24, 2009, "Puppet biker clubs tied to Hells Angels have top cops in B.C. worried" [online].

Aug. 14, 2010, "Boat load of almost 500 Sri Lankan illegal migrants lands off B.C. coast."

Mar. 24, 2011, "59 criminal gangs in Saskatchewan: Police" [online].

Aug. 28, 2012, "Hells Angels Kelowna clubhouse raided, seven arrested on drug offences" [online].

Oct. 25, 2012, "Vernon man faces 34 firearms counts after undercover gun trafficking probe" [online].

Nov. 1, 2012, "Amero and friends charged in massive cocaine ring out of Montreal" [online].

Nov. 3, 2012, "For second time this week, police break up major international drug network with Vancouver links" [online].

Apr. 6, 2013, "Six Hells Angels plead guilty to murder conspiracy" [online].

Jun. 4, 2013, "Police find another underground pot bunker linked to Hells Angels" [online].

Sep. 12, 2013, "Mounties seize 12,000 marijuana plants near Pemberton" [online].

Feb. 18, 2014, "RCMP argue medical marijuana regime breeds criminal and safety concerns" [online].

Feb. 25, 2014, "Biker expert says Hells Angels selling their assets" [online].

VICE.COM

Dec. 5, 2012, "The RCMP were horribly wrong about crippling the White Boy Posse."

VICTORIA NEWS

Nov. 10, 2006, "Police shut down players in '99."

WALL STREET JOURNAL

Aug. 18, 1980, "Shakedown, N.Y."

Sep. 29, 1999, "Travelers offers insurance against stolen identities."

WASHINGTON POST

May 13, 1973, "Illegal immigrants and drug smuggling."

WESTERN REPORT

May 29, 1995, "The Natives are getting restless."

WINDSOR STAR

Oct. 26, 2007, "Stay east, police tell N.S. girls" [online].

Dec. 17, 2013, "The Pipeline: 'A lot of people in Canada want guns'" [online].

WINNIPEG FREE PRESS

Feb. 17, 2003, "Asian gangs moving in? Police concerned over big rise in sophisticated grow operations."

Sep. 9, 2005, "Grow op busts indicate farms are going to pot" [online].

Sep. 17, 2005, "Police credit neighbours' tips for pot busts" [online].

Jan. 6, 2010, "Indian Posse founder killed. Gang leader stabbed to death during brawl in penitentiary" [online].

Apr. 10, 2012, "Cops make life hell for Angels. Arrested even if they haven't done a crime" [online].

Jun. 6, 2017, "Gangs 'help fill a void.'"

WINNIPEG SUN

Oct. 22, 2004, "Busts of grow ops just drop in bucket, says union cop."

Apr. 24, 2012, "Manitoba Hells Angels associate arrested."

Jun. 8, 2012a, "Rarely used peace bond issued against Manitoba Hells Angels Member."

Jun. 8, 2012b, "Warriors collared in $32K coke bust 50."

Jul. 25, 2012, "Hells probe was off the hook."

YORK GUARDIAN

Dec. 1, 2015, "Toronto police display $12-million in counterfeit goods seized in Project Pace."

LEGAL CASES

R. v. Campbell, [1999] 1 S.C.R. 565

R. v. Carter, [1982] 1 S.C.R. 938 1982 CanLII 35

R. v. Cotroni, (sub nom. *Papalia v. R.*) [1979] 2 S.C.R. 256

R. v. Lindsay, 2005 CanLII 24240 (ON SC)

R. v. Stinchcombe, [1991] 3 S.C.R. 326

R. v. Terezakis, 2005 BCSC 1727

R. v. Terezakis, 2007 BCCA 384

Office of the Commissioner for Federal Judicial Affairs. (1999). *Veluppillai Pushpanathan (Applicant) v. The Minister of Citizenship and Immigration (Respondent)*. Indexed as: Pushpanathan v. Canada (Minister of Citizenship and Immigration) (T.D.) Trial Division, Sharlow J. Toronto, May 13.

ARCHIVAL MATERIAL

Archives of the City of Montreal, P43: Fonds de la Commission d'enquête présidée par le juge François Caron (1950–53), P43, S4, SS2, D7.

Archives of the Province of Ontario, RG 4-32: Attorney General Central Registry Criminal and Civil Files, File No: 1909-651, File title: "P.E. MacKenzie, Crown Attorney, Kenora: Complaint of black-hand gang at Fort Frances and query re deportation of certain Italians, 1909."

Archives of the Province of Ontario, RG 4-32: Attorney General Central Registry Criminal and Civil Files, File No: 1909-1705, File title: "J.B. McKillop, Crown Attorney, London: Re proceedings against sale of opium in London."

Archives of the Province of Ontario, RG 22: Criminal Assize Clerk criminal indictment files, Container 167, Criminal Assize Indictments, File No: RG-22-392-0-8947, File title: "Defendant: Italiano, Guiseppe; Charged with Sending threatening letters (2 counts); Robbery (3 counts); Conspiracy (2 counts), Welland County, 1928."

Archives of the Province of Ontario, RG 23: Records of the Ontario Provincial Police, File No: 23-26-39, File Title: "OPP Investigations—Narcotics Files (1912-1919)," File label: "Narcotics, 1917."

City of Toronto Archives, Fonds 15: Toronto Board of Commissioners of Police Fonds, Series 181: Transcripts of Inquiries, File 1, Box 109205, Folio 3: "In the matter of an enquiry by the Board of Police Commissioners into certain charges of neglect of duty on the part of the officers and members of the Toronto Police Force in connection with Gaming-houses in the city of Toronto, Nov. 12 to 23, 1901," pp. 65–68.

City of Vancouver Archives, MSS. 54: Major Matthews Collection, File No: 505-G-1 File 15, File title: Civic—Mayor's—L.D. Taylor—Correspondence.

City of Vancouver Archives, MSS. 69: Henry Herbert Stevens Fonds, Location: 509-D-8, File 1, Document cited: *Annual report, opium and narcotic drug branch for the fiscal year ended Mar. 31st, 1922*, p. 4.

City of Vancouver Archives, Vancouver Police Fonds, Series 181: Police Board General Files, Lennie Investigation Records, Volume 5, Location: 37-D-6, File 1, June 1–7, 1928, pp. 2064–65.

City of Vancouver Archives, Vancouver Police Fonds, Series 181: Police Board General Files, Lennie Investigation Records, Vol. 6, Location: 37-D-6, File 2, June 8–12, 1928, pp. 2570, 2572–73.

City of Vancouver Archives, Vancouver Police Fonds, Series 181: Police Board General Files, Lennie Investigation Records, Volume 9, Location: 37-D-8, File 3, June 21–27, 1928, pp. 4670–4674.

National Archives of Canada, RG 16: Records of the Department of National Revenue, Vol. 789, File No: 128256, File Title: "Operations of Mr. A.J. Gaudron, Superintendent of Criminal Investigation RCMP re: Border Patrol and Prevention of Smuggling." Document cited: Letter dated March 23, 1926, from RCMP Hamilton detachment to the Officer Commanding Western Ontario, re: R. Perry, No 106 Bay Street.

National Archives of Canada, RG 18: Files of the Royal Canadian Mounted Police, Volume 3167, File No. G494-1, File title: "Alleged Irregularities, Opium and Narcotic Drug Acts—Vancouver—Commission to investigate..."

National Archives of Canada, RG 18: Files of the Royal Canadian Mounted Police, Vol. 3291, File No: 1922-HQ-189-Q-1, File title: "Opium and Narcotic Drug Act—General—Miscellaneous Reports."

National Archives of Canada, RG 18: Files of the Royal Canadian Mounted Police, Volume 3288, File No. HQ-189-E-1, File Title: "Opium and Narcotic Drug Act—Vancouver, British Columbia—General—Miscellaneous."

National Archives of Canada, RG 18: Files of the Royal Canadian Mounted Police, Vol. 3313A, File No: HQ-189-O-1, File Title: "Rocco Perri (with alias) et al.—Hamilton—Opium and Narcotic Drug Act—Liquor Smuggling—Murder of wife Bessie Perri."

National Archives of Canada, RG 29: Files of the Department of Health and Welfare, Vol. 229, File no: 323-2-6 Part IV, File title: "Narcotics: Drug Traffic and Smuggling—United States and Canada Drug Traffic."

National Archives of Canada, RG 76: Records of the Department of Immigration and Citizenship, Series D-7 , Vol. 1445 File: 287-USA-1, Access code: 32 Parts: 1=1961/07/04-1968/12/07 2=1968/12/08-1969/12/31, File Title: Mafia (Cosa Nostra)—U.S.A.

National Archives of Canada, RG 76: Files of the Department of Immigration and Citizenship, Volume 1447, File No: 289-1-1, File Title: "Kung Lok Society."

Provincial Archives of British Columbia, GR-0429: Attorney General Fonds, Box 15, File 4, Reel No. B09823, Folio Nos: 3052/08, 3039/08, File title: "Re: Petitions of the citizens of Fernie. (1908)."

INDEX